Herrn W.M. Betz
mit herzlichem Dank & Gruß

Dieter Lange

Chicago, 20.10.06

V&R

In the spring of 1930

Nathan Söderblom

Brev – Lettres – Briefe – Letters
A selection from his correspondence

edited by

Dietz Lange

Vandenhoeck & Ruprecht

With 3 illustrations

Bibliografische Information Der Deutschen Bibliothek

Die Deutsche Bibliothek verzeichnet diese Publikation in der
Deutschen Nationalbibliografie; detaillierte bibliografische Daten sind
im Internet über <http://dnb.ddb.de> abrufbar.
ISBN 13: 978-3-525-60005-4
ISBN 10: 3-525-60005-4

Table of Contents

Note: Abbreviations used in the footnotes follow the reference work *Theologische Realenzyklo-pädie /Abkürzungsverzeichnis* by Siegfried M. Schwertner, 2nd ed., Berlin/ New York 1994.

Introduction

I

Nathan Söderblom (1866–1931) was one of the eminent historians of religion at the turn of the 20th century when this new field of research came to be based on a truly scientific footing, after the great speculative systems of 19th century philosophy of religion had given way to methodical empirical research. He, along with Einar Billing (1871–1939), was also one of the central figures of the Swedish Luther-Renaissance which preceded the corresponding rediscovery of Luther in Germany, linked with the name of Karl Holl, which for many later historians became known – incorrectly – as »the« Luther-Renaissance. Finally, Söderblom was a chief architect of the ecumenical movement and the driving force behind its first great conference in Stockholm in 1925. Without his clear theological sense of direction and stern determination, his patient and relentless prodding and his charm offensives, that conference never would have taken place. It was he who first provided the nascent ecumenical movement with its theological guidelines and helped it steer free of the fierce nationalism that poisoned the political climate in the years after World War I. His influence extended far beyond the church and his field of scholarly activity.

Yet remarkably little is known about him nowadays, even in church and theological circles. Literature on him has been rather sparse in recent decades. We do possess two good biographies. One was written by Tor Andrae, a historian of religion and successor to Söderblom on his Uppsala chair, who drew a lively portrait based on close personal knowledge and deep reverence for his great teacher. It reads exceedingly well. Its limitation lies in its concentration on the earlier years. The other is by Bengt Sundkler, African missionary and Uppsala professor of church history. It is written from a greater distance but conveys an invaluable wealth of information. Sundkler's focus is on Söderblom's ecumenical activities where his account is very detailed – one might say: sometimes too detailed.[1] He had planned to write a more elaborate two-volume biography in Swedish after his shorter English one but never got around to doing so before he died in 1995.[2] Neither work attempts an exhaustive account of Söderblom's theological

---

[1] Tor Andrae, *Nathan Söderblom*, Uppsala 1931, 5th ed. 1932, German tr. Berlin 1938 (from which the following references); Bengt Sundkler, *Nathan Söderblom. His Life and Work*, Uppsala 1968.

[2] Cf. op. cit., p. 10.

thought. This is all the more regrettable since no one has ever bothered to write a comprehensive monograph in that field.

This state of affairs is due to a variety of reasons. The most obvious one is Söderblom's own many-faceted work. Authors usually wrote on one aspect or another, apparently feeling that the scope of the whole was beyond their reach. In addition, Söderblom was no »system-builder«, as his sharp-sighted friend Nils Johan Göransson, professor of dogmatics in Uppsala, had observed early on [26. 27].[3] As a historian of religion, he had an empirical mind (though he had never done any field studies), which made him abandon the neat schematisms of abstract theories of an allegedly unified evolution of religion and let him lay great store by elaborating the unique collective individuality of every single religion. And then there is the simple fact that Söderblom often wrote his books in great haste. His enormous workload obviously had its effects on his literary production; moreover, he was a restless, spontaneous, impulsive personality.

On the other hand, Söderblom was of a man of the grand overview, never one prone to get lost in the maze of detail. His good friend Eivind Berggrav, primate of Oslo, in his fine eulogy rightly observed that what makes reading Söderblom fascinating is the fresh originality of his basic ideas, the glimpses of genius, and the surprising connections between phenomena seemingly quite apart from each other, that one encounters time and again (and it should be added: a marvelous Swedish style).[4] This should be enough to make one curious.

The particular mindset of Söderblom – and even more so his being a theologian – has made him seem hopelessly outdated for much of present day science of religion. The discipline of phenomenology of religion of which Söderblom can be considered the founder seems to be out of favor with most contemporary scholars who are more ethnologically and sociologically oriented. Eric J. Sharpe even calls him a competent but only average scientist although he does acknowledge his genius in his overall view of *The Living God*.[5] His theological thought, on the other hand, is virtually unknown today outside Scandinavia. His works on Luther have never been translated from the original Swedish. The same is true for some of his important works in systematic theology,[6] but even if they had been, Söderblom appears to have been considered an outsider in that field, history of

---

[3] Numbers in square brackets refer to numbers of letters in this edition.

[4] Eivind Berggrav, *Nathan Söderblom. Geni og karakter*, Oslo 1931, 51. 67.

[5] Eric J. Sharpe, »Nathan Söderblom,« in: *Klassiker der Religionswissenschaft von Friedrich Schleiermacher bis Mircea Eliade*, ed. by A. Michaels, Darmstadt 1997 (157–169), 168. The words in italics are the title of Söderblom's last book.

[6] There is a posthumous English translation of *Uppenbarelsereligion* (Stockholm 1903, 2nd ed. 1930) by F. E. Pamp: *The Nature of Revelation*, London 1933. However, that was a time when the stage set on the continent for this subject by the Dialectical theology and his conservative Lutheran counterparts in Germany left virtually no room for the way Söderblom had treated it. Another text available in a language other than Swedish is *Naturlig religion och religionshistoria*, Stockholm 1914. A shorter version of it had appeared in German a year earlier

religion being his professional preoccupation. Moreover, his concept of ecumenicity came to be overshadowed by burning political issues after World War II on the one hand, and by more recent endeavors in church policy to achieve even doctrinal and organizational unity on the other. Disappointments in the latter area have not led to reappraising the contribution of the »father of the ecumenical movement«.

Work on the present edition of Söderblom's letters is inspired by the conviction that, time-bound though many of his ideas certainly are, there is a lot this great man has to teach contemporary thought on religion. This concerns his work on the notion of the Holy, as well as his ideas on pluralism, both within the confines of the church and with regard to relations between the religions, intertwined as they are with his social and political ideas. He shared his thoughts with an incredibly large number of important people: church leaders, theologians, scholars of religion, historians, politicians, artists, journalists, and others from many countries, and he in turn seriously pondered what they had to say on their part. Söderblom's letters therefore make fascinating reading, both for becoming acquainted with one of the seminal personalities of the last century and for being drawn into the lively exchange of ideas in that momentous period of history.

It is generally agreed that Söderblom was a genius of communication. Even in an age prior to e-mails and SMS and with prohibiting costs and tedious procedures for long-distance phone calls, these letters are quite outstanding. Söderblom was a tireless letter-writer.[7] He would read incoming letters at the breakfast table and dictate the replies, dictate letters when walking on the street, riding in a car or train, in restaurants, during conferences, and even at night. Bengt Sundkler cites one busy day during a tour of church inspection in 1916 when no less than 42 letters went to the mail. And every letter is different. One may be authoritatively demanding a decision, the other gently prodding or patiently leaving room for reflection. There are long religious meditations and deliberations on political and social questions as well as crisp and concise notes immediately getting to the heart of the matter, or then again helpful words of counseling to persons in a conflict of conscience and moving letters of condolences after a tragic loss of life. We meet a person with a rare gift of empathy, someone who was able to talk to everyone, be it the king or a laborer, a little girl or an old lady, on an equal footing, a charming man with a wonderful sense of humor.[8] »He was a man of the people and wanted the church to be in the midst of the vil-

---

but in Stockholm, and it seems largely to have missed the German reading public. Other works like *Svenska kyrkans kropp och själ*, Stockholm 1916, have never been translated.

[7] For the following, cf. Bengt Sundkler, »Nathan Söderblom som brevskrivare,« in: *RoB* 30/1971, 3–16.

[8] It is no accident that Söderblom's most significant book on Luther accords humor a central position in Luther's faith: *Humor och melankoli och andra Lutherstudier* [Humor and melancholy and other Luther studies], Stockholm 1919.

lage and the people in the midst of the church,« a newpaper article says at the occasion of his funeral.[9]

The letters can also help to eradicate an inveterate prejudice which asserts that Söderblom was above all »a great actor«. It is true, he did love elaborate liturgies, ornate clerical gowns, grand public appearances. But that was not a sign of vaingloriousness. If he was an actor, he was one who was one with his role, who served his role and not himself. In the words of his life motto from Scripture which also appears on his tombstone in Uppsala Cathedral: »When you have done all that is commanded you, say: ›We are unworthy servants; we have only done what was our duty.‹« (Luke 17:10) This is what his letters unequivocally bear out.

Letters reflect their author's life. Therefore, a short biographical sketch is in order here, including a rough outline of the most important aspects of Söderblom's thinking. That is, of course, no substitute for a full-fledged monograph which remains a great desideratum in the history of modern theology. But it can serve to put the ideas discussed in the letters in their context in a somewhat more systematic fashion than mere footnotes are able to do. The third part of this introduction will inform the reader on the guiding principles of the present edition and the way they are implemented.

II

Lars Olof Jonathan Söderblom was born on January 15, 1866, to the pastor Jonas Söderblom (1823–1901) of Trönö in the province of Hälsingland and his spouse Sophia, nee Blume (1838–1913), daughter of a Danish doctor, as their second son (the first one had died in infancy). Five other children were born to the couple, one of whom, a little girl, also died as a child. Jonas Söderblom, son of a farmer, bore the imprint of the Swedish revival movement, a stern Lutheran pietist with a lively interest in foreign missions, a rigorous teetotaler, theologically very conservative but »burning« for the Gospel, not a legalist. He was harsh, of a volcanic temperament but with a tremendously forceful self-discipline, devoted to his family, with an ascetic streak and a tendency to excessive work to the point, it seems, of verging on a neurotic condition. He was proud of his son whose intellectual gifts he had well recognized, and he had high expectations in this regard. He also considered physical prowess important and let young Nathan work hard on the parish farm (something which later provided him with a natural understanding for hard-working manual laborers). One must also remember, however, that for Sweden, this was the pre-industrial time when poverty was widespread, with many people emigrating to the United States because

---

[9] *Svenska Dagbladet*, July 19, 1931, Part A, p. 13: »… han var folkets man och ville ha kyrkan mitt i byn och folket mitt i kyrkan.«

of the dire economic conditions at home. Pastors' salaries were modest, to say the least.

Sophia Söderblom was an entirely different personality. She was quiet and gentle, if somewhat passive, highly educated, poetic and humorous. Even though she came from a more worldly background, she accepted much of her husband's religious views. However, she frequently compensated for the Spartan principles of childrearing and the often rash measures her husband used to apply for this purpose, a loving mother to her children. The parents were Nathan's first teachers before he enrolled in school at the age of nine, but his mother was by far the better pedagogue, and he always remembered her empathy, her »diplomatic« skills, and her patience. Over the years, the difference in character led to a growing distance between Sophia and her husband. She more and more retreated to her own room, being further isolated by increasing deafness.

As has often been observed, Nathan Söderblom combined important elements of both his parents' heritage. Of his father, he had the deep faith, determination, strong sense of duty and iron self-discipline. Working and traveling indefatigably, doing at least two jobs at once for most of his lifetime, he was burned out at the age of 65 – leaving behind him a towering legacy of achievement. It stood under the motto that his father had bequeathed to him on his deathbed and that also became the theme of his charge as archbishop in 1914: »Not that we lord it over your faith, we work with you for your joy« (I Cor. 1:24). For him, this sentence must have contained at least as much of a reference to the amiability of his mother, her capacity for getting rapport with people, her talent for music and poetry. All of this not only made this church leader a personality who commanded great respect, but also won him the deep affection of men and women from all walks of life.

Söderblom received a solid classical education at school, with German and French as foreign languages (English was only optional). His particular fortes were Scripture and church history. After finishing school at the age of 17, he went on to Uppsala University where he received his *filosofie kandidat* (something like a B. A.) in 1886, with particularly good grades in the classical languages and Arabic. Then he turned to the study of theology. It was a time full of tension in Sweden. Late romanticism was on the wane, and great challenges were posed to the church by a philosophical monism based on the new discoveries of natural science, as well as by the rapidly rising movement of Pentecostalism. Sadly, the faculty was by no means up to the task. The only two teachers who were able to elicit greater interest in Söderblom were Professor Robert Sundelin (1847–1896) in church history and the Old Testament scholar Fredrik Fehr (1849–1895), pastor primarius in Stockholm and promoter of Albrecht Ritschl's theology. At the same time, Söderblom became acquainted with modern Biblical criticism such as Julius Wellhausen's *Prolegomena zur Geschichte Israels* and the latest theories on the Synoptic Gospels. These things fascinated him but also led to a deep intellectual and religious crisis. That was confounded by the strain which his preoccupation with liberal theology put on Söderblom's relationship to his pietistic father who had come to fear that his son would become a »freethinker«.

In this situation the Student Missionary Association, of which Söderblom was a founding member since 1884, may have provided some support in combining traditional piety with an international outlook. In the event though, it was a religious tract by the Scottish preacher W.P. Mackay which helped him overcome his religious doubts.[10] Around Christmas, 1889, Söderblom experienced a conversion. From now on his faith centered around a Christology of the cross. Somewhat later he discovered for himself Ritschl's basic idea that God's revelation consists in his works in history, above all in the person of Jesus Christ. It thus is not identical with the Bible which rather is the fundamental witness of faith.[11] This intertwining of religious experience and theological insight found its clear expression in Söderblom's first book on Luther[12] and remained characteristic of his thought. Deep piety and a sense of liberation by modern theology were no contradiction but an organic unity. So his conversion mollified the conflict with his father, but full reconciliation seems to have been accomplished only at the latter's deathbed in 1901.

From now on Söderblom's study of modern theology intensified. With his friends Samuel Fries and Nils Johan Göransson with whom he had met every Sunday since 1888 for reading and discussing poetry, he delved into the latest German theological works of the likes of Albrecht Ritschl, Adolf Harnack, Wilhelm Herrmann, Julius Kaftan, and Otto Pfleiderer. Ritschl had directed Söderblom's attention both to God's revelation in the Jesus of history and to Luther. Two other important figures must be mentioned. One is the romantic Swedish poet and philosopher Erik Gustaf Geijer (1783–1847), whose basic idea of the great personality, the genius (snille), was to play an important role in Söderblom's thinking, and whose love for provincial and national culture counterbalanced his wide international horizon. The other one is the leading Swedish historian of his time, Harald Hjärne (1848–1922) who was a staunch apologist of the Christian faith.

Already during his student days Söderblom discovered his rhetorical, journalistic, and organizational capabilities. From 1886 onwards he was a member of his fraternity's debating society. He edited the Student Christian Association's journal Meddelanden from 1888–1893. In 1892 he became president of the Uppsala Student Corps and chairman of the local YMCA. His nationwide fame as an orator was established when he served as a

---

[10] W.P. Mackay, Grace and Truth, London 1874; cf. Sundkler, op. cit., p.30. Cf. Söderblom's own account – in the third person singular – in his San Francisco sermon of Oct. 7, 1923: Från Uppsala till Rock Island. En predikofärd i nya världen, 2nd ed. Stockholm 1924, 21 f.

[11] Andrae, op. cit., p.13, ascribes this to Julius Kaftan's review of Willibald Beyschlag, Zur Verständigung über den christlichen Vorsehungsglauben, Halle 1888, in: ThLZ 14/1889, 375–378. In the last paragraph, 378, the reviewer stresses that Biblical texts can never directly serve as proof but must always be viewed in their specific historical context.

[12] Den lutherska reformationens grundtankar II: Luther's religion, Stockholm 1893.

speaker at the three-day national celebration of the 1593 Uppsala Synod's tercentenary. That Synod had declared the Augsburg Confession the foundation of the Swedish church, facing down both the efforts of the Polish and Swedish king Sigismund III. Vasa (1566-1632) at re-introducing Catholicism, and the Calvinist leanings of his uncle and successor Karl IX. (1550-1611). That independence from the throne continued to play a pivotal role in Söderblom's view of the church [e. g., 50. 108].

It was also as a student that Söderblom was able to make his first journey abroad. He was sent to the annual Student Christian Movement's conference in Northfield, Massachusetts in June 1890, where he came in contact with impressive leaders like John R. Mott (1865-1955) and Dwight L. Moody (1837-1899). He had been invited by a Congregational pastor to stay in North Haven, Connecticut for two months. The United States was not unfamiliar to him even before that, since an uncle and a brother of his lived in that country, and they regularly exchanged letters with the manse in Hälsingland. American openness and hospitality, practical mind and indomitable optimism made a great and lasting impression on the young student. As for church life, the atmosphere of tolerance between members of quite different denominations at the conference was a spur to him to work for a positive relationship of peaceful co-existence and cooperation of Christian churches the world over.

However, we have to return to Uppsala. It was in Harald Hjärne's lectures in 1891 that Söderblom met Anna Forsell (1870-1955), daughter of a sea captain and a student of history. They quickly fell in love with each other and became engaged in November of the following year, the day after Söderblom had taken his *teologie kandidat* (roughly equivalent to an S. T. M.) with the highest honors.

On March 5, 1893, Söderblom was ordained by the bishop of Lund, Gottfrid Billing, and began his church service as a chaplain at the psychiatric ward of Uppsala hospital. Besides, he was working on his doctoral thesis on eschatology in the ancient Persian religion; he had taken up the study of the Avesta in 1892 under Johan August Ekman (1845-1913) [1]. The first version of this thesis was not accepted; he rewrote it during the following years.

Meanwhile, another event radically changed his life. One day in the waiting room of the royal palace in June, 1893, he heard that the post of Swedish pastor in Paris would become vacant on May 1, 1894. Longing for a pastorate in its own right, and lured by the opportunity to continue his studies at the famous Sorbonne, he applied and was accepted, promising that he would continue to pursue his academic studies in his spare time.

Anna Forsell was just as enthusiastic about the prospect. They married on April 29, 1894, and after a honeymoon in Germany – in Berlin, among other places, where Söderblom visited Harnack – they moved to France. It was to be a long and happy marriage. The couple had eight sons and four daughters (one of whom died in infancy). They always had an open house with many guests. Mrs. Söderblom also was her husband's respected intellectual partner. After his death she spent all of the 24 years by which she survived him ordering the huge mountain of materials he had left behind.

Söderblom's pastorate included ministry to the 350 or so Swedes and Norwegians of the Paris congregation, mostly artisans, manual workers, domestic servants, a few artists and a small number of diplomats, as well the sailors' chaplaincy in Calais during the summer months. Church members in Paris lived scattered across the huge city, and they often had to work on Sundays. So worship attendance was disappointing at first [6]. That changed in time, not least due to Söderblom's unpretentious ways and genuine interest in the people. Social problems were rife, particularly among the sailors who were ruthlessly exploited. And the Scandinavians in the big city had the most outlandish requests for help, like the dancer in a night club who asked for money for a skirt (and got it). Söderblom helped where he could, becoming sort of a star beggar on behalf of the congregation (something he continued on a grand scale as archbishop when aid was needed for the European nations impoverished by the World War).

So the social question was pretty much at the center of attention. Söderblom was quite sympathetic with the labor movement, though not backing any one political party, and publicly pleaded for more social justice [28].[13] He was greatly impressed by Friedrich Naumann and Paul Göhre at a meeting of the *Evangelisch-sozialer Kongress* which he was able to attend in Erfurt in November, 1896 (just after Adolf Stoecker had left it [13]). That event may have been of crucial importance for his later activities in Life and Work. It was no accident either that he wrote a book on the Sermon on the Mount in Paris, in which he stressed the radicalness of Jesus' demands (inspired, among others, by Tolstoy).[14]

Naturally, the great social and political events of the day also engaged the Söderbloms, like the social upheavals in France in the 1890s and the great Socialist congress in 1900 [7. 28], and, even more, the Dreyfus affair which began in 1894, the very year in which they had moved to Paris. Söderblom reacted violently against the vile antisemitism reigning the day [18]. This should warn the modern reader, by the way, to condemn the view Söderblom sometimes expressed that the Germanic nations were culturally more advanced and had a deeper sense of religion than the French [7. 8. 9] as »racist«. In general, Söderblom much more adheres to the neo-romantic view which considers all nations equal, with each of them contributing its own specific forte. So for him, the superior French intellectual clarity conterbalances the »depth« of the Germanic nations. In fact, Söderblom has so frequently given expression to his fondness of French culture and language, amiability and sense of humor, that any kind of anti-French »racism« would rightly have seemed quite absurd to him.

The Söderbloms also met many Scandinavian artists in Paris and fre-

---

[13] Cf., e.g., his lecture *Die Religion und die soziale Entwicklung* (SgV 10), Freiburg 1898.
[14] *Jesu bärgspredikan och vår tid. En undersökning*, Stockholm 1898.

quently had them as their guests. One of them was August Strindberg who was in a very sad condition at that time and was clandestinely supported by Söderblom [10]. With others like the painter Anders Zorn (1860–1920) or the sculptor Carl Milles (1875–1955) he later continued to communicate in Sweden.

Another important personality Söderblom became acquainted with in France and held in high esteem was Alfred Loisy (1857–1940), the leading Roman Catholic modernist who had been excommunicated by the Vatican.[15] Söderblom respected Loisy for his scholarly achievements and his courageous stand, and Loisy's fate inspired him to write the book *Religionsproblemet i katolicism och protestantism* (Stockholm 1910), the larger part of which is a sympathetic yet critical account of modernism.[16]

Söderblom's theological reasoning did not make things easy for him at home. The ultra-orthodox pastor Elis Daniel Heümann (1859–1908) published a wildly polemical paper on Ritschl and his Swedish followers which had come to Söderblom's eyes in Paris. He wrote a pointed rebuke which laid bare the fundamental weakness of that article. The immediate consequence was that Söderblom was prevented from publishing his own articles in the conservative periodical *Kyrklig Tidskrift* and considered founding an independent »yearbook« with his friends [12]. Meanwhile, conservative circles in Sweden campaigned for Söderblom's removal from his post – unsuccessfully. All the while, Söderblom was no uncritical partisan of Ritschl. He never shared the latter's negative view of all mysticism, and he deplored Ritschl's bourgeois mindset which led to his complete lack of religious fervor and enthusiasm and to his intolerance regarding the piety of Francis of Assisi, much as he continued to appreciate the liberating effect that Ritschl's view of revelation had had upon him [15]. He remained true to both his pietistic heritage and his newly won insights with regard to the social problems of his time.

Apart from his professional duties, Söderblom made extensive use of the opportunities the Sorbonne had to offer. He pursued his reading in ancient Persian under Antoine Meillet (1866–1936) and studied history of religion under Albert Réville (1826–1906), and he got in contact with some of the leading historians of religion abroad, such as Pierre Daniel Chantepie de la Saussaye (1848–1920) in Amsterdam and Cornelius Petrus Tiele (1832–1902) in Leiden, the third and fourth editions of whose *Kompendium der Religionsgeschichte* he later revised and re-edited.[17] Together with his friend, Samuel Fries, he organized a conference on the history of religion in Stockholm in 1897. He also attended lectures and seminars at the Protestant theological faculty. Beside the Lutheran systematic theologian Eugène

---

[15] For the letters exchanged by the two men included in the present selection, see the index.
[16] *Religionsproblemet inom katolicism och protestantism*, Stockholm 1910. Its second chapter, dealing with John Henry Newman, was translated into French and appeared in *FV* 16/1913, 242. 248. 266–276.
[17] Breslau 1903, Berlin 1912.

Ménégoz (1838–1921) and Paul Sabatier (1858–1928), the biographer of St. Francis,[18] it was above all the Reformed systematic theologian Auguste Sabatier (1839–1901) who impressed him. It was he under whom Söderblom was to take his doctorate. When Sabatier published his *Esquisse d'une philosophie de la religion d'après la psychologie et l'histoire* in 1897, Söderblom's comments were enthusiastic [8. 14], and he immediately translated it into Swedish. Sabatier had a wide range of interests as an *homme de lettres*, reaching far beyond his field of theology; he made a name for himself also as a preacher and a journalist. There are two things which Söderblom particularly appreciated in his thought: the concept of religion as a prayer of the heart, and the conviction that religious propositions are always symbolic. This symbolo-fideism of the Paris school not only supported Söderblom's liberal theological views and his ecumenical open-mindedness, but also, as Andrae rightly points out, his strong inclination, exhibited especially in his later years as archbishop, to preserve organically grown traditions.[19] This latter trait later formed an important bridge to the Anglican church and to British mentality in general. He did find Sabatier somewhat too rational and too little essentially religious in the sense of »Germanic« depth [8. 9. 24], and lacking a concept of revelation which for Söderblom was basic. That did not, however, detract from his reverence for the man and his achievement.

Söderblom finished his doctoral thesis in the year 1900 – after having published a preliminary study on ancient Iranian ideas of death, *Les fravashis*, in 1898 [24] – and passed his exams with distinction. The programmatic title of the dissertation *La vie future d'après le mazdéisme à la lumière des croyances parallèles dans les autres religions*[20] announces a study not only on ancient Iran but on comparative religion. The second part of each chapter adduces a wide array of examples from most of the world's major religions. In this fashion, the book represents the first specimen of a phenomenology of religion which was to become Söderblom's main contribution to the field. His overriding concern was to point out the strengths of each religion, yet at the same time to demonstrate the superiority of the prophetic religions (including Mazdaism) in general, with their basic contrast between good and evil, and of the Christian religion in particular.[21] The study therefore reaches its climax in Jesus' message of eternal life beginning in the present, and in the treatment of Luther in its last chapter. Here Söderblom discovered the dialectic of judgment and grace, despair and trust, as essential for Luther – and in the final analysis, for any religion. This is another step towards a more theocentric kind of theology respectively theory of religion as compared to his earlier book on Luther. There he had been quite aware of

---

[18] On him, cf. letters no. 14 and 22.
[19] Op. cit., 124.
[20] Paris 1901.
[21] Cf. Andrae, »Nathan Söderblom som religionens historiker,« in: *Nathan Söderblom in memoriam*, ed. by N. Karlström, Stockholm 1931 (25–62), 49.

religion being a sense of the »unconditional« (II 4), an experience initiated by God rather than agreement to doctrine to be achieved by human reason (a contention he shared with Harnack and Wilhelm Herrmann), but at that time he had little to say about the »hidden God« (*Deus absconditus*), according to Ritschl an unfortunate nominalistic relic in Luther's thought.[22]

Meanwhile, word had come to Paris that J. A. Ekman had abandoned the chair of history of religion in Uppsala for the episcopacy of Västerås (and later the archsee in Uppsala). Söderblom applied for his succession and easily won the nomination as the best contender. So a new phase of his life began as a professor of »Theological prenotions and encyclopedia«, which was the somewhat weird-sounding designation of that chair. It had been founded in 1877 and was meant to comprise philosophy of religion, theology in comparison to other sciences, and the recent and still suspiciously eyed discipline of history of religion.

Söderblom's inaugural lecture on general history of religion and church theology of Sept. 24, 1901,[23] has rightly been called a milestone. Swedish theology did not have a significant role to play in the great debates of the day. It was almost totally dependent on German »imports«, the liberal part of which (Ritschl, Harnack) as well as the whole phalanx of critical exegetes met with fierce opposition by powerful conservative circles, in Uppsala more so than in Lund. This made Christian faith and modern theological research appear well-nigh incompatible. So theology did not seem an overly attractive field of study.

The lecture began by stating that religion cannot be understood without religious experience. That is the common ground of history of religion and theology. Now religion needs a supporting community. One obligation of that community is to develop doctrinal guidelines. Therefore, the question arises whether or not allegiance to a religion is compatible with its being subjected to scientific scrutiny. Söderblom's answer is an unequivocal yes. He agrees with Luther that freedom of thought is part and parcel of the Christian faith, and contends with Schleiermacher and Harnack that there is but one truth. Scientific research and religious devotion converge in their humble respect for reality – a central motif in Söderblom's thought.[24] This can be demonstrated, he continues, by the fact that recent research in the history of religion has tremendously enhanced the understanding of the essence and uniqueness of the Christian religion and the person of Jesus Christ.

This is why Söderblom strongly favors the inclusion of history of religion

---

[22] Albrecht Ritschl, »Geschichtliche Studien zur christlichen Lehre von Gott,« 2nd article, in: A. R., *GAufs* NF, Freiburg / Leipzig 1896, 65–107, esp. 84 f.

[23] »Den allmänna religionshistorien och den kyrkliga teologien, jämte Ord till de teologie studerande,« in: Nathan Söderblom, *Om studiet av religionen*, Lund 1951, 13–48.

[24] *Om studiet …*, p. 46. Cf. later: *Tre livsformer. Mystik, förtröstan, vetenskap*, Stockholm 1922, 104. 106 f. 116. 119 f. Scientific research has religious implications and is even called a kind of worship, ib. 123.

in the theological faculty, diverging in this point from Harnack who in his rector's address just a couple of months previously had pleaded firmly for that field to be part of the humanities.[25] Harnack's reasons were, that the sheer amount of material encompassed by the world religions and their respective cultural contexts would make their inclusion in the theological faculty unmanageable. Even more important for him was his belief that Christianity is the religion *par excellence* which contains all essential elements of religion in their most perfect form, so that anyone who understands Christianity will understand all religions (168), quite apart from the fact that the field of ancient oriental religions had become an indispensable part of Biblical studies anyway. Söderblom, however, wants the superiority of Christianity, in which he too believes, demonstrated by methodical comparison, while preserving the respect for alien traditions, for the good both of foreign missions and the educated class at home.[26] This implies both a more positive valuation of other religions than Harnack's more Ritschlian point of view can concede, and a greater significance of the missionary aspect. In this way Söderblom's effort to gain an overall picture of the history of religion by means of the phenomenological method supersedes even his lively interest in the collective individuality of each single religion – and seems to have made him feel immune to Harnack's warning of overcrowding the field of theological studies.

In his concluding »Word to the Students of Theology,« Söderblom congratulated them on their choice of study and encouraged them wholeheartedly to delve into »more, not less« scientific research, in spite of the religious crises they might have to go through, and he congratulated them on having chosen the service in the church as their profession. It was an inspiring address which did not fail to impress the listeners.

However, this did not go down well with the conservative majority of the faculty. Söderblom's rapport with his immediate colleagues remained limited, and he conversed far more with the luminaries in the humanities. The theologians did not nominate Söderblom's friend Samuel Fries, an outstanding exegetical scholar, to the vacant chair of New Testament in 1902 because they considered him too liberal, and the excellent doctoral thesis of his disciple Torgny Segerstedt on *The Origin of Polytheism* was rejected in 1903 because of a lack of »Christian substance«[27] – a scandal that for a while made Söderblom seriously consider resigning. Nonetheless – or even because of this – his lectures quickly became a magnet for the students.[28] The designation of his chair provided him with the liberty of covering a

---

[25] Adolf von Harnack, »Die Aufgaben der theologischen Fakultät und die allgemeine Religionsgeschichte, nebst einem Nachwort« (1901), in: A. v. H., *Reden und Aufsätze*, vol. 2, 2nd ed. Gießen 1906, 159–187.

[26] That reminiscence of Schleiermacher's *On Religion. Speeches to its Cultured Despisers* is no coincidence. Söderblom had lectured on its centenary in Uppsala two years previously.

[27] Cf. letter no. 40, n. 3.

[28] Cf. the lively description in Andrae's biography, 137–141.

wide variety of subjects, and he used it extensively, lecturing not only on the history and philosophy of religion, but also on the history of Swedish theology and on Luther. In all of this Söderblom was never exclusively dependent on German theology but opened the window to other European traditions, and in doing so, began to develop an original concept of his own.

Söderblom's first significant literary contribution in his new post was his little book *Uppenbarelsereligion.*[29] It was occasioned by the Bible-Babel debate of those years. Its thesis is that God reveals himself in all religions, but that this is more clearly the case in prophetic religions of history (among which also Zoroastrianism is counted) than in religions of nature or of culture, and most clearly of all in Jesus Christ. This categorical distinction between different kinds of religions is spelled out in a subordinate differentiation with regard to mysticism. A »mysticism of infinity,« absorbing the individual in the infinite as in Buddhism but also Hellenism, is juxtaposed to a »mysticism of personal life«, where the voice of the prophet summons the individual person to make religious and ethical decisions between good and evil. Here the religious geniuses play a pivotal role (an idea indebted to the romantic thinkers Erik Gustaf Geijer and Friedrich Schleiermacher). In this context, the revelation in Christ is considered final; yet it continues in subsequent »heroes«, particularly in Martin Luther.

In *Religionsproblemet inom katolicism och protestantism*, that distinction of two kinds of mysticism is supplemented by another one referring to the doctrine of justification by faith alone. That is the distinction between a »mysticism of exercise« by which the believer tries to approach God by means of ascetic endeavor, and »mysticism of conscience« according to which union with God is effected by God alone. The one is represented by Ignatius of Loyola, the other by Luther.[30]

Obviously, Söderblom had taken up here Auguste Sabatier's idea of the *Dieu intérieur*, but he developed it further and used it to repudiate Ritschl's wholesale rejection of mysticism. As it turned out, however, in the larger theological arena this proposal of Söderblom did not prevent the problematic yet far-reaching influence of Ritschl's diehard position in this matter which lasted throughout the period of the Dialectical theology and beyond.

Equally important, if not more so, is Söderblom's introduction of the category of holiness, years before Rudolf Otto wrote his famous book on the subject.[31] The Holy is the mysterious power of the transcendent affecting the human soul in seemingly contradictory ways, a reality which is at the

---

[29] Cf. note 6.

[30] *Religionsproblemet* (as in n. 16), 273. 281.

[31] Rudolf Otto, *Das Heilige*, Breslau 1917(English tr. *The Idea of the Holy* by J. W. Harvey, Oxford 1923, 2nd ed. 1950); Nathan Söderblom, Art. Holiness, *ERE* 6 (1913), 731–741; *Naturlig religion och religionshistoria*, Stockholm 1914 (German ed. *Natürliche Religion und Religionsgeschichte*, 1913).

same time inaccessible and inescapable.[32] This category was in Söderblom's view the hub of the phenomenology of religion that he had initiated, and all psychology and sociology of religion had to revolve around it.

Apart from his research and his teaching duties, Söderblom also was a prebendary at medieval *Trefaldighetskyrkan* (Trinity Church) in the vicinity of Uppsala's cathedral. During these years this church saw, as did the chapel of *La Charité* in Berlin in Schleiermacher's time, many an academic who had otherwise never dreamed of attending a worship service. Among his pastoral duties Söderblom also counted being a chaplain to his students. His manse in the suburb of Staby always was an open house. Every Monday evening students would meet there, discussing literature and burning issues of the time, singing and playing music. That manse thus became one of Uppsala's most important intellectual centers at the time.

Söderblom's ecclesiastical activities also involved him in the influential endeavor at renewing the Swedish folk church, the so-called Young Church Movement (*ungkyrkorörelse*), founded by Manfred Björkquist (1884–1985), bishop Johan Alfred Eklund (1863–1945), and Einar Billing among Uppsala students of theology in 1908, which was Lutheranism's positive reaction to the revival movement of the 19th century and the resulting inroads by the Free Churches, as well as to the rising tide of an aggressive anti-Christian materialism, inspired by the Uppsala philosopher Axel Hägerström (1868–1939). That church movement to which Söderblom gave his active if not unqualified support, soon took hold of the entire Swedish church and gained considerable influence on the culture of the country, especially after it had found its center at Sigtuna near Stockholm where church-sponsored conferences on urgent religious, cultural, and political problems continue to be held to this day.

Söderblom's reservations concern certain nationalistic tendencies in parts of the movement. His own initiatives regarding the church counterbalanced them by attempting to widen its international perspective. Three events stand out: One is the establishment of the Olaus-Petri-Foundation in 1907, funded by an endowment bequeathed by a wealthy lady. Its purpose is twofold: providing young students of theology with scholarships for study abroad in order to give them the opportunity to become acquainted with non-Christian religions, and inviting foreign scholars for guest lectures in Uppsala. Under Söderblom's aegis, this institution became the veritable counterpart to the famous Gifford lectures at Edinburgh. Scholars of world renown like Franz Cumont, Adolf Deißmann, Rudolf Eucken, Ignaz Goldziher, Adolf von Harnack, Friedrich Heiler, Rudolf Otto were invited by him.

The second point concerns the rapprochement with the Anglican communion which Söderblom pursued – not without resistance in his own church and in the Augustana Synod, the church of Swedish Lutherans in America.

---

[32] *Naturlig religion* …, 112 (109 in the German edition).

It was the initiation of a long process, beginning with a visit of Söderblom in England (the occasion was a conference on the history of religion in Oxford) in 1908 and an English delegation coming to Uppsala in the following year, leading up to the agreement on intercommunion between the two churches in 1922. This link, personified particularly by the Archbishop of Canterbury, Randall Davidson (1848-1930), proved to be an important part of Söderblom's ecumenical endeavor.

In the third place, we have to mention the conference of the World Student Christian Federation in Constantinople in 1911. There were orthodox students among the participants, and Söderblom became acquainted with Strenopoulos Germanos, director of the theological school at Halki and later metropolitan of Thyateira, who was to become one of his most important connections to the world of Greek orthodoxy. He also met John Mott, the Scottish theologian David S. Cairns, and many others who were likewise important collaborators in his later ecumenical efforts.

In the same year of 1911, a change in Söderblom's life on a different plane was foreshadowed by a visit of the Leipzig church historian Albert Hauck to Uppsala. This visit resulted in the call to the new chair of history of religion in Leipzig.[33] Söderblom accepted, on condition of keeping up his Uppsala position simultaneously. So he moved to Germany with his family in 1912. He had always held German literature, music, and intellectual tradition in high regard; after all, German culture had formed a significant part of his own education. So he does not seem to have had much of a problem acclimatizing. His inspiring way of teaching received an enthusiastic echo from many an able student. He also won friends among his colleagues. So in a way, he seems to have felt at home in this country. Yet at the same time, he utterly detested the rampant German nationalism of the time as downright idolatrous [54.58.64 f.].[34]

Leipzig saw two important publications. In *Naturlig religion och religionshistoria*, he expounds his idea of the history of religion as being constituted by God's revelations. There is no such thing as the Enlightenment's so-called natural religion, but only different ways of God's revealing his holiness in history, most clearly in the prophetic religions and culminating in the revelation in Christ (which is then considered absolute by faith, though not by science, 91). This being in large part a concise summary of his fundamental view of the essence of religion thus far developed, the other book is perhaps his greatest scholarly achievement: *Das Werden des Gottesglaubens*.[35] In it, Söderblom distinguishes three main types of religion: animism, the religion of Mana or power, and what he calls the religion of the originator. All of these exist simultaneously in various parts of the world, repre-

---

[33] Söderblom's name had previously been put on the list for a corresponding chair in Berlin, but the call had then gone out to Edvard Lehmann of Copenhagen instead [48. 49. 51. 52].

[34] Cf. also the article »De två gudarne,« in: *Vår lösen* 5/1914; enlarged version in his *När stundarna växla och skrida* Stockholm 1915, 118-130 ([2]1921: 124-136).

[35] *Das Werden des Gottesglaubens*, Leipzig 1916 (*Gudstrons uppkomst*, Stockholm 1914).

senting separate developments. This is a rebuke not only to the idea of an original monotheism that Wilhelm Schmidt had advocated,[36] but to any kind of theory deriving all religions from a single root. Rather, he views them as independent collective individualities, all of which contain elements of truth, and, as Tor Andrae rightly says, he then tries to mediate between them, being »a true ecumenic« even in his special field of research.[37] He does this by analyzing and comparing similar phenomena occurring in quite different cultural environments. That effort is reminiscent of his earlier book *La vie future*, but it is now based on a much broader foundation. So it is this later book which may be called the birth of the new discipline of phenomenology of religion.

Söderblom's academic career abruptly ended in 1914, due to a surprising development in his home church. On November 30, 1913, Archbishop Johan August Ekman of Uppsala had died. As his successor, Söderblom's name was one of those proposed. But in the election, he ended up a poor fourth, far behind the other three (the first place was shared by two candidates with an identical number of votes). Yet he had a strong supporter in the cabinet, Karl Gustaf Westman, the secretary of ecclesiastical affairs. On his advice the King appointed Söderblom, to the great dismay of conservative circles in the Swedish church, on May 20, 1914. So Söderblom knew that he would have to leave Leipzig at the end of the summer term of 1914. In the event, however, his departure had to be arranged in unexpected haste and under dramatic circumstances: War had broken out on August 1.

Even before his return to Sweden, Söderblom had taken part in the founding conference of the World Alliance for Promoting International Friendship through the Churches, a pacifist organization that was to become one of the germs of the ecumenical movement, in Constance (Konstanz), Germany, on the very day the war began. As soon as he was back in Sweden, one of the first measures of the archbishop-elect was to write the draft of a peace appeal. It was signed by the Scandinavian bishops and published at the end of November – not long after his consecration [75] – and promptly drew fire from both German and French quarters [79–81. 83. 86f.]. His position towards the belligerent nations was strictly neutral. However, this was not a silent but an outspoken neutrality, putting him between a rock and a hard place. At the outset of the war, he had a certain sympathy with the German point of view [69. 71. 72]. That may have to do with the old Swedish fear of the Russians, now Germany's enemies.[38] But soon he was greatly disappointed by a nationalistic appeal to Christians abroad issued by German intellectuals [85]. He also severely and repeatedly criticized the violation of Belgian neutrality and the sinking of the British passenger vessel Lusitania by the Germans, as well as their policy of

---

[36] Wilhelm Schmidt, *Der Ursprung der Gottesidee*, 12 vols., Münster 1912–1955.
[37] Tor Andrae, »Nathan Söderblom som religionens historiker« (cf. n. 21), 39f.
[38] Cf. Sundkler, *Nathan Söderblom*, 177.

scorched earth in Northern France. This was often held against him by Germans, whereas French and English nationals found fault with one of his sons having served in the German army – not being aware that his father had tried to dissuade him [89. 128. 130. 135. 207 n. 5]. Later on, Söderblom in no uncertain terms disapproved of the Versailles peace treaty of 1919 which crippled the German economy [284 n. 2], and of the French occupation of the Rhine and Ruhr area in 1923 which, as he astutely observed, bore in it the seed of a new war [195. 200. 207 n. 5],[39] but also repudiated the view of some German Lutherans that war was inevitable in principle [305]. He considered such public statements an essential part of his calling as a churchman. Theologically, Luther's doctrine of the two governances for him never meant a separation of spiritual and wordly affairs but their careful distinction as two aspects of one and the same Kingdom of God.[40]

Söderblom did not limit his peace activities to criticism of the war and its atrocities. He sent emissaries to prisoner-of-war camps in Russia and Germany, in close cooperation with the Swedish Red Cross. In 1917, when the United States entered the war and Russia was shaken up by its revolution, a silver lining seemed to appear on the horizon. Pope Benedict XV. admonished the belligerent nations to terminate hostilities. Söderblom immediately intensified his contacts with Quakers and other pacifist churchmen in Britain, and he was instrumental in issuing a renewed peace appeal by the World Alliance. And when the war was finally over, he in a way reactivated his Paris practice as his congregation's »premium beggar« by organizing relief efforts on a grand scale, such as inviting starved Austrian and German children to Sweden for recovery, starting in 1919 [154. 157. 158. 197].

Closer to home, the end of the war coincided with sharp socialist polemics against the Swedish church. The party program of the Social Democrats of 1920 demanded its separation from the state. Söderblom apparently did not consider this the right time for such a far-reaching measure, let alone under these auspices [132]. More importantly, he was of the opinion that a state church of the kind that existed in Sweden was a setup advantageous for everyone concerned, provided it would be able to retain its independence with regard to its internal affairs. For it was able to prevent the church from becoming a narrow-minded sect, and the state from succumbing to nationalistic idolatry [50].[41] Anyway, Söderblom succeeded in defusing the situation, among other things by a general church conference to which he invited leading Social Democrats like the new prime minister Hjalmar Branting and Fabian Månsson, a friend of his, to speak. How

---

[39] This was also the subject of an international appeal, issued by the Swedish bishops on Söderblom's initiative.

[40] He considered that Luther's original intention, though he thought that Luther had at times been inconsistent in his adherence to it, particularly in the Peasants' War of 1525; cf. Söderblom's most important book on Luther, *Humor och melankoli och andra Lutherstudier*, Stockholm 1919, 339–358.

[41] Cf. Nathan Söderblom, *Religionen och staten*, Stockholm 1918, 81–110. 183. 190–201.

firmly he was convinced of the Swedish model can be illustrated by his attempt at persuading the German emperor to introduce the office (not just the title) of bishop into the German church [106. 108. 111. 112]. The emperor was in no mood to give up his position as *summus episcopus*, as one could have expected. It is a tempting thought, however, to speculate on the golden opportunities the German churches might have had if Söderblom's advances had been crowned with success. The mere fact that he made this attempt, albeit with the slim chances of a foreigner, shows how deeply he must have felt the dangers the German system entailed for the church.

Even before that, Söderblom had begun to formulate the basic tenets of his theory of the church.[42] If the message of the Gospel has universal relevance, the church is essentially one in faith. That is the starting point. This essential unity consists in the Word of God on which it is founded and which is directed, first of all, to the individual person.[43] Of course, the church needs a »body«, in order to be effective as a social institution in this world.[44] This does not imply, however, that its unity should also be one of doctrine and church organization. On the contrary, that is (at least in the short and medium term) not even a desirable goal, because it could only be an enforced uniformity.[45] That would in effect be the model envisaged by the Vatican Council of 1870, unacceptable to all non-Roman churches [280]. The Swedish archbishop sometimes pointedly adds with Loisy that Jesus announced the Kingdom of God and did not found a church.[46] We simply have to acknowledge, he says, that the universality, or in his own terminology, the catholicity, of the church has taken on three different forms in the course of history: the Eastern Orthodox, the Roman, and the Evangelic[47] (Protestant) form, the latter being characterized by belief in justification by faith alone [97. 248. 263. 280]. These historically grown types of Christianity cannot be lumped together or amalgamated, neither can the way to visual unity be paved by some sort of compromise. Rather, visualized unity can for the foreseeable future only be one of practical cooperation in confronting the challenges of the modern world, particularly those arising from the material and spiritual misery caused by the war.[48]

---

[42] Cf. *Svenska kyrkans kropp och själ* (cf. n.6); »Evangelisk katolicitet,« in: *Kyrkans enhet* 7/1919, 65–126; »Evangelische Katholizität,« in: *FS Deißmann*, Tübingen 1927, 327–334.

[43] Cf. »Katolicitet« (as in n.42), 100. 110. 115.

[44] »Katolicitet,« 77 f. 115. Söderblom insists that the »body« belongs to the outward, worldly appearance of the church; it should correspond to its »soul« but is by no means identical with it, *Svenskars fromhet*, Stockholm 1933, 34.

[45] *Svenska kyrkan* ..., 142; »Katolicitet« (cf. n.42), 72. The limitation in parentheses reflects his position in his later years; cf. , e. g., his *Christliche Einheit!*, Berlin 1928, 70).

[46] *Svenska kyrkan* ..., 74. Cf. Alfred Loisy, *L'évangile et l'église* (1902), 5th ed. Paris 1930, 153.

[47] This is the English form Söderblom chose as translation of the Swedish *evangelisk* and the German *evangelisch*, because the English term »evangelical« denotes a narrow conservatism, an interpretation Söderblom wanted to avoid. Cf. Sundkler, op. cit. 263 f.

[48] Söderblom is here taking up a suggestion by Adolf von Harnack comparing the churches in the world to people inhabiting different homes in a garden which it is their common task to

Beyond that, the different churches can only coexist in peaceful contest (*tävlan*), true to their respective heritages, and respecting those of the others.[49]

After the World War, this ecclesiological outline in Söderblom's mind gradually took on a more concrete shape. That was his vision of a »League of Churches« as a spiritual analogy to the League of Nations. It was an idea soon to become common in World Alliance circles; it had already been promoted by the Holy Synod in Constantinople in 1919 when it decided (unsuccessfully) to convene a universal ecumenical conference with precisely that analogy in mind [141. 302].[50] Later that year, the idea of founding an »ecumenical council of churches« for the first time occurs in one of Söderblom's letters [144].[51] In a characteristic turn of his theological thought, he even hoped that such a church body could become something like a religious inspiration (»soul«) for the League of Nations [134]. Not surpisingly, as the parable of the leaven had always been one of his favorites.

Söderblom was quite aware of the fact that his concept of church unity, allowing as it did for a wide variety in both doctrine and church administration, was based on specifically Protestant presuppositions.[52] This acknowledgment did not deter him, however, from energetically pursuing his ecumenical endeavors; on the contrary, it reassured him that it was the specific task of Protestantism to lead the flock along the road to unity in Christian freedom. It should be noted though that this is all the more remarkable since the universal scope of this vision far exceeded anything his fellow Lutherans had hitherto dared to imagine.[53]

It was even before the end of the war that Söderblom planned his first invitation to an ecumenical conference. That was as early as December 14, 1917. Obviously the portents were not favorable at the time. Two more attempts were made during the year 1918. But both the difficulty of obtaining the permission for members of the belligerent nations to travel abroad and, even more so, prevailing wartime emotions thwarted these plans and caused them to be shelved until the conclusion of peace [113. 114. 119. 124].

Anyone reading about all these activities might be inclined to think that Söderblom must have neglected his specific duties as archbishop of his dio-

---

keep in good shape: »Protestantismus und Katholizismus in Deutschland« [1907], in: A. v. H., *Aus Wissenschaft und Leben*, vol. 1, Gießen 1911, 225–250; id., »Über den sogenannten ›Consensus quinquesaecularis‹ als Grundlage der Wiedervereinigung der Kirchen,« in: *Die Eiche* 13/1925, Sonderheft, 287–299 (also in: A. v. H., *Reden und Aufsätze* N. F. 5. *Aus der Werkstatt des Vollendeten*, ed. by Axel v. Harnack, Gießen 1930, 65–83). Cf. letter no. 251.

[49] *Svenska kyrkans kropp och själ*, (cf. n. 6) 58. Sundkler, *Nathan Söderblom*, 51. 69, has shown that this term is an adaptation of an idea fundamental to Benjamin Kidd's *Social Evolution*, London 1894.

[50] It is hard to tell whether the priority belongs to the members of the Synod or to Söderblom who first conceived the idea of a League of Churches in the same year; cf. »Katolicitet,« 119, and Sundkler, op. cit. 219. 248.

[51] Cf. also Sundkler, op. cit. 236.

[52] »Evangelische Katholizität« (cf. n. 42), 332.

[53] Cf. Sundkler, op. cit., 253 f.

cese. Nothing could be farther from the truth. Nor is it true that his introduction of colorful liturgical vestments replacing the traditional black gowns in any way stood in the foreground of his endeavors, as his detractors would have it. Crucial in his episcopal work were church inspections. Witnesses are unanimous in relating that his outspokenness, his personal charm, and his knack for encouraging people hardly ever failed to make a lasting impact on the congregations he visited. This may be underscored by an oft-reported anecdote. At one of those inspections, the pastor complained that he was working himself to death. »Well, that is completely all right,« Söderblom replied kindly but unmoved. »A pastor is *supposed* to be working himself to death – but slowly please, and with good sense!«

As for the guiding principles of his episcopal activities, one has to refer to Söderblom's close association with the Young Church Movement mentioned above. The renewal of the Swedish church was high on his agenda. True to the liberal part of his theological convictions, he wanted the church to open up to the secular world around her, and especially to tackle the urgent social problems created by an economy in the process of industrialization. At the same time, his pietistic heritage and his firm grounding in Lutheran theology convinced him that the church is not primarily a social agency but a religious institution, and therefore its first and foremost duty is to proclaim the Gospel. The sermon thus rightly is the center of the worship service. But the Lutheran church must beware of becoming a one-sidedly intellectual institution. This is why Söderblom considered an elaborate sung liturgy so important, a revised hymnal, colorful vestments: all of that was to be a vivid expression of the joy of faith. Basically, there was to be a close-knit interrelation of the three traditional tasks of the church, *martyria, leiturgia, diakonia*, which so easily drift apart.

In all of this, the archbishop more and more came to appreciate time-honored traditions. This is not just a sign of an age-related conservatism, still less of the kind of insidious clericalism so easily encroaching on high church officials in the course of time. Rather, it has to be seen in the context of Auguste Sabatier's symbolo-fideism that had so strongly influenced Söderblom: Even the church of the Word needs palpable symbols, and those which tradition provides should not lightheartedly be discarded unless their message is incompatible with Protestant Christendom.

Two more general remarks are in order at this point. One is the tribute due to Mrs. Anna Söderblom. With her husband completely absorbed by his professional work and ever so often gone for business to be pursued out of town, it was she who was primarily in charge of their large family and of the open house they continued to have as they had done in Paris. This must have involved an immense amount of work in spite of the servants it was common to have at the time. Nonetheless, Mrs. Söderblom not only saw to her household duties but also was her husband's reliable and independent intellectual partner, the most important critic of many of his speeches and sermons. It has often been said that he would never have been what he was without the support of his wife who certainly was a great personality in her own right.

The second thing to be mentioned here is the fact that Söderblom, for all his sense of the dignity of his high office, neither lost his common touch nor limited his interests to matters strictly ecclesiastical. He never hesitated to support a needy individual, be it by giving advice, money, or just a helping hand. Literally hundreds of anecdotes to that effect were circulating in Sweden at the time which cannot be reproduced here. On the other hand, his speeches and articles in periodicals and newspapers secured him a wide audience, and through the office of pro-chancellor of Uppsala university that a Swedish archbishop automatically holds, he also remained in close contact with academia. He had emerged early on as one of the leading figures in the Swedish intelligentsia. One sign of recognition of his far-flung intellectual activities was his appointment to the Swedish Academy in 1921.

Meanwhile, Söderblom continued his efforts toward an international ecumenical conference. At the meeting of the World Alliance in Oud Wassenaar, Netherlands, in October, 1919, the delegates were very much in favor of his suggestion although it was not within their authority to decide anything in this matter. Moreover, at a conference of the Faith and Order movement in Uppsala in June of that year, a controversy had arisen with regard to the overall ecumenical goals, which had to be ironed out. Söderblom, true to his own idea of ecumenicity, had pleaded for focusing on practical cooperation of the churches, leaving their differences of doctrine and forms of administration untouched. This could serve, he said, as a preparation for a universal conference on Faith and Order. The opponents were primarily Anglicans who stressed the importance of the sacraments and the apostolic succession for any kind of church unity. Then in August of 1920, no fewer than three relevant meetings took place in Geneva, all of which Söderblom attended: one organized by himself which then came to be called Life and Work, and immediately afterwards Faith and Order, as well as the World Alliance. At the first one, he was able to present the draft of a program for a »Universal Conference«, and a preparatory committee was formed for its implementation. His opponents were virtually absent here, and the Faith and Order meeting seems to have realized that its project was more long-term. Anyway, Söderblom succeeded in establishing the priority of Life and Work. The rift between the two factions of the ecumenical movement was not completely healed, but it did not prevent either Anglicans from coming to the great Life and Work conference in Stockholm in 1925 (though the Archbishop of Canterbury was conspicuously absent) or Söderblom from taking part in the Faith and Order conference in Lausanne 1927. The issues at stake acquired new relevance long after Söderblom's death, when at the end of the century Lutherans and Roman Catholics had entered talks on doctrinal union – but that lies beyond the scope of the present introduction.

It seems safe to assert that without Söderblom's decidedly Protestant vision, the ecumenical movement never would have come off the ground. Yet in spite of the solution reached within the ecumenical movement itself, the road to Stockholm proved to be long and arduous. The outward obstacles posed by the war had been removed. But the thorny question of which nation had caused it, still loomed large. The Versailles peace treaty of 1919 demanded that the Germans accept full responsibility. They in turn placed the guilt squarely on the Allies. Thus, wartime nationalistic feelings, which had been fueling hate sermons in the churches on either side, continued to smolder and even flare up time and again, and in Germany were further aggravated by the French occupation of the Ruhr area. This whole complex involved Söderblom in a frantic swell of correspondence not only with church leaders but also with leading statesmen of the Western world. It took his enormous diplomatic skills to persuade some of the most important churchmen, the persisting problems notwithstanding, to concur with his plan that he hoped would make a significant contribution to reconciliation between the churches and the nations. One condition that he pushed through and that proved to be vital for the conference to take place at all was that the question of guilt with regard to the war be excluded from the agenda and left for the political institutions to decide.

Another difficulty besetting this preparatory stage was the relationship to Roman Catholicism. The Eastern Orthodox church had, as was mentioned above, launched an inititative of its own and thus was easy to win over, particularly since Söderblom had been able to establish close personal contact to leading members of the hierarchy such as the Patriarch of Alexandria, Photios I. Perioglou. That in turn helped to overcome a certain hesitation on the part of some Anglican leaders. As for Rome, Söderblom did prevail in his determination to invite the Vatican to send delegates, over strong initial opposition in the preparatory committee. But the Pope was not in the position to overcome his principal objections to the whole enterprise. The declaration of infallibility of the papacy at the Vatican Council of 1870 and the subsequent struggle against the modernist movement within the church, ending with the excommunication of its chief representatives, had hardened the exclusive claim to being the one true church of Christ. In addition, Söderblom's own friendly relations with Loisy and other modernists, as well as his forthright criticism of the Roman Catholic understanding of the authority of the church in his earlier book *Religionsproblemet*, did not recommend him personally to the Pope as a negotiator.[54] So the replies to the two invitations of 1918 and 1921 [115. 176] given by Cardinal Gasparri [120. 179] were formal and evasive, and the explicit answer Pius XI. gave in his Encyclical *Mortalium animos* of 1928 [cf. 302], three years after the conference, was crystal clear in its rejection of the idea of an »evangelic catholicity« as a viable principle of any kind of ecumenical accord.

Nonetheless, the first great and truly comprehensive ecumenical conference finally did come about in Stockholm in 1925. This feat is above all else one of Söderblom's persistent and indefatigable endeavors in prodding the

---

[54] Cf. letter no. 212: he knew he was in disrepute, »illa anskriven«, in Rome.

reluctant, encouraging the hesitant, stimulating the cooperative. It was his active part in virtually every aspect of the preparations and his communicative genius and empathy for each single participant, as well as his skill in bridging contrary positions, that had the lion's share in making the conference a success. The letters of this time bear this out with such clarity that it does not seem necessary to name examples here. The driving force behind all this was his assured hope that, as a result of the war and its concomitant misery, a renewal of religion was under way in the Western world. To be more precise, he was expecting a renewal of Christianity as a religion of the Cross which would sever the church's ties to the worldly power of the state that had so fatefully entangled it in the nets of nationalism and implicated it in the war activities.[55] The situation of severe crisis was indeed conducive to such a development, as can be shown by the large variety of fresh starts in religious life in general and in church and theology in particular that these momentous years produced. In fact, it is not far-fetched to view the Stockholm conference itself as one of the features of this new religious awareness that Söderblom had been hoping for. The long-term prospects of this hope need not be discussed here; Söderblom can, of course, not be held accountable for not having presaged the formidable advances of secularism unfolding in the second half of the century.

Contemporary comments on the Stockholm conference were full of praise, but there was also severe criticism. Not only the Vatican but also ultra-conservative Protestants like Gustaf Johansson, the Finnish archbishop, decried it for lacking in genuine Christian substance [227. 230]. In actual fact, nothing could be farther from the truth. The catchword of a »Nicaea of Christian Ethics« which became the favorite epithet of Stockholm early on, as well as the dominance of ethical topics on its agenda, obviously had a misleading effect. But for one thing, this conference was, after all, on Life and Work, not on Faith and Order! Moreover, the basic significance of salvation through Christ was invoked at the worship services, which were an integral part of the conference, and at many other occasions. Of particularly high symbolic value were a common celebration of the Lord's Supper in St. Engelbrekt's church (even though not all participated), and the fact that it was the Patriarch of Alexandria who read the Nicene Creed in the worship service in the cathedral.

So inspiration by faith in Christ was the *sine qua non* of the whole conference, and must be the basis of any judgment on its achievements or shortcomings. This faith was understood in such a way that it necessitated brotherly love and social responsibility. Söderblom's maxim that the »two governances« must be distinguished but also held together, thus served as a bridge over a chasm very much in evidence at the conference, the chasm between Lutherans who stressed the otherworldly character of the Kingdom

---

[55] Cf. the booklet *Gå vi mot religionens förnyelse?*, Stockholm 1919 (German tr. by P. Katz: *Zur religiösen Lage der Gegenwart*, Leipzig 1921).

of God, and the Anglo-Saxons who saw it as a goal to be realized in history. This bridge did not, of course, permanently eliminate the basic difference between the two. Later ecumenical conferences witnessed an increasing dominance of the Anglo-Saxon – or, more generally speaking, Calvinist – tradition, due not least to the failure of much of German Lutheranism during the Nazi period. But there was also many an effort of achieving a synthesis in Söderblom's vein such as, for instance, the contribution of Reinhold Niebuhr at Amsterdam in 1948.[56]

A second problem the conference had to tackle, partly intertwined with the first one, was the remaining antagonism between members of the erstwhile belligerent nations. It had taken concentrated efforts to persuade particularly the French and the Germans to take part. When their delegations did arrive, the German group betrayed a considerable degree of internal tensions along the lines of opposing political convictions. They did observe group discipline among themselves. Yet inevitably some of their speeches rang with nationalist overtones. Due to the wise decision to exclude the question of guilt with regard to the war, as well as the spirit of Christian fellowship dominating the conference, the discussions could be carried on in a peaceful mood throughout. In many quarters even a degree of understanding for the motivation of the other party was achieved. Seen from a present day perspective, this may not seem much of an accomplishment, but at the time it was almost more than could have been hoped for.

A third result which is seldom mentioned but which is quite evident from subsequent developments is that the host country of Sweden experienced a hitherto unknown thrust of cosmopolitanism through the Stockholm conference, pulling the country out of its relative isolation. International relief work by the Swedish Red Cross had played an important role in this development too. Within the country itself, tolerance between the Lutheran state church and the free churches such as the Baptists and the Pentecostals was considerably enhanced.

In all, the Stockholm conference represented a giant step towards a better understanding among the churches worldwide. The scope of representation was such that the Roman Catholic church as the only one to decline the invitation had for some observers a sectarian appearance over against the newly formed ecumenical movement. The gathering also had a wider significance beyond the confines of the Christian church. Its strides towards peace and reconciliation between the nations, however limited and impeded, met with a deep desire in the whole world to overcome the devastations, both physical and mental, of the hitherto cruelest war in recorded history. This does not detract from Söderblom's credit; on the contrary, he

---

[56] Reinhold Niebuhr, »God's Design and the Present Disorder of Civilization,« in: *The Church and the Disorder of Society, Amsterdam Studies* vol. 3, New York 1948, 13–28. By the way, there is, to my knowledge, no evidence in Niebuhr's writings of a more intimate knowledge of Söderblom's work.

had sensed the most central need of his time and the church's obligation to try to meet it.

Stockholm clearly was the culmination of Söderblom's career. Honors were showered upon him. Honorary doctorates from several countries had been bestowed on him even before, and lecture and preaching tours such as the one to the United States in 1923 had been triumphant experiences. He was invited to preach at the 7th session of the League of Nations when Germany was admitted as a member in 1926. He actively supported initiatives by the World Alliance and other institutions directed at disarmament whenever he could. All this was crowned by the conferral of the Nobel Peace Prize in 1930.

As for himself, Söderblom considered Stockholm as just a beginning that opened new vistas for the church. So at his insistence a Continuation Committee (called Universal Christian Council for Life and Work, or Ecumenical Council, from its meeting in Chêxbres in 1930 onwards) was set up which was to make sure that the goals of the conference would be pursued further. An Ecumenical Institute was founded in 1928 whose first director was Adolf Keller in Zürich. Its task was to give the movement a solid basis in theology and social science. And there was of course the need to integrate the two branches of the ecumenical movement into an organizational unity under the aegis of an overarching Ecumenical Council of Churches. It was not least in the interest of this objective that Söderblom attended the Faith and Order Conference in Lausanne in 1927 where he was made one of the four vice-presidents. But this was »a conference of old men representing the old churches of Europe,« as one observer quipped.[57] It was divided and had no sense of urgency. So in spite of the blueprint for integration that Söderblom sent to the orthodox Metropolitan Germanos in 1928 [302], that objective was not reached before the Amsterdam conference in 1948.

In terms of Söderblom's theological thought, there were few new developments during these years. It was more a matter of clarifying ideas previously promoted. For instance, he kept up a debate in his correspondence on his concept of evangelic catholicity. Notably, he distinguished it from Heiler's more »catholic« institutional approach and from Rudolf Otto's theory of the three pillars, Protestantism, Anglicanism, and Orthodoxy, which for him were to form the overarching roof of the ecumenical movement [248. 261. 280. 312. 315]. In addition, Söderblom cautiously but clearly distanced himself from Otto's rather nebulous concept of an interreligious »Menschheitsbund« (league of humanity, as a parallel to the League of Nations) as something quite utopian in comparison with his own ecumenical endeavors.

What may seem most startling to the modern reader is the fact that there is virtually no serious discussion of Karl Barth and the so-called Dialectical theology. In this respect, Söderblom seems almost totally dependent on

---

[57] Quoted by Sundkler, op. cit., 406.

Torsten Bohlin's critical account of this movement [245][58] and on Rudolf Otto's and Friedrich Heiler's equally critical judgments [221. 222. 279. 309]. One must keep in mind two things, however. One is that this new school of thought was beginning to excite minds in Germany and Denmark, but was still far from holding sway over much of the world's Protestant theology. In particular, Sweden was left virtually untouched by it since it had experienced its own particular renewal in the form of its Luther-Renaissance and its church reform movement, both of which enjoyed Söderblom's active participation.[59] And the second factor is of course Söderblom's involvement in so many inescapable obligations that he could not possibly find the time for the thorough study an independent judgment would have required.

Söderblom did indeed keep up his grueling schedule in the years following the ecumenical conference, engaging, apart from his regular duties as archbishop and from problems arising in the aftermath of the conference itself, in a host of issues he deemed of crucial importance. Even before Stockholm, he had repeatedly raised his voice in the controversy concerning the activities of the Indian Christian mystic Sadhu Sundar Singh [203 n.4; 233]. He continued to be active for the World Alliance. He organized a conference on the history of religion in Lund in 1929, though in the event, he was not able to attend it because of health reasons. And last but not least, he experienced the great honor and satisfaction of being invited to give the famous Gifford Lectures in Edinburgh in 1931. He was able to deliver only their first part before his death. That appeared in print as *The Living God*. It was his intention to give a summary of his views on the history of religion. The part he was able to present contained chapters on primitive religion, Indian and Persian religions, Socrates, Judaism, and the beginning of his treatment of Christianity, which should have been continued in the second volume.

All these activities during the last years of his life, impressive as they are, were overshadowed by Söderblom's deteriorating health and his feeling that he was beginning to get old [309]. Increasingly, he had to delegate obligations to others. The exacting workload he had been shouldering throughout his life, and particularly in the heyday of his ecumenical activities, had taken its toll. His almost superhuman self-discipline was undaunted, and in his letters he still appears as the warm and humorous, outgoing personality he had always been. But he was actually tired and longing for rest. In July 1931, an acute intestinal illness made immediate surgery necessary. That proved too much for his heart that had been seriously damaged by repeated bouts of angina pectoris since 1922. He kept up seeing

---

[58] Torsten Bohlin, *Tro och uppenbarelse. En studie till teologiens kris och »krisens teologi«*, Stockholm 1926 (German transl.: *Glaube und Offenbarung*, Berlin 1928).

[59] Cf. Aleksander Radler, »Der Einfluß des theologischen Werkes von Karl Barth auf die skandinavische Theologie,« in: *NZSTh* 29/1987, 267–293; Dietz Lange, »Eine andere Luther-Renaissance,« in: *Luthers Erben*. FS J. Baur, Tübingen 2005, 245–274.

visitors, giving advice and counseling, almost to the very end. On his last day, he had found the title for his Gifford Lectures, and he added the words that have since become famous: »I know that there is a living God. I can prove it by the history of religion.« He died on July 12, 1931; his last words were: »This is eternity.«

III

Even among people only remotely acquainted with Scandinavian church history and theology, it has been common knowledge that the collection of Nathan Söderblom's papers in Carolina Rediviva, that is, Uppsala University Library, was a treasure waiting to be dug up. It is an exceptionally heavy treasure, though, consisting of approximately 38,000 letters, diary notes, and countless sketches for his literary production. All of this material is exceptionally well ordered, thanks to the efforts of Söderblom's wife and those of his grandson, Dr. Staffan Runestam, who spent ten years of hard work on it during his retirement. The letters are ordered according to authors respectively recipients, all with their dates of birth and death and their professional status indicated. As a result, a reader looking for some particular item will have no trouble finding it quickly. Yet the sheer mass of this material, much of it in Söderblom's bold and impressive, yet often hardly legible handwriting, can easily have a discouraging effect. Söderblom saved simply everything, weighty letters discussing important theological, political, or personal matters, as well as vacation postcards, birthday greetings, telegrams announcing an arrival by train, notes acknowledging receipt of the fee for a guest lecture, and so on and so forth. A letter was for him an outstretched hand, says his biographer.[60] And you just don't chop that off.

It is evident even from these mere hints that an edition of those letters can only be a selection, and a comparatively small one at that. Even so, it took six weeks of »reading with a fan« (both in a figurative and in a literal sense, as it was an unusually hot summer) in Uppsala's University Library in 2003, just to sort out those letters that should be copied for further consideration. Inevitably, such a procedure unwittingly will have left many an interesting source untapped in spite of strenuous efforts to penetrate even the nooks and crannies. For this, I can only apologize; there simply was no other way of getting the project off the ground.

It has been my objective to render the selection as many-faceted and representative as possible. Wherever feasible, I have taken up letters not only from, but also to Söderblom, in order to give an impression of the lively exchange. The selection extends from the first professional years (1893) until Söderblom's death (1931), leaving out completely all letters from childhood

---

[60] Bengt Sundkler, »Nathan Söderblom som brevskrivare«, (as note 7), 3.

and youth, these being mostly family letters which are not yet accessible for reproduction. The samples are arranged in chronological order. A reader looking for correspondence with a specific author may find him or her in the index.

The earliest letters (1893–1901) present Söderblom as a hospital chaplain in Uppsala and as a pastor and doctoral student in the history of religion in Paris. They bear witness to the development of his own theological position, his many-sided pastoral work, his growing family, cultural events and contemporary politics, the Dreyfus affair, for example. The following groups of letters, from the time when he was a professor in Uppsala and Leipzig (1901–1914) and Archbishop and ecumenical church leader in Uppsala (1914–1931), cover a wealth of different aspects. One important part concerns correspondence with renowned theologians, such as Gustaf Aulén, Torsten Bohlin, Wilhelm Bousset, Adolf von Harnack, Friedrich Heiler, Alfred Loisy, Rudolf Otto, Paul Sabatier, Ernst Troeltsch, and churchmen like the Archbishop of Canterbury, Randall Davidson, the Metropolitan of Thyateira, Strenopoulos Germanos, and others. These letters treat all manner of theological issues, like Biblical criticism, the interpretation of the Holy and of revelation, subjects from church history, particularly the Reformation and modern times, the nature of faith, of dogma, homiletics and liturgy, etc. As one would expect, particular emphasis is laid on both the concept and the institutional reality of the church, the idea of »evangelic catholicity« and its ecumenical implications, as well as on practical issues of church policy. This includes aid to prisoners of war, relief measures in the years immediately after 1918, peace initiatives, the threat of nationalism. While all of this concerns Söderblom as a public person, there is also a more private side: Söderblom as a pastoral counselor and as a friend.

There seem to be some conspicuous omissions. One concerns the historians of religion. The letters I have seen in this field are treating such highly specialized subjects that I considered it inadvisable to include them in a volume designed to give an overall impression. I did print a few though (Bousset, van der Leeuw, Troeltsch), as examples which can claim a somewhat more general interest. Another omission concerns one or the other important churchman of the time, Bishop Ammundsen of Copenhagen, to name just one. This is due to the fact that much of that correspondence is concerned with organizational matters like preparing some conference or winning a keynote speaker. At least among Scandinavian bishops, many of the weightier issues seem to have been discussed orally; they met quite often. Thirdly, there are philosophers like Henri Bergson or Rudolf Eucken. Söderblom's letters to them are invitations for a lecture on the Olaus Petri program (repeated but futile attempts in the case of Bergson), and thanks for books received, unfortunately not discussions of philosophical problems as one would have hoped. Neither are there any letters to Söderblom's teacher Auguste Sabatier. He died in 1901, the year Söderblom left Paris. Those few short notes that are extant concern matters like an invitation or the date of an exam. And finally, none of the letters to writers and

artists has been taken up, for the simple reason that it has proved exceed- ⌈ʈ
ingly difficult to get hold of any of these. One notable exception is the delightful correspondence with Selma Lagerlöf.

The scope of this correspondence is truly international, though, of
course, Sweden as Söderblom's home country plays a special role. Therefore the reading public which this edition will hopefully reach will be
spread across many countries too. This is why the present edition is predominantly in English: All letters written in one of the Scandinavian languages
or in French have been translated into that language, and not only this introduction but all the footnotes concerning the persons, events, literary
quotations, and allusions occurring in the letters are also in English. As a
matter of course, however, every letter is first reproduced in its original language. This is simply a requirement of scientific standard. Apart from that,
no translation ever matches the meaning and atmosphere of the original.
»Traduir c'est trahir«, as the saying goes, translating is a sort of treason.
Last but not least, Söderblom was a masterful Swedish stylist and wrote an
elegant French – that is part of the attractiveness of these letters. His German and English were fluent, too, but contained some charming peculiarities, both in spelling and in the choice of words. All of this has of course
been painstakingly preserved in the printed version.

There is one big exception to the rule: I did not translate the letters written in German, even though that would have presented me, being a German, with the least difficulty. The reason for this is quite simple: Too many
letters written in that language had to be part of this selection. Had I provided a translation of these as well, the volume simply would have become
far too bulky and thus would not have stood a chance of publication. A
further complication arises from the fact that Friedrich Heiler and Rudolf
Otto were both able to read Swedish but preferred to write in their own language while Söderblom from a certain point onwards wrote in Swedish. I
translated these letters into German, not English, because introducing a
third language into this mix would have been confusing, quite apart from
the fact that the bilinguality of these particular correspondences betrays a
very special air of confidentiality which must not be obscured. I am quite
aware of the difficulty with which this procedure will present those readers
who do not have a sufficient command of the German language, but I did
not see any other way out of the dilemma.

One more fact regarding this edition must be mentioned. Part of the correspondence with Harnack, Heiler, and Loisy has been published previously in other, more specialized collections. All three of these authors are
indispensable in any edition of Söderblom's letters that claims to be representative. So a certain repetition has proved unavoidable. Of course, I never
copied any of the other editions but in every single case went back to the
autographs, and my footnotes are based on my own research. Moreover,
my selection differs considerably from all three of those just mentioned in
that I am presenting only some of their samples and added a great many
others they have left untouched.

35

In order to present the full picture, I shall now give a somewhat more detailed account of this:

1° Friedrich Heiler's article »Erzbischof Nathan Söderblom. Religionsforscher und Herold christlicher Einheit (1866-1931),« in: *ÖE* 1/1948, 69-110, has an appendix (103-110), containing 7 letters from Söderblom to Harnack of which the following also occur in my edition: May 2, 1923; Sept. 12, 1923; Jan. 26, 1926; May 12, 1926; and Dec. 30, 1930 (to Amalie von Harnack), and one from Harnack (Aug. 20, 1925). There are two differences: My selection presents 24 letters of this correspondence and thus is considerably larger. And regarding Söderblom's own letters, Heiler's edition is based on the typewritten copies made in Uppsala, not on the autographs which are in the Berlin Staatsbibliothek. I have seen those copies; they are carefully made but not entirely free from errors.

2° Paul Misner published the selection: *Friedrich von Hügel – Nathan Söderblom – Friedrich Heiler, Briefwechsel 1909-1931* (KKSMI 14), Paderborn 1981. In my own edition, I did not take up von Hügel, Catholic modernism being sufficiently represented by Alfred Loisy. However, Söderblom's correspondence with Heiler is one of the most important ones, so here again, a certain parallelism could not be avoided. Of the 57 relevant letters Misner has selected for his volume, the following 19 occur in the present edition. From Heiler: Mar. 29, 1918; May 15, 1918; Oct. 1, 1918; Oct. 2, 1918; June 5, 1921; May 14, 1922; Feb. 15, 1923; July 9, 1924; Oct. 9, 1925; Jan. 12, 1926; Aug. 10, 1926. From Söderblom: May 4, 1918; Jan. 17, 1920; July 1, 1920; Jan. 23, 1923; Dec. 23, 1924; Aug. 4, 1926; Jan. 14, 1927; Dec. 1, 1927. In addition, there is one letter from Rudolf Otto which appears in an appendix to Misner's book (Jan. 12, 1920) and which is also included in the present book – as one out of a total of 25. A further difference concerns the fact that Misner omits the original Swedish version of Söderblom's letters which appears in the present edition; the translation of these is my own, as well as the footnotes. Many of these letters are quite long; I have abridged them somewhat more often, and at different places, than Misner. Moreover, my selection contains 28 letters Misner did not include.

3° Finally, there is a small collection by Alan Jones: »The Correspondence of Alfred Loisy and Nathan Söderblom,« in: *DR* 94/1976 (261-275), 266-274. The following letters from Loisy occur also in my edition: Aug. 26, 1924; Dec. 30, 1926; and from Söderblom: Dec. 18, 1926; Jan. 18, 1927. Jones rendered the French autographs just as I do; I add an English translation. My comments are again different and shorter. Besides, I have taken up 10 more letters not contained in Jones' collection.

A further collection of Söderblom letters previously published does not have a parallel here: Friedrich Siegmund-Schultze, *Nathan Söderblom. Briefe und Botschaften an einen deutschen Mitarbeiter* (SÖA 2), Marburg 1966. The function fulfilled by this collection is here taken care of by selected letters exchanged between Söderblom and Adolf Deißmann (16 letters) which were hitherto unpublished.

At the end of this introduction, there remains the pleasure of giving thanks to all those who in some way or other helped to make this edition possible. This is true first of all of Dr. Staffan Runestam who during my sojourn at Uppsala University Library spent several mornings introducing me to Nathan Söderblom's handwriting and on countless occasions then and in the following two years patiently and meticulously answered many an intricate question I needed to solve for my comments to the letters. He certainly is the most competent living Söderblom scholar. So I am extremely grateful for his invaluable and indispensable advice.

Many thanks are due to Riksbankens Jubileumsfond in Stockholm which generously provided the funds for my journey to, and stay in, Uppsala in 2003, and for the large number of copies I needed for my work.

I also wish to give my sincere thanks to Dr. Viveca Halldin Norberg and her colleagues in the Manuscript Department of Carolina Rediviva. I am well aware of the stress I caused them, ordering all those files of Söderblom papers in rapid succession. They have been lenient and courteous, and without their kind and swift cooperation, I would have run out of time long before my work was finished. It was this library that provided the vast majority of copies of the letters printed in this volume. Anna Söderblom had sent a circular after her husband's death, asking to submit his letters to this library either for copying or for keeping. In this way, it has come to own quite a few autographs of these, though of course in many cases they still had to be secured from libraries owning the recipients' papers.

I am greatly indebted too to the two gentlemen who have read the manuscript in order to correct its language. This is first fil. kand. Lars-Erik Hjertström Lappalainen in Malmö who corrected my translations of the Swedish and Norwegian letters. His job was quite laborious since I learned Swedish late in life, and my command of the language is far less secure than I wish it were. He did a very thorough reading of the texts and made a host of useful suggestions for their improvement. Secondly, the whole manuscript went to a friend from student days, Professor Gregory T. Armstrong in Sweet Briar, Virginia. He critically screened my English style and brought order into my rather chaotic punctuation. Remaining peculiarities are not his fault, of course, but owing to the fact that I am not a native speaker.

Thanks are further due to Mrs. Elisabet Wentz-Janacek in Lund for her generous gift of a unique collection of newspaper clips she had inherited from her father who had been personally acquainted with Söderblom. The clips contain articles from a wide variety of papers, written on the occasion of Söderblom's funeral in 1931, palpably rendering the profound personal impact the late Archbishop had on renowned contemporaries as well as ordinary people.

I also want to thank all those libraries that provided me with copies of Söderblom letters to recipients whose papers are in their possession. They are, in alphabetical order of their locations:

Historic Collections King's College, University of Aberdeen
Staatsbibliothek zu Berlin, Preußischer Kulturbesitz
Zentral-und Landesbibliothek Berlin
Landeskirchenarchiv der Evangelisch-Lutherischen Landeskirche Sachsens, Dresden
Niedersächsische Staats- und Universitätsbibliothek Göttingen
The Trustees of Lambeth Palace Library, London
Universitetsbiblioteket, Lunds Universitet
Universitätsbibliothek Marburg
Landeskirchliches Archiv der Evangelisch-Lutherischen Kirche in Bayern, Nürnberg
Riksarkivet, Oslo
Bibliothèque nationale de France, Paris
Carolina Rediviva, Uppsala Universitetsbibliotek.

A list of printing permissions for personal letters to Söderblom by authors who died less than 70 years ago can be found at the end of this book. I should like to express my thanks to the respective heirs for granting me that permission; without it the present edition would not have been possible.

Last but not least, I wish to express my gratitude to Dr. Arndt Ruprecht and Mr. Jörg Persch of the publishing house of Vandenhoeck & Ruprecht in Göttingen for accepting this rather voluminous book, and to the printers for their careful work on my floppy disks. Dr. Ruprecht has deserved well of Scandinavian theology over the years by publishing quite a few of those interesting hyperborean works in a German translation and thereby delivering them from their linguistic isolation, and I am happy that he agreed to continue this tradition.

It is my wish that this volume may contribute to reinvigorating the fading interest in the life and work of Nathan Söderblom, and that the freshness and relevance of his insights, especially regarding ecumenicity and the relations of Christianity to other religions, may spring to the reader's mind as it did to mine when I first began to study these fascinating texts. Along the way, the great churchman's warm humanity, generous liberal spirit, and deep religious faith will certainly not fail to elicit some of the reverence and enthusiasm he inspired during his lifetime. Hopefully, all of this may then induce one reader or another to turn to Söderblom's books for more systematic research.

Göttingen, in the fall of 2005   Dietz Lange

38

I The Pastor: Letters from Uppsala and Paris

1. To Nils Johan Göransson[1]

Upsala, 18. 2. 1893

Min käre Göran!

...

Jag är i Iran och i Persien ännu nätt och jämt orienterad. Det synes litet nationalekonomiskt underligt, att för docentafhandling forska i ngt så nytt, när jag är så pass bevandrad redan i t.ex. dogmhistoria. Men får jag hållas, så kan jag kanske häri göra något gagn. Jag anser det vara ett nyttigt komplement att använda den vetenskapliga frimodighet och glädje, som Ritschl gifvit mig genom sitt pekande på *vår* profet, den störste, på Kristus såsom den ende, till att arbeta hos de andre Guds uppenbarare på andra håll, som gifvit andre den praktiska lösningen af religionens problem. Om jag så en gång skulle hafva kommit till en konkret bild af *religionens* historia, så vore jag vid mitt stoltaste mål. Drömmar, säger du Göran. Lyckliga drömmar, svarar jag.

...

Helsa Anna F. Jag reser till Anna F.
Din
Nathan S

Uppsala, February 18, 1893

My dear Göran,
...[a longer treatment of several subjects of a more personal nature]
In Iran and Persia, I have only just taken my bearings. It may seem somewhat odd economically to be doing research for a doctoral thesis[2] on something so new, being already well versed, e.g., in the history of doctrine. But being left to my own devices, I may be able to achieve something worthwhile in that field. I consider it to be a useful complement applying the assurance and delight in scholarship Ritschl[3] pro-

---

[1] Nils Johan Göransson (1863–1940), pastor in Simtuna Karleby, 1898 in Karlsborg, 1906 lecturer and 1911 professor of dogmatics in Uppsala. At first a liberal theologian, he became quite conservative from about 1920 onwards. – Nathan Söderblom's collection of letters, to Swedes and foreigners, University Library Uppsala (=UUB), handwritten letter.

[2] Swedish: docentafhandling, thesis for the purpose of becoming lecturer. As a rule, at that time this was a post-doctoral thesis. However, if it was considered excellent by the faculty, the author's doctoral thesis would immediately admit him to a lecturership (information from Lars-Erik Hjertström). So apparently Söderblom counts on such a success for the doctoral thesis he is contemplating here.

[3] Albrecht Ritschl (1822–1889) was the most influential German theologian in the second half of the 19th century, also widely read in Sweden. Opposing preceding efforts of speculative German idealism and its theological followers, he stressed the historical and comprehensible if

vided me with by pointing to our own prophet, the greatest, Christ the unique, to the study of other revealers of God elsewhere who provided others with the practical solution to the problem of religion. Should I thereby arrive at a concrete picture of the history of *religion* one of these days, I would have attained my proudest goal. Dreams, you say, Göran. Happy dreams, I reply.

...

Regards to Anna F. I shall travel to Anna F.[4]
Yours,
Nathan S

2. To Nils Johan Göransson[1]

Upsala, hospitalet, 26.11.93
Käre Göran!

...

Schrempf vill ju *saken*, lif och omvändelse, se i »Wahrheit«. Jag ser i honom ett föredöme ss. en evangeliets predikare för vår tid. Han kan som ingen af mig känd beskrifva de religiösa förloppen utan judisk offerlära och hellensk spekulation. Jag har för afsikt att till våren utge ett häfte »Schrempf«. Fehr tycker det är betänkligt. Men jag förmenar att vi icke ha råd afvara en dylik personlighet. Har du sett, att Schrempf i Wahrheit häft 3 lemnar ett positivt förslag till enande mellan »positive« och »freie« i apostolikum-striden? Detta utgör ju ett väsentligt framsteg framur den rent negativa hållning till kyrkan, som han förut visade.

...

Helsa Siri. När kommer du till oss här?
Din Nathan Sm

Uppsala, Hospital, November 26, 1893
Dear Göran,
... (Some fairly general remarks on homiletics)
Schrempf[2] wants to look at *reality*, life and conversion, see *Wahrheit*. I see in him a model as a preacher of the gospel for our time. He is able like no one else

---

supernatural character of God's revelation in Christ, recognizable in the »value judgment« of the believer. One focus of his »elliptical« concept is the Reformation doctrine of justification by faith alone, interpreted in a radically anti-pietistic way. The other focus is human dominion over the world, realized in one's »calling« in society. Söderblom was particularly indebted to Ritschl for his first encounter with Luther.

[4] The second »Anna F.« is Söderblom's fiancée Anna Forsell (1870–1955) whom he married in 1894.

[1] N.J. Göransson's collection, UUB, handwritten letter.
[2] Christoph Schrempf (1860–1944), pastor in Leuzendorf / Württemberg. By refusing to use the Apostles' Creed in baptism in 1892, he provoked the so-called *Apostolikumsstreit* (dispute on the Apostles' Creed) which became famous through Adolf von Harnack's intervention. This did not prevent, however, his dismissal from the ministry in the same year. (That explains the riskiness of Söderblom's plan of writing on him, cf. below.) *Die Wahrheit* is a periodical he edited between 1893 and 1897. »Reality« is oppsed here to ancient dogmatic formulae.

Гоs

known to me to describe the religious course of events without a Jewish doctrine of sacrifice and Hellenic speculation. I am planning to publish a brochure *Schrempf* in the spring[3]. Fehr[4] considers this as hazardous. I presume, however, that we cannot afford to do without such a personality. Did you notice that Schrempf in the 3rd issue of *Wahrheit* submits a positive suggestion for uniting »Positive« and »Freie«[5] in the dispute about the Apostles' Creed? This represents substantial progress, to be sure, over against the purely negative attitude toward the church which he previously displayed.

... [A series of short remarks on a variety of issues]

Regards to Siri. When will you come to us here?

Yours, Nathan Sm

3. From Nils Johan Göransson[1]

Simtuna Karleby den 28/11 1893

Käre Nathan!

Innerligt tack för dagens bref och talet på Gustaf Adolfs-dagen! Jag har nu också läst Ditt tal ett par g:r. Det är ju en litterär konstprodukt och skall bedömas estetiskt! Jag förvånas öfver Din mångsidighet och rika begåfvning min käre Nathan. Men, vet Du, jag kände icke fullt igen Dig i detta tal. Kanske jag redan börjat »ligga af mig« på bondlandet! Om felet är mitt eller hur det kan förhålla sig vet jag ej, men jag kände mig »unheimlich« som tysken säger, vid läsningen första gången. Andra gången märkte jag, huru mycket det är i detalj att verkligen beundra, men som går förloradt om man ej är uppmärksam. Du får icke bli ledsen Nathan, om jag säger, att jag tyckte mig äfven andra gången finna en imitation af Hjärnes stil, hvilket gjorde att jag ej kände igän *Dig*. Du har naturlig fallenhet för en rask, på sak rakt gående stil, som ofta kan bli lekande, ja sprittande, men ej får denna af idéer rent af jäsande framställning, där tankegångens framsteg döljes af den yppiga idérikedomen. Fäst icke för mycket afseende vid hvad jag säger, ty det kan vara enfaldigt. Men jag är så rädd för att Du icke skall bli just Du själf. Om Du blifver Dig själf i vår literatur, så blifver Du helt säkert en storhet af första ordningen. Då jag är öfvertygad därom, förstår Du nog att jag känner mig »unheimlich« till mods, då jag t.o.m. blott anar imitation af Dig i stilistiskt afseende. – Schrempf har jag sista tiden lärt mig

---

[3] Lacking in Söderblom's bibliography; apparently he has not carried out his intention. Among his papers at UUB there is only an undated manuscript from the 1890s entitled *Förord till Schrempf* (Preface to Schrempf). Information from Staffan Runestam.

[4] Dr. Fredrik Fehr (1849–1895), pastor primarius in Stockholm, was an Old Testament scholar and chief advocate of Ritschl's theology in Sweden. He had great influence on Söderblom. Besides, Anna Söderblom had been confirmed by him, and she and her husband were married by him in 1894.

[5] Contemporary German terms for conservative and liberal theology.

[1] N. Söderblom's collection of letters, from Swedes, UUB, handwritten letter.

sätta högre än sedan jag skref till Dig. Att samma tanke skulle uppstå hos oss båda! Äfven jag har tänkt ge ut ett häfte Schrempf. Jag har tänkt och äfven något börjat att skrifva en uppsats om honom såsom inledning till några föredrag som jag tänkt öfversätta. Jag lemnar då detta, ty jag är viss på att Du gör det mycket, mycket bättre än jag. Jag ser i Schrempf en ande nästan jämförlig med Fichte i sedlig och religiös kraft och allvar. Han är verkligen mera positiv än jag först trodde. Också är han psykolog af första rang. Det gör att han kan bättre än de flesta nå människohjärtat. Han är heller icke Kierkegaards lärjunge förgäfves.

...

Nu skall Du varmt och innerligt helsa Sam och Din Anna.

Din tilgifne Göran

Simtuna Karleby, November 28, 1893

Dear Nathan,

Sincere thanks for today's letter and your speech on Gustaf Adolf's Day![2] Meanwhile, I read your speech several times. It really is a product of literary art and must be appraised in terms of aesthetics! I am astonished by your many-sidedness and rich talents, my dear Nathan. But you know, I did not fully recognize you in that speech. Maybe I have already begun to »turn stale« in the countryside! Whether it is my fault or what else the reason may be, I do not know; I did feel »unheimlich« [uneasy], however, as the Germans would say, when I first read it. The second time I noticed how much there really is to be admired in detail, but which gets lost if one does not pay attention. You should not be sorry, Nathan, if I say that even when I read it for the second time, I felt I had discovered an imitation of Hjärne's[3] style, which is why I did not recognize *you*. You have a natural bent for a brisk style immediately getting down to brass tacks, which often can be playful, even sparkling, but it never becomes that sort of exposition which is downright bubbling with ideas, in which the progress of thought is being disguised by the exuberant wealth of ideas. Don't give too much weight to what I am saying, for it may be simple-minded. I am only so afraid that you may not remain just yourself. If you do remain yourself in our literature, you will most certainly obtain first-rate greatness. As I am convinced of this, you may understand that I feel »unheimlich« at the mere surmise of a stylistic imitation by you. – As concerns Schrempf, I have recently learned to rate him more highly than I did when I wrote to you. That the same thought should arise in both of us! I too have thought of publishing a pamphlet on Schrempf. I have thought of it and even begun to write a paper on him as an introduction to some lectures I had thought of translating. I shall now give it up, for I am sure that you will be doing a much, much better job than I would. I see in Schrempf a spirit almost comparable to Fichte with regard to moral and religious strength and seriousness.[4] He really is more positive than I had first supposed. He also is a first rate psycholo-

---

[2] Nov. 7, the day commemorating Gustaf II Adolf's death 1632.

[3] Harald Hjärne (1848–1922), renowned professor of history at Uppsala university, under whom both Anna and Nathan Söderblom had studied.

[4] Johann Gottlieb Fichte (1762–1814), renowned German idealistic philosopher, known particularly for his basic philosophy in *Wissenschaftslehre* (1798. 1804. 1810), his rigorous ethics of duty in his *Sittenlehre* (1798), and his philosophy of religion in *Anweisung zum seligen Leben* (1806).

gist. That makes him better able than most people to reach the human heart. Not for nothing is he a disciple of Kierkegaard.[5]

Please give my warm and heartfelt regards to Sam[6] and your Anna.

Yours, Göran.

4. To Gottfrid Billing[1]

Upsala, hospitalet 18. 12. 1893

Herr Biskop!

Jag har en stark åstundan att kunna ge Biskopen intryck af den tacksamhet jag känner för Biskopens bref. När jag tog mig dristigheten att sända min skrift om Luther, skedde det med den rätt jag visste mig ega i min tacksamhet till Eder, särskildt riktad på hvad hr Biskopen vid prestvigningen i Ersta gaf mig. Nu vet jag, att Biskopen så mottagit min bok.

När jag lemnat ut den till en vidsträckt allmänhet, har det skett med fruktan och bäfvan. Känslan af det oafslutade i allt studium och rädslan att med profana händer behandla något af det, som hör till en människas heligaste har stridt med önskan att meddela något, som jag undfått. Nu kan det ej vara min mening att här meddela de för mig gamla eller nya tankar, som Biskopens bref väckt till lif. Blott ett vill jag beröra: Biskopens ord om förlåtelse och skuld, fällda med tanke på min korta teckning af Luthers grundläggande erfarenhet. Orsaken, hvarför jag upptager denna punkt, är icke nu dess vikt i och för sig såsom tillhörande själva kärnan i religionen, utan orsaken därtill är den, att hvad Biskopen antyder, just tillhört min erfarenhets dyraste egendom. Att det i den framställning, Biskopen åsyftar, ej kommit tydligt till sin rätt, är en ofullständighet i framställningen af hvad jag eger. Om jag förnekade detsamma skulle det vara ett brott mot hvad jag dyrast fått och har.

Att *förlåtelse* är just raka motsatsen till att *se igenom fingrarna med*, och att Jesu värf med afseende på syndaförlåtelsen är något helt annat och mer än en undervisares, hoppas jag emellertid med tydlighet skall framgå af min följande framställning. Eljes vore ju tron visserligen icke det, som jag återgifvit såsom Luthers tro, utan »en blott tanke om Gud«, II,2b som ej kunde i världen gifva evigt lif. Låt mig hänvisa allenast till sid II,10!

Jag menar, att Guds kärlek är det tillräckliga vilkoret för syndaförlåtelsen. Men häri ligger, så vidt jag förstår, ingen saklig åtskilnad mot hvad

---

[5] Søren Kierkegaard (1813-1855), Danish Christian philosopher, student and later opponent of Hegel, vehement critic of what he felt was the complacency of mainstream Danish church life. He came to be a forerunner both of existential philosophy and the so-called dialectical theology of Karl Barth and Rudolf Bultmann. Schrempf translated Kierkegaard's works into German and thereby became one of the first men to make him known beyond Scandinavia.

[6] Samuel Fries, cf. letter no. 5.

[1] Gottfrid Billing (1841-1925), Bishop in Lund. N. Söderblom's collection of letters, to Swedes and foreigners, UUB, typed copy of handwritten letter. The original is missing in the Billing collection in Lund.

Biskopen anför. Ty till kärlekens väsen hör just att taga riktig notis om synden, som skall förlåtas. Den som ej stort bryr sig om synden hos den älskade, uppvisar därmed brist i sin kärlek. Lika vis[s]t som det är, att skilnaden mellan Guds kärlek och vår af synden förstörda känsla är väsentlig, lika vis[s]t är det, att vi redan mänskor emellan få erfara, både hvilket svårt och mödosamt värf det är att förlåta, och huru långt det är emellan att ega *utsago[r]* om förlåtelse och verkligen *ega förlåtelse.* Vilkoret för en verklig förlåtelse är, att den förlåtande erfar och besinnar hela djupet och vidden af brottet. Eljes skulle ju misstanken finnas kvar: ack, om han riktigt visste och kände hela det förskräckliga jag gjort, skulle han icke förlåta. Han tror mig om bättre än hvad jag är. Ju innerligare och renare kärleken är, desto mer svidande och djup måste smärtan kännas öfver den älskades synd, desto mer *afgjord och klar måste domen falla därefter.* Så kommer det ytterst därpå om ändock kärleken är stark nog att öfvervinna.

Nu kan det för mig tröstefulla korteligen utsägas så, att hos Jesus har den guddomliga kärleken öfvervunnit, varit starkare, än den, i af oss oföreställbar fullhet, erfarna smärtan af och fällda domen öfver mänsklighetens, det är för mig min synd.

Innan jag skref detta om Luther, hade jag i annat sammanhang omtalat denna min erfarenhet af skuld och förlåtelse. Däraf måhända dess relativa tillbakaträdande i denna bok.

Det har nu varit mig angeläget att upptaga Biskopens tid med detta uttalande, för att därmed ge innehåll åt det, som jag alltsedan invigningen i Ersta velat säga till Biskopen: ett tack, för att Biskopen då gaf det *utan all hänsyn och jämkning stränga* evangelium[2] och därför *utan allt förbehåll eller slapphet hugsvalande evangelium*, som det är min af Gud förlånade uppgift att i lif och gärning, i tal och skrift förkunna.

Biskopens värdnadsfullt tillgifne
Nathan Söderblom

Uppsala, Hospital, December 18, 1893
Your Grace,
I heartily wish to give you an impression of the gratitude I feel for your letter. When I had the audacity of sending my publication on Luther,[3] this was done with the right I knew I possessed because of my gratitude to you, concerning in particular what your Grace bestowed on me at my ordination at Ersta. Now I know that you have received my book.

When I let it go out to a widespread public, this was done in fear and trembling. The sense of the uncompleted in all study and the apprehension to treat with profane hands something of the sort that belongs to mankind's most sacred had been in conflict with the desire to communicate something I had received. Now it cannot be my intention here to communicate the thoughts your letter aroused to life, may they

---

[2] Thus in the copied letter; one would expect »den ... lagen« at this point.
[3] Nathan Söderblom, *Luthers religion* (= *Den lutherska reformationens grundtankar* II) Stockholm 1893.

44

have been familiar or new to me. Only one thing I should like to touch upon: your words on forgiveness and guilt, uttered with regard to my short sketch of Luther's basic experience. The reason why I am taking up this point is not its weight as such as belonging to the very core of religion; rather, the reason is that what your Grace is indicating has been part of my own experience's dearest possessions all along. That it is not clearly being done justice to in the presentation to which your Grace refers, is an incompleteness in presenting what I do possess. If I denied it, that would be an offence against the dearest I have received and still own.

I do hope, however, that it will clearly appear from the following presentation that *forgiveness* is the exact contrary of *looking through one's fingers*, and that Jesus' activity with regard to the forgiveness of sins is something entirely different from, and more than, that of a teacher. Otherwise faith would certainly not be what I presented as Luther's faith, but »a mere thought about God,« II,2b, that in no way could provide eternal life. Let me only refer to p. II,10!

I think that God's love is the sufficient condition for the forgiveness of sins. But as far as I understand, this does not constitute a material difference to what your Grace is suggesting. For it belongs to the essence of love that it really takes note of the sin that is to be forgiven. Someone who does not care about a loved one's sin thereby displays a lack of love. Certain as it is that the difference between God's love and our feelings which are extinguished by sin is essential, it is just as certain that already between humans we experience both what a difficult and hard achievement forgiveness really is, and how far removed possessing mere *statements* about forgiveness is from actually *possessing forgiveness.* The condition for real forgiveness is that the forgiving person experiences and reflects upon the whole depth and extension of the offence. Otherwise the suspicion would remain: Oh, if he really knew and felt the horrifying thing I have perpetrated, he would not forgive me. He deems me to be better than I am. The more intimate and pure love is, the more burning and deep the distress about the loved one's sin must be felt and the more *decisive and clear the judgment must be passed afterwards.* So in the end everything depends on whether love is nonetheless strong enough to prevail.

Now what is comforting for me can shortly be put thus: in Jesus divine love has prevailed, been stronger than the distress which for us is unimaginable in its depth and the judgment passed on humankind's sin, which for me is my own sin.

Before I wrote this on Luther, I had treated this experience of mine of guilt and forgiveness in a different context. Therefore perhaps its relatively background position in this book.

It has been my concern to take up your Grace's time with this statement in order to lend substance to what I had already wanted to convey to your Grace in Ersta: my thanks that your Grace at that occasion expounded the *relentlessly and unremittingly strict* Gospel[4] and therefore [the] *unreservedly and without any weakness comforting* Gospel, which to proclaim in life and deeds, in speech and writing it is my duty bestowed on me by God.

Sincerely and reverentially yours,
Nathan Söderblom

---

[4] Thus in the copied letter; one would expect »Law« at this point.

5. To Samuel Fries[1]

Paris, rue Rodier 59, 11.6.94

Samuel!

...

Hvar skall jag börja. I Berlin traf jag Harnack i hans hem, hörde ett två timmars seminarieföredrag af Kaftan, som gjorde det med stor pedagogisk skicklighet men som ej imponerade, närvar vid en föreläsning, klar och briljant, af Pfleiderer, om Schleiermacher och Hegel. Harnack var härlig. Luther och Lessing prydde hans skrifbord. Jag tänkte här är oss godt att vara, låtom oss göra tre hyddor, en för Samuel, en för Göran, en för mig.

Lund passerade jag på nedvägen. Domprosten Eklund, renässangsman. Jag tycker om lundensarne. Där blåser en frisk vind. I Berlin träffade jag två unga lundensare, som hade fart i sig och som voro entusiastiska för Harnack.

Paris. Ett är visst att Paris är världsstaden. Här är ett underligt lif. Det kännes godt att ha det starka stödet af en fordrande och stor uppgift midt i detta brokiga och slitsamma lif. Denna min uppgift i den kring hela Paris spridda, till stor del fattiga församlingen, har lagt beslag på min varelse, och bekantskapen med Paris i allmänhet får ske mycket småningom. För dig skall jag nämna, att jag formerat bekantskap med fakultetens dekan prof. Menegoz, att jag mötte åtskilliga protestantiska präster, som äro hängifna i sitt kall och ega mer studier än våra präster, men bland hvilka namnet Ritschl har en dålig klang. I allmänhet kan väl sägas att des protestantiska prästerskapet här i Paris är mönstergillt.

...

Din vän
Nathan Söderblom

Paris, rue Rodier 59, June 11, 1894

Samuel,

... [The letter begins with some remarks on Fries' activities and continues with a report on a trip to Berlin and first impressions of Paris.]

Where shall I begin? In Berlin I met Harnack in his home,[2] heard a two-hour seminar lecture by Kaftan[3] who went about it with great pedagogic skill but without being impressive, attended a lecture, clear and brilliant, by Pfleiderer,[4] on Schleier-

---

[1] Samuel Fries (1867–1914), pastor in Stockholm and Old Testament scholar. Samuel Fries' collection, UUB, handwritten letter.

[2] Adolf von Harnack (1851–1930), leading German church historian of his time. Söderblom owed much of his own knowledge of the history of theology to Harnack's *Lehrbuch der Dogmengeschichte* (1st ed. *Grundriß der Dogmengeschichte*, Tübingen 1889).

[3] Julius Kaftan (1848–1926), systematic theologian of the Ritschl school, wrote a widely read *Dogmatik*, Tübingen 1897 (7th/8th ed. 1920).

[4] Otto Pfleiderer (1839–1908), liberal systematic theologian with a particular interest in the philosophy of religion (*Religionsphilosophie auf geschichtlicher Grundlage*, 2 vols., Berlin 1883/1884). He was influential also in the Anglo-Saxon world. By comparing Christianity to other religions, he tried to prove that it represented the highest degree of perfection.

macher and Hegel. Harnack was marvelous. Luther and Lessing[5] graced his desk. I thought: it is good for us to be here, let us make three tabernacles, one for Samuel, one for Göran, one for myself.[6]

Through Lund I passed on the way down here. Dean Eklund,[7] man of the Renaissance. I like the Lundensians. A fresh wind is blowing there.[8] In Berlin I met two young Lundensians who had real vigor and who were enthusiastic about Harnack.

Paris. One thing is for sure: Paris is the world's great city. Here life is curious. It feels good to have the strong support of an exacting and great task in the midst of this varied and strenuous life. This asssignment of mine in that congregation, spread all over Paris and for the most part poor, has taken hold of my whole being, and getting acquainted with Paris in general will have to happen very gradually. For you I shall mention that I have become acquainted with the dean of the faculty, Prof. Ménégoz,[9] that I met several Protestant pastors who are dedicated to their call and possess more learning than our pastors, but among whom the name of Ritschl has a bad ring to it. In general it may well be said that the Protestant clergy here in Paris are exemplary.

... [Here follows a description of Söderblom's pastoral work; the next letter provides a more vivid version of that.]

Your friend
Nathan Söderblom

6. To HERMAN PALMGREN[1]

Paris, rue Rodier 59, 18.6.94

Broder!
Hjärtligt tack för ditt bref ...

Jag har ej kunnat fatta, hur dagarne flugit. Faktum är, att mina vänner i hemlandet fått förgäves vänta på bref. Svårigheten med denna brefskrifning är en embrarras de richesse. Jag skulle kunna förtälja något om resan. En dag i Lund, en i Berlin. Mycket att se och någon reströtthet. Här i Paris ha vi blifvit utmärkt vänligt mottagna. Den skandinaviska kolonien – jag har nämligen äfven [att] göra med danskar och i synnerhet norrmän – änskönt spridd öfverallt i det väldiga Paris, bildar något liknande en svensk vänlig småstad, där allas angelägenheter äro så kända och omtalade. Mina närmaste hjälpare, en svensk och en norsk trämänniska – »hommes de bois

---

[5] Gotthold Ephraim Lessing (1729–1781), playwright and philosopher, one of the main representatives of the Enlightenment in Germany and advocate or religious tolerance (cf. his play *Nathan der Weise*, and the essay *Die Erziehung des Menschengeschlechts*).

[6] Cf. Mark 9:5.

[7] Pehr Eklund (1846–1911), Dean (domprost) and professor of theology at Lund University.

[8] The theological faculty at Lund was more liberal than Uppsala at the time.

[9] Eugène Ménégoz (1838–1920), Lutheran professor of theology (cf. letter no. 8, n. 2).

[1] Herman Palmgren (1865–1933), public servant (regeringsråd). N. Söderblom's collection of letters, to Swedes and foreigners, UUB, handwritten letter.

et fer« - äro de bästa jag kunde önska mig, arbetsamma och trofasta och utan någon opålitlig och svårhandterlig pietistisk anstrykning. Min företrädare har lemnat mig i arf en kolossalt svår uppgift däri att hans arbete och duglighet äro oöfverträffliga. Däri ligger också ett stöd. Jag kan än fortsätta och finner öfverallt den hjälp, som ligger i en allmän stor respekt för pastors uppgift och värf. Här föreligga också en mängd rent praktiska frågor. Fattigvården tar en god del af min tid. Alla besök hos sjuka och fattiga äro så tidsödande, emedan afstånden i Paris äro så dryga. Det tar t. ex. ungefär en timme med omnibus från Montmartre, där jag bor, till Montparnasse, där jag haft att göra fem besök.

Predikotjänsten är nedslående. Få i kyrkan, som är kanske Paris' vackraste protestantiska kyrka, men mycket aflägsen. De fattige arbeta oftast på söndagen, kunna ej komma. De rike gå gärna till fransyska celebriteter, i synnerhet de, som ej så länge varit i Paris. Det är ej uppmuntrande att predika för på sin höjd en 30–40 människor.

...

I förra veckan voro vi på K. F. U. M. i London. Skilnaden var högst intressant mellan det mångdubbelt större, solida, äfven ståtliga London – jag var ej i de fattiga kvarteren – och med den dysterhet och mörker och detta ljusa, härliga Paris. Men du skall själf se det, när du kommer nästa sommar.

...

Anna helsar dig. Din tilgifne
Nathan Söderblom

Paris, rue Rodier 59, June 18, 1894

Dear friend,
Sincere thanks for your letter ...
I just could not grasp how the days have flown past. The fact is that my friends back home have had to wait for letters in vain. The difficulty with that letterwriting is an *embarras de richesse*. I should be able to relate something about the journey. One day in Lund, one in Berlin. Much to be seen and some tiredness from traveling. Here in Paris, we have been received with exquisite kindness. The Scandinavian colony – for I also have to work with Danes and particularly with Norwegians –, even though spread all over the huge city of Paris, forms something like a friendly small Swedish town where everyone's affairs are known and talked about. My closest associates, a Swedish and a Norwegian woodman – Nordic »hommes de bois et fer« – are the best ones I could have wished for, hard-working, faithful and without any unreliable and unmanageable pietistic touch. My predecessor has left me with an immensely difficult task in that his work and capability are unsurpassable. This also means relief[, however]. I can still continue [in his footsteps], and I am finding everywhere the support inherent in a generally great respect for a pastor's task and profession. There are also lots of purely practical matters here. Assistance to the poor is taking up a goodly portion of my time. All visits to the sick and poor are so time-consuming, as distances in Paris are so long. For example, it takes about an hour by bus from Montmartre where I live to Montparnasse where I had five visits to pay. Preaching is disheartening. Few in the church which is perhaps Paris' most beautiful Protestant church, but very remote. The poor most often work on Sundays

and cannot come. The well-to-do like to go to French celebrities, particularly those who have not been in Paris so long. It is not encouraging to preach for some 30–40 people at most.

...

Last week we were at the YMCA in London. The difference was highly interesting between the vastly larger, sturdy, even stately London – I have not been to the poor districts – with its gloominess and darkness and this wonderful beaming Paris. But you shall see for yourself when you come next summer.

...

Anna sends her regards. Sincerely,
Nathan Söderblom

7. To Nils Johan Göransson[1]

Calais, l'église suédoise 13.7.94

Min käre Göran!

Jag skrifver till dig i en underlig tid. Hela världen ryser och vredgas inför den väldiga förstörelsens makt, som fruktansvärdast uppenbarat sig i mordet på den franske republikens korrekte president. Under det att vi så få förnimma anarkismen, de längst framkastade förtrupperna i det sociala missnöjets här, börjar la grande armée att röra på sig i Amerika. Är det ej det sociala kriget som börjar där, i frihetens förlovade land. Man kan ej annat än stå i frågande förvåning öfver – ja hvarför i förvåning? – att det är världens två republiker, som äro skådeplatsen för begynnelserna till sekelslutets elände. Betecknande är det i sanning. Lika betecknande är det, att i Amerika själfva den massiva revolutionen af »arbetets riddare« skall ega rum, som att i Frankrike anarkismen skall värst grassera. Här uppe i Calais är det ju fjärran och lugnt. Men hvar skulle man i dessa dagar vara för att ej känna suckarne och våndan i vår civilisations gamla utlefvade lekamen. Och hvar skulle man vara för att ej känna att vi Germaniens nordliga söner i vårt det lyckligaste och friaste af jordens länder, ha en mission i denna stormuppfyllda tid. Det är som en vandring i en frisk och sval barrskog att läsa ngt från hemlandet, då man dvalts i det fransyska kvalmet.

Under allt detta ligger den gamle papa, som skådat djupare in i tiden än de fläste och vetat att väl styra sin kyrkas skepp i storm och bränning, för döden i Rom.

...

Ännu känner jag endast några pastorer af Paris' synnerligen högt stående protestantiska prästerskap. Det tyckes jag mig dock redan ha märkt att *religion* såsom en specifik storhet icke på samma djupa och särskilda sätt berör dessa, som oss germaner. Det blir så gärna blott moral, allvarlig och hängifven men att så säga, något tunn. Ritschl står ej högt i kurs, är väl föga

---

[1] N.J. Göransson's collection, UUB, handwritten letter.

förstådd. Men några äro fruktansvärdt liberala. Min plats ss svensk präst ger äfven i detta hänseende synbarligen stort anseende.

...

Helsningar från oss. Din tillgifne
Nathan Söderblom

Calais, The Swedish church, July 13, 1894

My dear Göran,

I am writing to you at an eerie time. The whole world is shuddering and enraged by the enormous power of destruction, most dreadfully manifested in the murder of France's proper president.[2] While we have come to experience the anarchism, the vanguard of the army of social dissatisfaction thrown farthest to the frontline, la grande armée is beginning to stir in America. Is it not the social war that is starting there, in the promised land of freedom? One cannot but be astounded – but why astounded? – at the fact that it is the world's two republics that are providing the stage for the beginning misery of the end of the century. It is significant as a matter of fact. It is equally significant that it is in America where the massive revolution of the »knights of labor«[3] should be taking place, and that in France anarchism should be rampant at its worst. Up here in Calais it is, of course, far removed and quiet. But where could one possibly be unaware these days of the groans and the agony in our civilization's old and decrepit body. And where could one be unaware of the fact that we, Germania's northernmost sons in the world's happiest and freest country, have a mission in this tempestuous time. Reading something from the home country feels like taking a walk in the fresh and cool air of a pine forest, when one is being numbed in this French closeness.

During all of this, the old Pope, who has had a more profound understanding of the times than most people and has known how to steer his church's ship well through storm and surge, is lying on his deathbed in Rome.[4]

... (The letter continues with news of the journey to Paris and the first impressions of the congregation.)

Thus far, I have come to know only a few of Paris' peculiarly excellent clergy. I do seem to have already become aware, however, that *religion* as a specific entity does not affect them in the same deep and special way as it does us Germanic folks. It is becoming so easily just morals, serious and dedicated, but, to put it thus, somewhat meager. Ritschl is not highly esteemed, probably hardly understood. But some of them are terribly liberal. My position as a Swedish pastor apparently generates great respect even in this regard.

... [Söderblom then relates news on an apartment he is going to rent.]

Greetings from us.

Sincerely yours,
Nathan Söderblom

---

[2] Marie François Sadi Carnot (1837–1894), President of France 1887–1894, assassinated by the Italian anarchist S. Caserio.

[3] Secret labor organization founded in the US in 1869 to secure the rights of industrial workers.

[4] This remark turned out to be erroneous: The pontificate of Leo XIII. continued until 1903.

8. To Nils Johan Göransson[1]

8 Villa Michon, Paris 19.12.94

Käre Göran!

...

Jag börjar känna teologerna här. I dag hade jag ett långt o. mycket intressant samtal med prof. Menegoz och åhörde sedan en i sanning lysande föreläsning af fakultetens prydnad Sabatier. Den senare talade sant och hänsynslöst om protestantismens princip och emot all yttre auktoritet. Han visade huru protestantismen ödelägger sig genom sina många otroheter mot sin princip. Och han talade med rifvande hänförelse och frisk trosfrimodighet om protestantismens anspråk på oss och om dess väldiga framtidsutsikter. »Gån på med tro och sanningskärlek. Frågen ej hvart I kommen. Gud sörjer därför.« Prof. Menegoz inledde i går i det teol. sällskapet diskussion om det bibliska begreppet »under«. En hans uppsats härom har emot honom uppväckt en storm, emedan han säger, att motsägelse mot naturlagen är ett nonsens och att det för oss religiöst hållbara i N.T.s underbegrepp är dess egenskap af att vara bönhörelse. I denna mening ss bönhörelse förekommer religiösa under i hvar kristens lif. Under ss. »naturunder« ha i och för sig intet att betyda. I går skulle han förklara sig. Det är lif i fransmäns diskussioner. När jag såg desse män undrade jag ej på att den dem i mänsklig bildning så underlägsna hopen i kammaren använder handgripligheter. – Där fanns »ortodoxiens« målsmän: de båda präktiga lutheranerne Weber (Norrby) och Appia m.fl. De generaliserade och talade om rationalism. Du förstår väl hvilka inkonsekvenser de gjorde sig skyldige till. Där talade ock den gammaldags liberalismen, klar o. tunn i Coquerels person. Menegoz liksom Sabatier och andra – majoriteten i fakulteten – tillhöra afgjordt den moderna historiska teologiska riktningen. De beundra Harnack. Sin ståndpunkt behandla de icke »teologiskt« utan snarare såsom ett föremål för bekännelse. Deras arbeten äro klara, rakt på sak, orädda och duktiga – och mästerliga ss. literatur. I ett afseende stå de mycket högt. De känna sin samtid och äro angelägna om att ej mista kontakten med tidens ideer. De vilja arbeta för de moderna människorne. Men de äro ej germaner. Måhända sammanhänger härmed ock, att de icke synas så, som vi begynna att göra, se och märka Jesu persons sanna härlighet och kraft. Jag saknar i predikningar och allt något, som jag kallar för i egentligaste mening religion.

...

Må vi alltid känna oss i Guds händer! Edra vänner
Nathan o Anna

---

[1] N.J. Göransson's collection, UUB, handwritten letter.

8 Villa Michon, Paris, December 19, 1894

Dear Göran,
...
[The letter first talks about plans Göransson's brother had of studying in Paris.]

I am about to know the theologians here. Today I had a long and very interesting conversation with Prof. Ménégoz and then heard a truly brilliant lecture of the faculty's luminary, Sabatier[2]. The latter spoke truthfully and relentlessly on the principle of Protestantism and against all extraneous authority. He demonstrated how Protestantism is ruining itself by its frequent lack of faithfulness towards its principle. And he spoke with vigorous dedication and refreshing certitude of faith on Protestantism's claim on us and its great outlook for the future. »Go on with faith and love of truth. Do not ask where this will get you. God will take care of that.« Prof. Ménégoz yesterday introduced a discussion of the Biblical notion of »miracle« in the theological society. One of his articles on this subject has aroused a storm against him, because he says that a contradiction to the law of nature is nonsense and that that which is religiously tenable for us in the New Testament's concept of miracle is its quality of being an answer to prayer. In this sense, as an answer to prayer, religious miracles occur in every Christian's life. Miracles as »miracles of nature,« properly considered, do not mean anything. Yesterday he was to vindicate his views. There is liveliness in Frenchmen's discussions. When I saw these men, I was not astonished that the crowd assembled in parliament which is inferior to them in terms of humane education would resort to violence. There were the champions of »orthodoxy,« the two splendid Lutherans Weber (Norrby) and Appia[3] among others. They generalized and talked about rationalism. You can imagine which inconsistencies they committed. Old-fashioned liberalism was also raising its voice, clear and meager in the person of Coquerel.[4] Ménégoz like Sabatier and others – the majority of the faculty – decidedly belong to the modern historical-theological school. They admire Harnack. They do not treat their point of view »theologically« but rather as a matter of confession. Their writings are clear, to the point, unafraid and sound – and masterly as literature. In one respect they are quite outstanding. They know the age in which they live, and they take great strides in order not to lose contact with the ideas of the age. They want to work for modern man. However, they are not Germanic. It might also be due to this that they do not seem to see, and take note of, the true glory and strength of the person of Jesus in the way we are beginning to do.[5] In sermons and in everything I am missing what I call religion in its proper sense.
...
May we always be feeling to be in God's hands! Your friends,
Nathan and Anna

---

[2] Eugène Ménégoz (cf. letter no.5, n.7) and Auguste Sabatier (1839–1901), the Lutheran and the Reformed professors of systematic theology, were both representatives of symbolofideism, according to which faith is independent of both ecclesiastical authority and modern science, and all theological statements are symbolic in nature. Sabatier's philosophy of religion took its point of departure in psychology and history, not in dogma. Under him Söderblom later took his doctorate.

[3] Adolphe Weber (1897–1913) and Louis Appia (1863–1938), supervising church officials (inspecteurs ecclésiastiques), Paris.

[4] I have not been able to gather information about him. The editor.

[5] This is an indirect reference to the romantic poet and philosopher Erik Gustaf Geijer (1783–1847) whose central notion of the great personality greatly influenced Söderblom, as it did much of Swedish thought.

9. To Nils Johan Göransson[1]

Paris 8 Villa Michon, 11.1.95

Käre Göran!

Två bref ha kommit tillhanda sedan mitt sista. Det första hade mött mitt på vägen. Det andra kom till oss för några dagar sedan. Vi har med stor sorg läst om den förskräckliga o. hårda pröfning, som du o. din Siri hafva haft i hennes sjukdom. Vi fingo en sådan ljuflig julhälg. Det är tungt att tänka, att densamma för dig haft idel oro och bekymmer. Måtte [hon] bli återstäld fullkomligt. Må detta år fortsättas o. slutas bättre för Eder, än det begynt.

Vi hade en riktigt ljuflig Julhelg både hemma och i kyrkan. Anna min hade knogigt, men var rätt kry. Men nyåret har haft med sig för oss en stor sorg. Nu ligger min Anna här framför mig och i minst fjorton dagar skall det fortvara. Hon har ansträngt sig alltför häftigt den sista tiden, och det som var vårt hopp till någongång långt fram i vår har med sitt lif fått betala den barnfäst, som i söndags alltför mycket tog Annas möda. Det är någonting hemskt och innerligt bittert i denna erfarenhet af ett hastigt och våldsamt afklippt moders- och fadershopp, som jag önskar, att du aldrig må få erfara. Den värsta faran för Anna är öfver, men mattigheten är ängslande och blir långvarig och smärtorna äro stundtals svåra. I allt kan jag ej nog vara tacksam, att vi ega hvarandra o. få hjälpa hvarandra.

...

Den protestantiska, i någon mån verkligen protestantiska religiositeten härstädes har en annan bakgrund än hemma. Här framkommer densamma ur en »rationalism«, som var föga religiös, och den ser omkring sig som en tröstlös mur katolicismens svårförklarliga makt. Vi germaner äro tidens mest framskjutna släkt. Skola vi ega lifskraft o. ursprunglighet nog att alstra den nya religion, som tiden behöfver? I närvarande stund omgifvas vi af rivaliserande religionsformer, som i lifskraft vilja täfla med vår. Hvad skall bli af arbetarskarornas »socialistiska« tro? Det, du en gång skref om nödvändigheten för kristendomen att visa sin makt i den sociala nöden, har gifvit mig mycket att tänka på. Jag märker, att detta är ett i det stora hela obearbetadt ferment i mina religiösa intressen. Teorierna hota att göra en esoterisk i den meningen att den moderna bildningsvärlden kännes såsom så öfvervägande föremål för ens tankar och de väldiga skarorna, som gå ibland utan att vi känna dem, träda lika fullkomligt tillbaka, när jag ser på formen för framtidens tro, som de äro svåra att lära känna och komma åt. Den beröring, jag här stundom har med arbetare, är underlig. Jag möter en mig obekant, vidsträckt värld och blicken däri är egnad att ge förfäran.

Min gode Göran. Finner du det ej svårt att ordentligt studera, när det praktiska arbetet ligger öfver. Jar har längtan. Men hinner så litet. Kan jag i framtiden ej få mer tid, reser jag genast hem. Skriv till mig!

Dina vänner i Paris genom din tillgifne
Nathan

---

[1] N.J. Göransson's collection, UUB, handwritten letter.

Dear Göran,

Two letters have arrived since my last one. The first one crossed mine. The other one arrived a couple of days ago. We have been reading with great sadness about the dreadful and severe tribulation you and your Siri had to go through because of her illness. We had such a pleasant Christmas holiday. It is disheartening to think that for you, it has been filled with sheer anxiety and worry. May [she] recover completely. May this year continue and end for you better than it has begun.

We had a really pleasant Christmas holiday both at home and in the church. My Anna had a strenuous time but was quite well. New Year's Day, however, brought with it great sorrow for us. Now my Anna is lying in front of me, and this is going to continue for at least another two weeks. She has been exerting herself with far too much intensity recently, and what was our hope for some time far ahead in spring had to pay with its life for the children's festivity that craved far too much toil of Anna last Sunday.[2] There is something awful and profoundly bitter in this experience of a mother's and father's hope being suddenly and violently cut off, which I wish you may never have to experience. The worst hazard for Anna is over, but her feebleness is worrying and lingering, and the pain is sometimes great. In all, I cannot be grateful enough that we have each other and have a chance to support one another.

...

Protestant, in some way truly Protestant religiosity around here has a different background from that back home. Here it originates from a »rationalism« which was scarcely religious, and it perceives of Catholicism's hardly explicable sway as of a desolate wall around it. We Germanic folks are the most advanced people of this day and age. Shall we have sufficient vitality and originality to generate the new religion this era needs? Right now, we are surrounded by rivaling forms of religion competing with ours in terms of vitality. What is to become of the »socialist« faith of labor's droves? What you wrote some time ago on the necessity of Christendom's proving its potency in the face of social need has given me much to think about. I am aware that on the whole this is an undeveloped ferment in my religious interests. Theories threaten to make one esoteric in the sense that the modern world of learning seems to be such a predominant object of one's thoughts, and the huge crowds, moving in our midst without our knowing them, disappear as completely in the background when I look at the forms of future faith as they are difficult to get acquainted with and to approach. The contact I sometimes had with working men has been strange. I encounter an unacquainted, wide world, and looking into it is liable to cause fear.

Good old Göran. Don't you think it is difficult to study properly with practical work waiting to be done? I do long for it. But I am getting so little done. If I cannot find more time in the future, I shall go home immediately. Keep me posted!

In the name of your friends in Paris, yours sincerely,

Nathan

---

[2] Anna Söderblom had suffered a miscarriage.

10. To HERMAN PALMGREN[1]

Paris, 8 Villa Michon 11.1.95

Afhållne vän!

...

Vi ha förtjusande trefligt, fast trångt efter svenskt mått. Vi ha börjat att
samla en liten hop intressant folk omkring oss. Hvad intressanta och välvil-
liga människor angår, finnes här ingen brist. Det är af stort intresse att något lära känna artisternas lif. D.v.s. i vanliga fall får jag se den dystraste
sida. För ögonblicket har jag i uppdrag att tigga åt Strindberg, som är öf-
vergiven af sin andra fru, är sjuk och vill in på sjukhus, och för en svensk
skulptör af de allra förnämsta. Jonas Lie räknar jag till de roligaste be-
kantskaperna, vi gjort. Men bäst är det, när vi någongång råka en gammal
Upsalavän, såsom vi nu hvar dag vänta Axel Boman, som skall bli sjömans-
präst i Bordeaux.

...

... jag är din sedan gammalt tacksamme och tillgifne vän
Nathan Söderblom

Paris, 8 Villa Michon, Jan. 11, 95

Esteemed friend,

...

We have got an exquisitely pleasant home, though cramped by Swedish standards.
We have begun to gather a small flock of interesting people around ourselves. As far
as interesting people are concerned, there is no shortage here. It is of great interest
to get acquainted somewhat with the artists' life. That is to say, ordinarily I get to
see its darkest side. At the moment I am in charge of begging on behalf of Strindberg[2] who has been abandoned by his second wife, is ill and wants to get into the
hospital, as well as of one of the finest Swedish sculptors.[3] Jonas Lie[4] I consider to
be one of the nicest acquaintances we have made. The best thing is, however, to
meet an old friend from Uppsala some time, just as we are now awaiting Axel Boman[5] one of these days who is going to become a sailors' chaplain in Bordeaux.
... [Söderblom goes on to report on the tragic event described in the preceding letter.]
... I am your grateful and sincere friend of old,
Nathan Söderblom

---

[1] N. Söderblom's collection of letters, to Swedes and foreigners, UUB, handwritten.
[2] August Strindberg, Swedish poet (1849-1912), traveled restlessly across Europe from
1883 onwards.
[3] Söderblom probably refers to Christian Eriksson (1858-1935), as Staffan Runestam in-
forms me.
[4] Jonas Lie (1833-1908), Norwegian poet.
[5] Axel Boman (1860-1933), sailors' chaplain, later university lecturer.

11. To Nils Johan Göransson[1]

Käre Göran!

Ett par ord till dig här i kvällens stillhet. Först ett tack för ditt varma bref. Det andas ej teologi utan kristendom, d.ä. Kristi ande.

Jag har ingen rädsla för möjligheten, att Jesus [ej] finnes. Ty den är helt abstrakt, d.v.s. helt o. hållet spöke. Men många människor äro på *allvar* rädda därför – icke ss. t.ex. Sam, som i *logiskt* intresse räknar därmed. Dessa många skola vi hjälpa. Varaktigt går det endast genom att de få förnimma Kristi ande, så att de äro vissa om hans verklighet likasom om sitt eget lif. Men jag sätter också den profanhistoriska forskningen om honom mycket högt. För densamma är ju Jesu verklighet ett faktum, som man endast gör sig löjlig genom att förneka. Jag tror föröfrigt, att ingenting verkligt stort kan rent diktas. Alla de personer i dikten, som icke äro blotta marionetter liksom i röfvarromanerna har poëten verkligen sett. Ty lif kan icke diktas. Då blir det endast döda gestalter. Evangelierna visa oss ingen schablonmässig typ, utan ett hemlighetsfullt lif hos Kristus, förvecklat och i sitt sammanhang gåtfullt ss. lifvet är. Sådant kan ingen dikta. Detta resonnemang är en tankelinie utan anspråk eller stort värde. Men jag tror, att vi böra möta alla, som äro rädda och ängsliga, på halfva vägen. Och vi få aldrig tröttna att börja om och om igen med A.B.C.D. Till detta trons A.B.C.D. hör ock teologin. Den är icke mål. Men den kan göra god tjänst som medel att hjälpa själarne.

Den gångna veckan har varit mycket bråkig. Pastoralkonferensen: där talades om »försoningen«. Med yttre, men ej inre klarhet. Jag känner efter denna diskussion än innerligare, hurusom inga gamla häfdvunna, eller »kätterska« tankegrupper kunna lägga i dager den erfarenhet, som vi kalla »försoningen«, utan att något kommer till korta. Alla dessa läror ega för mig psykologiskt intresse i det de skvallra om den religiösa affekt, som de otympligt afspegla. Men min egen försoningslära innehåller blott satser, den är intet system.

Vidare ha här firats årsmöten af allehanda protestantiska »oeuvres«. Jag har haft två intressanta aftnar med de personer, som vilja en »congrès religieux« år 1900. Bland dem äro flere i bästa mening moderna människor. Denna kongress kommer att få en mer lekmannaartad o. direkt religiös prägel. Barrows, som ledde Chicagomötet, är nu i Paris. – I fredags öppnades konstutställningen, den ena, mera intressanta af de två årliga. Vi voro där många timmar. På denna den första utställningsdagen är »hela Paris« där, o. publiken är lika intresseväckande som taflorna. Utställningen i dess helhet gjorde ett intryck af större sundhet än förra året. De anspråksfulla, sjukliga fostren af en konstgjord fantasi voro färre. Största hopen stannade framför en tafla om nattvarden. Den var mycket vacker. En del af lärjungarnes typer såg man gärna länge på. Men Jesus var bedröfligt sentimental.

---

[1] N.J. Göransson's collection, UUB, handwritten letter.

Honom kunna de aldrig måla. Aldraminst de, som icke känna honom personligen.

Lägges därtill, att vår tjänstflicka insjuknat, att jag ingen enda kväll på öfver en vecka fått vara hemma före midnatt, så inser du att jag känt mig rätt missnöjd med allt jäkt och tacksam för söndagen i dag. Min Anna ber mig helsa Eder båda varmt o. innerligt. Måtte du nu ändtligen få ordinarie plats! – Eklund kom till Upsala.

Din vän Nathan Söderblom

Paris, April 25, 96

Käre Göran,

A few words to you here in the evening's quiet. First of all thanks for your cordial letter. It does not convey theology but Christianity, i. e., the spirit of Christ.

I am not at all afraid of the possibility that Jesus [did not] exist.[2] For it is entirely abstract, i. e., nothing but a specter. However, many people are afraid of it *in earnest*, not like Sam [Fries] who reckons with it in the interest of *logic*. We ought to succor these many. In a permanent way, this is possible only as they perceive the spirit of Christ, so that they are just as assured of his reality as they are of their own lives. But I also think very highly of secular historical research about him. For to it, the reality of Jesus is a fact whose denial would ridicule itself. Besides, I believe that nothing really great can be wholly fabricated. All personages in poetry which are not mere puppets, as in cheap novels, have really been seen by the poet. For life cannot be fabricated. It would only become dead masks. The Gospels do not present us with a stereotype but with a mysterious life in Christ, entangled and puzzling with regard to its coherence, as life happens to be. Something like that cannot be fabricated. This kind of reasoning represents a line of thought without any pretension or great value. But I think we should go halfway to meet all those who are afraid or anxious. And we should never get tired of starting with the ABCs time and again. Theology also belongs to the ABCs of faith. Theology is not a goal. But it can be of good service towards succoring souls.

This past week has been very restless. Pastors' conference: »Reconciliation« was discussed there, but with outer, not inner clarity. After this discussion, I feel all the more profoundly that no time-honored or »heretic« set of ideas can bring to light the experience we call »reconciliation« without curtailing something. All these doctrines are of psychological interest to me in that they chat about the religious emotion which they only awkwardly reflect. But my own doctrine of reconciliation contains only propositions; it is not a system.

Furthermore, annual meetings of all sorts of Protestant »oeuvres« have been celebrated here. I had two interesting evenings with those people who want a »congrès religieux« in 1900. Among them are several modern people in the best sense of the word. This conference will be of a character much more oriented towards laymen and more explicitly religious. Barrows who led the Chicago meeting[3] is now in Paris. – Last Friday the art exhibition opened, the more interesting of the two an-

---

[2] Conjecture: Söderblom refers to the claim made by Bruno Bauer in his *Christus und die Cäsaren*, Berlin 1877, that the person of Christ was the product of mere fantasy.

[3] John Henry Barrows (1847–1902), Chicago Presbyterian minister (1899 president of Oberlin College), organizer and chairman of the World Parliament of Religions in Chicago 1893.

nual ones. We spent many hours there. On this first day of the exhibition »all of Paris« is there, and the public is just as interesting as the paintings. The exhibition as a whole made an impression of greater soundness than last year. There was less of that pretentious, sickly offspring of an artificial fantasy. The largest crowd was standing in front of a painting of the Lord's Supper. It was very beautiful. Some of the types of disciples one would love to look at for a long time. But Jesus was deplorably sentimental. Him they just never can paint. Least of all those who do not know him personally.

If you add to this that our servant has become sick, that I was not able to be home before midnight one single evening, you will understand that I felt quite dissatisfied with all this bustle and grateful for Sunday today. My Anna asks me to send her warm and sincere regards to both of you. May you now at last get a full professorship! Eklund[4] went to Uppsala.

Your friend Nathan Söderblom

12. To Nils Johan Göransson[1]

[Date at the end of the letter]

Min käre Göran!

Tack för ditt sköna, varma och sanna bref!

...

Vårt Land har trakasserat mig på det mest utstuderadt retsamma sätt och Kyrklig Tidskrift sänder tillbaka med tacksamhet ett par små manuskript, det ena en rec[ension] af Koetsvelds klassiska arbete om liknelserna, som i bibelkritiken är alldeles konservativ, sålunda af K. Tidskrifts o. icke af min ståndpunkt, det andra en uppsats om ev. sociala rörelsen i Tyskland i an-l[edning] af Göhres bok. Mot uppsatsernas innehåll anmärkes ingenting. De äro intressanta och innehålla ingen propaganda. Men kunna ej intagas, ty mitt *namn* anses kätterskt, och namnet gör mer än saken. Detta samtidigt med att de hos mig fördömda meningarne under andras namn gå i Kyrklig Tidskrift. Skola vi ta skeden i vackra hand och tiga? Nej, får jag ej med de andra gå, får jag väl ensam gå. Äfven sådana teologer i vår kyrka som du o. Sam o. Personne o. Bosson o. Lundborg o. Freidenfelt och jag kunna ha ngt nyttigt att säga. Jag är glad öfver årsboken.

... Vi samarbeta i årsboken icke för att formulera satser utan för att tala, så det begripes äfven af dem, som ej tränats in i den fromma klicken, om religionens verkligheter.

Isolering, – och isolerad är jag i viss mån äfven här – verkar en stark och allt öfvergripande känsla för det väsentliga. Men man glömmer lätt dagens nödtorft. Och jag får hemifrån gång på gång obehagliga påminnelser om, att mycket rödjingsarbete är nödvändigt för sådden. Och jag har gång på gång blifvit dragen ut från en slags esoterism, där jag endast känner den

---

[4] Pehr Eklund (1846–1911), until then professor of systematic theology at Lund university.

[1] N.J. Göransson's collection, UUB, handwritten letter.

djupa enheten och samarbetet med alla dem som tro, ut i ett kyligt rum, där mina ord missförstås, eller öfverröstas af bullersamma stämmor, som icke vilja låta mig komma till tals, emedan de ha sanningen omhand. Sam känner, där han sitter, starkare än vi två, nödvändigheten af hvad han kallar »reformarbete«, af att icke ignorera, utan taga allvarligt itu med de mäktiga företeelser, som i evangeliets eget namn – dölja det för många af vår samtid o. försvaga dess kraft. Vi få icke optimistiskt inbilla oss, att man för vår tros o. kärleks skull förlåter oss vårt begär att fritt tänka o. tala.

Vill du, om du ej kan öfvervinna dina betänkligheter mot medverkan i årsboken, säga mig ett ord till, innan du beslutar dig. ...

Må årsboken bli icke en partipublikation jämte de andra, utan må man där kunna andas friare luft och äfven förnimma innerligare värme.

Anna min helsar Eder!

Din vän är Nathan Sm

Paris 6/10 96

My dear Göran,

Thank you for your beautiful, cordial, and truthful letter!

... [on problems of getting manuscripts accepted by conservative theological journals] *Vårt Land* has been pestering me in the most cunningly annoying way, and *Kyrklig Tidskrift* gratefully sends back some small manuscripts, one a review of Koetsveld's classic work on the parables[2], which is quite conservative in terms of Biblical criticism, thus in accordance with *K. Tidskrift's*, not with my view, the other a paper on the Protestant social movement in Germany, occasioned by Göhre's book[3]. Against the content of the papers no remarks were made. They are interesting and do not contain any propaganda, but they cannot be accepted because my *name* is considered heretical, and the name matters more than the subject.[4] This simultaneously with the opinions being condemned in my case being published under other names in *Kyrklig Tidskrift*. Are we to retire into the shade and keep silent? No! If I can't go with others, so I shall have to go by myself. Even such theologians in our church as Sam [Fries] and Personne and Bosson and Lundborg and Freidenfelt and myself might have something useful to say. I am glad about the yearbook.[5]

... [A lengthy passage on a conflict that had arisen between N.J. Göransson and

---

[2] C.E. Koetsveld, *De Gelijkenissen van den Zaligmaker*, 2 vols., Schoonhoven 1869; German transl. by O. Kohlschmidt, [2]1896.

[3] Paul Göhre, *Die ev.-soziale Bewegung, ihre Geschichte und ihre Ziele*, Leipzig 1896.

[4] The background to this is Söderblom's brochure *Hedendomen i helgedomen. Ett ord till ... E.D. Heüman i anledning af hans skrift: »Ritschlianismen och församlingen eller Hedendomen i helgedomen ...«*, Stockholm [2]1895, which in no uncertain terms rebuked Heüman's excessive polemic against Ritschl and his school. Elis Daniel Heüman (1859–1908) was an ultraconservative pastor and politician (member of the Swedish Diet), who was vehemently opposed to modern theology, socialism, and what he considered softness towards Norway (united with Sweden at the time).

[5] Samuel Fries: cf. letter no.5 note 1; Johan Vilhelm Personne (1849–1926), dean at Linköping cathedral 1897, and bishop there from 1910 until his death; Trued Bosson (1833–1916), dean i Vemmenhög (Lund diocese); Matheus Lundborg (1860–1935), pastor in Kristianstad 1907, dean in Villand (Lund diocese) 1911; Samuel Freidenfelt (1869–1901), assistant pastor. The »yearbook« is a journal planned by Söderblom and others.

Sam Fries, trying to mediate between them. That conflict would even have touched the planned yearbook.]

We cooperate in the yearbook not in order to formulate principles but in order to talk about the realities of religion in a way understood even by those who have not been trained into the pious clique.

Isolation – and isolated I am too here after a fashion – brings about a strong and comprehensive sense of that which is essential. But one easily forgets the daily needs. And time and again I get from back home unpleasant reminders that much clearing work is necessary for the sake of sowing. And time and again have I been pulled out of a sort of esotericism where I only feel the deep unity and cooperation with all the faithful, into a chilly place where my words are being misunderstood or drowned out by boisterous voices that do not want me to start talking because they are in charge of the truth. Sam at his place is feeling more than the two of us the need for what he calls »reform work,« of not ignoring but seriously tackling the mighty manifestations which – in its very name – disguise the Gospel for many contemporaries and weaken its force. We must not fancy optimistically that because of our faith and love we shall be forgiven our desire to think and talk freely.

If you cannot get over your misgivings with regard to the yearbook, would you please drop one more word to me before you make up your mind. ...

May the yearbook not become a partisan publication like the others, but may one be able to breathe more of an air of freedom and also perceive a warmer atmosphere.

My Anna sends her regards to both of you.

Your friend is Nathan Sm

Paris, October 6, 96

13. To NILS JOHAN GÖRANSSON[1]

Erfurt, Hôtel Silber, den 23 nov. 1896

Käre Göran!

Jag fick ditt bref mig tillsändt hit och läste det i dag på e.m. midt under den hetaste diskussionen om det nationelt-socialistiska partiets program. Du skall ha tack! Märk, att jag är med på hvad du säger o. känner i denna sak, i saken om tro o. vetenskap. Jag har känt det så starkt under dagarne i Giessen och Marburg. Det är blott applikationen på vår käre Sam, som jag finner tillspetsad. Jag tror, att gemytet hos honom har större plats än så.

Fattigdomen hos Ritschl framträder mer hos hans efterföljare. Kattenbusch var from o. snäll, nyttig för prästkandidaterna, men beatus possidens i sin färdiga värld. Stade är ju öfverlägsen såsom historisk vetenskapsman. Baldensperger var min man. Han har varit publicist, förstår konst o. förefaller de andra besynnerlig. Är också lite nervös. Men har den rätta Jesustron o. är för resten – därför – fri.

I Marburg hörde jag Herrmann. Han är mer än Kattenbusch. Jag känner för honom samma beundran och sympati som tillförene. Hans föreläsningar

---

[1] N.J. Göranssons collection, UUB, handwritten letter. Söderblom wrote it on an educational journey through Germany.

är mycket besökta. Där träffade jag – Freidenfelt. Vi hade tillsammans hög-tidsstunder. Jag har ju talat om för dig, att min vän Norlin bjudit mig på två veckors resa. Sedan sågo vi Wartburg – Luther – den härliga Thüringerwald – o. Weimar – Goethe, Schiller, Herder. Men från de döda till de lefvande kommo vi här i Erfurt. Jag mötes här af en kristendom, sådan jag vill den, handlingskraftig men ej metodistiskt, manlig, icke braskande, innerlig, icke gudlig. Naumann är en väldig människa. Jag tror, att han kan komma att göra stora ting. Han har redan samlat de lekmän o. teologer, som äro leds-na på det teologiska käbblet o. kyrkopolitiken, i en enig, kraftig vilja att hjälpa i samhällets nöd. Sådana män behöfva vi. Då får basunen en viss klang.

...

De Upsalapedanterna! Här kan man andas och värmas i själen.
Din
Nathan Sm

Erfurt, Hôtel Silber, November 23, 1896

Dear Göran,
I received your letter which was forwarded here and read it this afternoon during the hottest discussion on the program of the National Socialist party.[2] You shall have thanks! Note that I agree to what you are saying and feeling in this matter, the matter of faith and science. I have felt it very strongly during these days in Gießen and Marburg. It is only the application [of your criticism] to our dear Sam which I think is too sharp. I think that good-naturedness has a more prominent place with him than you make it out to have.

Ritschl's meagerness stands out more clearly in his followers. Kattenbusch was devout and friendly, helpful for the candidates for the ministry, but *beatus possidens* in his ready-made world. Stade is, of course, superior as a scholar of history. Bal-densperger was my man. He has been a journalist, is versed in the arts and appears odd to the others. Is a little nervous, too. But has the true faith in Jesus and is by the way – therefore – free. In Marburg I heard Herrmann.[3] He is more than Katten-busch. I have the same admiration and liking for him as I did before. His lectures are well attended. There I met – Freidenfelt. We had a grand time together. I told you, didn't I, that my friend Norlin[4] has invited me for a two week trip. Then we saw the Wartburg – Luther – the marvelous Thüringerwald – and Weimar – Goethe, Schiller, Herder. But from the dead we have here in Erfurt come to the living. I am being received here by a kind of Christianity as I want it, energetic but not Metho-dist, manly, not ostentatious, hearty, not goody-goody. Naumann[5] is a terrific per-

---

[2] Friedrich Naumann's »Nationalsozialer Verein«, a liberal socialist grouping; no link with Hitler's infamous National Socialist party.

[3] Ferdinand Kattenbusch (1852–1935), systematic theologian, known particularly for his *Konfessionskunde*; Bernhard Stade (1848–1906), Old Testament scholar; Guillaume Balden-sperger (1856–1936), historical-critical New Testament scholar (disciple of H. J. Holtzmann's) – all of these were teaching at Gießen University at the time of Söderblom's visit; Wilhelm Herrmann (1846–1922), Marburg systematic theologian who later became the teacher of both Karl Barth and Rudolf Bultmann.

[4] Christopher Norlin (1851–1911), businessman.

[5] Friedrich Naumann (1860–1919), very influential in liberating Protestant ethics from its

son. I believe he will be able to do great things. He has already collected those laymen and theologians who are sick of the theological bickering and church politics in
a united, strong will to help in society's misery. We need such men. Then the trom-
bone will have a certain timbre.

...

These Uppsala pedants! Here you can breathe and have your soul warmed up.
Yours,
Nathan Sm

14. To NILS JOHAN GÖRANSSON[1]

Paris, 2 rue Maleville, 2/2 97

Käre Göran!

Har icke en hel månad o. mer gått af det nya året, innan jag skrifvar och
säger dig tack för ditt nyårsbref.

...

Ett ord dock till hvad du skrifver om personlighet o. programarbete på
tal om de kristligt sociale. Jag lemnar nu dessa ur räkningen – där kan nog
vara många reservationer att göra vid deras verk o. uppträdande. Men jag
är bestämdt af annan mening än du rörande den store mannens eller låt oss
säga den betydande mannens uppgift. Han skall verka personligt, fritt, o.
ha till sitt mål att bilda personligheter. Sant. Men hvem skall då ändra sakerna? Ty äfven de behöfva ändras, grundligt ändras ibland. Skall den
verkligen betydande människan anse det vara under sin värdighet att befatta sig med sådana ting, som lagar o. ordningar, hvilka ingå i samhällslifvets
oundgängliga maskineri? Skola då endast de underlägsna befatta sig med
dylikt? Men för att göra något i dessa ting behöfves parti. Jag gläder mig
öfver att öfverlägsna sedliga viljor gå in i det arbetet. Där äro de sannerligen af nöden.

Men låt mig tala nu för dig om A. Sabatiers nya bok. Ménégoz kallar den
för det mest betydande franska teologiska (prot[estantiska]) arbete efter
Calvin, och Ménégoz känner den saken. Jag läser o. fröjdas. Boken heter
»Esquisse d'une philosophie de la religion«. Nog saknar jag ett par ting –
men det är barbari att tala därom, när det gäller ett mästerverk, helgjutet af
en stor och lefvande o. varm personlighet i en skön o. fulländad form. Detta
arbete synes mig – för mig personligen – det märkligaste, som kommit efter
Ritschl o. Harnacks Dogmengesch[ichte]. Men Sabatier är ss. personlighet
mycket rikare än Ritschl o. hans uppfattning af dogmen är mindre »dogmatisk« än Harnacks. Detta arbete kommer att verka djupt, särdeles, na-
turligen, så långt det franska språket når. Det kan nämnas i raden: Pascal,

---

bonds to social conservatism by means of his activities first as a member of the *Evangelisch-sozialer Kongress* (cf. letter no. 14, n. 2), later as a politician and writer.

[1] N.J. Göransson's collection, UUB, handwritten letter.

Vinet. Framförallt känner sig Sabatier såsom Pauli o. Pascals lärjunge. Den gamle Sabatier är för öfvrigt en härlig människa. Af alla jag sett representerar han för mig närmast idealet för en teolog. Ingen skulle jag så vilja likna. Kanske beror detta i hög grad på hans »mänsklighet«. Han är en lefvande människa, icke en stofil af finare eller klumpigare slag. Inga människor, vore de än aldrig så ortodoxa eller liberalistiska eller hvad det än månde vara, så anser han sig icke för god att på ramaste allvar inlåta sig med dem, blott de äro uppriktiga. Vi teologer bli eljes lätt högfärdiga af för mycken skolvisdom.

Sabatiers hemlighet är det nu, att vara teolog – historiker o. dogmatiker – o. literaturkännare o. tidningsman utan att på något af dessa områden vara dilettant.

Paul Sabatier, den i hast berömde förf. till »den hel[ige] Franciskus' lif« är en lärjunge till Aug. Sabatier; denne Paul S. råkade jag här för en tid sedan. Han är uppriktig »franciskan« mer än kalvinist o. lutheran – o. hvarför skulle han [icke] få o. kunna vara det till välsignelse äfven i protestantismen?

Jag sänder i dag min embetsberättelse. Det skall glädja dig att höra, att antalet kyrkobesökande o. nattvardsgäster i fjol var betydligt större än under något föregående år. Tro ej, att jag gör för mycket däraf i mina pastorala förhoppningar. Men det gläder mig. Det har ej skett i ett slag.

...

Din N. Sm

Paris, 2 rue Maleville, February 2, 1897

Dear Göran,

Has not a whole month and more of the new year gone by until I have written and said thanks to you for your New Year's letter?

...[The first paragraph speaks of a Swedish acquaintance Söderblom happened to meet on the street after a concert.]

One word though on what you write about personality and programmatic work with regard to the Christian Socials.[2] I shall for now leave those people out of account – many reservations could certainly be voiced concerning their work and performance. But I am definitely differing from your opinion as regards the great man's or shall we say the outstanding man's task. He is to act in a personal and free way and to aim at educating personalities. True. But who is then to change the order of things? For that too needs to be changed, sometimes to be changed thoroughly. Should the really outstanding person consider it to be below his dignity to concern

---

[2] The Christian Social Movement was founded in Germany in 1848 by Johann Hinrich Wichern (1808–1881) in the form of *Innere Mission*, an organization for home missions and social work. Its second phase is represented by the *Evangelisch-Sozialer Kongress*, initiated by Adolf Stoecker (1835–1909) and others in 1890, which began to view the »social question« as a political problem. The reservations Söderblom is hinting at may concern paternalistic remnants as well as Stoecker's well-known anti-semitism. However, Stoecker and the conservatives had left the *Kongress* in 1896, making room for the more progressive wing under Friedrich Naumann, for whom cf. previous letter, notes 2 and 5.

himself with such things as laws and statutes which are part and parcel of society's indispensable machinery? Should only the inferior concern themselves with that kind of thing? But in order to do something about these things, a firm position is required. I am glad that superior moral wills are taking part in that kind of work. They are truly needed there.

But let me now tell you about A. Sabatier's new book. Ménégoz calls it the most significant French theological (Protestant) work after Calvin, and Ménégoz knows these things. I read [it] and am delighted. The book is called »Esquisse d'une philosophie de la religion«.[3] I'm certainly missing a few things – but talking about that is barbarian when a masterwork is concerned, molded in a beautiful and consummate shape by a great and lively and warm personality. This work seems to me – to me personally – to be the most remarkable one since Ritschl and Harnack's *History of Dogma*. But Sabatier as a personality is much richer than Ritschl and his view of dogma is less »dogmatic« than Harnack's. This work will have a profound impact, in particular, of course, within the range of the French language. It can be mentioned in the same breath with Pascal, Vinet[4]. Sabatier conceives of himself primarily as St. Paul's and Pascal's disciple. Besides, old Sabatier is a wonderful person. Of all those I have come to know, for me he comes closest to representing the ideal of a theologian. There is no one I would so much want to be like. This is perhaps to a high degree due to his »humanity.« He is a lively human being, no old fogy of a more subtle or more clumsy kind. There is no person, be he ever so orthodox or so liberalistic or whatever else, that he would consider beneath himself to deal in absolute seriousness, if only he is sincere. We theologians otherwise become so easily conceited from too much scholastic wisdom.

It is now Sabatier's secret being a theologian – historian and dogmatician – and an expert in literature and a journalist without being an dilettante in any of those fields.

Paul Sabatier, the suddenly famous author of *Life of St. Francis*,[5] is a disciple of Aug. Sabatier's; I met this Paul S. some time ago. He is a sincere »Franciscan«, more than a Calvinist or a Lutheran – and why should he [not] be allowed to be that and be a blessing even within Protestantism?

I send my official report today. You will be glad to hear that the number of churchgoers and participants in the Lord's Supper was considerably higher last year than in any previous year. Don't think that I make too much of that in my pastoral aspirations. But I am glad about it. It did not happen all at once.

...

Yours, N. Sm

---

[3] For Auguste Sabatier, see letter no. 8, note 2. *Esquisse* ... appeared in 1897 and is the one book by Sabatier that most profoundly influenced Söderblom.

[4] Alexandre Vinet (1797–1847), practical theologian at Lausanne and prolific writer, with a particular forte in the psychology of religion.

[5] Paul Sabatier (1858–1928), church historian with close contacts to Catholic modernists. His *Vie de St. François d'Assise* was published in 1893, appeared in no less than 42 editions until 1931, and was translated into several other languages.

15. To Nils Johan Göransson[1]

Paris 4/3 1897

Käre, trofaste vän!

. . .

Ritschls biografi har jag senast läst med stor ifver, och mycket har klarnat för mig i Rs åskådning. Bland annat har jag känt, huru kyrklig han från början var, under det att hans kunskapsteoretiska utredningar kommo mycket sent. »Kyrkolärare« synes mig vara ett namn, som passar honom bättre än de fleste. Men hvad jag saknar hos honom är det entusiastiska, urkristna, det rent individuelt religiösa i sina spontana, ofta besynnerliga, men dock gripande yttringar. Allt är så ordnadt. Måhända tillåter du mig att kalla, hvad jag saknar hos R., för den vilda, otämjda, oreflekterade religionsdriften. Den fanns hos pietismen. Utan den kommer kyrkan nog trots all regelrätt och normal fromhet att lefva på svältkost. Blir protestantismen för borgerlig, så kan den icke konkurrera med katolicismen. Ritschl var för snäf, när han beröfvade Frans af Assisis fromhet existensrätt i den evangeliska kyrkan. Där sammansnörpte han samma kyrkobegrepp, som han gjort sig så mycken tackvärd möda att utvidga ifrån renlärighetens trånghet.

Din tilgifne
Nathan Söderblom

Paris, March 4, 1897

Dear faithful friend,

. . . [on Göransson's professional outlook, and on having little time for a scholarly contribution Söderblom had promised to write]

I very eagerly read Ritschl's biography recently, and much about R's views has become clearer for me. Among other things, I have felt what a churchman he was from the beginning, while his epistemological analyses came very late. »Teacher of the church« seems to me to be an epithet that suits him better than most others. What I am missing in him, however, is the enthusiastic, original Christian, the purely individual religious in its spontaneous, often strange but moving manifestations. Everything is so orderly. Perhaps you will allow me to call what I miss in R. the wild, untamed, unreflected religious drive. Pietism had it. Without it the church, in spite of all its regular and normal piety, will doubtless live on a starvation diet. If Protestantism becomes too bourgeois, it will not be able to compete with Catholicism. Ritschl was too blunt when he denied Francis of Assisi's piety the right to exist in the Protestant church. Thereby he constricted the very concept of the church which he had taken such pains, deserving of gratitude, to widen beyond orthodoxy's narrow confines.

Yours sincerely,
Nathan Söderblom

---

[1] N.J. Göransson's collection, UUB, handwritten letter.

16. To Nils Johan Göransson[1]

Paris 7/6 97

Käre trofaste vän Göran!

. . .

Hvad du säger om kongresserna såsom tidstecken synes mig slå hufvudet på spiken. Men jag är mindre skeptisk rörande gagnet af dem. Jag tror, att personligheterna kunna komma fram där, och att många kunna komma i en intensiv beröring med en stor personlighet, som därefter får lättare att tala till dem i skrift. Dessa kongresser skola ock väcka många sofvande. Faran för att de skola skapa enhetliga, allmängiltiga förnuftssatser i den religiösa erfarenhetshemlighetens ställe, är ej stor. Mångfalden är för rik. Och det finnes vetenskapsmän äfven i teologi med karaktärfull och lefvande fromhet. . . .

I lördags kväll voro vi hos Jonas Lie. Under samtalet med honom om religiösa ting och våra kyrkors vilkor stärktes jag i min öfvertygelse om, att vi protestanter ha två angelägna ting i striden mot den katolska kyrkan. Jag menar i den andliga tvekamp mellan kyrkorna som alltjämt drar in nya människor af vårt släkt till att beundra och sympatisera med Rom. Det är frågorna om under o. auktoritet. Det är en olycka, att protestanterna möta Rom med förståndskritik. Den verkar på de sinnen, som skulle påverkas, snarare motsatsen mot hvad den är ämnad att verka. Misstanken om att protestantismen är en kritiskt afkortad katolicism är allmän äfven hos andligen myndige protestanter, och den jagar de innerlige, religionstörstande sinnena till Rom. I fråga om undret måste det ske en Auseinandersetzung med Rom från religiös synpunkt. Vi måste ega medvetandet om religionens under klarare än de katolske, eljes ha vi ingen rätt att kalla oss evangeliske, kristne i en äktare mening än de. Mig synes att katolicismen i själfva verket har fördolt o. förfuskat det stora undret = Guds nåd, genom en mängd förklaringar och genom att sönderplocka det på en mängd småunder. Vi ha genom Luther fått det klart o. enkelt ställdt framför oss. Det gäller, att icke fördölja det eller göra det plausiblare genom vare sig barbariska försoningsteorier eller någon slags rationel förklaring af modernare snitt.

Vi, »moderne« teologer, tro oss göra samtiden en tjänst med att vältra undan stötestenarne och göra en slät väg åt det mänskliga förnuftet ända in i det allra heligaste. Men de moderne människorna äro trötta på tänkande o. resonnemang. De vilja möta en auktoritet, något riktigt påtagligt att hålla sig vid – en gåfva, ty en riktig auktoritet är en gåfva, ett Guds verk för oss. Skola vi lyckas att göra *Jesus* riktigt verklig o. närvarande för dem? Det är en klentrogen fråga. Men en allvarlig. De ortodoxe förstå denna sak bättre än de kritiske herrarne. Grundtvig har besinnat protestantismens behof i detta stycke. Ritschl bättre än någon jag känner.

. . .

---

[1] N.J. Göransson's collection, UUB, handwritten letter.

Jag beräknar få lite tid i juli för Karl Marx' evangelium. Hans verk om »kapitalet« är uppbyggelsebok för tusenden, i original eller i oändliga mängder af återgifningar.

Alla de mina sofva. Gud vare med dem och oss alla! Helsa din egen Siri.

Din vän

Nathan Söderblom

Dear faithful friend Göran,

... [Some short remarks on private matters]

What you are saying about conferences as a sign of the times hits the nail on the head. However, I am less sceptical with regard to their usefulness. I believe that personalities can emerge there, and that many can get in close contact with a great personality, who afterwards has an easier time speaking to them in written form. These conferences shall also wake up many who are asleep. The risk that they will create uniform, generally valid rational propositions [taking] the place of the mystery of religious experience is not great. The diversity is too rich. There are also in theology men of science with a steadfast and living piety.

... [On Sabatier]

On Saturday afternoon, we were at Jonas Lie's. In the course of our conversation with him on religious matters and our churches' condition, my conviction was reinforced that we Protestants have two pressing issues in our struggle with the Catholic church. I mean in the spiritual duel between the churches which continually lures new people of our kin into admiring, and sympathizing with, Rome. It's all about the questions of miracles and authority. It is unfortunate that Protestants encounter Rome by means of rational criticism. The effect of that on the minds to be influenced is rather contrary to what it is intended to be. The suspicion that Protestantism is Catholicism curtailed by criticism is common even among spiritually mature Protestants, and it drives the minds that are devoted to and thirsting for religion to Rome. As far as miracles are concerned, there must be an *Auseinandersetzung* [debate] with Rome from a religious point of view. We must have a consciousness of the miracle of religion clearer than the Catholics, or else we don't have any right to call ourselves Protestants[2], Christians in a more genuine sense than they are. It appears to me that Catholicism has indeed disguised and spoiled the great miracle = God's grace, by means of a multitude of explanations and by breaking it down into lots of petty miracles. We have had it put before us by Luther in a clear and simple fashion. It is paramount not to disguise it or make it more plausible, be it by barbarian theories of reconciliation, be it by some sort of rational explanation of a more modern design.

We »modern« theologians believe we are doing our contemporaries a favor by rolling away the stumbling blocks and paving a smooth passage for human reason even into the holy of holies. Modern man is, however, tired of thinking and reasoning. He wants to encounter an authority, something really tangible to adhere to – a gift, for real authority is a gift, wrought by God for us. Will we succeed in making *Jesus* truly real and present for them? That is an incredulous question. But a serious one. The orthodox understand these things better than the critical gentlemen.

---

[2] The Swedish original has *evangeliske* which makes better sense than Protestant as it is derived from the Greek euangelion, Gospel. However, »evangelical« in English has come to mean conservative Christian, which would miss the point here.

Grundtvig contemplated Protestantism's need in this respect.[3] Ritschl better than anyone I know.

...

I reckon to have some time in July for Karl Marx's Gospel. His *Das Kapital* is the edifying book for thousands, in the original or in an infinite host of renderings.

All of my folks are asleep. May God keep them and all of us! Regards to your Siri.

Your friend,
Nathan Söderblom

17. From RUDOLF OTTO[1]

Paris, le 8. Juni 1897

Sehr geehrter Herr Pastor!

Erinnern Sie sich meiner noch vom Erfurter Parteitage der »National-Sozialen« her? Ich erzählte Ihnen damals, dass ich mich um die deutsche Pfarre, (rue blanche, 25) bewerben wolle. Jetzt bin ich auf 8 Tage hier in Paris um mir die Verhältnisse anzusehen und würde mich sehr freuen, Sie wiederzusehen. Würde ich Sie nicht stören, wenn ich Sie Donnerstag Nachmittag etwa um 5 1/2-6 Uhr besuchen würde? Bitte geben Sie mir doch kurz an obige Adresse Nachricht.

Mit ergebenem Grusse
Ihr hochachtungsvoller
R. Otto, cand. min
(Stiftsinspector, Göttingen.)

18. To HERMAN PALMGREN[1]

Paris 19/12 97

Käre vän! ...

»Le Grelot« utsäger min mening i Dreyfusaffären, Scheurer-Kestner etc

---

[3] Nikolaj Frederik Grundtvig (1783-1872), Danish pastor, historian, and educator. At first an adherent to Romanticism, he later turned to a conservative Lutheran version of the faith, with a characteristic emphasis on the doctrine of creation: »a human being first, then a Christian.« The basic fact of Christianity is for him God's encounter with the believers in the congregation. Their response is the confession of faith as expressed in the Apostles' Creed which, he thought, was bequeathed to the church by Jesus himself.

[1] Rudolf Otto (1869-1937), later professor of systematic theology in Breslau (today: Wroclaw) 1914 and in Marburg 1917-1929. He became famous through his book *Das Heilige*, Breslau 1917; according to its central thesis, the a priori category of the Holy mediates religious experience with rationality. Widely traveled and a charismatic personality, he was well versed in the history of religions to which he devoted a number of important books. – N. Söderbloms collection of letters, from foreigners, UUB, handwritten letter.

[1] N. Söderblom's collection of letters, to Swedes and foreigners, UUB, handwritten letter.

vilja uppriktigt dra fram sanningen. Men Dinmont, La libre Parole o. hela den antisemitiska hydran vill släcka ut ljuset, och Rochefort, L'Intransigeants redaktör, med sin yfviga lugg, gör allt hvad han kan för att förhindra la justice militaire att se något.

Aldrig har jag sett den franska chauvinismen o. judehatet i så ömklig och retsam skepnad.

Må du ha en god jul, o. måtte det nya året bringa med sig uppfyllelse af dina förhoppningar!...

Din tillgifne tacksamme vän
Nathan Söderblom

Paris, December 19, 1897

Dear friend,

... [Söderblom regrets having had so little time to see Palmgren during a short visit to Sweden]

Le Grelot expresses my opinion with regard to the Dreyfus affair.[2] Scheurer-Kestner[3] etc. honestly want to bring the truth to light. But Dinmont, *La libre Parole*, and the whole antisemitic hydra want to extinguish the light, and Rochefort, *L'Intransigeant*'s editor with his bushy forelock,[4] is doing all he can to prevent *la justice militaire* from seeing something.

Never have I seen French chauvinism and hatred of Jews in such a deplorable and exasperating shape.

May you have a merry Christmas, and may the New Year bring to you fulfillment of your hopes!...

Sincerely, your grateful friend
Nathan Söderblom

19. To NILS JOHAN GÖRANSSON[1]

2 rue Maleville 11.1.98

Käre Göran!

...

Däremot delar jag alls icke din pessimistiska åskådning af församlingen. Min egen erfarenhet lär mig annat. Visserligen är personligheten medelpunkt för allt mänskligt lif; att det ytterst kommer an på personerne äfven i

---

[2] Alfred Dreyfus (1859–1935), Jewish Alsatian captain, was expelled from the French army in 1894 on the false charge of high treason. His case aroused political passions across the board. The affair kept dragging on for years; only in 1906 was Dreyfus definitively acquitted and rehabilitated.

[3] Auguste Scheurer-Kestner (1833–1899), Protestant, liberal politician, Vice-President of the Senate, tried to obtain retrial for Dreyfus.

[4] I have not found any data for Dinmont. Victor-Henri de Rochefort-Luçai (1831–1913) was an extremely polemical journalist and radical conservative politician. For his criticism of Napoleon III. as well as of later governments, he had to go into exile several times. His comments on the Dreyfus affair were harshly anti-semitic and anti-paliamentarian.

[1] N.J. Göransson's collection, UUB, handwritten letter.

den [sic, l.: det] sociala, har jag med all tydlighet och temligen fullständigt utredt i mitt föredrag (F. A. Johanson [sic] finner i Kyrklig Tidskrift att jag gjort det för *mycket*; dock vill jag säga, att jag icke i värde ens vill jämföra hans antipodiska kritik med din). Men institutioner betyda också något i världen. Och hvad du kallar den moderna idealiseringen af församlingen är enligt min tanke ett ytterst glädjande fenomen, den enda motvikt mot den desslikes moderna hyperindividualismen, som är af något ruckligt värde för den protestantiska kristenheten. Själf har jag sett t.ex. i Helsingland, min hemtrakt, hvilken makt ett någorlunda godt och lefvande församlingsmedvetande har. Ett dylikt församlingsmedvetande kan öfvervintra under mången underhaltig prästs tid. Och en dylik församling har kristligt omdöme. Jämför ett prästval i Helsingland med ett i Stockholm, skall du förstå, hvad jag menar med församling. Jag ville komplettera dina ord med detta: en religiös personlighet, som icke är församlingsbildande, har däri ett märke på sin underlägsenhet.

...

Din tillgifne
Nathan Söderblom

2 rue Maleville, January 11, 1898

Dear Göran,

...[On Göransson's suitability for an academic career and on criticism of a paper of Söderblom's which he accepts.]

I do not, however, share your pessimistic view of the congregation. My own experience teaches me otherwise. Certainly the personality is the focal point of all human life; that in the final analysis, everything depends on the persons, even in social life, I expounded quite plainly and fairly completely in my paper (F. A. Johansson[2] in *Kyrklig Tidskrift* holds that I *overdid* it; I may say, however, that I don't even want to compare the value of his antipodal criticism with yours). But institutions are also of significance in the world. And what you call the modern idealization of the community[3], is in my thinking an utterly pleasing phenomenon, the only counterweight to the likewise modern hyperindividualism, which has a destabilizing impact on Protestant Christianity. I myself have seen e. g. in Hälsingland, my home area, the power a fairly good and vivid communal consciousness [of a congregation] has. Such a communal consciousness is able to hibernate during many a deficient minister's time. And such a congregation possesses Christian judgment. Compare a minister's election in Hälsingland with one in Stockholm, and you will understand what I mean by congregation. I would complete your words by the following: a religious personality not forming a congregation is thereby characterized as inferior.

... [Some family news, such as the Söderbloms expecting their third child]

Yours sincerely,
Nathan Söderblom

---

[2] Frans August Johansson (1850–1910), professor of dogmatics and Christian ethics in Uppsala 1892; of exegetical theology in Lund 1896 and simultaneously pastor in Stora Uppåkra, founded *Kyrklig tidskrift* in 1895.
[3] The Swedish word församling can be rendered both by congregation and community.

20. To MAGNUS PFANNENSTILL[1]
Svenske Pastorn i Paris   2, rue Maleville, den 12.3.1898
Käre broder!
...
Ditt storartade verk om Gudsbelätet, till hvilket jag måste lyckönska vår
teologi. Och beundrar jag dig, som midt under en mångfaldig, trägen
tjänstgöring fått tid till ett så omfattande arbete. Jag längtar att få tillfälle
till en ordentlig genomläsning. Nu har jag endast kunnat kasta en flyktig
blick på uppställningen och skönja grundtankarne. Njutningen förminskas
ej däraf, att jag finner dig lägga vikt vid en hel del data i den traditionella
dogmatiken, hvilkas värde jag ej kan inse, ex. ett rel[igiöst] fullkomlighe-
tens tillstånd och ett syndafall i begynnelsen. Någon som helst lösning på
problemet om syndens ursprung ger mig ej denna supposition, den endast
flyttar problemet längre ifrån mig. Däremot är berättelsen om fallet mig
mycket värdefull ss. illustration till en alltid upprepad psykologisk process.
Skulle vi leta efter grunderna till att en sådan legend uppkommit, skulle vi
väl till sist stanna vid två moment: dels den religiösa erfarenheten af syndens makt och list, dels ett spekulativt intresse att förklara dess uppkomst.
Den förra är beståndande och fordjupas för oss i Nya förbundet. Men det
senare synes mig ej längre kunna nöja sig med en quasilösning, som endast
är ett aflägsnande af frågan och ej tar någon hänsyn till människans faktis-
ka beskaffenhet, sådan vi känna den.
    Emellertid, jag har ännu ej sett det hela af din tankegång. Men jag gläder
mig, att du skänkt oss en så mogen och närkraftig frukt af din tanke o. dina
studier. Gud gifve, att man äfven i Upsala sloge sig med allvar på bekännelseskrifterna. Billing och du ären goda exempel.
    ... Din varmt tilgifne
    N. Söderblom

The Swedish pastor in Paris   2 rue Maleville, March 12, 1898
Dear Brother,
    ... [On a short paper by Pfannenstill]
    Now to your magnificent work on the image of God[2] for which I must congratu-
late our theology. And I admire you who in the midst of a manifold assiduous service found time for such a comprehensive work. I am yearning to get a chance for a
careful reading. As for now, I have only been able to cast a cursory glimpse at the
outline and to identify the basic ideas. The enjoyment is not diminished by my finding you to give weight to quite a number of data in traditional dogmatics the value
of which I cannot discern, e.g. a rel[igious] state of perfection and a fall in the beginning. This supposition does not provide me with any solution whatsoever to the
problem of the origin of sin; it only removes the problem further away from me. On
the other hand, the narrative of the fall is very valuable for me as an illustration of a

---

[1] Magnus Pfannenstill (1858–1940), professor of systematic theology in Lund; collection
Pfannenstill. M., Lund University Library, handwritten letter.
[2] Magnus Pfannenstill, *Om Gudsbelätet (Imago Dei): en dogmatiskethisk undersökning på de
lutherska bekännelseskrifternas område*, Lund 1897.

continually repeated psychological process. If we were to search for the reasons why such a legend should have come up, I suppose we would finally arrive at two elements: on the one hand religious experience of the power and guile of sin, on the other hand a speculative interest to explain its origin. The former is invariable and is being deepened for us in the New Covenant. But as regards the latter, it seems to me we can no longer be satisfied with a quasi-solution which only eliminates the question and does not take into consideration man's actual nature as we know it.

However, I have not seen the whole of your line of thought as yet. But I am glad that you have presented us with such a ripe and nourishing fruit of your thought and your studies. May God grant that even in Uppsala they devote themselves in earnest to the Reformation Creeds. Billing[3] and you are good examples.

...

Yours very sincerely,
N. Söderblom

21. To Samuel Fries[1]

2, rue de Maleville, den 14.3.1898

Käre broder!

...

Ett bevis på värdet af personlig med[d]elelse af privat art har jag nu ock i ditt bref. Där ser jag nämligen tydligt, hvad jag anat och hvad jag funnit hos andra än dig, nämligen att du ej forstår väsendet i den teologiska grundriktning, hvarom vi tala. Du jämför den moderna teologin med din egen skepsis, som fört dig steg för steg till noll. Detta är en stor förvexling. Den nyare teologin är ej skepsis utan position, och denne dess karaktär framträder i sin fulla kraft hos Ritschl. Äfven jag vet, hvad skepsis och samvetsnöd vill säga. Jag har befunnit mig på det sluttande planet och med förfäran märkt, hurusom de fästen, man hade gifvit mig och som man erbjöd mig alltfort, gledo lika ohjälpligt som jag. Men Gud [har] hört bön och gaf mig en fast grund Jesus Kristus. Först behöfde allt det andra ramla. Det är i den moderna teologin, jag har funnit denna protestantiska position uttalad. Och så länge du med den stora hopen af utomstående icke förmår se i vår position annat än en grad af skepsis, så länge måste ditt omdöme bli lika besynnerligt som recensionen af Sabatier. Och då kan jag förklara psykologiskt din känsla af beatus possidens gentemot honom. Men dess fundament är falskt. Och vi skola, om Gud ger oss lif o helsa, strida om själarne. De, isynnerhet de blifvande prästerna o. teologerna, kunna ej bygga på »Tiefsinn« och en slags estetiskt försonande identitetsfilosofi, de måste ha en *fast*

---

[3] Einar Billing (1871-1939), 1908-1920 professor of dogmatics and Christian ethics in Uppsala, then bishop of Västerås. Initiator of the rediscovery of Luther in Sweden (*Luthers lära om staten*, Stockholm 1900, [2]1971), before the so-called Luther-Renaissance in Germany, and author of equally important books on the idea of folk church (*Den svenska folkkyrkan*, Stockholm 1930, [2]1963). His considerable influence was limited to his native country.

[1] Samuel Fries collection, UUB, handwritten letter.

grund, en sådan, som enligt min erfarenhet endast kan skänkas genom det djärfva språnget, som den moderna teologin har gjort. För den, som hissnar vid anblicken, ser det vådligt [ut]. Den, som står på terra firma efter språnget, skall aldrig, så länge det finnes kärlek och lif i honom, upphöra att visa för dem, som tilläfventyrs äro i den själanöd, han erfarit, på det fäste han funnit – såsom din tillgifne vän

Nathan Söderblom

2, rue de Maleville, March 14, 1898

Dear friend,

...

Proof of the value of personal communication of a private kind is what I also have in your letter. For I see in it clearly what I had divined and what I found in others than you, namely that you do not understand the essence of the theological school we are talking about. You compare modern theology to your own scepticism which has led you, step by step, towards naught. This is a big confusion. Recent theology is not scepticism but position, and this character stands out in its full force in Ritschl. I too know what scepticism and a troubled conscience mean. I found myself on the slope and became frightfully aware of how the stronghold that I had been given and that I had been constantly offered was sliding equally helplessly as I did myself. But God heard my prayer and gave me a firm foundation, Jesus Christ. First everything else had to collapse. It is in modern theology that I have found this Protestant position articulated. And as long as you, along with the whole crowd of outsiders, are unable to see in our position anything but a degree of scepticism, your judgment is bound to be just as awkward as the Sabatier review. And then I can explain psychologically the feeling of *beatus possidens* you are harboring against him. But its basis is false. And if God gives life and health, we are supposed to fight for the souls. *They*, in particular future ministers and theologians, cannot build upon »*Tiefsinn*« [»profoundness«] and some kind of esthetically conciliatory philosophy of identity[2]; they must have a *firm* foundation, one that according to my experience can only be granted as a gift by means of the audacious leap[3] modern theology has made. For anyone who feels dizzy at the sight it looks perilous. Anyone who stands on *terra firma* after the leap will never, as long as there is love and life in him, cease to refer those who happen to experience the troubled conscience he has had, to the stronghold he has found, like your sincere friend

Nathan Söderblom

---

[2] This refers to 19th century German speculative philosophy, esp. that of Friedrich Wilhelm Joseph Schelling (1775–1854).

[3] Allusion to Søren Kierkegaard's notion of leap of faith, which means that the certitude of faith cannot be reached by an intellectual conclusion but only by an existential venture. This is the theme of his *Concluding Unscientific Postscript to Philosophical Fragments* (1846), transl. by H. N. and E. H. Hong, Princeton 1992.

22. To Nils Johan Göransson[1]

2 rue Maleville 28.5.98

Käre Göran!

...

Jag läser sedan ett par dagar den älsta lefnadsteckning, som finnes af Frans af Assisi, författad af hans kamrat o. biktfader Leo samma år som Frans dog – nu först utgifven af Paul Sabatier, samme unge prot. präst, som skrifvit en till svenska öfversatt bok om Frans. I denna enkla latinska berättelse är Frans en människa, ej ett helgon med affilade drag och banal glans. Så mycket större och skönare framstår han. Kristi arf är rikt. Och ingen har det till fideikomiss. Frans och Luther stå som de två typerna för de två historiska huvudsätten att ärfva honom. Det är välgörande att lyftas upp ur allt det elände, som man här ser i den katolska kyrkan på nära håll, till den sköna idealbilden. Jag kan säga, att katolicismen var för mig en terra incognita i djupare mening, när jag kom hit ut. Nu har jag sett en ömkligare allmän vidskepelse, lägre gängse moralbegrepp, särdeles i fråga om könslifvet och sanningsenlighet och ett mycket ohyggligare tyranni på samvetena än jag kunnat drömma om. Jag gick i natt till öfver midnatt o. talade med en curé, som måste bryta för sitt samvetes skull. Och det är inga tilltalande interiörer man får ifrån pastoralvård och kyrkostyrelse, när det så en gång förunnas att lyfta på förlåten. Men å andra sidan har jag lärt mig förstå katolicismen. Den dödas icke med katolikfräternes godtköpspolemik. Jag tror icke någon evangelisk teolog i någon tid *känt* katolicismen så som Ritschl. I hans temperament låg dock en viss omöjlighet att fullt *uppskatta* den. Men han har haft den härliga tron att emot katolicismen uppställa ett helt konsekvent lifsideal utan beblandelse eller kompromiss. Jag har en svagare, mindre djärf tro. Jag skulle ej vilja utdrifva Frans, om han funnes i vår kyrka, fastän jag ej vill efterlefva eller predika hans ideal i dess egendomliga form. Men sinnena äro så olika. Och Kristus är så rik. – Det bedröfliga kriget är sannerligen ej till protestanternas förmån, om man nu skall med den kortsynt[a] massan bedöma det som religionskrig. En katolik sade en gång till mig: de latinska katolska folken äro mindre egoistiska än de angelsachsiska protestantiska. Jag tror, det ligger någon sanning häri. Vi bedrifva inom protestantismen gärna afguderi med vår kultur och fria tankeodling. Ytterst gäller det ju dock kärleken.

I morgon Pingst, snart juni, snart halfva året gånget till de många. Och jag är ännu en nybörjare i konsten att lefva.

Helsa hjärtligt din Siri från oss!

Din varmt tilgifne

Nathan Söderblom

---

[1] N.J. Göransson's collection, UUB, handwritten letter.

Dear Göran,

... [Congratulations to Göransson who had moved into his first parsonage]

Since a couple of days, I have been reading the oldest biography there is of Francis of Assisi, written by his companion and confessor Leo in the year Francis died – now first edited by Paul Sabatier,[2] the same young Prot[estant] pastor who wrote a book on Francis which has been translated into Swedish. In this simple Latin narrative Francis is a human being, not a saint with polished features and trivial gloss. He comes out so much more superior and graceful. Christ's heritage is rich. And no one owns it like an inalienable right. Francis and Luther represent the two main types in history of being heirs to him. It is refreshing to be raised above all the misery one is seeing here at close range in the Catholic church, to the beautiful ideal image. I can say that Catholicism was for me a *terra incognita* in a more profound sense when I came out here. Now I have seen a more pitiful common superstition, lower prevalent notions of morality, especially with regard to sex life and truthfulness, and a much more appalling tyranny over the consciences than I could have dreamed of. Tonight I went to a *curé* and talked to him till after midnight, a man who had to break away for the sake of his conscience. It is really no attractive picture you get of pastoral care and church administration once you get a chance to lift the curtain. But on the other hand, I have learned to understand Catholicism. It will not be put to death by Catholic-bashers' cheap polemics. I don't think any Protestant theologian at any time has *known* Catholicism like Ritschl. Yet in his temperament there was a certain inability fully to *appreciate* it. But he had the marvelous faith to establish against Catholicism a completely consistent ideal of life without adulteration or compromise. I have a weaker, less audacious faith. I would not want to expel Francis if he were to be found in our church even though I do not want to live after, or preach, his ideal in its particular form. But minds are so different. And Christ is so rich. – The deplorable war truly is not to the advantage of Protestants if one, with the short-sighted masses, really is to consider it a religious war. A Catholic once said to me: The Latin Catholic nations are less egoistic than the Anglo-Saxon Protestant ones. I think there is some truth in that. Within Protestantism we like to commit idolatry with our culture and our cultivation of free thinking. In the end, however, it is all about love.

Tomorrow Whitsunday, soon June, soon half of the year gone to the many [others]. And I am still a beginner in the art of living.

Kind regards to your Siri from us!

Yours very sincerely,

Nathan Söderblom

---

[2] Paul Sabatier (cf. letter no. 14, n. 4), ed., *Speculum perfectionis seu legenda antiquissima sancti Francisci auctore Leone*, Paris 1898.

23. To Samuel Fries[1]

2. rue de Maleville 10.10.1898

K[äre] B[roder]

...

Aldrig har jag så lifligt känt, hvad Ritschl har gjort åt den kristna kyrkan, än öga mot öga inför denna i grunden sterila liberalism, som kan göra
en mörkrädd, när man betänker, att den har prästbildningen i sin hand.
Brandt, med hvilken jag gick till botten på deras åskådning, motsåg den
tid, då bibelns historier och historietter icke längre kunna intressera ett mer
upplyst släkte, då prästen läser bibeln som Homer, och för rästen predikar
moral + *poesi*. En sådan man leder öfvningarne i predikoskrifning.

...

Hvad Upsala angår, tänka vi så här: det gör ju ingen för när, att vi gå
och drömma en smula, så länge det är möjligt. För min egen del är jag fullkomligt på det klara med, att min kallelse kanske lika väl är på annat håll.
Kan jag någorlunda hedersamt komma till ända med mina arbeten, så må
det sedan gå, hur det vill. Ju mer jag tänker på saken, desto orimligare synes
det mig, att Upsalagubbarne skulle kunna upptaga mig i sin midt.

[...] Din vän

Nathan Sm

---

2 rue de Maleville, October 10, 1898

Dear friend

... [Söderblom tells about a visit to Leiden where he saw Chantepie de la Saussaye.[2]
The visit is the occasion for some critical remarks on the polarization between the
»orthodox« and the »moderns,« i.e., liberals, in Dutch theology. This is the context
of what follows.] Never have I so vividly felt what Ritschl did for the Christian
church, as when I encountered that basically sterile liberalism eyeball-to-eyeball, a
liberalism which can deeply frighten you when you think of the fact that it is holding the education of pastors in its hands. Brandt,[3] with whom I got to the bottom of
their views, anticipated the time when the Bible's stories and short stories will no
longer attract the interest of a more enlightened generation, when the pastor reads
the Bible like Homer and besides preaches morals + *poetry*. Such a man is leading
the exercises in writing sermons.

... [on a review of a book by Erik Stave, professor of Old Testament in Uppsala,
and on a possible German translation of the second edition of Söderblom's own
book on the Sermon on the Mount which was to be published in 1899]

... As regards Uppsala, we are thinking in this way: it would not be stepping on anyone's toes if we dream a little, as long as it is possible. As far as I myself am con-

---

[1] Samuel Fries collection, UUB, handwritten letter.

[2] Pierre Daniel Chantepie de la Saussaye (1848–1920), professor of the history of religion
in Amsterdam 1878, in Leiden 1899–1916. He was a specialist in Germanic religion and co-
founder of the new discipline of phenomenology of religion, along with Söderblom and others.
He also worked for religious tolerance in general and for the reconciliation of the Christian
churches in particular.

[3] Wilhelm Brandt (1855–1915), orientalist in Amsterdam.

cerned, it is completely clear for me that my calling might just as well lie elsewhere. If I can somehow conclude my works with honors, then things may turn out however they will. The more I come to think of the matter, the more preposterous it seems to me that the old Uppsala guys would admit me into their midst.[4]

...

[On an offer of a traveling scholarship to Palestine and Egypt for the sake of writing a scientific book for the general public, and a request to find a student who could assist Söderblom in his congregation.]

Your friend,

Nathan Sm

24. To Nils Johan Göransson[1]

Paris 15.11.98

Käre Göran!

Du och de par tre vänner, som trofast skrifven mig till, har i år mer anledning till klagomål än vanligt. Ditt kära bref af 27.9 är ännu obesvaradt.

Du läser Sabatier. Jag finner med dig, att han ibland skattar åt en slags utvecklingslära, som ej ger rätt åt verkligheten. Men Max Müllers Vedaentusiasm synes mig än betänkligare, om man ej vill frånsäga sig anspråket på att förstå historiskt och i stället, hvilket också är värdefullt och när det gäller den egna religionen mer eller mindre nödvändigt, använda alla religiösa uttryck som ett slags chifferspråk, som vi ifylla med våra tankar. Sabatier har en viss fransk benägenhet att utarbeta begreppen, tills de få en klarhet och en symmetri, som kommer oss att tro, att vi veta mer, än vi veta. Den beprisade franska klarheten har sin frånsida äfven den. Ett annat exempel är det, du nämner. Han gör ej alls rättvisa åt de mer onormala, våldsamma formerna af inspiration och uppenbarelse. Ett annat ex. Han tror, att tillit till Gud är karakteristisk för det högsta stadiet, medan fruktan härskade på de lägsta stadierna. Där har önskan att få en rak och tydlig utvecklingslinie åter spelat honom ett spratt.

Men han är härlig. Jag ville hafva dig med hos honom en kväll.

Här är nu redan så mycket att göra, att jag får ringa tid till ngt eget, få se, om jag får ut en student till hjälp. Eljes blir det svårt at afsluta något. Jag trycker nu *om bärgspredikan*. La Section des sciences religieuses de l'École des hautes Études har tillerkänt mig sitt diplom för mitt arbete: »Les Fravashis«, om spåren af en äldre föreställning om de döda i Avesta. Detta innebär ju ett välvilligt uttalande af kompetente män. Dessutom tryckes min afhandling gratis. Granskningen af mitt arbete var anförtrodd åt A. Réville, prof. i rel. historia o. Foucher, prof. i sanskrit.

---

[4] The paragraph refers to the idea of applying for a professorship in Uppsala; S. thinks that the conservative majority of the faculty would not tolerate his more liberal stance.

[1] N.J. Göransson's collection, UUB, handwritten letter.

Dreyfusbråket lugnar sig trots alla ansträngningar från de »patriotiske« galningarne.

Nu går posten. Helsa din Siri! Anna helsar Eder!

Din Nathan Sm

...

Dear Göran,

You and the two or three friends who have faithfully written to me have more reason for complaint this year than usual. Your dear letter of September 27 has still not been answered.

You are reading Sabatier. I believe with you that he sometimes pays tribute to a kind of theory of evolution which does not give reality its due. However, Max Müller's enthusiasm for the Vedas[2] seems to me still more questionable, unless you want to deny every claim to historical understanding and instead (which is also valuable and with regard to one's own religion more or less necessary) use all religious expressions as a sort of cipher language which we fill in with our thoughts. Sabatier has a certain French inclination to work out his concepts to the extent that they receive a clarity and symmetry which leads us to believe that we know more than we know. Even that praised French clarity has its reverse side. Another example is the one mentioned by you. He does not at all do justice to the less normal, violent forms of inspiration and revelation. Another example. He believes that trust in God is characteristic of the highest stage, whereas fear was dominant at the lowest stages. There the desire to get a straight and clear line of evolution played him a trick once again.

But he is marvelous. I should like to have you with me at his place some evening.

There is already so much to be done here that I have little time for something of my own; let's see if I can get a student out here to help me. Otherwise it would become difficult to finish something. I am having the *Sermon on the Mount* reprinted.[3] La Section des sciences religieuses de l'École des hautes Études has awarded its diploma to me for my work *Les Fravashis*, on traces of a more ancient idea of the dead in the Avesta.[4] This of course implies a well-meaning pronouncement by competent men. Moreover, my treatise is going to be printed gratis. The evaluation of my thesis had been assigned to A. Réville, professor of the history of religions, and Foucher, professor of Sanskrit.[5]

The Dreyfus row is calming down, in spite of all the efforts of the »patriotic« maniacs.

Now the mail is leaving. Regards to your Siri! Anna sends her regards to you all!

Yours, Nathan Sm

... [P.S.: Request to write a book review.]

⌐ri

[2] Max Müller (1823-1900), orientalist in Oxford. The Vedas are the authoritative writings of Hinduism.

[3] *Jesu bärgspredikan*, 2nd ed. Stockholm 1899.

[4] *Les Fravashis. Étude sur les traces dans le mazdéisme d'une ancienne conception sur la survivance des morts. Thèse*, Paris 1899; also in RHR 39/1899, 229-260. 373-418.

[5] Albert Réville (1826-1906); Alfred Foucher (1865-1952).

25. From ERNST TROELTSCH[1]

Heidelberg 5 VIII 1900

Hochgeehrter Herr Pastor!

Erst das Ende des Semesters giebt mir Zeit, Ihre vortreffliche Abhandlung über die Fravashis zu lesen und Ihnen für die gütige Übersendung zu danken. Sie gestatten, dass ich das in deutscher Sprache thue, da ich bei französischem Ausdruck mich vor Fehlern scheue. Freilich bin ich kein Fachmann in iranischer Philologie, aber die religionsgeschichtliche Seite der Sache glaube ich würdigen zu können. Sie haben mit ausgezeichneter Klarheit und einleuchtendem Geschick die These durchgeführt, die Rohde für die Griechen und Caland wie Oldenberg für Indien bereits veranschaulicht haben.[2] Freilich bleiben Fragen. Die Beziehung der Geister zu Wasser, Pflanzen, Sternen und die spätere Behandlung derselben als Schutzgeister machen einige Bedenken gegen reine Erklärung aus Ahnenkult. Aber hier bleibt wohl viel ... [»imer« = für immer?] dunkel

Mit ausgezeichneter Hochachtung
Ihr ganz ergebener Dr E. Troeltsch

26. To NILS JOHAN GÖRANSSON[1]

Paris, 2 rue Maleville 28.8.1900

Käre Göran!

Jag hade hört ett och annat om Din recension af min bok om Jesu bärgspredikan men trodde ej, att den skulle publiceras för[e] Upsalasakens afgörande, då det ju är sed att medsökande ej bedömes eller, såsom anledning var i detta fall, skarpt kritiseras af medsökande. Nu kommer den emellertid som ett bref från Dig med alldeles öfvermåttan vänliga uttalanden å ena sidan och den kritik, som jag känner från Dina vänskapliga och kärkomna meddelanden å den andra. Jag skyndar att säga, att det intryck, någon (*icke* Sam) haft af den, att den andas ovänlighet och en nervös stämning, icke på något sätt delas af mig, när jag läst den. Jag känner min käre Göran så väl. Tacksammast är jag, när recensenter referera. I Ditt referat kan jag egentligen känna igen min bok i allt, utom när det gäller »Luthers« och »Jesu tolkning«. Du går skarpt åt min stackars »vetenskaplighet«, hvilket jag förstår. Du vet, att jag känner vid min svaghet i spekulation. Men jag räknar till vetenskapen med fullaste rätt äfven iakttagelse o. ordnande af fakta. Eljes blir systemet lätt perfekt, men den stackars verkligheten kommer till korta. Så hafva väl de tänkt, som unnat mig ett arbetsfält inom vetenskapen.

---

[1] N. Söderblom's collection of letters, from foreigners, UUB, handwritten postcard.

[2] Vgl. Erwin Rohde, *Psyche. Seelencult und Unsterblichkeitsglaube der Griechen*, 2 vols., Tübingen 1890.1894, [2]1897; Willem Caland, *Altindischer Ahnenkult*, Leiden 1893; Hermann Oldenberg, *Die Religion des Veda*, Berlin 1894.

[1] N. J. Göransson's collection, UUB, handwritten letter.

I Upsala teol. fakultet är det några, som ej göra det, åtminstone ej i Upsala, och Dina ord skola bli dem en söt lukt, (hvilket naturligtvis icke är ngn som helst anledning att icke skrifva en redlig och nyttig kritik, som Du gjort). Men de t.ex. Danell i K[yrklig] Tidskrift, ha då antydt, att den praktiska prästerliga tjänsten med hvad därtill hör, vore min pennas o. min persons plats. Nytt är det, att Du snarare hänvisar mig till journalistiken, hvilket ypperligt bekräftas af att jag i samma häfte för den lumpna förtjänstens skull ritat två lappriartiklar. Det rådet kommer jag kanske i någon mån att följa. Men först skall jag, om jag lever och ej djävulen släppas lös, bli ärligen gjord till teol. Doktor af universitetet i Paris och tryckt i »Annales du Musée Guimet«.

Det händer rätt ofta, att människor själfva ta miste om, hvad som är deras egentliga styrka.

. . .

Jag har fått en skur beröm i ett par publikationer, så att det kännes skönt att få lite kritik. Alltför mycket sötsaker blir vämjeligt. Nu har jag en rätt allvarlig konflikt med ett par rika o. mäktiga kaxar här.

Gud hjälpe oss att i allt vara hänsynslöst redliga och sanna mot oss själfva och hvarandra, till stöd för kärleken!

. . .

Din vän
Nathan Söderblom

På kuvertet: K. B. När Du, som jag hoppas, snart skrifver, säg mig följande. Det är väl på redaktionens uppmaning, Du recenserat min bok?
Tuus N. Sm

Paris, 2 rue Maleville, August 28, 1900

Dear Göran,
I have heard a thing or two about your review of my book on Jesus' Sermon on the Mount[2] but did not believe that it would be published before the Uppsala affair had been decided, since the custom is that competing candidates are not reviewed or, as on this occasion, sharply criticized by their rivals.[3] Now, however, it has come like a letter from you, downright overflowing with friendly utterances on the one hand and the criticism I know from your amicable and welcome notes on the other. I hasten to say that the impression someone (*not* Sam) had of it, that it has an air of unfriendliness and a nervous mood, was not by any means shared by me when I read it. I know my dear Göran so well. I am the most grateful when reviewers are reproducing the content. In your rendering I can in fact recognize my book in every respect, except insofar as »Luther's« and »Jesus' interpretation« is concerned. You are passing rigorous judgment on my pitiable »scientific method« which I understand. You know that I acknowledge my speculative weakness. But I also count observation and the ordering of facts as science with complete legitimacy. Otherwise the

---

[2] *Jesu bärgspredikan*, 2nd ed. Stockholm 1899. Göransson had reviewed the book in the culture journal *Ord och Bild* 9/1900, 425–428.
[3] Göransson had applied for the same professorship at Uppsala University as Söderblom.

system easily becomes perfect – but poor reality is cut short. This is probably what those thought who allowed me to occupy a field of work within the realm of science. In the theological faculty of Uppsala there are some who will not do that, at least not in Uppsala, and your words will have a sweet smell for them (which is of course no reason at all for not writing an honest and useful criticism such as you did). However, they, e. g. Danell[4] in *Kyrklig Tidskrift*, hinted that the practical pastoral ministry and its activities would be the proper place for my pen and my person. What is new is that you show me the door to journalism, which is splendidly confirmed by the fact that for the sake of shabby profit I wrote two trivial articles in the same issue. That advice I shall perhaps follow in some way or other.[5] But first, in case I am alive and the devil is not let loose, I shall honestly be made a doctor of theology of the university in Paris and printed in *Annales du Musée Guimet*.[6]

It quite often happens that people themselves fail to assess what their actual forte is.

... [A few short notes on personal matters are tossed in]

I have been showered with praise in a couple of publications so that it feels good to receive a little criticism. All too many sweets is disgusting. Now I am involved in a quite serious conflict with a couple of wealthy and influential bigwigs here.

May God help us in being uncompromisingly honest and true to ourselves and to each other, as a confirmation of love!

...

Your friend,
Nathan Söderblom

On the envelope: Dear G. When you, as I hope, write soon, tell me the following. It is probably on request of the editor that you reviewed my book?
Yours, N. Sm

---

[4] Hjalmar Danell (1860–1938), at the time professor of dogmatics in Uppsala (1905–1935 bishop of Skara) in: *Kyrklig Tidskrift* 5/1899, 343–351.

[5] The review in itself would indeed seem fair enough, praising as it does Söderblom's interpretative insight, his wide reading in both theology and literature, his keen interest in the developments of his own time, his judicious and differentiated way of thinking, his fine Swedish style – and rightly stating, that systematic thought in the strict sense of the word is not his forte, that he is lively and impulsive and sometimes not cautious enough. He is lauded for writing both for the scholarly and the general public; his having a journalistic vein does not seem to be meant as a reproach. However, he seems to be quite right in fearing that the faculty could read it as such, and Göransson does not seem sufficiently to take into account the situation of a pending decision on a professorship for Söderblom, especially as he was himself one of the contenders.

[6] Söderblom's doctoral thesis was published as: *La vie future d'après le Mazdéisme à la lumière des croyances parallèles dans les autres religions. Étude d'eschatologie comparée*, Paris 1901.

27. From Nils Johan Göransson[1]

Karlsborg, Ulfstigen d. 2 september 1900

Käre Nathan.

...

Det var mycket vänligt af Dig att skrifva så snällt om min anmälan af Din utläggn. af bergspredikan. Att Du talar om kritik och skarp sådan till och med, det förstår jag icke. Jag har ju där bedömt Dig uteslutande ur allmän litterär synpunkt. Fackkritiken ansåg jag icke vara på sin plats i Ord & Bild, liksom det ju heller icke varit rätt af mig att under nuvarande förhållanden dissikera [sic] Din bok. Att jag uttalade min tanke om Din speciella anläggning och att jag påpekade att Du egentligen icke åsyftar att framträda som filosof med ett nytt system, torde icke rättvisligen böra kännetecknas som kritik. Icke heller anser jag mig ha gått det ringaste hårdt åt Din vetenskaplighet, ty med detta ord förstår jag ingalunda blott det framställningssätt som är filosofens egendomliga syn på tingen. Mina studier och min anläggning ha nog gjort, att jag vid studiet af denna Din bok uppställde frågor, som Du nog aldrig gjort Dig, eller om Du gjort dem, aldrig ämnat att besvara. Men tro för all del icke, att jag därför tänker lågt om Ditt arbete eller att jag skulle vilja vara med om att neka Dig en plats på det »vetenskapliga« arbetsfältet. Där behöfves för visso alla begåfningar. Och för Din begåfning vill jag vara med om att tacka Gud, liksom jag också alltjämt vill beundra densamma. Att mina uttalanden icke äro så superlativa som andras, beror däraf, att jag för egen del vämjes vid beröm, som icke åtföljes af de reservationer, som all mänsklig begränsning kräfver. Du skall icke tro, att min recension blir någon söt lukt i vissa upsalaprofessorers näsa, ty de förstå nog, att den begränsning, jag betonat för Ditt författarskap, äfven gäller både Eklund och Bergström, och att hvad min egen ringa person angår så är jag förskräckligt mycket mera begränsad.

...

Din tillgifne
N. J. Göransson
P. S. Recensionen af Din bok skrefs på grund af särskild anhållan från O. & B.

Karlsborg, Ulfstigen, September 2, 1900

Dear Nathan.
... [Some personal news]
    You were very kind to write in such a nice way about my review of your interpretation of the Sermon on the Mount. That you are talking about criticism, and even a sharp one, that I do not understand. After all, I appraised you there exclusively from a general literary point of view. A more technical critique I did not think was appropriate in Ord & Bild, just as it would not have been right, under prevailing circumstances, for me to dissect your book. That I uttered my thoughts on your parti-

---

[1] N. Söderblom's collection, from Swedes, UUB, handwritten.

cular disposition and that I pointed out that you did not really intend to present yourself as a philosopher with a new system, this could not justly be characterized as criticism. Neither do I think that I have in the least been hard on your scientific method, for this term by no means denotes for me only the kind of exposition representing the philosopher's particular way of looking at things. My line of studies and my disposition probably induced me, while reading your book, to ask questions you may have never put to yourself – or, if you did, never intended to answer. In any case, do not believe that I therefore hold your work in low esteem or that I would agree to denying you a place in the field of »scientific« work. Certainly all talents are needed there. And for your talent I will join in to thank God, just as I shall always admire it. That my statements have not turned out as superlative as those from others, has to do with the fact that for my part, I am disgusted by praise that is not accompanied by those reservations which all human limitation demands. You should not think that my review will be a sweet smell in certain Uppsala professors' noses, for they understand quite well that the limitation I stressed with regard to your writings is valid also for Eklund and Bergström[2], and as far as my own lowly person is concerned, I am frightfully more limited.

... [Göransson expresses his astonishment that the outside verdicts on which the faculty's selection for the chair is to be based take so long in arriving; some remarks on a professor of mathematics; an invitation to Söderblom to see him in Karlsborg.]

Yours sincerely,

N.J. Göransson

P.S. The review of your book was written at the express solicitation from *O. & B.*

28. To Samuel Fries[1]

Paris 28.9.1900

Kära vänner!

...

Här pågår nu en märklig kongress: socialisternas. Det är en väldig makt, ungdomsfrisk, beundransvärdt ordnad och med en stor fond idealism i sig. En del af dem ega något både af urkristendomens entusiasm och af dess känsla af solidaritet. Vandervelde, belgarnes chef, ville, att socialisterna skulle göra skäl för: »se hur de älska hvarandra«. De ha tagit i arf liberalismens från evangeliet hemtade ideal om människovärde och människorätt och gjort det till själen i en lekamen som är full af blod och lifskraft. I Dreyfusaffären fanns i Frankrike intet stort folkligt parti som ej sviktade, utom den autentiska socialismen. Inga män stå den evangeliska kristendomen närmare i det moderna Frankrike än socialisterna af en Jean Jaurès' idealistiska läggning. Gentemot de verkligen förödande makterna i tiden, de må kallas anarkism eller imperialism – klerikalism – nationalism, vet jag

---

[2] Ludvik Bergström (1857–1932), and Johan Alfred Eklund (1863–1945), two other contenders for the same professorship.

[1] Samuel Fries' collection, UUB, handwritten letter.

utom den evangeliska kristendomen ingen mer betryggande företeelse än den organiserade socialistiska arbetarrörelsen. Gud gifve åt densamma goda uppfostrare, så att det går framåt som det börjat från »magfrågan« mot intresse för alla de högsta lifsfrågorna. Gud gifve åt kyrkans män klarsynthet och mod att tillämpa Jesu ord: »Den som ej är mot oss, han är med oss.«

...

Eder tillgifne
Nathan Söderblom

Paris, September 28, 1900

Dear friends,

... [Remembering Fries' visit to Paris; on the argument with Göransson regarding his review (cf. letters no. 27 and 28) and the latest developments concerning the Uppsala professorship Söderblom had applied for; on the question of whether his Swedish translation of Harnack's *Das Wesen des Christentums* (The Essence of Christianity) would need a preface]

A peculiar conference is under way here: the socialists'. This is a mighty force, youthful, admirably organized and containing a great treasure of idealism. A number of them have something both of early Christianity's enthusiasm and its sense of solidarity. Vandervelde, their Belgian leader,[2] wanted the socialists to prove worthy of [the exclamation]: »behold how they love each other«. They have inherited liberalism's ideal, originating in the Gospel, of man's worth and human rights and made it the soul of a body which is replete with [fresh] blood and stamina. In the Dreyfus affair, there was no large popular party in France which did not waver, apart from authentic socialism. Nobody is closer to Protestant Christianity in modern France than the socialists of the idealistic mind-set of a Jean Jaurès.[3] Over against those really destructive forces of our time, may they be called anarchism or imperialism – clericalism – nationalism, I know of no more reassuring phenomenon, apart from Protestant Christianity, than the organized socialist labor movement. May God grant it good educators, so that things will move forward as they have already begun, from the »stomach issue« to an interest in all of life's ultimate concerns. May God grant churchmen the clear sight and courage to apply Jesus' saying: »He who is not against us is on our side.«[4]

... [On the idea of a journey to Palestine]

Yours sincerely,
Nathan Söderblom

---

[2] Émile Vandervelde (1866–1938), leader of the Belgian Labor Party, 1900–1914 President of the Second International, between 1914 and 1937 various positions in Belgian cabinets.

[3] Jean Jaurès (1859–1914), philosopher and politician, 1893–98 and 1902–14 socialist deputy, actively engaged for a retrial of Dreyfus. His political orientation within the socialist movement was revisionist and pacifist. He was assassinated by a nationalist fanatic in 1914.

[4] Mark 9:40.

29. To Nils Johan Göransson[1]

Paris 19.12.1900

Käre Göran!
Tack för Ditt goda bref af den 27 nov! Jag har dröjt och kommer nu lagom till julen, må den bli Eder en upplifvande och ljuflig fröjdefäst!
I fråga om bibelkritiken är det icke de elementära satser, som jag skref i N[ya] D[agligt] A[llehanda] apropos Personne's skrift, som egentligen sysselsatt och sysselsätta mig på sista tiden. Det har fastmer gällt ett problem, där äfven jag inser en konflikt mellan trons kraf på obetingad och fullkomlig trygghet – och vetenskapen, ifråga om Jesu person. Jag kan icke se, att någon formel kan lösa det dilemmat, och jag kan i det stycket hvarken ge Sabatier eller Harnack rätt. Något hade jag ock börjat skrifva om saken. Men det får ligga, det förlorar i alla händelser ej därpå. Harnacks bok kan jag icke värdera så högt som jag önskade, men jag anser mycket däri förträffligt och utredande. Först afböjde jag att skrifva företal ss. onödigt, men då förläggaren ändå vidhöll sin önskan, skref jag några sidor med svårighet. Att bara annonsera, är ledsamt. Hvad skall man i sådant fall skrifva!

...

Detta må äfven bli nyårsönskan till Eder! Tack för ännu ett år tillsammans, Göran! Om en sak, som därunder förekommit mellan oss, ville jag säga följande. Jag kan värdera den sträfvan efter opartiskhet och redlighet, som jag fann i Din recension af min bok. Att jag ej kan finna ett o. annat berättigadt däri, har jag sagt Dig. Men det finnes ju så många olika meningar och tycken. *Framförallt*, måtte Du alltid och alltfort anse mig värd, att Du tar notis om mig och *rent ut* säger mig hvad Du tänker om mina förehafvanden. Min Anna undantagen, vet jag ingen af mina vänner, af hvars skarpsinnighet jag haft så mycket reellt gagn som af Din. Du har i omdömen om, hvad jag skrifvit, yttrat sådan kritik, som mer än en gång synts mig träffande och som vidgat mina insikter. Måtte det få fortfara!

...

Din vän
Nathan Söderblom

Paris, December 19, 1900

Dear Göran,
Thank you for your good letter of Nov. 27! I have been tardy, and now I am coming just in time for Christmas. May it be a cheerful and pleasant, joyful celebration for you!
As for the problem of Biblical criticism, it is not the elementary propositions that have been and are occupying my mind, as I wrote in *N[ya] D[agligt] A[llehanda]* on the occasion of Personne's book.[2] It rather was a problem which even I realize to

---

[1] N.J. Göransson's collection, UUB, handwritten letter.
[2] Johan Vilhelm Personne, *Bibelkritiken*, 1900, a book which is open for Biblical criticism. *Nya Dagligt Allehanda* is a newspaper which had a moderately conservative stance at that time.

imply a conflict between faith's requirement of unconditional and complete trust –
and science, concerning the person of Jesus. I cannot see that some sort of formula
could solve that dilemma, and on this issue I cannot agree with either Sabatier or
Harnack. I had also started to write something on this issue. But that will have to
wait; nothing will be lost thereby. I cannot esteem Harnack's book[3] as highly as I
would have wished, but I do consider much in it excellent and clarifying. At first I
declined to write a preface as unnecessary, but when the publisher nonetheless adhered to his request I wrote a few pages with difficulty. Just announcing [it] is tedious. What do you write in such a case!

... [A few lines on the new book by Émile Boutroux, *Pascal*, Paris 1900]

This may also be [our best] wishes for the New Year to you! Thank you for yet
another year together, Göran! About one event that occurred between us in its
course, I would like to say the following. I can appreciate the striving for impartial-
ity and honesty that I found in your review of my book. That there is a thing or two
in it which I cannot deem justified, that I told you. But there are so many opinions
and likings. *Above all*, may you at all times and furthermore consider me worth
your taking note of me and telling me *straightforwardly* what you think of my undertakings. Apart from my Anna, I don't know of any of my friends by whose astute-
ness I have profited so much. In your judgment about what I wrote, you uttered
such criticism as more than once seemed pertinent to me and broadened my view.
May that continue to be so!

...

Your friend,
Nathan Söderblom

30. From NILS JOHAN GÖRANSSON[1]

Ulfstigen, Karlsborg d. 28/12 1900

Käre Nathan.

Hjärtligt tack för Ditt vänliga bref med de kära julhälsningarne. Nu vilja vi
alla här sända Eder alla de varmaste lyckönskningar till det nya året. Måtte
det bereda Eder tillfälle att få komma hit hem och här i Sverige få en för
Dig tilltalande verksamhet! Ja, *allt godt* önska vi Eder alla.

Du nämde något om bibelkritiken. Jag vill då omtala för Dig, att jag blef
en smula förvånad, då jag läste Personnes skrift. Han synes nämligen icke
alls ha förstått hvad som egentligen gömmer sig i denna fråga. Jag trodde
att han var en skarpsinnigare person än hvad denna skrift ger vid handen.
Det stora flertalet prester förstå nog heller icke detta stora problem, men
de ana dock instinktmessigt, att det i sig innesluter en konflikt ej blott mellan en äldre och en nyare inspirationsteori utan hvad allvarsammare är mellan tvenne olika slags bildningsarter. Det tjänar till intet att sluta sina ögon
till för det faktum, att »bibelkritiken« är en makt i den moderna kulturen,
som Personne icke alls karaktäriseradt. Den slags bibelkritik, som han pro-

---

[3] Adolf von Harnack, *Das Wesen des Christentums*, Leipzig 1900.

[1] N. Söderblom's collection of letters, from Swedes, UUB, handwritten letter.

tegerar inför den svenska allmänheten, är helt beskedlig. Man blir icke klok på den, emedan den icke vet hvad den vill, den förstår icke sina egna premisser.

»Den moderna vetenskapligheten« är visserligen ännu icke fullt medveten om sig själf i alla sina representanter; men så vida som vi skola räkna med den såsom en *makt*, så kan den betecknas såsom en fruktansvärd motståndare till hvarje religiös lifsåskådning. Dess metod bortser från alla dessa faktorer i lifvets stora drama, genom hvilka den gudomliga providensen gör sig gällande. Dessa faktorer betraktas som tillfälligheter, och man märker icke, att man härigenom blott åtkommer det allra allmännaste i företeelserna, och när man ändock i historien har behof att individualisera och fatta de innersta och afgörande motiven, så förstår man icke, att man här då måste sätta det medelmåttigt mänskliga i stället för det underbart gudomliga. På sådant sätt synes visserligen enskildheterna i den religiösa historien bli mycket klara äfven för ytliga hufvuden, emedan den befinnes vara analog med hvarje annan hvardaglighet, men det hela blir oförklarligt.

Redan Fichte d. y. har påpekat den strid, som måste utkämpas mellan den religiösa världsåskådningen och den *profana*, som får sitt uttryck i den moderna s. k. »vetenskapligheten«. Det är en delikat uppgift att i denna strid från början intaga den rätta ställningen. Ty naturligtvis är nästan allting i den åskådning, som såväl katoliker som protestanter hittils utarbetadt, otillfredställande formuleradt, ehuru grundidéerna nog äro riktiga.

Nu de varmaste och hjärtligaste helsningar. Mona sitter hos sin Mamma midt emot mig och jollrar. Det är skönt att höra.

Din tillgifne
N.J.Grn.

Ulfstigen, Karlsborg, December 28, 1900

Dear Nathan.

Thanks a lot for your kind letter with its good wishes for Christmas. Now all of us will send you our warmest best wishes for the New Year. May it present you with a chance to come back home and to find an attractive field of activity for yourself. Yes, we wish all of you the *very best.*

You mentioned something about Biblical criticism. I will therefore tell you that I was a bit astonished when I read Personne's book. For he does not seem at all to have understood what is actually implied in this question. I had thought he would be a more astute person than this book indicates. The large majority of ministers certainly do not understand this big problem either; they do, however, suspect instinctively that it implies a conflict not only between an older and a more recent theory of inspiration but, which is more serious, between two different kinds of education. It serves no purpose to close your eyes before the fact that »Biblical criticism« is a force in modern culture which Personne did not delineate at all. The kind of Biblical criticism he advocates before the Swedish general public is a very mild one. You cannot make heads or tails of it since it does not know what it wants, it does not understand its own premises.

»The modern scientific mind« is surely not altogether conscious of itself in all its representatives, but inasmuch as we have to account for it as a *force*, it can be characterized as a formidable adversary to every kind of religious view of life. Its method disregards all those factors in life's great drama through which divine providence asserts itself. These factors are viewed as accidental, and one does not notice that thereby only the most general facts about the phenomena can be grasped; if one nevertheless in history feels the need to individualize and to grasp the innermost and decisive motives, one does not realize that the miraculously divine will then necessarily be replaced by the mediocre human. In this way, the details in religious history certainly seem to become very clear even for superficial minds since it is considered analogous with any other triviality, but its totality becomes inexplicable.

It was already the younger Fichte[2] who pointed out the dispute which must be fought out between the religious world view and the *secular* which finds its expression in the modern so-called »scientific mind«. Taking the right position in this dispute from the very beginning is a delicate task. For of course, almost everything in that view that both Catholics and Protestants have worked out, is thus far formulated in an unsatisfactory fashion even though the basic ideas are probably correct.

Now the warmest and most cordial regards. Mona is sitting by her mother face to face with me, babbling. That is wonderful to hear.

Yours sincerely,
N. J. Grn.

31. To Nils Johan Göransson[1]

Paris den 1 febr. 1901

Käre Göran!

Tack så hjärtligt för bådas Edra lyckönskningar och goda önskningar! Och tack dessförinnan för julhelsning och för vänskaplig skrifvelse af 28/12. För mig är det alltid af stort intresse att få del af Din tankegång och jag längtar efter mer däraf än Du i detta bref ger mig. Dock vill jag hemställa, om Du inte möjligen själf skapar den för religionen ödesdigra bibelkritik, som Du sätter upp emot den af Personne hyllade, mer beskedliga d:o. Jag frågar mig själf: hvilka kritiker och hvilka arbeten tänker Göran härvid på? »Bibelkritiken« är den direkta fortsättningen af den bibelforskning, som funnits i kyrkan alltsedan de stora alexandrinerna och de mindre konstruerande o. mer nyktra antiokenerna. Dess mål är att med alla medel få kännedom om den historia, Bibeln vittnar om. Du behöfver endast taga en af de talrika »Handkommentarer«, som nu äro allmänt använda o. som alla tillhöra den bibelkritiska metoden, för att förvissa Dig därom. Till denna verklighet, som bibelkritiken med mer eller mindre framgång söker utforska, hör också Guds uppenbarelse, som för oss står som ett oförklarligt un-

---

[2] Immanuel Hermann Fichte (1796–1879), one of a group of philosophers called speculative theists, who tried to mediate between the speculative philosophy of Hegelian stamp and the more modern spirit of the natural sciences. Göransson here refers to *Die theologische Weltsicht und ihre Berechtigung. Ein kritisches Manifest an ihre Gegner und Bericht über die Hauptaufgaben gegenwärtiger Speculation*, Leipzig 1873, esp. pp. 1–11.

[1] N. J. Göransson's collection, UUB, handwritten letter.

der. Nog kan en och annan frestas att göra allt till »medelmåttigt män-skligt« i stället för »underbart gudomligt«. Porphyrius studerade ju Bibeln för att kunna fördöma dess »fabler«. Och mer än en ledes kanske, ja, säkert i dessa våra dagar vid sin bibelkritik af naturalistiska förutsättningar. Men märk väl: detta ligger ej i bibelforskningens *väsen*, utan är en metod, som tarfligt karrikerar o. konstruerar verkligheten i st. för att respektera den. Tag en bibelkritikens storman o. autentiske målsman sådan som Wellhau-sen. Läs om hans passus om profeternas kallelse t.ex.! Säger han ej, att där är ett under af människans förening med och lyssnande till Gud, som vi ej kunna med vår analys komma åt? Framstår ej detta, uppenbarelsens under hos profeterna o. Jesus, mycket skarpare i den klarare bild, »bibelkritiken« gifvit oss af vår religions förhistoria, än i synagogans häfdvunna uppfatt-ning, där underbarheten låder vid boken o. bokstafven som sådan? Gör för all del inte Bibelkritiken farligare än hon är! Verkligheten står sig nog. Och det är ju den, kritiken vill nå. – En härlig bok vill jag rekommendera åt Dig af *Boutroux*. Den heter »*Pascal*« kostar 2 frcs. Du skulle njuta däraf. *Du* passar till att studera Pascal. Boutroux har ngt som påminner om Dig.

Helsa Siri o. Mona från oss!
Din tillgifne
N. Söderblom

Paris, Feb. 1, 1901

Dear Göran!
Thank you so heartily for the good wishes from the two of you! And thanks for your earlier Christmas greetings and kind letter of Dec. 28. It is always of great in-terest for me to be able to take part in your line of thought, and I am longing for more of it than you are presenting me with in your letter. Let me suggest though the possibility that it is yourself who creates the kind of Biblical criticism so fatal for re-ligion which you are putting up against the milder one cherished by Personne. I am asking myself: Which critics and which literary works is Göran thinking of? »Bibli-cal criticism« is the direct continuation of the Bible research that has been pursued in the church ever since the great Alexandrians and the less [artificially] construct-ing and more sober Antiochians. Its goal is by all [available] means to attain knowl-edge of the history the Bible testifies to. You only have to take one of those numer-ous »hand commentaries« being in use now everywhere, all of which adhere to the method of Biblical criticism, in order to ascertain that. To this reality which Biblical criticism with more or less success seeks to investigate also belongs God's revelation which stands before us as an inexplicable miracle. Of course, someone or other can be tempted to turn everything into »mediocre human« instead of »miraculously di-vine«. Porphyrius[2] indeed studied the Bible in order to be able to condemn its »fa-bles«. And in our day and age, more than one person is perhaps, nay certainly, guided by naturalistic preconceptions. But note: this is not part of the *essence* of Bib-lical criticism but a method caricaturing and [artificially] constructing reality in a vulgar way instead of respecting it. Just take a great and authentic champion of Bib-lical criticism like Wellhausen. Read once more, e. g., his passage on the prophets'

---

[2] Porphyrius (233–204 B.C.), incisive neo-Platonic critic of Christianity.

calling![3] Doesn't he say that there is a miracle of man's union with, and listening to, God which is beyond the reach of our analysis? Does not this miracle of revelation in the prophets and in Jesus stand out much more sharply within that clearer picture of our religion's previous history which »Biblical criticism« has provided us with than in the time-honored interpretation of the synagogue according to which a miraculous character is attached to the book and the letter as such? Do not in any case make Biblical criticism more dangerous than it is! Reality will surely stand firm. And reality is what criticism seeks to attain. – There is a magnificent book I want to recommend to you by *Boutroux*. Its title is *Pascal*, and it costs 2 francs.[4] You would enjoy reading it. *You* are the right kind of person to be studying Pascal. Boutroux has something that reminds me of you.

Regards to Siri and Mona from us!
Yours sincerely,
N. Söderblom

32. From NILS JOHAN GÖRANSSON[1]

Ulfstigen, Karlsborg d. 4/2 1901

Käre Broder Nathan.

Hjärtligt tack för det vänliga brefvet af den 1 dennes liksom ock för brefkortet från Anna. Och trefaldt tack för att Du såsom skett vill utbyta tankar med mig. Jag skyndar mig nu att säga, att Du icke alls får tänka, att jag skulle önska, att de bibliska skrifterna ej blefve vetenskapligt undersökta. Vare det långt från mig! Endast det ville jag säga, att när man talar om bibelkritiken, så bör man veta, att den utgör yttringarne af en metod, som fått en makt i samtiden. Det är icke fråga om *vetenskaplighet* rätt och slätt utan det handlar, om jag så får uttrycka mig, om en *idériktning*. Du har rätt däri, att kyrkan bör vara angelägen om att bevara och omhulda en historisk förståelse af sina skrifter och att uppmuntra visdomens tillväxt och utbredande. För närvarande hjelpes hon ock betydligt i första stycket af hela den profana bildningen, som kan sägas vara den makt, som skapat bibelkriti-ken. De, som förstå kristendomen och älska den, böra lägga mycken vigt vid detta sakförhållande. Men man bör därvid icke glömma, att den profana vetenskapens oerhörda framsteg framkallat en uppfattning af vetenskaplighet, som rent af är fientlig mot den visdom, som allena förtjänar heder och värdighet af sann vetenskaplighet. Det är denna i grunden profana och irreligiösa metod, som vanligen möter en i moderna s.k. bibelkritiska arbeten och som gjort ett pinsamt intryck på mig. Jag har för Dig icke gjort någon hemlighet af att jag t.o.m. funnit betydande spår af en sådan företeelse i vår vän S[amuel] A. F[ries]'s skrifter. ... Själasörjaren ser måhända detta i

---

[3] Cf. Julius Wellhausen, *Israelitische und jüdische Geschichte*, 3rd ed., Berlin 1897, 125–135 (esp. 125, on Isaiah).

[4] Söderblom had enthusiastically attended the lectures on which this book was based in 1896/97.

[1] N. Söderblom's collection of letters, from Swedes, UUB, handwritten letter.

ett skarpare ljus än den, som arbetar teoretiskt utan hänsyn till sina med-
människor. Hur ofta har jag t.ex icke märkt, att de s.k. bildade, som med
intresse omfattar den bibelkritiska forskningen, äro fullständigt urståndsat-
ta att hemta någon uppbyggelse ur bibeln, helt enke[l]t därför att de se den
såsom något relativt.

... Jag tror att ingen blir vetenskapsman i ordets verkligt stora betydelse,
utan att han ödmjukt och stilla vill lyssna till Guds uppenbarelse. Hvad
Wellhausen beträffar är nog han en utomordentlig förmåga, men han är för
våldsom, brutal, skulle jag vilja säga, för att kunna hedras som vetenskapsman. Hans ord om profeterna torde i mycket få räknas till retoriken. At-
minstone verkade hela den af Dig citerade passus i en af hans böcker på
mig som ett retoriskt mästerstycke snarare än som uttrycket af en djup tros-
visshet.

... Ibland frågar jag mig, om meningen verkligen skall vara den, att de
bibliska skrifterna snart spelat ut sin roll *såsom trosauktoritet*, och att de
germanska folkens religiösa anlag skall fritt få göra sig gällande i sin egen
riktning för att skapa något väsentligen nytt. ...
...
Din tillgifne
N.J.Göransson.

Ulfstigen, Karlsborg, February 4, 1901
Dear friend Nathan.
Many thanks for your kind letter of the 1st of the current month and likewise for
Anna's postcard. And threefold thanks that you will, as you did, exchange ideas
with me. [The following lengthy exposition has been somewhat abridged here.] I
hasten to say now that you must not think by any means that I did not want the Biblical Scriptures to be investigated scientifically. That be far from me! All I wanted to
say was that when you talk about Biblical criticism, you must be aware of the fact
that it consists of manifestations of a method which has become a powerful force in
our time. The question is not about the *scientific mind* [scholarliness[2]] as such but,
if I may so express myself, about a *school of thought.* You are right in saying that the
church should be desirous to preserve and cherish an historical understanding of its
Scriptures and to encourage the growth and spreading of wisdom. In the former respect, it is at present indeed being helped to a considerable extent by all the secular
scholarship which can be said to be the force which created Biblical criticism. Those
who understand and love Christianity must give great weight to this state of affairs.
However, at the same time one must not forget that the enormous progress of secular scholarship has occasioned a view of the scientific mind which is definitely hostile to that wisdom which alone deserves the honor and dignity of true scholarship.
It is this basically secular and irreligious method which one usually encounters in
modern so-called works of Biblical criticism and which have made a painful impression on me. I have made no secret for you of the fact that I have found considerable
traces of such an appearance even in our common friend S[amuel] A. F[ries]'s writ-

---

[2] The Swedish word *vetenskaplighet* can be rendered both by »scientific mind« and »scho-
larliness«. In this letter, it is oscillating between the two. See also the following.

ings. ... The minister in his counseling work perhaps sees this in a brighter light than one who works in the field of theory without taking his fellow men into consideration. How often have I not noticed, for example, that so-called educated people who with [great] interest embrace research in Biblical criticism have been rendered completely incapable of getting edification out of the Bible simply because they consider it as something relative? ...

... I think that no one becomes a scholar in the really great sense of the word, unless he will humbly and quietly listen to God's revelation. As for Wellhausen, he is certainly an extraordinary talent, but he is too violent, brutal, I should like to say, to be honored as a man of science. His words concerning the prophets could in many ways be counted as rhetoric. At least the whole passage in one of his books that you quoted made on me the impression of a rhetorical masterpiece rather than of the manifestation of a profound certitude of faith.

... I sometimes ask myself whether or not the bottom line really will be that Biblical Scriptures will soon have exhausted their role *as the authority for faith*, and that the religious bent of the Germanic nations will freely assert itself in pursuing its own course towards creating something substantially new. ...

...

Yours sincerely,
N. J. Göransson.

33. To Alfred Loisy[1]

Paris, légation de Suède et Norvège, 58 av. Marceau, le 8 juillet 1901
Très honoré Monsieur,
Voilà des semaines que j'ai calculé pour aller vous rendre une visite un jeudi et vous prier en même temps de recevoir mon volume sur la Vie Future, que je vous envoie en même temps que cette lettre. Peutêtre serez-vous assez aimable de consacrer quelques lignes à mon livre dans la Revue critique. ...

Je reviens de la Suède où j'ai pu recevoir le dernier message personnel de mon cher vieux père mourant. En revenant je reçois la nouvelle de ma nomination à la chaire de philosophie de la Religion et de l'Histoire des Religions á l'Université d'Upsal. Je dois donc bientôt quitter Paris. Voilà pourquoi je dois me priver pour cette fois du grand privilège d'aller vous voir dans votre intimité.
Que Dieu vous soutienne et qu'il bénisse votre travail!
Votre tout dévoué en N. Seigneur,
Nathan Söderblom

---

[1] Alfred Loisy (1857–1940), eminent French Roman Catholic modernist, pioneer in historical-critical exegesis. He lost his chair as professor of exegesis at the Institut Catholique in Paris in 1893. From 1900–1904 he taught at the École pratique des Hautes Études, thereafter till 1926 at the Collège de France. He was excommunicated in 1908. His most famous work is *L'évangile et l'église*, Paris 1902. – Alfred Loisy's papers, Bibliothèque nationale de France, n. a. f. 15661, fol. 419–420, handwritten letter.

Paris, Embassy of Sweden and Norway, 58 av. Marceau, July 8, 1901
Highly revered Sir,
Now these are the weeks I had thought [I would use] for paying you a visit some
Thursday and at the same time asking you to accept my volume on *La vie future*[2]
which I am sending you simultaneously with this letter. Perhaps you will be so kind
as to devote a few lines to my book in the *Revue critique*. ...

I am returning from Sweden where I was able to receive the last personal message
from my dear old father on his deathbed. On my return, I receive the news of my
nomination to the chair of philosophy of religion and history of religions at Uppsala University. I shall therefore soon have to leave Paris. This is why I must for the
time being deprive myself of the great privilege of going to see you at your home.

May God keep you, and may he bless your work!

Yours very affectionately in Our Lord,

Nathan Söderblom

34. From Alfred Loisy[1]

Bellevue, 11 juillet 1901

Monsieur,

Je prends une part très sincère à votre deuil, et je regrette que vous soyez
obligé de quitter Paris si promptement. Je comprends d'ailleurs que votre
nouvelle situation vous rappelle au plus tôt dans votre patrie. Vous allez ho-
norer la chaire qu'on vous confie, et la France aura droit aussi d'être fière
de vos succès. J'ai commencé à lire votre ouvrage et je ne puis vous dire
combien j'y trouve satisfaction et profit. La compétence me manque en
grande partie pour en parler dignement dans la *Revue critique*; mais la
bonne volonté y suppléera. Quand j'aurai terminé ma lecture, je ferai le
compte rendu que vous me demandez. On voit que votre travail est le fruit
de beaucoup de recherches; mais vous avez classé vos matériaux avec mé-
thode, et vous traitez dans un esprit religieux et scientifique un sujet qui importe encore plus à la religion qu'à la science. Vous ne pouviez mieux inau-
gurer votre carrière professorale. Vous me permettez d'exprimer un souhait,
puisque vous avez commencé d'écrire en français: c'est que vous continuez à
faire de vos travaux ultérieurs une édition dans notre langue.

Veuillez agréer, Monsieur, l'expression de ma cordiale sympathie et de
mes sentiments respectueuses.

A. Loisy

P. S. Je vous envoie à titre de document – et de souvenir – une petite brochure de caractère plutôt théologique, où vous pourrez voir comment la
question biblique se pose maintenant chez les catholiques.

---

[2] Söderblom's doctoral thesis, *La vie future d'après le Mazdéisme*, Paris 1901.

[1] Nathan Söderbloms collection of letters, from foreigners, UUB, handwritten letter.

Bellevue, July 11, 1901

Sir,

I feel very sincere sympathy with you in your mourning,[2] and I regret that you are obliged to leave Paris so quickly. I understand, however, that your new situation calls you back to your home country as soon as possible. You are going to bring honor to the chair that is being entrusted to you, and France too can rightly be proud of your successes. I have begun to read your work, and I cannot tell you how much satisfaction and profit I am drawing from it. In large measure, I lack the competence to speak of it adequately in the *Revue critique*; but good intention will compensate for it. When I have finished my reading, I shall write the review you requested of me. One can see that your work is the fruit of much research; but you have classified your material methodically, and you are treating in a religious and scientific spirit a subject which is of more significance for religion than for science. You could not inaugurate your professorial career in a better way. Permit me to express a request, as you have started to write in French: that is that you continue to make an edition in our language of your future works.

May I express to you, Sir, my cordial affection and my sentiments of respect.

A. Loisy

P.S. I am sending you as a document – and as a souvenir – a little brochure of a more theological character[3], where you can see how the Biblical question is nowadays posed among Catholics.

---

[2] Jonas Söderblom (1823–1901), Nathan Söderblom's father, had passed away in June.
[3] Alfred Loisy, *Études bibliques*, 2nd ed. Paris 1901.

94

II The Professor: Letters from Uppsala and Leipzig

35. To Nils Johan Göransson[1]

Uppsala Staby 5.12.01

Käre Göran!

...

Jag tror att det redan är en stor och viktig sak, om den komp[arativa] rel[igionshistoriska] forsk[ningen] kan uppvisa Jesu öfverlägsenhet, enastående art och olikhet mot allt annat i rel[igionen]s historia. Jag tror t.o.m. att denna forskning föres ett steg längre inför Jesus – till inseendet af otillräckligheten af sin psykologiska »förklaring«. Men den verkliga uppskattningen af Jesus och hans andliga goda kan göras endast på en helt annan väg, som jag, ändock den så strider mot »vetenskaplighet«, dock ej tvekar att räkna såsom en nödvändig faktor för hvarje rel[igions]vetenskap, som vill höja sig öfver en blott ordnad beskrifning. Den vägen är erfarenhet af egen själanöd, som tvingar till trons oförnuftiga djärfva språng in i den förlåtelsens och kärlekens o. helighetens värld, där Jesus är hemma och dit han för oss in, ja, alldeles som Du skrifver: *erfarenhet af mörker o. skuld, som ej kunna hjälpas af annat än uppenbarelse o. försoning.* ... Jag söker uppmuntra rel[igions]psykologi, där anlag finnas. Tror Du ej, att analys af de andliga tillstånden, lyssnandet till siarnes skildringar, äro en god väg, för att ögonen må öppnas och denna andliga värld bli synlig, som ingen »vetenskaplig« operation kan tvinga till att se o. erkänna, men som, sedd, blir det vissaste o. värdefullaste i världen? Jag hör nog i bra mycket till de naive. Men nu börjar jag tänka, att det kanske ej skadar ungdomen, att så är, när jag håller mig strängt vid uppriktigheten. – Ack, om Du visste, hur ljufligt det kännes att få lemna det resonnerande och allvetande Upsala o. gå ut till Staby. Gudi tack för ungdomen, som finnes här! Af professorerna känner jag mig mest dragen till Noreen.

...

Din vän
Nathan Sm

---

[1] N.J. Göransson's collection, UUB, handwritten letter.

Dear Göran,

... [On the Old Testament professor Erik Stave who had been accused of plagiarism]

I think it already is a big and important achievement if comparative religious research can establish Jesus' superiority, uniqueness, and unlikeness in comparison to everything else in the history of religion. I even believe that this research is getting one step closer to Jesus – toward the realization of the insufficiency of its psychological »explanation«. True estimation of him and his spiritual goodness can, however, only be attained on an entirely different path which, even though it is so adverse to »scientific method,« I would not hesitate to count as a necessary factor in every science of religion that is to rise above mere orderly description. That path is the experience of one's own soul's tribulations which compels the unreasonable, audacious leap of faith into the world of forgiveness and love and holiness where Jesus is at home and whither he leads us, yea, just as you write: *experience of darkness and guilt which cannot be remedied other than by revelation and reconciliation.* ... I seek to encourage psychology of religion where there is talent for it. Don't you believe that an analysis of the spiritual states of mind, listening to the seers' tales, are an excellent method by which the eyes may be opened and this spiritual world may become visible, which no »scientific« operation can force [one] to see and acknowledge, yet which, once seen, will be the most certain and valuable thing in the world? I may belong to the naive people in quite a few respects. But I am beginning to think that it perhaps is not harmful for the youth that this is so, as long as I strictly keep to sincerity. Oh, if you knew how pleasant it feels to be able to leave arguing and omniscient Uppsala and go out to Staby[2]. Thank God for the youth that is here! As for the professors, I am attracted most by Noreen[3].

...

Your friend,
Nathan Sm

36. To ALFRED LOISY[1]

Upsala, Suède, le 8 janvier 1902

Cher et très honoré Monsieur,

Voici une réponse bien tardive mais très reconnaissante de votre sympatique [sic] lettre du 11 juillet et de vos Études bibliques, que j'ai lues avec un vif interêt. La cause que vous y plaidez avec tant d'autorité et de sagesse, m'est chère, c'est la cause d'une saine et féconde étude historique au sens de notre litterature canonique, une étude pourvue d'un véritable sens pour la vie de l'histoire et pour les réalités de la religion et sevrée ainsi de tout rationalisme dogmatique, qui met la formule au dessus du mouvement et de la vie. Vos articles m'ont fourni maintes excellentes remarques et maintes valuables

---

[2] Today: Stabby, a village W of Uppsala (now part of the suburb of Luthagen) where Söderblom lived.

[3] Adolf Noreen (1854–1925), professor of Scandinavian languages.

[1] N. Söderblom's collection of letters, to Swedes and foreigners, UUB, handwritten letter.

citations sur cette question brûlante. Dans un seul de vos article [sic] j'ai une opinion essentiellement différente, c'est sur le caractère du 4me évangile, où je vois à côté de, et sous le mysticisme et le symbolisme une nouvelle source authentique des faits de la vie de Jésus, source supérieure à bien des égards aux Synoptiques.

Votre livre sur La religion d'Israel m'a beaucoup appris et m'a aussi confirmé dans certains doutes que j'ai vis à vis des idées critiques géneralement reçues. Par exemple sur l'origine du monothéisme prophétique le seul monotéisme authentique, que connaisse l'histoire des religions. Il m'est incompréhensible qu'il soit sorti d'un polythéisme. Je serait [sic] fortement tenté de croire avec vous que l'exclusivisme de Yahvé ait été préché déjà par Moïse et qu'il fut chez Moïse une continuation de la monolatrie naive d'une tribu nomade. La véritable tradition religieuse en Israel n'a jamais passé par la porte qui conduit au polythéisme. Car la religion qui y entre rien sort jamais sans briser son évolution.

– Merci de votre promesse de vouloir bien sacrifier quelques lignes dans la Revue critique à mon volume sur l'eschatologie. Je les liront [?] avec gratitude.

– Il m'a été pénible de devoir quitter Paris juste [sic] lorsque j'aurais pu profiter de mes rapports avec vous pour vous parler et vous connaitre. Je le considère comme un des grands avantages de la vie que de connaitre des hommes qui partagent mon amour pour le Christ et mon sincère désir d'être loyal en toute récherche de la verité sans partager mes traditions ecclésiastiques et théologiques. Celles ci me sont chères et précieuses, mais je veux comprendre celles des autres. Ainsi la vue s'élargit et le coeur s'enrichit.

Que Dieu vous bénisse, vous et votre oeuvre, pendant l'année qui vient de commencer! Que je serais heureux de vous montrer notre vieil Upsal, où je suis à côté de ma tâche principale comme professeur de théologie à l'Université, membre du Chapitre et où j'ai une vieille petite église qui vous plairait. Cela fait trop d'occupations donner du temps pour les travaux personnels. Mais j'ai de longues vacances d'été.

Votre dévoué
Nathan Söderblom

Uppsala, Sweden, January 8, 1902

Dear and revered Sir,

Here is a pretty late but very grateful reply to your nice letter of July 11 and to your *Études bibliques*[2] which I have read with vivid interest. The cause you are pleading there with such authority and wisdom is dear to me, that is the cause of a sane and creative historical study in line with our canonical literature, a study endowed with a veritable sense of the life of history and of the realities of religion and thus bereft of all dogmatic rationalism which fits the formula ›above movement and life.‹ Your articles have provided me with many an excellent remark and many a valuable quote with regard to this burning issue. It is in only one of your articles that I am of an es-

---

[2] Alfred Loisy, *Études bibliques*, Paris (1894) [2]1901.

sentially different opinion; that concerns the character of the fourth Gospel, where I discern beside, and beneath, the mysticism and the symbolism a new authentic source regarding the facts of the life of Jesus, a source superior in quite a few respects to the Synoptics.

Your book *La religion d'Israel*[3] has taught me much and has also confirmed certain doubts I have concerning some generally accepted critical ideas. For instance with regard to prophetic monotheism as the only authentitic monotheism the history of religion knows of. It is incomprehensible to me that it should have arisen from polytheism. I would very much like to believe with you that the exclusivism of Yahweh was already preached by Moses and that in Moses it was a continuation of the naive monolatry of a nomadic tribe. Genuine religious tradition in Israel has never passed through the door leading to polytheism. For the religion which enters through it one bit will never return without disrupting its evolution.

– Thank you for your promise to devote some lines in the *Revue critique* to my volume on eschatology. I shall read them with gratitude.

– It was hard for me having to leave Paris just when I could have profited from my relations with you by talking to you and knowing you. I consider it one of the great advantages of life knowing people who share my love of Christ and my sincere desire to be faithful in all search for truth, without sharing my own ecclesiastical and theological traditions. These are dear and precious to me, but I want to understand those of others. That way, the view is enlarged and the heart enriched.

May God bless you, you and your work, during the year which has just begun! How glad I would be to show you our old Uppsala where I am, apart from my principal task as a professor of theology, a member of the Chapter and where I have an ancient little church[4] which would appeal to you. All this entails too many chores to leave time for personal work. But I have long summer vacations.

Yours affectionately,
Nathan Söderblom

37. From Alfred Loisy[1]

Bellevue, 19 janvier 1902.

Cher et très honoré Monsieur,

Je vous remercie de votre excellente lettre, et j'ai été très touché des sentiments que vous y exprimez. Les détails que vous me donnez à la fin sur votre situation actuelle m'ont fait grand plaisir. Vous vous plaignez un peu de vos occupations, mais on sent que vous êtes heureux et que, après le temps d'études un peu arides que vous avez passé à Paris, vous jouissez doublement et de votre foyer et de votre patrie. Avouez que si vous avez bien travaillé, la Providence est bonne aussi pour vous. Qu'Elle continue à bénir votre oeuvre et votre vie.

---

[3] Alfred Loisy, *La religion d'Israel*, Paris 1901.

[4] *Trefaldighetskyrkan* (Trinity church), in the immediate vicinity of Uppsala cathedral, where Söderblom served as pastor of the congregation during the years of his professorship.

[1] N. Söderblom's collection of letters, from foreigners, UUB, handwritten letter.

Vous aurez sans doute lu mon compte rendu de votre livre dans la *Revue critique*. En le relisant je me suis reproché de ne m'être pas plus étendu sur le mérite de l'ouvrage et d'avoir tant parlé du quatrième Evangile. J'admets la grande valeur religieuse de ce livre, mais je ne vois pas que cela change rien à sa condition devant la critique et l'histoire. Il me parait extrêmement dangereux de lui sacrifier les Synoptiques pour ce qui est des traditions de fait et d'enseignement. Je sais bien que les protestants répugnent à admettre que le christianisme doive quelque chose à la tradition; c'est pourtant la tradition qui nous donne le Christ, et dans le quatrième Evangile, elle l'explique. Je crois, ailleurs, que la seule Oraison dominicale contient le christianisme sous une forme aussi haute, aussi pure, et je dirais volontiers plus haute et plus pure que le quatrième Evangile. Vous aimez Jean parce qu'il vous ressemble; cela prouve seulement qu'il est bon, mais non qu'il se fonde sur une tradition historique indépendante de la Synopse.

Bien respectueusement à vous,

A. Loisy.

P. S. Vous savez certainement qu'on ne m'a pas attribué la succession de M. Sabatier à l'Ecole des Hautes Etudes. Je fais mon cours cette année, sur les paraboles evangéliques, dans les mêmes conditions que l'année dernière, comme conférencier libre.

Bellevue, January 19, 1902.

Dear and very honorable Sir,

I thank you for your excellent letter, and I am quite moved by the sentiments you are expressing in it. I enjoyed very much the details you are relating to me at the end concerning your present situation. You are complaining a bit about your chores, but one senses that you are glad and that, after the time of somewhat barren studies you have spent in Paris, you are feeling double joy over both your home and your country. Admit that if you may have been working a good deal, Providence has been good to you too. May It continue to bless your work and your life.

You will certainly have read my review of your book in the *Revue critique*.[2] When rereading it, I reproached myself for not having written more extensively about the book's merits and for having talked so much on the fourth Gospel. I acknowledge the great religious value of that book, but I do not see how this would change anything concerning its status in the face of criticism and history. It seems extremely dangerous to me to sacrifice the Synoptics for it, with regard to the traditions of facts and of knowledge. I know quite well that Protestants recoil from admitting that Christianity should owe something to tradition; it is tradition, however, which gives us Christ, and in the fourth Gospel, it explains him. Besides I believe that the Lord's Prayer alone contains Christianity in a form so superb, so pure, and I would like to say more superb and more pure than the fourth Gospel. You love [the Gospel

---

[2] *Revue critique d'histoire et de littérature*, N. S. vol. 52, année 35/1901, 507–509. Loisy considers Söderblom's book a first-rate scholarly achievement, but thinks that his treatment of Christianity is a trifle too »dogmatic« for an historical treatise, due to an unwarranted trust in the historical value of St. John's Gospel.

of] John because he resembles you; that only proves that he is good but not that he is grounded in a historical tradition independent of the Synopsis.

Respectfully yours,

A. Loisy.

P.S. You certainly know that they have not appointed me to succeed Monsieur Sabatier at the Ecole des Hautes Études.[3] I am giving my course this year, on the Parables of the Gospels, under the same conditions as last year, as a freelance lecturer.

38. To Alfred Loisy[1]

Upsala 22 XII 02

Cher et très honoré Monsieur,

Depuis presqu'un an j'ai à vous remercier d'une excellente et aimable lettre et du compte rendu que vous avez bien voulu donner de mon livre »La vie future« dans la Revue critique. En relisant votre lettre je renouvelle chez moi le sentiment de regret que j'ai éprouvé de ne pas avoir eu plutôt le privilège de vous connaître à Paris et de vous parler. Entre tout ce que je dois à la science j'apprécie comme un insigne bienfait qu'elle m'a mis en rapport avec des hommes éminents, issus d'une autre tradition religieuse que la mienne et qu'il m'est, à cause de cela, doublement profitable de connaitre.

Aussi dans mon appréciation de l'Evangile dit selon St Jean vous devinez une conséquence d'une manière de voir protestante. Dans ce cas particulier je ne le crois guère. J'ai moi-même eu précisément la même opinion sur le quatrième évangile que vous. J'y ai vu un chef d'oeuvre de la spéculation sur le Christ, nullement une source authentique de sa vie. Mais il m'a paru, que cette explication, qui rend sans aucun doute bien compte de toute une série de phénomènes dans le 4 E., je dirai, de toute une grande partie de ce livre, est trop simpliste pour nous faire comprendre d'autres singularités d'un tout autre caractère, singularités, auxquelles je n'ai pas encore trouvé d'autre explication satisfaisante que celle-ci: nous avons au fond de ce livre si spiritualiste et si spiritualisant un récit tour réaliste, parfois racontant des paroles de Jésus qui n'ont pas été conservées par la tradition synoptique. Il faut toujours une hypothèse pour tâcher de comprendre les phénomènes, ici les récits du 4me évangile. Il y en a que l'idée courante ne m'explique pas, mais qui s'expliqueront facilement par l'hypothèse d'un témoin oculaire. J'admets donc pour le 4me évangile une histoire littéraire assez compliquée, depuis une source, dont la valeur historique égale pour moi celle des Synoptiques, jusqu' à la forme actuelle de ce livre. Et je vois que plus d'un exégète de ceux, qui ne sont pas atteints par la maladie apologétique, s'arrêtent de nouveau devant le problème johannique que nous croyions il y a quelques ans résolu dans ses grandes lignes d'une manière définitive. –

---

[3] Auguste Sabatier had died the year before.

[1] N. Söderblom's collection of letters, to Swedes and foreigners, UUB, handwritten letter.

Il a été une déception pour moi d'apprendre que vous n'avez pas été nominé successeur de Mr [= M.] A. Sabatier. Cela ne vous empêchera pas, j'espère, de nous donner de nouveaux ouvrages sur les questions bibliques. Mes meilleurs voeux pour le nouvel an!

Bien respectueusement à vous

Nathan Söderblom

Upsala 22 XII 02

Dear and very revered Sir,

It has been for almost a year that I have to thank you for an excellent and gracious letter and for the review of my book *La vie future* which you kindly wrote in the *Revue critique*. Rereading your letter revives in me the feeling of regret I had sensed that I have no longer had the privilege to know you in Paris and to talk to you. Among all the things I owe to science, I consider it an outstanding benefit that it has brought me into contact with eminent people originating from a religious tradition different from mine, and whom, because of this, it is doubly profitable for me to know.

Also in my interpretation of the Gospel called according to St. John you divine a consequence of a Protestant way of viewing things.[2] In this particular instance, I hardly believe this to be the case. I have myself held precisely the same opinion concerning the fourth Gospel as you. I have seen in it a masterpiece of speculation on Christ, in no way an authentic source for his life. It seemed to me, however, that this explanation which indubitably well takes into account a whole series of phenomena in the fourth Gospel, I shall say a large part of the whole book, is too simplistic to help us understand other peculiarities of an entirely different character, peculiarities for which I have as yet found no satisfactory explanation other than this one: we have at the bottom of this book, so spiritualistic and spiritualizing, quite a realistic story, sometimes relating words of Jesus which have not been preserved by the Synoptic tradition. You always need a hypothesis for trying to understand the phenomena, in this case the stories of the fourth Gospel. There are such [phenomena] that the prevailing view does not explain to me, but which will easily be explained by the hypothesis of an eyewitness. I thus admit for the fourth Gospel a pretty complicated literary history, from a source whose historical value for me equals that of the Synoptics down to the present shape of this book. And I see more than one exegete among those not afflicted by the apologetic disease, who once more pauses before the Johannine problem which a couple of years ago we had considered definitively solved in its main outlines.

It was a disappointment for me to learn that you have not been nominated as Mr. A. Sabatier's successor. That will not prevent you, I hope, from presenting us with new works on the Biblical questions. My best wishes for the new year!

Very respectfully yours,

Nathan Söderblom

---

[2] Cf. letter no. 37, n. 2 on Loisy's review of Söderblom's book.

39. To Wilhelm Bousset[1]

Upsala 10 IV 03

Sehr geehrter Herr College,

Schon vor Wochen hätte ich Ihnen für Ihr prächtiges, überaus ausgiebiges und besonders für die Untersuchung des parsistischen Einflusses auf das Judentum hochbedeutsames Werk[2] danken müssen. Ich hatte gehofft, meine Dankbarkeit sogleich durch eine ausführliche Besprechung in RHR Ihnen bezeugen zu können. Das ist durch die Umstände verzögert worden. Erst nach ein paar Wochen werde ich die Recension schreiben können.

Meinen Studenten habe ich das große Buch ebenso wie die treffliche Broschüre[3] auf das wärmste empfohlen. Sie fallen ja in das Gebiet meines Collegen Stave[4]. Aber ausser den theologischen Studenten habe ich etliche der phil. Facultät, die sich der Rel[igions]geschichte gänzlich oder hauptsächlig widmen und welche auch für die isr[aelitisch] jüdische Religion die religionsgeschichtlich bedeutsamsten Arbeiten kennen müssen.

Was unsere Meinungsverschiedenheit betrifft, ist wohl kaum in jeder dieser Fragen etwas ganz gesichertes zu sagen. Ich finde, dass der Weltbrand in die jüd[ische] Apokalyptik zurückzudatieren ist.[5] Aber eben diese ganze Weltbrandfrage scheint mir mehr compliziert als vorher. Mit Interesse erwarte ich die weiteren Untersuchungen A. Olriks[6] über die nordische Eschatologie. Es scheint als ob sie die These von dem Weltbrand als eine uralte allgemein arische Vorstellung bekräftigen sollen. Allerdings bleibt es fraglich, ob nicht der jüd[isch] apok[alyptische] Weltbrand z. B. in den Sib[yllinischen Büchern] ebensogut wie bei Philo auf hellenistischer Einwirkung beruht.

– Hier in Upsala habe ich eine traurige Geschichte zu einregistrieren. Kolmodin[7], frommer aber wissenschaftlich unbegabter Mensch, typisch »apologetisch«, ist anstatt des tüchtigen P[astors] S.A. Fries in Stockholm zum prof. der biblischen (neut[estamentlichen]) Exegese ernannt worden. Das bedeutet für das neutestam[entliche] Studium ein entschiedener Rückschritt in Upsala. Aber es soll kirchenpolitisch klug sein!!

Mit ehrfurchtsvollem Gruss an Frau Bousset, Ihr dankbarer und ergebener Nathan Söderblom

---

[1] Wilhelm Bousset (1865–1920), one of the chief representatives of the *Religionsgeschichtliche Schule* in Germany (on Bousset: Johann Michael Schmidt in TRE 7, 97–101); Cod. Ms. Bousset 119 Söderblom (1903/15), Univ. Library Göttingen, handwritten letter.

[2] Wilhelm Bousset, *Die Religion des Judentums im neutestamentlichen Zeitalter*, Berlin 1903.

[3] This is probably: *Frömmigkeit und Schriftgelehrtentum. Antwort auf Herrn Perles' Kritik meiner Religion des Judentums im N. T. Zeitalter*, Berlin 1903.

[4] Erik Stave (1857–1932), professor of Old Testament in Uppsala.

[5] Söderblom in his doctoral thesis, *La vie future d'après le Mazdéisme*, Paris 1901, 280–290, had pleaded for a late date for the idea of an eschatological cosmic conflagration in Jewish apocalypticism; Bousset objected in his review of this book (*ThLZ* 26/1901, col. 520), pointing to its very early, probably Iranian origin.

[6] Axel Olrik (1864–1917), professor of ethnology in Copenhagen.

[7] Adolf Kolmodin (1855–1928), professor of New Testament in Uppsala.

40. From Nils Johan Göransson[1]

Ulfstigen d. 14 juni 1903

Käre Nathan!

...

Du säger att, man ej får skilja mellan det intryck Kristus gör och hvem han är, eller vill Du säga att det måste vara det intryck, som Kristus gör på mig, som uteslutande influerar på den tanke jag har om hvem han är. Du menar med andra ord, att vi icke behöfva någon hjelpidé för vår uppskattning af honom, utan att denna alltjämt skall vara resultatet af det omedelbara intryck, som hans ord och arten af hans verk gifva oss.

Man kan återföra striden mellan den gamla och den nyare teologien till denna olikhet i tankegång. Och när jag på denna punkt tänker öfver de principiella olikheterna, känner jag att jag ej öfvervunnit den gamla teologiens ståndpunkt. Jag tror att vi behöfva hjälpideer för att klargöra vårt inre inför Kristus. Jag tror att vi förlora honom, om vi ej kunna fasthålla någon sådan hjälpidé.

Vi behöfva hjälpideer för uppskattningen af hvarje personlighet, men gemenligen taga vi dem från de personliga kulturvärden, som slagit an i tiden och som behärskat oss. Det gifves olika personliga ideal; och mer eller mindre betjäna vi oss af den utarbetning, som de fått inom den kultur vi tillhöra, när en person möter oss. Det intryck han gör modifieras eller förböjes af dylika ideal. Allteftersom vi göras mottagliga för dem, omsättes de personliga intrycken till omdömen, som få betydelse inom vårt eget personliga lif.

Barnet behöfver föreställningen om faders och moders myndighet, om den särskilda ställning de skola intaga och om barns allmänna pligter o.s.v. Det är en hjälpidé, som har en lång och vigtig historia, men utan den skulle barnauppfostran ännu befinna sig på barbariets ståndpunkt.

Kristus-idén var en hjälpidé i Israel, och utan den skulle Jesus antagligen vara okänd för världen i denna dag. Vi se ju af Nya Testam[ente]t, att Jesus själf uppbygde sitt verk på denna idé och att han lade den största vigt vid, att lärjungarne orienterade sig angående hans betydelse efter denna idé. Att han gick varsamt tillväga berodde ju derpå, att han såg, att den måste fördjupas och renas; men att han ville, att denna idé skulle ligga till grund för åskådningarne, som hans intryck skapade, se vi af sådana ställen som Mc. 8,27 [sic! läs: 29]: »Och I hvem sägen I mig vara? Petrus svarade Du är Kristus.«

Då jag talade om den bibliska åskådningen, då menade jag företrädesvis dessa hjälpidéer, som de första kristna betjänade sig af för att orientera sig angående Jesus. Kristenheten begagnar sig ju ännu af dem, om vi se bort från enskilda teologers uttalande. Och det är det jag fruktar, att om denna komplex af hjälpidéer, som betecknats med ordet *orientalism*, utbytes mot andra, som en modern vetenskap kan skapa, så förlora vi Jesus. Vi förlora

---

[1] N. Söderblom's collection of letters, from Swedes, UUB, handwritten letter.

honom i betydelsen af Kristus, ty denna idé »Kristus« är för vetenskapen ett krux. Vi kunna tilläfventyrs behålla Jesus i betydelsen af en människa, som är djupt genomträngd af den himmelske faderstanken och som offrar allt för sin öfvertygelse, men det blir någon ting annat än »Kristendom«. Ty en sådan människa var t.ex. Spinoza.

...

Din tillgifne
Göran

Ulfstigen d. 14 juni 1903

Dear Nathan,
... [A somewhat lengthy introduction]
You are saying that one should not distinguish between the impression Jesus makes and who he is, or you want to say that it must be the impression Jesus makes on me which exclusively influences the idea I have of who he is. In other words, you mean that we do not need some auxiliary idea for our estimation of him, which should rather be the result of the immediate impression that his words and the nature of his activity give us.

You can trace back the struggle between ancient and more recent theology to this divergence in lines of thought. And when I ponder the principal divergences regarding this issue, I feel that I have not overcome the point of view of ancient theology. I believe that we need auxiliary ideas in order to elucidate our souls before Christ. I believe that we lose him if we cannot cling to some such auxiliary idea.

We need auxiliary ideas for the estimation of any personality, but usually we take them from the personal cultural values that have left their imprint in [our] time and which have been dominating us. There are different personal ideals; and we more or less make use of the elaboration they have received within the culture we belong to, when a person meets us. The impression he makes is modified or distorted by such ideals. Gradually we are being made susceptible for them, those personal impressions are transformed into judgments which become significant within our own personal lives.

The child needs the notion of father's and mother's authority, of the special position they are supposed to occupy and of a child's general duties, etc. That is an auxiliary idea which has a long and important history, but without it child rearing would still remain at the stage of barbarism.

The Christ-idea was an auxiliary idea in Israel, and without it Jesus would probably be unknown to the world in this day and age. We see in the New Testament, to be sure, that Jesus himself built his activity upon that idea, and that he gave greatest weight to the disciples' being guided by this idea with regard to his significance. The fact that he proceeded with care is of course due to his being aware that the idea had to be deepened and purified; but that he wanted the views which the impression of his person evoked to be based on this idea, we can conclude from such passages as Mark 8:27 [sic! read: 29]: »And you, who do you say I am? Peter replied: You are Christ.«

When talking about the Biblical view, I meant primarily these auxiliary ideas which the first Christians made use of in order to orient themselves with regard to Jesus. Christendom still continues to employ them, if we leave the statements of individual theologians out of account. And that is what I am afraid of, that if this complex of auxiliary ideas which has been dubbed by the term *orientalism* is exchanged for others which modern science might create, we shall lose Jesus. We lose him in the sense of Christ, for the idea of »Christ« is a crux for science. We may perchance keep Jesus in the sense of a human being who is deeply imbued with the concept of the heavenly father and who sacrifices everything for his conviction, but that is going to be something different from »Christianity«. Spinoza, for example, was such a man.

... [Some personal remarks and good wishes for Söderblom and his standing in the faculty]

Yours sincerely,
Göran

41. To Nils Johan Göransson[1]

Upsala 19 VI 03

Käre Göran!

Tack för Ditt mycket värdefulla o. utredande bref! Jag menar, att de två höra tillsammans: hvad Jesus gjort och gör *och* hvem han är. Men jag kan ej stanna vid det första och nöja mig med någon som helst beskrifning af det intryck, Jesus gör på mig. För att säga, hvem han är, behöfvas hjälpidéer. Sådana ger han oss själf i talet om sin enastående medlareställning. Det väsentligaste i den bibliska åskådningen är väl detta: Gud utför ett frälsande verk för människors barn. Jesus är dess redskap o. fullbordare. Jesus har en ställning öfver alla o. skild från alla i Guds regering.

Messiasidén var ju för judarne en den ypperstahjälpidé, så äfven enligt min tanke för Jesus själf. Likaledes logos-idén för grekerna. Dessa idéer kunna vi teologer förstå och uppskatta. Men fråga är, om de värkligen i vår tid äro *hjälp*idéer. Det synes mig vara en oafvislig uppgift för att söka finna i vår tids tänkande idéer, som kunna hjälpa till att ge Jesus en plats som motsvarar hans anspråk o. församlingens tro. Du svarar: Detta går ej, ty vår tids tänkande är ej religiöst, utan uteslutar hvarje moment, som kunde tjäna till kommentar åt uppenbarelsen. Ja och nej. Vi talade om ett sådant; personlighetens originalitet och under, högre upp: det skapande snillets under, högst upp Jesus det ojämförligt rikaste o. direktaste utflödet från skapelsekällan. Ett annat moment är historien, dess sammanhang, dess mening, dess underliga sammanknytning i Jesus, historiens filosofi måste ge honom en alldeles ensam plats. – Jag tror ej att vi kunna eller böra lösrycka Jesus från hans sammanhang med profeterna o. hans omgifning. Men jag kan ej släppa hoppet om en formulering af, hvem han är, som för de sökande i tiden är tillnärmelsevis lika uttrycksfull och upplysande som det då var att Jesus är Kristus. Men Du kan vara viss om, att jag ej skall vara med på en tolkning af honom, som stryker det väsentliga i de bibliska hjälpidéerna. Tror Du inte, att metafysiken, som nu dyker upp i teologin, kommer att ge åt Kristus en plats, som bättre motsvarar kristendomens heliga

---

[1] N.J. Göransson's collection, UUB, handwritten letter.

historia, än fallet varit med de moderna Kristustolkningarna? Det ser så ut. Du skall utföra det problem, Du nu tänker på o. ge oss en bok därom!

...

Har Du sett *Eduard Geismar*, Kristendom og Udvikling. En alldeles förträfflig bok, som t.o.m. begriper en smula, att de G.T. profeterna ej voro bara moralister. Du kommer att tycka mycket om den. – Helsa!

Din N. Sm

Uppsala, June 19, 03

Dear Göran,

Thank you for your most valuable and clarifying letter! I think that the two belong together: what Jesus did and does *and* who he is. But I cannot stop at the former and be content with any description whatsoever of the impression Jesus makes on me. In order to say who he is, auxiliary ideas are needed. He himself provides us with such ideas when speaking about his unique position as mediator. What is most essential in the Biblical view would seem to be this: God performs a work of redemption for the children of man. Jesus is its tool and consummator. Jesus has a position above all [men] and distinguished from all [men] in God's governance.

The idea of Messiah was for Jews the supreme of auxiliary ideas, and in my opinion also for Jesus himself. The same is true of the Logos idea for Greeks. We theologians are able to understand and appreciate these ideas. However, the question is whether or not they really are *auxiliary* [helpful] ideas in our time. It seems to me to be an irrefutable task to try to find in contemporary thought [such] ideas as can help to accord to Jesus a position, which corresponds to his claims and to the beliefs of the [Christian] communion. You reply: that is impossible, for contemporary thought is not religious, it rather excludes every element that could serve as a commentary to revelation. Yes and no. We have been talking about one such [element] before; the originality and miracle of personality – higher up: the miracle of the creative genius, highest up Jesus, the incomparably richest and most immediate emanation from the source of creation. Another element is history, its coherence, its significance, the wondrous convergence [of its lines of development] in Jesus: philosophy of history must accord him a completely unique position. – I do not believe that we could or should isolate Jesus from his connection with the prophets and from his environment. However, I cannot give up hope for a formulation of who he is which for those searching [for meaning] in our time is approximately as expressive and enlightening as it was then that Jesus is the Christ. But you can be assured that I shall not take part in an interpretation of him which eliminates what is essential in Biblical auxiliary ideas. Don't you think that the metaphysics now emerging in theology[2] will accord a position to Christ which better corresponds to Christianity's holy history than was the case with modern interpretations of Christ? It would seem so. You should expound the problem you are now contemplating, and present us with a book on it!

... [On Stave's role in the Segerstedt affair.[3]]

---

[2] Söderblom is referring here to Kristoffer Jakob Boström's (1797–1866) and Viktor Rydberg's (1828–1895) school of philosophical idealism (based on Platonic and Hegelian elements) to which Göransson adhered; Söderblom's own philosophical preference was E.G. Geijer (cf. letter no. 9, n. 4).

[3] Torgny Segerstedt (1876–1945) was a disciple of Söderblom's whose doctoral thesis was

106

Have you seen Eduard Geismar, *Kristendom og Udvikling*[4]. Quite an excellent book, which even in a way understands that the O.T. prophets were no mere moralists. You will appreciate it quite a bit. Greetings!
Yours, N. Sm

42. From WILHELM BOUSSET[1]

Nybyholm, 28.8.03

Lieber Herr Kollege
Lassen Sie mich Ihnen und Ihrer Frau Gemahlin noch einmal danken für die schönen Stunden, die ich bei Ihnen verlebt habe. Es hat immer etwas stärkendes und erhebendes, Geistesverwandten und in gleichem Kampfe stehenden zu begegnen. Ganz besonders aber habe ich bei dem Besuch in Upsala und in Staby diese Empfindung gehabt, wie auf der ganzen Linie – dvs [Swedish for »i.e.«] zum hohen Norden hin – ein frischer Zug durch unsre gemeinsame Arbeit geht. Jetzt werde ich noch mit ganz anderm Interesse Ihre künftigen Schriften lesen, da Sie mir dann persönlich gegenwärtig sein werden in Ihrem freundlichen und so künstlerisch ausgestatteten ländlichen Pfarrhaus, Ihrer grossen Bibliothek an der Seite Ihrer verehrten Frau Gemahlin und Ihrer lustigen Kinder, die mit so viel Phantasie zu spielen verstehen.

Auf der Reise las ich Ihre kleine Schrift über die »Kleider« Jesu[2] mit großem Interesse und weitgehendster Zustimmung. Hat Sie auch seiner Zeit Carlyles Sartor Resartus[3] so hingerissen wie mich? In Gedanke und Haltung erinnert vieles an ihn. Mir ist diese Kleiderphilosophie so ausserordentlich sympathisch. Sie ermöglicht uns beides: Ehrfurcht und Pietät vor der Vergangenheit nebst vollkommener Freiheit von ihren Formeln.

Ganz kann ich nicht mitgehen, wenn Sie Jesus so ganz aus der Reihe alles menschlichen herausstellen. Das Johanneische: »er von oben, wir von un-

---

rejected by the conservative majority of the faculty in 1903, apparently on purely doctrinal grounds, an event which annoyed Söderblom to the extent that he considered leaving the faculty. Segerstedt was nonetheless after this affair invited to teach in the faculty of Lund as a lecturer. (Cf. Eva Strohlander Axelson, *Ett brännglas för tidens strålar. Striden om Torgny Segerstedts docentur 1903* [BTP 66], Lund 2001, doctoral thesis, esp. 210 f.222.) After his application there for a professorship in 1913 failed because of Bishop Gottfrid Billing's objection, he was granted a professor's chair ad personam in Uppsala. From 1917 until his death in 1945, he was the editor in chief of Göteborgs Handels- och Sjöfartstidning and as such one of the most scathing critics of the Nazis. But he also turned against Söderblom's ecumenical activities, esp. against the Stockholm conference of 1925. Cf. Bengt Sundkler, *Nathan Söderblom. His Life and Work*, Lund 1968, 419 f. – Söderblom was disappointed with Stave's unhelpful activities in this affair, particularly since that influential colleague had been instrumental in bringing about Söderblom's appointment in 1901.

[4] Eduard Geismar, *Kristendom og Udvikling*, København 1903.

[1] N. Söderblom's collection of letters, from foreigners, UUB, handwritten letter.
[2] *Jesu kläder. Betraktelse*, in: *Vintersol* 6/1898, 91–117.
[3] Thomas Carlyle, *Sartor Resartus*, London 1838.

ten« kann ich nicht unbedingt unterschreiben. Ich sehe darin den Ansatzpunkt für alle christologische Dogmatik, die an diesem Punkte immer wieder einzusetzen und die menschliche Einfachheit des evangelischen Jesus uns zu zerstören droht. Ich kann auch nicht so schlechthin die Formel von der »Sündlosigkeit« Jesu gebrauchen. Das ist auch noch johanneische Betrachtung, bei der man das synoptische und sicher echte Jesuswort: Niemand ist gut als Gott allein, vergisst. Gewiss Jesus hat uns ein sittlich vollkommenes Lebenswerk hinterlassen. Aber er steht mit alledem an der *Spitze*, auf der *Höhe* menschlich sittlicher Vollkommenheit und nicht im ausschliessenden *Gegensatz* gegen menschliches Wesen. Gegen die letztere dogmatische Betrachtungsweise protestiert sein schlichtes u[nd] einfaches Menschenbild. Wie er zur Taufe des Täufers (εἰς ἄφεσιν ἁμαρτιῶν!) kam, so hat er m.E. auch mit seinen Jüngern das Vaterunser, einschliesslich der fünften Bitte gebetet.

Doch das sind Nuancen in der Betrachtungsweise. Ich glaube in dem Worte, dass er der Weg, die Wahrheit und das Leben sei, können wir uns bei alledem einigen.

Und so danke ich Ihnen noch einmal für die große Freude, die Sie mir mit Ihrem Aufsatz gemacht. Ich hatte mich in diese Gedankenreihen so vertieft, daß ich fast versäumt hätte in Station Enköping auszusteigen.

... [A couple of remarks concerning financial matters]

Mit nochmaligem herzl[ichem] Dank und Gruß an Ihre verehrte Frau Gemahlin u[nd] Sie

Ihr

Wilhelm Bousset

43. To Wilhelm Bousset[1]

Upsala 6 X 03

Lieber Herr Kollege

Wir bewahren beide, meine Frau und ich, Ihren freundlichen Besuch in sehr dankbarer Erinnerung. Es war erfrischend und wertvoll, Sie persönlich zu sehen und zu hören. Haben wir doch in unsren Bestrebungen und Hoffnungen so viel gemein.

Ich habe soeben dem Stockholms Dagblad geschrieben, Ihnen meinen Artikel über Ihr »Wesen der Religion« zu senden. Für eine Uebersetzung in schwedisch schien eine hiesige Dame, die das Buch mit lebhaftem Entusiasmus gelesen hatte, interessiert. Es gibt doch Verleger zu kriegen. Noch ist nichts bestimmt. Darf ich Sie bitten, Ihrem Herrn Bruder für das Exemplar und den guten Brief zu danken!

Ihr freundliches Schreiben vom 28 8 hat mich gefreut. Die Predigt von

---

[1] Cod. Ms. Bousset 119 Söderblom (1903/15), Univ. Library Göttingen, handwritten letter.

Heitmüller[2] habe ich soeben gelesen. Sie ist wirklich schön und modern im besten Sinn des Wortes, fromm und kräftig an derselben Zeit.

Ich wusste ja, dass Sie Carlyle lieben. Es fiel mir ein, eben an Jesus seine Kleiderphilosophie anzuwenden.

– Allerdings sind wir über die Stellung Jesu nicht ganz einig. Natürlicherweise will ich ihn nicht von dem menschlichen entfernen. Aber ich finde es klärend, seine wunderbare Sonderstellung scharf klar zu legen. »Sündlosigkeit« ist ein Terminus mit welchem viel Unfug betrieben worden ist. Mir sagt er schlechthin ein einziges: Jesus hat kein Schuldbewusstsein gezeigt. Ich finde nimmer in den Evangelien, dass er sich mit den Jüngern im Gebete um Vergebung oder überhaupt in der Anrufung an »unsren Vater« zusammengeworfen hat.

Er spricht ja immer von »meinem himmlischen Vater« und »eurem himmlischen Vater«. Ich finde die Sonderstellung die Jesus beansprucht oder einfach ausübt, sehr auffallend und ohne Analogie. Aber ich kann nicht umhin, sie zu sehen. Werden wir in diesem Probleme einmal klarer sehen!

Einige Kleinigkeiten hoffe ich Ihnen bald senden zu können. Kann ich einmal ein grösseres Werk fertig bringen, so wird es wohl über jüngere schwedische Theologie sein. Aber das wird zögern.

Alle die meinigen, kleine und große, senden Ihnen viele gute Grüsse.

Ihr herzlich ergebener

Nathan Söderblom

44. From Gustaf Aulén[1]

[Heidelberg, 20 juli 1908]

Käre professor! Med stor glädje hörde jag genom Gabrielsson, att Du befinner Dig väl af Karlsbadvistelsen. Nu har jag hunnit till Heidelberg efter att först i Halle ha lärt åtskilligt af gamle Kähler – ej egentligen det principiella, men hvad han sjelf kallar »angewandte Dogmen« är hans styrka – och efter att redan i 4 veckor ha uppbyggt min panna med att höra Herrmann predika med oförminskad kraft. Nu fröjder jag mig för tillfället åt Troeltschs fullkomligt glänsande dogmhistoriska öfversikter samt åt hans instruktiva föreläsningar i religionsfilosofi (kunskapsteori). Många intres-

---

[2] Wilhelm Heitmüller (1869–1926), member of the *Religionsgeschichtliche Schule* (school of history of religions), taught New Testament in Göttingen, from 1908 professor in Marburg, Bonn, and Tübingen. He was a specialist in Hellenistic history of religion.

[1] Gustaf Aulén (1879–1977), student of Einar Billing and Nathan Söderblom. Professor of dogmatics in Lund 1913–1933, one of the founders of the so-called Lund School that closely linked research in the history of theology, esp. on Luther, with systematic theology. Bishop in Strängnäs 1933–1952. Also known as a church musician. His books include *Christus victor* (*Den kristna försoningstanken*, 1930 and 19 more editions), London 1970, and *The Faith of the Christian Church* (*Den allmänneliga kristna tron*, 6 editions 1923–1965), London 1961. – N. Söderblom's collection of letters, from Swedes, UUB, handwritten postcard.

santa samtal och bekantskapen ha också gifvit innehåll åt min resa. – I Marburg hörde jag af H-n [Herrmann], att han blifvit vidtalad af Dig att komma till Upsala, och att han ämnade sig till oss i okt., hvartill jag naturligtvis styrkte honom. Hoppas det blir af. Hjärtligaste hälsningar från min fru som jag nu fått ned till mig, och från mig sjelf Din tilgifne Gustaf Aulén

[Heidelberg, July 20, 1908]
Dear professor, With great joy I learned from Gabrielsson[2] that your stay at Karlsbad is doing you good[3]. Now I have made it to Heidelberg, after first having learned a lot from old Kähler[4] in Halle – actually it is not so much the fundamentals but rather what he himself calls »angewandte Dogmen« [applied dogmas] that are his forte – and after for as much as 4 weeks having edified my head by hearing Herrmann preach with undiminished force. Just now I am enjoying Troeltsch's perfectly brilliant overviews of the history of dogma as well as his instructive lectures on the philosophy of religion (epistemology). Many interesting conversations and acquaintances have also lent meaning to my journey. – In Marburg I heard from H-n [Herrrmann] that you have made arrangements for him to come to Uppsala and that he intended to come to us in October, in which, of course, I fortified him. Hope it will work out. Most cordial regards from my wife whom I now have with me down here, and from myself,
Sincerely yours,
Gustaf Aulén.

45. To Adolf Deissmann[1]

Upsala den 19 nov. 1908
Hochgeehrter Herr College!
Seit mehr als drei Monaten verdanke ich Ihnen ein wertvolles und sehr geschätztes Schreiben, mit Ihrem Versprechen, wenn nichts hindernd dazwischentritt, die Olaus-Petri-Vorlesungen im Frühjahr 1910 an der Universität in Upsala zu halten. Im Namen der Stiftung danke ich Ihnen herzlichst dafür. Persönlich freue ich mich sehr, Ihren Paulus näher kennen zu können. Die einzige Vorlesung, der ich Ende von Juni in Berlin beigewohnt habe, sagte mir ganz besonders zu. Und was ich von Ihrem Vortrag über Paulus vor einer grösseren Versammlung gelesen habe, hat diesen Eindruck bestätigt und bereichert. Auch jetzt, in diesen Tagen, wenn von »Methode« in

[2] Samuel Gabrielsson (1881–1968), later dean in Rättvik, Dalarna.
[3] Söderblom had to drink the waters there because of an intestinal ulcer.
[4] Martin Kähler (1835–1912), professor of systematic theology in Halle.

[1] Adolf Deißmann (1866–1937), professor of New Testament in Berlin, discovered the significance of the Egyptian papyrus finds for the text of the New Testament. His *Evangelische Wochenbriefe* (1914–1921, English translation 1914–1917), a weekly publication commenting on contemporary events, became quite influential. He became increasingly involved in ecumenical affairs, was engaged in an extensive correspondence with Söderblom, and published the German report on the Stockholm conference of 1925. – Zentral- und Landesbibliothek Berlin, Deißmann's papers – letters; handwritten letter.

einem abergläubischen und dilettantischen Sinne öfters gesprochen wird, brauchen wir doch am Ende in der Religionswissenschaft vor allem 1. neue, exakte Kenntnisse und 2. geniale Auffassung, besonders Auffassung für das Ausserordentliche und für die Ausserordentlichen. Sie, Herr Professor, gehören den wenigen Glücklichen, die das Beide geliefert haben und liefern können. –

...

Die Olaus-Petri-Stiftung ist ganz neu. Aber doch die erste und bis jetzt die einzige in ihrer Art an unsrer Universität. Es gilt erst recht die Traditionen zu schaffen. Es wird vorgeschrieben, hervorragende Persönlichkeiten der Religion oder der Religionswissenschaft zu rufen. Bisher sind berufen: R. Eucken, W. Herrmann, A. Deissmann, Fr. Cumont, F. C. Burkitt und die Schweden H. Hjärne, V. Norström und M. Pfannenstill[2]. Harnack war schon im letzten Herbst in Schweden. Hoffentlich wird es ihm später einmal möglich sein, für die Olaus-Petri-Stiftung eine Serie von Vorlesungen zu halten. Ausdrücklich wird in den Statuten der Stiftung betont, dass keine Richtung als solche bevorzugt werden darf. Nur soll man wirklich Bedeutendes erstreben.

Mit gutem Grusse
Ihr ergebenster
Nathan Söderblom

46. To Paul Sabatier[1]

Upsala 21 IV 1909

Cher Monsieur,

...

J'ai consacré une bonne partie de ce semestre au modernisme. Et il m'a été tout particulièrement intéressant de remarquer la situation différente que le problème religieux actuel a dans le catolicisme et dans le protestantisme. Rien ne me semble plus favorable pour montrer le caractère essentiel et idéal du catolicisme que le mouvement moderniste. Si je ne puis pas m'y rallier complètement, cela ne signifie aucune critique des principes modernistes mais seulement le fait que ma conception de la religion appartient, si je puis dire ainsi, à la famille protestante du christianisme. J'ai été profondément intéressé par les deux gros volumes du Baron von Hügel. Personne n'a attaqué le problème du mysticisme avec plus de compétence – à ma connaissance. Seulement – il veut rester avant le concile de Trente – comme Tyrrell

---

[2] Rudolf Eucken (1846–1926), philosopher in Jena; Wilhelm Herrmann: cf. letter no. 15, n. 3; Franz Cumont (1868–1947), archeologist and historian of religion in Brussels; Francis Crawford Burkitt (1864–1935), exegete and orientalist in Oxford; Harald Hjärne: cf. letter no. 3, n. 3; Vitalis Norström (1856–1916), philosopher in Göteborg (Gothenburg).

[1] Cf. letter no. 14, n. 4. N. Söderblom's collection of letters, to Swedes and foreigners, UUB, handwritten letter.

veut rester avant le concile Vatican. Mais le temps, même dans les églises, ne marche jamais à retours. Il faut avancer.

...

Votre à tout coeur dévoué
Nathan Söderblom

Uppsala, April 21, 1909

Dear Sir,
... [Thanks for sending a book]
I have devoted a large part of this term to modernism. And it has been particularly interesting for me in the process to take note of the different position the contemporary religious problem has in Catholicism and Protestantism. Nothing seems to me better suited for demonstrating the essential and ideal character of Catholicism than the modernist movement. If I cannnot be completely at one with it, that does not reflect any criticism of the modernist principles but only the fact that my concept of religion belongs, if I may say so, to the Protestant family of Christianity. I have been deeply interested in the two large volumes by Baron von Hügel[2]. No one is tackling the problem of mysticism more competently – as far as I know. Only – he wants to stop before the Council of Trent – just as Tyrrell[3] wants to stop before the Vatican Council. But time, even in the churches, never runs backwards. We must go forward.
... [request to name an address for a colleague who wants to do research in France]
Yours very sincerely,
Nathan Söderblom

47. To Alfred Loisy[1]

Upsala / pro tempore Lund / 27 V 09

Monsieur et très honoré Collègue,
Je vous dois deux bonnes lettres et votre Leçon d'ouverture depuis que je vous aie écrit. Vous comprenez, que j'ai été tout particulièrement curieux de voir votre jugement sur l'école sociologique à Paris. Elle est certainement une des lignes les plus fortement tracées de l'étude de la religion. Mais je suis parfaitement d'accord avec vous sur l'exagération paradoxe et – insensée à laquelle ces messieurs portent leur programme, d'ailleurs tout à fait remarquable.

---

[2] Friedrich Freiherr von Hügel, *The Mystical Element of Religion as Studied in St. Catherine of Genoa and Her Friends*, 2 vols., London 1908.
[3] George Tyrrell (1861–1909), Irish Jesuit (converted to Catholicism in 1879) and modernist (excommunicated 1907).

[1] Alfred Loisy's papers, letters, Bibliothèque nationale Paris, n.a.f. 15661, fol. 415–417, handwritten letter.

Quant au Sacrifice, je suis d'autant plus heureux de vous écrire que j'ai dirigé les travaux de plusieurs de mes élèves dans cette direction depuis des années. ...

– Enfin, vous y êtes, dans le Collège de France. Pour l'autorité, vous en avez plus que toutes les chaires du Collège en peuvent conférer. Pour votre position, vous savez vivre en érémite. Mais Dieu soit loué que vous avez, enfin, un lieu de travail sûr et honoré. Il est une véritable satisfaction morale d'y songer.

Votre dévoué
Nathan Söderblom

Uppsala / pro tempore Lund, May 27, 1909

Sir and highly revered Colleague,

I am indebted to you for two good letters and your opening lecture since I last wrote to you. You will understand that I was particularly curious about seeing your judgment on the sociological school in Paris.[2] That is certainly one of the lines most vigorously pursued in the study of religion. But I completely agree with you on the paradoxical and – senseless exaggeration to which these gentlemen carry their program, which is otherwise quite remarkable.

As to sacrifice,[3] I am all the happier for writing you that I have directed the work of several of my students in this direction for years. ... [Examples, and some indications of further literature for which Loisy had asked.]

– Finally, you have arrived, at the Collège de France. As for authority, you command more of it than all the chairs of the Collège could confer. As for your situation, you know how to live as a hermit. But praise be to God that finally, you have a safe and honorable place of work. It is a veritable moral satisfaction to contemplate that.

Yours affectionately,
Nathan Söderblom

48. To Gustaf Aulén[1]

Berlin S.W., den 1 VII 1909

Käre Broder!

Jag kom att nämna för Dig i vintras om Lehmanns o[ch] min besynnerliga, omedvetna konkurrens här i Berlin. Hoppas, saken ej därför får spridning. Sedan en fak[ultets] medlem nu på eget initiativ berättar mig följande, är jag skyldig Dig ett beriktigande.

För ett halft år sedan föreslog fak[ulteten] Troeltsch, men ej enhälligt. Samtidigt förordades alternativt ren religionshistoria, och däri föreslogos

---

[2] Reference to Émile Durkheim (1858–1917), one of the founders of modern sociology of religion, professor at the Sorbonne since 1902. His main work is *Les formes élémentaires de la vie religieuse*, Paris 1912. The central idea is that society (based on solidarity) is the soul of religion, and the essential fact about religion is its social function.

[3] Subject of Loisy's current lecture.

[1] Collection Aulén. G., University Library Lund, handwritten letter.

enhälligt, utan meningsskiljaktighet jag och Lehmann – fast på olikas förslag. Endast emeriti – B. Weiss o[ch] någon till, de rösta med – önskade
hela professurens ombildning. Min sagesman ansåg mig ha bättre utsikter.
Jag önskar uppriktigt, han ej måtte bli sannspådd, och har nu äfven skrif-
tligt till honom framlagt mina betänkligheter.

– Trist att lemna Er. *Låt ej Upsala och Lund gå isär!* Utan sammansvetsas
till Guds redskap!

Hälsa Din Fru och vännerna!

Tillgifne

Nathan Sm

Berlin S. W. 1 VII 1909

Dear friend,

Last winter, I happened to mention to you Lehmann's[2] and my strange and unwit-
ting competition here in Berlin. Hopefully things won't therefore be spread. Since a
member of the faculty now of his own initiative tells me the following, I owe you a
correction.

Half a year ago, the faculty nominated Troeltsch, but not unanimously. At the
same time pure history of religion was recommended as an alternative, and in that
connection Lehmann and I were nominated *unanimously, without any difference of
opinion* – even though on proposals made by different persons. Only emeriti – B.
Weiss and someone else, they [the emeriti] take part in the vote[3] – wished that the
whole chair be transformed.[4] My informant considered me to stand a better chance.
I sincerely wish he may not be proven true, and I have now even in written form put
forward my reservations to him.

Sad to leave you. *Do not let Uppsala and Lund come apart!* But welded together,
to be God's tools!

Regards to your wife and the friends!

Sincerely,

Nathan Sm

49. To Adolf Deissmann[1]

Berlin S. W., den 1 juli 1909

Hochverehrter Herr College,

...

Wenn ein Ruf kommt – auf der einen Seite ein starkes sachliches Interesse
für die Religionsgeschichte, die wirklich gegenwärtig meines Erachtens für
die Wissenschaft vom Christentum, für die allgemeine Bildung und für die
Kirche eine riesige, aber öfters unbeholfen dilettantisch aufgefasste Aufga-

---

[2] Edvard Lehmann (1862–1930), did receive the call as the first professor of the history of
religion in Germany and taught in Berlin 1910–1913, then returned to Copenhagen.

[3] Bernhard Weiß (1827–1918), conservative professor of New Testament. – As a rule, only
the active members of a faculty would be entitled to vote.

[4] Transformed: i.e. to be returned to systematic theology. See letter no.52, n.2.

[1] N. Söderblom's collection of letters, to Swedes and foreigners, UUB, handwritten letter.

be hat. Im nächsten Herbstsemester werde ich eben einen in einer neuen Weise angelegten Aufbau der Religionsgeschichte versuchen. Auch ein lebhaftes persönliches Interesse: das wissenschaftliche Leben[,] die Berliner Fakultät! Ich würde jedenfalls einen Ruf als die grösste Ehre, die mir zum Theil kommen kann, betrachten.

Auf der anderen Seite. Wie tief bin ich im akademischen, geistlichen, nationalen, kirchlichen, künstlerischen Leben Schweden[s] eingewurzelt. Wie kurz ist das Leben, und wie nothwendig ist es, dem um unsrer Persöhnlickheit wachsenden Beruf jede Kraft zu geben. 5 Knaben, 3 Mädchen. Ich habe ein immer stärkeres Gefühl, dass unsres Leben von einer eisernen aber doch liebesvollen Hand geleitet wird. Und ich werde sicherlich, wenn die Sache wirklich herankommt, auch hier gewiss einen klaren Entschluss und einen vorgezeichneten Weg finden. Aber, wenn ein Ausländer wirklich gerufen wird, gönne ich es aufrichtig lieber meinem lieben und prächtigen Freunde Lehmann, der die Aufgabe glänzend erledigen wird, und der im heimatlichen Boden nicht so fest eingewurzelt ist.

Ihr ergebener
Nathan Söderblom

50. To Paul Sabatier[1]

Upsala 12 déc 1909

Cher Monsieur,
En effet, ils sont drôles, quelques-uns de ces snobs anglicans en matière ecclésiastique. La conférence à Upsal 21–23 Septembre fût un grand succès. Les méfiances furent vaincues par l'excellent choix de représentatives anglicans. Et j'espère qu'il nous réussit en partie de revendiquer devant eux l'indépendance de notre église, qui n'a jamais accepté un régime césaro-papiste et qui n'a jamais permis aucun iconoclasme soit dans la liturgie soit dans les églises. On cherchera en vain chez nous aucun document de quelque autorité contenant des mots analogues à ceux placés en tête des »39 Articles on Religion«: »We (the King) are supreme Governor of the Church«. Notre église épiscopale et nationale accentua en 1593 dans le Concile d'Upsala son luthéranisme contre le roi catholique – Sigismond – et contre le duc Charles calviniste!

...

Mille remerciments!
Votre de tout coeur dévoué
Nathan Söderblom

---

[1] N. Söderblom's collection of letters, to Swedes and foreigners, UUB, handwritten letter.

Dear Sir,

Indeed, they are funny, some of these Anglican snobs in church matters. The Uppsala conference of Sept. 21–23[2] has been a great success. The suspicions were overcome by the excellent selection of Anglican representatives. And I hope that we will succeed in part in maintaining over against them the independence of our church, which has never accepted a cesaro-papist regime and which has never permitted any iconoclasm, be it in liturgy, be it in the churches. You will search in vain, with us, in any document of some authority for words analogous to those heading the *39 Articles on Religion*: »We (the King) are supreme Governor of the Church«. Our episcopal and national church affirmed its Lutheranism at the Council of Uppsala in 1593 against the Catholic king – Sigismund – and the Calvinist duke Charles![3]

... [Hints at »the interesting antecedents« of the recent conference to be told some time later on, and some general remarks on Tyrrell]

Thanks a lot!

Yours very sincerely,

Nathan Söderblom

51. From ADOLF VON HARNACK[1]

WB. [?] 23.12.09.

Hochgeehrter Herr College!

Haben Sie vielen Dank für die freundliche Zusendung ihrer Abhandlungen.

Unsere religionsgeschichtliche Professur wird Dr. Lehmann – Kopenhagen erhalten. Ich freue mich, dass er kommt, aber ich hätte Sie noch lieber hier begrüsst. Dieser Wunsch hat sich nun nicht erfüllt; aber es wird Sie jedenfalls freuen, dass Sie pari passu mit Lehmann auf unsrer Liste gestanden haben; möge der Pangermanismus – im guten, nicht im chauvinistischen Sinn des Worts – in den engen Beziehungen der schwedischen, dänischen, norwegischen, niederländischen und deutschen Gelehrten immer stärker zum Ausdruck kommen! Ich nehme die englischen und amerikanischen hinzu. Zwar gilt die wissenschaftliche wie die religiöse Botschaft allen hominibus bonae voluntatis, und sie sind alle willkommen, aber die Wissenschaft u[nd] die Religion haben auch ihre »Heimlichkeiten« der Race.

---

[2] The conference had been deliberating intercommunion between the Anglican and the Swedish churches and even practiced it for the first time. The Swedish church, being both Lutheran and episcopal, has considered itself as a natural bridge between Protestantism and Anglicanism ever since. On the conference and its background, cf. Sundkler, op. cit., 88–98.

[3] The Polish king Zygmunt (Sigismund) III. Wasa (1566–1632, Swedish king 1592–1599) wanted to return the country to Roman catholicism; his uncle, Duke Karl of Södermanland (1550–1611) became king in 1603 as Karl IX., turned against him, and convened the Synod of Uppsala mentioned above. The synod confirmed Archbishop Laurentius Petri's Lutheran line, declaring the Augsburg Confession of 1530 the basis of doctrine, and thus induced even Karl with his Calvinist leanings to give in.

[1] N. Söderblom's collection of letters, from foreigners, UUB, handwritten letter.

Mit herzlichem Gruss u. besten Empfehlungen an Ihre Frau Gemahlin
Ihr
AHarnack

52. To ADOLF VON HARNACK[1]

Hochverehrter Herr Professor!
Ich verdanke Ihnen zwei gütige und hochgeschätzte Briefe. Immer werde
ich es als eine der grössten Auszeichnungen die mir im Leben zu Teil kommen können, betrachten, dass die Berlinerfakultät beim Aufnehmen der allgemeinen Religionsgeschichte an mich neben E. Lehmann gedacht hat. Aber
noch höher schätze ich die Gewissheit, die mir Ihre freundlichen Worte gegeben haben, dass Ihr Wille, Herr Professor, dabei beteiligt gewesen ist.
Weniger denke ich dabei an den Klang, den der Name Adolf Harnack in
der Kulturwelt hat, als an die geistige Befreiung und Aufklärung und an die
wissenschaftliche Erweckung, die ich Ihren Schriften verdanke, und an den
ganz besonderen und schwer zu beschreibenden Reiz und Werth Ihrer persönlichen wissenschaftlichen Art. Ist ja Wissenschaft doch wohl auch eine
hohe Form des Lebens, nicht nur ein Weg zu »Resultaten«. In bedauerlicher
Weise wird das auch bei sehr tüchtiger und moderner Theologie allzu oft
vermisst.
Von ganzem Herzen freue ich mich über die Anstellung E. Lehmanns.
Wir sind Busenfreunde. Trotz grossem Unterschied der Umgebung, des
Temperaments und der Aufgaben haben sich bei uns sehr nahe befreundete
Principien ausgebildet, besonders was die Gesamtorientation und Aufgabe
der allg[emeinen] und vergleichenden Rel[igions]wisssenschaft anbetrifft,
Principien, welche die sog. »religionsgeschichtliche Methode« kaum ahnt.
Ich bin stolz darauf, dass es mir gleich nach dem Tode Pfleiderers[2] fest-
stand, dass Lehmann der rechte Mann ist. Auch seine vier Jahre an deutschen Universitäten, um die ich ihn beneide, machen ihn für diese herrliche
Aufgabe besonders befähigt.
Mir wäre es ausserdem trotz der überaus, ach, allzu verlockenden wissenschaftlichen Umgebung in Berlin, überaus schwierig gewesen, Upsala
ganz zu verlassen. Und mit einer Verteilung wie die z. B. Westermarck zwischen Helsingfors und London gemacht hat[3], wäre weder Berlin noch Upsala gedient worden. Wir sind zu wenige in unserem langen Lande. Halb
öffnete sich mir eine Tür in das Land der Zukunft, der Arbeit und des Wil-

---

[1] Staatsbibliothek zu Berlin, Preußischer Kulturbesitz, Harnack's papers – letters; handwritten letter.
[2] Otto Pfleiderer's (cf. letter no. 5, n. 4) chair of systematic theology was converted to history of religion.
[3] Eduard Alexander Westermarck (1862–1939), Finnish social anthropologist and moral
philosopher.

lens zum Leben – aber mein ganzes Dasein ist mehr und mehr mit dem geistigen, kirchlichen und nationalen Lebens Schwedens unauflöslich verwachsen.

Von drei jungen nordischen Theologen, die eigentümlicher Weise von einander ganz unabhängig vor zwanzig Jahren sich der allgemeinen Religionsgeschichte zu widmen beschlossen und zwar durch dieselbe Eingangspforte, das Avestastudium, die allg[emeine] Rel[igions]wissenschaft antraten, hatten die zwei anderen den ungemeinen Vortheil mehrere Jahre unverkürzt den betreffenden philologischen Studien in Deutschland und Holland widmen zu können – während ich in Paris von einem – zwar *menschlich sehr bereichernden* aber mannigfältigen und mühsamen Pfarramt Stunden und Tage für die Wissenschaft abzuzwingen hatte. Jetzt hat der Norweger, Brede Kristensen[4], – der philologisch am gründlichsten und vielseitigsten ausgebildete – nach C. P. Tiele in Leiden[5] den Lehrstuhl der rel[igions]gesch[ichtlichen] Tradition inne, wo auch Lehmann und ich von der Fakultät vorgeschlagen waren. Der Däne, genialer Schriftsteller und Vorleser und ein Mann gewaltiger Leistungsfähigkeit, hat die vornehm[s]te Professur, wo er nach meiner Überzeugung Ihre Erwartungen glänzend erfüllen wird. Ich, der Schwede, allein habe den – zwar durch mannigfaltige andere Aufgaben auf die rein wissenschaftliche Arbeit beeinträchtigenden – Vortheil, in meinem Vaterlande wirken zu können. – Mit den besten Neujahrswünschen auch von meiner Frau, Ihr dankbar und ehrfurchtsvoll sehr ergebener
Nathan Söderblom

53. To David Cairns[1]

Upsala 3 Oktober 1912

My Dear Professor Cairns,

If I have not sent you earlier a letter with thanks for two inspiring and beautiful letters and for the warmly appreciated gift from the Liverpool Conference, that does not mean, that you have not been very often and in very intimate thought present to my mind.

...

It is very foolish to consider, with the last generation of anthropologists and historians of religion, animism and everything in the primitive human-

---

[4] William Brede Kristensen (1867–1953), egyptologist in Leiden.

[5] Cornelis Petrus Tiele (1830–1902), author of a much-used *Geschiedenis van den godsdienst tot aan de heerschappij der wereldsgodsdiensten* (1876), whose German translation *Kompendium der Religionsgeschichte* (1880) in its later editions (until the 6th, 1931) was revised by Söderblom.

[1] David Cairns (1862–1946), Principal of United Free Church College and professor of apologetics and systematic theology in Aberdeen; N. Söderblom's collection of letters, to Swedes and foreigners, UUB, handwritten letter, draft. The actual letter is missing in Cairns' papers at King's College Library, Aberdeen.

ity as sheer superstition and curiosa. Then we are sheer superstition and curiosa ourselves, because there is nothing in the actual civilization, which cannot be traced back to primitive man. He had no flying machine – but he used the instrument for several purposes. He had not the Christian belief, but he dimly conceived the Supernatural and he knew High Beings, who have made everything. By the fact, it is more natural to consider the evolution of religion, as we consider other branches of human knowledge, as a long and painful history of ignorance and mistakes, but also as a growing acquaintance with reality. I have treated this problem in a course of lectures during the second half of September. And I have become more convinced than before, that the three chief beginnings of the idea of God to be found in primitive belief: 1) »Makers«, »Allfathers« (Andrew Lang[2]), Bajamee, Nzambe etc etc, 2) the Mana, Orenda, Wakanda etc, the »Power«, the unusual, not-to-be-treated lightly, tabu, »supernatural[«], 3) animism = soul, spirit, volitional and thinking unity, individuality; these three dim apperceptions of the Divine have been developped in different way in the three great civilizations: 1) the »deistic« Shang-ti in China, 2) the impersonal Brahman in India, 3) the will-power Jahveh in O.T and God in Christianity.

On Monday we go to Leipzic with the largest part of the family. The Saxon government asked me to come and take a new chair to be founded from 1 oct. for Religionsgeschichte [history of religion]. The Theol. Faculty in Leipsic let me know, that they knew, that I had declared three years ago in behalf of Pfleiderers vacant chair ... [the remainder of the letter is missing]

54. To Gustaf Ribbing[1]

Leipzig G 15 III 1913

Gode, käre vän!

...

Här drar man nu en lättnadens suck i följd af demobilisering och fredsutsikt. Åtminstone de af våra bekanta, som ha söner i första uppbådet. Frankrikes vanvettiga revanchhets och Times' synnerligen kloka och kraftiga artiklar däremot ha nog en smula påverkat stämningen här i god riktning. Eljes är man fruktansvärd [sic] krigisk och Englandshatande. Vi träffade her[r] Lamprecht ägaren af Leipcigs förnämsta tidning, som några dagar tidigare kallat Kung Edward »einen Commis-voyageur in Deutschen Hass.« Jag kunde inte hålla mig från att fråga, om sådant språk förekommer i engelsk press och är värdigt en stor nation. Vederbörande tog i mycket hett,

---

[2] Andrew Lang, *The Making of Religion*, London 1898.

[1] Gustaf Ribbing (1849–1942), district judge; N. Söderblom's collection of letters, to Swedes and foreigners, UUB, handwritten letter.

men lugnade sig, då jag föreslog honom att Tyskland och England borde i allsköns ro dela den ännu disponibla delen af världen. Tyskland kunde gärna ta brorslotten.

...

Jag fortsätter detta bref i Gatersleben nära Quedlinburg hos kyrkoherden Radlach, en lärd och from man, som redigerar provinsen Sachsens historiska tidskrift och är en intensiv Gustaf-Adolfs-kännare och beundrare. Vi ha idag Palmsöndag[.] Staffan och jag varit med om konfirmationen, hjärtligt och rättframt. De tänka och tala om sin preussiska historia något i samma stil som 1600talets svenskar kände och talade om sin historia. Trakten är rik, jorden ypperlig. Men armarna gå till industrin – och hvar vår komma 200 à 300,000 polacker bara för provinsen Sachsen, lefva sammanfösta i kaserner och så och skörda åt det germanska herrefolket. Hur går det med kultur och kyrka, när de behöfvas hela året, bli bofasta och draga med sig sina själasörjare? Vi ha nyss beskådat den sk. domänen, som Johan Banér en gång utarrenderade för 6 år.

... Din tillgifne
Nathan Söderblom

Leipzig Gohlis, March 15, 1913
Dear good friend,
[Thanks for Ribbing's letter, plans of coming to see him]
Here one is now heaving a sigh of relief as a consequence of demobilization and the chance for peace. At least those of our acquaintances who have sons first in line for conscription. France's raving agitation for revenge and *The Times'* extraordinarily judicious and sound articles against it have certainly somewhat swayed the mood in a good direction. Otherwise one is frighteningly warlike and hating Britain. We met Mr. Lamprecht, owner of Leipzig's most distinguished newspaper,[2] who a couple of days previously had called King Edward »einen Commis-voyageur in Deutschen Hass« [a commercial traveler in hatred of Germans].[3] I could not help asking him if such language occurred in the English press and if it was worthy of a great nation. This man became very excited and angry, but calmed down when I suggested to him that Germany and Britain should in peace and quietness distribute the still disposable part of the world among themselves. Germany might readily take the lion's share.
... [on a controversial speech of the Kaiser to the Bund der Landwirte, an ultra-conservative farmers' organization]
I am continuing this letter in Gatersleben near Quedlinburg in the home of pastor Radlach[4], a learned and pious man who is the editor of the province of Sachsen's historical journal and who is a well-versed expert on, and admirer of, Gustaf Adolf.

---

[2] I have not been able to secure more information about him. The editor.

[3] King Edward VII. (1841–1910), King of Great Britain and Ireland 1901–1910, since 1901 Emperor of India. The above invective refers to the goodwill tours abroad that he had made as a crown prince, which helped to bring about the Entente cordiale between Britain and France in 1904. This accord at first concerned the colonies of the two countries, later the eventuality of a war against Germany.

[4] Heinrich Radlach (1882–1927), pastor in Gatersleben.

Today is Palm Sunday. Staffan and I took part in the confirmation service, hearty and straightforward. They think and talk about their Prussian history in the same manner as 17th century Swedes felt and talked about their history. The region is rich, the soil superb. But the poor go to work in industry – and every spring 200 to 300,000 Poles are coming to the province of Sachsen alone; they live crowded in barracks and the like and then harvest for the Germanic master race. What is to become of culture and church when they are needed the year around, settle down and bring their clergy with them? We recently visited the so-called domain that Johan Banér[5] once had leased for 6 years.

... Yours sincerely,

Nathan Söderblom

55. To Alfred Loisy[1]

Paris, le 14 avril 1913

Cher Monsieur et Collègue,

Votre livre, si émouvant, si révélateur, si unique dans la complication tragique de circonstances intérieures et extérieures et dans la voie tracée à travers elles – j'ai été touché de l'amitié de me l'envoyer. Je l'ai reçu à Upsal, je l'ai lu entre Hambourg et Cologne. Et j'aimerais bien vous en remercier de vive voix à Paris.

Il me semble qu'il est très difficile de dire, dans cet ordre des choses morales, ce qui est erreur ou peine perdue. Personne ne peut calculer ce que l'âme humaine et les âmes humaines en tirent pour leur profit. Il y a ici un mystère de solidarité, que l'église a tâché à exprimer – mais qui, certainement, est plus facile de constater pour celui qui n'a pas lui-même porté les souffrances.

Merci – et surtout de la préface et de votre indépendance toujours gardée en dépit de toutes les dogmatiques.

Avez vous un instant pour moi un de ces jours? Quand vous dérangerai-je le moins? Nous resterons, Madame Söderblom et moi, jusqu'au mardi 22, et nous demeurons chez le Consul général Nordling. J'espère de pouvoir entendre un de vos cours.

Votre de tout coeur dévoué

Nathan Söderblom

Paris, April 14, 1913

Dear Sir and colleague,

Your book,[2] so moving, so revealing, so unique in the tragic complication of interior and exterior circumstances and in the path you have traced through them. I was

---

[5] Johan Banér (1596–1641), Swedish field marshal under Gustaf II. Adolf, governor of Pomerania 1638–1641.

[1] N. Söderblom's collection of letters, to Swedes and foreigners, UUB, handwritten letter.

[2] Loisy's autobiography *Choses passées*, Paris 1913.

moved by your kindness of sending it to me. I received it in Uppsala and read it between Hamburg and Cologne. And I would very much like to thank you for it personally in Paris.

It seems to me that it is very difficult to tell, in this category of moral affairs, what is an error or futile endeavor. No one can estimate what kind of profit the human soul and the human souls will draw from it. There is a mystery of solidarity here which the Church has tried to express – but which it is certainly easier to confirm for one who has not himself borne the sufferings.

Thank you – particularly for the preface and for the independence you have always preserved in spite of all dogmatics.

Are you going to have a spare moment for me one of these days? When shall I least disturb you? We shall stay, Mrs. Söderblom and myself, until Tuesday the 22nd, and we are lodging with the Consul General, Nordling.[3] I hope to be able to listen to one of your courses.

Yours very sincerely,
Nathan Söderblom

56. From ALFRED LOISY[1]

Ceffonds, 18 avril 1913

Monsieur et cher Collègue,

Votre lettre m'arrive dans mon trou de campagne où je suis rentré depuis huit jours. Mes cours sont terminés. Comme Paris me fatigue, je me suis éclipsé immédiatement. Je regrette beaucoup que cette fugue me prive du plaisir de vous voir.

Mon petit livre a au moins un mérite, celui de n'être pas une apologie ni un plaidoyer. Ce serait plutôt une confession publique. J'ai fait en sorte de ne pas faire la confession d'autrui, ce qui arrive quelquefois.

Bien cordialement à vous, avec mes sentiments respectueuses pour Madame Söderblom.

Alfred Loisy

Ceffonds, April 18, 1913

Sir and dear colleague,

Your letter has reached me in my country hole where I returned a week ago. As I got tired of Paris, I decamped immediately. I very much regret that this running away deprives me of the pleasure of seeing you.

My little book has at least one merit, that of being neither an apology nor a defence. It would rather be a public confession. I have done it in such a way as not to present a confession of someone else, as it sometimes happens.

Very cordially yours, and with my sentiments of respect for Mrs. Söderblom,
Alfred Loisy

---

[3] Gustaf Nordling (1853–1916), Swedish Consul General in Paris 1898–1915.

[1] N. Söderblom's collection of letters, from foreigners, UUB, handwritten letter.

57. To Alfred Loisy[1]

Paris 29 IV 1913

Monsieur et cher Collègue,
Merci de vos aimables lignes. J'aurais un grand intérêt et grand profit, certainement, de pouvoir m'entretenir avec vous au sujet du Sacrifice, dont on a fait trop de théories et trop peu d'analyse. –

Oui, en effet, votre autobiographie ne ressemble à aucune des autres confessions. Son originalité est, à coté de l'accent individuel de votre tempérament, la passion de l'exactitude et le courage de la vérité telle qu'elle. Vous n'êtes clément ni pour vous, ni pour les autres. Mais comme je vous ai dit, vous n'avez pas seulement fourni un moyen de se rendre compte de certaines évenements compliqués et tristes et de la nature d'un système plus facile à condamner qu'à remplacer: on sort de votre livre avec le sentiment sacré d'avoir assisté à un grand effort moral.

J'espère que vour garderez les forces nécessaires pour réaliser le plan d'études comparées que vous voulez [?] être proposé – et surtout je vous souhaite beaucoup plus de soleil que nous n'ayons à Paris en ce moment.
Votre de tout coeur dévoué
Nathan Söderblom

Paris, April 29, 1913

Sir and dear colleague,
Thank you for your amiable lines. I would be very much interested in, and certainly greatly profit from, being able to talk with you on the subject of Sacrifice,[2] on which too many theories have been put forward and too little analysis. –

Yes indeed, your autobiography does not resemble any of the other confessions. Its originality lies, apart from the personal accent of your temperament, in the passion for precision and the courage of [pursuing] the truth for its own sake. You are not lenient either toward yourself or toward others. But as I told you, you have not only displayed a means of giving account of certain complicated and sad events and of the nature of a system which it is easier to condemn than to replace: one leaves your book with the feeling of having witnessed a great moral effort.

I hope you are going to spare the energy necessary for realizing the plan of the comparative studies you want [?] to be presented – and above all, I wish you much more sunshine than we are having in Paris at the moment.
Very sincerely yours,
Nathan Söderblom

---

[1] N. Söderblom's collection of letters, to Swedes and foreigners, UUB, handwritten letter.
[2] Loisy had long been interested in this subject (cf. letter no. 47, n. 3) and finally wrote a well-known book on it: *Essai historique sur le sacrifice*, Paris 1920.

58. To Ulrik Quensel[1]

Käre Broder!

...

Jag skrifver nu på hygglig svenska en sak, som jag – dumt – först skref på tyska. Sedan låter jag en herre med ledning af båda göra tyskan läsbar. I seminariet äro duktiga ynglingar. Deras arbetsförmåga är foredömlig. – Emot den tyska nationalguden reagera vi våldsamt.

Märkvärdigt, så länge människan och nationen knoga i uppförsbacken, äro de mycket tilltalande. Men bli de beati possidentes, äro de outhärdliga – åtminstone innan de hunnit få sådana säkra fasoner, som engelsmännen ha. – Tack för Helge!

– Hälsa! Tillgifne
Nathan Söderblom

Leipzig Gohlis, June 6, 1913

Dear friend,
... [On Quensel's two sons who had come to Leipzig as exchange high school students in order to learn German]

I am now writing in decent Swedish something I – stupidly – first wrote in German[2]. I shall then let a gentleman with a command of both [languages] make the German readable. In my seminar there are capable young men. Their capacity for work is exemplary. – Against the German national deity we are reacting violently.

Strange, as long as man and nation are struggling uphill, they are quite attractive. But once they become *beati possidentes*, they are unbearable – at least before they have managed to acquire such assured manners as the English. Thanks for Helge![3]

Greetings! Sincerely,
Nathan Söderblom

59. From Adolf Deissmann[1]

Berlin-Wilmersdorf, 12. Nov. 1913

Verehrter und lieber Freund! Heute komme ich mit einer Sache, die mir sehr am Herzen liegt und die ich gleich ohne Zögern vortrage: würde *irgend welche Aussicht* vorhanden sein, dass Sie einem Ruf in unsere Berliner Fakultät folgeleisteten?[2] Allgemein sagt man: »Söderblom kann nicht kom-

---

[1] Ulrik Quensel (1863–1944), pathologist at Uppsala University and Söderblom's physician. N. Söderblom's collection of letters, to Swedes and foreigners, UUB, handwritten letter.
[2] *Das Werden des Gottesglaubens*, revised and enlarged translation, revision of the German text by R. Stübe, Leipzig 1916; the Swedish edition was published first: *Gudstrons uppkomst*, Stockholm 1914.
[3] Söderblom's son who had stayed in Uppsala and whom the Quensels were taking care of.

[1] N. Söderblom's ecumenical collection A 6, UUB, handwritten letter.
[2] Edvard Lehmann had left Berlin again for Copenhagen; cf. letter no. 48, n. 2.

men, er muss nach Schweden zurück«, ich möchte aber doch gern den Versuch machen, mich authentisch zu informieren. Falls irgend eine Möglichkeit besteht, dass Sie zu uns kommen, würde ich in der Fakultät beantragen, dass wir Sie vorschlagen, und ich glaube, alle würden freudig zustimmen. Wie sehr würde ich mich persönlich freuen, wenn Sie eine ernsthafte Hoffnung machen könnten, dass die Möglichkeit eines Eintritts in unseren Kreis besteht.

Mit der Bitte, mich sobald Sie können zu informieren und mit vielen Grüßen von Haus zu Haus

Ihr

treu ergebener

Adolf Deißmann.

60. To HARALD HJÄRNE[1]

Vördade, käre Lärare och Broder!

Afskedsuppvaktning. Afsked från Uppsala kan Du ej taga, ens om Du ville det. Så evigt som något mänskligt kan vara, så fast sitter Du i Upsala. Jag menar förstås inte »stenarne och marken« och allt det där, som en primitiv eller dekadent religiositet kan hålla heligt. Utan jag menar verkligen Anden. Den Helige Ande är liksom allt lefvande stadd i tillväxt i tiderna, Och Han har en historia. Och det har varit Dig af gudomlig nåd förunnadt att i mångas bröst, här är två, inlägga en vetskap och en fordringsfull underkunnighet om Anden i vissa hans yttringar, som vi utan Dig ej skulle ega. En försakelse är i alla fall att ej få vara med om lördag. Du afskyr med rätta sentimentalitet. Någon gång kan det ändå vara välgörande att få gifva känslorna fritt lopp. –

Här är beklämmande att vara så långt från medelpunkten i denna tid. I allt annat är mycket hugnesamt att förtälja. Locktonerna ljuda igen från Berlin. Äfven om jag vore tysk, skulle de för mig icke spela någon roll, då jag här har och kan ytterligen få det vida bättre än i Berlin. Nu är ju saken den, att jag senast sommaren 1915 vill och måste vara på allvar installerad i Upsala. Men det ser ut, som om dörrar öppnade sig för sträfvandena. Och det är alltid angenämt att konstatera utsiktslösheten i försöken att inrangera mina Upsalaläror på någon af de här gifna apotekshyllorna.

Men beklämmande äro hörsagor från och tankarna på fosterlandet. »Was ist eigentlich in Schweden los«? En regering, som kan göra huru mycket den än påfordrar för försvaret – och låter landet pinsamt vänta. Och denna allena s.k. konungamakt, som skall klämmas. Jag försäkrar, intrycket prins Vilhelm gjorde, går ej ur mig. Nog ha de syndat, inklusive underlåtenhetssynder, men nu får man för kungahuset en känsla som knap-

---

[1] Collection Harald Hjärne 1p, UUB, handwritten letter.

past förr. Här undra alla öfver, att icke Sverige knyter fastare band med Tyskland. – Apropos, Du måste låta Hohenzollern – Vasa komma för tysk publik. – De fräcka tjeckiska barbarerna och Rosegger! Nu vore det ju nästan synd, om han icke finge priset – fast den andre är så mycket, mycket förmer. ...

Din N. S-m

Leipzig-Gohlis, November 13, 1913

Esteemed, dear Teacher and friend,

Farewell respects.[2] You cannot say farewell to Uppsala, even if you wanted to. As eternally as anything human can be, so stuck you are in Uppsala. Of course, I don't mean »the stones and the soil«[3] and things like that which a primitive or decadent religiosity can regard as sacred. Rather, I really mean the Spirit. The Holy Spirit is, like everything alive, continually growing in the course of time, and He has a history. And it has been granted to you by Divine grace to plant in many a heart – here are two [of them][4] – a knowledge and demanding awareness of certain of the Spirit's manifestations, which we would not possess without you.[5] One loss is, in any event, not to be able to be present on Saturday. You rightly detest sentimentality. Sometimes, however, it can be beneficial to let feelings take their course.

It is disheartening to be so far from the center [of things] at this time. In every other respect there is much to report that is pleasant. Enticing sounds are again to be heard from Berlin.[6] Even If I were a German, they would not play a role for me, as I am having and can continue to have a far better life here than in Berlin. Now the fact of the matter is that I want to and have to get settled in earnest in Uppsala in the summer of 1915 at the latest.[7] But it looks as though doors were opening for aspirations. And it is always pleasing to recognize how hopeless it is trying to fit my Uppsala teachings into one of the pharmacy shelves being supplied here.[8]

But what is disheartening is hearsay from and thoughts about the home country. »Was ist eigentlich in Schweden los?« [What really is the matter in Sweden?] A government that can do as much as it is demanding for defence – and lets the country wait in an embarrassing way.[9] And that only so-called royal power which is to be

---

[2] Hjärne was about to retire.

[3] Allusion to Verner von Heidenstam's (1859–1940) poem *Ensamhetens tankar* IV (Thoughts of loneliness) in his first collection, *Vallfart och vandringar* (Pilgrimage and wanderings) of 1888, 114, lines 4 and 5: »Jag längtar marken, jag längtar stenarna där barn jag lekt« (I long for the soil, I long for the stones where I had played as a child), Samlade verk, ed. by K. Bang and Fr. Böök, vol. 1, Stockholm 1943. Von Heidenstam was longing for home which he had left because of a conflict with his father; he therefore longed »not for people« but for the soil. Söderblom, however, refers to the poet's neoromanticism which he disliked; he felt von Heidenstam's generation deviated from the highly esteemed master August Strindberg (1849–1912). Information from Erik Aurelius.

[4] Söderblom here refers to his wife who had also studied under Hjärne.

[5] Hjärne was a fervent defender of the Christian faith.

[6] Cf. letter no. 59 from Adolf Deißmann concerning a possible call to a professorship there.

[7] Söderblom had accepted the Leipzig chair only for a limited period of time. Since he had simultaneously maintained his Uppsala chair, he now felt he had to make up his mind.

[8] In Uppsala, he had to put up with intense opposition by the strong orthodox wing of the faculty against his leanings towards Ritschl.

[9] There had been an intense debate concerning defence expenditures which the right wing of parliament wanted to increase considerably – particularly in order to build armored battle-

squeezed. I assure you that the impression Prince Vilhelm made does not leave my mind.[10] Surely they have sinned, including sins of omission, but now one is beginning to feel about the royalty like hardly ever before. Here everybody is wondering why Sweden does not forge closer links with Germany. – By the way, you must make Hohenzollern – Vasa known to the German public.[11] – The brash Czech barbarians and Rosegger! Now it would almost be a pity if he did not receive the prize – though the other one is so very, very superior.[12] ... [Regards to the family, etc.]

Yours, N. S-m

61. To GUSTAF AULÉN[1]

Leipzig Gohlis, 17 XII 1913

Käre vän!

Icke kunde jag tänka att det någonsin skulle bli svårt att skrifva ett bref till Dig. Med ingen af de unga, kära Upsalavännerna, hvilkas tillvaro upplyser och förklarar lefnadsstigen, kan jag friare och oförbehållsamare tala om allt. Det har på sista tiden blifvit för sällan. Tankarna ha städse varit hos Er under den onaturligt utdragna tiden af spänning och ovisshet. Nu kom från Malmö, dit Malin telefonerat, Annas oroande ord på ett brefkort om det tunga att lemna Upsala, då våra närmaste vänner äro djupt försänkta i sorg. Tankarna irrade. Nu är Anna här. Intet sorgebud kunde träffa alla ända till Bror Carl ömmare. Två älskade, speglande – Edert hems tro och lycka speglande – barnaögon slutna före Jul till eviga ron. Vi minnas hans moders sköna, moderliga tapperhet och möda och så mycket osagdt, anadt, i hoppet inlagdt, som blifvit för föreställningen en gloria kring min ljuse, klare vän Gustaf Auléns och hans hugvarma makas förstfödde. Anna berättar om lördagen, hur Du gjorde den så underbart vacker, för Thyra hjälprik, ehuru Du själf var rätt hårdt medtagen. När Ni icke skulle få behålla honom härnere, var det en Guds nåd, att den ohyggliga sjukdomen icke fick länge plåga och härja honom, utan att barnaögonen fingo genast slockna för att slåss upp lika klara i Guds värld hinsides. Men det är ingen tröst, in-

ships – in order to counter what they perceived to be a serious threat from Russia (in view of Russification endeavors in Finland, etc.). Söderblom and Hjärne, being quite progressive in social matters, sided with the conservatives on this point, though by no means in the fashion of Sven Hedin's influential, nationalistic brochures on the issue. Incidentally, Söderblom, in all his later work for peace, never questioned the right of national self-defense.

[10] Prince Vilhelm (1884–1965) was a son of King Gustaf V Adolf (1858–1950). Söderblom apparently refers to a speech the prince had made.

[11] I have not been able to verify whether this remark refers to a lecture or to one of Hjärnes many Swedish publications.

[12] Peter Rosegger (1843–1918), popular Austrian writer, was a candidate for the Nobel prize in literature in 1913 but did not receive it. Some Czechs seem to have been instrumental in this. »The other one« who did receive the prize is Rabindranath Tagore (1861–1941), Indian philosopher of culture and poet from a Bengali Brahman family, whom Söderblom highly esteemed.

[1] Collection Aulén. G., University Library Lund, handwritten letter.

för det oändligt smärtsamma, som drabbade Er två afhållna renhjärtade medarbetare och vänner. Det känns kyligt att vara långt borta, när sådant hemsöker vännerna. Lifvet är en gång, icke mer, och när det sammanpressas till det väsentliga, är den själfvalda som plikt fattade exilen mycket känbar [sic].

Maktlösa, innerliga känslor kunna endast bedja: Gud uppehålle Er, goda båda föräldrar! Gud välsigne Edra små, den hemkallade store bror, som därför ej skilts från Edra böner, lilla syster och den väntade. Jul med tårar! Men ändå Jul, Kristus verklig, Guds barmhertighet.

Eder Nathan Sm

Leipzig-Gohlis, December 17, 1913

Dear friend,

Never would I have thought that writing a letter to you would become hard. With no one of the young dear friends in Uppsala, whose presence enlightens and elucidates the course of life, can I talk more frankly and unreservedly about everything. This has happened too seldom in recent times. My thoughts have continually been with you during the unnaturally extended time of suspense and uncertainty.[2] Now I have received a letter-card from Malmö where Malin had phoned to, with Anna's worrying word about the hardship of leaving Uppsala, at a time when our nearest friends are deeply submerged in mourning. Thoughts wandered about. Now Anna is here. No mournful tidings could have struck everyone, including brother Carl, in a more painful way. Two beloved child's mirroring eyes – mirroring your home's faith and bliss – closed unto eternal peace before Christmas. We remember his mother's wonderful motherly bravery and toil and so much unsaid, divined, wrapped up in hope, which for the imagination has become a halo around my bright friend Gustaf Aulén's and his warmhearted wife's firstborn. Anna tells about Saturday, how you made it so extremely beautiful, and helpful for Thyra, even though you were quite exhausted yourself. Since you were not to keep him here below, it was by God's mercy that the terrible illness did not get to torment and harass him for long, but that the child's eyes were allowed to be closed instantly in order to be opened, being just as clear, in God's world beyond. But that is no comfort in the face of the immensely painful [event] that struck you two beloved, pure-hearted co-workers and friends. It feels chilling to be far away when something like this haunts one's friends. Life is being lived once, no more, and when it is condensed to what is essential, the self-chosen exile, conceived as a duty, is making itself severely felt.

Powerless, warm feelings can only pray: May God keep you two good parents! May God bless your little ones, the big brother [whom God] called home, who is not thereby removed from your prayers, the little sister and the expected one. Christmas with tears! And yet Christmas, Christ real, God's mercy.

Yours,
Nathan Sm

---

[2] Aulén had applied for a professorship in Lund. For a long time his chances had been quite uncertain, yet he was still hoping to succeed.

62. From GUSTAF AULÉN[1]

[between Dec. 18 and 23, 1913]

Kära, goda vänner

Från oss båda till Eder båda ett hjärtevarmt tack för värme och styrka, som strömmat oss till mötes, och för de vackraste renaste blomster[.] Högtids-stunden på kyrkogården slutade med, att solens sista klara strålar lyste på den lilla hvita kistan, när den sänktes ned. Nu skall den lille käre, ljuse gestalten alltid lysa öfver vår lefnadsväg, hvart den bär

God jul till Eder alla

Eder

Gustaf Aulén

[between Dec. 18 and 23, 1913]

Dear friends

From the two of us to the two of you hearty thanks for warmth and strength which poured upon us, and for the most beautiful immaculate flowers. The funeral ended with the sun's last rays shining upon the little white coffin as it was lowered. Now the little beloved, bright figure shall for ever shine over our path through life, wherever it may lead.

Merry Christmas to all of you.

Yours,

Gustaf Aulén

63. To GUSTAF AULÉN[1]

Leipzig-G., 27 XII 1913

Käre vän!

De sköna orden på Ditt svartkantade kort ha stått framför mina ögon. I dag är de spädas dag. Tankarna, som ej lemna Er, få än starkare lif. Gudi tack, att I egen hvarandra!

Till min mycket stora glädje kom från Stockholm tidender, att Dina utsikter till Lund skola vara mycket goda. Kanske afgöres saken i dag? Det vore en gärd åt rättvisan. ...

Till Din Fru, vår afhållna väninna, och till Dig och Edra goda nyårsönskningar. Din tillgifne

Nathan Sm

---

[1] N. Söderblom's collection of letters, from Swedes, UUB, handwritten card.

[1] Collection Aulén. G., University Library Lund, handwritten letter.

Leipzig-G., December 27, 1913

Dear friend,

The beautiful words on your black-framed card have been standing before my eyes. Today is Infants' Day. My thoughts which are not leaving you become even more lively. Thank God that you have each other!

To my very great joy, word came from Stockholm today that your chances for Lund were very good. Maybe things are decided on today? That would be an act towards justice....

To your wife, our beloved friend, and to you and your folks best wishes for the new Year. Sincerely yours,

Nathan Sm

64. To HARALD HJÄRNE[1]

Leipzig-Gohlis, 11 I 1914

Käre Broder!

Mycken tack för Dina två sista bref. ...

Jag känner också igen det puritanska inslaget i Din ande i ogillandet af, äfven de högsta, efterbibliska helgonnamn. Jag tror dock att isoleringen af den bibliska epoken ej saknar våda. Kyrkan måste igenkänna Andens verk äfven i senare män. Och profeter och apostlar voro icke mer gudomligt påverkade än Luther och Bunyan.

... Här lefva vi under intrycket af Zabern och tyska rikets blifvande härskares telegramverksamhet. I Professorenzimmer reagerar man starkt. Men studenterna, äfven allvarliga, finna det sehr schön både med hans sehnlichster Wunsch: en rytteriattack, och med hans fromma blick på die Armee droben.[2] Stackars oss civila. Nej, jag börjar fatta något af betänkligheterna mot detta Preussen. Må vi kunna stå på egna ben!

... Min hustru är med och hälsar Dig, Eder.

Din tillgifne

Nathan Söderblom

Leipzig-Gohlis, January 11, 1914

Dear friend,

Many thanks for your two last letters.

... [A passage concerning Mrs. Hjärne who was seriously ill at the time]

I also recognize the puritan woof in your mind in the disapproval of the name of saint [for persons in] post-biblical [times], even the most egregious ones. I believe, however, that the isolation of the biblical epoch is not without jeopardy. The church must recognize the work of the Spirit also in later men. And prophets and apostles were not acted upon by God any more than Luther and Bunyan.[3]

---

[1] Collection Harald Hjärne 1p, UUB, handwritten letter.

[2] Mixture of Swedish and German in the original.

[3] John Bunyan (1628–1688), English Baptist preacher and author (*The Pilgrim's Progress*, London 1678. 1684).

... [A remark on a lecture by Hjärne] Here we are living under the impression of Zabern and the telegraphic activities of the present sovereign of the German empire.[4] In the professors' room, they react strongly. But the students, even serious ones, find it *sehr schön* [very nice], both his *sehnlichster Wunsch* [dearest wish]: a cavalry attack, and his pious look to *die Armee droben* [the army up there]. We poor civilians. No, I am beginning to grasp something of the misgivings about this Prussia. May we be able to stand on our own feet!

My wife joins me by sending her regards to you.

Sincerely yours,
Nathan Söderblom

65. To HARALD HJÄRNE[1]

Leipzig-Gohlis, 28 I 1914

Käre Broder!
Mycken tack för Ditt bref af den 13 januari. ...
Här minnas vi i dag Karl den store. I går hyllades fredskäjsaren med skollof – också ett sätt att stärka konungsliga känslor. Inför förödmjukelsen i Konstantinopel fråga sig tyska patrioter, om icke vissheten om hans fredlighet låta Ryssland etc. snart våga hvad som helst. Detta är en ond värld, där dygd ej alltid belönas. Man sörjer öfver allt som nedsätter detta stora rikes prestige, därför äfven öfver Zabern och de konservativas oresonliga rabalder mot Bethmann-Hollweg. Men opinionen hemma lider i fråga om Tyskland ej sällan af det felet att alldeles ignorera måttstockarna. Här blir den omedvetet hög därför är man kritisk. Men man blir arg, när så

---

[4] In early November, 1913, a young lieutenant of the regiment stationed in the little Alsatian town of Zabern had ordered his soldiers to use armed force when encountering street brawls among civilians and used an insulting nickname for the Alsatians in that context. Not only were officers forbidden to use such insults, but the army had no business mingling in police affairs. When the incident was published in the local newspaper, there was uproar. People had been mistrustful all along of an army that had failed to connect with the population, and resentful of the autocratic way Alsace-Lorraine was ruled: In spite of having been granted a constitution and a measure of autonomy in 1911, it was in effect still treated pretty much as the occupied territory German troops had conquered in the 1870/71 war. The larger context was the pivileged position of the military in the German empire as a state within the state. In Zabern, the situation escalated, and the army illegally arrested a group of demonstrators. So the affair reached the Reichstag where it led to a vote of no confidence against the chancellor, Theobald von Bethmann-Hollweg, by the bourgeois majority on Dec. 3/4, 1913, and to a similar procedure in the Prussian House of Delegates on Jan. 10, 1914, the day before the above letter was written. But such was the power of the military (supported by the Emperor) that these votes entailed no consequences. The lieutenant and his colonel were tried by court martial but acquitted on Jan. 10, 1914. So the military was vindicated. Worst of all, this was a huge encouragement for the highly influential reactionaries on the far right who for some time had considered war inevitable and wanted it sooner rather than later. – The telegrams referred to were sent not by the Emperor but by the rather immature crown prince. – Cf. Wolfgang Mommsen, *Bürgerstolz und Weltmachtstreben. Deutschland unter Wilhelm II. 1890-1918*, = PWG VII/2, Berlin 1995, 440-446.

[1] Collection Harald Hjärne 1p, UUB, handwritten letter.

folk utan vidare sammanställer Nordschlesvigs med Finlands öde och i allmänhet tyska förhållanden med ryska uselheter. Det är därför man drar sig
för att offentligt hemma alltför mycket syna tyska svagheter, hur lifligt man
än måste reagera särdeles mot deras själfgoda världslighet i religionen.
Man blir mörkrädd, när man ser, hur nationalismen får förgrofva allt. Det
är väl dess barnsjukdom. Engelsmännen ha kommit öfver den – om de någonsin ha haft den? Hos oss hemma är nöden för dörren. Det ger ett helt
annat innehåll åt nationella sträfvandet. Bara det inte stannar i tillställning
och paroxysmer. Vi ha en olycklig benägenhet att tro oss ha uträttat något,
när vi demonstrerat och bråkat och fästat en smula. –
    Hur hafven I det i denna stund, vänner och kära hemsökta människor?
Anna hälsar Eder båda, Eder tre! Din tillgifne
    Nathan S-m

Leipzig- Gohlis, January 28, 1914

Dear friend,
Many thanks for your letter of January 13. … [On Mrs. Hjärne's illness which had
worsened]
    Here we are commemorating Charlemagne[2] today. Yesterday, the emperor of
peace[3] was paid homage by means of a school holiday – another way of reinforcing
royal sentiments. In view of the humiliation in Constantinople[4], German patriots
ask themselves whether the assurance of his peacefulness might not induce Russia
etc. soon to dare anything whatsoever. This is an evil world where virtue is not always rewarded. One worries over everything that diminishes the prestige of this
great empire, therefore also over Zabern and the conservatives' obstinate row with
Bethmann-Hollweg.[5] But opinion at home with regard to Germany not infrequently
suffers from the error of completely ignoring the [question of] standards. Here it is
instinctively set high, therefore one is critical. But one becomes angry when people
simply lump together Northern Schleswig's and Finland's lot,[6] and generally German conditions and Russian meanness. That is why one hesitates too much to scruti-

---

    [2] The 1100th anniversary of Charlemagne's (742–814, German emperor 800–814) death.
    [3] Ironic reference to Wilhelm II.'s favorite epithet.
    [4] The peace treaty of Constantinople of Sept. 29, 1913, which ended the second Balkan
war by a new distribution of the formerly Osman territories, effectively blocked the access to
the Dardanelles Russia had been coveting for a long time.
    [5] Cf. previous letter, n.3. Bethmann-Hollweg (1856–1921), German Chancellor and Prus-
sian prime minister 1909–1917, was considered weak and vacillating by the conservatives. Actually, he was caught between the two horns of a dilemma: his desire for political moderation
and loyalty to the Kaiser who backed the privileged military caste. He failed to stop the huge
effort initiated by Admiral Tirpitz to increase the size of the German navy. After 1914 he resisted the annexionist demands of the far right but succumbed to the military brass in terms of
political leadership. He was forced to resign in 1917.
    [6] Prussia and Austria had conquered Schleswig from Denmark in the war of 1864; it be-
came a Prussian province in 1867. Schleswig's northern part had a large Danish population.
There was at first a gradual integration policy which in the 1880s became more aggressive but
not violent. In effect, it enhanced Danish awareness which resulted in a thoroughgoing organization of the Danish-speaking population. In a plebiscite in 1920, Northern Schleswig opted
for Denmark and has been a Danish province ever since. – Finland was ceded to Russia by Sweden in 1809. Russia subsequently tried to »Russify« the country by coercion.

nize German weaknesses publicly at home, however vigorously one must react to their complacent worldliness in religion.[7] One becomes deeply frightened when seeing how nationalism makes everything more coarse. That seems to be its children's ailment. The English have overcome it - if they ever had it? For us at home, emergency is at the doorstep. That lends a totally different content to national ambition. If only it will not stop at celebrations and paroxysms.We have an unfortunate inclination to believing that we have achieved something when we have demonstrated and blustered and celebrated a bit. -

How are you doing these days, friends and dear afflicted people? Anna is sending her regards to both of you, to the three of you!

Yours sincerely,

N. S-m

66. From WILHELM BOUSSET[1]

Gt [Göttingen] 10 5. 1914

L[ieber] H[err] Kollege. Ich möchte Ihnen doch noch nachträglich meinen Dank für die Übersendung Ihres neuesten Werkes[2] aussprechen. Und zugleich meine herzlichste Bewunderung. Sie bringen wirklich Ordnung in das Chaos u[nd] Licht in ein Gebiet, auf dem es bisher finster war. - Ich habe mich seit langen Jahren von aller Arbeit an d[er] Religion d[er] Primitiven zurückgezogen, weil mir das Meer uferlos erschien. Ihre Arbeit hat mir beinahe Lust gemacht, wieder mitzuarbeiten. - Wenn man nur zu allem Zeit hätte! *Das* ist Religionsgeschichte in grossem Stil. Und wie Sie die Linien hinaufzuziehen wissen in die chinesische und die indische Religion! Die letzten Kapitel nur empfinde ich mit ihrer vielleicht zu grossen Ausführlichkeit als eine Belastung d[es] Buches. Statt dieser Linienführung bis in die *moderne* Zeit hätte ich lieber noch einen Abschnitt über die Welt des *Synkretismus* in d[er] hellen[istisch] röm[ischen] Kulturwelt u[nd] Umgegend. Urmenschenmythos, Schöpfungssagen, Mysterienwesen, Taburiten bis in d[en] Manichäismus hinein! Da wäre wohl manches zu holen. - Aber warum erschien gerade dieses Buch *schwedisch? Haben Sie schon über eine deutsche Übersetz[ung] verhandelt?* Ich bin von Ruprechts ermächtigt Ihnen mitzuteilen, dass Sie [sic! lies: sie] bereit seien, d[ie] Übersetzung zu übernehmen (Angebot M. 600 f[ür] d[en] schwedischen Verlag).[3] - Meine Frau

---

[7] This refers to an influential school of thought in German church and theology which later came to be known as culture Protestantism (*Kulturprotestantismus*).

[1] Cod. Ms. Bousset 119 Söderblom (1903/15), Univ. Library Göttingen, handwritten postcard.

[2] *Gudstrons uppkomst. Studier*, Stockholm 1914.

[3] The Ruprecht family, owners of the publishing house Vandenhoeck & Ruprecht in Göttingen. What Bousset could not know at this stage is that Söderblom's book was actually first written in German (cf. letter no. 52, note 2 in the present edition). The revision of this version (enlarged, not only stylistically improved, cf. preface) was already being prepared, and the Leipzig publisher J.C. Hinrichs had even begun with the printing procedure. It finally came out in 1916 as *Das Werden des Gottesglaubens*.

133

trägt sich fast m[it] d[em] Gedanken, sich an d[er] Übersetzung zu versuchen. Sie würde es, des Schwedischen ziemlich mächtig, können, zumal ich
fachmännischen Rat geben könnte. Allerdings fürchtet sie, doch wegen viel-
facher Beschäftigung i[n] d[er] Frauenfrage keine Zeit zu haben Wie würden Sie über den Plan denken?

Mit Dank u[nd] herzl[ichem] Gruß Ihr Bousset

67. To HARALD HJÄRNE[1]

Leipzig-Gohlis, 18 V 1914

Käre Broder!

... Ärkebiskopssaken har ej tagit en timme från mitt sinneslugn och min arbetstid. Mirabile dictu hörde jag häromdagen indirekt från eckl[iastisk]
mun, att Billings energiska agitation hos kungen och drottningen är det
enda, som skulle fördröja min utnämning. Billing har rätt. Jag passar bättre
som episcopus in partibus (om än inte precis infidelium). Och det ligger
onekligen ett stycke tro i hans önskan att få Eklund framför Danell. Den
som blir skall få en vacker bild af domkyrkan i Sens, där jag i april tänkte
mig in i situationen för 750 år sedan.

Med många hälsningar från Anna Din tillgifne
Nathan Söderblom

Leipzig-Gohlis, May 18, 1914

Dear friend,

... [On Hjärnes son Erland who was staying with the Söderbloms]

The archbishop affair has not taken away one hour from my peace of mind and
my working time. *Mirabile dictu* [wonderful to relate], I indirectly heard from an
ecclesiastical mouth these days that Billing's energetic agitation at the king's and the
queen's is the only thing which might delay my appointment. Billing is right. I am
better suited for *episcopus in partibus* (if not downright *infidelium*)[2].
And there is undeniably a bit of faith in his desire to get Eklund rather than Danell.[3]
The one that becomes [archbishop] shall receive a beautiful picture of the cathedral
in Sens, where in April I contemplated the situation of 750 years ago.[4]

With many regards from Anna,
sincerely yours,
Nathan Söderblom

---

[1] Collection Harald Hjärne 1p, UUB, handwritten letter.

[2] Titular bishop, officiating only in an auxiliary function. From the 14th century onwards,
such bishops were consecrated for dioceses which after the crusades had reverted to the »infi-
dels«. Söderblom here alludes to his being considered by many in the Swedish church as far too
liberal for the post.

[3] Johan Alfred Eklund and Hjalmar Danell were two of the other contenders who both appeared on the list submitted to the king in the first place. Herman Lundström (1858–1917) was
second, and Söderblom third (Sundkler, op. cit., 104). Yet he was the one to be appointed by
the king.

[4] The first archbishop of Uppsala was consecrated in the cathedral of Sens in 1164.

68. From Ernst Troeltsch[1]

Heidelberg 10 VI 14

Sehr verehrter Herr Kollege!

Erst jetzt habe ich die Zeit gefunden Ihre mir gütigst übersandte Arbeit über die natürliche Theologie[2] eingehend zu lesen und danke Ihnen nun ganz ergebenst. Das Buch hat in der Gesamtauffassung (bis auf S. 87) meine volle Zustimmung, wie Ihnen ja bekannt ist, und ich freue mich über die vielen feinen und lehrreichen Einzelbemerkungen. Möchte sich diese Auffassung doch durchsetzen.

Gleichzeitig gratuliere ich Ihnen herzlichst zu der hohen Auszeichnung, die Ihnen Ihr König hat zu Teil werden lassen. Hätten wir nur auch solche Erzbischöfe.

Ihr ganz ergebener E. Troeltsch

69. To Gottfrid Billing[1]

Leipzig-Gohlis 1 VIII 1914

Högt vördade Broder,

Jag är då tacksam för den 17 aug. – om jag ej i följd af nu hotande krig äfven för oss uppenbarar mig förr. En massa saker äro här att ordna. Och min hustru ligger med bråkande hjärta, dock ger oss läkare godt hopp. Är det möjligt, stannar jag därför och kommer till Lund den 17 ds, är tacksam att få samtala efter föredraget kl. 2 och reser med natttåget till Upsala.

Redan i pingstveckan lofvade jag biskop Löfgren att förmedla hans förslag, att biskoparna måtte rikta en vädjan till Sveriges kyrkofolk och präster att på tacksägelsedagen 11 okt. frambära tack för den hundraåriga freden. Det är djupt förödmjukande att tänka på, hur uselt vi användt nådatiden, och det är nu osäkrare än någonsin, om vår fred skall räcka i hundra år, d.v.s. till den 14 augusti. Men visst måste vi erkänna Guds oförtjänta långmodighet. Och uppmaningen bör då komma ut i tid, icke sedan alla möjliga och omöjliga fredsfirningar egt rum. Löfgrens mening var nog en utförligare, gemensam vädjan. Men dels synes det mig utsiktslöst att förenas om sådan. Dels kan mer än en känna behofvet att i denna sak dessutom säga något mer ingående till sitt stift. Kan man tänka sig, att biskoparna skulle vilja i senare hälften af augusti utsända en gemensam kort uppmaning af t.ex. hosföljande lydelse eller af en lydelse, som jag vågar bedja Dig godhetsfullt affatta? Innan jag fullgör mitt löfte till Löfgren, inväntar jag ett råd från Lund.

---

[1] N. Söderblom's ecumenical collection A 24, UUB, handwritten postcard.
[2] *Natürliche Theologie und Religionsgeschichte* (BRW 1 [1913/14], 1st issue, Stockholm 1913. The enlarged Swedish version is *Naturlig teologi och religionshistoria. En historik och ett program*, Stockholm 1914.

[1] Collection Billing. G., Lund University Library, handwritten letter.

Det var icke med lätt hjärta jag i går e.m. afslutade den härliga verksamheten ss. universitetslärare, besynnerligt nog i ett främmande land och på en fruktansvärdt allvarlig historisk dag. Det var med uppriktigt hjärta och under en djupt allvarlig stämning i auditoriet, som jag slutade med bönen, att Gud måtte bevara Tyskland som fredens och den kristna kulturens värn. Imponerande verkar den lugna beslutsamheten och den tunga ansvarskänslan i denna nation.

...

Gud hjälpe!
Med goda önskningar vördnadsfullt tilgifne
N Söderblom

Bilaga:
Sveriges biskopar rikta härmed till vårt lands prästerskap och kyrkofolk en uppmaning att på årets tacksägelsedag den 11 oktober frambära gemensamt tack och lof till Gud, för att riket förskonats från krig och fått åtnjuta yttre fred i hundra år.

Leipzig-Gohlis 1 VIII 1914

Highly esteemed Brother,
I am now grateful for the 17th of August – unless I turn up earlier due to the war threatening even us. A lot of things have to be taken care of here. And my wife lies ill with heart trouble; however, doctors give us hope. I shall therefore stay on, if possible, and come to Lund on the 17th, would be grateful for getting a chance to talk to you after my lecture at 2 o'clock, and shall travel to Uppsala by night train.

I promised Bishop Lövgren[2] that I would already in the week after Whitsunday serve as an intermediary for his suggestion that the bishops issue an appeal to Sweden's churchfolk and pastors, to give thanks for the one hundred years of peace on Thanksgiving Day, the 11th of October. It is deeply humiliating to think of what poor use we have made of that respite; and it is now less certain than ever whether our peace will really have lasted one hundred years, i.e. until the 14th of August.[3] But certainly we must recognize God's undeserved forbearance. And the exhortation must get out in time, not after all kinds of peace celebrations have taken place. Lövgren's idea presumably was a detailed common appeal. But on the one hand, agreeing on something like that seems hopeless to me. On the other hand, more than one bishop might feel the need to say something more profound to his diocese on this matter. Is it conceivable that the bishops would be willing to dispatch in the second half of August a short common exhortation, e.g. in the wording attached to this letter, or in a wording which I would dare to ask you kindly to draft? Before I fulfill my promise to Lövgren, I expect advice from Lund.

It was not lightheartedly that I quit the wonderful activity as a university teacher yesterday in the afternoon, oddly enough in a foreign country and on a terribly se-

---

[2] Nils Lövgren (1852–1920) became bishop of Västerås in 1900. (Misspelled as Löfgren in the original.)

[3] The last armed conflict Sweden was involved in ended on Aug. 14, 1814 in the Moss Convention, when Denmark ceded Norway to Sweden to which it had been previously accorded in the Kiel peace treaty of Jan. 14, 1814. The union of the two countries ended peacefully in 1905.

rious historic day. It was with all sincerity and in a deeply serious mood that I concluded with the prayer that God may keep Germany as a bulwark of peace and Christian culture. What is making [a deep] impression is the quiet determination and the profound sense of responsibility in this nation.

...

May God help!
With best wishes,
reverentially,
N Söderblom

Attachment
Sweden's bishops hereby direct to clergy and churchfolk of our country an exhortation to give thanks and praise to God together on this year's thanksgiving day, October 11, that the nation has been saved from war and granted the enjoyment of outward peace for one hundred years.

70. To Nils Johan Göransson[1]

[Leipzig, 5.8.1914]
Lieber Göran! Diese Woche nur Militärzüge. Angstvoll in dieser Zeit nicht zu Hause zu sein – obwohl wir ja hier bei den treuesten Menschen sind. Anna noch zu Bett, beginnt sich ein wenig kleiden zu können. Gern möchte ich sie mitnehmen. Unter allen Umständen reise ich sobald wie möglich. Der Weltbrand ist entfacht. Wie werden nicht alle Erzeugnisse der Kultur, geistige und materielle, unter den Füssen getreten. Englands Kriegserklärung war ein furchtbarer Schlag. Italien abwartend. Deutschland – Oesterreich ungefähr allein gegen eine Welt. Alles schlimmer als die pessimistischsten Erwartungen. Du kannst nicht denken wie peinlich es ist, in dieser Schicksalstunde nicht zu Hause zu sein. Hoffe Beginn nächster Woche in Upsala zu sein.
Grüsse! Dein N. Söderblom

[Leipzig, 5.8.1914]
Dear Göran! This week only military trains. Frightening not to be at home these days – even though, of course, we are living here with the most reliable of people. Anna, still in bed, is beginning to be somewhat able to dress. I would be glad to take her with me. In all circumstances I shall travel as soon as possible. The world conflagration has been ignited. How all products of culture, spiritual and material, are being trodden under foot. England's declaration of war was a terrible blow. Italy reserved. Germany – Austria just about alone against the world. Everything worse than the most pessimistic expectations. You can't imagine how embarrassing it is not to be at home in this fateful hour. Hope to be in Uppsala at the beginning of next week.
Regards! Yours, N. Söderblom

---

[1] N. Söderblom's collection of letters, to Swedes and foreigners, UUB, handwritten postcard. Written in German because military censorship would have refused mail written in a foreign language.

No. 70

71. To Nils Johan Göransson[1]

Lund den 12 augusti 1914

Käre Göran!

Tack för Ditt bref i soliga juli. Vemodigt var att höra om Siris klenhet. Ack, hvad ha vi ej sedan dess upplefvat. Sedan Napoleon har Västerlandet ej sett en så våldsam katastrof i ett slag. Våra stamförvandter och trosbröder i Tyskland ha fått öfver sig en öfvermänsklig uppgift. De vilja lösa den och ännu hålla riket vid makt, kosta hvad det vill. Historien har ej sett ett sådant skådespel: ett världsrike, där hvar medborgare och hvarje parti villigt bringar de tyngsta offer i en lugn heroism. Det var en underlig kontrast att komma från en nation, som spänner hvarje muskel i enig målmedvetenhet

---

[1] N.J. Göransson's collection, UUB, handwitten letter.

138

No. 70

till detta idylliska land, där partikifvet för tillfället nedtystas af vapenbra-
ket rundt omkring, men där man fortfarande tror på metoden att prata och
icke handla. Tänk om David, Jakob et C:i nu hade setat vid makten! Frisin-
nets besynnerliga ryssfjäsk tycks emellertid fortfara.

Oändligt ljufligt är att vara på svensk botten. Vi våga knappast tro, att
det är sannt. Så orimligt såg det ut med Annas klenhet och allt. Men inför
svårigheter blir hennes spänstighet större. Gud ske lof, att jag har henne
lefvande här. Nu ligger hon på sjukhuset. Hjärtat pustar, blodet ringa och
dåligt det som är. Den onaturliga ansträngningen är nu öfver. Gud hjälpe
oss! Vi hade tänkt få resa lördag. Men doktorn är betänksam. Brita, J[an]
Olof, Bror Carl med Hildur kokerskan och Emma, småflickorna och Lag
sändas i två repriser förut till Staby. Helge o. Staffan ännu här. Fredag råkar jag biskop Billing.

Din, Eder tillgifne Nathan Söderblom

139

Dear Göran,
Thanks for your letter in sunny July. It was saddening to hear of Siri's poor health.
Alas, what have we not experienced since then! Since Napoleon the occident has not
seen such a raging catastrophe in one single blow. Our kinsmen and fellow Christians in Germany have had a superhuman charge cast upon them. They want to fulfill it and yet keep the Empire in power at all costs. History has never seen such a
spectacle: a world power where each citizen and each party readily make the most
burdensome sacrifices in quiet heroism. It was a strange contrast to be coming from
a nation which is straining each muscle in unanimous pusposefulness to this idyllic
land where for the moment party strife is silenced by the clash of arms but where
the method of talking without acting is still believed in. Think if David, Jacob etc.
had now been in power! Liberalism's strange adulation for the Russians, however,
seems to continue.

It's immensely delightful being on Swedish soil. We hardly dare believe that it is
true. It had seemed so unlikely in view of Anna's poor health and all that. But in the
face of hardship her vigor increases. Praise be to God that I have her here alive.
Now she lies in the hospital. Her heart pants, blood is scarce and what there is, is
bad. The unnatural stress is over now. God help us! We had intended to travel on
Saturday. But the doctor is wary. Brita, Jan Olof, Brother Carl with Hildur, the
cook, and Emma, the little girls and Lag will be sent to Staby in two turns. Helge
and Staffan are still here. On Friday I shall meet Bishop Billing.

Yours sincerely, Nathan Söderblom

72. To Samuel Fries[1]

Lund 12.VIII.1914

Käre Sam!
Säkerligen ären I nu, goda vänner, i någon landtlig luft. Men jag hoppas
detta tack skall nå Dig för de ömma vänskapsorden med blyerts. Ett under
är att vi äro helbregda hemma. Anna, öfver höfvan ansträngd och blodfattig, ligger här på sjukhuset. Jag väntar till lördag.

Sista veckan var öfverväldigande. Ett stort folk, enigt, villigt till de tyngsta offer för sin ära och rikets framtid. För första gången ser världen en
medborgarhär i egentlig mening. Det är fruktansvärdt, att detta härliga
folk skall åderlåtas på detta vis af ett Europa, hvars fred tyske käisaren
tryggat. Och vi, vi se på. Det är ju önskligt att slippa krig. Får se, hur man
sedan behandlar oss i freden. Inte begriper jag, att man här hemma kan så
föga beröras af dånet från de apokalyptiska ryttarna och af faran som
hvarje försvagning af Tyskland för oss innebär.

Hälsa Din Anna från oss!
Din tillgifne
N. Söderblom

---

[1] S. Fries' collection, UUB, handwitten letter.

Lund, August 12, 1914

Dear Sam,

You, good friends, will probably be [enjoying] some good country air. I hope this note of thanks for your kind penciled words of friendship will reach you anyway. It is a miracle that we are safely back home. Anna, excessively strained and anemic, lies in the hospital. I shall wait until Saturday.

The last week [over there] was overwhelming. A great nation, united, willing to make the most burdensome sacrifices for its honor and the future of the Empire. For the first time the world is witnessing a citizens' army in the true sense of the word. It is frightening that this wonderful people shall suffer bloodletting in this way by a Europe whose peace the German Emperor had safeguarded. And we, we are looking on. Of course, it is desirable to escape war. Let's see how we will then be treated in peacetime. By no means do I understand that here at home we are being so little affected by the rumbling of the apocalyptic riders and by the danger every weakening of Germany entails for us.

Regards to your Anna from us!
Sincerely yours,
N. Söderblom

73. From NILS JOHAN GÖRANSSON[1]

Danmarks prästg[ård] d. 14/8 1914.

Käre Nathan.

För Ditt vänliga bref som jag erhöll i går kväll tackar jag med varmt hjärta. Jag har så mycket tänkt på Eder, särsklidt har jag med ängslan tänkt på Eder hemresa, då jag visste hur klen Anna var. För en åtta dar sedan råkade jag Tyra Quensel, som berättade, att Fru Zorn fått telegram från Er, att Anna fortfarande låg. Måtte nu hemresan icke alldeles ha brutit hennes kraft. Hon är utomordentlig i sin viljestyrka och i sin andliga kraft. Men det fysiska underlaget kan icke i längden undvaras. Jag hoppas innerligt att Ni nu icke reser från Lund, förrän hon återvunnit så mycket krafter, att den återstående resan icke medför någonsomhelst risk för henne. Du själf behöfver väl också hvila ut. Hädanefter måste Du mer tänka på Dig själf än hvad Du hittils gjort, ty Din kraft har nog också sina gränser.

Det måste ha varit storartadt att se detta präktiga tyska folk i dessa ögonblick af det djupaste allvar. Sådant glömmer man nog icke. Vårt folk börjar väl också nu känna något af lifvets allvar, men nog fattas det ännu mycket. Den lättsinniga optimismen sitter hos oss mycket djupt. Vi behöfva tuktan, och den kanske nog också tyvärr snart kommer.

...

Ja, käre Nathan, måtte nu Guds välsignelse på allt sätt följa Dig och de Dina. Särskildt ligger mig Annas snara tillfriskande varmt om hjärtat. –

---

[1] N. Söderblom's collection of letters, from Swedes, UUB, handwritten letter.

Här är sig likt. Siri icke sämre, men heller icke bättre. Vi förena oss i de varmaste helsningar.

Din Göran.

Denmark's parsonage, August 14, 1914

Dear Nathan.

Thank you wholeheartedly for your kind letter which I received last night. I have been thinking of you so much, and in particular did I think with apprehension of your journey back home since I knew how poor Anna's health was. About a week ago I met Tyra Quensel who told me that Mrs. Zorn[2] had received a cable from you, that Anna was still in bed. Hopefully the journey home has not broken her strength altogether. She is extraordinary in her willpower and spiritual strength. But the physical basis cannot in the long run be dispensed with. I now fervently hope that you won't travel from Lund before she has regained sufficient strength so that the remaining trip will not entail any risk for her whatsoever. I guess you too would certainly need some rest. From now on, you will have to think more of yourself than you have hitherto done, for your strength surely has its limits too.

It must have been magnificent seeing that splendid German nation in these moments of utmost seriousness. One will certainly never forget something like that. Our nation is probably also beginning to feel life's seriousness, but it is still pretty much lacking. That lighthearted optimism is deeply rooted in us. We need chastisement, and alas, that will perhaps happen soon, too.

... [On remuneration for the Archbishop, and on his mansion]

Well, dear Nathan, may now God's blessing be with you and your folks in every way. In particular, I have at heart Anna's quick recovery. – Here it is as usual. Siri not worse, but not better either. All of us send warmest greetings.

Yours, Göran.

74. To Robert Gardiner[1]

Upsala August 25 1914

My dear Mr. Gardiner!

Who could dream such a reason for not meeting in September. The apokalyptic horrors of this epoch absorb every interest. And the Church of Christ suffers as seldom before. I have thrown away sometimes the possibility of war between the two great christian Powers of Europe, England and Germany, as a nightmare. The fact is worse than any dreams. What will it mean to christian Missions and to the cause of Religion and Western Civilization in every respect! Even such a true and old admirer of English culture and Churchlife as myself has some difficulty in understanding, why England

---

[2] Tyra Quensel, wife of Ulrike Quensel (cf. letter no. 58, n. 1); Mrs. Zorn, wife of the painter Anders Zorn (1860–1920).

[1] Robert H. Gardiner (1855–1924), General Secretary of the World Conference of Faith and Order; N. Söderblom's collection of letters, to Swedes and foreigners, UUB, handwritten letter.

could not share the glorious position of the United States as a safeguard of Humanity in this conflagration, and why Asiatic and (through France) African peoples should be set on to the nation of Erasm[us] and Luther, Bach, Kant and Goethe and of the german science. Poor and beloved France must suffer horribly for its humiliating alliance with the Moscovite. Then, in France, as well as in Germany, nobody wished the war. We ask ourselves, not without anxiety, if in England as in Russia internal troubles made the war desirable. And we say to ourselves, that the only great christian Power, which is left, will not allow asiatic and halfasiatic influence to overwhelm Western civilization. I think, that the friends of peace and the members of the Church and of Christian thought have never seen more clearly the grand mission of the United States in the complicated system of this poor Humanity.

It would be a good thing, if the Churches could issue a common protest against this slaughter. The wellmeaning but powerless Tsar Nicolaus said the other day, that »the God of Russia is a mighty God.« I think, that the Father of our Lord Jesus Christ is still mightier. But now He hides His face. Matth. 24,6–7.13. With hearty thanks for your letter,

Sincerely Yours
Nathan Söderblom

III The Archbishop

75. PEACE APPEAL[1]

For Peace and Christian Fellowship.

The War is causing untold distress. Christ's Body, the Church, suffers and mourns. Mankind in its need cries out: O Lord, how long?

The tangle of underlying and active causes which have accumulated in the course of time, and the proximate events which have led to the breaking of peace, are left to history to unravel. God alone sees and judges the intents and thoughts of the heart.

We, the servants of the Church, address to all those who have power or influence in the matter an earnest appeal seriously to keep peace before their eyes, in order that blood-shed may soon cease.

We remind especially our Christian brethren of various nations that war cannot sunder the bond of internal union that Christ holds in us. Sure it is that every nation and every realm has its vocation in the divine plan of the world, and must, even in the face of heavy sacrifices, fulfill its duty, as far as the events indicate it and according to the dim conception of man. Our Faith perceives what the eye cannot always see: the strife of nations must finally serve the dispensation of the Almighty, and all the faithful in Christ are one. Let us therefore call upon God that he may destroy hate and enmity, and in mercy ordain peace for us. His will be done!

76. From DAVID CAIRNS[1]

62, Hamilton Place, Aberdeen, 11th Sept.,1914.

My dear Dr. Söderblom,

I hardly know how to address you since your elevation, but I just want to

---

[1] As one of the first measures after his return from Germany, Archbishop-elect Söderblom sent this Appeal for Peace in Swedish, English, French and German to church leaders in neutral as well as belligerent countries in September, 1914. After intensive discussion, it was published in November. The text is here taken from Bengt Sundkler, *Nathan Söderblom. His Life and Work*, Lund 1968, 163.

[1] N. Söderbloms collection of letters, from foreigners, UUB, typewritten letter. Unfortunately, only very few letters from Söderblom have survived in Cairns' papers in Aberdeen. There is none among them that corresponds to the one from Cairns printed above.

write and congratulate you with all my heart on the honours which have come so thickly and so fast upon you. It is a re-assurance about the World to find one who deserves it so well, accompanied by »Love, Honour, troops of friends« as our poet[2] has it. Your elevation to the Primacy is not only an honour to yourself, but to your country. It is a great regret to me that I did not see you when I was in Upsala last summer, but I heard a great deal about you, from Fries, and Westmann[3], and many another and I saw that lovely church near Stockholm in whose plan, as I gathered from Fröken Wikander, you had a part. It was as if you spoke to me, as I entered into its noble design. Upsala interested me intensely, and I shall never forget two visits which I paid to Old Upsala, and the prospect over the wide plain in the morning light. Sweden, in fact, captured my imagination and my heart, and in happier times I hope to return and renew the acquaintance with it, which I have begun, but how can one think of anything just now except of those tremendous tragic events which are hurrying on to us so fast? It is a very startling thing to feel that one is living among some of the greatest events of human history, and must do his puny best to play his part therein.

I got a week or so ago a copy of a Leipzig newspaper, containing the report of the fateful day in the Reichstag, which I read with the deepest interest. It bore the Upsala postmark. I do not know if it came from you, but I am grateful to whoever sent it. I have sent on to you, by post, the English White Book[4], and I send with this a Supplementary Paper. We are quite content to rest our case with any impartial witness on these documents. I quite admit that the Policy which led up to them is more open to criticism. I do not think that our Country has sufficiently appreciated the German case for expansion, but as the thing shaped itself in the last weeks of July and the beginning of August, I cannot see that we had any honourable alternative. What has absolutely united opinion in our Country and silenced those of us who have all along been friends of Germany, has been her treatment of Belgium[5]. To condone that would, it seems to me, mean the end of international morality as well as of the independence and freedom of all the smaller States of Europe, and we who are Scotsmen, believe in what are known as the smaller States with all our souls. I can quite understand that the peculiar position in which you stand in Sweden may incline your sympathies to Germany. Russia is a dangerous neighbour. Personally, I believe, that England has taken guarantees for Sweden and Norway before entering

---

[2] Willliam Shakespeare, *Macbeth*, V,3, 24–26: »And that which should accompany old age,/ As honour, love, obedience, troops of friends,/ I must not look to have ...«

[3] Knut Bernhard Westman (1881–1967), professor of church history in Uppsala, friend of Söderblom's.

[4] Cairns possibly means the British *Blue Book* which, analogous to the German *White Book*, proclaimed the meaning and goals of the war.

[5] Handwritten footnote by Cairns: »I took part in two protests against war with Germany, prior to the fatal denouement of her crossing the Belgian frontier. We took precisely the same line in 1870 under the Gladstone Ministry.« – William Ewart Gladstone (1809–1898) was British prime minister 1868–1874; in 1870, Germany declared war against France.

into an Alliance with her, but I cannot produce documentary proof of the fact as yet. If I can get it, I will let you know. Our Country is absolutely united, and has never wavered in its conviction that powerful as Germany is, there can be but one end to this conflict, but the way to it may be long and terrible. It is the end of an epoch. May it be the birth pangs of a new World! I only wish I could see you, and get your full mind about it all, but I hope to keep in touch with you, and to send on to you anything of importance that bears upon the changing phases of the struggle.

Excuse this hurried letter, Give my *hommage* to your wife, accept it for yourself, and believe me,

Very truly yours,

David S. Cairns

[Handwritten postscript:] I see that Herrmann, Eucken, Naumann, the Axenfelds, & my valued friend Le Seur, with whom I spent a happy ten days in his home in Berlin & in Stockholm in June have all issued a protest against the wrongs done to Germany.[6] Belgium is accused of inexcusable enormities against the Fatherland. I suppose we are all a little mad when patriotic feeling is roused. It almost makes me feel that Tolstoy is right when he denounces it! My own Country has committed crimes enough in its name. But nothing will ever make me believe that it can be right to treat a Country in a way that would be shameful if the Country were a man. When are [we] to have the recognition of an international morality & faith in God as ruler of the peoples? ... I have been greatly delighted lately with the works of Selma Lagerlöf.

77. From ROBERT GARDINER[1]

September 11, 1914.

Dear Professor Söderblom:

Truly this horrible war in Europe is almost apocalyptic! I cannot help hoping, however, that, dreadful as it is, it will be overruled for good, and that the world will recognize that our Christianity must be vastly more vital and

---

[6] The manifesto is entitled *Aufruf deutscher Kirchenmännner und Professoren: An die evangelischen Christen im Ausland* and is dated Sept. 4, 1914. The names not mentioned thus far: Paul Le Seur (1877–1963), minister in Berlin; Karl Axenfeld (1869–1924), director of missions, later *Generalsuperintendent* of Kurmark; Theodor Axenfeld (1867–1930), ophthalmologist. Other signers were Adolf Deißmann, Adolf von Harnack – not Naumann; here Cairns' memory failed him. Nor does this manifesto echo the German war propaganda about Belgium's alleged »enormities« , but asserts that Belgian neutrality had first been breached by the Allies. It claims that Germany was completely innocent, that it had to ward off the Russian aggressor's Asian barbarism, was encircled by the Western allies, etc. Yes, God was calling even Germany to repentance – but it was not guilty. The document only just stops short of claiming God as a German ally. The text is printed in Gerhard Besier, *Die protestantischen Kirchen Europas im Ersten Weltkrieg. Ein Quellen- und Arbeitsbuch*, Göttingen 1984, 40.42–45.

[1] N. Söderblom's collection of letters, from foreigners, UUB, typewritten letter.

practical than it has ever been. Hitherto our service has been altogether too much merely that of the lips. We must now, however, cease to profess to be Christians, or else we must make the laws of the Prince of Peace absolutely the determining influence of our lives, and we must preach Christ with a fervor and intensity hitherto unknown. If our hearts could only be stirred to a real desire for the establishment of His Kingdom, our differences would soon melt away and we should be united in Him and go forward in His strength.

...

It seemed to me that England realized pretty clearly that the struggle is one of life and death between civilization and true democracy on the one hand and of military despotism on the other. ...

Very sincerely yours,
Robert H. Gardiner

78. To Hermann von Bezzel[1]

Upsala 24 IX 1914

Exzellenz,

In der Überzeugung, dass Sie die in diesem Aufruf ausgedrückten Gefühle und Wünsche teilen, und dass Sie dringende Notwendigkeit empfinden in dieser harten Zeit dem Zusammenhang und der Gemeinschaft der Christen einen Ausdruck zu geben, bitte ich Sie, neben den auf der beigelegten Liste aufgerechneten Kirchenmännern, Ihren Namen unter dem Aufruf zeichnen zu wollen. Die Welt muss sehen, dass Christus noch lebt.

Darf ich Sie bitten mir sobald es Ihnen angenehm ist Nachricht zu geben, und zwar spätestens vor dem 5 Oktober. Wenn alle Antworten gekommen sind, werde ich gleichzeitige Veröffentlichung des Dokuments in Deutschland, Österreich-Ungarn, Frankreich, England, Russland, den Vereinigten Staaten und den kleineren Ländern besorgen. Wenn Sie Ihren Namen senden und gleichzeitig den Wunsch aussprechen, werde ich Ihnen telegraphieren, wenn das Ganze für die Veröffentlichung fertig sein wird.

Mit herzlichen Wünschen für Ihre herrliche Nation, die ein in der Geschichte einzig dastehendes Beispiel von Einigkeit und Opferfreudigkeit gegeben hat –

und in der Hoffnung, dass das evang[elische] Christentum sich stärker zeigen wird als alle nationale Gegensätze,

bin ich Ew Exzellenz sehr ergebener
Nathan Söderblom

---

[1] Hermann von Bezzel (1861–1917), Oberkonsistorialpräsident in Munich; Landeskirchliches Archiv Nürnberg, LKAN Pers. XI (Hermann von Bezzel) Nr. 19, handwritten letter.

79. From ERNST VON DRYANDER[1] to Hermann von Bezzel

Berlin, den 29. 9. 14

Verehrte Exzellenz!
Sie haben, wie ich, ein Schreiben des designierten Erzbischofs von Upsala Dr. Söderblom erhalten mit der Bitte um Unterzeichnung eines für die Oeffentlichkeit des In- und Auslands bestimmten Aufrufs.

In dem dringendem [sic] Wunsche, dass unsere Antworten, wie verschieden immer motiviert, sachlich nicht auseinander gehen möchten, in der brennenden Sorge auch, das falls dies geschähe, ein schmerzlicher Riss in die Einigkeit unseres Volkes in der Beurteilung des Krieges hineintreten könne, fasse ich den Mut, Ihnen die Antwort, die ich dem Herrn Erzbischof zu geben beabsichtige, anbei abschriftlich mitzuteilen. Ich wäre innig dankbar, wenn ich, selbstredend abgesehen von der Stellung, in der ich durch die beiden ergebenst beigefügten Publikationen mich befinde, doch im Resultat mir Ihren Anschauungen und Ihrer Entscheidung zusammentreffen würde.

In der furchtbaren Not des Krieges, Sie, unser Volk, unsere Kirche und die Sache des Reiches Gottes dem lebendigen Herrn befehlend, der auch in dieser wilden Zeit seine Friedensgedanken verwirklichen wird.
Ihr
In warmer Verehrung ergebener
Dryander
[handwritten postscript: Ich würde außerordentlich dankbar sein, wenn Sie in der Lage wären, prinzipiell zuzustimmen, für eine kürzeste telegrafische Nachricht.

80. From ERNST VON DRYANDER[1]

Berlin, N. 24, den 29. 9. 14

Hochwürdiger Herr Erzbischof!
Euer Bischhöflichen [sic] Gnaden danke ich herzlich für den Brief vom 24. 9. Und das darin zutage tretende mich ehrende Vertrauen. Ich habe Ihre Bitte reiflich erwogen und beehre mich folgendes zu erwiedern [sic]:

Wie ich zu dem Gedanken eines Aufrufs an die christlichen kriegsführenden Mächte stehe und stehen muss, wollen Sie gütigst der anliegenden Antwort auf einen Brief entnehmen, den ein mir bekannter, von mir auf das Wärmste verehrter und ehrwürdiger französischer Geistlicher schon vor

---

[1] Ernst von Dryander (1843–1922), 1892 Generalsuperintendent of Kurmark, 1898 Prussian court chaplain (Oberhofprediger), 1906–1918 Vice President of the United Church of Prussia (Altpreußische Union); Landeskirchliches Archiv Nürnberg, LKAN Pers. XI (Hermann von Bezzel) Nr. 19; circular letter (typewritten).

[1] Landeskirchliches Archiv Nürnberg, LKAN Pers. XI (Hermann von Bezzel) Nr. 19; carbon copy of typewritten letter.

Beginn der Schlachten an mich gerichtet hatte, der aber erst vor kurzem in meine Hände gelangt ist. Er verfolgt den gleichen Gedanken wie Ihre Erklärung. Die inzwischen völlig veränderte Situation hat auch den Ton der Antwort verändert und uns aus bestimmten Gründen die weitere Veröffentlichung, in der alles Persönliche unterdrückt ist, nahe gelegt.

Ich bin hiernach – wie Sie sehen – auch Ihrer Aufforderung gegenüber durch eine bereits ausgesprochene Stellungnahme gebunden. Aber auch wenn ich das nicht wäre, so vermöchte ich in dem gegenwärtigen Augenblicke nicht Ihrer Mahnung Folge zu geben.

So ungeteilt ich dem in Absatz 1 ausgeführten Gedanken zustimme, so würde ich ausser Stande sein, den 2. Satz mir anzueignen. Gewiss wird die Geschichte vieles in anderem Lichte zeigen, was wir nur durch die trübende Staubwolke der Arena des Tages sehen. Aber dass sie nur umso heller – wie bereits geschehen – die Gerechtigkeit unserer Sache ans Licht bringen werde –: auf dieser für uns unerschütterlichen Ueberzeugung ruht unser gutes Gewissen, unsere Freudigkeit und unsere Entschlossenheit in der furchtbaren Bedrängnis der Gegenwart. Es ist für mich unmöglich, auch nur *ein* Wort zu unterzeichnen, das einem Zweifel an dieser Ueberzeugung Raum gäbe.

Noch stärker aber, wenn das anders möglich ist, müsste ich mich gegen den dritten Absatz der Erklärung wenden. Wer von vier Seiten überfallen, sein Leben verteidigt, handelt im Stande der Notwehr und vollzieht eine christliche Pflicht. In dieser Lage sind wir. Nie könnte ich es über das Herz bringen, irgend jemand, der für diesen Kampf verantwortlich ist, in diesem Augenblicke »nachdrücklich an seine Pflicht zu mahnen«, den Gedanken des Friedens ins Auge zu fassen. Eben weil wir »für unseren göttlichen Beruf im Weltenplan« kämpfen, dürfen wir, wie es vor wenig Tagen unser Reichskanzler ausgesprochen hat, um unserer christlich-sittlichen Pflicht, ja um der Liebe zu unserem Volke willen nicht eher die Waffen niederlegen als bis uns ein Friede gesichert ist, der künftigen schmählichen Friedensbruch unmöglich macht und uns die Ausübung jenes Berufs sichert.

So wollen Sie, hochwürdiger Herr Erzbischof, mit dem Verständnis, das Ihnen aus der genauen Kenntnis des deutschen Volkes erwächst, die Gründe würdigen, aus denen ich trotz voller Würdigung Ihrer Absichten und trotz völligen Einsseins mit Ihnen im Glauben, in der Liebe zu den Brüdern und den daraus für den Krieg sich ergebenden Folgerungen doch meine Unterschrift versagen muss. Sie werden es umso eher können, jemehr Sie sich in die Empfindungen eines Volkes versetzen, das vom Könige bis zum geringsten Manne darüber einig ist, dass es gegenüber tückischem Ueberfall um seine heiligsten Güter, um Sein oder Nichtsein ringt und täglich dafür, ohne zu klagen, die unerhörtesten Opfer darbringt.

Aber Sie wollen mir gestatten einen anderen Gedanken hinzuzufügen. Ich weiss nicht, welche Antwort Sie von den anderen Brüdern, an die Ihre Bitte sich richtet, erhalten werden. Dennoch könnte ich mir denken, dass letztere einen offenern Zugang zu einer anderen späteren Zeit finden könnte. Ich erlaube mir darum, den Gedanken Ihrer gütigen Erwägung zu unterbreiten, ob vielleicht in einem künftigen Moment ein deutlicher, von Gott gewiesener Fingerzeig für eine ähnliche Mahnung sich ergeben könnte.

Ich vereinige mich von Herzen mit Ihnen in der Bitte, dass in dieser Zeit des Opferns, der Tränen und des Jammers, von dem ich täglich umgeben bin, der grosse Herr des Friedens der Welt Seinen Frieden[2], Hass und Feindschaft überwinden und ein neugeborenes Christenvolk aus den Wehen der Kriegeszeit hervorgehen lassen wolle, als Ihr Ihnen in Christo verbundener

Dryander

81. From HERMANN VON BEZZEL[1]

München, den 30. September 1914

Hochwürdigster Herr Erzbischof,
hochzuverehrender Bruder in Christo!

Sie gestatten mir auf die gestern und heute an mich ergangene Zuschrift mit der Freimütigkeit zu antworten, die unter Männern und Bekennern des gleichen teuren Glaubens nütze und not ist.

Mit Ihnen beklage ich den furchtbaren Völkerkrieg und erflehe mit Ihnen einen lauteren, ernsten und wahren Frieden, der durch Gottes Gnade geeignet sein möchte, den ersten Anfang zu einen [sic] Völkerfrieden zu bilden, wie ihn die Gemeinde Jesu Christi ihren Friedefürsten entgegen erhofft.

Wenn die am Krieg nicht beteiligten Völker so der Klage über den Krieg wie dem Wunsch nach Frieden öffentlich Ausdruck geben, kann das nur begrüßt werden. Aber ich, als Glied des deutschen Volkes, das wie die Geschichte nicht erst herausstellen *wird*, sondern jetzt schon klärlich zeigt, zu Unrecht angegriffen und mit wahrhaft infernalen Lügen bekämpft wird, kann nicht meinen Namen unter ein Schriftstück setzen, das wenigstens in seinen [sic] ersten Teil meinem Volksempfinden wie meiner christlichen Überzeugung nicht ganz gerecht wird.

Genehmigen Sie, hochwürdiger Herr Erzbischof, die Versicherung meiner Verehrung und den Wunsch gemeinsamer Arbeit zu Ehren Christi und der lutherischen Kirche

Ihr ergebenster
D Dr von Bezzel

---

[2] Probably to be added: »schenken«.

[1] N. Söderblom's collection of letters, from foreigners, UUB; handwritten letter.

82. To ROBERT GARDINER[1]

Upsala October 13th 1914.

My dear Mr Gardiner,

Thank you very much for your letter and the enclosed documents. The pastoral letters of the Bishop of Winchester are models of pastoral wisdom and true Christian charity. I am most obliged to you for having sent them.

As to the war, the question is more complicated than a fight between democracy and militarisme. You can hardly mean that Russia is the champion of democracy. You may for instance realize the treatment of Finland by the Russian governement and its consequences with regard to freedom and civilisation. Law and order have been entirely spoilt in the former most loyal country of Finland by illegal acts, issued from the governement in the later years, and especially directed against the old administration and culture of the country.[2] On the other hand you may admit that no European country has a more democratic legislation than Germany with its old-age-pension[3] and its progressive taxation, which has broken the hegemony of money, which is the bosom sin of the modern world; and at last the universal conscription, a most democratic institution which represents to the world the edifying sight of princes, farmers and labourers fighting and falling side by side for their country. And besides all these, who have to serve according to the military Law, (that is every man in the age of 21–45 years) there are about 1 1/4 million of volunteers of all classes who have enrolled themselves without any call. The type of civilisation is certainly finer and higher in France and England, but education is more spread and more democratic in Germany.

It would be an irreparable loss for the world if the British Empire would lose something of its useful authority in all parts of the world. But it will certainly win nothing by unfounded and bitter accusations against Germany. To me, who love France more than any other country except my own, and who see in England and Germany besides the U.S.A. the strongholds of Western civilisation, this cruel war and hatred between the great nations seems a tragic event, which cannot but weaken Europe. But let us hope that, although we do not understand how, good may be brought out of evil.

Very sincerely yours
N Söderblom

---

[1] N. Söderblom's collection of letters, to Swedes and foreigners, UUB, handwritten letter.

[2] Finland was an autonomous Russian grand-duchy from 1809–1917. In 1899, Czar Nicholas II. abolished autonomy. The Finns rebelled against Russification; in 1904, the Russian governor was assassinated. When the revolution of 1905 spread to Finland, the Czar restored autonomy to the country.

[3] Old age insurance was introduced by Bismarck in 1889 as part of a series of social security legislative measures from 1883–1889 which was quite avant-garde at the time.

83. From Jean Meyer[1]

Paris, le 14 Octobre 1914

Monsieur l'archevêque,
très honoré et cher frère,

J'ai reçu il y a trois jours la lettre par laquelle vous voulez bien m'inviter à nouveau et avec une insistance qui me touche profondément, à venir assister à votre consécration. J'ai tenu à consulter mes collègues. Ils ont été d'avis, comme moi-même, que je ne pouvais m'absenter en ce moment.

Songez donc que la moitié de nos pasteurs sont mobilisés et qu'il faut pourvoir à tous les services; puis, bien que l'ennemi ait été repoussé loin de Paris et qu'un retour offensif de sa part vers la capitale ne paraisse pas possible, il n'a cependant pas encore été chassé de notre territoire; enfin les deuils se multiplient autour de nous, – notre cher ami, le doyen Vaucher, vient de perdre son fils aîné, tué dans un combat. En de telles circonstances, un voyage de moi qui durerait de trois à quatre semaines produisait, dans l'Eglise et dans ma paroisse, plus que de l'étonnement.

Je le regrette profondément, car je m'étais fait une grande joie de me rendre à Upsal pour cet évènement sollennel, et de prier avec vous et pour vous le souverain chef de l'Eglise de répandre sur vous ses bénédictions. Nous en serons réduits à nous joindre à vous de loin le 8 Novembre. Nous songerons cependant à vous envoyer, pour me remplacer et nous représenter, un homme qui nous paraît bien qualifié et que vous verrez certainement avec plaisir. Je ne puis le nommer encore, la décision n'étant pas définitivement arrêtée.

Pour ce qui est de votre appel concernant la paix je l'ai reçu *aujourd'hui* seulement. J'ai pu consulter, à ce sujet aussi, plusieurs de mes collègues. Ils ont été, cette fois encore, unanimes avec moi pour penser que je ne pouvais pas signer cette pièce. Vous ne vous rendez pas compte de la situation dans laquelle nous sommes. Les allemands non seulement combattent contre nos troupes, mais ils couvrent une partie de notre pays, comme la Belgique, de ruines et de sang innocent; ils brûlent et massacrent, ils commettent des atrocités sans nom et sans nombre; à l'étranger, beaucoup ne le croient pas et pourtant cela est vrai, trop vrai. Un fait seulement: le régiment dans lequel sert mon fils a vu des allemands allumer des meules de paille, puis prendre des blessés par les bras et les jambes et les jeter, malgré leurs cris de détresse, dans les flammes; hélas, nos gens, qui n'étaient sans doute pas en force, ne pouvaient aller au secours des ces malheureux! ... Et nous irions nous associer à une demande de paix, au fond désirée par l'empereur d'Allemagne, qui prétendrait cependant la dicter, quitte à recommencer la guerre dans dix ans, lorsqu'il se croirait plus sûr encore que cette fois de nous écraser. Mais, autour de nous, on nous considérerait comme traîtres à la patrie, et, vous le savez, dans notre pays, il ne manque pas de gens qui seraient trop

[1] Jean Meyer (1849–1932), inspecteur ecclésiastique de l'église évangélique luthérienne de France; N. Söderblom's ecumenical collection A 17, UUB, handwritten letter.

heureux de nous représenter comme tels. Ce n'est pas, sans doute, que nous ne souhaitions pas la paix, mais le moment n'est pas venu d'en parler. Ce n'est pas non plus que nous soyons inspirés par des pensées de haine; non, c'est simplement la prudence qui nous commande de nous abstenir. Ici encore, je regrette, – mais ma voie est nettement tracée.

Laissez-moi vous remercier encore très chaudement pour l'affection que vous témoignez à notre cher pays. J'y suis extrêmement sensible, surtout dans ces jours si sombres où nous sommes.

Pardonnez cette trop longue lettre et croyez-moi, Monsieur l'archevêque et bien cher frère, votre respectueusement affectionné et dévoué

Jean Meyer, past-r,

Insp-r ecclésiastique.

P. S. Je me permets d'inclure une coupure de journal qui exprime l'état d'esprit des alliés dans cette question de la paix.

Paris, October 14, 1914

Lord Archbishop, highly esteemed and dear Brother,

Three days ago, I received the letter by which you would like to invite me once more and with a profoundly moving urgency to come and assist in your consecration. I set store by consulting my colleagues. They were, like myself, of the opinion that I could not set out for a journey at this moment.

Just think that half of our ministers have been conscripted and that all the worship services must be taken care of; moreover, even though the enemy has been repulsed far from Paris and a return offensive from his part does not seem possible, he has nevertheless not been expelled from our territory yet; finally, bereavements are multiplying around us, – our dear friend, Dean Vaucher,[2] has just lost his elder son, killed in action. Under such circumstances, a journey by me which would last between three and four weeks would entail more than astonishment, both in the Church and in my parish.

I profoundly regret this, as it would have been a great joy for me to travel to Uppsala for this solemn event and to pray with you and on your behalf to the supreme Head of the Church that he may bestow his blessing upon you. We shall be reduced to joining you from afar on the 8th of November. We do consider, however, sending to you a highly qualified man you will certainly be pleased to see, in order to substitute for me and to represent us. I cannot tell you his name as yet, the decision not having been finalized.

As for your appeal for peace, I have received it only *today*. I have been able to consult several of my colleagues on this subject, too. They were, once again, in complete agreement with me that I could not sign this document. You are not taking into account the situation in which we are. The Germans are not only combating our troops, they are also covering part of our country, like Belgium, with ruins and innocent blood; they are burning and massacring, they are committing unspeakable and innumerable atrocities; many people abroad do not believe it, and yet, it is true, only too true. Just one fact: the regiment in which my son is serving saw Germans setting alight piles of straw, then pulling some injured [soldiers] by their legs and

---

[2] Édouard Vaucher (1847–1920), Lutheran pastor, teacher of theology at the Protestant theological Faculty at the Sorbonne in Paris since 1879, and Dean since 1909.

arms and throwing them into the flames, despite their cries of anguish; alas, our people who doubtless were not in sufficient force could not come to the rescue of these hapless men! ... Besides, we would join a demand for peace actually desired by the emperor of Germany who would, however, pretend to be dictating it, at the risk of taking up the war again after ten years when he would feel more secure that this time around, he could crush us. In our own environment, though, we would be considered traitors of our nation, and as you know, in our country, there is no shortage of people who would be only too happy to paint us as such. It is doubtless not because we did not desire peace, but the time for talking about it has not come. Nor is it because we were inspired by thoughts of hatred; no, it is simply prudence which commands us to abstain. Here again, I regret, – but my route has been clearly staked out.

Let me give you my heartfelt thanks once again for the affection you show for our dear country. I am extremely sensitive concerning this, particularly in somber days such as these.

Excuse this overly long letter and consider me, Lord archbishop and very dear brother, yours respectfully affectionate and dedicated

Jean Meyer, pastor,

Church President

P.S. Permit me to enclose a newspaper clip which expresses the state of mind of those united on this issue of peace.

84. To Hermann von Bezzel[1]

Upsala 17 X 1914.

Exzellenz und hochwürdigster Kollege,

Herzlich danke ich Ihnen für Ihre aufrichtige und mir völlig verständliche Antwort. Die Brüder in den neutralen Staaten haben alle den Aufruf mit herzlicher Beteiligung unterzeichnet – diejenigen die bisher geantwortet haben, ich erwarte die letzten Antworte in der nächsten Woche. Auch einige unserer Brüder in führender kirchlicher Stellung in den am Krieg beteiligten Ländern haben den ganzen Aufruf unterschrieben. Aber Anderen haben die Stücke 2 und 3 wie Ihnen Schwierigkeiten gemacht.

Die Formulierung war aus den folgenden Gründen gewählt worden. Niemand kann lebhafter als ich von der deutschen Friedensliebe beim Ausbruch des Krieges überzeugt sein. Da aber aufrichtige Brüder in Christo in anderen Ländern einen anderen Gesichtspunkt einnehmen, und da die Vorgeschichte eines Krieges immer in der Weltgeschichte ein verwickeltes Problem gewesen ist, muss im Aufruf die Frage von den Ursachen des Krieges allgemein formuliert werden: wer seines Rechtes gewiss ist, kann an die Geschichte ruhig appellieren.

Aus Ihrem Briefe wie aus demjenigen Dr. Dryanders und anderer führenden Kirchenmännern in den vom Kriege heimgesuchten Nationen geht in

---

[1] Landeskirchliches Archiv Nürnberg, LKAN Pers. XI (Hermann von Bezzel) Nr. 19; handwritten letter.

wohltuender Weise hervor, dass Sie ein wahrhaft pastorales Herz haben, und dass Sie den ersten und vierten Teil des Schriftstückes daher billigen. Wie mir schon nahe gelegt worden ist, schlage ich somit Ihnen wie Dr. Dryander vor, dass Sie – wie z. B. der Erzbischof von Canterbury – *ausdrücklich nur Stück 1 und 4 des Aufrufs* unterzeichnen, was für die betreffenden Herren genau und deutlich vermerkt werden wird. Es wäre besonders für Amerika, wo Legenden über den vermeintlichen Furor teutonicus in gewissen Kreisen geglaubt werden, misslich, wenn in diesem Zusammenhange die autoritativsten deutschen Namen gänzlich fehlten, aber auch hier würde eine deutsche Beteiligung an den Sätzen des Stückes *4* des Aufrufs viele Augen öffnen, die jetzt durch falsche Auslegungen verblindet sind. Der von feindlicher Seite energisch gemachte Versuch Deutschland geistig zu isolieren darf nicht gelingen. Hier kann etwas dagegen ausgerichtet werden.

Ich bin, hochzuverehrender Herr Kollege, Ihr in herzlicher Dankbarkeit für Ihre guten Wünschen, im Dienste der evangelischen Kirche ergebenst verbundener

Nathan Söderblom

85. To Randall Davidson[1]

Upsala 19.X.1914.

My dear Archbishop,

The answer, issued by You and other British Churchmen, must needs make an excellent impression on every Christian heart. I do not think, that Treitschke and Bernhardi[2] mean much in the present war. But the dignified and thoughtful Christian comity and earnest goodwill of the document are most efficacious. I know, how grieved the Germans felt. But their appeal »to the evangelical Christians abroad«[3] was to me a grave disappointment, although several of the signers are my dear personal friends and all of them are most honourable and, partly, eminent Christians. Their appeal has, however, not served the cause of christian fellowship. When I read the British answer in the Times, I had the impression, that it must be allowed to accomplish its blessed mission during some weeks before publishing the manifestation of Christian fellowship in spite of the war, in behalf of which I

---

[1] Randall Thomas Davidson (1848–1930), Archbishop of Canterbury 1903–1928; N. Söderblom's collection of letters, from foreigners, UUB; copy.

[2] Heinrich von Treitschke (1834–1896), influential German historian (*Deutsche Geschichte im 19. Jahrhundert*, 5 vol., new ed. Leipzig 1927) of extremely conservative views. He advocated strengthening the executive at the expense of parliament and an aggressive policy of colonisation; Friedrich von Bernhardi, Prussian general and writer on military affairs, whose book *Deutschland und der nächste Krieg*, Stuttgart/Berlin 1912, considered war inevitable; Germany had, in his view, no other choice than either becoming a world power or suffering defeat.

[3] As for its content, cf. letter no. 76 note 6.

have had the honour of receiving two letters from you, one of which will be published together with the mentioned manifestation.

I thank you most heartily for these beautiful and most valuable letters, one private, one for publication, and for the prayer, that I shall reproduce in my Pastoral letter. The brothers, asked to sign, in neutral countries and some ones in the fighting nations have signed the entire manifest[4] with hearfelt conviction. But I understand, that the parts (2 and) 3 make difficulty to you as well as to some other most honoured leading Churchmen. Therefore I take the liberty of proposing to you as well as to the two most authoritative men in Germany, to our French brethren and to the Archbishop of York and the Moderator of the Presbyterian Church in Scotland to sign *only the points 1 and 4* of the proclamation in accordance with the several letters, that I have received. ...

With warm gratitude for Your Grace's good pastoral wishes I have the honour of being most sincerely Your servant

Nathan Söderblom

86. From HERMANN VON BEZZEL[1]

München, den 20. X. 1914

Reverendissime,

ich vermag trotz guten Willens kein neues Moment aufzufinden oder anzuerkennen, das mich auch nur berechtigen könnte, den Aufruf – ob auch mit Verwahrung – zu unterzeichnen.

Ihre und meine Auffassung von der Lage der Dinge, der causa belli u[nd] den ihr innewohnenden Berechtigungen vor dem heiligen Gott, geht zu weit auseinander. Ihnen erscheint noch als Aufgabe, was mir bereits als Voraussetzung der Kriegsführung vorkommt. Und jetzt in der groszen Not, die wir als ein nicht aus eignem Wirken geschnitztes, sondern aus Gottes Willen uns auferlegtes Kreuz im Gehorsam tragend durchkämpfen wollen, gilt mein ganzes Gebet lediglich der Gabe christlicher Beharrlichkeit, deren Hauptmoment die Klarheit ist.

Unbezweifelt sind in dem Aufrufe Sätze, die mich mit Ihnen und nicht nur mit Ihnen, hochwuerdigster Herr, verbinden, aber es sind christliche, evangelische Axiome, die meiner unterschriftlichen Bezeugung wahrlich nicht beduerfen.

Gerne denke ich an September 1911 u[nd] an den Frieden von Upsala nicht ohne Heimweh zurück. Gott wird den über allem Erdenweh fortwirkenden Frieden uns erhalten.

In Ehrerbietung

D Bezzel

---

[4] See above, no. 75.

[1] N. Söderblom's collection of letters, from foreigners, UUB; handwritten letter.

87. From Jean Meyer[1]

Monsieur l'archevêque,
Cher et honoré frère,

... Sans doute je partage les sentiments que vous exprimez dans votre manifeste; je suis un homme de paix, je crois nécessaire d'affirmer l'union des enfants de Dieu, en dépit de l'horrible oeuvre de Satan dont nous sommes les témoins. Mais je crains qu'une manifestation publique de notre part, dans notre pays à l'heure présente, non seulement n'eût pas été comprise, mais eût agi à l'encontre de ce que nous aurions souhaité.

Pardonnez-moi si je reviens sur ce que je vous ai précédemment écri. Les allemands ont commis et commettent encore journellement des atrocités sans nom, telles qu'on ne peut presque pas le croire, avec le but avoué d'exterminer la race française. Vous pouvez vous imaginer les sentiments de colère, d'horreur de notre peuple tout entier contre de tels sauvages. Les journaux catholiques écrivent complaisamment: c'est l'empereur *luthérien* qui fait cela. Et je pourrais vous citer tels propos d'un homme, qui n'est pas le premier venu, puisqu'il est professeur au Collège de France et ancien membre de notre Constistoire, qui me disait: »Une Eglise luthérienne en France, il n'en faut plus! Qu'il y ait une Eglise protestante française, mais plus de luthériens! Je prendrai la chose en main, j'écrirai pour cela; et, si l'on ne m'écoute pas, je quitterai l'Eglise luthérienne, j'entrerai dans l'Eglise réformée.« ... J'ai eu beau lui dire que Guillaume II n'est précisément pas luthérien et que ses ancêtres ont établi par la force en Prusse exactement l'Eglise qu'il voudrait créer en France; il n'a rien voulu entendre. On ne raisonne pas avec la passion. Que l'archevêque de Cantorbéry signe, je puis le comprendre. Sa situation est très différente de la nôtre. D'abord, son pays n'est pas été envahi et dévasté d'une manière systématique, avec accompagnement de massacres; puis il est le chef d'une Eglise de majorité, dans un pays où les divers partis religieux sont en paix et où, d'une manière générale, on prend les choses avec sang-froid. Moi, je suis à la tête d'une Eglise d'infime minorité, facilement soupçonnée et même menacée, et cela dans un pays où l'on se gouverne trop souvent par la passion plus que par la raison. Ai-je besoin d'ajouter que si, néanmoins, j'avais cru de mon devoir de signer, je l'aurais fait, mais, encore une fois, je ne voyais pas que le manifeste, du moins pour ce qui nous concerne, pût avoir un effet utile.

Pardonnez-moi de vous avoir encore donné si longuement tous ces détails, mais je tenais à vous prouver qu'il n'y a eu, de ma part, aucune mauvaise volonté.

Agréer, encore ici, l'expression de mes très vifs regrets pour l'autre impossibilité, celle d'être au milieu de vous le 8 Novembre, et veuillez me croire, cher et honoré frère, votre respectueusement dévoué
Jean Meyer

---

[1] N. Söderblom's ecumenical collection A 17, UUB, handwritten letter.

Lord Archbishop, dear and esteemed Brother,

... [Thanks for two letters] I share beyond doubt the sentiments you are expressing in your manifesto; I am a man of peace, I deem it necessary to affirm the unity of the children of God, in spite of the horrible work of Satan we are witnesses of. But I am afraid that a public proclamation on our part, in our country at the present hour, would not only not be understood but would effect the contrary of what we would have desired.

Excuse me for returning to what I previously wrote to you. The Germans have committed and continue to commit unspeakable atrocities every day, such as one almost cannot believe, with the express aim to exterminate the French race. You can imagine the sentiments of wrath, of horror of our whole nation against such savages. The Catholic papers complacently write: That's the *Lutheran* emperor who is doing this. And I could quote for you such proposals by a man who is not the first to come, since he is a professor at the Collège de France and an ancient member of our Church Council, who said to me: »A Lutheran church in France, that is no longer necessary! If there only were a French Protestant church, but no more Lutherans! I shall take care of the matter, I shall write for that cause; and if I am not listened to, I shall leave the Lutheran church, I shall join the Reformed church.« ... I could easily tell him that Wilhelm II is precisely not a Lutheran and that his ancestors forcibly established in Prussia exactly the church he wanted to create in France; he did not want to hear any of that. You don't argue against passion. If the archbishop of Canterbury signs, I can understand him. His situation is quite different from ours. First, his country has not been invaded and devastated in a systematic fashion, accompanied by massacres; then, he is the head of a majority church, in a country where the various religious parties are living in peace and where, in general, things are being taken in cold blood. I am at the head of a Church of a tiny minority, easily suspected and even threatened, and that in a country where people are all too often guided by passion rather than by reason. Do I have to add that if I nonetheless had considered it my duty to sign, I would have done it, but, once more, I did not see that the manifesto, at least as far as it concerns us, could have had a useful effect.

Excuse me for having given you once more all these lengthy details, but I set store by proving to you that there is no ill will on my part.

Please accept, once more, the expression of my very lively regrets for the other impossibility, that of not being in your midst on the 8th of November, and believe me, dear and esteemed Brother, your respectfully dedicated

Jean Meyer

88. From David Cairns[1]

62, Hamilton Place, Aberdeen, 18th January, 1915.

My dear Archbishop,

I have again to thank you for your kindness and courtesy in sending me your Appeal for Peace. I cannot help hoping that when the storm has cleared away, you will have a very great deal to do in bringing the Churches

---

[1] N. Söderblom's collection of letters, from foreigners, UUB; typewritten letter.

and the divided nations together again, and whether this endeavour on your part meets with present success or failure, it is of vital importance as publicly initiating your further mission. It is a great act of faith, and faith is always »a going against appearances«. I cannot believe such acts done in real faith can be lost, for in their very nature, they are a part of that future, which will supersede the past and present alike. The great difficulty, as I have no doubt you realise, with many here, is summed up in one word, – Belgium. We believe ourselves bound in honour to conclude no peace, which shall not contain as one of its terms, complete reparation to Belgium, nor can I see any outlook at all for the future peace and stability of Europe, if Germany's action toward Belgium is to be condoned. Were it to be so condoned, as Maximilian Harden[2] said, Europe would simply accept the fact of the reign of the stronger, and its whole international morality would at once sink to a lower plane. I have carefully examined many German statements of their case regarding Belgium, and possess the State papers of Britain, France, Belgium, Germany and Russia, and the facts seem to me perfectly plain and the conclusion unescapeable. The whole necessity of war is indescribably hateful, and the present war peculiarly calamitous, but unless I become a convert to the principles of Tolstoy and the Quakers, I cannot see that we have any moral alternative except to continue fighting until this plain act of justice is done. I quite appreciate the necessity of your Country remaining neutral. I think that much of the influence for good, which you will have afterwards will depend upon the reality of that neutrality now. I think on the other hand, it is our duty to state our difficulty to you quite frankly, first, that you may understand it, and second that you may have the chance of removing it, if you think our view onesided or can bring any new fact to light that is not as yet within our horizon. ... It is really that [i. e., the violation of Belgian neutrality] and also, I say it with profound sorrow, the light which many of us believe it has thrown on the whole mind of official Germany, that has made the worst trouble here. Indeed it has been one of the greatest and most terrible surprises of my whole life, for the Germany of today is not the Germany that I knew as a student and which I have long loved and reverenced. I have no doubt that this point of view is perfectly familiar to you. It does not exclude my own conviction of great national shortcomings on our part, and I trust a very heartfelt repentance for them. But I cannot, unfortunately, find the smallest trace, in any writings from Germany that have come to my hand, of any indication whatever that they recognise that any wrong has been done to the weaker Country, or are willing to make the smallest reparation. As I reflect, I remember that there are two exceptions to this, some of the Social Democrats and Martin Rade of the »Christliche Welt«[3]. If you can help me, or any of

---

[2] Maximilian Harden (1861–1927), German writer and journalist, favoring German imperialism before World War I but turned pacifist when the war had begun.

[3] Martin Rade (1857–1940), Protestant minister, from 1900 professor of sytematic theology in Marburg, editor of the leading liberal Protestant journal *Christliche Welt*, one of the

us, over this »foul broad ditch«[4], I shall be grateful. I know how overburdened you are, and I do not expect a reply to this letter. You seem to me, if I may say so, predestined, above most other men in Europe, to take a leading part in the great work of reconciliation. You have made so many of us your debtors in matters of scholarship and religious faith; your own Country has singled you out to be her representative in matters of Religion, and you are so intimately related and understand so well the life of the Student Federation, that one naturally looks to you to lead in this great work of reconciliation and reconstruction. Hence I feel it incumbent upon me to put before you what to me is the greatest moral obstacle in the way of realising the ideal of your message. It may be that God will reveal to you the message which will deliver us all. Meanwhile those of us in the warring nations, who have come together in the work of the Student Federation, must pray for one another, and keep our personal friendships alive and warm, and trust in Almighty God. There is a great saying of Luther which has been much in my mind during the past month, »It is impossible for a man who trusts in God not to rejoice. Though the whole world should fall to pieces around him, the ruins will strike him undismayed.«[5]

With all grateful and friendly wishes for the New Year, for yourself, your wife and household.

I am, my dear Archbishop,
Most truly yours,
David S. Cairns

89. To David Cairns[1]

Upsala, March 10th 1915

Reverend and dear Sir,
I owe you an answer to your most earnest and valuable letter. I have not the slightest doubt, that the public opinion amongst Christian people in Great Britain would never have approved of the war, if Germany had not committed the wrong and mistake – because a wrong is always a mistake – of violating the neutrality of Belgium. But it is never the less an obvious fact that this was not the real reason for England's partaking in this detestable war. This is proved already by the terrible accusation, brought by Mr. Salandra[2] in his great speech in the beginning of this year in Rome against the inferiority and blindness of German diplomacy. He said, that he had tele-

---

founders of the »Evangelisch-Sozialer Kongress« and one of the few Protestant theologians who supported the fledgling German democracy in 1918.

[4] An allusion to Dante, *Inferno*, Canto XII: »the deep foul valley trembled« (verses 40 f.), and »the broad ditch« near which the poet sees centaurs armed with arrows, verses 52–57.

[5] I have been unable to identify this quotation. The editor.

[1] Historic Collections King's College Aberdeen, MS 3384/3/6.1893–1906, handwritten letter.

graphed to Berlin and Vienna, telling that the English government was sure not to keep peace, if the war should break out. ... [Further details on the contemporary debate] Now I cannot but hope, ... that England and Germany will win, during the fighting, each other's respect.

Anyhow, I cannot but keep my *praeterea censeo* in the words of the prophet Jesaia ch. XIX: 24–25.[3]

I am most sincerely yours in community of faith and prayer
Nathan Söderblom

90. To David Cairns[1]

Upsala, March 19th 1915.

Reverend and dear Sir,
I just received this letter from a student, that used to be my famulus in Leipzig. It will give to you a fair idea of the sentiments prevailing in the army of the »huns« – as *you* don't call them. If one is to believe the fighting nations themselves, there is a striking difference between the brutal egoism of Germany and the idealistic and altruistic motives of the other peoples. England fights for the sanctity of treaties and the neutrality of Belgium, and for the protection of the small nations, France for the deliverance of Alsace-Lorraine etc, and in order to crush German militarism for the benefit of mankind, Russia very openly tells, that she struggles for liberty and in order to afford to more people the blessing of belonging to the Holy Russian Empire; meanwhile Germany very prosaically says, that it fights only for its existence in order not to become crushed between the overwhelming multitudes on each side.

I am sure that every acute reader of the public and private utterances from the different countries must make the same observation. With men as e. g. you and Deissmann the bonds of Christian fellowship between Great Britain and Germany cannot be long broken.

I remain with hearty greetings and wishes from Mrs. Söderblom
Yours affectionately
N Söderblom
I see, that the Editorial of the Times of 8 March very strongly proves, that the violation of Belgium was not the real cause of Englands partaking in the war.
Yours N S-m

---

[2] Antonio Salandra (1853–1931), Italian jurist and politician, prime minister 1914–1916. He led Italy into the war in 1915 by joining the Entente.

[3] »When that day comes Israel shall rank with Egypt and Assyria, those three, and shall be a blessing in the center of the world. So the Lord of Hosts will bless them: A blessing be upon Egypt my people, upon Assyria the work of my hands, and upon Israel my possession.«

[1] Historic Collections King's College Aberdeen, MS 3384/3/6.1893–1906, handwritten letter.

91. From David Cairns[1]

Aberdeen, 27th March, 1915.

Dear Archbishop Söderblom,

I am greatly indebted to you for your two kind letters, and for the deeply interesting and touching enclosure, which I herewith return. It is such letters from the field which bring home to one the deep pathos of the whole story. ... [Some loosely connected ideas on the war situation]

I am not at all disposed to claim that Britain is clear of blame for the situation that culminated last July, or that her motives, however sound they may be in the main, are wholly ideal and pure. I rather pray »God forgive us all«! On the other hand unless we are to hold the Quaker view, or the more logical Tolstoyan view of War, and of the whole coercive element in society, I am simply unable to see how we could have done anything else than take up arms. »Truth«, as the proverb says, »lies at the bottom of a well«. In this case it is an ocean. ... It must be strange indeed for you to look from your neutral ground and to see all your friends a little off their heads, (and some not a little), all protesting their innocence, and their devotion to the highest ideals! It must be like looking into a madhouse! Yet is it not, when all is said too simple a solution to conclude, – »Six of the one and half a dozen of the other«. All human affairs, as history shows, are desperately entangled matters, but in great controversies is there not usually a broad issue, however entangled the presentment of it may be. Is it really the case that Germany only wanted the right to live peaceably with her neighbours and to be let alone? I once was inclined to think so. I have done some little work for peace, and am a vice-president of the British Peace Society, but I cannot help now remembering that she has steadily resisted the extension of arbitration proposals, and for years has blocked, still more, movements for disarmament ... Now they may have been right in this general attitude regarding arbitration. National expansion may have demanded it. But they cannot have it both ways. It will not do at the same time to plead national expansion, and to claim that they only wish to be let alone. Whatever we may have to say, history will have something to say later. Further one cannot help seeing now that Germany was *far* better prepared than the Allies for the War. Does that really look like [sic] as if the Allies were the aggressors? ...

Now as regards Belgium, I am exceedingly glad to find that we are at one here as to the German action. It is mournful and strange to find Harnack and so many of one's friends in Germany, so many noble names, scholars, saints and thinkers, still defending this action. ... What makes it worse is the evidence that for years past this violation of neutrality had been resolved upon, I do not say by these men, but by the governing powers of Germany. It is this that makes some of us wonder if we had been wrong in condemning the darker view which our militarists have all along taken of

---

[1] N. Söderblom's collection of letters, from foreigners, UUB; typewritten letter.

162

the German intentions. I shall be glad to have the shadow lifted by you or by anyone. Personally I cling to the faith that the Kaiser did not deliberately plan what happened, but permitted these measures as a possible emergency alternative. But taking things as they have shaped themselves, it is not simply the violation of Belgian neutrality, it is the ruthlessness with which the subjugation of the country has been carried through, and the apparent absence of any sense on the part even of the religious leaders of Germany that anything *wrong* has been done, that is so disquieting. Is the Germany that practically with one voice now justifies the national action against Belgium the real Germany? If it is, can you or I or anyone condemn the Entente? That is the problem that our friends, »The Evangelical Theologians« are forcing upon us by their impassioned defence of their country in the matter of Belgium.[2] Suppose that Germany won this War, can any human being suppose that they will stop with Belgium? These doctrines, vindicated by success, will certainly be in time be applied to Holland, and probably next to Scandinavia and German Switzerland. What hope is there for a just and stable international order in Europe if they should prevail? What chance is there for the smaller states?

Now as regards the reasons why England came into the quarrel, these were of course two – the engagements with France involved in the Entente, and the invasion of Belgium ... Would we have gone into the War had it not been for the attack on Belgium? I cannot say. ... I believe that you underestimate the influence that the Belgium matter has had here. There are two nations in Britain. We have our *Junkers* and our *Volkspartei*, cavaliers and puritans, social reactionaries and social reformers. At first the militarists were a small minority in this matter, though they were in positions of great military and diplomatic importance, and made a good deal of noise in the press. ... Many of us were absolutely opposed to the whole campaign of Junker opinion, warning the nation against German intentions, of which it was one expression. We remembered the Germany of our student days and our many friendships there. We resented what was said about her as a wicked slander. But if even then any German had said to me »What will England do if we invade Belgium?« *I could have told him that it would mean war with England.* ... It was the violation of the Belgian frontier that closed the ranks.

There is no doubt that the real reason for our joining the Entente at the first was the creation of the German fleet, along with the belief (rooted in the memories of 1864, 1866, and 1870,[3] fostered by the Kaiser's speeches ..., ... and by the incitements of our Junker press) that it was aimed directly at our sea power. This, in view of the oversea character of the British Empire, meant a blow at the heart. I did not share that view, and thought that the German case for building their fleet as stated by Bülow

---

[2] This probably refers to the manifesto mentioned in letter no. 76, n. 6.
[3] The Prussian wars against Denmark and Austria and the German-French war.

was a good one.[4] It is one which we shall have to recognise when the time comes for peace. But the whole German idea of the reason for our taking part in the War being the wish to destroy their trade is, I believe, a mere nightmare dream. Of course our business men found their competition annoying, but there went with that annoyance a very sincere respect and admiration for what they were doing in business, and we should never have dreamed of war on that ground. As a nation we certainly did not want war. ... But we did want to keep what we had got, and to be free from the fate which Germany has brought upon Belgium. What has brought about the trouble is clear enough. The Junker party in both countries has for the time triumphed. Our share of the guilt, lies so far as the past is concerned, in the *damnosa hereditas* of centuries of grasping at oversea dominion, and, in the present, in a want of ready and general appreciation of Germany's real claims to a place in the sun. Germany's share I need not further particularise. There is to me a clear element of megalomania in their national mind at present. All their manifestos are touched with the marks of *abnormal* feeling. The suspicion of a world conspiracy, idée fixe, etc., etc. seem to me plain enough proofs of a pathological condition.[5] We have suffered enough from that madness in the past to recognise its signs too well in others. That sad truth is that no nation has sought *first* the Kingdom of God, and no nation has been willing to allow Christ to control its international relations. ...

... [On the Student Christian Movement people in all countries being less bitter than the majority of their populations] I have written you an enormously long letter, but there is one thing more that I should like to say. Dark as the sky may be at present and vast and terrible as is the immediate tragedy, I cannot say that I at all despair. I believe that God will bring some great good out of the human evil. Nor surely need we suppose that that great good will be slow in realising itself, if only the Church awakens to its hour. ... May it be yours, my honoured friend, to take your own great part in that new day of God!

Will you express my heartiest greetings to your wife. Accept them for yourself, and believe me with grateful thanks for all your great kindness and courtesy.

Affectionately yours,
David S. Cairns.

---

[4] Bernhard Heinrich Martin Fürst (since 1905) von Bülow, conservative German Chancellor 1900–1909, oversaw the acquisition of overseas colonies by Germany in 1897 and enforced a great enlargement of the German fleet. Both developments contributed to the Germany's international isolation. Bülow's undoing came in 1908. The Kaiser had given an interview to the Daily Telegraph asserting that he, as one of the few of England's friends in Germany, had presented the English Queen with a strategic plan for the war against the Boers in South Africa. Bülow saw the text and let it pass. The British considered the interview a provocation, and the resulting row in the German parliament where the Kaiser's highhandedness was severely criticized, eventually led to Bülow's resignation.

[5] The last two sentences have been marked by Söderblom on the margin by: !!?

92. From ADOLF DEISSMANN[1]

Berlin-Wilmersdorf, Prinzregentenstrasse 6, II, 13. April 1915.
Hochverehrter Herr Erzbischof, lieber Freund!
Sogleich nach Empfang Ihres ersten Briefes vom 15.3. habe ich mich mit
dem Kriegsministerium in Verbindung gesetzt. ... Ich fand sofort (trotz der
durch die Anwesenheit von etwa 850 000 Gefangenen in Deutschland be-
greiflichen Überlastung der Leiter der betreffenden Abteilung des Kriegs-
ministeriums) ein überaus freundliches Entgegenkommen. Der eine der
maßgebenden Herren, der die Verhandlung führte, musste dann eine längere Revisionsreise durch die Gefangenenlager machen, lud mich aber sofort
nach seiner Rückkehr auf heute früh zu einer Konferenz im Kriegsministerium, Dieselbe ist sehr befriedigend verlaufen. Der Herr, Hauptmann von
Lübbers,[2] ist eine hochgebildete, vornehme Persönlichkeit, mit der sofort
der Kontakt unbedingten Vertrauens hergestellt ist. Herr von Lübbers war
über Ihr Interesse sehr erfreut und lässt Ihnen dafür seinen herzlichen Dank
aussprechen.

... [citing the decree of the war ministry on the treatment of POWs and a
report of Prof. Carl Stange from Göttingen[3] who worked as a counselor to
the prisoners, both of which documents had originally been attached to this
letter.]

Von mir aus glaube ich versichern zu dürfen, dass der peinlich-honette
Geist unserer deutschen Verwaltung für die praktische Verwirklichung der
oben genannten Grundsätze überall sorgt. Aber es finden fortwährend
durch die amerikanische und spanische Botschaft, durch das Rote Kreuz in
Genf, durch philanthropische Organisationen Besuche und Prüfungen unserer Lager statt, die stets ein günstiges Urteil im Gefolge haben. Unter
850 000 Menschen aus den Dreckhöhlen, Londons, den Dschungeln Indiens, den Fiebersümpfen Senegambiens, den Steppen Rußlands, den
Schlössern Frankreichs finden sich natürlich immer einige, die Beschwerden
haben; aber alle berechtigten Beschwerden werden sofort abgestellt. Wie
diabolisch gelogen wird, ... zeige Ihnen beifolgender Artikel ... [apparent-
ly lost]

Herr von Lübbers hat mich dann ermächtigt, Ihnen mitzuteilen, dass Sie,
falls Sie selbst (oder ein Vertrauensmann von Ihnen) sich durch den Augen-
schein von den Zuständen in den Lagern überzeugen wollten, herzlich willkommen sein werden.

Einen dahingehenden Wunsch Ihrerseits würde ich sehr gern an das Ministerium übermitteln.

Bei der Beurteilung unserer Gefangenenfürsorge dürfen die ungeheueren
Schwierigkeiten nicht übersehen werden, die schon allein auf hygienischem

---

[1] N. Söderblom's collection of letters, from foreigners, UUB; handwritten letter.
[2] I have not been able to identify him. The ed.
[3] Carl Stange (1870–1959), professor of systematic and practical theology in Göttingen
1912. He was theologically close to the Luther-Renaissance initiated by Karl Holl.

Gebiete bestehen. Nicht nur die zum guten Teil aus den niedersten (bei uns *so* überhaupt nicht mehr vorhandenen) Schichten des Lumpenproletariats stammenden englischen Gefangenen sind oft furchtbar verlaust, sondern ganz besonders die Russen haben entsetzliche Seuchen mitgebracht, z. B. Flecktyphus, dem bereits mehrere unserer bedeutenden Ärzte in heldenhafter Pflichterfüllung zum Opfer gefallen sind. Da heisst es natürlich: »primum vivere, deinde philosophari«,[4] was man 1915 übersetzen könnte: erst Kampf gegen die Läuse und den Typhuserreger, dann Seelenpflege. Und was die Verpflegung betrifft, so hat Ihre Gattin ganz recht, wenn sie schreibt, dass manches deutsche Pfarrhaus nicht so reichlich und kräftig isst, wie die Kriegsgefangenen es können.

Herr Hauptmann von Lübbers ersuchte mich, Ihnen noch eine Bitte vorzutragen. Der Weltbund der Christl. Vereine junger Männer hat auch in Russland die Absicht, sich der Gefangenen anzunehmen, findet dort aber dem Vernehmen nach bis jetzt kein Entgegenkommen bei den Behörden. Könnten Sie Ihren Einfluss vielleicht zugunsten der Bestrebungen des Weltbundes geltend machen? ...

Ich stehe, verehrtester Freund, auch in Zukunft gern zu Ihren Diensten, wenn Sie Ihr außerordentlich gütiges Interesse für die Gefangenen betätigen wollen und verbleibe mit den herzlichsten Grüßen von Haus zu Haus

Ihr
treu ergebener
Adolf Deißmann.

93. To Eivind Berggrav[1]

Upsala den 27 juli 1915

Ärade Herr Redaktör!

De tvänne spörsmål Ni framställer rörande de nordiska kyrkornas inbördes närmande få genom tidslägets tyngd ett ännu större eftertryck. Kraftigare än på länge påminnas vi i Norden om vår samhörighet. Och det är en väl-

---

[4] Life first, philosophy later (Latin); origin unknown.

[1] Eivind Berggrav (1884–1959), from 1909 to 1959 editor of the influential Norwegian periodical *Kirke og kultur*, from 1914 till 1919 teacher in various positions, 1919–1924 pastor in a remote village, 1925 prison chaplain in Oslo; participation in the ecumenical conference at Stockholm. After taking his doctorate with a thesis on *Religionens terskel* (Oslo 1924; German transl. *Der Durchbruch der Religion im menschlichen Seelenleben*, Göttingen 1929), he lectured in Oslo. In 1929, he became bishop of Hålogaland in Tromsø and in 1937 bishop of Oslo, where he had to resign for health reasons in 1951. Berggrav was the courageous leader of the church opposition against the Quisling regime which collaborated with the German occupation force after 1940. He based these activities theologically on Luther's doctrine of the two governances in that it determines the limits of obedience to the authorities (*Staten og menesket*, Oslo 1945, German transl. by W. Lindenthal, *Der Staat und der Mensch*, Hamburg 1946). B. also criticized the modern welfare state as potentially totalitarian. – N. Söderbloms collection of letters, from foreigners, UUB, handwritten letter.

⊢to

signad gärning att bringa å bane en allvarligare klarhet öfver vår ställning till hvarandra.

Det är icke sagdt, att grannskap och blodsband garantera verklig andlig gemenskap. Onekligen hafva Nordens kyrkor i högre grad mottagit inflytelser hvar för sig från den evangeliska lutherdomens moderland och, hvad nyare folkliga religiösa strömningar angår, från den anglosaxiska Västern, än från hvarandra. För mig personligen är det en källa till uppriktig glädje att på senare tid spåra sträfvanden till ett närmande mellan Nordens kyrkor, hvilket besjälas af en verklig öfvertygelse att vi ha att lära af hvarandra. Och när jag tänker på utbytet af att under ett par alltför upptagna novemberdagar i fjol ha fått råka Själlands biskop och Kristiania biskop, kan jag ej undgå att hoppas på flera och grundligare sammanträffanden.

Jag är viss på, att Ni, Herr Redaktör, träffat det rätta, då Ni hänvisar till ökad kunskap. Skandinaviska möten af kyrklig och religiös art hafva i allmänhet lidit af bristande förkunskaper hos deltagarna. Huru många känna till de nordiska grannkyrkornas psalmböcker, historia, i mer tillfälliga eller varaktiga uttryck utpräglade egendomligheter och lifsrörelser? Först ett intresseradt studium kan skapa förutsättningar för önskvärd växelverkan. Och ingen som inlåter sig på slikt studium får skäl att ångra det.

Eder med utmärkt aktning
Nathan Söderblom

Uppsala, July 27, 1915

Dear Editor,

The two issues you are putting forward with regard to the mutual rapprochement of the Nordic churches are made still weightier by the gravity of the present situation. We in the North are being reminded of our belonging together more strongly than we had been for a long time. And it is a well-deserving feat to bring about a more serious clarity in our mutual relations.

It does not go without saying that proximity and ties of blood guarantee true spiritual communion. Undoubtedly the churches in the North have each by itself taken in a considerably higher degree of influence from the motherland of evangelic Lutheranism, and as far as more recent popular religious currents are concerned, from the Anlo-Saxon West, than from each other. For me personally, discovering endeavors lately at mutual rapprochement between the churches of the North, inspired by a genuine conviction that we have to learn from each other, has been a source of heartfelt joy. And when I come to think of the benefit of having had the opportunity to meet Zealand's bishop and Oslo's bishop[2] during a few far too busy November days last year, I cannot help hoping for more, and more intensive, meetings.

I am sure that you, Mr. Editor, have hit the mark by pointing to increased knowledge. Scandinavian ecclesiastical and religious meetings have generally been suffering from a lack of preparatory knowledge on the part of those attending. How many people know their neighbor churches' hymnals, their history, their peculiar characteristics and expressions of vitality in their more accidental or more enduring manifestations? Only devoted study would create the requisite conditions for the

---

[2] Harald Ostenfeld, Zealand, cf. letter no. 195, n. 4; Jens Tandberg (1852–1922), Oslo.

desirable reciprocity. And no one who engages in such a study will find reason for regret.

Yours with high respect,
Nathan Söderblom

94. To Erik Rinman[1]

Ups. 2 VIII 1915

Broder!

Ifråga om hätskheten mot främmande nationer och dess bekämpande måste erkännas, att detta senare icke är en tacksam uppgift. Det är mera omtyckt att tjuta med ulvarna. Men det offentliga ordet har nu, om någonsin, hos oss den stora och grannlaga uppgiften att främja upplysning och besinning, icke hatets förmörkelse.

...

Skall det vara någon idé med att predika, bör ju någon känna sig träffad. Tyvärr var mitt ord mot hätskheten alltför träffande. Det gäller England och Tyskland. Och mot det närmare föremålet blir känslan våldsammare. Det finns, dessvärre, i vida kretsar fördomar mot England, som behöva skingras. Men ingen klok människa här i landet tror, att en enda röst höjts till offentlig gensaga, om jag särskilt hade omnämnt hat mot England. Annorlunda med Tyskland. Få vi icke hata Tyskland i fred? Det är, som om man ville beröva människor en dyrbar och oförytterlig rättighet.

Jag är ändå nog barnslig att mena, att vi böra bruka förnuftet så långt vi orka, och icke låta oss ryckas med av hatets svallvågor, som gå höga i världen såväl i den centraleuropeiska opinionen som på ententeopinionens väldiga världshav. Hatets herravälde är skadligt för vårt nationella väl och vår nationella värdighet.

Men isynnerhet tänker jag på kyrkans plikt att föra kärlekens talan, även när lidelserna rasa. Och jag tror fortfarande på vår svenska kyrkas heliga uppgift att genom trohet mot sig själv utgöra en fast föreningspunkt för trosförvanter, som nu äro grymt åtskilda, men som måste återfinna eller finna varandra, när de skola uppleva en morgondag efter hatets och förödelsens mörker.

...

Nathan Söderblom

Uppsala, August 2, 1915

Dear friend,

As far as hostility against foreign nations and combating it is concerned, it must be admitted that the latter is no rewarding task. Howling with the wolves is more pop-

---

[1] Erik Rinman (1870–1932), historian who, like Söderblom, had studied under Harald Hjärne (cf. letter no. 3, n. 2); editor of the liberal newspaper Stockholms-Tidningen; N. Söderblom's collection of letters, to Swedes and foreigners, UUB; handwritten draft.

ular. But if at any time, it is now that public speech has the great and delicate task to promote enlightenment and deliberation, not the obscurantism of hatred.

... [On a speech of S. on the occasion of a tour of inspection in his diocese]

If there is any point in preaching, someone must of course feel hurt. Unfortunately my talk against hostility was only too much hitting home. That refers to both Britain and Germany. And with regard to the closer object, feelings are more acrimonious. Alas, prejudice against Britain is widespread and must be dispelled. But no judicious person in this country believes that a single voice would be raised in public protest if I had singled out hatred against Britain. Different with regard to Germany. Should we not be undisturbed in our hatred of Germany? That is as if you would deprive people of a precious and inalienable right.

Nonetheless I am sufficiently childish to think that we should make use of reason as far as we are able to, and not be carried away by the surge of hatred which runs high in the world, both in central European opinion and in the huge ocean of Entente opinion. The domination of hatred is detrimental for our national weal and our national dignity.

But I am thinking in particular of the duty of the church to plead for love, even when passions are raging. And I continue to think of the sacred task of our Swedish church, in being true to itself, to serve as a reliable rallying point for our brothers in faith who at present are so fiercely divided but who must find again, or [begin to] find each other if they are to experience a tomorrow after the darkness of hatred and destruction.

...

Nathan Söderblom

95. From ADOLF VON HARNACK[1]

Berlin NW 7, den 21. Dezember 1915

Hochwürdiger Herr Erzbischof!
Hochverehrter Herr!

Ihr geehrtes Schreiben vom 14. d. M. die Armenier betreffend[2] habe ich dort eingereicht, wo ich mir den relativ größten Erfolg verspreche. Wie Euer Hochwürden bekannt ist, ist es nicht leicht möglich, auf die inneren Verhältnisse eines befreundeten Staates Einfluß auszuüben; dennoch hoffe ich, dass unsere fortgesetzten Bemühungen in dieser Angelegenheit einen gewissen Erfolg haben werden und bedaure gleichzeitig lebhaft, dass anscheinend weder England noch Amerika es wagen, auf die Verhältnisse der Juden in Rußland einzuwirken.

Verehrungsvoll
v. Harnack

---

[1] N. Söderblom's collection of letters, from foreigners, UUB, typewritten letter.

[2] I have not been able to find this letter. The issue in question is the bloody prosecution by Turkey of the Armenian part of its population.

96. To Adolf von Harnack[1]

4 Januar 1916

Exzellenz!

Für die entgegenkommende, Ihnen und einem wahrhaftigen, christlichen Kulturinteresse würdige Weise, in welcher Sie die Güte gehabt haben, meinen letzten Brief zu beantworten und weiter zu befördern, sage ich Ihnen meinen ehrerbietigen Dank. Wir, die Nachbarn der Finländer, haben mit Gram und Ärgernis gesehen, wie die russischen Ungeheuerlichkeiten gegen die finländische Rechts- und Staatskultur[2], welche während des Krieges nur geschärft worden sind, von englischer und französischer Seite stillschweigend gutgeheissen wurden und werden. Dazu kommen die barbarischen Methoden den Juden gegenüber. Solche Tatsachen hebe ich besonders meinen englischen Korrespondenten hervor. Einige empfinden den Schmach. Andere besitzen den glücklichen Panzer der undurchdringlichen Unwissenheit.

Mit guten Wünschen für Sie, Exzellenz, die Ihrigen und Ihr grosses Vaterland während des neuen Jahres verbleibe ich Ihr
verehrungsvoll ergebener
Nathan Söderblom

97. To Gustaf Aulén[1]

18 I 1916

Käre kyrkovetare och vän!

Det var förträffligt, att Du tänkt igenom kyrkobegreppet till den klarhet och enkelhet, som Din bok har. Så långt hade den teologiska formuleringen ännu icke nått. Men den är nödvändig, för att det kyrkobegrepp som hänför oss och som måste vara evangeliets och uppenbarelsehistoriens enda autentiska samfundsprincip, må kunna förverkligas. Endast därigenom kan en evangelisk katolicitet komma till stånd. Ett symptom på, att Du verkligen fört spörsmålet framåt, ligger i att Ditt sätt att bestämma romersk och reformert kyrklighet eger ett positivt innehåll och icke nöjer sig med den vanliga skematismen. Jag lyckönskar Dig till den sköna och upplysande bilden Sid. 40: den transparenta taflan, och till åtskilligt annat i denna lilla, men alltigenom innehållsrika, fängslande och vetenskapligt genomtänkta afhandling. Och vad kan jag säga annat än af hjärtat tack till den mycket stora heder, som den käre vännen sedan så månget år och Pehrs värdiga ef-

---

[1] Harnack's papers – letters, Staatsbibliothek zu Berlin, Preußischer Kulturbesitz, handwritten letter.

[2] Cf. letter no. 82, n. 2.

[1] Samling Aulén. G., University Library Lund, handwritten letter.

terträdare bevisat mig genom att låta mitt namn förbindas med en så bety-
delsefull dogmatisk traktat i en för kyrkoregementet grundläggande fråga.
Tack! Till Din maka och barnen allas våra goda hälsningar!
  Din tillgifne
  Nathan Söderblom

January 18, 1916
Dear church scholar and friend,
It is indeed splendid that you have elaborated the notion of the church to the degree
of clarity and simplicity that your book[2] exhibits. Thus far, theological formula-
tions have not achieved that. This is necessary, however, in order that the notion of
the church, which engages us and which must be the only authentic social principle
of the Gospel and of the history of revelation, may be realized. Only in this way an
evangelic catholicity[3] can be brought about. One symptom for your really having
furthered the debate is that your way of determining Roman and Reformation
churchliness has a positive content and is not satisfied with the usual schematism. I
congratulate you on the beautiful and elucidating image, p. 40, of a transparent
painting, and on several other things in this small but altogether informative, captivating, scientifically thought out treatise. And what else than thanks from all my
heart can I say about the very great honor which the dear friend of so many years
and Pehr's[4] worthy successor has bestowed upon me by letting my name be connected with such a significant dogmatic treatise on a question so essential for church
administration. Thanks! To your wife and children good wishes from all of us!
  Yours sincerely,
  Nathan Söderblom

---

[2] Gustaf Aulén, *Evangelisk kyrklighet*, Uppsala 1916 (74 pp.). Better known is Auléns earlier book *Till belysning af den lutherska kyrkoidéen, dess historia och dess värde*, Uppsala and
Leipzig 1912 (238 pp.). This is probably the one to which the somewhat facetious address of
this letter alludes.

[3] This expression goes back to Johann Gerhard's *Confessio Catholica. In qua Doctrina Catholica et Evangelica, Quam Ecclesiae Augustanae Confessionis addictae profitentur, ex Romano-
Catholicorum Scriptorum Suffragiis confirmatur*, Jena 1634–1637. Söderblom first introduced it
into the modern debate in *Svenska kyrkans kropp och själ*, Stockholm 1916, 142 (Cf. »Evangelisk
katolicitet,« in: *Kyrkans enhet* 7/1919, 65–126). He distinguishes between Roman, Greek Orthodox, and evangelic catholicity, the characteristic of the latter being the insistence on justification
by faith alone. The three are not identical with church bodies but with forms of Christian piety;
they are supposed to interact in peaceful contest. – The form »evangelic« was used by Söderblom
in English in order to distinguish it from »evangelical« in the sense of ultra-conservative Protestantism; cf. Sundkler, op. cit., 263f. For more background information, cf. Nils Karlström,
Nathan Söderblom. Seine Entwicklung zum ökumenischen Kirchenführer (German tr. by F. Siegmund-Schultze), SÖA 5, Soest 1968, 84f.

[4] Pehr Eklund, cf. letter no. 5, n. 6.

98. From WILHELM BOUSSET[1]

Göttingen 10. III 16

Sehr verehrter Freund.

Mitten in meinem Umzug von Göttingen nach Giessen begriffen bin ich noch immer nicht dazu gekommen, Ihnen für Ihre freundliche und wertvolle Gabe, die Sie mir mit der Übersetzung Ihres Werkes[2] gemacht haben zu danken. Doch ehe ich nun definitiv meine Schiffe hier abbreche, soll diese Dankespflicht abgetragen werden.

Ich habe, als ich Ihr Werk im deutschen Gewande noch einmal las, einen noch stärkeren Eindruck gewonnen von dessen Bedeutung, Grosszügigkeit und der Fülle des darin verarbeiteten Materials. Die Disposition und der ganze Gedankengang ist allerdings durch die Einarbeitung des neuen Materials in der Übersetzung weniger straff und übersichtlich. Aber wer das Werk im ersten Wurf gelesen, freut sich doch der reichen Zusätze.

Wenn ich mir kurz ein paar Fragen und Bemerkungen gestatten darf, so scheint es mir denn doch, als wenn wir im »*Präanimismus*« wirklich eine ältere *Stufe* der Religion erreicht haben, während Sie Spiritismus resp. Animismus, Präanimismus, Urheberglaube als verschiedene Möglichkeiten neben -einander stellen. Führt uns nicht der Präanimismus in eine Zeit und Welt zurück, wo der Mensch sich eigentlich noch gar nicht als Ichwesen erfasst und fast noch ein träumendes Bewusstsein hatte? Ist er daher nicht so schwer verständlich? Freilich der Übergang von einer Stufe zur andern erfolgte an den einzelnen Stellen – oft wohl an demselben Ort – zu sehr verschiedener Zeit. Reinlich abgrenzen lässt sich hier nirgends. Doch meine ich, könnte man prinzipiell ordnen: Präanimismus – Animismus (Spiritismus).

Andererseits möchte ich den *Urheberglauben* und *Schöpfer-Glauben* noch weniger, als Sie es geneigt sind, als Religion gelten lassen, als eine Form, die *neben* Präanimismus und Animismus stände. Was wir hier haben, ist doch nichts Unmittelbares sondern früheste Gnosis, Theologie in Urform, Befriedigung eines religiösen Neugier-Dranges. Noch stärker als früher ist mir durch ihr Werk die Tatsache deutlich geworden, dass diese religiösen Phantasien eigentlich nirgends aus sich heraus und ohne Verbindung mit andern Prämissen einen Kult erzeugen. Damit ist für mich die Frage entschieden. Denn »Religion« ist m. E. nur da wo »Beziehung« vorhanden ist, und »Beziehung« zur Gottheit giebt es nicht ohne Kult – wenigstens nicht im primitiven Zeitalter. So möchte ich der grossen »Missionars«-Entdeckung noch weniger Recht und Bedeutung beimessen, als Sie es zu tun geneigt sind.

Ihr Buch hat mir starke Anregungen für mein eigenes Gebiet gegeben. Ich bin jetzt dabei die Begriffe πνεῦμα – Ruach unter präanimistischen Ge-

---

[1] N. Söderblom's collection of letters, from foreigners, UUB, handwritten letter.
[2] Nathan Söderblom, *Das Werden des Gottesglaubens. Untersuchungen über die Anfänge der Religion* (dt. Bearbeitung hg. v. R. Stübe, Leipzig 1916; Swedish: *Gudstrons uppkomst. Studier*, Stockholm 1914).

172

sichtspunkten durchzuarbeiten. Wenn irgendwo haben wir in der *Ruach* des alten Testaments so eine primitive Reliquie. Um sie zu verstehen muß man ganz absehen von allem Spiritismus, Beziehung zu Jahve, zur Geisterwelt, zur menschlichen Psyche (zu der »Nephesch« u. »Leb« in viel engerer Beziehung stehen). Das Besondere ist hier nur, dass hier das Göttliche »Mana« »Orenda« in fast ausschliesslicher Beziehung zu den Erscheinungen der Ekstase gesetzt erscheint. Aber Ruach ist auch die ruhende Kraft, die sich im Besitz des Magiers (Gottesmannes) befindet u. Ruach ist die wunderbare Lebenskraft wie etwa das Tondi der Battaks. Und dieses Urwüchsige Primitive an der Ruach-Pneuma Idee bricht immer wieder durch; bis in die Geisteswelt des Mönchstums wirkt sie nach.

Auch der Urheber und Schöpferglaube wäre in das synkretistische Gebiet um das neue Testament zu verfolgen. Gayomarth, der Urmensch im Manichäismus, der Anthropos der Gnostiker u. der Hermetiker, der Adam der Pseudoklementinen, – das alles rückt mir nun in einen neuen »primitiven« Zusammenhang.

Besonders interessant waren mir noch ihre Ausführungen über »Hvareno«. Das Ineinanderklingen der Begriffe, die der Grieche δόξα und δύναμις nennen würde ist ausserordentlich interessant und verlockt zu weiteren Kombinationen.

Haben Sie nochmals herzlichen Dank. Sie sehen, dass Sie in meinem religionsgeschichtlichen Denken eine kleine Revolution angerichtet haben. Möge etwas Gutes dabei herauskommen.

. . .

Für Ihr treues Gedenken an das deutsche Volk in seiner ernsten u. grossen Zeit haben Sie herzl[ichen] Dank.

Ihr aufrichtig ergebener

W. Bousset

99. From Adolf Deissmann[1]

Berlin-Wilmersdorf, Prinzregentenstr. 6.II, 2. 8. 16.

Hochverehrter Freund! Darf ich Ihre gütige Hilfe für eine unglückliche Mutter (Pfarrers-Witwe) erbitten?

Am 16. Juli 1916 geriet bei Pustamyty in russische Gefangenschaft, durch Kopfschuss verwundet:

Vizefeldwebel Hans Wittenberg, 7. Komp., Reserve-Inf.=Regt. 203. Die Mutter hofft, dass er noch lebt; vielleicht könnten Sie beim Russ. Roten Kreuz Auskunft erbitten? Oder beim Schwedischen R. Kreuz.

Im Voraus herzlichst dankend & mit vielen Empfehlungen

Ihr treu verbundener

Adolf Deißmann.

---

[1] N. Söderblom's collection of letters, from foreigners, UUB, handwritten postcard.

100. An Adolf von Harnack[1]

Upsala, den 27. Oktober 1916 [date at the end of the letter]

Excellenz.

Ich komme heute in einer Angelegenheit, die für die Deutschen und Österreichischen Kriegsgefangenen sowohl als für die Russischen Kriegsgefangenen in Deutschland und Österreich von der grössten Wichtigkeit ist.

Seit Beginn des Krieges ist der Wunsch vorhanden gewesen, für die Kriegsgefangenen Gottesdienst und sonstige seelsorgerliche Bedienung zu Stande bringen zu können. In Deutschland und Österreich ist schon viel in dieser Hinsicht geleistet worden. Ich habe selbst bewundern können, mit welcher christlichen Gesinnung und Opferfreudigkeit die Deutsche Kriegsgefangenenhilfe dafür eingetreten ist, und es ist mir eine ganz besondere Freude zu wissen, dass mein junger Freund, der Träger dieses Schreibens, Pastor Herman Neander, Vikar von Ockelbo in der Erzdiözese Upsala, in dieser Arbeit im vorigen Jahr mit geschätztem Erfolg tätig gewesen ist.[2]

Das grosse, durch ausserordentliche Vertrauensbeweise bezeugte Ansehen, das er durch diese Tätigkeit für die Religionsausübung der Russischen Kriegesgefangenen, beim Hofe, unter der Höchsten Geistlichkeit und in sonstigen Kreisen in Russland gewonnen hat, ist ihm im höchsten Masse zu gute gekommen in seiner späteren Tätigkeit unter den Deutschen und Österreichischen Kriegsgefangenen in Russland; und da er nach seiner durch übertriebene Anstrengung und Spannung gewirkten Krankheit ziemlich erholt jene Liebesarbeit wieder aufnimmt, hat er besondere Voraussetzungen, das erreichen zu können, was leider trotz der Beschlüsse der Roten-Kreuzkonferenz in Stockholm durch verschiedene Hindernisse bisher nicht verwirklicht werden konnte. Das Bedürfnis seelsorgerlicher Bedienung wird für die Kriegsgefangenen mit jedem Monat stärker, kann aber in befriedigender Weise nur durch dazu befähigte Geistliche der betreffenden Kirchen erfüllt werden. Von Russischer Seite scheint jetzt einige Möglichkeit vorhanden zu sein, Deutsche und Österreichische evangelische und katholische Geistliche in die Gefangenenlager zuzulassen unter der Bedingung, dass eine analoge Anzahl Russischer Popen in den Deutschen und österreichischen Kriegsgefangenenlagern unter nötiger Kontrolle wirken dürfen. Ich handle daher im Interesse der Deutschen Kriegsgefangenen in Russland und Sibirien, wenn ich Ew. Excellenz ergebenst bitte, bei den betreffenden hohen Behörden befürworten zu wollen, das dreissig (30) Russische Priester für ihre Landesleute in Deutschland und Österreich zugelassen werden dürfen unter der Bedingung, dass die Russische Regierung in ähnlicher Weise die gleiche Zahl (z. Beispiel 10 Deutsche, Evangelische und Katholi-

---

[1] N. Söderblom's collection of letters, to Swedes and foreigners, UUB, handwritten copy (the original seems to be lost).

[2] Herman Neander (1885–1953), an internationally well-versed churchman (Olaus-Petri-scholar in Greece, Palestine, and Russia 1910–1911), worked in POW camps in Germany, Siberia, and Japan in World War I (partly in cooperation with Elsa Brändström). Cf. also letter no. 273, n. 4.

sche, 10 österreichische und 10 ungarische) zulässt. Der Austausch könnte dann, wenn einmal ein Erlaubnis von Deutscher und österreichischer Seite vorliegt, durch Schwedische Vermittlung ausgeführt werden.

Mit den besten Wünschen verbleibe ich Ew. Excellenz
ehrerbietigst und treu ergebener
Nathan Söderblom

101. From ADOLF DEISSMANN[1]

Berlin-Wilmersdorf, Prinzregentenstr. 6.II, 9. Nov. 16.
Hochverehrter, lieber Freund!
Haben Sie vielen Dank für Ihre gütige Auskunft vom 6. Nov.! Darf ich heute etwas anderes vorbringen? Ich soll Ende Nov. & im Dez. in mehreren Großstädten über das Thema reden: »Der religiöse Ertrag des Krieges«. Ein großes Material aus unserem & den anderen kriegführenden Ländern steht mir zugebote; ich wüßte aber gern etwas über die jetzige religiöse Lage & Temperatur in den skand[inavischen] Ländern; z. B. ob die auch dort am Kriegsanfang erkennbare religiöse Erschütterung noch nachwirkt, ob der Krieg seither im ganzen mehr erweckend oder mehr erschlaffend gewirkt hat für das religiöse Leben u.s.w. Ich brauche keine langen Betrachtungen, aber vielleicht könnten Sie im Telegrammstil nur mit einigen Stichworten mich ungefähr orientieren oder orientieren lassen. Ich wäre Ihnen sehr zu Dank verpflichtet.

In treuer Verbundenheit Ihr
Adolf Deißmann

102. From PAUL SABATIER[1]

La Maisonnette par St-Sauveur-de-Montagut (Ardèche), 11 novembre 1916
Monseigneur et cher ami.
Voici de long mois que je veux vous remercier pour vos bonnes lignes du début de 1915, mais la reprise des fonctions pastorales n'a pas été facile pour moi…

Après plus de deux ans de guerre la tenue de nos populations est la même qu'au début avec plus de décision, de résolution, d'obstination. C'est vraiment la conscience du pays dans ce qu'elle a de plus profond qui lutte non seulement contre l'hégémonie politique de l'Allemagne, mais surtout contre son hégémonie spirituelle. La Prusse asservissant la science et la foi pour les associer à un gigantesque effort, d'inspiration toute matérialiste, a réveillé en nous le vieux levain d'idéalisme, et si l'âme de la France sent que les vieil-

---

[1] N. Söderblom's collection of letters, from foreigners, UUB, handwritten postcard.

[1] N. Söderblom's collection of letters, from foreigners, UUB, handwritten letter.

les organisations religieuses sont devenues sourdes et muettes elle finira bien par en créer de nouvelles.

...

Veuillez agréer, Monseigneur et cher ami, l'expression de mon respectueux et bien cordial dévouement

Paul Sabatier

Vour trouverez si-joint une carte postale de la Maisonnette. C'est simplement pour vous redire combien on souhaiterait vous y voir et vous y avoir. Il y a place pour vous et tous les membres de votre famille. Il y a une chapelle où Mgr. Lacroix a célébré cet été.

La Maisonnette par St-Sauveur-de-Montagut (Ardèche), November 11, 1916

Sir and dear friend,

It has been for long months that I have wanted to thank you for your kind words from the beginning of 1915; but taking up pastoral duties again has not been easy for me...

... [Comments on a number of publications being sent along with this letter]

After two years of war, the morale of our population is the same as it was at the beginning, with more determination, resolution, obstinacy. It really is the conscience of the country which is most profound in those who fight not only against the political hegemony of Germany but primarily against its spiritual hegemony. Prussia, by subjugating science and faith in order to have them participate in a gigantic effort, in a totally materialistic vein, has reinvigorated in us the old leaven of idealism, and if the soul of France feels that the old religious organizations have become deaf and speechless, it will end up by creating new ones for itself.

... [on a couple of documents Sabatier received, urging the unity of the Christian church]

Sir and dear friend, please accept the expression of my respectful and cordial affection

Paul Sabatier.

Please find enclosed a postcard depicting la Maisonnette. This is simply to repeat how much I would wish to see you here and to have you here. There is [sufficient] space here for you and all the members of your family. There is a chapel where Mgr. Lacroix has been reading Mass this summer.[2]

103. To ADOLF DEISSMANN[1]

Upsala, den 17 Nov. 1916

Hochgeehrter, lieber Freund!

Von der religiösen Erschütterungen [sic], die beim Kriegsanbruch durch unser Volk ging und einige Monate lang Kirchen füllte, ist gegenwärtig nicht viel zu spüren. Mammon hat in vielen Herzen seine Herrschaft befe-

---

[2] I have not been able to identify him. The ed.

[1] Deißmann papers, Zentral- u. Landesbibl. Berlin, handwritten letter.

stigt; vor dem Phariseismus der Neutralen habe ich öffentlich gewarnt;[2] aber es gibt auch solche, die über den Ernst der Zeit und des Lebens nachdenklich geworden sind, und im allgemeinen darf man sagen, dass die Tatsachen der Religion in diesen letzten zwei Jahren für die Menschen in weiten Kreisen wirklicher als zuvor geworden und ihnen näher gebracht worden sind.

Mit herzlichem Gruss
Ihr sehr ergebener
Nathan Söderblom

104. To Paul Sabatier[1]

Upsala 28 XII 1916

Cher et très estimé ami!
Devant moi l'image si invitant de Votre Maisonnette, dans ma tête les paroles si amicales et si chaudement appréciées de votre lettre. Quand une fois la paix sera établie, mon premier devoir épiscopal tant désiré est d'installer les nouveaux curés des paroisses suédoises à Londres et à Paris. Laissez-moi chérir l'espérance de pouvoir à cette occasion vous voir chez vous.

... Malgré la brillance éblouissante et des détails tout ce qu'il y a de ... [mot illisible] touchants j'ai été moins pleinement satisfait du discours de M Barrès à Londres sur *Les Traits essentiels de la France*. Il y a certainement beaucoup de vrai là dedans. Mais je ne comprends aucune apothéose de la guerre, soit française soit allemande.

La saine et vigoureuse véridicité et la précision toute française de votre lettre et de vos jugements m'ont procuré une heure de pure jouissance intellectuelle et morale. Rien n'est plus évident dans l'épreuve terrible de cette guerre que la grandeur – pour beaucoup inattendue – de l'âme française qui se manifeste dans la domaine religieuse avec une simplicité héroïque dangereuse seulement pour le vieil Adam, même s'il apparait en sectaire ecclésiastique.

Parmi mes chers et excellents correspondants vous êtes celui qui me laisse le plus entrevoir la réalité et l'interieur des choses actuelles en France. Je vous en remercie – et des documents que vous voudrez bien m'envoyer encore.

Avec mes voeux ardents pour vous, les votre[s] et l'Honneur de votre héroïque Patrie
Votre dévoué
Nathan Söderblom

---

[2] N. Söderblom, »Neutral egenrättfärdighet. Botdagspredikan,« in: *Kristendom i vår tid* 11/1916, 116–122; English transl.: »Our Spiritual Peril as Neutrals,« in: *The Constructive Quarterly* 5/1917, 91–96.

[1] N. Söderblom's collection of letters, to Swedes and foreigners, UUB, handwritten letter.

Upsala, December 28, 1916

Dear and esteemed friend,

In front of me the very inviting picture of your Maisonnette, in my mind the words of your letter which are so friendly and so warmly appreciated. When peace is established, my first episcopal duty for which I am longing so much will be to install the new pastors of the Swedish congregations in London and Paris. Let me cherish the hope to be able at that occasion to see you at your home.

... [Thanks for the brochures Sabatier had sent him] In spite of its brilliance and the details concerning all the moving ... [illegible word], I am less fully satisfied with the address of Mr. Barrès[2] in London on *The essential Traits of France*. There is certainly a lot of truth in it. But I do not understand any apotheosis of the war, be it French or German.

The healthy and vigorous truthfulness and the typically French precision of your letter and your judgments has presented me with an hour of pure joy, both intellectual and moral. Nothing is more evident in the terrible afflliction of this war than the greatness – for many unexpected – of the French soul which manifests itself in the religious sphere with a heroic simplicity, dangerous only for the old Adam, even if he appears as a churchly fanatic.

Among my dear and excellent French correspondents, you are the one who lets me sense the most of the basic reality of the present situation in France. I thank you for that – and for the papers you are kindly still going to send me.

With my best wishes for you, your family, and the Honor of your heroic Country,

Yours sincerely,
Nathan Söderblom

105. From KARL HOLL[1]

Charlottenburg, Mommsenstr. 13   16. V. 17

Hochgeehrter Herr Erzbischof,   darf ich als persönlich Unbekannter es wagen, mich mit einem Anliegen an Sie zu wenden? In der Theol[ogischen] Lit[eratur] Z[eitung] Nr 8/9 war unter der neuesten Literatur genannt: »Solo[v]jev, Der gegenwärtige Krieg in seinem Verhältnis zur religiösen Erkenntnis«.

Die Schrift wäre mir für einen Vortrag, den ich in den nächsten Wochen hier zu halten habe, von ganz außerordentlichem Wert. Aber es besteht zur Zeit keine Möglichkeit, sie in Deutschland aufzutreiben. Wäre es nicht Ih-

---

[2] Maurice Barrès (1862–1923), French writer and literary critic. He propagated nationalist views at the time quite akin to those of Paul Sabatier.

[1] Karl Holl (1866–1926), professor of church history in Berlin, renowned both as a patristic and a Luther scholar (»Was verstand Luther unter Religion,« *GAufs zur Kirchengeschichte I, Luther*, 6th ed. Tübingen 1932, 1–110), influential also through his conservative views of the German nation and the meaning of war (»Die Bedeutung der großen Kriege für das religiöse und kirchliche Leben innerhalb des deutschen Protestantismus,« *GAufs III, Der Westen*, 1928, 302–384). – N. Söderblom's collection of letters, from foreigners, UUB, handwritten postcard. Söderblom's reply, as indeed any letters to Holl he may have written, did not survive World War II.

178

nen möglich, sie zu erlangen u[nd] sie mir zuzusenden? Sie würden mich damit in besonderem Maße verpflichten. Denn Sie werden begreifen, wie viel uns deutschen Protestanten, vollends in diesem Lutherjahr, daran liegen muß, auf dem Boden der Frömmigkeit unsren Standpunkt zu befestigen und zu vertiefen. Verzeihen Sie daher, wenn ich mir die Freiheit genommen habe, Sie zu stören. Es handelt sich für uns beide doch zuletzt um eine große, gemeinsame Sache.

In ausgezeichneter Hochachtung
Ihr ergebenster
Prof. Karl Holl

106. To Adolf von Harnack[1]

Uppsala 4/10/17

Excellenz,

Ich kann nicht umhin, Ihnen für den hohen, geistigen Genuß und für die reiche Belehrung, welche mir Ihre wundervolle Abhandlung über die Reformation[2] bereitet hat meinen ergebendsten Dank zu sagen. Während der Lesung habe ich, wie ich glaube, die sehr unvernünftige Äußerung sogar laut gemacht:»Warum schreiben eigentlich andere über die Reformation?«

Verzeihen Sie, wenn ich in diesem Zusammenhang eine Angelegenheit bespreche, welche in Vergleich mit den großen Werten der Religion und der Reformation eine Kleinigkeit ist. Öfters wollte ich während der letzten 10 Jahren die betreffenden hohen Stellen in Deutschland wegen des erwünschten Bischofsamtes der evangelischen Kirche befragen. Ihre Bemerkung darüber giebt mir den Anlaß Ihnen anheimzustellen, ob es seiner Majestät dem König von Preussen wohl möglich ist z. B. die Generalsuperintendenten zu Bischöfe zu machen. Eine wirkliche äußere Parität mit der katholischen Kirche wird erst dann möglich sein, und das Bischofsamt würde der evangelischen Christenheit des Mutterlandes der Reformation einen deutlichen und wertvollen Ausdruck der OEcumenicität und Selbständigkeit der Kirche geben. Wäre ich impulsiv und dreist genug, würde ich mir den Mut holen an seine Majestät den Kaiser und König über diese Sache zu schreiben, was ich auch wirklich tun werde. – Es wird wohltuend sein, die Wiedergabe Ihrer großen Worte über die Übernationalität des Evangeliums in der englischen Presse, wie ich beabsichtige, zu veranlassen.

Ich verbleibe, Excellenz, Ihr mit lebhafter Dankbarkeit und den besten Wünschen sehr ergebener
Nathan Söderblom

---

[1] N. Söderblom's collection of letters, to Swedes and foreigners, UUB, handwritten draft by secretary, signed by Söderblom (the original of the actual letter seems to be lost).
[2] Adolf von Harnack, »Die Reformation,« in: *IMW* 11/1916–17, 1281–1364; as »Die Reformation und ihre Voraussetzung« also in: A. von Harnack, *Erforschtes und Erlebtes. Reden und Aufsätze* NF Bd. 4, Gießen 1923, 72–140. Harnack dedicated this volume to Söderblom.

107. From ADOLF VON HARNACK[1]

Berlin-Grunewald, 16.10.17.
Hochwürdiger und hochverehrter Herr Erzbischof!
Aufrichtigen und herzlichen Dank sage ich Ihnen für Ihr freundliches Ur-
theil über meine Abhandlung »Reformation«, mit dem Sie mich sehr erfreut
haben: es ist mir von hohem Werte zu wissen, dass die Anschauung, die ich
mir von Luther u. der Reformation gebildet habe, die Anerkennung eines
Fachgenossen findet, der in der ganzen Religionsgeschichte, wie kein Anderer, heimisch ist und zugleich die gegenwärtigen Kirchen, wie kein Anderer, aus eigener Anschauung kennt.

Die Wiederherstellung des Bischofsamtes *zusammen mit der Organisation
als wirklicher Gemeinde= und Volkskirche* in den evangelischen Kirchen
Deutschlands zu besorgen – das ist ein Ziel, auf's innigste zu wünschen!
Aber ich fürchte, die Macht des Unverstandes und der Gewöhnung an das
Unzulängliche ist schon zu gross! Ich glaube, wir vertragen dieses Heilmit-
tel nicht mehr, weil wir schon zu schwach sind. Vielleicht kommt die Hilfe
von anderer Seite!
In besonderer Verehrung
Ew. Hochwürden ergebenster
A. v. Harnack

108. To WILHELM II.[1]

[1917, between Oct. 2 and 20]
Majestät!
Der wundervolle Gesang des Domchors Eurer Majestät gibt mir den Mut
bei Eurer Majestät eine Frage zu erwähnen, welche mich seit vielen Jahren
lebhaft beschäftigt, und welche auch seine Excellenz Adolf von Harnack in
der neulich erschienenen, grosszügigen Abhandlung über die Reformation
in der »Internationalen Monatsschrift«[2] erwähnt, obwohl diese Sache neben den Hauptsachen des Evangeliums und der Reformation eine Kleinigkeit ist. Nach einem schönen Hymnus erblickten die lieben Knaben und
Herren des Domchors[3] in meinem Hause an der Wand ein Bild Friedrich

---

[1] N. Söderblom's collection of letters, from foreigners, UUB, handwritten postcard.

[1] Wilhelm II. (1859-1941), German Emperor and King of Prussia (1888-1918). – N. Söderblom's collection of letters, to Swedes and foreigners, UUB, typewritten copy. This undated
letter was published, along with the Denkschrift of the Evangelischer Oberkirchenrat, in *Hundert Jahre Evangelischer Oberkirchenrat der Altpreußischen Union 1850-1950*, ed. by O. Söhn-
gen, Berlin 1950, 195-208. For further information, cf. Staffan Runestam, »Nathan Söderblom, kejsaren och biskopsämbetet,« in: *STK* 72/1996, 49-58.
[2] Cf. letter no.106, n.2.
[3] The »Königlicher Hof- und Domchor« (choir of the Royal court and the cathedral) had
given a concert in Uppsala cathedral on the 30th of September, 1917.

Wilhelms IV.[4] – des Begründers des Domchors – der zugleich für diese kirchliche Angelegenheit ein Interesse hatte. Das Bischofsamt drückt ja wie kein zweites die Oekumenizität und die dem Staate und dem Reiche gegenüber loyale Selbständigkeit der christlichen Kirche aus[5]; sogar Luther hat ja persönlich zwei Bischöfe feierlich geweiht[6], obwohl die große Mehrzahl der damaligen Bischöfe leider seiner Erneuerung der Kirche abhold waren. Kann von einer wirklichen Parität der zwei grossen Kirchengemeinschaften der deutschen Christenheit – der evangelischen und der katholischen – gesprochen werden, so lange die evangelische Kirche kein Bischofsamt besitzt? Ich weiss nicht, in wie fern es Eurer Majestät und der evangelischen Kirche im Königreiche Eurer Majestät erwünscht scheint oder inwiefern es möglich ist die Generalsuperintendenten zu Bischöfen bzw. in Magdeburg, Berlin, Strassburg und anderen Mittelpunkten des kirchlichen Lebens zu Erzbischöfen zu ernennen.

Aber ich darf hoffen, dass Eure Majestät meine offene und allerehrerbietigste Anheimstellung mir verzeihen werde, da sie einem tiefen und aufrichtigen Eifer für die Kraft und Gesundheit des evangelischen Kirchenwesens entspringt.[7]

In tiefster Ehrerbietigkeit

---

[4] Friedrich Wilhelm IV. (1795–1861), Prussian king since 1840; great-uncle of the Kaiser.

[5] This is because the Swedish Reformation had been able to win over the existing bishops for its cause and thus to form a church governance of its own, even under the conditions of a state church. Thus the Swedish church was able, at its Uppsala meeting of 1593, to assert its independence over against the Catholic king of Poland, Sigismund III. Vasa, in Polish: Zygmunt Wasa (1566-1632) who from 1592 to 1599 simultaneously was king of Sweden, as well as over against Sigismund's uncle and successor Karl IX. (1550-1611, king 1603) who had Calvinist leanings. Söderblom desired such independence also for the German church. But the ministry of culture as well as the highest representatives of the church were firmly opposed; see the following letter.

[6] These two were Nikolaus von Amsdorff (1483-1565), installed (not consecrated!) as bishop of Naumburg on Jan. 20, 1542, and Georg III. of Anhalt (1507-1533), installed as bishop of Merseburg on Aug. 2, 1545. Cf. Martin Brecht, *Martin Luther*, vol. III, Stuttgart 1987, 296-303. Luther would actually have much preferred the episcopacy to the kind of state church which developed from what he had meant to be just a preliminary service by the princes to help keep external order in the church in the emergency situation when the Catholic bishops could not be persuaded to join the Reformation movement. See Karl Holl, »Luther und das landesherrliche Kirchenregiment,« in: id., *GAufs zur Kirchengeschichte I. Luther*, Tübingen 1932, 326-380, esp. 372-376.

[7] This letter does not mention the real reason for Söderblom's initiative, since that was the mere rumor that the Kaiser had intended to honor certain eminent church leaders by conferring the title of bishop upon them, cf. letter no., 311.

109. To Alfred Loisy[1]

Upsal. 6.12.1917.

Cher Monsieur et très honoré Collègue,
Parmi les nombreux et intéressants livres qui viennent sur ma table je vois que je distingue trois differentes classes: 1. Il y en a que je mets dans la bibliotèque pour les consulter plus tard pour une raison particulière quelleconque, 2. Il y a d'autres que je feuillète avec un vif désir de les lire aussitôt que possible, 3. mais quelques fois un livre me vient entre les mains qu'il est impossible de ne pas lire aussitôt, comme un savoure la lettre d'un bon ami ou d'un rémarquable corréspondent, malgré les occupations qui s'amassent quelques fois écrasantes sur la tâche moins enviable qu'importante qu'on m'a imposé sans me demander[.] Il était ainsi avec le volume sur la Réligion que j'ai eu le privilège de recevoir il y a quelques mois. Comme conception générale de la réligion et de son évolution je me demande, si j'ai jamais lu un livre, dont l'idée directrice et les résultats décisifs coincide si étroitement avec l'image que mes études ont formé du problème réligieux. Ce que vous dites de l'importance essentielle du sentiment d'obligation apparant déjà dans le tabou et indispensable même pour la plus haute civilisation jusque à sa fin, sur le rôle de l'élément religieux et morale dans la discipline humaine etc. me paraissent être des vérités trop peu reconnues, mais qui ont été dévéloppées dans les leçons que je regrette de ne plus devoir donné [sic; lis: donner] aux étudiants. Cette harmonie dans les vues générales est pour moi un preuve de ce que l'étude moderne historique et comparée de la religion a déjà atteint chez quelques uns indépendemment quelques conclusions de la plus haute importance pour la conception réligieuse. J'ai mis quelques points d'interrogation, par exemple page 72 sur la prétendue confiance de la réligion la plus rudimentaire, page 80 sur le rôle de taoisme, page 147 sur l'aspect réligieux de cette guerre affreuse – malgré ma sympathie profonde pour la France, plus intime et plus irréflechie que pour aucun autre pays bélligérent[,] le problème de cette guerre est pour moi plus compliquée, et page 299 où le rôle de la prière individuelle ne me parait pas être assez appréciée.

Je vois des différences plus importantes 1. quand [sic; lis: quant] au côté métaphysique et transcendant, pour moi indispensable, de la réligion, 2. dans la place attribuée par moi et par la tradition religieuse, dans laquelle je me trouve en différence de celle d'où vous êtes sorti, à l'individu dans la réligion. Cepandant tout ceci me parait être secondaire à côté des vérités lucides et pénétrantes que votre livre donne sur l'histoire réligieuse.

»Ceffonds« sur votre carte éveille un agréable souvenir. Les animaux mentionnées page 97 en bas ne sont ils pas vos poules?

Croyez moi cher Monsieur avec les voeux les plus sincères votre du tout coeur dévoué
Nathan Söderblom

---

[1] Alfred Loisy's papers, letters, Bibliothèque nationale de France, Paris, n.a.f. 15661, fol. 425–426; handwritten letter (not Söderblom's own handwriting).

Dear Sir and highly revered Colleague,

Among the numerous and interesting books getting on my table, I see that I distinguish three different classes: 1° There are those that I put into the library in order to consult them later on for a specific reason, 2° there are others that I browse through with a vivid desire to read them as soon as possible, 3° but sometimes a book gets into my hands which it is impossible not to read at once, as one savors the letter of a good friend or of a remarkable correspondent, despite the occupations accumulating overwhelmingly upon a task less enviable than important that one has imposed on me without asking me. That is the way it was with the volume on *La religion*[2] which I had the privilege of receiving a couple of months ago. As a general concept of religion and its evolution, I wonder if I have ever read a book whose guiding principle and decisive results so closely coincide with the image my studies have shaped of the problem of religion. What you are saying about the crucial importance of the sense of obligation already appearing in the taboo and indispensable even for the highest civilization until its end, about the role of the religious and moral element in the human enterprise, etc., seem to me to be truths too little recognized, but which have been developed in the lectures I regret no longer to be obliged to deliver to the students. That harmony in the general views is for me proof that modern historical and comparative study of religion has already attained in some [people], independent from each other, some conclusions of utmost importance for the concept of religion. I have put some question marks, for instance on page 72 concerning the alleged certitude of the most rudimentary religion, on page 80 concerning Taoism, on page 147 concerning the religious aspect of this horrible war – in spite of my deep sympathy for France, much more intimate and much less reflected upon than for any other belligerent country, the problem of this war is for me more complicated, and on page 299 where the role of individual prayer does not seem to me to be sufficiently appreciated.

I see more important differences 1° with regard to the metaphysical and transcendent aspect of religion, indispensable for me,[3] 2° in the place attributed by me and by the religious tradition in which I find myself, as distinguished from that from which you originate, to the individual in religion. However, all this appears to me to be secondary beside the lucid and penetrating truths your book presents about the history of religion.

»Ceffonds« on your postcard evokes a pleasant memory. The animals mentioned at the bottom of page 97, are they not they your chickens?

Believe me, dear Sir, with the most sincere wishes, yours with all my heart devoted,

Nathan Söderblom

---

[2] Alfred Loisy, *La religion*, Paris 1917 (2nd ed. 1924).
[3] In his later years, Loisy's religion more and more became a kind of ethical humanism.

110. To Albert Hellerström[1]

Uppsala den 19/12 1917

B[äste] B[roder]

Hjärtlig tack för bref och telegram, som lämnat synnerligen värdefulla upp-lysningar. Neutrala konferensen har gått öfver förväntan bra och visat, att man kan behandla dessa frågor utan att alls beröra politiken. Vi skildes med fast föresats och tro att ekumeniska konferensen skall komma till stånd i april. Jag ber Dig nu efter inhämtade upplysningar ytterligare till-skrifva mig rörande 1) plats, 2) sammansättning och 3) program.

Först bör förutskickas, att t.ex. för Ungern officiella delegerade redan utsetts. England och Tyskland äro de viktigaste. Tyskland har äfven den passvårighet, som ligger i vissa mäktiga kretsars veto mot hvarje samman-träffande med krigförande från andra sidan, men känslan för nödvändighe-ten af betygande af kristendomens enhet är så stark hos behjärtade kyrko-män, att jag fått visshet om möjlighet för den mest representativa deputa-tion, som man kan tänka sig, bl. a. generalsuperintendent Lahusen, som 1915 höll den uppmärksammade predikan mot hatet mot England, Deis-mann (Wochenbriefe), t.o.m. den vördnadsvärde exc[ellensen] Dryander, som hela kriget strängt iakttagit evangelii bud.

Katolikerna hänvisa till påfven, som nu får formlig inbjudan. Ryska och amerikanska delegerade ha vi anledning att vänta m.fl., m.fl.

I. Inbjudan föreligger från samtliga fem neutrala länder. Ditt telegram föredrager Schweiz, emellertid stannade konferensen i stort sedt vid den öfvertygelsen, att om *Uppsala* eller *Göteborg* öfvergifvas, Kristiania är lämp-ligaste, ja enda lämpliga plats. Här i Norden uppbäres konferensen af ett starkt deltagande från kyrkorna och deras män i dess helhet, och vi hafva genom biskopsämbetet dels en rörelsefrihet, dels särskildt för anglikansk och svensk uppfattning af kyrkan en anknytning, som saknas i Schweiz. En svårighet ligger ock däri, att hvarken jag eller Danmarks eller Norges pri-mas under kriget få aflägsna oss så långt som till Schweiz. Och en betryg-gande neutral ledning torde från Schweiz vara svårare att erhålla. Jag ber Dig sondera vederbörande och uppriktigt säga; verkar Sverige (Uppsala, ev. Göteborg) på våra engelska bröder i denna stund mindre inbjudande? Eller är det uteslutande Nordsjön man på goda grunder vill undvika? I för-ra fallet bör Kristiania tagas, ehuru konferensen i Uppsala (eller Göteborg) skulle erhålla större helgd, värdighet och kunna på ett för våra krigförande, särskildt engelska bröder, mer betryggande sätt anordnas. I senare fallet måste, ehuru med afsaknad, Schweiz tillgripas såsom nödfallsutväg, helst Bern eller Neuchatel. Vi skola då göra vårt bästa där, men ekumeniska kyr-

---

[1] Albert Hellerström (1881–1972), Swedish pastor in London 1915–1930 who was the chief mediator between Söderblom and the Church of England. Hellerström later was pastor in Danderyd, northeast of Stockholm, (1930–1952) where he became dean in 1948. – Nathan Sö-derblom's ecumenical collection B 3, UUB, typewritten letter with handwritten additions and corrections.

kokonferensen blir en kongress bland andra. I Uppsala eller Göteborg blir den hvad Challenge vill. Naturligtvis får platsen ej bli hinder för våra engelska bröder. Utan jämförelse för öfvrigt har Norden och Stockholm aldrig ansetts för resans skull svårtillgängligt under kriget. Både Holland, Schweiz och Danmark torde till sist föredraga Uppsala eller Göteborg (Lund är för nära Tyskland). Äfven normännen insågo trots sin vänliga gästfrihet till sist Uppsalas afgjorda fördelar.

II. För sammansättningen föreligga tre möjligheter. 1;o) officiellt kyrklig, hvilket inbjudarna nu beslutat; 2;o) Worlds alliance (kyrkliga världsförbundet) och 3;o) en officiell konferens med rätt för världsförbundet att hafva ombud. Worlds alliance har hos oss fått en kyrklig, nästan officiös, prägel; i Sverige är jag, i Danmark Själlands biskop ordförande, med betydande kyrkomän i styrelsen. Jag förstår, att man på en hel del neutrala håll och äfven i Tyskland och England på vissa håll föredrager en ny Worlds alliance konferens, såsom det ringare men säkrare, framför den större planen. Vi gå på den senare.

Canterburys bref, som först ett par dagar före konferensen kom mig tillhanda, är sådant, att ny förhandling väl kan upptagas.

III. Jag medsänder förslagsvis programpunkter. Neutrala konferensens uttalanden visa i hvad anda de behandlats. Skulle från vederhäftigt engelskt håll modifikation önskas, så sänd mig godhetsfullt med första uppgift därom. »Disarmament«, som Canterbury fäst sig vid, anföres i vår inbjudan ur påfvens budskap, såsom af veterligt alla ledande statsmän enstämmigt förordad åtgärd (rustningarnas inskränkning), men ej som ärende på konferensen, som fast mer skulle behandla den sedligt religiösa förutsättningen för mellanfolkligt samförstånd. Jag medsänder den nya, för tidens skull redan till Amerika afsända, inbjudan, som emellertid efter konferensen kan och skall bli och nu är närmare fixerad. Jag medsänder äfven lista på redan inbjudna. Vi skola äfven därvidlag i möjligaste mån tillmötesgå önskningar, som uttalas.

Först efter Ditt svar fixeras den nya inbjudan – om ej kurirposten går för långsamt.

Med hjärtliga hälsningar till grefve Wrangel och andra
Din tillgifne
Nathan Söderblom

Uppsala, Dec. 19, 1917

Dear Brother,

Many thanks for your letter and cable which conveyed particularly valuable information. The conference of the neutrals has passed well beyond expectations and shown that one can treat these questions without for once touching on politics. We left with the firm resolve and trust that the ecumenical conference will take place in April. I now ask you to write to me, after having collected further information, on 1) location, 2) composition, and 3) program.

First it ought to be mentioned that, e.g., for Hungary, official delegates have already been appointed. England and Germany are the most important [countries].

Germany has the additional passport difficulty which lies in the veto of certain powerful circles against any meeting with belligerents from the other side; but the sense for the necessity of witnessing to Christianity's unity is so strong in courageous churchmen, that I have been assured with regard to the possibility of the most representative deputation you can think of, among others Generalsuperintendent Lahusen,[2] who in 1915 preached the well publicized sermon against hatred of England, Deißmann (Wochenbriefe)[3], even the venerable Excellency Dryander who during the whole course of the war strictly adhered to the Gospel's commandment.

The Catholics point to the Pope who will now receive the formal invitation. We have reason to expect Russian and American delegates, etc. etc.

I. An invitation has been pronounced by all five neutral countries. Your cable prefers Switzerland; however, the conference on the whole stuck to the conviction that if *Uppsala* or *Gothenburg* must be abandoned, Oslo is the most suitable, even the only suitable location. Here in the North, the conference is being supported by a strong participation of the churches and its men as a whole, and by means of the episcopacy, we have on the one hand a freedom of movement, on the other a connection particularly with the Anglican and Swedish understanding of the church, which is lacking in Switzerland. Another difficulty lies in the fact that neither I nor Denmark's or Norway's primates can afford to be as far away as Switzerland during the war. And satisfactory neutral leadership would be more difficult to obtain from Switzerland. I ask you to inquire about these matters and to tell me frankly: Does Sweden (Uppsala, possibly Gothenburg) seem to be less inviting to our English brethren at the present time? Or is it only the North Sea that one for good reasons wants to avoid? In the former case, Oslo should be chosen, even though a conference in Uppsala (or Gothenburg) would be vested with more sanctity and dignity, and could be organized more safely for our belligerent, particularly English, brethren. In the latter case, Switzerland must be resorted to as an emergency makeshift, albeit with regret, preferably Berne or Neuchâtel. We shall then do our best there, but the ecumenical church conference becomes one assembly among others. In Uppsala or Gothenburg it becomes what *Challenge*[4] wants it to be. Of course, the location must not become an impediment for our English brethren. As a matter of fact, by comparison, the North and Stockholm have never been considered hardly accessible for travel during the war. In the final analysis, the Netherlands as well as Switzerland and Denmark would prefer Uppsala or Gothenburg (Lund is too close to Germany). Even the Norwegians at last realized Uppsala's decisive advantages, in spite of their kind hospitality.

II. As to the composition, there are three possibilities. 1) Officially ecclesiastical, which the inviters have now decided; 2) World Alliance[5], and 3) an official conference with the World Alliance's right of being represented. The World Alliance in this country has a sort of semi-official church character; in Sweden, I am its chairman, in Denmark, it is Zealand's bishop, with important churchmen on its board. I

---

[2] Christoph Friedrich Lahusen (1851–1927), 1911 Generalsuperintendent in Berlin, 1918–1921 Vice President of the United Church of Prussia (Altpreußische Union).

[3] See letter no. 45, n. 1.

[4] English journal.

[5] The World Alliance for Promoting International Friendship through the Churches, Social Gospel inspired pacifist organization and one of the germs of the ecumenical movement, was founded at a conference in Constance (Konstanz) on August 1, 1914, the day of the outbreak of World War I. During the war, it arranged aid for prisoners of war; after 1918, it worked for the reconciliation of the belligerent nations.

understand that in quite a few neutral quarters and in certain quarters also in Germany and England a new World's Alliance conference is being preferred to the larger plan as the lesser but more secure alternative. We go for the larger one.

Canterbury's letter which reached me only a couple of days before the conference is such that fresh negotiations may well be entered upon.

III. I am enclosing suggestions as to items of the program. The pronouncements of the neutrals' conference show in which spirit they have been treated. If from authoritative English quarters modification is desired, please be so kind as to include some first information on that. »Disarmament« which Canterbury has attached such importance to is cited in our invitation from the Pope's message as a measure unanimously recommended, as far as we know, by all statesmen, but not as a subject [to be discussed] at the conference, which should instead treat the moral and religious prerequisites for international understanding. I am enclosing the new invitation which for timesaving reasons has already been sent to America, which can and will, however, become fixed in more detail after the conference, and now is. I am also enclosing a list of those already invited. In this respect too, we should meet requests as far as possible that may be voiced.

Only after your reply the new invitation will be fixed – unless express delivery is too slow.

With kind regards to Count Wrangel[6] and others,
sincerely yours,
Nathan Söderblom

111. From WILHELM II.[1]

Hochwürdiger Herr Erzbischof!
Ihr freundliches Schreiben mit dem warmherzigen Bekenntnis zu einer die landeskirchlichen Unterschiede überragenden inneren Einheit der evangelischen Gesamtkirche habe Ich gern entgegengenommen. Es berührt sich mit Gedankengängen, die auch Mir vertraut sind, und die Mich wiederholt, zuletzt bei der Einweihung des Berliner Doms, veranlaßt haben, die ersten Geistlichen aller evangelischen Kirchen zu gegenseitigem Meinungsaustausch zu versammeln. Es hat Mich deshalb auch gefreut, dass sich die Beziehungen deutscher und schwedischer Geistlicher unter Ihrer hervorragenden Mitwirkung in letzter Zeit vertieft und in gemeinsamer Liebesarbeit für unsere Gefangenen in Rußland bewährt haben.

Aus solcher Anschauung heraus würdige Ich Ihre Anregung, die innere Einheit auch in der äußeren landeskirchlichen Form zum Ausdruck zu bringen und zu diesem Zweck den in vielen evangelischen Kirchen hergebrachten, altchristlichen Bischofstitel auch den leitenden Geistlichen unserer

---

[6] Anton Magnus Herman Wrangel, Count of Sauss (1857–1934) 1906 Swedish ambassador in London, Minister of foreign affairs 1920–1921.

[1] N. Söderblom's collection of letters, from royal persons, UUB, typewritten letter. The actual author entrusted with writing this letter was the Geheime Oberregierungsrat Gottfried von Dryander (1876–1951), who most probably discussed it with his father, Ernst von Dryander (1843–1922), Generalsuperintendent of Kurmark.

Landeskirche zu verleihen. Der gleiche Gedanke ist bei uns aus einer andern Wurzel, nämlich aus dem Wunsch erwachsen, die Aufgaben unserer ersten Geistlichen durch Verleihung einer schlichteren, volkstümlicheren und deutscheren Amtsbezeichnung zu fördern. Auch kann der Gedanke an die geschichtliche Tatsache anknüpfen, dass in unserer altpreußischen Landeskirche, und zwar in Zeiten ihrer höchsten Bewährung vor und nach den Freiheitskriegen, eine Reihe ihrer hervorragendsten Diener den evangelischen Bischofs- oder Erzbischofstitel geführt hat. Es würde sich dabei naturgemäß nur um Verleihung eines *Titels*, nicht etwa um die Einführung der in schwedischen Verhältnissen begründeten und bewährten bischöflichen Verfassung handeln können. In Deutschland hat schon die Reformationszeit, wie Ihnen bekannt sein wird, den Landesherrn und seine Kirchenbehörden zu Trägern der Kirchengewalt gemacht und dieses landesherrliche Kirchenregiment, das ein Bistum nach schwedischem Vorbild seiner Natur nach ausschließt, hat sich in Deutschland in vierhundertjähriger Geschichte als ein für Staat und Kirche gleich segensreiches Band bewährt.

Im Rahmen dieser geschichtlich gewordenen Kirchenverfassung die gesegnete Wirksamkeit unserer Kirche zu fördern, ist Mir als Träger der Kirchengewalt ein Herzensanliegen, das mit den Traditionen Meines Hauses eng zusammenhängt. Darüber hinaus wird es Mir auch ferner eine besonders gern erfüllte Aufgabe sein, die Beziehungen unserer Landeskirchen zu den verwandten Bruderkirchen des Auslands, insbesondere zu der uns seit den Tagen Gustav Adolphs engverbundenen schwedischen Kirche zu pflegen und zu vertiefen. Möchte die Gemeinschaft der Kirchen, die am 31 Oktober trotz des Weltkriegs durch den Aufblick zu den großen Gestalten der Reformationsgeschichte verbunden waren, sich auch in den Anschauungen der Völker und bei den Aufgaben bewähren, die die ernsten und arbeitsreichen Jahre der nächsten Zukunft uns allen an heilender und versöhnender Liebesarbeit stellen werden!

Großes Hauptquartier,
den 30 Dezember 1917.

Wilhelm

I[mperator] R[ex]

Seiner Erzbischöflichen Hochwürden Herrn Erzbischof D. S o e d e r b l o m
Upsala.

112. To Wilhelm II.[1]

Upsala den 15.I.1918.

...

Die Absicht Ew. Majestät gewissen kirchlichen Aemtern von metropolitischen Charakter den altchristlichen Bischofs- oder Erzbischofsnamen im evangelischer Sinne ... zu verleihen, wird ohne Zweifel, wie ich dem gnädigen Schreiben entnehme, unbeschadet des geschichtlich begründeten Unterschiedes der evang[elischen] Kirchenverfassungen in Deutschland und Schweden, für das allgemein christliche Bewusstsein, für die volkstümlichen grossen Aufgaben der leitenden Geistlichen und für die wahrhaftige Katholicität und Oekumenicität der evangelischen Christenheit ... eine Bedeutung gewinnen ...

Nathan Söderblom

113. From Randall Davidson[1]

Lambeth Palace, S.E.1.   12 February 1918

My dear Archbishop and Friend,

Your Grace's important letter of December 27th 1917 has been the subject of most careful consideration by myself and by others with whom I have taken counsel. I am anxious to assure you of the eager desire which we entertain that nothing should be left undone which might contribute to the securing for Europe of a just, an honourable, and a lasting peace. That this may be attained is the object of our continuous prayer and effort.

We appreciate to the full the importance of the invitation you extend to representatives of various Christian communions to meet at Upsala, or at Christiania, or even at Berne, for united prayer and for conference, not about the conditions of peace or about the International differences as such, but about the spirit which we desire as Christians to extend and deepen among the peoples of Europe. We note the information you give as to the bodies of persons to whom an invitation has been extended. The list is long and varied, and I observe that the Roman Catholic Church appears as one item, though of course it is noted that its followers are in many lands and that the co-operation of different ecclesiastical leaders would be required if that branch of the Church Catholic is to be properly represented. I am myself particularly anxious that we should not in any way seem to underrate the importance of your proposal or the true spirit of loyalty to Our Lord and Master Jesus Christ which underlies it. The value and significance of such a gathering, however, must in large measure depend on its constituent elements, and a meeting which consisted in great measure of representa-

---

[1] N. Söderblom's collection of letters, to Swedes and foreigners, UUB, abridged typewritten copy.

[1] N. Söderblom's ecumenical collection A 5, UUB, typewritten letter.

tives from the small and scattered denominations, Evangelical and Protestant, on the Continent of Europe, without the great central Churches, would not bear the character which you rightly desire such a Conference to have. If you are able to tell me that the invitation is accepted by the authorities of the Roman Catholic Church, that the Pope gives it his benediction, and that duly accredited Roman Catholic representatives from such countries as France, Italy, Austria, Spain, and the United States of America, will officially attend it, we shoud feel it to be both a privilege and a duty that the Church of England should bear its part. Similarly we should desire to see duly accredited representatives from the Eastern Churches in Russia, in the Turkish Empire, and in Greece. We should not feel it to be possible to send representatives to a gathering which, while claiming to represent the organised forces of the Church of Christ in Europe (you even use the word Oecumenical), was without accredited spokesmen belonging to the Roman Catholic Church or belonging to the Orthodox Church of the East. Upon that point therefore I ask you to give me reassurance and information before I could be justified in asking delegates belonging to the Church of England to attend in that capacity.

There is another point: In the careful arrangements which you have foreshadowed you suggest that the representatives of belligerent countries attending such a Conference should be lodged apart, and should not, according to your plan, meet one another either for devotion or for conference, though each of them would meet representatives of the Neutral Powers. To me and to others whom I have consulted it seems impossible to anticipate that such an arrangement could work satisfactorily if the representatives of belligerent countries are in the same place, whether it be Upsala, Christiania or Berne, at the same time. The arrangement you contemplate would work more satisfactorily were the representatives of the belligerent nations to meet the representatives of Neutral Powers in successive weeks, the opposing belligerent Powers not being represented in the town at the same time. This is a matter which would require careful consideration, but the principle to which I have already given expression – namely, that if we are to be part in such a Conference it must be a Conference of the chief organised Christian communions – is the supreme question, and is in our judgment vital to the true significance and usefulness of such a gathering.

Let me again, my dear Archbishop, assure you of our deep appreciation of your endeavour to promote the true spirit of Christian peace in Europe and of your kindness in writing to me as you have written.

[handwritten:] I remain, with fraternal greeting
Your faithful brother & servant
Randall Cantuar:

114. From Édouard Gruner[1]

Messieurs et honorés frères,

Votre lettre nous a profondément émus, et nous sommes pressés de rendre un respectueux hommage aux sentiments si vraiment chrétiens qui vous l'ont inspirée. Vos coeurs saignent et vos consciences sont bouleversées à la vue d'une chrétienté déchirée, en lutte contre elle-même, si peu conforme aux volontés du Christ. Nous comprenons que vous en souffriez à ce point. Mais vous comprendrez que nous en souffrions encore plus que vous, nous qui ne sommes pas de simples spectateurs de ce qui se passe, mais qui sommes acteurs dans ce drame et qui sommes torturés dans notre chair et dans notre âme.

Si touchés que nous soyons par votre appel et soucieux de répondre dignement à vos intentions fraternelles, notre premier devoir est de rester plus que jamais en communion avec notre peuple, victime d'une injuste aggression, et avec nos soldats qui luttent, peinent et meurent pour la libération de notre pays en même temps que pour le rétablissement total du droit.

A l'heure où nous sommes défendus par nos combattants héroïques, nous ne saurions supporter l'idée d'aller, à l'abri de leurs poitrines, entrer en conversation, même d'une façon détournée, et serait-ce par des intermédiaires bien intentionnés et affectueusement ingénieux, avec d'autres hommes dont les soldats tirent sur nos fils et sur nos frères et occupent encore des parcelles du sol sacré de la Patrie. Cet acte paraîtrait à beaucoup de concitoyens et à nous-mêmes mériter un nom que nous ne voulons pas écrire dans une lettre adressée par des chrétiens à d'autres chrétiens. Vous ne pouvez voir les choses comme nous, et nous ne nous permettrons pas de vous le reprocher. Mais nous vous prions, de conscience à consciences, de comprendre le scrupule invincible qui nous lie.

Vous avez raison de vous demander avec angoisse comment la communion spirituelle pourra être rétablie entre les chrétiens. Nous aussi, nous avons beaucoup médité sur ce problème douloureux, et nous sommes arrivés, devant Dieu, à une conviction que nous avons le devoir de vous communiquer.

La communion spirituelle, pour n'être pas un vain simulâcre, pour être une réalité profonde, a pour condition essentielle l'élimination de tous les griefs sous-entendus, de toutes les pensées inexprimées, de tous les sentiments inavoués, la confession des responsabilités encourues et la répudiation formelle des injustices commises. Les coupables, quels qu'ils soient, doivent être déclarés coupables. Un silence honteux sur tous ces points ne serait qu'un mensonge; et la chrétienté, sous une apparence d'unité, restant divisée dans son fond, serait sans rayonnement autour d'elle. La vie religieuse est minée par les interdits et, pour se développer, pour simplement se

---

[1] Édouard Gruner (1849–1933), president of the Fédération protestante de France; N. Söderblom's ecumenical collection A 9, UUB, typewritten letter.

maintenir, il faut à tout prix qu'elle s'en débarrasse. C'est l'expérience des collectivités comme des individus. La chrétienté ne redeviendra saine et forte que dans et par la recherche loyale de la vérité, dans et par la proclamation de la vérité.

C'est pourquoi nous estimons qu'il ne suffira pas à l'honneur de Dieu et à l'honneur du Christ que la paix soit faite un jour, c'est-à-dire que les hostilités prennent fin, et que les hommes retournent à leurs affaires. Nous demanderons alors, au nom même de cet honneur de Dieu, au nom de cet honneur du Christ que la lumière complète soit faite sur les causes de la guerre et sur la façon dont elle a été déclarée et engagée. Nous demanderons à l'humanité d'appeler le bien: bien et le mal: mal. Nous lui demanderons de condamner solennellement tout mépris, par raison d'Etat, de la parole donnée et des engagements internationaux. Nous lui demanderons de proclamer que la force ne prime jamais le droit, que l'oppression du droit, aussi longtemps que des hommes en souffrent, ne connaît pas de prescription et que toutes les violations doivent en être réparées.

Si ces principes élémentaires ne s'imposaient à la conscience chrétienne, elle serait inférieure à celle de l'honnête homme le plus banal, et nous n'accepterons pas cette humiliation pour Celui que nous appelons le Saint et le Juste.

Messieurs et honorés frères, vous nous avez adressé un appel affectueux. Nous sommes tentés de vous en adresser, de notre côté, un autre qui vous marquera la haute estime que nous avons pour l'autorité de vos caractères et l'importance de votre action possible.

Pour tout dire en un mot, nous sommes persuadés que les chrétiens des nations neutres pourront jouer un rôle capital dans le rétablissement de la communion spirituelle. Ils en seront les meilleurs ouvriers, non pas en invitant les belligérants à ne pas soulever le problème des responsabilités, mais en posant eux-mêmes ce problème; en s'attachant à le résoudre avec une sainte passion de sincérité intransigeante, en jetant des flots de lumière sur tout ce qui doit être connu, en aidant les âmes à se libérer des ignorances complaisantes et des solidarités coupables. De grandes et belles choses seront possibles sur cette terre ensanglantée, le jour où ces chrétiens des nations neutres, revenants aux audaces sacrées, prenant au tragique pour eux-mêmes l'objet de leur intercession rediront la prière du Christ: »Sanctifie-les par la vérité«.

Nous attendons ce jour. Nous avons trop de confiance dans les destinées de l'Evangile pour douter de sa venue, et nous vous prions, chers et honorés frères, de croire toujours à notre plus profond respect et à tout notre dévouement.

LE PRESIDENT,
E. Gruner

LES VICE-PRESIDENTS,
Jules Pfender, pasteur
A. Juncker
Raoul Allier

192

Paris, February 26, 1918

Sirs and revered Brothers,

Your letter has moved us profoundly, and we feel obliged to express our respectful esteem for the truly Christian sentiments motivating it. Your hearts are bleeding and your consciences are troubled at the sight of a Christianity torn apart, fighting against itself, so little in conformity with Christ's commandments. We understand that you are suffering from that at this point. But you will understand that we are suffering even more than you, we who are not simple spectators of the things happening, but actors in this drama and who are being tortured by it in our bodies and in our souls.

Much as we are moved by your appeal and keen to respond in a way worthy of your brotherly intentions, our first duty is to remain more than otherwise united with our people, victim of an unjust aggression, and with our soldiers who are fighting, toiling, and dying for the liberation of our country and likewise for the total reestablishment of the law.

At a time when we are being defended by our heroic fighters, we are unable to support the idea of going, under the protection of their bodies, to enter a conversation, if in a twisted fashion, and be it by intermediaries with good intentions and ingenious in matters of tact, with other people whose soldiers shoot our sons and our brothers and are still occupying parts of the sacred soil of our native land. Such an action would seem to many of our fellow citizens and to ourselves to deserve a name we do not want to write in a letter directed from Christians to other Christians. You are not able to see things the way we do, and we will not permit ourselves to blame you for it. But we beg you, from conscience to conscience, to understand the invincible scruples that bind us.

You are right in asking yourselves with anxiety how the spiritual communion can be reestablished between Christians. We too have meditated a great deal on this painful problem, and we have arrived before God at a conviction which it is our duty to convey to you.

For spiritual communion, if it is not to be an airy mirage, the essential prerequisite is the elimination of all tacit grievances, all unexpressed thoughts, all undisclosed sentiments, the acknowledgment of the responsibilities incurred and the formal repudiation of the injustices committed. The guilty, whoever they are, must be declared guilty.[2] Ignominious silence on all these points would be nothing but deceit; and Christianity, under the [mere] appearance of unity remaining divided at base would lack illuminating power. Religious life is undermined by taboos, and in order to develop, or simply to maintain its position, it is necessary at all costs to get rid of them. This is the experience of collectives as well as of individuals. Christianity will not become healthy and strong again but in and by faithful search for the truth, and by the proclamation of the truth.

That is why we consider it not sufficient for the honor of God and the honor of Christ that peace should be made one day, i.e., that hostilities come to an end and that people return to their business. We shall therefore demand in the name of that honor of God, in the name of that honor of Christ that the causes of the war and the way it was declared and begun be completely uncovered. We shall demand from

---

[2] The question of who was guilty of the war was to remain the thorniest issue right up to the final stages of planning of the Uppsala conference in 1925. It was then decided painstakingly to avoid it as it had become obvious that otherwise, the conference could not have been convened at all.

193

humanity to call the good good and the bad bad. We shall demand from it to condemn solemnly every disregard, for the sake of national interest, of a given promise and of international obligations. We shall demand from it the proclamation that force never override the law, that the suppression of the law, as long as people are suffering from it, not be subject to superannuation, and that all violations of it must be repaired.

If these basic principles are not imposed on the Christian conscience, it will be inferior to that of the most ordinary gentleman, and we do not accept this humiliation because of Him whom we call the Holy one and the Just one.

Sirs and revered brothers, you have directed to us a cordial appeal. We are eager to direct, from our side, another one indicating the high esteem in which we are holding the authority of your personalities and the importance of your possible action.

In a word, we are convinced that Christians of the neutral nations will be able to play a crucial role in the reestablishment of the spiritual communion. They will be the best agents in this feat, not by inviting the belligerents not to raise the problem of responsibilities, but by posing that problem themselves; by endeavoring to solve it with a holy passion of uncompromising sincerity, by casting floods of light upon everything that must be known, by assisting the souls in liberating themselves from complacent ignorance and from culpable solidarity. Great and beautiful things will be possible on this bloodstained earth on the day the neutral nations, returning to a holy audacity, taking seriously the subject of their intercession, will repeat the prayer of Christ: »Sanctify them by the truth«[3].

We are looking forward to that day. We have too much confidence in the destiny of the Gospel to doubt its arrival, and we beg you, dear and revered brothers, always to believe in our most profound respect and in our affection.

THE PRESIDENT
E. Gruner

THE VICE PRESIDENTS
Jules Pfender, pastor
A. Juncker
Raoul Allier

115. To Pope Benedict XV.[1]

[March 11, 1918]

Sanctitatem Vestram
cum qua decet reverentia invitare ausi sumus, ut pro parte Romanae Ecclesiae mitterentur legati cum eis congressuri, qui de ex nonnullis Ecclesiis et terris tam bello implicatis quam pacem agentibus die VIII mensis Septem-

---

[3] John 17:17.

[1] Benedict XV. (1854–1922), pope 1914–1922. Joint letter by Bishops Harald Ostenfeld of Copenhagen, Jens Tandberg of Oslo, and Nathan Söderblom, set up in Latin by Yngve Brilioth, Söderblom's personal secretary. The text above is the final draft, in Brilioth's handwriting. The letter was answered by Cardinal Gasparri, cf. letter no. 117. – Nathan Söderblom's ecumenical collection, UUB.

bris Upsaliam convenire statuerunt, ut de quibusdam rebus ad statum Ecclesiae Christi diro ac diuturno bello turbatum pertinentibus deliberarent. Quod si alius locus posthac fuerit constitutus, Sanctitatem Vestram certiorem facere nobis liceat.

Quam sit necesse civitates mundi, sive regna sive respublicae, in futurum novam viam ineant lites inter se coortas arbitrio componendi necum ingentibus bellandi apparatibus modum statuendi, non solum ex diversis partibus gravius in dies monetur, sed prope jam inter omnes constat. Quod imprimis ipsa Sanctitas Vestra, pacis vindex, nomine universae Christianae Ecclesiae bis jam eloquentissime asseruit. Sed novam hanc mundi atque humanae societatis formam, quam gratia Spiritus Sancti quasi mentis oculis jam surgentem cernere videmur, redintegrata et firmata conscientia unitatis illius, qua in Christo conjungimur, fulciri oportet. Praesens igitur omnium rerum status magna quadam voce poscere quodammodo videtur, ut insigni ac singulari indicio manifestetur spiritus ille Christianae fraternitatis, qui cuilibet propriae patriae amori et pietati praestare debet et excellere. Quare id ante omnia agendum videtur, idque solum nos agimus, ut de rebus Ecclesiae fraterna concordia consultemus. Quae enim ad res mundi civitatumque negotia pertinent, ea, ut a nobis aliena, non videtur nostrum esse tractare.

Cui concilio cum piis precibus adesse tum vero legatis missis interesse si Sanctitas Vestra dignata erit, egregium nobis fuerit subsidium.

Datum Havniae, Christianiae, Upsaliae die XI mensis Martii A.D MCMXVIII.

<table>
<tr><td>H. Ostenfeld</td><td>Jens Tandberg</td></tr>
<tr><td>Episcopus Havniensis</td><td>Episcopus Christianiensis</td></tr>
<tr><td>manu Y. B.</td><td>manu Y. B.</td></tr>
</table>

Nathan Söderblom
Archiepiscopus Upsaliensis
manu propria

[March 11, 1918]

With the appropriate reverence, we dare to request

Your Holiness

that on behalf of the Roman Church delegates be sent who shall meet with those who have decided that [persons] from several Churches and countries who have either been involved in the war or have kept the peace, convene in Uppsala on the 8th of September, in order to deliberate on certain issues pertaining to the state of the Church of Christ which has become perturbed by the horrible and long drawn-out war. If another location should be determined later on, may we be allowed to inform Your Holiness accordingly.

How necessary it is that the nations of the world, be they monarchies or republics, henceforth find a new way of resolving conflicts arising between them by negotiation [and] of setting a limit to the huge killing machineries of warfare, [that] is not only being enjoined with daily increasing urgency from various quarters, but is already agreed upon by virtually everyone. It is in particular Your Holiness Himself, the guardian of peace, who in the name of the whole Christian Church already twice pronounced this in the most eloquent way.[2] However, the new order of the world and of human society, the emergence of which we already seem to discern by the grace of the Holy Spirit, must be reinforced by the renewed and confirmed consent on that unity by which we are conjoined in Christ. The present overall state of affairs therefore seems to demand with a loud voice, as it were, that by way of a conspicuous and specific declaration that spirit of Christian brotherhood be manifested which must exceed and surpass any love and patriotic devotion to one's own country. Therefore what is to be promoted above all, and what alone we are promoting, is to confer in brotherly accord regarding ecclesiastical concerns. For what pertains to worldly things and to the affairs of society, being alien to us, does not seem to be our business to treat.

If Your Holiness pleases not only to be present at this Council through devout prayers, but more particularly to take part in it through delegates sent, that would be an enormous support for us.

Given in Copenhagen, Oslo, and Uppsala on March 11, 1918.

H. Ostenfeld   Jens Tandberg
Bishop of Copenhagen   Bishop of Oslo
through Y[ngve] B[rilioth]   through Y[ngve] B[rilioth]

Nathan Söderblom
Archbishop of Uppsala
with his own hand

116. From FRIEDRICH HEILER[1]

München (Wörthstr. 13), 29.3.18

Hochwürdigster Herr Erzbischof!

Verzeihen Sie mir gütigst, wenn ich mir die Freiheit nehme mein Werk über das Gebet zu übersenden. Ich fühle mich dazu aus tiefstem Herzen verpflichtet, da ich (wie ich auch im Vorwort hervorgehoben habe) gerade aus dem Studium Ihrer Schriften die wertvollsten Anregungen für meine Untersuchungen empfangen habe. Mein Plan, die Universität Leipzig zu beziehen, um Ihr persönlicher Schüler zu werden, wurde leider durch Ihre Beru-

---

[2] The Pope had been engaged in efforts to restore the peace almost from the beginning. The most notable effort is his memorandum of August 1, 1917, addressed to the heads of government of the belligerent nations.

[1] Friedrich Heiler (1892–1967), converted from Roman Catholicism to Protestantism by receiving the Lord's Supper in Vadstena, Sweden, in 1919 (he had been invited by Söderblom to take part in a church conference there). In 1920, he became associate professor of history of religions and philosophy of religion in Marburg, thanks to support by Rudolf Otto, and full professor in 1922. The Nazis transferred him »for diciplinary reasons« in 1934 because he had criticized the ouster of Jewish professors and civil servants from office. After the war, Heiler became a chief proponent of the Una Sancta movement and a leading participant in interdenominational talks. – Sending his doctoral thesis, *Das Gebet*, Munich 1918, to Söderblom (cf. above), the book that was to make him famous, marked the beginning of a longstanding close relationship between the two men. N. Söderblom's collection of letters, from foreigners, UUB, handwritten letter.

fung nach Uppsala vereitelt. Zugleich gestatte ich mir meinen (von H. Oldenberg in den Gött[ingischen] Gel[ehrten] Anz[eigen] anerkennend beur-
teilten) Aufsatz[2] über die buddhistischen Versenkungsstufen beizulegen,
auf den in meinem Werke wiederholt verwiesen ist und dessen Schlußaus-
führungen Sie interessieren dürften. Da ich Ihr Urteil ganz besonders hoch
schätze, so wäre ich Ihnen für nichts dankbarer als für eine Besprechung
meines Buches in einer schwedischen oder außerschwedischen Zeitschrift.
Doch wage ich es nicht, Sie ausdrücklich darum zu bitten, da ich weiß, dass
Sie durch Ihr Amt voll in Anspruch genommen wind.

Mein Verleger Herr Ernst Reinhardt, früher Buchhändler in Paris, der
Ihnen von Ihrem dortigen Aufenthalt wohlbekannt ist, hat mich gebeten,
Ihnen seine Empfehlungen zu übermitteln. Mit dem Ausdruck der größten
Hochschätzung bin ich

Ew. Exzellenz dankbar ergebener

Dr. phil. Friedr. Heiler.

Die Zensurvorschriften verbieten es, Postpaketen briefliche Mitteilungen
beizulegen, weshalb ich den Brief gesondert schicken muß.

117. To Friedrich Heiler[1]

Upsala 4 V 1918

Sehr geehrter Herr Doktor!

Was ich von Ihrem schönen Werke denke, können Sie meinem Artikel[2] entnehmen. Leider verbietet mich gegenwärtig die Zeit, eine eingehende wissenschaftliche Recension und Würdigung zu schreiben. Sie haben mir [je]-
doch durch diese wunderbare Gabe aus dem Wunderland des Gebets die
Wohltat bewiesen, wenigstens zu nötigen ein Buch zu lesen, was mir durch
die Überhäufung von religiösen, kirchlichen, akademischen, nationalen
und internationalen Pflichten und Liebeswerken sonst jetzt verboten wird –
leider. Erst im Frieden kann ich hoffen die ersehnte Forschungsarbeit wieder mal aufzunehmen.

Es giebt im Gebiete unsrer Studien wenige solche Arbeiten wie die Ihrige,
welche mit einem so umfassenden Gegenstand ernste Methode und eine feste religionsgeschichtliche und -psychologische Orientierung verbinden und
einen unbefangenen kritischen Blick mit wahrem Sinn für das Geheimnis
der Religion vereinigen. Was für eine Freude Sie mir durch Ihr Opus Ma-

---

[2] Friedrich Heiler, »Die buddhistischen Versenkungsstufen,« in: *Aufsätze zur Kultur-und
Sprachgeschichte des Orients*, FS Ernst Kuhn, Breslau 1916, 357-387; Hermann Oldenberg
(1854-1920), from 1908 professor in Göttingen, was one of the best-known indologists of his
time. His above-mentioned review appeared in GGA 179/1917, 170f.

[1] Fr. Heiler's papers (Ms. 999), UB Marburg, handwritten letter.
[2] Nathan Söderblom, »Bönen. För Bönsöndagen,« in: *Stockholms Dagblad* May 5, 1918; cf.
P. Misner (ed.), *Friedrich von Hügel – Nathan Söderblom – Friedrich Heiler: Briefwechsel 1909-
1931*, in: KKSMI 14, Paderborn 1981, 79 note 1.

gnum bereitet haben, Erquickung, Belehrung und Anregung und Dankbarkeit für die liebevoll eindringende Weise in welcher Sie meine Arbeiten verwertet haben – ja, das kann ich Ihnen nicht sagen. Ich beglückwünsche unsre gemeinsame Wissenschaft und die Zukunft der Religionsgeschichte an den deutschen Universitäten zu der ebenso überraschenden als erfreulichen Erscheinung eines bei jungen Jahren schon reifen und durch eine gewaltige wissenschaftliche Leistung vollbewährten Forschers. Wäre das Buch vor vier Jahren erschienen, wären Sie auf dem Vorschlag zu meiner Nachfolge in Leipzig sicherlich aufgeführt worden. ...

Ich habe schon eine schwedische, vielleicht etwas verkürzte Übersetzung angeregt ... [Remarks on some printing errors and a couple of details concerning the content of the book]

Mir bleibt auch ein embarras de richesse, wenn ich die Stellen verzeichnen sollte, die ich mit besonderer Genugtuung las oder wo ich eine neue und treffende Beobachtung fand. Wohltuend wirkt z. B. in der Frage von Zauber und Gebet und sonst Ihre Selbständigkeit landläufigen Theorien gegenüber.

... Hoffentlich besuchen Sie mich einmal in Upsala. Wir werden die Sache so ordnen, dass ich Sie einlade, als Gast der Olaus Petri Stiftung der Universität[3], an der Universität in einigen Jahren eine Reihe von Vorlesungen zu halten. Senden Sie mir, bitte, einstweilen Ihre Photographie.

Morgen – schon heute! – ist Vocem, Bönsöndag. Ich werde in Stockholm bei der Einführung eines Pfarrers vom Gebet reden. Ihnen verdanke ich neue Anregung. Im Heiligtum der Religion weilt Ihr Buch. Gottes Segen wünsche ich, darum bete ich für Sie und für Ihren weiteren Gottesdienst, der darin besteht, die Religion mit unermüdlichem Fleiss, kritischer Wahrheitsliebe und kongenialem Sinn zu erforschen.

Ich bin, mein lieber und hochgeschätzter Herr Doktor, Ihr in tiefer Sympathie und warmer Dankbarkeit ergebenster

Nathan Söderblom
Grüßen Sie bestens Ihren Herrn Verleger
N. S-m

118. From Friedrich Heiler[1]

München, Wörthstr. 13, 15. V. [1918]

Hochverehrter Hochwürdigster Herr Erzbischof!

Für die übergroße Freundlichkeit, die Sie mir und meinem Buche zuteil werden ließen, die so anerkennende, lange Besprechung meines Werkes,

---

[3] A lectureship foundation at the University of Uppsala. Söderblom, who was, like all Swedish archbishops until 1950, also Vice-Chancellor of the University, frequently used such invitations for promoting the ecumenical idea.

[1] N. Söderblom's collection of letters, from foreigners, UUB, handwritten letter.

den überaus herzlichen Brief, die gütige Widmung mehrerer Ihrer wertvollen Schriften, sage ich Ihnen meinen herzlichsten Dank. Sie haben mir eine Freude bereitet, wie ich sie mir nie erträumt hätte, eine Freude, für die ich Ihnen nicht genug danken kann. Ihre Besprechung meines Buches ist, was mich besonders freut, die *erste*, die erschien; erst am 11. Mai kam die zweite aus der Feder des Univ[ersitäts-] Prof. Hugo Koch[2]. Ich glaube, Sie haben mir zuviel des Lobes gespendet, ich bin ja erst ein Anfänger. Meine eigene Leistung ist schließlich doch nur ein unermüdlicher Sammeleifer. Die großen religionsgeschichtlichen Richtlinien verdanke ich ja dem Studium Ihrer Schriften, gerade in der Sonderung der beiden religiösen Haupttypen[3], die Sie mit Recht als den Schwerpunkt des ganzen Werkes bezeichnet haben, bin ich ganz besonders von den Resultaten Ihrer Untersuchungen abhängig. Desgleichen schulde ich die Gewinnung des richtigen Ausgangspunktes für die Geschichte des Gebets Ihren Abhandlungen über die primitive Religion[4]. Wenn ich aber das im Gebet sich offenbarende religiöse Leben richtig erfaßt und verdolmetscht habe, so verdanke ich das persönlichen Gotteserfahrungen, also göttlicher Gnade. Ich selbst halte mein Buch nur für eine Vorarbeit zu einer monumentalen Geschichte des Gebets, an die sich, wie ich hoffe, die künftige Religionswissenschaft heranwagen wird.

...

Sie wunderten sich, daß ich als Katholik Luthers Persönlichkeit wie der evangelischen Frömmigkeit mit so verständnisvoller Sympathie gegenüberstehe. Dies gibt mir Anlaß, Ihnen einiges aus meiner inneren Entwicklung mitzuteilen. Ich entstamme einer streng katholischen Familie, nahm von Jugend an eifrig am katholischen Gottesdienstleben teil und kannte keinen höheren Wunsch als katholischer Geistlicher zu werden. In den letzten Jahren meiner Gymnasialzeit begann die religiöse Krisis; ich beschäftigte mich damals ständig mit dem griechischen Neuen Testament, was zur Folge hatte, daß mir die bibelkritischen und dogmengeschichtlichen Probleme in ihrer ganzen Schwere aufgingen; die Fundamente der katholischen Dogmatik gerieten für mich ins Wanken. In dieser Zeit kam von Rom die Forderung des Antimodernisteneides; zahlreiche meiner Freunde und Bekannten waren damals in schwerer Gewissensnot; aber sie halfen sich mit Reserva-

---

[2] Hugo Koch (1869–1940), professor of church history and canonical law at the Academy (state-sponsored Roman Catholic theological faculty) of Braunsberg/East Prussia 1904–1910. He was dismissed as a modernist because of a critical examination of Cyprian's writings. He then pursued patristic studies in Munich. His review of Heiler's book appeared in the Süddeutsche Zeitung, signed »H.K.« (cf. Misner, l. cit., 87 note 1).

[3] Söderblom distinguishes between mysticism of infinity and mysticism of personality; the latter can also be called prophetic religion or religion of revelation; see esp. his *Uppenbarelsereligion*, Uppsala 1903, 2nd enlarged ed. Stockholm 1930. Heiler accepts this distinction in principle but prefers to limit the term mysticism to the former: *Das Gebet*, 4th ed. Munich 1921, 250–255.255–257.

[4] Cf. Nathan Söderblom, *Das Werden des Gottesglaubens*, Leipzig 1916 (enlarged German translation of *Gudstrons uppkomst*, Stockholm 1914).

tionen und Interpretierungen und schworen, nicht mit Preisgabe ihrer Überzeugung, wie vielfach geglaubt wird, sondern weil sie den Bruch mit der Kirche und das Scheiden von ihrem Beruf nicht wagten. Für mich selbst begann nun ein stetes qualvolles Schwanken in der Berufsfrage; mit der stärksten Neigung zum theologischen Studium und zum Priesterberuf rang der innere Widerspruch gegen das offizielle Kirchensystem. In dieser zwiespältigen Seelenstimmung begann ich meine Universitätsstudien. Ich studierte erst semitische und arische Philologie, dann Philosophie und Psychologie, fand aber nirgends rechte Befriedigung. Mein Lieblingsstudium war immer Theologie. In der Hoffnung, mit der Kirche doch wenigstens zu einem äußeren Kompromiss zu kommen, ließ ich mich von meinem 3. Universitätsjahre als Theologe immatrikulieren. Vorlesungen hörte ich aber meist nur bei dem mir geistig nahestehenden Prof. Adam[5], wohl dem tüchtigsten katholischen Dogmenhistoriker Deutschlands, und dem kritischen alttestamentlichen Exegeten Goettsberger[6]. Alle anderen Vorlesungen waren mir eine Qual: nur tote Dogmatik. (Nur die Anstandspflicht erforderte es, diese Theologen, die mir innerlich ganz fremd blieben, in meiner Dissertation aufzuführen). So stillte ich meinen theologischen Heißhunger im privaten Studium der protestantischen Theologie. In meinem 2. Universitätsjahre fiel mir Ihre Neubearbeitung des Tiele'schen Kompendiums[7] in die Hand; es hatte für mich einen solchen Reiz, dass ich es halb auswendig lernte. Dieses Buch wies mir den Weg zu Ihren anderen Schriften und zu der vergleichenden Religionswissenschaft, die meinen Neigungen zusagte. Im Frühjahr 1914 nahm sich Aloys Fischer[8] meiner an und erklärte, mir den Weg zur Habilitation für Religionswissenschaft in der philosophischen Fakultät ebnen zu wollen. Er veranlaßte damals dieses Werk. Fischer als Psychologe dachte an eine psychologische Arbeit; ich selbst bin kein großer Freund von der eigentlichen Religionspsychologie; ich schuf ein religionsgeschichtliches Werk; nur Fischer zu liebe habe ich dem Untertitel »religionspsychologisch« eingefügt ... Trotzdem sich durch die Beschäftigung mit dem Gegenstand meine religiösen und wissenschaftlichen Anschauungen geklärt hatten, trug ich mich noch im verflossenen Herbst ernstlich mit dem Gedanken, mich zum Priester weihen zu lassen und mich der Seelsorge zuzuwenden; denn ich habe ein unausrottbares Bedürfnis nach dem Dienst im Heiligtum; ich beneide jeden, der mit ehrlicher religionswissenschaftlicher Forscherarbeit die Verkündigung des Evangeliums verbinden darf. Der Plan scheiterte aber schon daran, dass ich dann auf die Veröffentlichung meines Buches in der jetzigen Form hätte verzichten müssen, was ich nie über mich gebracht hätte. Jetzt sind die Brücken mit der katholischen

---

[5] Karl Adam (1876–1966), church historian in Munich until 1915, then in Strasbourg, from 1919 in Tübingen.

[6] Johann Baptist Goettsberger (1868–1958), professor in Munich from 1903–1935.

[7] Cornelis Petrus Tiele, *Kompendium der Religionsgeschichte* (übers. von F. W. T. Weber), 4th ed., completely revised by N. Söderblom, Berlin 1912.

[8] Aloys Fischer (1880–1937), psychologist and educationist, devout Catholic.

Theologie endgültig abgebrochen, da mein Buch in katholischen Kreisen, wie ich nicht anders erwartet habe, nicht geringen Anstoß erregt hat. Es läuft, obgleich unbeabsichtigt, von selbst auf eine Apologie des evangelischen Frömmigkeitsgeistes hinaus.

Den Gedanken eines Übertrittes in eine evangelische Landeskirche habe ich oft erwogen. Was mich davon zurückhält, ist einmal Pietät gegen meine Eltern, ferner die Neigung zum Sakramentalismus, die ich mit Tyrrell[9] teile und die der Protestantismus nicht befriedigen kann. Ich bin im Grunde evangelischer Christ; trotz aller Sympathie für die Mystik bin ich selbst kein eigentlicher katholischer Mystiker, wie es die echten katholischen Modernisten sind (Hügel und meine Freunde Phil. Funk, früher Redakteur des »Neuen Jahrhunderts« und Jos. Bernhart[10], ein hochbegabter jetzt aus dem Kirchenamt ausgeschiedener Geistlicher). Sie haben hierin in »Religionsproblemet«[11] den Nagel auf den Kopf getroffen.) Aber der *äußere Rahmen* meines persönlichen Christentums ist das mystisch-sakramentale Gottesdienstleben der katholischen Kirche. Mit dem starren Dogmatismus und dem politisch-hierarchischen Institut der katholischen Kirche habe ich völlig gebrochen. Aber das eucharistische Mysterium, der Mittelpunkt ihres Gottesdienstlebens, fesselt mich an diese Kirche, der ich doch sonst so entfremdet bin. Vom Standpunkt des Kirchenrechtes aus bin ich natürlich als exkommuniziert zu betrachten. Doch dieser Konflikt, den ich klar und scharf sehe, hindert mich nicht – so wenig wie den sterbenden Tyrrell – weiterhin an dem sakramentalen Leben der katholischen Kirche teilzunehmen. Die Halbheit und Inkonsequenz dieses Standpunktes erkenne ich wohl. Aber vielleicht wird dieses merkwürdige mixtum von katholischer und evangelischer Frömmigkeit irgendwann und irgendwo noch in der Geschichte realisiert werden. Mich beschleicht bisweilen die stille Hoffnung, dass im Laufe der Zeit noch eine Synthese zwischen dem echten evangelischen *Geist* und den wertvollen religiösen *Formen* der katholischen Kirche gefunden werden wird. Das Herz des Christentums freilich muß biblisch-evangelisch sein; aber der sakramentale Symbolismus und das universalistische Ideal der una sancta lassen sich, wie ich glaube, in den Dienst des inneren Christentums stellen, ohne dass dieses (wie es im Katholizismus aller Jahrhunderte der Fall war) dadurch ständig bedroht wird.

Ich will mich noch in diesem Sommer an der philosophischen Fakultät der hiesigen Universität mit einer größeren Monographie über die buddhistische Versenkung für Religionswissenschaft habilitieren. Falls das bayrische Kultusministerium aus prinzipiellen Gründen Schwierigkeiten machen

[9] George Tyrrell (1861–1909), Irish Catholic theologian and mystic who became a leading modernist. He was excommunicated because of his criticism of the Encyclical *Pascendi dominici gregis* of 1907. He did receive the extreme unction but was denied a church burial.

[10] Friedrich Freiherr von Hügel (1852–1925), Roman Catholic layman theologian and friend of Tyrrell, sympathizing with the modernists; Philipp Funk (1884–1937), a reform-minded Roman Catholic and modernist; Josef Bernhart (1881–1969), Catholic writer.

[11] Cf. Nathan Söderblom, *Religionsproblemet inom katolicism och protestantism*, Stockholm 1910, 1–372, esp. 331–372.

sollte, steht mir nach der Zusage von Prof. Krüger (Nachfolger von Wundt)[12] die Habilitation in Leipzig offen. Ich hoffe in der religionsgeschichtlichen Lehrtätigkeit einen Ersatz für die theologisch-kirchliche Wirksamkeit zu finden, die mir versagt blieb.

... [On Söderblom's suggestion to have Heiler's book translated into Swedish and on Heiler's own idea to translate Söderblom's *Religionsproblemet* into German]

Nochmals sage ich Ihnen vielen Dank für Ihre große Liebenswürdigkeit und bin mit dem Ausdruck der größten Verehrung   Ihr ergebenster   Friedrich Heiler

119. From CHARLES S. MACFARLAND[1]

New York, June 4, 1918

My dear Archbishop Soderblom:

I thank you for your good letter of May 1 and the accompanying document relative to the proposed conference.

I am reporting your communications at each monthly meeting of the Administrative Committee and I assure you that the Committee will give them the most thoughtful consideration.

I expect to sail for France within a few days and perhaps when I am there I can get more light on the situation.

The brethren of our Administrative Committee, up to the present time, however, feel that the Constituent bodies of the Federal Council would not approve taking any action.

We are all in the deepest sympathy with the purposes you have in mind and at heart.

The almost universal feeling here, however, is that no acction must be taken which would in any way impair the great world movement for crushing militarism.

I earnestly wish that we were near enough so that I could talk these great matters over with you.

With our affectionate good will,

Faithfully yours,

Charles S. Macfarland

General Secretary

---

[12] Felix Krüger (1874–1948), professor of philosophy; Wilhelm Wundt (1832–1920), philosopher and empirical psychologist, best known for his 10-volume *Völkerpsychologie*, Leipzig [3]1911–1920.

[1] Charles Macfarland (1866–1956), General Secretary of the Federal Council of the Churches of Christ in America. He was born in Härnosand, Sweden, of Scottish parents. N. Söderblom's collection of letters, from foreigners, UUB, typewritten letter.

120. From Pietro Cardinal Gasparri[1]

DAL VATICANO, die 19 Junii 1918

Perillustres Viri,

Libenter quidem Sanctitas Sua accepit vestras obsequentes epistolas de Congressu die VIII mensis Septembris eo proposito Upsaliae habendo, ut in hominum Societate, immani hoc bello ad finem tandem adducto, christianae caritatis magis magisque vincula firmentur.

Beatissimo Patri pergrata fuerunt humanitatis officia quae iisdem epistolis continebantur. Ipse vero persuasum habet civilem societatem plena constantique pace et tranquillitate frui non posse, nisi christianae fraternitatis praecepta rite serventur. Quare in hac tanta odii conflagratione quidquid huc spectat, quidquid ad hunc finem adstruitur, Augusto Pontifici et iucundum et optabile est, idque eo magis quod viam sternit ad assequendum votum evangelicis illis contentum verbis: »Fiat unum ovile et unus pastor.«

Haec pro mumere [sic; lege: munere] Vobiscum, Illustrissimi Viri, communicans, ea qua par est obeservantia sum et permanere gaudeo

Vobis addictissimus

P. Card. Gasparri

FROM THE VATICAN, June 19, 1918

Most illustrious men,

His Holiness has gladly received your polite letter on the conference to be held in Uppsala on Sept. 8, with the aim that in human society the bonds of Christian charity be more and more reinforced, when this horrible war will finally have drawn to a close.

The obligingness toward humanity contained in that same letter has been most warmly appreciated by the Holy Father. He is himself truly convinced that civil society cannot enjoy full and permanent peace and tranquillity, unless the commandments of Christian brotherhood are duly observed. Therefore whatever leads there in this great conflagration of hatred, whatever is designed towards that end, is pleasing and desirable to the August Pontifex, all the more so because it paves the way for obtaining the [fulfillment of the] promise contained in those words of the Gospel: »May there be one flock, one shepherd.«[2]

In dutifully communicating this to you, most illustrious men, I am with due respect and glad to remain

yours most sincerely

P. Card. Gasparri

---

[1] Pietro Gasparri (1852–1934), Cardinal Secretary of State 1914–1930. This letter is the Vatican's reply to the joint request by the three Nordic bishops to the Pope of March 11, to send delegates to an ecumenical conference (cf. above, letter no. 112). N. Söderblom's ecumenical collection A 8, UUB, typewritten letter.

[2] John 10:16; the original text has a future tense instead of a present subjunctive.

121. To Adolf Deissmann[1]

Hemsjö d. 9. 7. 1918

Sehr geehrter, lieber Freund!
Aus dieser Sommerfrische, wo wir bei lieben Freunden die Nöten der Welt
vergessen könnten, wenn nicht von aussen tägliche neue Erinnerungen zu
uns kämen, möchte ich der Einladung unserer Olaus-Petri-Stiftung das fol-
gende hinzufügen.

Aus verschiedenen Gründen sind wir jetzt überzeugt, dass, wie Sie mir
schon längst geschrieben haben, unsere ekumeniche Konferenz nicht in
Sept. sondern zuerst im nächsten Jahre stattfinden kann. Die stattliche Reihe der Vorlesungen über die Einheit der Kirche aus dem Gesichtspunkt verschiedener religiösen gemeinschaften, werden doch ein Zeugnis ablegen,
dass eine bedeutsame Tat der Kirchengeschichte ausmachen wird. Die
Konferenz können wir zugleich persönlich vorbereiten. Am Jahrestag des
Kriegsausbroches [sic] werden viele Gedanken und Gebeten in unseren
neutralen Ländern wie auch, wie ich höre, in Gross-Brittannien, wo es doch
viele echt-christliche Persöhnen [sic] gibt, die vor dem Baal nicht Knie ge-
beugt haben, sich sammeln um die Aufmerksamkeit auf das Ziel ekumeni-
chen Konferenz zu konzentrieren, d. h. für die Wiederherstellung der Einheit der Kirche, für die Verwirklichung Christlicher Grundsätze im inneren
und äusseren Leben der Nation und auch, wie ich persöhnlich hinzufügen
möchte, gegen die sittlichen Gefahren und Greul, welche zu dem Unheil
dieser harten Zeit gehören.

Ich weiss nicht, ob Sie es wertvoll finden, beim Anfang des 5. Kriegsjahres
die Gedanken unsere Mitchristen auch auf diese Angelegenheiten zu lenken.

Gott gebe, dass die Stimmen der Vernunft, die jetzt in den Ländern der
Entente den Gedanken an Frieden nicht mehr verhöhnen und welche hinter
sich eine Gewaltige aber unterdrückte Folkstimmung haben, auch in der
Politik etwas ausristen können werden.

Mit den besten Grüssen von Haus zu Haus
Ihr sehr ergebener

122. From Friedrich Heiler[1]

München Wörthstr. 13/I, 1. Okt. 18

Hochverehrter Hochwürdiger Herr Erzbischof!
Seit meinem letzten Brief vom 15. Mai, in dem ich Ihnen meinen inneren
Entwicklungsgang und meinen damaligen religiösen Standpunkt ausführlich darlegte, haben sich bedeutsame innere und äußere Wandlungen abge-
spielt. Die phil. Fak. der hiesigen Univ. hat meine Habilitationsschrift über

---

[1] N. Söderblom's ecumenical collection B 2, UUB, typewritten letter (carbon copy).

[1] N. Söderblom's collection of letters, from foreigners, UUB, handwritten letter.

»Die buddhistische Versenkung«[2], die Ihnen in diesen Tagen vom Verlag (entsprechend den neuen Zensurvorschriften) zugehen wird, angenommen. Ich werde in 14 Tagen meine Probevorlesung halten und noch in diesem Semester meine akademische Lehrtätigkeit eröffnen können. Wichtiger als diese äußeren Ereignisse sind die inneren Erkenntnisse und Erlebnisse, die mir die letzten Wochen brachten. Nach langen inneren Kämpfen hat sich die Entscheidung für mein künftiges Leben vorbereitet; unter Schmerzen und Wehen wird in mir der Entschluß geboren, meine Mutterkirche zu verlassen und mich der evangelischen Theologie und dem evangelischen Kirchendienst zu weihen. Die entscheidenden Gründe sind rein religiöse, doch darf ich nicht verhehlen, daß die äußeren wirtschaftlichen Schwierigkeiten, mit denen ich zu kämpfen habe, mir die rein wissenschaftliche und akademische Tätigkeit auf die Dauer nicht ermöglichen. ... Dieses lebhafte religiös-theologische Interesse, das mich in meiner isolierten Stellung als überkonfessioneller Gelehrter stets quälte, spüre ich gerade jetzt am stärksten, da ich im Begriffe bin meine Dozententätigkeit an der philosophischen Fakultät zu beginnen. Ich fühle, daß eine Lehrkanzel in der phil. Fak. nicht der rechte Platz für mich ist, wegen des Hörerkreises wie wegen des Lehrerkollegiums. Meine Vorlesungen werden wohl nur von religiös oder philosophisch interessierten Laien besucht werden. Den Theologiestudierenden wird jedoch wegen meines nichtkatholischen Standpunktes die Teilnahme verwehrt sein. Ich aber möchte zu Theologen reden, möchte junge Theologenherzen wecken und zünden, möchte, dass der Same meines Wortes auf fruchtbares Ackerland, nicht auf die Straße falle. Weil ich mich als christlicher Theologe nicht als Vertreter einer farblos-neutralen Religionswissenschaft fühle und bekenne, darum begegnet mein wissenschaftliches Streben bei manchen Mitgliedern der philosophischen Fakultät – trotz des liebenswürdigen Entgegenkommens, das man mir bewiesen hat und das ich dankbar anerkenne – nicht dem von mir gewünschten Verständnis. Manche wollen aus mir einen Religions*archäologen*, andere einen Religions*philologen* machen, wieder andere einen Religions*psychologen* oder -*Philosophen*. Mir aber ist es nicht um Archäologie oder Philologie, nicht um Psychologie oder Philosophie zu tun, sondern um die Religion. Man wünscht, dass ich Religionswissenschaft als *Profan*wissenschaft betreibe, von einem möglichst untheologischen und areligiösen Standpunkt aus. Für mich aber ist Religionswissenschaft die Wissenschaft vom Heiligsten, das die Menschheit hat, und diese Wissenschaft können nur religiöse Menschen betreiben. Man wünscht, dass ich das Christentum möglichst beiseite lasse – denn das sei die Domäne der Theologen – und mich mit den außerchristlichen Religionen begnüge; für mich aber ist das Christentum das A und Ω aller meiner wissenschaftlichen Arbeiten; und wenn man mich auf die außerchristlichen Religionen abdrängt, hat man mir alle Freude an der Religionswissenschaft

---

[2] Friedrich Heiler, *Die buddhistische Versenkung. Eine religionsgeschichtliche Untersuchung*, Munich 1918.

genommen. Ein Religionsforscher, der die höchste und reichste Erscheinung der Religionsgeschichte beiseite rückt, behält nur ein Fragment von der Religion in Händen. Man ist von den persönlichen Bekenntnissen, mit denen ich mein »Gebet« und meine »buddhistische Versenkung« abschloß, etwas unlieb berührt; aber diese religiösen Bekenntnisse sind für mich die Formulierung des Endresultats meiner wissenschaftlichen Forschung.

So betrete ich denn die Lehrkanzel der phil. Fak. in dem Bewußtsein, meiner innersten Geistesart nach einer anderen Fakultät anzugehören. Aber meine tiefste Sehnsucht zielt gar nicht auf eine akademische Lehrkanzel, sondern auf eine Kirchenkanzel; die religiöse Verkündigung steht mir noch höher als das wissenschaftlich-theologische Lehramt. So sehr ich das streng wissenschaftliche Suchen und Forschen liebe und ihm all meine verfügbaren Kräfte weihe, so tiefe persönliche Befriedigung ich allzeit aus der wissenschaftlichen Arbeit geschöpft habe, so hungere und dürste ich doch nach dem Dienst am Gotteswort, nach Predigt und Seelsorge. Was ich seit Jahren fühlte und ahnte, daß mein Beruf nicht die Wissenschaft, sondern das Priestertum ist, das drängt sich mir nun mit voller Wucht auf. Aber der Weg zum Priestertum ist mir in der Kirche verschlossen, der ich von Geburt an angehörte und deren eifriges Glied ich – trotz aller Opposition gegen Dogma und Autorität – bis in die jüngste Zeit war. Der Weg ist mir verschlossen, weil ich durch mein Werk über das Gebet auch nach außen hin bezeugt habe, daß ich die »unfehlbare« Lehrautorität dieser Kirche nicht anerkenne, daß sie mir nicht die einzige ist, »außer der es kein Heil gibt«. Ich könnte mir die Pforte zum katholischen Priestertum nur öffnen, wenn ich meinen wissenschaftlichen Überzeugungen abschwören würde ... Eine solche Absage an meine wissenschaftlichen Prinzipien käme einer geistigen Selbstentmannung gleich. Und doch könnte ich mich dazu verstehen, wenn meine persönliche Frömmigkeit die Frömmigkeit der Kirche wäre, mit anderen Worten, wenn ich Mystiker wäre. Die Mystik ist die katholische Herzensfrömmigkeit, die Religion aller wahrhaft innerlichen Katholiken, sie ist es, die dem starren, dogmatischen und hierarchisch organisierten Gesetzeskirchentum Leben und Wärme einhaucht. »Ein Mystiker, der nicht katholisch wird, bleibt Dilettant« hat Harnack gesagt[3]. Ich möchte hinzufügen: »Wer Mystiker ist und nicht katholisch bleibt, würde die Wurzeln seiner Frömmigkeit zerstören.« Obgleich der Mystiker innerlich über alles Kirchentum erhaben ist, so braucht er doch die Kirche als die Stätte, in der er wohnt und Ruhe findet. ... Für mich hingegen ist die Rückkehr zur katholischen Theologie und der Eintritt ins katholische Priestertum eine Unmöglichkeit. Ich habe gewiß die größte Achtung vor der mystischen Frömmigkeit, die in der katholischen Kirche ihre Heimstätte und ihren Nährboden hat; sie offenbart ja eine Zartheit und Wärme, eine Innigkeit und Tiefe, die nur der ganz kennt, der sie einmal selbst gekostet hat. Aber ich bin nur

---

[3] Adolf von Harnack, *Lehrbuch der Dogmengeschichte*, Bd. 3, 4. Aufl. Tübingen 1910, 436: »... ein Mystiker, der nicht Katholik wird, ist ein Dilettant«.

kurze Zeit meines Lebens (vom 16. bis zum 19. Lebensjahr) ein eigentlicher Mystiker gewesen. Dann ging mir im Studium des Neuen Testamentes die ganze Größe und Herrlichkeit des biblisch-evangelischen Christentums auf; und von da an empfand ich die Mystik trotz aller Sympathie doch als ein Christentum mit heidnischem Zusatz. Trotz meiner bis in die jüngste Zeit währenden Hochschätzung des mit der Mystik verkoppelten Sakramentalismus habe ich seither doch stets als evangelischer Christ gedacht, gefühlt, gebetet. Aus meinem Werke ist auch ganz deutlich erkennbar, dass ich bei allem Verständnis für die Mystik mit Entschiedenheit auf der Seite des biblisch-prophetischen Frömmigkeitstypus stehe. ... Meine persönliche biblisch orientierte Religiosität richtet sich jedoch nicht nur gegen den verborgenen Lebensquell des Katholizismus: die Mystik, sondern auch gegen sein organisierendes Prinzip: den Synkretismus. Der Katholizismus hat sich mir nach langem und sorgfältigem Studium als complexio oppositorum zu erkennen gegeben, als eine grandiose Verschmelzung von Heidentum u. Christentum, von hellenistischer Mystik und biblischem Christentum, von primitivem Zauberkult und persönlicher geistig-sittlicher Religion, von Werkgerechtigkeit u. Gnadenglaube, von Autoritätsgehorsam und innerer Freiheit, von Individualismus und Herdengeist. Aus unendlich vielen und verschiedenartigen Elementen ist der Dom des Katholizismus aufgebaut; aber das Evangelium Jesu ist nur ein Baustein neben vielen anderen, nicht der Grundstein u. Eckstein. Aber gerade dieses ist für mich die höchste und inhaltsreichste Position, die ich in der ganzen Religionsgeschichte finde.[4]

Die Zensurbeschränkung der Briefe auf 8 Seiten zwingt mich hier für heute abzubrechen und die Gedanken in einem späteren Briefe fortzuführen. Die Hab[ilitations]Schrift ist heute vom Verlag an Sie abgesandt worden.
Mit dem Ausdruck der Verehrung und Dankbarkeit
Ihr ergebenster   Fr. Heiler.

123. From FRIEDRICH HEILER[1]

München, Wörthstr. 13/I, 2. Oktober 1918
Hochverehrter Hochwürdigster Herr Erzbischof!
... (repetition of some of the main themes from the letter of the day before, and a short reflection on the possibility of joining the Old Catholic Church which Heiler rejects out of hand.]
Andererseits habe ich in der letzten Zeit ein volles Verständnis für das alles Magisch-Dingliche aus dem Kult verbannende evangelische Persönlichkeitsprinzip erlangt. Die tiefen Eindrücke, die ich während der Sommerferien in evangelischen Pfarrhäusern des Schwabenlandes und in evangeli-

---

[4] Cf. Friedrich Heiler, *Das Wesen des Katholizismus. Sechs Vorträge*, Munich 1920; revised and enlarged as *Der Katholizismus und seine Erscheinung*, Munich 1923.

[1] N. Söderblom's collection of letters, from foreigners, UUB, handwritten letter.

schen Kirchen empfing, haben mir den Blick für die hohen Werte des keuschen, geistig-persönlichen Wortgottesdienstes geöffnet, den ich (allerdings mehr unter massenpädagogischem Gesichtspunkte) in meinem Werke über das Gebet noch kritisiert hatte; die in nicht zu ferner Zeit zu erwartende Neuauflage wird in diesem Punkte (wie auch in anderen) bedeutsame Änderungen bringen. So hat sich auch die letzte Verbindung mit dem Katholizismus gelöst und ich glaube mich *ganz* als evangelischer Christ betrachten zu dürfen. Seit kurzer Zeit habe ich aufgehört am liturgischen Leben der katholischen Kirche teilzunehmen und besuche nun den evangelischen Gottesdienst. Und ich habe erfahren, dass man auch ohne Sakramente, ohne Beichte, Eucharistie und Tabernakel ein ernstes und kräftiges Frömmigkeitsleben pflegen kann, ja dass der rein geistige, aller sinnlichen Stützen entbehrende Gottesumgang, der Glaube, der Gott nur in den Tiefen des persönlichen Innenlebens gegenwärtig weiß, viel höher steht als die am Sakrament sich nährende Frömmigkeit. Der innere religiöse Aufschwung, den ich gerade in dem Augenblick erfuhr, da ich mit dem mystischen Sakramentalismus der katholischen Kirche brach, ist mir ein Zeugnis des Geistes, dafür, dass ich auf der rechten Bahn wandle.

So ist es denn eine Reihe von Motiven, die mich zum Übertritt in die evangelische Kirche drängen. Der lang gehegte Wunsch, als Theologe zu forschen und zu lehren, als Diener Christi und seiner Gemeinde zu predigen und zu wirken, scheint sich nun der Erfüllung zu nähern. Die deutschen Landeskirchen haben jetzt bitteren Mangel an Geistlichen; der Krieg hat fürchterliche Lücken in die Reihen der jungen Theologen gerissen. Und doch sind in dieser schweren Zeit Männer, die mit der ganzen Kraft der Persönlichkeit und der ganzen Liebe ihres Herzens sich für die religiösen und kirchlichen Aufgaben einsetzen, doppelt nötig. Ich würde mir einen Gewissensvorwurf machen, wollte ich jetzt nicht auf die Stimme der Zeit hören und mich der reinen Wissenschaft widmen, da der Herr um Verkünder seines Evangeliums wirbt. »Wehe mir, wenn ich nicht das Evangelium predige!« (1 Kor 9 16).

Gewiß sind die evangelischen Landeskirchen nicht das Ideal der christlichen Kirche, aber sie machen auch gar keinen Anspruch auf Absolutheit und Unfehlbarkeit. Gewiß habe ich, der frühere Katholik und der Religionshistoriker, ein offenes Auge für die Mängel und Schattenseiten der evangelischen Kirchen. Aber der Protestantismus scheint mir das zu bieten, was im Katholizismus unmöglich ist – und ich darf wohl hinzufügen, was in keiner Religionsgemeinschaft der Erde möglich ist, die Verbindung von freier und kritischer Religionsforschung mit lebendiger Frömmigkeit. In der evangelischen Kirche kann man bei der ehrlichsten und wahrhaftigsten wissenschaftlichen Arbeit zugleich Priester im Heiligtum der Religion sein, Diener Jesu Christi, Verkünder seines Evangeliums und Helfer seiner Gemeinde. Das ist es, was ich in der evangelischen Theologie und Kirche zu finden glaube und aus diesem Grunde wünsche ich in ihre Dienste zu treten.

… [On the possible effect of Heiler's plans on his Roman Catholic parents; on the practical problems of joining the Protestant church]

Eine weitere Frage ist, in *welche* deutsche Landeskirche ich übergehen soll. Nun stehe ich *religiös* der »orthodoxen« Theologie näher als der typisch »liberalen«. *Wissenschaftlich* freilich d. h. methodisch stehe ich entschieden auf dem Boden der *kritischen* Theologie. Ich möchte darum nicht eine Orthodoxie mit einer anderen vertauschen. – In all den vielen Fragen, die ich Ihnen ausgesprochen habe, den inneren wie den äußeren, erbitte ich nun, Hochverehrter Herr Erzbischof, Ihren geschätzten Rat, Vielleicht ist es nicht unbescheiden, wenn ich zugleich heute schon um Ihre Vermittlung bei deutschen Theologen und Kirchenmännern Sie bitte. Vielleicht ist es Ihnen möglich mit H[errn] Prof. Deißmann, der demnächst nach Upsala kommt und der mich literarisch u. brieflich kennt, über diese Angelegenheit zu sprechen. Mit der Bitte, meine langen Ausführungen zu entschuldigen und mit dem Ausdruck der größten Dankbarkeit und Hochschätzung bin ich

Ihr ganz ergebener   Friedrich Heiler.

124. To Randall Davidson[1]

Upsala 6th November 1918

Your Grace,

... [Söderblom asks Davidson to comment on the propositions of the Conference of the Neutrals in Uppsala of Dec. 14 and 15, 1917 and to suggest a possible date for a comprehensive ecumenical conference]

The war is drawing to an end rapidly. Amongst our correspondents there has been only one opinion as to the necessity of such a conference when peace is in sight or after peace has been concluded. Referring to the conditions you deemed desirable in your honoured letter of 12 Febr. this year, we are happy to inform Your Grace, that Benedict XV has expressed his sympathy with our action through a letter from Cardinal Gasparri, Secr. of State[2], and that the oecumenical Patriarch of Constantinopel and his Holy Synod (as well as the new Metropolite of Athens) have given their complete adherence to the Conference. Difficulties as to passports made by the Turkish government having been removed, the Patriarch has delegated three distinguished Churchmen ... to give lectures in the University of Upsala, and if possible to stay and act as his representatives at the Conference. We are in relation with the Patriarch of Muscow.[3] The well-known Editor of the Orthodox Encyclopædia, Professor Glubokowsky of Petrograd[4] is here as

---

[1] Lambeth Palace Library, Davidson vol. 498, ff.9r-11v, handwritten letter.

[2] Cf. letter no. 120.

[3] Tichon (Vassily Ivanovich Be[l]lavin) (1865–1925), Patriarch of Moscow 1917–1923, was severely persecuted by the Soviet government but nonetheless tried to find a *modus vivendi.*

[4] Nikolai N. Glubokowsky (1863–1937), professor in St. Petersburg and, after the Russian revolution of 1917, in Belgrad and Sofia. One of the speakers at the conference in Uppsala in 1925.

the guest of the Olaus Petri Foundation, finishing his work on the History of the Russian Theology, which Les Archives Orientales (Uppsala) will publish in English. He will be useful at the Conference as a leading scholar of the Orthodox Faith.

February 1919 has been proposed from England and from one of us (Copenhagen[5]). Before settling definitely the date of the Conference, we ask to be favoured by your advice. Will you allow Rev. Hellerström[6] to cable it to us?

In the Preparatory Committee which must begin to work as soon as possible, we should like to have, besides neutrals, one member of the Anglican Church (or of English Christendom) as the only representative of the belligerent countries. Could Your Grace afford to appoint and send a man on this invitation of ours?

Having witnessed the excellent and wholesome effects of Dr A.J. Carlyle's (Oxford)[7] visit and lectures in our countries, I am convinced that Your Grace would add a new significant service rendered to the holy cause of Christian fellowship – so mightily advanced by You during the war – in appointing a Churchman and theologian to come on our invitation and to be my guest as early as possible in the next year, if he is not able to spend Christmas with us. Such a delegate of Yours to our Scandinavian countries and to the Preparatory Committee for the Oecumenical Conference would have an important and beautiful task just now. –

– »Från uppror och tvedräkt,
bevara oss, Milde Herre Gud«![8] –

[Note at the margin of the page:] These words in our Litany have got a terrible significance for poor old Europe.

In the name of the three brothers in Christiania, Copenhagen and Upsala[9], who have invited the Conference, I am, Dear and revered Archbishop, in the common service of Christ, sincerely yours

Nathan Söderblom

125. From ADOLF DEISSMANN[1]

In weiten christlichen Kreisen aller kriegführenden Länder ersehnt man nach den Schrecken des Kampfes ein Zeitalter gegenseitiger Vergebung und

---

[5] Harald Ostenfeld (1864–1934), bishop of Sjælland (Zealand), Denmark, 1911–1934.

[6] See letter no.110, n.1.

[7] Alexander James Carlyle (1861–1943), church historian.

[8] Beware us from uproar and discord, oh gentle God.

[9] Bishops Jens Tandberg (1852–1922) of Oslo, Harald Ostenfeld of Copenhagen, and Söderblom.

[1] Telegram of Nov. 15, 1918, which Deißmann asked Söderblom to forward to England and America. Söderblom sent it, in an English translation, to Archbishop Davidson on Nov. 19; N. Söderblom's ecumenical collection A 6, UUB, typewritten telegram.

Versöhnung um die furchtbaren Folgeerscheinungen des Krieges gemeinsam zu bekämpfen und dem moralischen Aufstieg der Völker und der Menschheit zu dienen. Das deutsche Volk sieht jedoch, nachdem es sich zu weitgehenden Opfern und Wiedergutmachung bereiterklärt hat, in den ihm auferlegten Waffenstillstandsbedingungen ein Anzeichen dafür, dass ihm ein Friede bevorsteht der nicht Versöhnung sondern Verelendung bedeutet. Millionen der Schwächsten und Unschuldigsten wären nach vierjährigem Hungerkriege aufs neue für unabsehbare Zeit gefährdet und die dadurch entstehende tiefe Bitterkeit würde die Verwirklichung aller Ideale christlicher und menschheitlicher Solidarität für Generationen hindern. Niemals aber ist die seelische Lage bei uns für eine Völkerversöhnung günstiger gewesen als jetzt. Gleichzeitig mit dem Abschluss des Waffenstillstandes hat sich eine mit elementarer Wucht emporstossende Volksbewegung angeschickt politische Grundlagen für unser Vaterland zu schaffen. Ihre auf den sozialen Fortschritt und die Stärkung der brüderlichen Solidarität aller Volksgenossen und aller Völker gerichteten Bestrebungen finden mitarbeitsfreudigen Widerhall auch in den Herzen unzähliger deutscher Christen. Diese verheißungsvolle Lage durch rücksichtslose Geltendmachung des brutalen Machtgedankens zu stören wäre eine unverzeihliche Sünde gegen den durch die Menschheit gehenden neuen Geist der in seinen edelsten Triebkräften dem Evangelium verwandt ist. Dass dieser Geist auch bei unseren Gegnern vorhanden ist haben Kundgebungen ernster christlicher Führer namentlich der angelsächsischen Kirchen bezeugt, allen voran das Manifest des Federal Council der protestantischen Kirchen von Nordamerika vom Mai 1917. Seit Kriegsbeginn in der Arbeit international christlicher Verständigung stehend halte ich es am Kriegsende für meine Pflicht an die mir bekannten christlichen Führer der seither mit uns kriegführenden Länder den Appell zu richten dass sie ihren ganzen Einfluss dahin geltend machen, dass der bevorstehende Weltfriede nicht den Keim neuer Weltkatastrophen enthalte sondern Volk zu Volk alle nur möglichen versöhnenden und aufbauenden Kräfte entbinde. Ich bitte Sie dieses Telegramm dem Erzbischof von Canterbury und dem Nordamerikanischen Federal Council übermitteln zu wollen.

Professor Adolf Deissmann, Universität Berlin

126. From Randall Davidson[1]

Lambeth Palace. S.E.1.   25th November 1918.

My dear Archbishop,

Mr. Hellerstrom has I believe sent to you by telegram a message acknowledging the receipt of your very important letter of November 6th respecting the holding of a Conference at Upsala or elsewhere in connexion with the

---

[1] N. Söderblom's ecumenical collection A 6, UUB, typewritten letter.

promotion of Christian well-being among the Nations in the coming years,. In your letter you write that you and others are strongly of opinion »as to the necessity of such a Conference when Peace is in sight or after Peace has been concluded«. I am sure that the second of these two alternatives which you suggest is the right one. Such Conference, if it took place at all, should be held after Peace has been concluded and not during the discussions and deliberations preceding the conclusion of Peace. A Conference held during these diplomatic and international negotiations would undoubtedly be regarded, however mistakenly, as an attempt to intervene in the negotiations themselves. To this I could not be a party, for I am sure that the position of those who represent Christian Churches and religious influences would be misunderstood were such a Christian Conference held concurrently with the State negotiations. Christian Churches and Communities will be able to speak both more freely and with greater weight after the conclusion of Peace when the process of reconstruction under new conditions is going on. I do not wish at present to undertake definitely that the Church of England will certainly take part in such a Conference even after the conclusion of Peace: that must depend upon the character of the Conference and the knowledge of who are to be represented at it. Consequently I should not think it desirable that the Church of England should take part in the private and preparatory conference or committee to which your letter refers, but I think it probable that we should be ready and even anxious in the subsequent Conference to share in the discussions about the responsibilities which would then be common to Christian communities and Christian leaders and Christian individuals everywhere. I do not think that this differs from what you have yourself suggested. Mr. Hellerstrom told me that there is some possibility that you may yourself be paying a visit to England before long. If so, it would be most important and most agreeable to me that we should have full conversation upon the subject. But in any case this letter will I hope make my own position clear – namely, that Christian conference of any formal kind wherein the belligerents on both sides are represented can only take place advantageously after Peace has been concluded. It may of course happen that after the formal settlement of Peace Preliminaries and acceptance by the nations of the main conditions certain points may be reserved for more detailed and prolonged discussions, and I do not mean to imply that no Christian conference can usefully take place until all these details have been finally decided. Formal acceptance of Peace conditions following upon the conclusion of the Armistice may I hope place the nations in a position on which a conference of representatives belonging to Christian churches can usefully be held. Where it should be held is a different question. I should myself have thought that some place more central that [sic; read: than] Upsala would be better. But this is a matter which can I think easily be arranged, and it need not disturb us at present.

I am
Your faithful brother in our Lord Jesus Christ,
Randall Cantuar

212

127. From RANDALL DAVIDSON[1]

Lambeth Palace. S. E. 1.   25th November 1918.

My dear Archbishop and brother,

I have received your telegram embodying the full message which Professor Adolf Deissmann asks you to convey to me in relation to the approaching Conference about a Peace settlement. It would not be easy to answer such a message by telegram as I find myself under the necessity of explaining my position rather fully. I can do this better in the form of a letter and as Professor Deissmann invites you to be the intermediary I hope that you may be able to communicate to him what I desire to say. Professor Deissmann's statement as to the present situation is not one which I can accept as correct. He speaks of the European situation as though all that is needed, on the part of Christian circles in the belligerent nations, were »mutual forgiveness and conciliation in order to fight in unison against the terrible consequences of the war and to serve the moral improvement of the nations and of mankind«. This form of statement ignores, as it seems to me, both the historic origin of the war and the manner in which Germany has conducted it. I called attention to these essential matters in a long letter which I wrote to Professor Deissmann on September 22, 1915. To that letter he sent no reply except a verbal acknowledgment. We in England did not choose this war. On the contrary every possible endeavour to prevent it was made by our statesmen up to the very latest moment. Upon that subject no fairminded or impartial man can entertain any doubt. We were forced into the war, though unprepared for it, because a grave wrong had been done which cut at the very root of international honour and of faith to plighted word, and ran counter to the principles which must regulate the conduct of Christian Nations. Our object was the vindication of freedom and justice and the ultimate securing of a righteous peace which should make war with all its horrors impossible of recurrence. We have fought without hatred and, so far as possible, without passion, and now that victory crowns the cause for which we fought we desire to be equally free from hatred and passion in the course which we follow as victors. But we cannot forget the terrible crime wrought against humanity and civilisation when this stupendous war with its irreparable agony and cruelty was let loose in Europe. Nor can we possibly ignore the savagery which the German high command has displayed in carrying on the war. The outrages in Belgium in the early months and indeed ever since: the character of the devastation wrought in France, including the inhuman deportation of innocent citizens: the submarine warfare against passenger ships like the Lusitania[2] and the rejoicings which ensued in Germany: the unspeakable cruelties exercised on defenseless prisoners down to the very

---

[1] N. Söderblom's ecumenical collection A 6, UUB, typewritten letter.

[2] Davidson refers to the violation of Belgian neutrality by German troops in August, 1914 and the sinking of the British passenger boat Lusitania (which had been transporting arms from America to Britain) by a German submarine on May 7, 1915.

end, including even the last few weeks: all these things compel the authorities of the allied powers to take security against the repetition of such a crime. The position would be different had there been on the part of the Christian circles in Germany any public protest against these gross wrongs, or any repudiation of their perpetrators.

The conditions of the armistice offer the best preliminary guarantees against a renewal of hostilities and a consequent postponement of peace. There is, I firmly believe, no spirit of mere bitterness or vindictiveness in the hearts of those who are imposing these conditions. The peace we hope to achieve must be a peace, not of hate or revenge, the fruits of which might be further and even more terrible strife. We wish by every means to avert that possibility. But righteousness must be vindicated, even although the vindication involves sternness. And the making good (wiedergutmachung) to which Professor Deissmann refers must be genuine, and, so far as is possible, complete. There is however, as I need hardly say, no wish on the part of the allied nations to crush or destroy the peoples of Germany. Evidence to the contrary is happily abundant. I thankfully repeat to Professor Deissmann, what I wrote to him in September 1915, my firm assurance that, in spite even of the horrors of this world war, we recognise the sacred ties which bind together in ultimate unity the children of Our Father who is in Heaven, the deep and enduring ties of Christian fellowship. That fellowship may be broken or impaired, but it cannot perish, and it is my hope and prayer that when the right and necessary reparation has been made, we may be enabled once more to lay hold of that fellowship and to make it mutually operative anew. It is in proportion as that Christian fellowship is sincerely maintained among the Christian people of all lands that the sorrows of the world can be healed, and true peace and goodwill established unbreakably among men. To that sacred end you are yourself, my dear Archbishop and brother, labouring, and I therein join you with my whole heart. Pray let Professor Deissmann be assured that that is not only my hope and prayer but that it will be the ultimate object of my untiring effort.

[in handwriting:] I remain, with warm respect & regard,
Your faithful brother in Christ
Randall Cantuar

128. To Albert Hellerström[1]

Upsala, 29/11 1918
K[äre] Br[oder]
... Arma Tyskland. Hybris straffar. Tragiskt med dem i Tyskland, som lidit outsägligt av Belgien, Lusitania, men i borgfredens namn tegat. Nu får Tyskland smaka förödmjukelsens bittraste kalk.

---

[1] N. Söderblom's collection of letters, to Swedes and foreigners, UUB, typewritten letter.

Dear Brother,

... Poor Germany. Hubris punishes itself. Tragic for those in Germany who suffered unspeakably because of Belgium, Lusitania[2] but kept silent in the name of cessation of party strife. Now Germany must taste the bitterest chalice of humiliation.

...

129. From ALBERT HELLERSTRÖM[1]

London, den 30 november 1918

Herr Doktor och Ärkebiskop!

Jag hade ett längre, mycket intressant samtal med Canterbury förra fredagen. Det har icke gått någon kurir sedan dess. Det slog mig, hur fullkomligt främmande vi i många fall stå till engelsk uppfattning av händelserna. Canterbury kan nog tas som uttryck för vad de mera sansade engelsmännen i allmänhet tänka. Hans uppfatning av kriget utgår från att tyskarna genom att angripa Belgiem [sic] gjorde sig skyldiga till ett brott, som England fann sig nödsakat att beivra. Tyskarna äro från och med denna handling criminals, och deras senare handlingar ha bestyrkt detta. Han uppräknar i det närslutna brevet till Deissmann åtskilliga förbrytelser. Det tycks inte vara fråga om att icke detta är en allvarlig övertygelse, och det finns ingen möjlighet för dessa engelsmän att se några förmildrande omständigheter för tyskarna. Då England sålunda är rättfärdighetens förkämpe, så bli neutrala, som icke velat ställa sig på Englands sida icke blott politiska fiender under [? förmodligen: utan] i grunden fiender till rättfärdigheten. Att tala om att det kristna folket nu skulle söka arbeta för att få till stånd en försoning är i själva verket okristligt, så länge straff icke blivit utkrävt av förbrytarna. »Professor Deissmann tala[r] om ömsesidig förlåtelse,« sade Canterbury; »det är en orimlighet; kristendomens plikt för tillfället är icke att förlåta utan att kräva rättfärdighet.« »Do you mean that the only [thing] Christianity has to do now, is to impose punishment«. He replied: »Punishment is not exactly the word I would use, but it comes very near.«[2] Först när brottslingarna blivit straffade, kan det bli tal om ett närmande. Varje försök att tala om hovsamhet avvisas som ett försök att hindra rättfärdigheten.

Canterbury avböjde bestämt varje sammanträffande med tyskar innan fred (åtminstone en preliminär och bindande) slutits. Orsakerna har han ju framställt i brevet, fast i mildare form. 1) Konferensen kunde få sken av att inverka eller vilja inverka på de politiska underhandlingarna; 2) omöjligt att träffa samman med brottslingar innan straff blivit utkrävt; 3) oklokt om

---

[2] See letter no. 127, n. 2.

[1] N. Söderblom's ecumenical collection A 10, UUB, typewritten letter.
[2] Handwritten note by Hellerström, citing the journal *Challenge* on the issue.

kristenheten skulle rycka segerns frukter ur händerna på segrarna; kristenheten skulle därigenom förlora i popularitet (ungefär så, fast försiktigare formulerat).

Som synes av brevet vill han icke bestämt binda sig för deltagande även efter kriget; han synes dock vara allvarligt intresserad av att något skall komma till stånd då.

Jag nämnde till Canterbury, att Ärkebiskopen, efter vad jag hoppades, inom en icke alltför avlägsen tid skulle komma över till England. Han förklarade, att han själv skulle vara mycket glad att i så fall överlägga med Ärkebiskopen om en del punkter. Men han framkastade också den förmodan, att ett besök av Ärkebiskopen innan fredsslutet skulle hos många uppfattas som avsett att skaffa Tyskland lindrigare villkor och därför betraktas med misstänksamhet. Många här i landet hålla före, att Ärkebiskopen är progerman. Canterbury sade, att han själv icke hade den uppfattningen, men frågade mig vad jag uppriktigt tänkte om saken. Jag svarade honom, att jag icke funnit något annat än att Ärkebiskopen sökte hävda vad som enligt Ärkebiskopens uppfattning var en opartisk och kristlig synpunkt och att det var oriktigt att stämpla Ärkebiskopen som progerman. – Men med tanke på detta resonnemang är jag dock icke säker på, om det vore vist, om Ärkebiskopens besök här kom före fredsslutet. I många avseenden skulle ett besök efteråt, när den värsta oron i sinnena lagt sig, kunna ha långt större praktiska följder, och Ärkebiskopen kunde få ett mera officiellt mottagande, än vad annars skulle bliva fallet. International Christian Meeting är som jag nämnde [i] förra brevet, mycket intresserat av att Ärkebiskopen skulle komma över så snart som möjligt, och Lord Parmoor har inbjudit Ärkebiskopen, att i så fall bo hos honom. Jag är dock rädd för att, om Ärkebiskopen bodde hos honom, resan skulle kunna misstydas just på det sätt som Canterbury antydde. Misstänksamheten här i landet är stor och just nu kanske större än någonsin. Jag vill därför med anledning, av vad jag nu vet om situationen icke hålla på mitt förslag i förra brevet utan hellre frånråda en resa just nu.

Jag vet icke om Ärkebiskopen fått Canterbury's båda svar utan närslutar dem. Jag har talat med en del personer om förslaget att ha en engelsman med i den förberedande kommittén. Det förefaller mig synnerligen viktigt, då, om konferensen kommer efter fredsslutet, en hel del nya frågor böra tagas upp och dessa böra vara fastslagna i kallelsen (eftersom väl inga nya frågor böra väckas på konferensen). Eftersom Canterbury inte vill skicka någon, borde man kunna få någon annan av auktoritet och god kännedom om ställningen här och helst tillhörande the Anglican Church att resa. Jag tänkte på William Temple, men han säger att han icke kan finna tid för det. Möjligen Deanen av Worcester eller Cannon [sic] Newsom. Hoppas vi skall kunna få fatt i någon lämplig.

Metropoliten av Athen är i England och vi ämna försöka att få fatt i honom för att begagna hans inflytande, då han ju är välvillig mot konferensen.

– Vi skall fira Karl XII i eftermiddag.

Med vördsam tillgivenhet

A. O. T. Hellerström

Dear Doctor and Archbishop,

I had an extensive, very interesting conversation with Canterbury last Friday. No courier has left since then. It struck me how completely alien is for us in many instances the English outlook on events. Canterbury can certainly be taken as an example of what more reasonable Englishmen in general think. His view of the war basically is that the Germans by attacking Belgium became guilty of a crime which England felt compelled to proceed against. From that feat on, the Germans have been criminals, and their later actions confirmed this. He enumerates several offenses in the enclosed letter to Deißmann. It seems to be beyond doubt that this is a serious conviction, and there is no way for these Englishmen to envisage extenuating circumstances for the Germans. Since England thus is the champion of righteousness, neutrals who did not want to side with it are not only political enemies but at bottom enemies of righteousness. Talking about Christian people now having to engage in achieving reconciliation is actually unchristian as long as punishment has not been demanded by the criminals. »Professor Deißmann talks of mutual forgiveness,« said Canterbury; »that is preposterous; Christianity's duty at this moment is not to forgive but to demand righteousness.« »Do you mean that the only [thing] Christianity has to do now is to impose punishment?« He replied: »Punishment is not exactly the word I would use, but it comes very near.« Only when the criminals have been punished can there be talk of rapprochement. Every attempt to speak about moderation is rebuked as an attempt to prevent righteousness.

Canterbury resolutely refused any meeting with Germans before peace (at least a preliminary and binding one) has been established. He has listed the reasons in his letter, even though in a milder form. 1) The conference could appear to influence or to intend to influence the political negotiations; 2) impossible to meet with criminals before punishment has been demanded; 3) unwise if Christianity should wrest the fruits of victory from the hands of the victors; Christianity would thereby lose popularity (something like this, though more carefully phrased).

It seems from the letter as though he does not want to commit himself to participation even after the war; he does seem, however, to be seriously interested in making something happen by then.

I mentioned to Canterbury that the Archbishop[3], as I was hoping, would come over to England in the not too distant future. He declared that in this case he would be very glad to deliberate a number of issues with the Archbishop. But he also put forward the surmise that a visit by the Archbishop before the conclusion of peace would be understood by many as intended to obtain more lenient terms for the Germans, and would therefore be viewed with suspicion. Many in this country are of the opinion that the Archbishop is pro-German. Canterbury said that he himself was not of this opinion, but asked me how I frankly felt about the matter. I replied that I was not aware of anything other than that the Archbishop was trying to advocate what he considered to be an impartial and Christian point of view and that it was incorrect to brand the Archbishop as pro-German. – However, in view of this reasoning, I am really not sure as to whether it would be wise if the Archbishop's visit here took place before the conclusion of peace. In many respects, a visit afterwards, when the worst agitation of minds has been relieved, could produce much more significant practical results, and the Archbishop could receive a more official

---

[3] This is the Swedish way of reverently addressing a person; in plain English, it would be »you«.

welcome than would otherwise be the case. International Christian Meeting is, as I mentioned in my previous letter, very much interested in the Archbishop's coming over as soon as possible, and Lord Parmoor has invited the Archbishop to lodge in his home then.[4] I am afraid though that if the Archbishop did lodge with him, the journey could be misinterpreted in exactly the way Canterbury intimated. Suspicion in this country is running high, right now perhaps higher than ever. Therefore, on the basis of what I now know about the situation, I would not uphold my suggestion in my previous letter but rather advise against a journey at this moment.

I do not know if the Archbishop has received both Canterbury's replies,[5] so I am enclosing them. I spoke to quite a few people about the suggestion of having an Englishman take part in the preparatory committee. This seems to me to be particularly important since, if the conference takes place after the conclusion of peace, a host of new problems will have to be taken up, and they will have to be defined in the call (as no new problems should be raised at the conference). Since Canterbury does not want to send someone, one should be able to induce someone else with authority and good knowledge of the state of affairs here to make the trip, preferably someone belonging to the Anglican church. I had thought of William Temple,[6] but he told me he could not find time for it. Perhaps the Dean of Worcester or Canon Newsom.[7] Let us hope that we shall be able to find someone suitable.

The Patriarch of Athens[8] is in England, and we aim to get hold of him in order to make use of his influence, because he is benevolent towards the conference.

– We shall celebrate Karl XII this afternoon.[9]

Respectfully yours

A. O. T. Hellerström

130. To RANDALL DAVIDSON[1]

Upsala 10th Dec 1918

My dear and most Reverend Lord Archbishop,

As the world tragedy is drawing to an end, which will mean, as we hope and ardently pray, a juster and safer and better settlement of international

---

[4] The British Council for the Promotion of an International Christian Meeting was initiated by Quakers in July 1917. Söderblom had been in contact with the group behind it since 1914. Charles Alfred Cripps, 1st Baron of Parmoor (1852–1941), British politician, became one of its leading figures. Cf. Bengt Sundkler, op.cit., 189.

[5] Letters no. 126 and 127.

[6] William Temple (1881–1944), Canon of Westminster Abbey 1917–1918; Bishop of Manchester 1921–1929, Archbishop of York 1929–1942, and of Canterbury 1942–1944.

[7] George Ernest Newsom (1871–1934), Newcastle; later professor at Oxford.

[8] Meletios Metaxakis (1871–1935), Metropolitan of Athens 1918–1920; became Ecumenical Patriarch 1922–1923 under dubious circumstances; Patriarch of Alexandria 1926.

[9] Karl XII. (1682–1718), King 1697–1718, most famous and most controversial of Sweden's kings. He extended the Swedish empire in several wars until he was defeated in the battle of Poltava in 1709. He was killed in the battle of the fortress of Fredrikshald in Norway on November 30, 1718, so this was the 200th anniversary of his death.

[1] N. Söderblom's ecumenical collection B 2, UUB, handwritten draft. This letter is not to be found among Archbishop Davidson's papers at the Lambeth Palace Library; it probably was never sent to him.

affairs into a commonwealth of nations as well as profound renewal of society after christian principles, it may be of some use to state to your Lordship in a few words I [Roman numeral] what may be called the national swedish point of view, and II my view as a christian on the situation.

I   Since more than 200 years Russia used to be the only serious danger to our national independance. It took nearly the half of our area, Finland (not to speak of other parts where swedish civilization was not introduced in the same way as in Finland, which has an entirely swedish civilization and about 400,000 Swedes, but no indigenous Russians). Russia exercised in later years the most comprehensive espionage in Sweden, built strategic railways against Sweden etc.

The fall of Russia and its future control by the western Powers, until the poor, great and pious Russian people can get a lawful order and a liberal government of its own, means a turning point in Swedish history, a wonderful deliverance from an imminent danger and an enormous reason for gratitude –, in the hope that bolshevism may be overcome.

II   Far more important is to me the opinion I have as a member of Christendom.

The initial and atrocious crime with Belgium loaded this war from the beginning with a pathetic moral sense. The fact confessed by Bethmann-Hollweg: »Heute werden wir ein grosses Unrecht gegen das Völkerrecht begehen« and other crimes became necessarily fatal to the German Empire. [Addition at the margin of the page: I sympathize with *those* Germans, who said in their sermons that after such criminal arrogance God must severely rebuke the nation in order to save it. Superbia]

But to treat Germany and all Germans therefore in a way analogous *mutatis mutandis* to the way in which Christendom has treated the Jews, because some of their leading men put our Saviour to death – *sit venia comparationi*[2] – would at the length [for Swedish *i längden*, i.e., in the long run] be as disastrous as the treatment of the Jews.

Of course I know, that you in no wise desire anything like that. To put an end to the dreadful starvation, which succeeded to organized hunger in Germany and to unorganized hunger in Austria, is not only a human duty but also politically wise, since starvation feeds bolshevism, and it cannot imply any danger, since famine and arms have won the most complete victory. I see, that important steps have already been taken by the Allies in that direction, and I understand, that there is wonderful readiness to help from english and american side. If the French have partly another disposition, it is easy to comprehend after their terrible sufferings.

– Looking at all the numerous wars of the last tenths [sic; read: tens] of years one is tempted to become pessimistic. But you have given a strong and strengthening example to all divisions of the Church and to all Churchmen in advocating, from a Christian point of view, the Commonwealth of Na-

---

[2] Latin for: the comparison may be excused.

tions, where each nation has to sacrifice something of its full independence for the universal security. May God grant to you, and to the Church power to contribute mightily to that high aim!

Believe me, my dear and most revered Archbishop, sincerely and brotherly yours in our Lord Jesus Christ

Nathan Söderblom

131. To Randall Davidson[1]

My dear Archbishop!

Your weighty and welcome letter on the Oecumenical Conference is in my hands. My gratitude implies also that of my colleagues, who will get copies of that auspicious document. We were already quite unanimous that the Conference must wait until peace has been concluded.

Of course the Church of Christ ought to have such a moral authority and derive from faithfulness to Christ such a religious strenght, notwithstanding cruel divisions of sin and hatred, that its Catholic Universalism could be embodied in a praying, interceding and truthseeking gathering during the weeks of political negotiations. That will be possible, we hope, for the Church of the future. Seeing how God has used you for promoting real and wellfounded unity and how mightily He is using you for that purpose now, I dare hope, that He will grant to you and to all of us to see some form of working Unity of the evangelical and the orthodox parts of the Church – I mean of the Holy, Catholic Church, but I think we shall have to wait longer for its Roman part –, before you shut your eyes.

Now the Conference can gather a really representativ expression of Christendom only after peace. – May the Conference be able to utilize fully the experiences painfully won during the war and create a sharply defined, inspiring and unifying religious action of the Church against war, for the Commonwealth of Nations and for the social and ethical renewal of Society!

Of course, there will be difficulties, not, as far as order can be restored, as it seems from the Orthodox Christendom. And why should not Anglo Saxon Christendom take a share corresponding to its leading position in the world? I understand, that our French friends will take another attitude now than during the German invasion. Hungary and the slavic populations will scarcely make any difficulties. But the parts of Christendom in Germany that have always refused will certainly not come now. And although we know almost nothing about Church things in Germany after the revolution, it seems more than likely that some of those, who promised to come or to send men to the Conference (in most cases under strict guarantees

---

[1] Lambeth Palace Library, Davidson vol. 498 ff. 29r-32r, handwritten letter.

against the possibility of personal and political private talk and intercourse), will take the same attitude to it now as the French protestants used
to have. But we shall, no doubt, have excellent representatives of the Christianity, that has in Germany a promising future and a strong vitality.

[Here follows a paragraph on the question of location which ends: As
you say, this is a point of quite secondary importance.]

We regret very much, that you do not see your way for sending a man,
with whom we might study all the questions about the program, those to be
invited etc. It is a sensible [probably: sensitive] loss. –

Rev. Hellerström may have had two reasons for thinking, that I could
come to London soon. 1:o Installations and visitations ought to be made in
our parishes in London and Paris already in 1915, and they have been announced and postponed every year ever since.

Being personally, after my seven years' stay in Paris as aumonier [cha-
plain] and as a student at la Sorbonne, one of the champions of the higher
French culture in our country, and considering it (ever since I went to
America as a student, and especially after it was possible to have the bishop
of Kalmar[2] – my sainted [late] friend who ought to occupy this see instead
of myself – sent officially to you and to the Lambeth Conference in 1908)
as a chief and beautiful task of my short lifetime to revive old and holy traditions in strengthening our contact with English Church life, I regarded it
as a great privilege and as an introduction to my new responsability to be
conducted as soon as possible by pastoral duties to London and France
(where I had gone, after my election, to pray for the Unity of Christ's
Church in April 1914 at the High Altar in the Cathedral of Sens, where my
first predecessor as an archbishop of Upsala had been consecrated 750
years earlier[3]).

2:o I understand, that I am most kindly invited to England from highly
appreciated quarters.

Nevertheless, it will not be possible to me for several urgent reasons to
undertake such a voyage before spring, when peace has been concluded.
Most important matters are to be treated here during the next months, e.g.
the relation between Church and State.

That the new world to come requires a new efficiency of the Gospel is felt
also in our corner of the world. The Society for christianized organisation
of Society (on socialistic principles), the free and fraternal unions between
priests and modern idealistic thinkers and popular leaders, our two new
brotherhoods, Sigtunastiftelsen,[4] close cooperation in due matters with

---

[2] Henry Tottie (1856–1913).

[3] Archbishop Stefan (date of birth unknown, deceased ca. 1185), a Cistercian monk who
had originally come from England, consecrated in 1164.

[4] The »new brotherhoods« are Stiftelse for Sverige och kristen tro (Foundation for Sweden
and Christian Faith), founded in 1916, and the more important and far more successful Sigtu-
nastiftelse, founded by Manfred Björkquist (1884–1985), N. Söderblom and Bishops J.A. Eklund and Einar Billing in 1917 on the premises of a former Dominican monastery in Sigtuna,
near Uppsala. Its background is the reform-minded Young Church Movement (with close con-

Nonconformists, the increase of gifts for missions etc. ... [on the amounts donated for various purposes]

But on the other hand such great tasks imposed by the new conditions of the world make us long still more than before for personal intercourse with and experienced counsels from responsable men from other parts of Christendom. We know that our prayers and Our Lords superhuman love and might will make the impossible – real: a united Christendom, already realized by Gods true people in all lands.

I shall take the liberty of writing in a few days on another matter, that ought to be put before your eyes,[5] and I am, with hopeful prayers and wishes for the New Year and for your personal strength and welfare as well as for the Conference,

Your true servant and brother in Christ's service
Nathan Söderblom

132. To Gottfrid Billing[1]

Upsala den 12 dec 1918

Högt vördade Broder!
Från skilda håll komma önskningar om biskopskonferens. Tiderna äro otrygga. Efter Första Kammarens nygestaltning uppkomma kraven på skilsmässa mellan stat och kyrka med förnyad kraft. Enligt min tanke bör man icke genom sådana förberedelser, som påyrkas, giva på hand, att skilsmässa skall ske. Men nog är det lönt att biskoparna överlägga om saken.

Skulle någon dag i slutet av januari passa Dig till biskopskonferens?

...

Din vördnadsfullt tillgivne
Nathan Söderblom

Uppsala, Dec. 12, 1918

Highly esteemed Brother,
From different quarters the desire has been voiced to have a bishops' conference. The times are insecure. After the reform of the First Chamber [of the Diet][2], de-

---

nections to the World's Student Christian Federation, founded in Vadstena in 1895, whose first president was the American John Mott). Its guiding principles were the idea of folk church (Christianizing the newly industrialized Swedish society) and the interpretation of the Bible on the basis of modern exegesis along Söderblom's lines. Sigtuna with its *folkhögskola* (people's high school) is even today an important meeting place for church-sponsored conferences on religious, social, political, and cultural issues, with participants from different ideological backgrounds.

[5] Söderblom probably refers here to the draft printed in the present edition as no.130 which in the end was never mailed.

[1] Collection Billing. G., University Library Lund, handwritten letter.

[2] General and equal suffrage was introduced in Sweden in principle in 1918 (definitively in 1919 and 1921), after long debates and not least under the influence of the news of the German

mands for separation of state and church have been coming up with renewed force[3]. In my view, one should not, by means of such preparations as are being urged, make it appear as if that separation will happen. But the matter is certainly worth deliberating for the bishops. Would some day at the end of January be suitable for you for a bishops' conference?

... [On the person of a candidate for ordination]
Respectfully yours,
Nathan Söderblom

133. From GOTTFRID BILLING[1]

Käre Broder
Hjärtligt tack för ditt bref af d. 12de. För egen del kan jag ej förstå, att frågan om eventuel skilsmässa mellan kyrka och stat står på dagordningen, och jag är alls icke ens om, att den blir aktuel genom väntad ny sammansättning af 1a kammaren. Därför är jag mest böjd för att anse ärendets diskussion å en biskopskonferens vara en för tidigt väckt fråga. Jag har verkligen betänklighet mot det väckta förslaget; därför att en sådan diskussion efter all erfarenhet ej skulle kunna förbli en hemlighet men notis om den skulle kunna vara ägnat till väcka björnen på ett och annat håll.

Af hvad jag sagt framgår, att jag anser önskvärdt vara, att ej någon konferens rörande detta ärende komme att hållas. Sammankallas sådan vill jag ej utan laga hinder hålla mig undan. Och i så fall kan slutet af Januari ej vara oläggligare än någon annan tid. Blott beder jag att den då komme att hållas annan dag än tisdag, onsdag, thorsdag.

Lund 15/12 1918

Din tillgifne
Gottfrid Billing

Dear Brother,
Many thanks for your letter of the 12th. As far as I am concerned, I do not see why the question of a possible separation between church and state should be part of the agenda, and I do not at all agree that it will come to the fore because of the expected new composition of the First Chamber. That is why I am most inclined to consider a discussion of the matter on a bishops' conference to be a question raised prematurely. I actually do have misgivings about the suggestion you made, because such a discussion according to all experience could not remain a secret, but news about it would be likely to wake sleeping dogs in one quarter or another.

It is obvious from what I said that I deem it desirable that no conference be held on this matter. If one is summoned, I shall not stay away without a valid excuse. In

revolution of Nov. 9, 1918. The First chamber thereby lost its aristocratic and plutocratic character. Cf. Sten Carlsson/Jerker Rosén, *Svensk historia*, vol. II, Stockholm 1961, 642 f.646.

[3] It did not actually happen until the year 2000.

[1] N. Söderblom's collection of letters, from Swedes, UUB, handwritten letter.

that case the end of January would not be less suitable than any other time. I would only ask you that it then be held on a day other than Tuesday, Wednesday, Thursday.

Lund, Dec. 15, 1918

Sincerely yours
Gottfrid Billing

134. To Albert Hellerström[1]

Upsala 20 Jan 1919

K[äre] Br[oder]

Ännu har jag ej tackat Dig för upplysande brevet av 30 XI. Jag förstår, att konferensen måste avvakta freden. Karl Fries råkar Dig i London. Jag hoppas, att även Du blir med om World Alliance's möte. Där bör, icke minst genom John Mott, bli klart, när och hur konferensen kan hållas, samt i sin mån varest. London skulle betyda uteslutande a priori av alla kristna från Centralmakterna. Återstår ett neutralt land. Vi hålla på Upsala (el. Christiania) även i följd av vikten att stärka de kyrkliga förbindelserna mellan Skandinavien och England.

De tre huvudfrågorna bör väl:

1:o Rel[igiöst] sedliga förutsättningar för folkens förbund, gemensam kristen förkunnelse därom, kristen lära om institutionellt broderskap och intern[ationell] rättsordning.

2:o Kristna principer i den sociala nydaningen.

3:o Vittnesbörd om enheten kring Korset. Och om möjligt förberedelse för en allmänkyrklig = »katolsk« representation med patriarken i Konstantinopel och Canterbury ss. alternerande ordf. och v[ice] ordf. och ett antal medlemmar. Ngt i Canon Mastermans anda.

...

Ungern mister väl Siebenbürgen tyvärr till det okunnigaste och oredligaste folket i Europa. Väl vore om Rumänien måste lemna garantier för religionsfrihet åt protestanterna.

Tyskland är inne på smala vägen som drager till livet. Nu kommer där religiös väckelse i nödens djup – nya underbara löner. Gud har sina vägar.

Tillgivne
Nathan S-m

Till konferensen kunna endast repr[esentanter] från det nya rel[igiösa] Tyskland komma, som grämt sig under kriget åt mycket men nu talar ut.

Upsala, January 20, 1919

Dear Brother,

As yet I have not thanked you for your informative letter of Nov. 30. I understand that the conference must await the peace. Karl Fries[2] will meet you in London. I

---

[1] N. Söderblom's ecumenical collection B 3, UUB, handwritten letter.
[2] Karl Fries (1861–1943), secretary of the Swedish committee of the World Alliance.

hope that you too will attend World Alliance's meeting. There it shall become clear, not least through John Mott[3], when and how the conference can be held, as well as where, to some extent. London would mean excluding a priori all Christians from the Central Powers. Remaining: a neutral country. We stick to Uppsala (or Oslo), not least with respect to its relative importance for reinforcing the connections between Scandinavia and England.

The three main areas of concern should certainly be:

1. Religious and moral requirements for the League of Nations, common Christian preaching on this subject, Christian doctrine on institutional brotherhood and international order of justice.

2. Christian principles in social reconstruction

3. Witness on unity round the Cross. And on a possible preparation for a universal = »catholic« representation of the church with the Patriarch in Constantinople and Canterbury as alternating chairmen and vice chairmen as well as on a number of members. Something in Canon Masterman's[4] spirit.

... [on further organizational details and on Söderblom's planned inspection of Hellerström's Swedish congregation in London]

Unfortunately, Hungary is likely to lose Siebenbürgen to the most ignorant and dishonest nation in Europe. It would be good if Romania had to furnish a guarantee for Protestants' religious freedom.

Germany now is on the narrow road which leads to life.[5] A religious awakening is now under way in the depths of misery – new, wondrous rewards. God has his ways.

Sincerely,

Nathan S-m

... Only repr[esentatives] from the new rel[igious] Germany will be able to come to the conference who were grieved about many things during the war but who now speak up.

135. To Albert Hellerström[1]

Upsala 25 I 1919

K[äre] Br[oder]

Ofrivilligt vållar jag nu Dig, mig och, vad värre är, vår gemensamma sak konferensen, extra obehag. Hjärne berättar, att Saturday Review nyligen attackerat min neutralitet, anförande min son och ngt yttrande om Lusitania.

Eventuellt efter samråd med Wrangel är det angeläget att Du avgör, om ändå icke till Saturday Review kunde sändas ett beriktigande av denna galenskap.

---

[3] John Mott (1865–1955), president of the YMCA and one of the key ecumenical figures in his time.

[4] John Howard Bertram Masterman (1867–1933), bishop of Plymouth 1922–1933. Member of the Church of England Peace League.

[5] Matth. 7:14.

[1] N. Söderblom's ecumenical collection B 3, UUB, handwritten letter.

För tids vinnande skulle då Du tillsända S.R. ett genmäle på min begäran. T. ex. The Archbishop of Upsala, who has heard that S.R. has questioned his neutrality in referring to his son having served in Germany and to some utterance about Lusitania requests me to give the necessary informations:

I. Vad angår Lusitania, så kan icke något annat yttrande avses, än det som fälldes i ett tal våren 1915 och där Titanic and Lusitania sammanställdes i följande ord om vilka läsaren själv må döma och se, att de utgöra ett skarpt klander: Stockholmtidningen återges ordagrannt.

(Jag vore tacksam återfå urklippet i och för kommande behov). [Tillägg i mindre skrift: Detta rykte om mitt bristande klander av Lusitania måste komma från någon illvillig skribent i någon tidning 1915.]

II It is well known that one of the seven sons of the Archbishop (whose younger brother entered the American army as a volunteer during the war and serves there as a captain of infantry) belongs to the numerous persons in neutral countries, who have considered the war as an opportunity of studying their business, in this case artillery. It is also well known, that the Archbishop was unwilling to let the young artillerist go and kept him waiting two years, until his military desire became too strong. Answering a question in the most pacifistic paper in Sweden, »Antikrigsordet«, the Archbishop published the following declaration.

III It is symptomatic, that the Archbishop har klandrats mer än en gång i Tyskland under kriget för sympatier med Belgien, för sitt fördömande av Lusitania, etc. och »för att han, som levt så länge i Frankrike, icke kan fatta tyska synpunkter.« [Tillägg på arkets marginal: Hur har legenden om Lusitania uppkommit? Samma mitt skarpa fördömande i detta tal har inhöstat åt mig obehag och klander från tyskt och svenskt tyskvänligt håll.]

Det kunde hänvisas till min broschyr redan år1914 i nov. »De två gudarne«, mot »den tyske guden«, för Bärgspredikans Gud. Och min botdagspredikan 1915 mot »Neutralas fariseism«, tryckt bl. a. i The Constructive Quarterly.

Däremot torde det kanske ej böra framdragas [tillägg bland linjerna: gör som Du tycker], att *min älste son, på väg till svensk konsulattjänst, nekades tyskt pass ett halft år på grund av »ententesympatier«.* [Tillägg i mindre skrift: Det kan gärna med, om Du tycker, apropos min son löjtnanten.]

Ja, avgör vad som bör göras. När denna visa, som härrör från någon ovilja mot mig från något svenskt håll, nu blivit så högljudd, torde det vara bäst att saken verkligen tages upp.

Min pojke satte mig i en smärtsam svårighet. Vad han ansåg vara en unik framtidsmöjlighet för ett äventyrsträngande på möda och farlighet insatt militärsinne, var för mig ännu en oerhörd svårighet i min förmedlande ställning. Pliktkollision, som kostat svår inre strid.

I nödfall må konferensplanen frikopplas från mitt deltagande, om det gagnar saken.

Jag kunde åberopa vad jag arbetat för franska familjers kommunikation med sina fångna i Tyskland, för ryska och polska krigsfångar.

Allt detta nämner jag endast för att Du må ur materialet ta det lämpliga.
Ja, lev nu väl! Måtte Gud välsigna mötet i London till enhetens främjande! Hälsa Mott, Ammundsen m. fl.
Din tillgivne
N Söderblom
Jag vågar mena, att efter reformationen ingen svensk kyrkoman gjort så mycket som jag för närmande till Church of England.

Upsala, Jan. 25, 1919

Dear Brother,

Now I am involuntarily causing you annoyance to you, to myself, and what is worse, to our common cause, the conference. Hjärne[2] tells me that Saturday Review recently attacked my neutrality, citing my son[3] and some utterance about Lusitania.

Possibly after consulting with Wrangel[4], it might be important that you decide if a correction of this nonsense could be sent to Saturday Review after all.

In that case, for the sake of saving time you should send a rejoinder to S. R. at my demand. For instance: [The following sentence was written in English by Söderblom himself.] The Archbishop of Upsala, who has heard that S. R. has questioned his neutrality in referring to his son having served in Germany and to some utterance about Lusitania, requests me to give the necessary informations:

I As for Lusitania, no other remark can be brought to bear than the one uttered in a speech in the spring of 1915, comparing Titanic and Lusitania in the following words, which the reader may judge for himself and see that they amount to a sharp condemnation: Stockholmstidningen reproduced literally:

(I would be grateful for your returning this clipping for future use[5]). [Addition in smaller handwriting: That rumor on my failure to condemn the Lusitania affair must originate from some malevolent penman in some newspaper of 1915.]

[Paragraphs II and partly III once again in Söderblom's own English]

II It is well known that one of the seven sons of the Archbishop (whose younger brother entered the American army as a volunteer during the war and serves there as a captain of infantry) belongs to the numerous persons in neutral countries, who have considered the war as an opportunity of studying their business, in this case artillery. It is also well known, that the Archbishop was unwilling to let the young artillerist go and kept him waiting two years, until his military desire became too

---

[2] Cf. letter no. 3, n. 2.
[3] The article is: »Neutrals at the Peace Conference,« in: *Saturday Review* 126/1918, 1124f (Dec. 7, 1918). It speaks among other countries of Sweden and of its »Activists [as opposed to the allegedly anti-German majority of the population], who were mad for war – on the German side!« and then states: »The Archbishop of Upsala defended the sinking of the Lusitania, and sent his son to serve in the Kaiser's Army.« Both assertions are false (cf. the text above). Söderblom's son Sven did join the 4th Prussian artillery regiment as an officer cadet in 1917 at the age of 19 and later took part in the war as a lieutenant – but was by no means »sent« by his father! Cf. Staffan Runestam, »Nathan Söderblom, ekumeniken och Europa,« *STK* 78/2002 (171–186), 175. Sven's motivation probably was provided by Russian advances in the Bukovina in 1916; Sweden had feared Russian aggession because of its policies in Finland, cf. letter no. 60, n. 8.
[4] Cf. letter no. 110, n. 5.
[5] Hellerström seems to have fulfilled this request, but the clipping referred to is missing in Söderblom's collection of letters.

227

strong. Answering a question in the most pacifistic paper in Sweden, *Antikrigsordet* [literally: The Anti-War Word], the Archbishop published the following declaration.

III It is symptomatic, that the Archbishop has been reprimanded in Germany more than once during the war for his sympathy with Belgium, for his condemnation of Lusitania, etc., as well as »for the fact that he who lived in France for so long, cannot comprehend German points of view.« [Addition in Swedish on the margin: How has the legend concerning Lusitania come up? It is just this sharp condemnation in that speech which made me reap annoyance and reprimand from German and pro-German Swedish sources.]

One could point to my brochure [written] already in November 1914 »De två gudarne« (The Two Gods)[6], against »the German God«, in favor of the God of the Sermon on the Mount. And to my sermon on the Day of Penance in 1915 against »The Phariseism of Neutrals«, printed in, among others, *The Constructive Quarterly.*[7]

On the other hand, one should probably not dig up [addition between the lines: do as you see fit] the fact that *my eldest son on his way to Swedish consular service was denied a German passport for half a year because of »sympathies for the Entente«.* [Addition in smaller writing: It may well be included if you think it should, in view of my son the lieutenant.]

Well, decide what should be done. Since this tune which originates from some animosity against me in some Swedish quarters has now become so loud, it would be best really to take up this matter.

My boy put me into a painfully difficult situation. What he viewed as a unique chance for the future of a military mind longing for adventure, intent on toil and danger, was for me another tremendous difficulty in my mediator's function. A conflict of duties craving severe inner struggle.

If necessary, the plan for the conference may have to be disentangled from my participation, if that benefits the cause.

I could refer to my work for the communication of French families with their prisoners in Germany, for Russian and Polish prisoners of war.

All of that has been mentioned only for you to select from the material what is suitable.

All right, farewell now! May God bless the meeting in London for the sake of furthering unity! Regards to Mott, Ammundsen, and others.[8]

Sincerely yours,

N Söderblom

I daresay that since the Reformation, no Swedish churchman has done as much as I have for a rapprochement to the Church of England.

---

[6] In: *Vår lösen* 5/1914, 252–255; enlarged in: N. Söderblom, *När stunderna växla och skrida* 3, Stockholm 1915, 118–130 ([2]1921, 124–136). It is not really a brochure but rather an article in a periodical.

[7] »Neutral egenrättfärdighet. Botdagspredikan,« in: *Kristendom och vår tid* 11/1916, 116–122 (offprint Lund 1916); English version: »Our Spiritual Peril as Neutrals,« in: *The Constructive Quarterly* 5/1917, 91–96.

[8] John Mott: cf. letter no. 134, n. 3; Valdemar Ammundsen (1875–1936), Bishop of Haderslev, Denmark.

136. From Albert Hellerström[1]

London den 11 februari 1919

Herr Doktor och Ärkebiskop!

... Dr Fries har jag träffat och rätt utförligt resonnerat med. Han synes mycket optimistisk på grund av de erfarenheter han gjort under resan. Alltför optimistisk, tror jag. Men han har ju också närmast kommit i beröring med folk av en försonlig stämning och inte med den stora genomsnittspubliken. För den är säkerligen för närvarande Lloyd George's valprogram den högsta politiska visheten. Arbetarna äro visserligen till en viss utsträckning konciliatoriska, men å ena siden sakna de stark organisation och å andra sidan hörs somliga av deras ledare mera än de betyda.

...

Greve Wrangel var hemma i går från fredskonferensen och jag kunde därför rådgöra med honom ang. Saturday Review's artikel. (Jag fick Ärkebiskopens brev därom i går.) Han ansåg bäst att för tillfället icke alls bry sig om saken, helst som Saturday Review inte är av synnerligen stor betydelse. Jag håller med honom däri, då i en tidningspolemik endast skulle röra upp och göra artikeln bekant i större kretsar. Det är inte alls säkert att tidningen skulle ta in något beriktigande, om jag skrev det. Och toge de in det kan [man] vara säker på att de gör det på ett sådant sätt att det vrids till deras förmån. Faktum att Ärkebiskopens son tog del i kriget kan man ju inte komma ifrån, och jag tror att det är för närvarande tämligen lönlöst att söka ge engelsmännen förklaringar om huru det tillgått. Skulle Ärkebiskopen dock anse att någon dementi bör göras ansåg Greve Wrangel att enda möjligheten skulle vara ett direkt meddelande från Ärkebiskopen till The Editor of Saturday Review, 10, King Street, Covent Garden, London, W.C.2.

...

Med vördsam tillgivenhet
A.O.T. Hellerström

London, Febr. 11, 1919

Dear Doctor and Archbishop,

...

I did meet Dr Fries and had quite an extensive discussion with him. He seems to be very optimistic because of the experiences he has had during his journey. Too optimistic, I believe. But of course, his closest contact was with folks of a conciliatory mood, not with the average public at large. For these people, Lloyd George's election platform certainly is the peak of political wisdom at the moment.[2] Industrial

---

[1] N. Söderblom's ecumenical collection A 10, UUB, typewritten letter.

[2] David Lloyd George (1863-1945), Liberal British prime minister 1916-1922. His election platform of 1918 promised sweeping reforms in housing, health, education, and transport, trying to avert social turbulence on account of the difficulties of gearing the economy back to peacetime conditions, of accommodating 4 million returning troops on the labor market, etc. As it turned out, however, his Tory coalition partners proved uncooperative, so he finally had

workers are surely conciliatory up to a point, but on the one hand they lack a strong organization, and on the other hand some of their leaders are more loud than important.

... [On a foolish article in a Swedish church paper concerning Söderblom, which had been sent to Archbishop Davidson and whose potentially detrimental effects Hellerström had been able to defuse]

Count Wrangel was back from the peace conference yesterday, so I was able to consult with him regarding *Saturday Review*'s article. (I received the Archbishop's letter on the subject yesterday.) He deemed it best not to worry about it at all at this point, particularly as *Saturday Review* is not of any great significance. I agree with him on that since a newspaper polemic would only stir up trouble and make the article more widely known. It is not at all sure that the paper would take up a correction if I wrote it. And if they did take it up, [one] could be sure that they would do it in such a way that it would be twisted to their advantage. The fact that the Archbishop's son took part in the war cannot be undone, and I think that at present it is quite useless to try to give explanations to the English as to how that came about. In case the Archbishop still thinks that some sort of denial must be given, Count Wrangel was of the opinion that the only way would be a direct letter by the Archbishop to The Editor of *Saturday Review*, 10, King Street, Covent Garden, London, W.C.2.

...

Respectfully yours,
A.O.T. Hellerström

137. From Édouard Gruner[1]

Paris, le 10 Avril 1919

Messieurs et honorés frères,

Vous avez bien voulu nous communiquer votre désir de convoquer, pour la date la plus proche possible, une conférence écclésiastique internationale pour manifester l'unité spirituelle de l'Eglise chrétienne, et vous nous demandez notre opinion sur l'opportunité de cette convocation. ...

Nous vous dirons, avec une franchise respectueuse et fraternelle, comment nous l'envisageons pour notre compte.

Au-dessus de tout, nous mettons l'honneur du Christ et l'intérêt de l'Evangile. Nous sentons avec un serrement de coeur combien est grande, dans les évènements actuels, la responsabilité des chrétiens qui n'ont pas su faire rayonner suffisament l'Evangile pour en pénétrer la société moderne, et nous ne nous représentons pas qu'un régime de justice et de fraternité puisse être construit sans que les principes de l'Evangile en soient le ciment.

---

to resign in 1922. At the Versailles peace conference Lloyd George clashed with George Clemenceau of France, whose demands on Germany he considered too harsh, and with Woodrow Wilson of the U.S. who he thought was too idealistic. He did exert a moderating influence. Nonetheless, he later regarded the Versailles peace treaty as a grave mistake, predicting another war within the next 20 years as a result.

[1] Nathan Söderblom's ecumenical collection, A 19, UUB, typewritten letter.

...

Tout ceci est bien élémentaire. Nous sommes heureux de sentir que vous vivez de la même conviction que nous et que nous communions avec vous dans la même certitude des triomphes réservés à l'Evangile et dans le même amour passionné du Christ. Vous demandez à vos frères du monde entier de se placer résolument devant le problème des problèmes: quel doit être le rôle des chrétiens dans la vie des sociétés humaines? Vous les invitez à dénoncer l'égoïsme responsable de tous les conflits entre les peuples, à lutter de toutes leurs forces contre les causes de guerre, à travailler à l'établissement de l'arbitrage international, à protester contre le mensonge qui proclame l'existence de deux morales différentes, une pour les individus, une autre pour les peuples. A ce programme nous adhérons de tout notre coeur, et nous sommes convaincus que, le jour où les Eglises s'entendront le réaliser, une immense bénédiction descendra sur les enfants des hommes. Mais une conférence écclésiastique internationale ne pourrait le prendre en main qu'à une condition: c'est qu'au préalable la conscience chrétienne se soit délivrée du fardeau qui l'oppresse et que, solennellement, le mal ait été appelé mal.

...

Le programme que vous nous avez adressé semble inviter tous les chrétiens à confesser qu'ils sont tous également responsables de ce qui s'est passé, et nous en sommes d'autant plus émus que nous retrouvons cette pensée, exprimée parfois avec insistance, dans les manifestations de certains chrétiens des pays neutres. Or, c'est là précisément ce qui est en question. On abuse d'une vérité religieuse que nous sommes les premiers à affirmer; à savoir que tous les hommes sont pécheurs et qu'ils sont tous appelés à la repentance. Il y a trop de simplisme dans la façon dont on rappelle ce principe. ... Oui, tous les hommes sont pécheurs devant Dieu; mais il ne faut pourtant pas mettre sur le même rang les prophètes qui parlent en son nom et les misérables qui les lapident. De même, entre les nations, sans qu'aucune puisse prétendre à la sainteté, il y en a de plus ou moins coupables, et le problème des responsabilités – de toutes les responsabilités – dans le présesnt cataclysme, ne saurait être esquivé sous aucun prétexte.

Quand nous réclamons la proclamation de la vérité, nous ne pensons pas à notre seul pays. La recherche des responsabilités, c'est la forme élémentaire de la justice. Cette justice, nous la réclamons pour tous notamment, pour les Serbes et pour les Belges. ...

Il ne s'agit pas, non plus, de tomber dans le pharisaïsme que le maître a dénoncé. Il serait mauvais que l'enquête nécessaire ait pour but d'arriver à une explosion d'orgueil et de propre justice. Mais il est certain qu'elle aboutira à autre chose. Elle fera comprendre à tous qu'une société nouvelle ne pourra être fondée que sur des principes tout à fait nouveaux. Il faut commencer par la dénonciation des crimes particuliers dont la guerre a été le lugubre déroulement. Mais il faut continuer par la mise en lumière de toutes les passions mauvaises, de tous les intérêts coupables, de toutes les préoccupations méchantes, de tous les préjugés meurtriers qui sont, trop souvent, dans la substruction de notre ordre social. Seule, l'élimination des toutes ces formes du mal permettra l'établissement de la justice et de la fraternité dans le monde.

Il nous en coûte de ne pas faire à votre invitation, dont nous apprécions hautement les motifs religieux, la réponse que vos coeurs souhaitaient. Il nous en coûte de causer peut-être de la peine à des chrétiens pour qui nous n'avons qu'affection et respect. Mais de même que nous comprenons parfaitement vos préoccupations, et ce qui les inspire, vous comprendrez les sentiments qui nous dominent et les convictions qui nous obligent. Vous ne sauriez trouver mal que nous répétions aujourd'hui, pour notre compte, la grande parole du Réformateur: »Il est dangereux d'agir contre sa conscience. . . Nous ne pouvons autrement«.

Nous attendons avec vous les temps bénis appelés par l'Eglise et nous vous prions, Messieurs et honorés frères, de croire toujours à nos sentiments respectueux et dévoués.

LES VICE-PRESIDENTS,   LE PRESIDENT,
A. Juncker   E. Gruner.

LE SECRETAIRE,
Raoul Allier   Bonnetfir [?]

Paris, April 10, 1919

Sirs and honorable Brothers,
You have kindly communicated to us your desire to convene, at the earliest possible date, an international church conference in order to manifest the spiritual unity of the Christian Church, and you ask us for our opinion on the appropriateness of that conference. . . .

We shall tell you, in respectful and brotherly frankness, how we envisage it from our point of view.

Above everything else, we put the honor of Christ and the advancement of the Gospel. We sense with an anxious heart in view of current events, how great the responsibility of Christians is who have not been able sufficiently to let the Gospel radiate in order to penetrate modern society with it, and we cannot imagine that a rule of justice and brotherhood could be established, unless the principles ot the Church are its cement.
. . .

All this is quite elementary. We are happy to know that you are of the same conviction as we are and that we share with you the same certitude of the triumphs destined for the Gospel and the same passionate love for Christ. You are demanding of your brethren throughout the world resolutely to face the problem of problems: What must be the role of Christians in the life of human societies? You are inviting them to denounce the egoism responsible for all the conflicts between the nations, to struggle with all their might against the causes of war, to work for the establishment of international arbitration, to protest against the lie that proclaims the existence of two different moralities, one for the individuals and another one for the nations. We wholeheartedly adhere to that program, and we are convinced that on the day the churches agree to realize it, an immense blessing will descend on the children of man. But an international church conference could take it into its hands only on one condition: that is that beforehand, the Christian conscience has relieved itself of the burden that suppresses it, and that evil is solemnly called evil.

[A lengthy passage on the necessity of determining the guilt of war]

The program you have sent us seems to invite all Christians to confess that they are all equally responsible for what has happened, and it has excited us all the more as we also encounter that idea, sometimes expressed forcefully, in the utterances of certain Christians from neutral countries. Now, this is precisely the point in question. This is abusing a religious truth which we are the first to affirm, that is that all humans are sinners and that they are all called upon to repent. It is too simplistic a way of reminding of that principle. ... Yes, all humans are sinners before God; but nonetheless one must not put the prophets who speak in his name on a level with the villains who stone them. Likewise, among the nations, even though none of them can pretend to sainthood, there are more or less guilty ones, and the problem of responsibilities – all responsibilities – in the present cataclysm cannot be eschewed under any pretext.

When we are claiming the proclamation of the truth, we are not thinking of our own country alone. The search for responsibilities is the elementary form of justice. That justice is what we are claiming for all, particularly for the Serbs and the Belgians. ...

Nor is this about falling prey to the Pharisaism which the Master denounced. It would be bad if the necessary inquiry had an explosion of pride and self-righteousness as its objective. But it is certain that it will lead to something different. It will make plain for everyone that a new society cannot be founded except on entirely new principles. One must begin by denouncing the particular crimes the war has unfolded in a sinister way. But one must continue by exposing all bad passions to the light of day, all the guilt-laden benefits, all the evil preoccupations, all the murderous prejudices which all too often are part of the substructure of our social order. Only the elimination of all these forms of evil will permit the establishment of justice and brotherliness in the world.

We are having a hard time not giving to your invitation, the religious motives of which we are holding in high esteem, the response that your hearts desired. We are having a hard time hurting perhaps the feelings of Christians for whom we feel nothing but affection and respect. But just as we perfectly understand your preoccupations and what inspires them, you will understand the sentiments that guide us and the convictions that oblige us. You will not be offended if we repeat today, on our account, the great word of the Reformer: »It is dangerous to act against your conscience. . . We cannot do otherwise.«

We are awaiting the blessed times called for by the Church, and we ask you, Sirs and honored Brothers, always to believe our respectful and devoted sentiments.

THE VICE-PRESIDENTS,   THE PRESIDENT

A. Juncker   E. Gruner.

THE SECRETARY,

Raoul Allier   Bonnetfir [?]

138. From FRIEDRICH HEILER[1]

München Wörthstr. 13/I, 26.6.19.

Hochverehrter Hochwürdigster Herr Erzbischof!

Gestatten Sie, dass ich den Mitteilungen vorgestrigen Briefes einige Zeilen über meine äußeren und inneren Erlebnisse der letzten Monate folgen lasse. Meine Habilitation fiel gerade in jene Zeit, da in mir der Entschluss des Übertrittes zum Protestantismus reifte. Die Fakultät wählte ganz wider mein Erwarten das vorgeschlagene Thema über Luther aus. So wurde denn meine Probevorlesung zum religiösen Bekenntnis, als solches wurde es auch von den anwesenden Professoren und Studenten aufgenommen. In der folgenden Diskussion hatte ich einen schweren Redekampf mit dem ultramontanen Historiker von Grauert[2] auszufechten, der mich mit großer Heftigkeit angriff. Er begann seine Gegenrede mit den bezeichnenden Worten: »Es ist ein Ereignis in den Annalen unserer Universität, dass ein solcher Vortrag gehalten werden konnte. Denn die Münchener Universität ist bekanntlich die Erbin der Ingolstädter Universität und Ingolstadt und Wittenberg standen in schärfstem Gegensatz.«[3] Seine der katholischen Durchschnittsapologetik entstammenden Einwände wies ich allesamt zurück, so daß er zuletzt erklärte: er sehe ein, dass er mit mir noch mehrere Stunden, ja Tage disputieren müßte, ohne daß auch dann eine Einigung zu erzielen wäre. Die Vorlesung erregte naturgemäß die katholischen Gemüter nicht wenig. Bereits am folgenden Tage erhielt ich von einem kath. Theologen einen persönlich verletzenden Brief, in dem er meinen Ausführungen jede Wissenschaftlichkeit absprach. »Wenn das Wissenschaft ist!« habe er sich bei meinem Vortrag sagen müssen. ... Die feindselige Haltung katholischer Kreise steigerte sich noch, als ich (neben einem Kolleg über die Geschichte der außerchristlichen Mystik) eine Vorlesung über Matthäus-Evangelium hielt, in der ich die von der protestantischen Theologie herausgestellten bibelkritischen und religionsgeschichtlichen Probleme beleuchtete. Den katholischen Theologiestudierenden wurden meine Vorlesungen verboten (ich doziere vor lauter Nichttheologen, von ein paar hier studierenden prot. Theologen abgesehen!), aber das genügte noch nicht! Auch die Nichttheologen wurden vor mir von kath. Geistlichen gewarnt. Ein Kollege der Theol. Fak. sagte wörtlich zu einer Studentin: »Wenn Sie zu Heiler gehen, dann ist es um Ihr Seelenheil geschehen.« All jene Verleumdungen und Vorwürfe, welche die katholischen Modernisten vor mir erlitten, muß auch ich ertragen. Ignorantia, superbia, curiositas[4] – das sind natürlich die psychologischen Motive meiner Ketzereien in den Augen der ultramontanen Katholi-

---

[1] Nathan Söderblom's collection of letters, from foreigners, UUB, handwritten letter.

[2] Hermann von Grauert (1850–1924), historian in Munich.

[3] The Ingolstadt professor Johann Eck (1483–1543) conducted a vehement public disputation with Martin Luther at Leipzig in 1519. Luther's firm stand there won him much further support.

[4] Latin for ignorance, arrogance, curiosity.

ken, die alles mit den Maßstäben der Encyclica Pascendi[5] messen. Ich lasse mich aber durch solche Anfechtungen in meiner objektiven Haltung gegenüber dem Katholizismus nicht beirren und fahre ruhig fort in meinen Vorlesungen und Schriften das Wertvolle, Tiefe und Schöne der katholischen Frömmigkeit darzustellen. Ich persönlich freilich stehe zum katholischen Frömmigkeits- und Gottesdienstleben in keinem inneren Verhältnis mehr. Nicht etwa, weil in mir alle katholischen Stimmungen und Ideale der Vergangenheit verschwunden wären. Ich habe im Gegenteil bei einem 14tägigen Aufenthalt in einem ev. Pfarrhaus in rein prot. Gegend gespürt, daß in mir noch viel Katholisches ist, das ich in unserem deutschen Protestantismus schwer vermisse. Ja ich hatte auf diese Erfahrung hin (Weihnachten 1918) sogar nochmals den Versuch gemacht mich dem Gottesdienstleben der kath. Kirche wieder zu nähern, aber es ging nicht. Es ist mir unmöglich vor dem eucharistischen »Mysterium« wie ehedem auf die Knie zu sinken und anzubeten; die katholische Mysterienliturgie ist für mich nicht mehr Gottesdienst im christlichen Sinne, die *Gebets*gemeinschaft mit der katholischen Kirche ist für mich abgebrochen und damit die religiöse Gemeinschaft mit ihr überhaupt. Ich empfinde darum ein weiteres Verbleiben im Katholizismus als einen inneren Widerspruch. Freilich ist mir der Eintritt in eine der *deutschen* Landeskirchen nicht so leicht, als es anfangs schien; wie ich bei näherer konkreter Beobachtung sah, ist hier viel Starres, Unlebendiges und andererseits Verwaschenes, Mattes und Rationalistisches. Mit Neid und Sehnsucht schaue ich stets auf *Ihre* Kirche, welche die evangelische Katholizität, mein christliches Kirchenideal, verkörpert.[6] Aber schließlich wird es für mich keine andere Möglichkeit geben, als eben in der unvollkommenen ev. Kirchengemeinschaft Deutschlands für jenes Kirchenideal zu werben und wirken. Ich habe mich darum wegen des praktischen Schrittes in diesem Frühjahr wieder mit verschiedenen prot. Theologen ins Benehmen gesetzt. Niebergall hat mir schon im Vorjahr von einem Konfessionswechsel entschieden abgeraten, Loofs dagegen zugeredet. Girgensohn, den ich hoch verehre, steht diesem Schritt sympathisch gegenüber.[7] Vor wenigen Tagen erhielt ich von einem Theologen (dessen Namen zu nennen vorläufig mir strenge Schweigepflicht verbietet) die Anfrage, ob ich bereit sei, sein sich wahrscheinlich bald erledigendes Ordinariat für Religionsphilosophie und systematische Theologie zu übernehmen, natürlich unter der Bedingung des sofortigen Übertrittes. Ich wollte zunächst rundweg ablehnen, da ich meinen Übertritt *spontan*, ohne irgendwelche Absicht auf einen Lehrstuhl, vollziehen wollte, damit die Katholiken mir nicht den Vorwurf

---

[5] *Pascendi dominici gregis*, antimodernist Encyclical promulgated by Pope Pius X. (1858–1914, Pope since 1903) in 1907.

[6] Cf. letter no. 97, n. 3.

[7] Friedrich Niebergall (1866–1932) a disciple of Ritschl's, professor of practical theology in Marburg; Friedrich Loofs (1858–1928) professor of church history in Halle; Karl Girgensohn (1875–1925), professor of systematic theology in Dorpat (Tartu) 1907–1919 and from then on in Leipzig. The latter two were conservative Lutherans.

machen, ich sei aus Versorgungsgründen apostasiert. Einstweilen verhandle ich mit dem betr[effenden] Herrn, ob nicht die Berufung ohne die offizielle Forderung des sofortigen Übertrittes möglich wäre. Wie ich mich entscheide, wenn das nicht der Fall ist, weiß ich noch nicht. Da ich aber von meiner hiesigen Lehrtätigkeit vor lauter Nichttheologen nicht befriedigt bin und andauernd den Impuls verspüre zu einer religiös-kirchlichen Wirksamkeit neben der wissenschaftlichen Forscherarbeit, sage ich schließlich zu und nehme jene Nachrede der Katholiken auf mich.

Beinahe hätte ich vergessen, Ihnen herzlichen Dank zu sagen für die Übersendung Ihres herrlichen Ostervortrages[8], der mir aus der Seele gesprochen ist. Ich habe [in] der Einleitungsvorlesung meines Kollegs über Leben-Jesu-Forschung, das ich z[ur] Z[eit] halte, ganz ähnliche Sätze gesprochen, die zum Teil bis in die Formulierung übereinstimmen. Ich freue mich gar sehr über diese Gemeinsamkeiten der Auffassung, muß aber dankbar bekennen, dass im Grunde Sie der Gebende und ich der Nehmende bin.

In der Hoffnung, dass sich meine Reise nach Schweden ermöglichen läßt, habe ich bereits um meine Beurlaubung für den August (in dem wegen des späten Semesterbeginns noch gelesen wird) nachgesucht und auch die ersten Schritte zur Erlangung eines Passes getan. Mit dem Ausdruck tiefster Verehrung und herzlicher Dankbarkeit   Ihr   Fr. Heiler

139. To FRIEDRICH HEILER[1]

Upsala den 3 juli 1919.

Bäste Herr Docent!

Hjärtligt tackar jag för Edra goda brev och för tillåtelsen att efter bästa förstånd till medmänniskors och medkristnas hjälp använda de erfarenheter, Ni gjort i Eder forskning och i Edert Gudsumgänge. Att Edert stora verk upplever en ny upplaga gläder mig mer, än jag kan säga. Den utomordentligt skarpsinniga analysen över buddhismens mystik har jag erhållit likaså det lilla föredraget om mystiken, vars tes verkligen uttrycker en övertygelse, som jag aldrig kunnat släppa, men som för mig icke utmynnat i en syntes utan snarare i den insikten, att den evangeliska förtröstan och den äkta mystiken måste få rum bredvid varandra i den kristna kyrkan och även i ett kristet hjärta, som behöver dem båda.

För att underlätta för Eder att erhålla pass sänder jag en formlig inbjudan till det allmänkyrkliga mötet i Vadstena, och beder Eder där hålla ett

---

[8] *Gå vi mot religionens förnyelse? Föredrag i Engelbrektskyrkan annandag påsk 1919* (Sveriges kristliga studentrörelsens skriftserie 101), Stockholm 1919 (1st and 2nd ed.); German transl.: »Gehen wir einer religiösen Erneuerung entgegen?« (In: N. Söderblom, *Zur religiösen Frage der Gegenwart. Zwei Vorträge,* 3–20; transl. by P. Katz), Leipzig 1921; English transl.: *Easter. A sermon preached in the Engelbrekt church, Stockholm, the day after Easter 1919* (transl. by D. Nyall), Chicago 1930.

[1] Fr. Heiler's papers (Ms. 999), UB Marburg, typewritten letter.

helt kort föredrag (en halv timma), t.ex. om evangelisk kristendom och
mystik. Jag hoppas, att Ni kan komma. Från det ögonblick, då Ni befinner
Eder i Vadstena, beder jag Eder vara min gäst till inemot den 1 oktober.
Den 9–18 augusti beder jag Eder åtfölja mig på en längre visitation i en
mycket stor församling, Bollnäs i Helsingland, så att Ni kan få en uppfattning av svenskt kyrkoliv på nära håll. Därefter måste jag resa till Danmark,
men under tiden beder jag Eder bo hos en av mina vänner. I september börjar universitetet, som kan intressera Eder. Och det Religionsvetenskapliga
sällskapet i Stockholm, liksom den teologiska föreningen i Upsala vilja under september få föredrag av Eder. Medel till Eder återresa erhåller Ni som
honorar. Kursen är så dålig, att Ni icke bör växla till Eder allt för mycket
svenska pängar. Har Ni en smula över (20 kronor), när Ni kommer till
Vadstena, skall jag sörja för resten. Vi behöva tala om många viktiga spörsmål, och vi kunna planera Olai Petri-föreläsningar åt Eder för ett kommande år.

Jag skickar Eder Svenska Kyrkans kropp och själ, dessutom en liten ka-
tekes och några små skrifter. Min adress är från den 7 till den 27 juli Hemsjö. ...

Jag beder Eder nu vara hjärtligt välkommen. Gud skydde Eder under resan och alltjämt! Eder med djup sympati och verklig beundran

Tillgivne

Nathan Söderblom

P. s. Då jag märker Eder sällsynta lätthet för språk, vill jag göra Eder följande förslag. Skriv Edert föredrag t.ex. om Stellung und Aufgabe des evangelischen Christentum in der Religionsgeschichte eller in der Zukunft eller
evangelium och mystik. Gör det kort, högst en halv timma. Sänd det sedan
till mig, adress Hemsjö, eller till Docent Tor Andrae, svenska legationen i
Berlin, och få det översatt till god svenska, samt föredrag det själv på svenska för det stora kyrkliga mötet. D. S.

N S-m

Uppsala, den 3. Juli 1919

Sehr geehrter Herr Dozent!

Herzlich danke ich Ihnen für Ihre guten Briefe und für die Erlaubnis, nach bester
Einsicht zum Nutzen von Mitmenschen und Mitchristen von den Erfahrungen Gebrauch zu machen, die Sie in Ihrer Forschung und in Ihrem Umgang mit Gott gemacht haben. Dass Ihr großes Werk eine neue Auflage erlebt,[2] freut mich mehr, als
ich sagen kann. Die außerordentlich scharfsinnige Analyse der Mystik des Buddhismus habe ich erhalten, ebenso den kleinen Vortrag über die Mystik[3], dessen These
wirklich eine Überzeugung zum Ausdruck bringt, die ich niemals aufgeben konnte,
die aber für mich nicht auf eine Synthese hinausgelaufen ist, sondern eher auf die
Einsicht, dass das evangelische Vertrauen und die echte Mystik nebeneinander

---

[2] Friedrich Heiler, *Das Gebet*, 2. Aufl. Munich 1920.
[3] Friedrich Heiler, *Die buddhistische Versenkung*, Munich 1918; *Die Bedeutung der Mystik
für die Weltreligionen. Vortrag*, Munich 1919.

Raum bekommen müssen in der christlichen Kirche und auch in einem christlichen Herzen, die beide brauchen.

Um es Ihnen zu erleichtern, einen Pass zu bekommen, schicke ich Ihnen eine förmliche Einladung zu der allgemeinen Kirchenkonferenz in Vadstena und bitte Sie, dort einen ganz kurzen Vortrag zu halten (eine halbe Stunde), z. B. über evangelisches Christentum und Mystik. Ich hoffe, dass Sie kommen können. Von dem Augenblick an, da Sie sich in Vadstena befinden, bitte ich Sie mein Gast zu sein bis ungefähr zum 1. Oktober. Vom 9. bis zum 18. August bitte ich Sie, mich auf einer längeren Visitation in einer sehr großen Gemeinde zu begleiten, Bollnäs in Helsingland, damit Sie sich aus der Nähe einen Begriff von schwedischem kirchlichem Leben machen können. Danach muss ich nach Dänemark reisen, aber während dieser Zeit bitte ich Sie, bei einem meiner Freunde zu wohnen. Im September beginnt die Universität, die Sie interessieren könnte. Und die Religionswissenschaftliche Gesellschaft in Stockholm ebenso wie die theologische Vereinigung in Uppsala wollen im September einen Vortrag von Ihnen haben. Mittel für Ihre Rückreise bekommen Sie als Honorar. Der Kurs ist so schlecht, dass Sie nicht zu viel schwedisches Geld eintauschen sollten. Wenn Sie ein bisschen übrig haben (20 Kronen), wenn Sie nach Vadstena kommen, werde ich für den Rest sorgen. Wir müssen über viele wichtige Fragen reden, und wir können für ein späteres Jahr Olaus-Petri-Vorlesungen für Sie planen.

Ich schicke Ihnen Svenska kyrkans kropp och själ,[4] außerdem eine kleine Katechese und einige kleine Schriften. Meine Adresse ist vom 7. bis zum 27. Juli Hemsjö.
...

Ich heiße Sie nun herzlich willkommen. Gott behüte Sie auf der Reise und allezeit! Mit Sympathie und wirklicher Bewunderung

Ihr

Nathan Söderblom

P.S. Da ich Ihr seltenes Geschick für Sprachen bemerke, will ich Ihnen den folgenden Vorschlag machen. Schreiben Sie Ihren Vortrag z. B. über Stellung und Aufgabe des evangelischen Christentums in der Religionsgeschichte oder in der Zukunft, oder Evangelium und Mystik. Machen Sie es kurz, höchstens eine halbe Stunde. Schicken Sie ihn dann an mich, Adresse Hemsjö, oder an Dozent Tor Andrae,[5] Schwedische Gesandtschaft in Berlin, lassen Sie ihn in gutes Schwedisch übersetzen, und tragen Sie ihn dann selbst vor der großen kirchlichen Versammlung auf Schwedisch vor.   D. O

N.S-m.

---

[4] Nathan Söderblom, *Svenska kyrkans kropp och själ*, Stockholm 1916.

[5] Tor Andrae (1885–1947), disciple of Söderblom's (specialist in Islam), lecturer at Uppsala University in 1917, professor of history of religions in Stockholm 1927. In 1929, he took over Söderblom's chair in Uppsala. Later (1937–1947), he was bishop of Linköping. He also wrote a biography of Söderblom: *Nathan Söderblom*, Uppsala 1931, 5th ed. 1932; German transl.: Berlin 1938.

140. From Friedrich Heiler[1]

München Wörthstr. 13/I, 10.Juli 1919.
Hochverehrter Hochwürdigster Herr Erzbischof!
Empfangen Sie meinen heißesten Dank für Ihren gütigen Brief und Ihre liebenswürdige Einladung, die mich mit der denkbar größten Freude erfüllt.
Es ist mir die höchste Ehre auf der Kirchenversammlung sprechen zu dürfen. Ich werde Ihnen in einigen Tagen das Manuskript des Themas: »Evangelisches Christentum und Mystik«[2] zusenden, damit es Ihrem Wunsche
gemäß übersetzt werden kann. Ich habe zwar noch nie schwedisch gesprochen oder sprechen hören, da ich diese wundervolle germanische Sprache
nur aus Büchern studierte, doch hoffe ich mir noch durch einige Stunden,
die ich hier nehmen will, eine korrektere Aussprache anzueignen. Es ist
freilich kein leichtes Wagnis, in einer Sprache, die man nicht voll be-
herrscht, öffentlich zu reden.
Das andere vorgeschlagene Thema über die Stellung des evangelischen
Christentums in der Religionsgeschichte hoffe ich dann in Upsala behandeln zu dürfen.[3] Was Ihre Stellung zu dem Problem: Evangelium und Mystik betrifft, so glaube ich mich *sachlich* in voller Übereinstimmung mit Ihnen zu befinden. Ich habe mich lediglich durch Prof. Rudolf *Otto*, mit dem
ich über diesen Gegenstand korrespondierte, dazu verleiten lassen den
nicht ganz glücklichen Ausdruck »Synthese« zu gebrauchen. Der Vorrang
gebührt unbestreitbar der biblisch-evangelischen Frömmigkeit, doch findet
diese eine wertvolle Ergänzung in der Mystik, soweit sie den für die Offen-
barungsreligion charakteristischen *persönlichen* Gottesumgang nicht anta-
stet. Das richtige Verhältnis zwischen mystischer und evangelischer Religion scheint mir bei Paulus, Johannes und Luther gefunden zu sein, deren
Frömmigkeit prophetisch-evangelisch mit mystischem Einschlag ist. Ihre
Verbindung von heilsgeschichtlichem Glauben und persönlicher Gotterfah-
rung erscheint mir unüberbietbar.
… [Dank für die übersandten Schriften und praktische Bemerkungen zu
der Reise]
Mit dem Ausdruck tiefsten Dankes und größter Verehrung bin ich
Ihr ergebenster
Friedrich Heiler

---

[1] N. Söderblom's collection of letters, from foreigners, UUB, handwritten letter.
[2] »Evangelisches Christentum und Mystik,« in: Fr. H., *Das Geheimnis des Gebets*, Munich
1919, 7–21.
[3] »Die Absolutheit des Christentums im Lichte der allgemeinen Religionsgeschichte,« in:
Fr. Heiler, *Das Wesen des Katholizismus. Sechs Vorträge, gehalten im Herbst 1919 in Schweden*,
Munich 1920, 116–137.

141. To ALBERT HELLERSTRÖM[1]

Upsala den 14.10.1919.

Käre vän!

Sedan Federal Council nu beslutat sig för ekumeniskt möte och tillsatt en kommitté för ändamålet, kommer saken säkert att förverkligas. Frågan är endast vilka som skola deltaga och vad som skall på mötet förekomma. Du kan av Rev. Bell få närmare underrättelser. Eftersom du är inne i saken frågar jag dig härmed om du kan i sällskap med Stadener, som reser härifrån, närvara vid mötet i Paris, som hålles i Federal Councils ämbetslokal, 8 rue de la Victoire den 10 november kl 9.30 f.m.. Som du vet innefatta våra önskemål särskilt tre ting:

1. Kyrkans plikt med hänsyn till mänsklighetens brödraskap och nationernas enighet gentemot krig.

2. Kyrkans och kristendomens uppgift i samhällets daning och den sociala omvälvningen.

3. Grundandet av ett ekumeniskt råd, som kan tala i kristenhetens namn.

Särskilt denna sista punkt kräver ju synnerligen omsorgsfullt övervägande. Som du vet har ekumeniska patriarkatet i Konstantinopel liksom även den heliga synoden i Atén utsett ombud till den ekumeniska konferens som aldrig blev hållen. Det är således lätt att få de ortodoxa med. Däremot tror jag att det är en illusion att vänta på Rom. Huvudsaken är att de evangeliska samfunden känna och uttrycka sin enighet »in testimony and action«.

4. Bland ytterligare frågor kan tänkas förhållandet mellan kyrkan och staten, där en gemensam uppfattning skulle vara värdefull, särskilt för folkkyrkorna i Europa. Säg mig per omgående om du kan resa och vad en resa skulle kosta, för att jag må söka tigga pengar. Jag skall göra mitt bästa att få en norrman med. Eljest kunna ev. Yngve Brilioth och du resa tillsammans med Stadener.

Platsen för den kommande ekumeniska konferensen är en underordnad fråga, men nog tala de förnämsta skälen för Norden, erkannerligen Upsala, där denna konferens kommer att få en plats i församlingens böner och medvetande som knappast på något annat ställe. Jag märkte att amerikanerna började något luta åt Upsala. Alla deltagarna skulle här åtnjuta gästfrihet och det hela skulle få en prägel värdig ett så stort företag.

Din tillgivne
Nathan Söderblom
[handskrivet tillägg:] Låt mig räkna säkert på Ditt deltagande!

Uppsala, Oct. 14, 1919

Dear friend,
Since the Federal Council has now decided to have an ecumenical meeting and installed a committee for that purpose, the plan will certainly be realized. The ques-

---

[1] N. Söderblom's ecumenical collection A 10, UUB, typewritten letter.

tion is only which persons are to participate and which issues should be raised at the meeting. You can receive further information from Rev. Bell[2]. As you are privy to the matter, I hereby ask you if you could be present, together with Stadener[3] who shall travel from here, at the Paris meeting which will be held at the Federal Council's office, 8 rue de la Victoire, on Nov. 10, at 9:30 a.m. As you know, our desiderations include three things in particular:

1. The obligation of the church regarding human brotherhood and unanimity of the nations against war.

2. The task of church and Christianity in the development of society and social upheaval.

3. The foundation of an ecumenical council which can speak in the name of Christianity.

Especially the last item, of course, requires careful deliberation. As you know, the Patriarchate in Constantinople as well as the Holy Synod in Athens had appointed representatives for the ecumenical conference which was never held.[4] It will therefore be easy to engage the orthodox. On the other hand, I believe that waiting for Rome is illusory. The chief concern is that the Protestant community feel and express its unity »in testimony and action«.

4. As for further issues, one could think of the relationship between church and state, where a common view would be of value, particularly for the state churches in Europe[5]. Tell me by return whether you can take the trip and what it is going to cost, so I can beg for money. I shall do my best to bring along a Norwegian. Otherwise Yngve Brilioth[6] and you can perhaps travel along with Stadener.

The location for the future conference is a secondary question. However, the weightiest reasons speak for the North, more particularly Uppsala, where that conference will have a place in the congregation's prayers and consciousness as hardly

---

[2] George Kennedy Allen Bell (1883-1958), at the time residential chaplain in charge of international and inter-church affairs to the Archbishop of Canterbury, Randall Davidson. He was a leading figure of the ecumenical movement, president of the World Alliance, and worked for reconciliation during World War I. He became Dean of Canterbury 1924, bishop of Chichester 1929-1957. A strong opponent of Hitler, he supported the German resistance movement (contact with Dietrich Bonhoeffer in Sigtuna, Sweden, in 1942) in its effort to topple the Nazi regime. Since he also took up the cause of alien (particularly Jewish) refugees in the UK and opposed saturation bombing of German cities during World War II, the good chances he originally had of becoming archbishop of Canterbury came to naught.
[3] Samuel Stadener (1872-1937), Söderblom's successor as embassy pastor in Paris 1901, liberal theologian and liberal politician. He was bishop of Strängnäs diocese 1927-1933 and Swedish secretary of church affairs 1930-1932.
[4] The Holy Synod of Constantinople had decided on Jan. 10, 1919, to issue an invitation to all churches, particularly the Anglicans, the Old Catholics and the Armenian church, to convene an ecumenical conference. Athens had joined in.
[5] There was a certain amount of debate on this issue in Sweden at the time (separation of church and state became § VI of the Social Democratic party program in 1920), which may be one of the reasons why this came to Söderblom's mind.
[6] Yngve Brilioth (1891-1959), 1914-1918 Söderblom's private secretary and later his son-in-law; 1919 lecturer in church history at Uppsala University, professor in Åbo 1925, professor of practical theology and Dean in Lund 1928, bishop in Växjö 1937, archbishop 1950-1958. He held leading positions in the World Council of Churches from 1947 until his death. His scholarly achievements include several important works on the Anglican church to which he established close ties. His most influential work is *Nattvarden i svenskt gudstjänstliv*, Stockholm 1926; English as *Eucharistic Faith and Practice Evangelical and Catholic*, London 1930.

anywhere else. I noticed that the Americans are beginning to be inclined towards Uppsala. All participants would enjoy hospitality here, and the whole would have a distinctive character worthy of such a great undertaking.

Yours sincerely,

Nathan Söderblom

[handwritten addition:] Let me count on your participation for sure!

142. From Rudolf Otto[1]

[Date at the end of the letter]

Hochgeehrter Herr Erzbischof.

Soeben vollende ich Ihr schönes Heft »Gå vi mot religionens förnyelse?«[2] Titius hat es mir zur Anzeige für die [Theologische] L[iteratur-]Z[eitung] zugesandt.[3] Ich habe einen jüngeren Bekannten, einen Pfarrer, der sehr gut schwedisch liest, u[nd] würde, da ich selber leider zu beschäftigt bin, durch diesen das Heft gerne ins Deutsche übersetzen lassen. Ich würde versuchen, die »Deutsche christliche Studentenvereinigung« zu veranlassen, es dann unter ihren Schriften herauszugeben. Sind Sie damit einverstanden?

Gerne würde ich dann selber ein Geleitwort schreiben oder Herrn Kollegen Herrmann[4] – was viel besser wäre –, veranlassen es zu tun. Doch wird noch zu überlegen sein, ob man das nicht doch lieber vermeidet, damit nicht der Schatten »der Marburger Theologie« auf das Schriftlein fällt.

Werden Sie nicht einmal wieder unser Land besuchen? Sollte es geschehen, so bitte ich sehr zu überlegen, ob Sie uns und unserer hiesigen Studentenschaft nicht eine Rede ähnlichen Inhaltes schenken möchten. Sie würden hier ein sehr dankbares Publikum finden.

Ich empfehle mich Ihnen mit ergebenen Grüßen. In aufrichtiger Verehrung

Ihr

R. Otto.

Marburg a.L.   Hainweg 6   1.10.19.

---

[1] N. Söderblom's collection of letters, from foreigners, UUB, handwritten letter.

[2] Cf. letter no. 137, n. 8.

[3] Arthur Titius (1864–1936), a liberal professor of systematic theology in Berlin, was one of the two editors at the time. He had a wide range of interests; his best known book is *Natur und Gott*, 2nd ed. Göttingen 1931. A former ardent monarchist, he was one of the few Protestant theologians who had become democrats, and this created him many foes; cf. Kurt Nowak, *Evangelische Kirche und Weimarer Republik. Zum politischen Weg des deutschen Protestantismus zwischen 1918 und 1932*, Göttingen 1981, 39.70.

[4] Cf. letter no. 13, n. 3.

143. To Rudolf Otto[1]

(13.10.1919)

Sehr geehrter Herr Professor
Nach einem interessanten Gespräch m[it] unserm gemeinsam[en] Gespräch
[? lies: Freund] Heiler habe ich soeben Ihren Br[ief] bekommen u[nd] be-
schleunige ich mich dafür zu danken – zu sagen, dass ich selbstver[ständ-
lich] mit der Übersetzung meiner Broschüre ganz einverstanden bin. Doch
möchte ich lieber die 2te jetzt erscheinend[e] durchgesehene Auflage ...
[abwarten] die ich Ihnen sofort senden werde[2]
Was Doc[ent] Dr Heiler betrifft hat er mit Genehmigung des amtieren-
den Bishofs von Skara in Vadstena am heiligen Abendmal in unserer Kirche
teilgenommen Das bedeutet nach unserer Teori und Praxis dass Dr Heiler
nicht mehr Römisch katolisch [ist] Wir haben nämlich in unserer Kirche
keine Form des Uebertrittes sondern nur diese schöne Auffassung der Bedeutung des heiligen Abenmals Wenn Sie wollen kan ich Ihnen diese Tatsache in mehr feierlicher Form besonders bestätigen.
Ihr sehr erg[ebener]

144. To Albert Hellerström[1]

Upsala 4.11.1919.

Käre broder!
Den ekumeniska konferensen behöver grundligt förberedas och jämförelsen med Edinburgh-konferensen är så till vida riktig, men dock föreligger
här en väsentlig skillnad. I Edinburgh gällde det att belysa och utreda en
massa diskussionsproblem och att över huvud skapa en grundlig översikt
över hela missionsväldet med dess viktiga problem. Däremot får ekumeniska konferensen sin största och sin egentliga betydelse just i det faktum, att
den sammanträder. Först när den sammanträder torde den kunna gå i författning om närmare utredning av alla de utomordentligt viktiga problem,
som måste sysselsätta det ekumeniska kyrkorådet. Mera belysande synes
mig därför jämförelsen med Lambethkonferensen vara. Den sammanträder
först, utser diverse utskott, tar sig en paus och sammanträder igen, när ut-
skotten gjort sitt arbete. På samma sätt borde, enligt min tanke, ekumeniska
konferensen sammanträda så snart den »Committee on an oecumenical conference«, som i Paris skall bildas, fått tillfälle att vända sig till kyrkosamfunden, och dessa hunnit utse (eller icke utse) delegater till ett sådant möte.

---

[1] N. Söderblom's collection of letters, from foreigners, UUB, draft in secretary's handwriting on empty space of foregoing letter. The actual letter has not been preserved.
[2] The second enlarged edition was published the same year, the German translation in 1921
(without a preface by either Otto or Herrmann). Otto's short review appeared in *ThLZ* 47/
1922, 407 f.

[1] N. Söderblom's ecumenical collection A 10, UUB, typewritten letter.

Naturligtvis bör då starkt betonas, att kyrkosamfundens trosbekännelse och författning, överhuvud deras inre liv, lämnas fullkomligt i fred och frihet i den åsyftade gemenskapen. Sedan dessa val skett, borde den ekumeniska konferensen egentligen så snart som möjligt sammanträda, nästa år, i samband med Studentvärldsförbundets konferens, eller möjligen 1921. Den får ett rikhaltigt program och kan konstituera det ekumeniska kyrkorådet, vilket väl måste anses vara dess kanske viktigaste uppgift. Vidare kan den ena sig i frågan om de praktiska uppgifter, som föreligga, och för vilket intill dess ett intensivt förarbete bör sättas i gång. Sedan torde närmare detaljer böra överlåtas åt det ekumeniska kyrkorådet, som när så kräves har möjlighet att rådfråga de organ, som de särskilda kyrkosamfunden för detta ändamål torde behöva utse, där de icke redan finnas i form av federationer, biskopsmöten, synoder etc. Ja, här föreligga viktiga problem, och jag är glad över att två så vederhäftiga kyrkomän som Stadener och Hellerström komma att behandla saken för Nordens vidkommande. Man kan fråga sig huruvida det icke vore lämpligt att inbjudan till den ekumeniska konferensen ävenledes utgår ifrån de grenar av kristenheten, som tagit initiativ i denna sak och som nu bliva företrädda i Paris.

Med varm önskan
din tillgivne
Nathan Söderblom

Upsala 4.11.1919

Dear Brother,

The ecumenical conference needs to be thoroughly prepared. Insofar, the comparison with the Edinburgh conference[2] is correct; there is, however, one crucial difference. In Edinburgh, the objective was to elucidate and analyze a host of problems to be discussed and above all, to produce an exhaustive survey of the whole realm of missions with its momentous problems. By contrast, the greatest and real significance of the ecumenical conference will lie in the mere fact of its convening. Only when it convenes, will it be able to make arrangements for analyzing all the extraordinarily important problems which must engage the ecumenical council of churches. Therefore, a comparison with the Lambeth conference seems to me to be more illuminating. That conference first assembles, appoints various committees, adjourns, and asssembles again when the committees have done their work. In the same fashion, according to my mind, the ecumenical conference should convene as soon as the »Committee on an ecumenical conference« to be formed in Paris will have had the opportunity of addressing the church bodies and these will have managed to appoint (or not to appoint) delegates to such a meeting. Of course, we shall then have to emphasize strongly that the confessions of faith of the church bodies, their constitutions, in fact all of their proper life, will be left completely unimpaired and free in the communion we are aiming at. When these selections have been made, the ecumenical conference should actually convene as soon as possible, next year, in connection with the World Student Christian Federation's conference, or possibly in 1921. It will have an ample program, and it can set up the ecumenical council of

---

[2] The World Missions Conference in 1910.

churches which perhaps must be considered its most important task. Moreover, it can agree on the subject of the practical obligations before us, something which requires intense preparatory work being under way until then. After that, further details should be left to the ecumenical council of churches which, if need be, will have the opportunity of consulting those agencies each single church body should appoint for this purpose inasmuch as they do not already exist in the form of federations, bishops' meetings, synods, etc. Oh yes, there are important problems ahead of us, and I am glad that two trustworthy churchmen like Stadener and Hellerström will tackle the matter as far as the North is concerned. One could ponder whether it might not be advisable to have the invitation for the ecumenical conference also go out from those branches of Christianity which took the initiative in this cause and which will now be represented in Paris.

With best wishes,
sincerely yours,
Nathan Söderblom

145. From GERARDUS VAN DER LEEUW[1]

Groningen, 15. XI. 19.

Sehr geehrter Herr Erzbischof – Es hat unserer hiesigen theol. Fakultät so sehr leid getan, dass Ihre Anwesenheit hier im Lande erst so spät zu unserer Kenntnis gekommen. Unsere Bitte, dass Sie auch unsere Universität mit einem Vortrage begünstigen möchten, ist noch unterwegs gewesen. Sie waren jedoch schon fort. Wir hoffen auf ein anderes Mal.

Gern hätten wir auch mit Ihnen gesprochen über die Möglichkeit eines Gedankens, der bei uns lebendig ist. ... [Scl. = scilicet?] ob nicht die skandinavischen Länder u[nd] Holland insbesondere sich dazu eignen Versuche zu machen zur Wiederanknüpfung des internationalen Verkehrs auf wissenschaftlichem, i.e. religionsgeschichtlichem Gebiete. Sollte nicht eine internat. religionswissenschaftliche Vereinigung, ausgehend von den neutralen Ländern, und dann allmählich sich auf die Belligerenten erstreckend eine lohnende Aufgabe finden? Scheint Ihnen dieser Gedanke irgendwie glücklich und zu verwirklichen, so hoffe ich auf ein Paar Zeilen.

Endlich muss ich Ihnen mein persönliches Bedauern aussprechen, dass ich den Autor der meine Gedanken so lebhaft und so verschiedlich angeregt hat, nicht gesehen habe, obwohl er im Lande. Auch ich persönlich hoffe, dass es ein nächstes Mal gibt.

Mit vorzüglicher Hochachtung
Ihr sehr ergebener
van der Leeuw

---

[1] Gerardus van der Leeuw (1890–1950), professor ot the history of religions in Groningen, Netherlands, 1918–1950. His most famous work is *Phänomenologie der Religion*, Tübingen 1933 (^{2}1956). N. Söderblom's collection of letters, from foreigners, UUB, handwritten letter.

146. To GERARDUS VAN DER LEEUW[1]

Upsala 28.11.1919.

Ärade Herr Professor!

Liknande strävan har sysselsatt oss här i Norden livligt under kriget. Det bästa torde vara att under loppet av nästa år söka få till stånd ett samarbete av kommittéer för de religionshistoriska kongresserna, vars medlem jag är, och därefter på någon konferens i ett neutralt land bilda en stor religionsvetenskaplig förening, som Ni anser. Med tack för de lärda verk jag haft förmånen mottaga från Eder

Eder aktningsfullt tillgivne

Uppsala, 28.11.1919

Sehr geehrter Herr Professor!

Ähnliche Bestrebungen haben uns hier im Norden während des Krieges lebhaft beschäftigt. Das Beste dürfte sein, im Laufe des nächsten Jahres zu versuchen, eine Zusammenarbeit von Komitees für die religionsgeschichtlichen Kongresse, denen ich angehöre, zustande zu bringen und danach auf einer Konferenz in einem neutralen Land eine große religionswissenschaftliche Vereinigung zu bilden, wie Sie sie befürworten. Mit Dank für die gelehrten Werke, die ich den Vorzug hatte von Ihnen zu bekommen

In Hochachtung Ihr ergebener

147. From FRIEDRICH HEILER[1]

Ockelbo, Prästgården [Pfarrhaus] 23. Dec. 1919.

Hochverehrter Hochwürdigster Herr Erzbischof!

Für die Gastfreundschaft, die ich vier Wochen in Ihrem Hause genießen durfte, sage ich Ihnen und Ihrer verehrten Frau Gemahlin den innigsten Dank. Mein Aufenthalt in Upsalas Ärkebiskopsgården [erzbischöflichem Palais] ist der Höhepunkt in meinem Aufenthalt in Schweden. Die meisten meiner Zukunftsträume sind unerfüllt geblieben, aber der eine Traum, den ich lange träumte: in Ihr Haus zu kommen und persönlichen Gedankenaustausch mit Ihnen zu pflegen, ist früher, als ich ahnte, in Erfüllung gegangen. Und dafür bin ich Ihnen von Herzen dankbar. Ich nehme aus Ihrem Hause so viele, schöne Eindrücke nach Deutschland mit, die ich nie vergessen werde. Von ihnen meinen deutschen Freunden erzählen zu können ist mir die größte Freude.

Die fünf Monate, die ich in Schweden verbrachte, bilden die inhaltsreichste Epoche meines Lebens. In diesem relativ kurzen Zeitraum drängte sich eine Fülle tiefer und bedeutungsvoller Erlebnisse zusammen. Mein Ide-

---

[1] N. Söderblom's collection of letters, to Swedes and foreigners, UUB, carbon copy of typewritten letter.

[1] N. Söderblom's collection of letters, from foreigners, UUB, handwritten letter.

al der evangelischen Katholizität hat hier immer festere Gestalt und deutli-
chere Züge gewonnen. Ich sehe das Problem: katholisches und evangelisches Christentum in viel schärferem Licht als früher. Mit vielen neuen Ide-
en und Impulsen kehre ich in meine Heimat zurück, dort wird das Vielerlei,
das jetzt sich in meiner Seele aufgehäuft hat, verarbeitet werden und Form
bekommen. Auch die Tragik, welche seit der dritten Augustwoche meinen
Aufenthalt in Schweden umschwebt, bedeutet eine ungewöhnliche Berei-
cherung meines Innenlebens. Sie sehen dieses mein Erlebnis in allzu rosigem
Schimmer, aber wenn Sie wüßten, wie kompliziert und verstrickt diese Erlebnisse waren, dann würden Sie mir glauben, dass ich nie in meinem Leben
so traurige Stunden hatte wie hier in Schweden. Ich wurde immer mehr in
die Mystik hineingetrieben, denn es gibt in solchen inneren Konflikten nur
einen Ausweg: die φυγὴ μόνου πρὸς μόνον.[2] Wenn ich nicht ebenso evangelisch fühlen würde wie mystisch und wenn ich nicht in Rom und dem Papst-
tum mit Luther antichristlichen Geist erkennen würde, würde ich das
braune Gewand des Poverello von Assisi anziehen und zu den Söhnen diesen [lies: dieses] größten katholischen Heiligen gehen. Denn sie sind »nihil
habentes omnia possidentes.«[3] Es gibt kein stärkeres Motiv zur Weltflucht
als eine unglückliche Liebe.-

Hier geht es mir besser als ich erwartet. Sie hatten, verehrter Herr Erzbischof, Recht, wenn Sie sagten, ich werde von Ockelbo leichteren Herzens
nach Deutschland zurückkehren. Ich hoffe nun, dass I. ohne Bitterkeit von
mir scheiden wird.[4]

Indem ich Ihnen und Ihrer ganzen Familie frohe Weihnacht wünsche,
verbleibe ich mit dem Ausdruck der Dankbarkeit und Verehrung

Ihr ergebenster
Friedrich Heiler

148. To FRIEDRICH HEILER[1]

Upsala Annandag Jul 1919

Käre vän!
Det är för mig en tillfredsställelse, att Ni icke reser hem i en stämning, som
hade en tillsats av bitterhet. Hur denna sak kommer att utveckla sig ligger i
Guds hand. I varje fall består den sanna kärleken däri, att någon ser sitt eget
självändmål [sic] i en annans självändamål. Skulle denna känsla icke delas,
så kvarstår dock kärlekens önskan och plikt att främja den älskades självändamål. Kanske innebär det för egen del en smärtsam, djupt ingripande för-

---

[2] The lone [soul's] fleeing to the Lone One: the soul's mystical union with ultimate reality,
Plotinus, *Enneads* VI 9, 11,51.
[3] Owning nothing and possessing everything; II Cor 6:10 in the Vulgate version.
[4] I. for Ingrid, a Swedish girl with whom Heiler had become friends during his visit in Sweden; the friendship ended in separation.

[1] Fr. Heiler's papers (Ms. 999), UB Marburg, handwritten letter.

sakelse. Men det gäller därvidlag att mista sitt eget liv för att vinna det. Det blir en bitter, men ändå i längden hälsosam undervisning i det svåraste som finnes, att *glömma oss själva och försaka oss själva* för kärleken till bröderna.

Väl förstår jag Eder känsla för poverello och hans bröder. Jag har förr skrivit: Jag hoppas Ni hör till de himlens pilgrimer, som aldrig bli fullt hemmastadda i någon jordisk organisation. Jag tror, att dessa som flytt in i munklivet besparas många av de lidanden men även de mänskliga och kristna erfarenheter, som samlivet med våra bröder och systrar förorsakar. Därför känna de nog också mindre av den livets rikedom och underbarhet, som visar sig för en uppriktig själ kanske mitt i tunga, ja marterande erfarenheter. I djupet bor som uti höjden Gud. Hans skola kan vara fruktansvärt svår. Det måste en evangelisk kristen veta. Men Gud döljer obeskrivlig nåd i besynnerliga höljen. Om vi blott troget hålla ut intill ändan. Den kommer snart. Maran atha. Gud välsigne Eder, käre vän och medkristen, och hjälpe Eder! Han vill lära Eder alltmer av sitt rikes hemlighet. I *livets* skola. Eder för alltid innerligt tillgivne

Nathan Söderblom

Uppsala, 26. 12. 1919

Lieber Freund!

Es ist eine Genugtuung für mich, dass Sie nicht in einer Stimmung heimreisen, die einen Beigeschmack von Bitterkeit hat. Wie diese Sache sich entwickeln wird, steht in Gottes Hand. In jedem Fall besteht die wahre Liebe darin, dass jemand seinen eigenen Selbstzweck im Selbstzweck eines anderen sieht. Sollte dieses Gefühl nicht geteilt werden, so bleibt doch der Wunsch und die Pflicht der Liebe bestehen, den Selbstzweck des geliebten Menschen zu befördern. Vielleicht bedeutet das für einen selbst einen schmerzlichen, tief einschneidenden Verzicht. Aber es gilt unter solchen Umständen, sein eigenes Leben zu verlieren, um es zu erhalten.[2] Das wird eine bittere, doch auf die Dauer heilsame Unterweisung in dem Schwersten, was es gibt, *uns selbst zu vergessen und preiszugeben* um der Liebe zu den Brüdern willen.

Gut verstehe ich Ihre Empfindungen für den poverello[3] und seine Brüder. Ich habe früher einmal geschrieben: Ich hoffe, dass Sie zu den Pilgern des Himmels gehören, die niemals in einer irdischen Organisation vollständig zu Hause sind. Ich glaube, dass denen, die ins Mönchsleben fliehen, viele von den Leiden, aber auch die menschlichen und christlichen Erfahrungen erspart bleiben, die das Zusammenleben mit unseren Brüdern und Schwestern verursacht. Deshalb kennen sie gewiss auch weniger von dem Reichtum und dem Wunderbaren des Lebens, das sich in einer aufrichtigen Seele vielleicht mitten in schweren, ja marternden Erfahrungen zeigt. In der Tiefe wohnt wie in der Höhe Gott. Seine Schule kann furchtbar schwer sein. Das muss ein evangelischer Christ wissen. Aber Gott verbirgt unbeschreibliche Gnade in sonderbaren Verhüllungen. Wenn wir nur treu bis zum Ende ausharren. Das kommt bald. Maran atha. Gott segne Sie, lieber Freund und Mitchrist, und helfe Ihnen! Er will Sie immer mehr von dem Geheimnis seines Reiches lehren. In der Schule *des Lebens.* Ihr Ihnen stets herzlich zugeneigter

Nathan Söderblom

---

[2] Mark 8:35.
[3] Francis of Assisi.

149. From FRIEDRICH HEILER[1]

München Wörthstr. 13 I, 5. Jan. 1920.
Hochverehrter Hochwürdigster Herr Erzbischof!
Verzeihen Sie, wenn ich meinem kurzen Telegramm erst heute einen aus-
führlicheren Brief folgen lasse. Aber ich wollte erst einige Eindrücke in der
Heimat gewinnen, ehe ich an Sie schrieb. Allererst sage ich Ihnen und Ihrer
verehrten Gattin nochmals innigen Dank für all die Güte und Fürsorge, die
ich in Ihrem Hause erfahren durfte. Besonderen Dank sage ich der Frau
Erzbischof für die Lebensmittel, die sie mir auf die Reise mitgab und die
mir sehr wertvoll waren, da auf den Zügen nichts zu bekommen war. Bisher
konnte ich mich in der Heimat noch nicht eingewöhnen. Ich hatte es – trotz
aller schmerzlichen Erlebnisse mit Ingrid – nie in meinem Leben so gut wie
in den fünf Monaten, die ich in Schweden zubrachte. Ich lebe nun ganz in
der Fülle schöner Erinnerungen, ich singe ständig schwedische Lieder um
die nordische Gefühlsstimmung in mir wachzuhalten. Ganz fremd geworden ist mir das katholische Milieu, in das ich nun plötzlich wieder zurück-
versetzt wurde. Darauf war ich nicht gefaßt, da ich im evangelischen Norden bisweilen die Katholizität vermißt habe. Ich hatte mich darauf gefreut
wieder einmal einen katholischen Gottesdienst zu sehen, und ging in solchen Erwartungen am Neujahrstag in ein katholisches Hochamt. Aber ich
fühlte mich ganz fremd und blieb innerlich ganz kalt, wurde nicht zur Andacht gestimmt. Die vollkommene Passivität der Gläubigen im Gottesdienste ist mir nie so zum Bewusstsein gekommen wie da. Im Gefühl völliger
Unbefriedigung ging ich schnurstracks von der katholischen Kirche in die
evangelische um hier im *Gemeinde*gottesdienst Erbauung zu suchen und zu
finden. Nun arbeite ich an der Druckfertigstellung meiner in Schweden ge-
haltenen Vorträge über Katholizismus usw.[2] Ich habe das Gefühl, dass ich
mit dieser Schrift eine Bombe gegen den Vatikan schleudere. Ich glaube
kaum, dass ich nach dem Erscheinen hier an der Universität noch bleiben
kann. Die Stimmung der Katholiken gegen mich ist ohnehin jetzt schon
feindselig, und diese verhaltene Feindseligkeit wird dann offen zum Ausdruck kommen, wenn diese Schrift veröffentlicht ist. Ich kann mich nur
deshalb zur Drucklegung in Deutschland entschließen, weil ich eine Propaganda für das Ideal der evangelischen Katholizität im gegenwärtigen Augenblick für dringend notwendig halte. Ich erhoffe mir von ihr eine Stärkung der ökumenischen und hochkirchlichen Bestrebungen im evangelischen Deutschland. Die religiösen Verhältnisse sind hier besser, als ich erwartet hatte. Der Kirchenbesuch ist ein sehr reger in den katholischen und
evangelischen Kirchen; in den kirchlichen Kreisen läßt sich keinerlei Ab-

---

[1] N. Söderblom's collection of letters, from foreigners, UUB, handwritten letter. The original bears the date Jan. 5, 1919. But that must be one of those early January errors, since the visit to Sweden and the lectures held there which Heiler is talking about took place only in the
summer and fall of 1919, cf. letter no. 147.
[2] Published as *Das Wesen des Katholizismus*, Munich 1920.

nahme des religiösen Lebens feststellen. Was Pastor Hasselrot in Dagens Tidning über die »leeren« deutschen Kirchen schrieb, ist absolut unzutreffend, wenigstens für Süddeutschland. Politisch macht sich ein starker Zug nach rechts geltend, der Sozialismus hat völlig Fiasko gemacht, die Hoffnungen, die man auf ihn gesetzt hat, sind kläglich enttäuscht. Man ruft allgemein nach einer starken Regierung, welche Deutschland aus seiner Notlage herauszuführen imstande ist. Die jetzige Regierung hat keine Autorität. In der Jugend zeigen sich kräftige monarchistische und nationale Tendenzen. Οὐκ ἀγαθὸν πολυκοιρανίη, εἷς κοίρανος ἔστω, εἷς βασιλεύς[3] – dieses Homerische Wort drückt am besten die Erfahrungen des letzten Jahres aus. Ich hoffe, dass der Ausfall der nächsten Wahl so ist, dass eine Volksabstimmung für die Wiedereinführung der Monarchie, wenn auch in der neuen Form eines freiheitlichen Volkskönigtums, möglich wird. Die Lebensmittelverhältnisse sind besser, als ich erwartet habe, doch gibt es keine Milch, Fett und Fleisch sind sehr knapp. Empfindlich ist der Kohlenmangel, der sich noch verschärfen wird, da die Entente nach der Ratifizierung des Friedens auf verdoppelter Kohlenlieferung besteht. Die Preise sind für alle Waren seit meiner Abreise erheblich gestiegen, in Berlin sind sie geradezu märchenhaft. Entsetzlich drückend sind die neuen Steuern (Einkommensteuer und Umsatzsteuer). Auf Schritt und Tritt spürt man, daß Deutschland ein Sklavenvolk geworden ist, das dem Ententekapitalismus Frondienste leisten muß. Die Bitterkeit gegen die grausame Unterdrückung und Ausbeutung durch die Entente ist groß. Als der Waffenstillstand geschlossen wurde, hatte niemand Haß- und Rachegefühle gegen die Feinde, weil man auf einen erträglichen Frieden hoffte. Auch war schon unter dem Kriege die Zahl der aufrichtigen Pazifisten eine sehr große. Jetzt sind die Pazifisten zu Nationalisten geworden. Man redet bereits vom künftigen Krieg – ich hörte das Wort, kaum nachdem ich Deutschlands Boden betreten hatte. Das ist tieftraurig, daß jetzt ein Revanchegefühl in die deutschen Herzen eingedrungen ist, das ihnen ursprünglich ganz fremd war, aber die Schuld daran fällt ausschließlich auf die, welche die Urheber des Versailler Friedensvertrages sind.

… (On his Swedish girl friend)

Nun sage ich nochmals Ihnen und den Ihrigen herzlichen Dank für alles, was ich während meines Aufenthaltes in Schweden von Ihnen empfing und grüße Sie, hochverehrter Herr Erzbischof, und Ihre ganze Familie herzlichst.

Ihr dankbar ergebener
Friedrich Heiler

---

[3] »Nichts Gutes ist die Herrschaft vieler; ein Herrscher sei, ein König«, Homer, *Ilias* 204 f.

150. From RUDOLF OTTO[1]

Marburg, Hainweg 6.   12.1.20.

Sehr geehrter Herr Erzbischof.

[On Fr. Heiler's future plans, thanks for a couple of brochures from Söderblom]

Mit Spannung verfolge ich Ihre zwischen=kirchlichen Bemühungen. Dr. Cramer aus dem Haag sandte mir die Protokolle von Wassenaer.[2] Wenn Sie bei diesen Bemühungen Marburger Hilfe brauchen, so stehen wir Ihnen ganz zur Verfügung.

Herr Wendte aus Boston[3] fragte bei Rade[4] an, ob jemand aus Deutschland zu dem wiedereröffneten »Kongress für freiheitliches Christentum«[5] kommen wolle, der im Herbste in Amerika tagen soll. Ich stehe der Sache zweifelnd gegenüber. Die Führung durch die Unitarier gefällt mir nicht. Eine Führung durch Kongregationalisten oder modern gerichtete Episkopate wäre mir lieber. Auch scheint mir der Mischmasch mit Gott=bestreitenden Buddhisten, mit fantastischen Bahaisten u. drgl. [dergleichen] romantischen Gruppen bedenklich. Andererseits wäre ein Zusammenarbeiten vorwärtstreibender Gruppen der verschiedenen großen christlichen Parteien in zwischenvölklichem Zusammenhange grade heute sehr wichtig. Vielleicht wäre grade Schweden berufen, hier die Führung zu nehmen. Auch die Anregung der japanischen »Bischöfe« vor dem Kriege zu einer Zusammenarbeit aller religiösen großen Gemeinschaften überhaupt in Bezug auf Menschheits=Ethik und allgemeine zwischen=völkliche und zwischen=staatliche Aufgaben wäre erwägenswert.[6] ...

Ich bitte um einen Gruß an Dr. Heiler u. Herrn Kollegen Billing. Vor längerer Zeit ließ ich durch den Verlag meine Schrift »das Heilige«[7] an Sie

---

[1] N. Söderblom's collection of letters, from foreigners, UUB, handwritten letter.

[2] World Alliance conference in Oud Wassenaer, Oct 1–3, 1919; Dr. Cramer probably is Jan Anthony Cramer, 1864–1952, later professor of church history in Utrecht.

[3] Charles William Wendte (1844–1931), Unitarian minister in Boston MA, first secretary of the International Association for Religious Freedom (for 20 years), which was founded in 1900 by Unitarians and other liberals. Wendte had helped to organize the Parliament of the World's Religions in Chicago in 1893.

[4] Martin Rade (1857–1940), liberal theologian, editor of the influential journal for church and theology, *Die Christliche Welt* (1886–1931), one of the founders of the *Evangelisch-Sozialer Kongress*. In the Weimar Republic, Rade was one of the few German Protestant theologians welcoming the new democratic state. He was professor of systematic theology in Marburg since 1900.

[5] The 5th Congress of Free Christianity and Religious Progress of the IARF (see note 3) had taken place in Berlin, with such speakers as Adolf von Harnack, Ernst Troeltsch, and the American Social Gospel theologian Walter Rauschenbuch (1861–1918). In the following years, the IARF became increasingly interfaith-oriented. The last meeting before World War I took place in 1913 in Paris, the next one convened in Boston in October 1920. In 1930, the IARF became permanently institutionalized under the name of International Association of Liberal Christianity and Religious Freedom.

[6] The idea of a covenant of the religions of humanity for the solution of the great moral obligations of human civilization was to become one of Otto's preoccupations after World War I. This did not imply minimizing the differences between the religions.

senden. Hoffentlich haben die Postwirren es doch in Ihre Hände kommen lassen.

Mit den besten Wünschen zum 1920 in Verehrung Ihr ergebener

R. Otto, Prof.

151. To Friedrich Heiler[1]

Upsala 17. 1. 1920.

Käre Docent och vän!

Tack för Edert brev, så tilltalande som vanligt, genom sin personliga uppriktighet och genom den klarhet, varmed såväl inre som ytttre forhållanden framläggas. Det har behagat Gud att föra Eder på en svår väg. Under alla omständigheter är det en vansklig och smärtsam sak att byta om hem, men i synnerhet är detta fallet, när et gäller själens andliga hemvist i Kristi kyrka. Dock har Ni icke bytt om hem, utan, så vitt jag kan förstå, har Eder utveckling följt alldeles följdriktigt ur kristendomens förutsättningar. Ni har följt vägen framåt enligt Guds anvisning och Kristi evangelium och Ni har därigenom kommit in på nya marker, in i evangeliet och det profetiska Gudsumgängets livsform. Väl förstår jag Edra svårigheter och ber Gud att han må så som hittils hjälpa Eder fram på den väg, som hans vilja utstakar. Smärtsamt är det i sanning att Ni måste känna Eder främmande i den romerska gudstjänsten. Men det kan icke vara annorlunda. Säkerligen har Gud menat, att Ni skall förhjälpa uppriktiga och fromma själar till att se vad som är kärnan i Kristi verk och vår tro och sålunda inifrån förverkliga den evangeliska katoliciteten, för vilken vi äro satta att troget arbeta först och främst genom andens verk i våra egna hjärtan, därnäst genom ord och gärning.

Jag har skrivit till filosofiska fakultetens dekanat om Edra framtidsutsikter, och jag frågar samtidigt professor Otto om han har bestämda planer för Eder ev. framtid i Marburg. [handskrivet tillägg på marginalen: Vad säger Ni om Kina?] Jag tänker att morgondagens omsorg skall med Guds hjälp lösas utan svårighet. Under årets lopp motse vi besök av Eder både i vår och till hösten.

...

Med allas våra goda hälsningar och innerliga tillönskan om frid, klarhet och välsignelse och i förhoppning att snart få höra vidare om Eder

Eder tillgivne

Nathan Söderblom

---

[7] Rudolf Otto, *Das Heilige*, Breslau 1917, 4th ed. 1920. The concepts of »mysterium tremendum« and »fascinans« which, according to Otto, are constitutive for religion, is preceded by Söderblom's concepts of »oåtkomlig« and »oundkomlig«, inaccessible and inescapable, *Naturlig religion och religionshistoria*, Stockholm 1914, 112 German ed.: *Natürliche Religion und Religionsgeschichte*, Stockholm 1913, 109).

[1] Fr. Heiler's papers (Ms. 999), Univ. Library Marburg, typewritten letter.

252

Lieber Dozent und Freund!

Danke für Ihren Brief, so ansprechend wie stets, durch seine persönliche Aufrichtigkeit und durch die Klarheit, mit der sowohl innere als auch äußere Verhältnisse dargestellt werden. Es hat Gott gefallen, Sie einen schweren Weg zu führen. Es ist in jedem Fall eine schwierige und schmerzliche Sache, die Heimat zu wechseln, aber ganz besonders ist das der Fall, wenn es um die geistige Heimstatt der Seele in Christi Kirche geht. Jedoch haben Sie nicht die Heimat gewechselt, sondern, soweit ich es verstehen kann, hat Ihre Entwicklung sich ganz folgerichtig aus den Voraussetzungen des Christentums ergeben. Sie sind dem Weg nach vorn gefolgt nach Gottes Anweisung und Christi Evangelium, und Sie sind dadurch auf einen neuen Boden geraten, in das Evangelium und die Lebensform des prophetischen Umgangs mit Gott hinein. Ich verstehe durchaus Ihre Schwierigkeiten und bitte Gott, dass er Ihnen so wie bisher auf dem Weg weiterhelfen möge, den sein Wille absteckt. Schmerzhaft ist es wahrlich, dass Sie sich im römischen Gottesdienst fremd fühlen. Aber das kann nicht anders sein. Sicherlich hat Gott die Absicht, dass Sie aufrichtigen und frommen Seelen dazu helfen sollen zu sehen, was der Kern des Werkes Christi und unseres Glaubens ist, und so von innen heraus die evangelische Katholizität zu verwirklichen, für die wir eingesetzt sind zu treuer Arbeit, zuerst durch das Werk des Geistes in unserem eigenen Herzen, danach durch Wort und Tat.

Ich habe an das Dekanat der philosophischen Fakultät geschrieben wegen Ihrer Zukunftsaussichten, und ich frage gleichzeitig Professor Otto, ob er bestimmte Pläne für Ihre eventuelle Zukunft in Marburg hat. [Handgeschriebener Zusatz am Rand: Was sagen Sie zu China?[2]] Ich denke, dass die Sorge des morgigen Tages mit Gottes Hilfe sich ohne Schwierigkeit lösen wird. Im Laufe des Jahres sehen wir Besuchen von Ihnen entgegen, sowohl im Frühjahr als auch zum Herbst hin.

... [Kurze Bemerkungen über eine Reihe von Themen, unter anderem über 77 unterernährte österreichische Kinder, für die Söderblom einen Erholungsaufenthalt in Schweden organisiert hatte]

Mit guten Grüßen von uns allen und dem innigen Wunsch für Frieden, Klarheit und Segen, und in der Hoffnung, bald wieder von Ihnen zu hören

Ihr Ihnen verbundener
Nathan Söderblom

152. To FRIEDRICH HEILER[1]

Upsala 5.2.1920.

Käre Docent och vän!

Jag erhåller ifrån Dekanus i Münchens filosofiska fakultet en synnerligen vänlig underrättelse om vad som gjorts för Eder därstädes. Låt mig veta hur det går med Marburg. Kanske kan då Münchener-universitetet göra ansträngningar för Eder framtid därstädes. Jag skall icke neka till att en anställning vid vårt universitet i Hankau i Kina för 5 år eller något mer skulle erbjuda Eder unika tillfällen för Eder religionshistoriska forskning.

---

[2] See next letter.

[1] Fr. Heiler's papers (Ms. 999), Univ. Library Marburg, typewritten letter.

...

Vad angår Religionsproblemet, så vill jag icke att Eder dyrbara arbetstid skall för mycket tagas i anspråk därmed. Men såsom Ni yttrade, skulle nog därav kunna göras en mindre tysk bok med ett slutkapitel om modernistepisodens anslutning. Om en sådan bok skall utkomma, borde det vara i år. Kanske kunde den göra något gagn och uppklara problemet för åtskilliga tänkande människor. Mycket tacksam är jag för Edra vänliga åtgärder i detta stycke och vill naturligtvis be att få till fullo ersätta Edert arbete.

...

Eder med varm tillgivenhet och ständig förbön förbundne
N. Söderblom

Upsala 5. 2. 1920

Lieber Dozent und Freund!
Ich bekomme vom Dekan der Münchener Philosophischen Fakultät eine ausnehmend freundliche Auskunft über das, was man dort für Sie getan hat. Lassen Sie mich wissen, wie es mit Marburg weitergeht. Vielleicht kann die Münchener Universität sich dann um Ihre Zukunft dort bemühen. Ich will nicht verhehlen, dass eine Anstellung an unserer Universität in Hankau in China für 5 Jahre oder etwas länger Ihnen eine einmalige Gelegenheit für Ihre religionsgeschichtliche Forschung bieten würde
[Über Ergänzungen von Heiler zur neuen Auflage des Kompendiums für Religionsgeschichte von Tiele / Söderblom und sein Angebot, die Korrekturlesung zu übernehmen]
Was *Religionsproblemet*[2] angeht, so möchte ich nicht, dass Ihre kostbare Arbeitszeit dadurch über Gebühr in Anspruch genommen wird. Aber wie Sie geäußert haben, sollte sich daraus durchaus ein kleineres deutsches Buch mit einem Schlusskapitel über den Anschluss der Modernisten-Episode machen lassen. Wenn ein solches Buch herauskommen sollte, so müsste es in diesem Jahr sein. Vielleicht könnte es einigen Nutzen bringen und das Problem für viele denkende Menschen klären. Sehr dankbar bin ich für Ihre freundlichen Unternehmungen in dieser Sache, und ich möchte natürlich darum bitten, Ihnen Ihre Arbeit vollständig vergüten zu dürfen.

...

Ihr Ihnen in herzlicher Freundschaft und in ständiger Fürbitte verbundener
N. Söderblom

153. From FRIEDRICH HEILER[1]

München Wörthstr. 13, 8. II. 1920

Hochverehrter Hochwürdigster Herr Erzbischof!
Herzlichsten Dank sage ich Ihnen für Ihren freundlichen Brief, der mir Ermunterung und Erquickung war, desgleichen danke ich besonders für das

---

[2] Nathan Söderblom, *Religionsproblemet inom katolicism och protestantism*, Stockholm 1910. Heiler had offered to translate this book, but the translation was never finished.

[1] N. Söderblom's collection of letters, from foreigners, UUB, handwritten letter.

schwedische Choralbuch, das mir besondere Freude machte. Ich kann nun nach Herzenslust nicht nur profane, sondern auch heilige schwedische Weisen singen. Als Gegengabe erlaubte ich mir Ihnen unser »schwäbisches« Choralbuch samt dem Textbüchlein zu schicken. Sie werden in ihm viele schöne Melodien und fromme Texte finden und können in ihm die deutsche katholische Frömmigkeit näher kennen lernen: viel echtes und tiefes Christentum, aber ebenso – zumal in den Marienliedern – halbheidnische Religion.

Wie Sie, hochverehrter Herr Erzbischof, vielleicht schon durch Prof. R. Otto gehört haben, bin ich von der Marburger theol[ogischen] Fakultät als Extraordinarius für *Religionsgeschichte* vorgeschlagen worden. Das wäre eine sehr passende Stelle für mich und ein sehr schöner Wirkungskreis, da Marburg eine der größten theol. Fakultäten hat. Die hiesige phil[osophische] Fakultät will mich zwar nicht ziehen lassen und sucht mich zu halten; aber ich selbst verlange von hier fort, da ich die stete Spannung mit den Katholiken nicht ertragen kann. Ich habe sehr unter der Feindseligkeit zu leiden, vor ein paar Tagen hat die hiesige katholische Zeitung mich in ganz häßlicher Weise angegriffen. Ich kann nicht verstehen, daß die religiöse Toleranz sich nicht Bahn brechen kann. Dagegen bewundere ich die Weitherzigkeit und das Verständnis meines Vaters, der mich ruhig meine Wege wandern läßt und mich sogar gegenüber den Katholiken verteidigt.

Unser Vaterland ist jetzt in der denkbar schwierigsten Lage. Die niederträchtige Auslieferungsforderung der Entente hat eine unbeschreibliche Bitterkeit erweckt. Aus Hass und Rachsucht geboren, muß sie erhöhten Haß und Racheverlangen im deutschen Volke erzeugen. Beim Abschluß des Waffenstillstandes hat das kriegsmüde deutsche Volk keinerlei Rachegefühle gekannt, aber jetzt *müssen* diese naturnotwendig aufsteigen. Wären wir nicht militärisch und wirtschaftlich ohnmächtig, wir würden gewiß die Waffen zum Verzweiflungskampf gegen unsere brutalen Unterdrücker erheben. Das μὴ ἀντιστῆναι τῷ πονηρῷ der Bergpredigt[2] kann auch in den deutschen Christen nicht mehr die natürliche[n] Leidenschaften niederhalten. Wie soll da das Werk der Völkerversöhnung und Kircheneinigung fortschreiten! Können Sie, hochverehrter Herr Erzbischof, nichts tun, daß wenigstens die englischen und amerikanischen Christen Einspruch erheben gegen diese Politik des Hasses und der Unterdrückung?

Die wirtschaftlichen Verhältnisse verschlechtern sich zusehends. Wir müssen fürchten, dass auch wir Münchener Wiener Zustände bekommen. Der niedere Valutastand macht es Deutschland unmöglich Lebensmittel aus dem Ausland zu beziehen. Alle Preise schnellen sprunghaft in die Höhe, die Geldgier der deutschen Kaufleute kennt keine Grenzen, Wucher und Schiebertum blühen. Ich habe Ihr gedankentiefes Böndagsplakat [Bußtagsplakat] mit tiefer Ergriffenheit gelesen; aber einen Hunger haben Sie nicht genannt, der unter den meisten Menschen der größte ist, größer als der nach

---

[2] Matth. 5:39.

Brot, Liebe und Ewigkeit – *auri sacra fames*[3]. Arbeiter und Kapitalisten, Bauern und Geschäftsleute, alles ist von einem Taumel der Geldgier ergriffen; der Mammonismus erstickt alles höhere Streben und erzeugt eine Genußsucht, die keine Schranken kennt. Wäre das nicht, dann könnte das deutsche Volke trotz aller Not genesen. Ich denke oft mit Beschämung an die ehrenden Worte über Deutschland, die ich so oft in Schweden gehört habe; denn wenn man die Entsittlichung weitester Schichten sieht, dann muß man sagen, daß das *heutige* Deutschland diese hohe Achtung leider nicht mehr verdient[.] Infolge der Agitation der unabhängigen Sozialisten[4] greift auch hier die Kirchenaustrittsbewegung in erschreckendem Maße um sich. Die Kirchen selbst tragen ihre Schuld daran, weil sie so starr und unbeweglich sind und auf die Zeichen der Zeit so wenig achten. Gerade in unserer bayerischen Landeskirche herrscht ein schrecklich enger und unfruchtbarer Geist; ich hörte von befreundeten evangelischen Pfarrern sehr bittere Klagen.

Zu allem allgemeinen Leid hat unsere Familie noch ein schwerer Schlag getroffen. Mein Bruder ist infolge des Zusammenwirkens verschiedener Gründe (Kriegsdienst, schlechte Ernährung und geistiger Überanstrengung) geisteskrank geworden und mußte in eine Irrenanstalt verbracht werden. Es besteht sehr wenig Hoffnung auf Heilung. Wenn ich einmal wieder nach Schweden komme, werde ich Ihnen all die näheren tragischen Umstände erzählen. Ich selbst erlitt bei seinem letzten Wahnsinnsanfall einen leichten Nervenschock. Meine Eltern zwingen mich nun meinen wissenschaftlichen Arbeitseifer etwas zu mäßigen, weil sie fürchten, dass geistige Überanstrengung bei ungenügender Ernährung auch bei mir zur Erkrankung führen könnte. Ich selbst muß zuversichtlich und froh sein um nicht dem Trübsinn nachzugeben. »Und ob es währt bis an die Nacht...[«].[5]

Einen Brief meines Verlegers gestatte ich mir beizulegen. Er kann mein Gebet, das einen riesigen Absatz gefunden hat, nicht in weiterer Auflage herausgeben, weil es an Papier fehlt und meint, durch Lieferung fertiger Exemplare von Schweden Papier eintauschen zu können. Vielleicht wissen Sie Rat.

Grüßen Sie herzlich Ihre hochverehrte Frau und Ihre liebe Familie und seien Sie selbst herzlichst und verehrungsvollst gegrüßt von Ihrem dankbaren Jünger

Friedrich Heiler

---

[3] Vergil, *Aeneis* 3,57: »der verfluchte Hunger nach Gold« (the cursed hunger for gold).

[4] *Unabhängige sozialdemokratische Partei Deutschlands* (USPD), radical Marxist wing of the Social Democrats which broke away from the party in 1917 in order to pursue an uncompromising course against the continuation of the war effort.

[5] Fourth stanza of Luther's hymn *Aus tiefer Not schrei ich zu dir* (From depths of woe I cry to Thee): »Und ob es währt bis in die Nacht/ Und wieder an den Morgen,/ Doch soll mein Herz an Gottes Macht/ Verzweifeln nicht noch sorgen.« In the hymnal currently in use in the Protestant churches of Germany, *Evangelisches Gesangbuch*, Nr. 299. Benjamin Latrobe's translation is a bit shallow: »Like those who watch for midnight's hour/ To hail the dawning morrow,/ I wait for Thee, I trust Thy power,/ Unmoved by doubt and sorrow.«

154. To Rudolf Kittel[1]

Upsala 12.2.1920

Hochverehrter Herr Professor und Freund!
Für Ihre Briefe herzlichst dankend teile Ich mit, dass wir gern in Upsala und Umgebung 100 notleidende Kinder aus Leipzig und Sachsen im Allgemeinen nehmen möchten. Vielleicht ist es bei Ihnen, wie in Wien, das Fall, dass intellektuelle Kreise, Universitätslehrer-, Pfarrer-, Beamten-Familien wenigstens ebenso bedürftig sind als andere Familien. Jedenfalls fragen wir ob Sie die rechte Personen damit beauftragen wollen 100 darbende Kinder aus Sachsen für uns auszuwählen. Zunächst dürfen wir nicht ältere Kinder als 14 Jahre nehmen. Für Knaben (Schüler) können aber Ausnahme gemacht werden. Der Unterricht macht Schwierigkeit. Kann der junge Heinrici[2] den der Prorektor Quensel[3] einladet, damit behilflich sein? Wir möchten sonst auch gern einen Lehrer einladen, aber die Kinder wohnen zum grösser Teil auf dem Lande. Selbstverständlich wird der Unterricht sehr mangelhaft sein. Vielleicht wäre es daher Ihnen eben so lieb entweder ganz kleine Kinder zu senden oder auch bis zum Sommer zu warten. Bitte sagen Sie mir was wir am besten tun können.
Wir freuen uns Sie selbst in April hören zu dürfen. Können Sie früher kommen, wäre es unter den jetzigen Umständen noch besser wenn die Vorlesungen schon am 9 oder 12 April beginnen könnten. Ist das Ihnen möglich?
Vielleicht kann Ich auf der Durchreise nach Genf am 23 oder 24 Februar Leipzig besuchen.
Mit herzliche Grüsse an die Fakultät und alle Freunde
Ihr sehr ergebener

155. From Rudolf Otto[1]

Marburg, 15.2.20

Verehrter Herr Erzbischof.
Morgen geht der Antrag meiner Fakultät an das Ministerium, Dr. Heiler nach Marburg für Religionsgeschichte zu berufen. – [On persons to be sent to India for research in Hinduism]
Meine Vorschläge über den »religiösen Menschheitsbund neben politischem Völkerbund« werden Sie in der nächsten »Christlichen Welt« lesen.[2]

---

[1] Rudolf Kittel (1853–1929), professor of Old Testament in Leipzig. N. Söderblom's collection of letters, to Swedes and foreigners, UUB, typewritten letter (carbon copy).
[2] A son of Georg Heinrici (1844–1915), professor of New Testament in Leipzig.
[3] Cf. letter no. 58, n. 1.

[1] N. Söderblom's collection of letters, from foreigners, UUB, handwritten letter.
[2] Rudolf Otto, »Religiöser Menschheitsbund neben politischem Völkerbund,« in: *ChW* 34/1920, 133–135. Otto's intention was the creation of a »world conscience« on an interreligious basis in order to promote international justice and peace. Similar organizations were created in the US, e. g. the Universal Religious Alliance. The first meeting of the *Menschheitsbund*

Harnack schrieb mir dazu Zustimmendes. Natürlich hält er die Sache für schwierig, aber doch vielleicht für leichter als den Zusammenschluß der christlichen Konfessionen im gleichen Sinne. Ich meine, dass der Papst sich vielleicht nicht ungern auf einen allgemeinen religiösen Menschheitsbund einlassen würde, in dem er ganz von selbst die größte Rolle spielen würde, während er zum Zusammengehen mit den andern *christlichen* Konfessionen nie zu haben sein wird. Das größte sachliche Interesse an meinem Plane müßte unter heutigen Verhältnissen aber der Khalif in Konstantinopel haben. Und es würde lohnen, etwa durch den türkischen Gesandten in Stockholm einmal Fühlung zu nehmen. Ich wagte nicht, diesen Hinweis in meinem Aufsatze zu deutlich zu machen, da das zunächst viele abgeschreckt hätte. Aber die Sache liegt auf der Hand. Mein »Menschheitsbund« ist ja zunächst stark im Interesse aller *kleinen*, aller *neutralen*, und aller jetzt vergewaltigten Völkerschaften. Sobald dieses eingesehen wird, müssen die islamischen und die indischen Gruppen den großen Nutzen des Gedankens einsehen. Der Anstoß zur Sache kann nur oder doch am besten von einer Kirchenschaft einer *neutralen* Macht ausgehen. Und darum muß ich alles weitere in Ihre Hände legen. Außerdem sind unsere deutschen Kirchenbehörden alle so durchaus subaltern und in engsten Ortsinteressen befangen (außer den Katholischen), daß von dieser Seite erst etwas zu erwarten ist, wenn der Anstoß von außen kommt. Ihre Stimme würde bei unserem *Luthertum* sehr von Bedeutung sein.

[A lengthy passage on lectures Otto held in Japan and on the connections he had been able to establish there.]

Für Ihre freundlichen Worte über mein »Heiliges« (das ich soeben in der 4ten Auflage, aber unverändert drucke) besten Dank.[3] Die Verwandschaft [sic] in unserem Denken hatte ich immer gefühlt und bin sehr erfreut, dass Sie sie bestätigen.

Große Freude habe ich an dem jungen Forell[4], der jetzt bei uns studiert und der mir fleißig schwedische Bücher und Zeitungen bringt. Die gewaltige Regung in Ihrem kirchlichen Leben erstaunt und erfreut mich zugleich trotz mancher offenbar recht radikalen Ausbrüche. Es ist doch offenbar eine gewaltige geistige Spannung bei Ihnen, die leider bei uns längst nicht so zu bemerken ist.

Mit ergebenem Gruße, in Verehrung

Ihr

R. Otto

Für Indien käme für meinen interreligiösen Menschheitsbund Rabindra-

---

took place in Berlin in 1922, but it was dissolved in 1933. As can be concluded from the next letter, Söderblom considered the idea an illusion. Cf. *RGG*, 4th ed., vol. 5, 1100.

[3] Rudolf Otto, *Das Heilige. Über das Irrationale in der Idee des Göttlichen und sein Verhältnis zum Rationalen*, 1st ed. Breslau 1917.

[4] Birger Forell (1893–1958). He was a sailors' chaplain in Rotterdam 1921–1926. In 1928, he traveled to India with Rudolf Otto where Mahatma Gandhi fascinated him. He then became the Swedish pastor in Berlin (1929–1942); after 1945 he was in charge of German prisoners of war in the UK and of refugees in Espelkamp. All the while, he was active in ecumenical affairs.

nāth Thagur[5] in Frage. Er würde ganz Bengalen und Halb=Indien hinter sich haben. Mit Ihnen, dem Khalifen und Thagur wäre der Menschheitsbund gesichert. Ich habe Th. in Kalkutta kennen lernen u. wollte schon vor dem Kriege die Gruppe der Freunde der Christlichen Welt veranlassen, ihn nach Deutschland einzuladen. Es würde jetzt noch viel zeitgemäßer sein, ihn einmal nach Europa einzuladen. Da er Träger des Nobelpreises ist, so würde er gewiß mit Freuden nach Schweden kommen und dann auch nach hier. Und wenn Sie ihn für die Idee des »religiösen Menschheitsbundes« gewönnen, so würde er sogleich in seinen Vorträgen der wirksamste Apostel dafür sein. [On talks Otto had with Turkish officials and on a medal he received from the Sultan]

156. To Rudolf Otto[1]

Upsala 24.2.1920.

H[ans] H[ögvördighet] Professor Dr. Otto
Marburg

För Eder vänliga skrivelse tackar jag hjärtligast!

Det gläder mig att Docent Heiler får ägna sig åt religionshistorien i fred, men jag är övertygad om att han genom fem års vistelse vid vårt universitet i Kina skulle erhållit en utbildning, som han icke i Europa kan finna. ...

Med livligt intresse tager jag del av Eder storslagna plan. Sänd mig några exemplar av uppsatsen i Christliche Welt. Det skall glädja Eder att höra att under tiden arbetet för den ekumeniska konferensen (som nu, sedan amerikanska Federal Council, representerande 50–60 millioner evangeliska kristna, formligen beslutat att med oss, Schweiz o.s.v. genomföra saken, verkligen kommer till stånd så småningom) betydligt gått framåt. ... När jag fått Eder artikel och studerat den och närmare tänkt mig in i saken skall jag återkomma. Ett sådant företag som detta får icke ha bråttom. För min del ser jag i den ekumeniska konferensen en närmare liggande uppgift, som för mig blivit någonting av den Guds dårskap, som jag måste söka vara med om att förverkliga i världen.

...

Både min hustru och jag erinra oss livligt Edert besök hos oss i Paris och hoppas vi mottaga Eder härstädes.

Eder med utmärkt aktning

Nathan Söderblom

---

[5] Rabindranath Tagore (1861–1941), Indian philosopher of culture and poet from a Bengali Brahman family, received the Nobel prize for literature in 1913. He was open for modernization, e. g., by opposing the caste system.

[1] Ms. OA 1461 Bibliothek Religionswissenschaft Marburg, R.-Otto-Archiv, typewritten letter.

Hochwohlgeboren Professor Dr. Rudolf Otto
Marburg

Für Ihr freundliches Schreiben danke ich aufs Herzlichste!
Es freut mich, dass Dozent Heiler sich in Ruhe der Religionswissenschaft widmen kann, aber ich bin überzeugt, dass er durch einen fünfjährigen Aufenthalt an unserer Universität in China eine Ausbildung bekommen hätte, die er in Europa nicht finden kann. ... [Reply to Otto's question concerning persons to be sent to India]
Mit lebhaftem Interesse nehme ich Anteil an Ihrem großartigen Plan. Schicken Sie mir einige Exemplare des Aufsatzes in der Christlichen Welt. Es wird Sie freuen zu hören, dass unterdessen die Arbeit für die ökumenische Konferenz (die jetzt tatsächlich nach und nach zustande kommt, nachdem der Federal Council, der 50–60 Millionen evangelischer Christen repräsentiert, förmlich beschlossen hat, mit uns, der Schweiz usw. die Sache durchzuführen) erheblich weiter fortgeschritten ist. ... [On inquiries by Islamic dignitaries whether Muslims should not also be invited to the planned ecumenical conference, as well as on previous promoters of the idea to convene members of all monotheistic religions] Wenn ich Ihren Artikel bekomme, ihn studiert und mich genauer in die Sache hineingedacht habe, werde ich darauf zurückkommen. Eine solche Unternehmung muss keine Eile haben. Was mich angeht, so sehe ich in der ökumenischen Konferenz eine näher liegende Aufgabe, die für mich etwas von Gottes Torheit hat, an deren [scil. der Torheit] Verwirklichung in dieser Welt ich mich beteiligen muss.
... [A few remarks on the Swedish *attaché honoraire* Johannes Kolmodin, and on Otto's and Söderblom's own connections with Japan)
Meine Frau und ich erinnern uns lebhaft an Ihren Besuch bei uns in Paris und hoffen, Sie hier empfangen zu können.
Mit ausgezeichneter Hochachtung Ihr
Nathan Söderblom

157. From RUDOLF KITTEL[1]

Leipzig, den 7. III 20

Verehrter Erzbischof & Freund!
Besten Dank für Ihren jüngsten Brief. Der *Paß* ist angekommen, die Einreisemöglichkeit also gesichert. Dass ich am *12. April* ganz gut beginnen kann, schrieb ich schon, ich nehme an, der Brief sei inzwischen angekommen.[2] Ebenso dass ich vorläufig den *Rektor* & den *Superintendenten* um Benachrichtigung der Kollegen und Pastoren gebeten habe. Von den Kollegen sind schon eine ganze Anzahl Meldungen eingegangen. Das Anerbieten wird augenscheinlich mit *großem Danke* angenommen & es wird gar keine Schwierigkeit haben, die 100 Kinder zusammenzubringen.

---

[1] N. Söderblom's collection of letters, from foreigners, UUB, handwritten letter.
[2] This concerns the invitation to lecture in Uppsala mentioned in the letter no. 154 of this collection. The letter Kittel refers to was written on March 1 and is part of the collection at UUB.

Die eine Frage ist noch offen betreffs *der Zeit.* Ich schrieb Ihnen, daß wegen der Schule von manchen Seiten der Juli gewünscht werde. Inzwischen höre ich, besonders auch von ärztlicher Seite, dass man hier zum Mai und Juni besondere Knappheit der Ernährung fürchtet, da die Vorräte zu Ende gehen & zur Einfuhr kein Geld im Lande ist; es sei deshalb ein möglichst früher Termin erwünscht. Im Juli gebe es Frühfrüchte & Gemüse. Was meinen Sie dazu? Zur Entscheidung der Frage müßte man erst wissen, wie *lange* Zeit als Aufenthalt in Aussicht genommen ist; 4 Wochen? 6 Wochen? 8 Wochen? Ich habe keine Ahnung, wie Sie und Ihre Freunde darüber denken. Aber nehme ich z. B. 6 Wochen an, so könnte wohl als Anfang Mitte oder gegen *Ende Juni* gewählt werden & als Ende das Ferienende. So viel Schulverlust würden gewiß alle ertragen. Vielleicht denken Sie darüber nach & lassen mich Ihre Gedanken wissen.

Dann noch eines. Es ist heikel, aber nicht zu umgehen. Heute teilt mir mein älterer Sohn, der im Eisenbahnministerium in Berlin ist, mit, dass die Fahrkarte Trölleborg [=Trelleborg] – Stockholm II. Kl. ohne Bettkarte 1600 M mit Bett 1950 M kostet. – Ebenso natürlich die Rückfahrt, wozu noch Leipzig = Trölleborg kommt. Zusammen ohne Bettkarte rund 3500–4000 M. Nun werden die Kinder in III. Klasse ja wesentlich billiger fahren. Aber 1800–2000 Mark scheint mir das Mindeste. Ich halte für ganz ausgeschlossen, daß die Eltern das aufbringen können. Bei normalen Valutaverhältnissen ginge es ja wohl, da wäre mit 100–120 M ja viel zu machen gewesen. Aber so!! Ich fürchte, die ganze Sache werde dadurch zum Scheitern gebracht. Denn den hochherzigen Spendern auch noch das Opfer freier Reise in Schweden zuzumuten, kann niemand in den Sinn kommen. Schon der Gedanke würde mich beschweren. Aber ob vielleicht Ihre *Regierung* für den guten Zweck Freifahrt oder erhebliche Ermäßigung in Aussicht stellen könnte? Verzeihen Sie die Offenheit. Aber es ist nicht meine private Sache.

Mit herzlichen Grüßen
Ihr
Kittel.

158. To Rudolf Kittel[1]

Professor Kittel, Rosentalgasse, Leipzig. Hundert Kinder sofort willkommen können fünf Monate bleiben wir bezahlen Reise Sassnitz Upsala hin und zurück. Wann können Kinder Sassnitz kommen wo wir abholen.

---

[1] N. Söderblom's collection of letters, from foreigners, UUB, undated draft of telegram, handwritten on free space of previous letter.

159. From FRIEDRICH HEILER[1]

München Wörthstr. 13, 8. III. 20.

Hochverehrter Hochwürdigster Herr Erzbischof!

Haben Sie vielen herzlichen Dank für Ihren gütigen Brief. Die Korrekturen besorge ich alle, ich lese jeden Bogen zweimal und hoffe so, dass keine sinnstörenden Fehler stehen bleiben. Gestern traf meine Ernennung zum Extraordinarius der vergleichenden Religionsgeschichte vom preuß. Ministerium ein. Vor 8 Tagen hatte ich nach langem Schwanken mich dazu entschlossen die Berufung anzunehmen. Es ist mir sehr schwer gefallen durch diesen Schritt endgültig den Katholizismus zu verlassen; denn ich kenne und liebe all das Große, Tiefe und Reine, das in ihm neben dem Niederen, Häßlichen und Unchristlichen wohnt. Und ich kenne auch die ganze religiöse Armut, Schwäche und Halbheit, die gerade dem deutschen Protestantismus eigen ist. Aber ich sah in dieser Berufung einen Fingerzeig Gottes, eine Aufforderung zu neuer Wirksamkeit und so beschreite ich entschlossen die Bahn, auf die Er mich geführt hat, im Vertrauen, dass ich auf ihr zum Ziele gelangen werde.

Die Stelle ist nicht etatsmäßig, darum sehr schlecht besoldet, so dass ich als Einzelstehender gerade knapp damit leben kann. Doch hoffe ich in nicht zu ferner Zeit in eine bessere Stelle einzurücken. Dagegen ist die Lehrverpflichtung größer als mir erwünscht ist. Ich fürchte an meiner Übersetzung Ihres »Religionsproblemets« sehr gehindert zu werden, da meine Arbeitszeit nun durch die Vorbereitung auf die Vorlesungen absorbiert werden wird. Hier hatte ich es wesentlich leichter, da ich immer ein neutestamentliches Kolleg las, was nicht viel Vorbereitung erfordert. Ende April werde ich nach Marburg übersiedeln, das Sommersemester dauert bis Ende Juli. Vorher werde ich nicht nach Schweden kommen können. Durch die Annahme des Rufes nach Marburg werden auch meine China-Pläne hinfällig. Der Aufenthalt dort wäre ja sehr lehrreich für mich gewesen, aber ich glaube, daß meine schwache Gesundheit das Klima in Hangkau nicht vertragen hätte, auch wären meine Eltern sehr unglücklich darüber, wenn ich auf so lange Zeit Europa verlassen würde. ...

[On translations of Heiler's book *Das Gebet*]

Grüßen Sie herzlichst Ihre verehrte Frau und Ihre Kinder. In Dankbarkeit und Verehrung verbleibe ich

Ihr ergebenster
Friedrich Heiler

---

[1] N. Söderblom's collection of letters, from foreigners, UUB, handwritten letter.

160. From RUDOLF OTTO[1]

Marburg. 9. 3. 20.

Hochgeehrter Herr Erzbischof.

… [On an article Otto had written, and on a leading Indian Muslim]
Zu Ihren schönen Erfolgen betreffs die öcumenische Konferenz beglückwünsche ich Sie und hoffe viel davon. – Für Ihre freundlichen Schlußworte
meinen besten Dank. Ich bin vor 17 Jahren einmal in Schweden gewesen
und habe oft den Wunsch gehabt, das schöne und liebenswürdige Land wiederzusehen. Aber das wird für viele Jahre unmöglich sein. Wir sind jetzt alle
wie in einem Käfig eingeschlossen. Umso mehr hoffen wir, Sie einmal in *unserer* Heimat wieder begrüßen zu können und haben bedauert, dass Sie Ihre
Reise nach Genf, bei der Sie gewiß unser Marburg besucht hätten, nicht
ausführen konnten. – Herzliche Freude habe ich an Ihrem Schüler und Ver-
ehrer, cand. Forell. Er hat so warmes Interesse an unseren Verhältnissen
und versteht sich so ausgezeichnet darauf, dass ich sehr wünschen möchte,
dass er einmal einige Jahre in Deutschland eine Anstellung finden könnte.
Er würde mit der Zeit ein treffliches Bindeglied zwischen hüben und drüben
werden können. –
… [On the renowned Frankfurt sinologist Richard Wilhelm]
Empfehlen Sie mich Ihrer verehrten Frau Gemahlin, die sich so freundlich meiner erinnert. Die Begegnung in Paris ist mir in lieber Erinnerung.
In Verehrung Ihr ergebener
R. Otto.

161. To FRIEDRICH HEILER[1]

Upsala 15/3 1920

gott segne ihren geraden weg = aerkebiskopen

162. To FRIEDRICH HEILER[1]

Upsala 17.3.1920.

Käre forskare, evangelist och vän!
Hjärtligt deltager jag och alla Upsalavänner i glädjen över Eder framgång.
Det är välförtjänt och jag tror att Marburg blir ett utmärkt arbetsfält. För
min del skulle jag föredragit Kina under de närmaste fem åren. Men särskilt
kroppslig svaghet måste tagas i betraktande. Gud välsigne Eder verksamhet

---

[1] N. Söderblom's ecumenical collection A 19, UUB, handwritten letter.

[1] Fr. Heiler's papers (Ms. 999), Univ. Library Marburg, telegram.

[1] Fr. Heiler's papers (Ms. 999), Univ. Library Marburg, typewritten letter.

i den evangeliska teologins fortsatta tjänst. Jag hoppas att Ni snart besöker oss i Sverige.

Boksändningen, som även omfattar böcker om modernismen, har jag nyss mottagit och längtar efter vårt stora kyrkliga möte taga i tu med den. Tack för ovärderlig hjälp med korrektur. Jag behöver icke se korrekturen utom i det fall att Ni är tveksam. Till England och Amerika har jag sänt Das Gebet och hoppas att en översättning kan komma till stånd. Menegoz i Strassburg är sedan gammalt min vän. Hans onkel, Fideismens bekante upphovsman i Paris, hör till mina äldsta och bästa franska vänner. Tänk om vi hade Eder här i maj, då Albert Schweitzer under en månad gäster vårt hus. Jag hoppas få närmare underrättelser om hur det gestaltar sig för Eder i Marburg. När Eder semester där är slut, så kom över ett slag och vila i Sverige.

Med hjärtliga hälsningar från hela familjen, som jublar över *professor* Heiler och från fröken Rodling

Eder tillgivne

Nathan Söderblom

Uppsala, March 17, 1920

Lieber Forscher, Evangelist und Freund!

Herzlich nehmen ich und alle Freunde in Uppsala teil an der Freude über Ihren Erfolg. Das ist wohlverdient, und ich glaube, Marburg wird ein ausgezeichnetes Arbeitsfeld. Ich persönlich hätte China während der nächsten fünf Jahre vorgezogen. Aber körperliche Schwäche muss hier besonders in Betracht gezogen werden. Gott segne Ihre Wirksamkeit im weiteren Dienst für die evangelische Theologie. Ich hoffe, dass Sie uns bald in Schweden besuchen werden.

Die Büchersendung, die auch Bücher über den Modernismus enthält, habe ich neulich bekommen, und ich sehne mich danach, sie nach unserer großen Kirchenkonferenz in Angriff zu nehmen. Danke für unschätzbare Hilfe bei der Korrektur. Ich brauche die Korrektur nicht zu sehen außer für den Fall, dass Sie Bedenken haben.

Nach England und Amerika habe ich *Das Gebet* geschickt und hoffe, dass eine Übersetzung zustande kommen kann. Ménégoz in Strasbourg ist seit alters mein Freund. Sein Onkel, der bekannte Begründer des Fideismus in Paris, gehört zu meinen ältesten und besten französischen Freunden.[2] Dass wir Sie doch im Mai hier hätten, wenn Albert Schweitzer einen Monat lang in unserem Hause zu Gast ist! Ich hoffe, weitere Nachricht zu bekommen, wie sich die Dinge für Sie in Marburg gestalten werden. Wenn Ihr Semester zu Ende ist, kommen Sie doch einmal herüber und ruhen Sie sich in Schweden aus.

Mit herzlichen Grüßen von der ganzen Familie, die über *Professor* Heiler jubelt, und von Fräulein Rodling[3]

Ihr Ihnen verbundener

Nathan Söderblom

---

[2] Fernand Ménégoz (1873-1944), professor of systematic theology in Strasbourg; as for his uncle, Eugène Ménégoz (1838-1920), see letter no. 8, note 2.
[3] Gerda Rodling (1895-1993), Söderblom's secretary.

163. From ADOLF DEISSMANN[1]

Berlin-Wilmersdorf, den 23. 3. 1920

Verehrter, teurer Freund!

Soeben erhalte ich von Dr. Paul Rohrbach[2] die Nachricht, dass Sie für die notleidenden Dorpater Kollegen dreihundert Kronen aufgebracht haben. Es ist mir das eine ganz große Freude, und ich möchte nicht verfehlen, Ihnen sofort herzlichst dafür zu danken. –

Leider liege ich seit 14 Tagen schwer erkrankt danieder; Darmblutungen haben mich ausserordentlich entkräftet. Ich werde wohl längere Zeit ganz fest liegen müssen. Die unerwartete Musse lässt oftmals meine Gedanken über Land und Meer schweifen, besonders oft zu Ihnen und ihrem mir so teuren Lande.

Ich wäre Ihnen sehr dankbar, wenn Sie freundlichst fortfahren würden, an mich deutsch zu schrieben, da mir das Schwedische immer noch Schwierigkeiten macht. –

Der wahnwitzige Putsch Kapp und Genossen, der ein grosses Unglück für unser Volk war, scheint nun glücklich abgewehrt zu sein.[3]

… [On a book about the Jewish catacomb in Rome]

Zum bevorstehenden Osterfest gedenken wir Ihrer und Ihres ganzen lieben Hauses mit den besten Wünschen. Mit den herzlichsten Grüssen

Ihr treu verbundener
Adolf Deißmann

164. To ADOLF DEISSMANN[1]

Hochverehrter teurer Freund

Wie traurig das Sie eben in dieser Zeit von einer so ernsten Krankheit heimgesucht wurden. I[ch] kenne aus eigener Erfarung das man nach solchen Magenblutungen lange Ruhe und besonders gut gewälte [sic, lies: gewählte] Nahrung braucht[.] Wenn wir nur Sie hier haben könnten mit Ihrer lieben Familie um Sie zu pflegen[.] Das kleine das gesandt werden kann reicht nicht viel aus Aber wenn sie einmal das Bett verlassen dürfen könnten Sie nicht zu uns kommen um erholung zu finden Ich möchte dann bitten Reisegeld senden zu dürfen

Mit herzl[ichen] Osterngrüssen

Ihr

---

[1] N. Söderblom's collection of letters, from foreigners, UUB, typewritten letter.

[2] Paul Rohrbach (1869–1956), writer in Berlin.

[3] In 1920, Wolfgang Kapp (1858–1922), a politician on the far right, and others staged a revolt against the German government. The labor unions reacted with a general strike. The revolt, though being an ominous symptom of the strength of anti-democratic sentiment in the Weimar republic, could quickly be quelled.

[1] N. Söderblom's collection of letters, from foreigners, UUB, undated draft of reply, in secretary's handwriting, on empty space of previous letter. I have not found the actual letter.

165. To Friedrich Heiler[1]

Upsala 7.5.1920.

...

Just nu erhåller jag det vänliga brevkortet från Marburg och önskar Eder Guds välsignelse i den nya verksamheten. Hälsa professor R. Otto, en bland de få teologer, som fatta kristendomens väsen ur religionens väsen och uppbygga en universell åskådning och strävan icke på rationalismen utan på grundvalen av religionens egentliga väsen. Hur är det med hans hälsa? Gärna skulle jag vilja bereda honom en vilotid här i Sverige. ...

Eder tillgivne.

Nathan Söderblom

Das Wesen des Katholicismus, för vilken jag hjärtligt tackar, betyder en högst väsentlig fördjupning av vår uppfattning och borde leda till en mindre tillfällig och ytlig[,] mera väsentlig och fruktbringande broderlig diskussion mellan den romerska och den evangeliska delen av Kristi kyrka.

Uppsala, 7.5.1920

Lieber Professor und Freund!

[On a person who would be willing to translate Heiler's *Das Gebet* into English, and on a couple of footnotes left out in the draft of the new edition of Söderblom/ Tiele, *Einführung in die Religionsgeschichte*]

Eben erhalte ich die freundliche Karte aus Marburg und wünsche Ihnen Gottes Segen für die neue Tätigkeit. Grüßen Sie Professor R. Otto, einen der wenigen Theologen, die das Wesen des Christentums aus dem Wesen der Religion heraus begreifen und eine universale Anschauung und Zielrichtung nicht aus dem Rationalismus, sondern auf der Grundlage des eigentlichen Wesens der Religion entwickeln. Wie steht es mit seiner Gesundheit? Gerne würde ich ihm eine Erholungszeit hier in Schweden bereiten. ...

Ihr Ihnen verbundener

Nathan Söderblom

Das Wesen des Katholizismus, für das ich herzlich danke, bedeutet eine ganz wesentliche Vertiefung unseres Verständnisses und sollte zu einer weniger zufälligen und äußerlichen, mehr am Wesentlichen orientierten und fruchtbringenderen brüderlichen Diskussion zwischen dem römischen und dem evangelischen Teil der Kirche Christi führen.

166. From Friedrich Heiler[1]

Marburg a/Lahn, Gisselbergstr. 21. 14.5.1920

Hochverehrter Herr Erzbischof!

Nun habe ich glücklich die Übersiedlung von meiner Heimatstadt in das schöne Marburg vollzogen, wo ich mich bereits einzugewöhnen beginne.

---

[1] Fr. Heiler's papers (Ms. 999), Univ. Library Marburg, typewritten letter.

[1] N. Söderblom's collection of letters, from foreigners, UUB, handwritten postcard.

An Professor R. Otto, einem Theologen von wundervollem religiösen Feinsinn, habe ich bereits einen freundlichen Führer gefunden. – Die gewünschten Korrekturen und Einfügungen für »Einführung in die Rel[igions]-Gesch[ichte]« habe ich besorgt entsprechend der schwed[ischen] Ausgabe. Sobald ich ganz eingerichtet bin, folgt ein ausführlicher Brief. Bis dahin grüße ich Sie und Ihre ganze Familie aufs herzlichste. In Dankbarkeit und Verehrung Friedrich Heiler

167. From RUDOLF OTTO[1]

Marburg a. L. Hainweg 6.   20.5.20.

Verehrter Herr Erzbischof.

[On Richard Wilhelm, cf. letter no.188, n.10]

Ich höre, daß die schwedische Pfarrstelle in Berlin frei wird. Darf ich Ihnen für ihre Wiederbesetzung meinen jungen Freund Birger Forell recht angelegentlich empfehlen? Er ist noch jung, aber ungewöhnlich gereift, hat sich während seiner zwei Semester in Deutschland eine große Kenntnis unserer Sprache und unserer Verhältnisse erworben und hat in der Berliner schwedischen Gemeinde während seiner letzten Ferien in Berlin schon Freunde gefunden und auch einige Gottesdienste gehalten. Er würde sein Examen im September oder November machen und seinen praktischen Kursus in Uppsala im Herbste erledigen. Aber vor dem 1ten Januar würde man den Platz in Berlin wohl kaum besetzen und ihn inzwischen vikarisch verwalten lassen. Mir scheint Forell für diesen Platz so ungewöhnlich gut geeignet zu sein, daß ich bedauern würde, wenn er ihn nicht erhielte. Durch langen Umgang habe ich ihn als einen Menschen schnellster Fassungsgabe, glücklichen Ausdruckes, bezwingender Liebenswürdigkeit und tief lauteren Charakters kennen lernen. Dabei hat er eine Gewandtheit und Sicherheit des Umganges und einen praktischen Takt, der in Erstaunen setzt. Er hat diese Gaben grade eben noch bewiesen auf einer großen Reise für meinen »religiösen Menschheitsbund«. Da hat er mit Hoch und Niedrig, mit Jesuitenvätern und Professoren verkehrt und überall vortrefflich abgeschnitten. Er ist bereits längere Zeit Prädikant gewesen, in seiner Heimat; hier hat er mit größestem Fleiße studiert. Die Stelle in Berlin hat doch gleichsam eine eigene Mission, die einen eigenen Mann erfordert. Und der scheint mir Forell zu sein. Er gehört zur »Helsinge Nation«,[2] und da werden gewiß alle seine persönlichen Verhältnisse gut zu erfahren sein. Seine Zeugnisse half ich ihm ins Deutsche übersetzen: sie waren vortrefflich. Er gehört hier der Christlichen Studenten Vereinigung an, teilt deren religiösen Ernst, aber ist den meisten an theologischem Weitblick überlegen. Seine stark socialen In-

---

[1] N. Söderblom's ecumenical collection, A 19, UUB, handwritten letter.
[2] Fraternity of students hailing from the province of Hälsingland.

teressen würde er in Berlin bei seinem Freunde Siegismund Schultze[3] noch besonders gut pflegen können.

Mir ist er ein treuer Helfer beim »religiösen Menschheitsbunde«. Hierüber noch ein Wort. Das Interesse dafür wächst. Aus England senden mir die Quaker ihre Boten. Auch die Church of England leage [= League] of peace sandte mir ein Schreiben. Lord Haldane[4] lies [sic] mir sein Interesse aussprechen. Ich hoffe, dass sich nun auch einige unserer Kirchenmänner an die Sache machen werden. Sehr möchte ich Sie bitten, sich mit dafür zu interessieren; und besonders im August, in Genf, dafür einzutreten. Vom 1-11. September soll dann in Leyden, an der Universität, eine »international school« gehalten werden, wo die Probleme der Internationale von Gelehrten und angesehenen Führern aller Länder verhandelt werden sollen. Wir erwarten Lord Cecil[5], Harnack, Deißmann und viele andere. Ich habe auch Rabindranath Tagore einladen lassen. Ich selber spreche über »Internationale und Religion«, und will dabei auch den R. M. B. vorschlagen. – Uns liegt sehr daran, daß Sie und viele andere vom Genfer Concil[6] auch nach Leyden kommen möchten. Ich bitte sehr darum.

Wenn Sie nach Genf reisen, so vergessen Sie nicht daß Marburg am Wege liegt. Es gäbe so vieles zu erörtern, wozu der Brief nicht ausreicht, und die Gelegenheit ist für Sie ja so sehr günstig.

Wir beneiden Sie um die Orgelspiele und Vorträge von Schweizer [Albert Schweitzer] und hätten ihn sehr gerne hier. Herr Forell stellt in Aussicht daß auch Herr Billing und Linderholm[7] einmal zu uns kommen könnten. Je mehr, je lieber. – Fünf junge Schweden werden demnächst bei uns studieren. Forell hat schon begonnen, deutschen Studenten schwedischen Unterricht zu geben. Möchten diese Freundesbande immer enger werden.

Heiler ist nun Freund und Kollege hier, und hat sich mit großem Erfolge bei uns eingeführt. So jung und schon so gelehrt und vertieft! Wir kommen uns in unseren Anschauungen sehr nahe. Die Studenten sind für ihn begei-

---

[3] Friedrich Siegmund-Schultze (1885–1969), socially active German churchman and a co-founder of the World Alliance for Promoting International Friendship through the Churches in 1914 (cf. letter no. 110, n. 4). He became a chief advocate of the ecumenical movement and an important collaborator of Söderblom's; cf. the latter's letters to him: *Nathan Söderblom. Briefe und Botschaften an einen deutschen Mitarbeiter*, ed. bei Fr. Siegmund-Schultze (SÖA II), Marburg 1966.

[4] Richard Burdon First Viscount Haldane of Cloan (1856–1928), English statesman, Secretary of War 1905–1912. He tried to mediate between the UK and Germany in 1912 (Haldane mission) but failed because of German prestige thinking. Later, he was twice Lord Chancelor (1912–1915 and 1924).

[5] Robert Cecil First Viscount of Chelwood (1864–1958), British parliamentarian and cabinet minister, one of the chief architects and proponents of the League of Nations.

[6] Otto refers to the first meeting of Life and Work which was to take place in August 1920.

[7] Einar Billing, co-founder of the Sigtuna Foundation and bishop of Växjö 1920–1939: cf. letter no. 21 n. 3 and 131, n. 4; Emanuel Linderholm (1872–1937), professor of the history of religion and church history in Uppsala. His theological views were liberal; cf. his book *Från dogmat till evangelium* (From Dogma to Gospel), Stockholm 1918. He also took a lively interest in liturgical reforms, cf. his *Svensk högmässa*, Stockholm 1926.

stert. Er selber ist für Schweden begeistert, und besonders für dessen Erzbischof.

Meine besten Grüße, auch an die Frau Ärkebiskopin.

In Ergebenheit Ihr

R. Otto, Prof.

Ich wäre dankbar für ein Programm oder einen Aufsatz über die Genfer Tagung.

168. From Friedrich Heiler[1]

Marburg a. d. Lahn, Gisselbergerstr. 21, 20. Juni 1920.

Hochverehrter Hochwürdiger Herr Erzbischof!

Schon längst wollte ich an Sie schreiben, aber teils war ich von vieler Arbeit überbürdet, teils war ich in schmerzliche innere Kämpfe verstrickt, die es mir schwer machten zu schreiben. Was ich bisher hier erfuhr, war eine Kette bitterer Enttäuschungen. Tief niedergedrückt hat mich vom Anfang meines Hierseins an die Verkümmerung des religiösen Lebens, die mir im norddeutschen Protestantismus entgegentrat. Nicht nur die Laien, sondern auch die Theologen sind dieser Verarmung anheimgefallen. Ich sehe mit tiefem Schmerz, wie wenig religiös meine Studenten sind, wie ihnen alles tiefere Frömmigkeitsleben eine fremde Welt ist, wie sie mit der evangelischen »Weltoffenheit« den Mangel religiöser Tiefe noch zu rechtfertigen wagen. In den theol. Hörsälen der Universität herrscht zumeist ein flacher Rationalismus und ein kritischer Radikalismus, der in vielen jungen Theologen die Reste evangelischer Frömmigkeit, die sie aus dem Heimathause noch mitbringen, zerstört. Ich tue in meinen Vorlesungen alles um Verständnis für echte und tiefe Frömmigkeit zu wecken, aber die Folge davon ist, dass man mir Propaganda für den Katholizismus vorwirft. Daran ist ja das eine richtig, dass ich das Gute und Schöne am Katholizismus heute mehr schätze denn je und dass ich oft tiefes Heimweh nach der Kirche meiner Jugend empfinde, wo trotz aller Entstellung doch noch warmes religiöses Lebens [sic] pulsiert und Sinn für das Heilige vorhanden ist. (Hier habe ich das Gefühl, in einem religiösen Vacuum mich zu befinden.) Die Folge dieser »katholisierenden« Wirksamkeit ist ein Konflikt, nicht nur mit einem großen Teil meiner Hörer, sondern auch mit meinen Kollegen. Prof. Heitmüller[2] polemisiert offen in seinen Vorlesungen gegen meine Auffassungen. Darin liegt gewiß eine Tragik, daß ich, ausgestoßen aus meiner Mutterkirche und befehdet von meinen früheren Glaubensgenossen, keine neue Heimat im Protestantismus finden kann, sondern derselben Vereinsamung anheimfalle, die den von mir so hoch verehrten Tyrrell[3] traf. Aber ich muß in all dem, was ich hier erfuhr, eine Führung Gottes erkennen und glaube, dass

---

[1] N. Söderblom's collection of letters, from foreigners, UUB, handwritten letter.

[2] For Wilhelm Heitmüller, cf. letter no. 43, n. 2.

[3] George Tyrrell (1861–1909), Irish Catholic modernist.

auch aus solchen Leiden und Konflikten Früchte des Segens für die Kirche Christi reifen können. Vielleicht gilt für solche vereinsamte Kämpfer das Wort: victor quia victima.[4]

Im Einverständnis mit Prof. Rudolf Otto, dem einzigen von meinen Kollegen, der mich versteht, werde ich um weitere Reibungen zu vermeiden Marburg wieder verlassen und meine akademische Tätigkeit auf dem neutralen Boden der philosophischen Fakultät fortsetzen. Es ist noch nicht entschieden, ob ich nach Berlin berufen werden kann oder ob ich wieder in meine alte Stellung in München zurückkehre. Ich habe ja oft bereut Schweden verlassen zu haben, da mir dann wohl alle diese schmerzlichen Konflikte erspart geblieben wären. Denn dort hat der Rationalismus das religiöse Leben nicht so zerfressen wie hier in Norddeutschland. Ich gestehe, dass ich, zumal seit eine Reihe junger Schweden hier sind, starke Sehnsucht nach dem Norden habe. Ich sehne mich darnach wieder die frische Luft evangelischer Frömmigkeit zu atmen, die hier gänzlich fehlt. Die Schwierigkeit liegt aber in der Valuta, welche die Reise furchtbar teuer macht. Zumal dann, wenn ich wieder in die schlecht besoldete Münchener Stellung zurückkehre, muß ich sehr sparen um bei der argen Teuerung auskommen zu können. Wäre es vielleicht möglich, daß ich ein paar Vorträge in Stockholm und Upsala hielte um die Reisekosten ersetzt zu bekommen? Jedenfalls würde es mich sehr freuen, wenn ich nach all den trüben Marburger Wochen wieder Sonnenschein in Schweden schauen könnte. Auch wäre mir eine Aussprache mit Ihnen über alle diese neuen Erkenntnisse und Enttäuschungen sehr erwünscht. Ich beurteile die Lage des deutschen Protestantismus nach meinen hiesigen Erfahrungen für sehr, sehr ernst. Man muß von einer allgemeinen Auflösung sprechen; noch eine politische Krise wie im November 1918 und die Katastrophe ist unvermeidlich. Das sind bittere Erkenntnisse, aber man darf dem Ernst der Tatsachen sich nicht verschließen.

... [On proofreading]

Mit dem Ausdruck tiefer Dankbarkeit und Verehrung und mit der Bitte Ihre ganze Familie und Frl. Rodling zu grüßen bleibe ich

Ihr ganz ergebener

Friedrich Heiler

169. To Friedrich Heiler[1]

Upsala 1.7.1920.

Käre Professor och vän!

Edert djupt vemodiga brev är för mig egendomligt nog ingen överraskning. Som jag flera gånger skrivit till Eder och sagt Eder och andra, hör Ni till dem, som äro dömda att vara pilgrimer i världen. Inget yttre kyrkosamfund

---

[4] Victor because victim, Augustinus on Christ: *Confessiones* X, 43,69.

[1] Fr. Heiler's papers (Ms. 999), Univ. Library Marburg, typewritten letter.

kan fullt motsvara själens innersta behov. Hade Ni varit född inom den evangeliska kristenheten, så hade detta faktum icke behövt hos Eder framkalla en så smärtsam erfarenhet, ty då hade Ni haft frihet till gudsumgänge och andlig självständighet i det heligas samfund utan att samvetet behövt råka i konflikt. Som det nu är, ber jag Eder att fullfölja Eder evangeliska katolska linje rakt fram. Skulle Ni hava känt Eder tillfredsställd i Eder nya omgivning, skulle jag däri hava sett en viss otrohet emot Eder själv. Det är självklart att Ni icke heller hos oss i Sverige kan äga den andliga hemkänsla som Ni nu en gång för alla är, liksom många andra av Kristi kyrkas söner, berövad. Men detta förminskar icke Eder uppgift, och egentligen har Ni ju en dubbel rikedom genom att Eder själ har öppnat sig för evangelium och för mystisk innerlighet även i annan form. Eder rika erfarenhet vid unga år bör betyda en Guds gåva till Edert kall såsom religionens utforskare, men framför allt såsom ett av Guds nådefullt och barmhärtigt upptagna barn.

När skulle Ni eventuellt kunna göra ett besök här i Upsala eller annorstädes i Sverige för att vinna nya krafter? Med resekostnaden blir det väl någon råd.

Vad angår den nordtyska evangeliska kristenheten, så har den nog, trots sin fattigdom på andakt och känsla, dock säkerligen stora gåvor från evangelium i form av obetingad respekt för sanningen, samvetsgrannhet, karaktärsstyrka, kallelsetrohet och gudsförtröstan. Gärna ville jag med Eder tala om de problem, som den nuvarande ställningen uppställer för oss.

Med förnyad hjärtlig tacksägelse för Eder hjälp med mina nya upplagor, med lyckönskan till Das Gebets enastående framgång och med en innerlig förbön samt med anhållan att Ni också måtte bedja för mig i mitt svåra kall, Eder för alltid
 tillgivne
 Nathan Söderblom

Uppsala, 1.7.1920

Lieber Professor und Freund!

Ihr tief wehmütiger Brief ist für mich, seltsam genug, keine Überraschung. Wie ich Ihnen mehrmals geschrieben und Ihnen und anderen gesagt habe, gehören Sie zu denen, die dazu verurteilt sind, Pilger in der Welt zu sein. Kein äußeres Kirchentum kann dem innersten Bedürfnis der Seele völlig entsprechen. Wären Sie innerhalb der evangelischen Christenheit geboren, so hätte dieses Faktum bei Ihnen nicht eine so schmerzliche Erfahrung hervorrufen müssen, denn dann hätten Sie Freiheit zum Umgang mit Gott und geistliche Selbstständigkeit in der Gemeinschaft der Heiligen gehabt, ohne dass das Gewissen hätte in Konflikt geraten müssen. Wie die Dinge nun einmal sind, bitte ich Sie, Ihre evangelisch-katholische Richtung geradlinig weiter zu verfolgen. Hätten Sie sich in Ihrer neuen Umgebung zufrieden gefühlt, so hätte ich darin eine gewisse Untreue Ihnen selbst gegenüber gesehen. Es versteht sich von selbst, dass Sie auch bei uns in Schweden nicht das geistliche Heimatgefühl haben können, dessen Sie jetzt ein für allemal, wie viele andere von den Söhnen der Kirche Christi, beraubt sind. Aber das macht Ihre Aufgabe nicht geringer, und eigentlich haben Sie ja einen doppelten Reichtum, dadurch dass Ihre Seele sich für das Evangelium und für mystische Innerlichkeit auch in anderer Form geöffnet hat.

Ihre reiche Erfahrung in jungen Jahren muss eine Gabe Gottes für Ihre Berufung als Erforscher der Religion, vor allem aber als eines von Gottes gnädig und barmherzig aufgenommenen Kindern bedeuten.

Wann würden Sie eventuell einen Besuch hier in Uppsala oder woanders in Schweden machen können, um neue Kraft zu schöpfen? Mit den Reisekosten wird sich wohl ein Weg finden.

Was die norddeutsche evangelische Christenheit angeht, so hat sie doch wohl trotz ihrer Armut in Andacht und Gefühl ganz gewiss große Gaben vom Evangelium in Gestalt unbedingter Achtung für die Wahrheit, Gewissenhaftigkeit, Charakterstärke, Berufstreue und Gottvertrauen. Gerne will ich mit Ihnen über die Probleme sprechen, welche die gegenwärtige Lage uns stellt.

Mit neuerlicher herzlicher Danksagung für Ihre Hilfe bei meinen neuen Auflagen, mit Glückwünschen zu dem einzigartigen Erfolg von *Das Gebet* und mit inniger Fürbitte sowie der Bitte, dass Sie auch für mich beten in meinem schweren Amt, stets Ihr Ihnen verbundener

Nathan Söderblom

170. From FRIEDRICH HEILER[1]

Marburg, Gisselbergerstr. 21, 8. Juli 1920.

Hochverehrter Hochwürdigster Herr Erzbischof!

Herzlichen Dank sage ich Ihnen für Ihren tröstenden und ermunternden Brief. Das Dunkel, das bisher über meinem Marburger Aufenthalt lag, hellt sich nun auf. Das quälende Heimweh nach der Kirche meiner Jugend verliert sich, da ich durch Gottes Hilfe nun hier einen frommen Gemeinschaftskreis gefunden habe, in dem Heimatgefühl aufkommt. Ich habe nunmehr in diesem meist aus Studenten bestehenden Kreise selbst eine intensive religiöse Tätigkeit begonnen und schätze mich glücklich etwas für die so dringend nötige Auffrischung des religiösen Lebens wirken zu können. Ich halte abwechselnd mit ein paar Freunden jeden Tag einen Morgengottesdienst, der sich großer Beliebtheit erfreut. Von den neuen liturgischen Bahnen, die wir dabei einschlagen, werde ich Ihnen ausführlich erzählen. Einen solchen Anschluß und eine solche religiöse Tätigkeit brauchte ich neben meiner Kathedertätigkeit; hätte ich sie gleich gefunden, als ich hierher kam, so wären mir viele furchtbar schwere Stunden erspart worden.

Durch Vermittlung von Troeltsch ist das disharmonische Verhältnis zu meinen Kollegen wenigstens äußerlich etwas gebessert worden. Innerlich freilich stehe ich nahezu allen fremd. Auch Rudolf Otto ist trotz seines Buches über das Heilige stark vom Rationalismus beeinflußt und ich kann nicht sagen, daß ich zu ihm in einen inneren Kontakt gekommen sei. Dagegen verstehe ich mich allmählich sehr gut mit meinen Studenten[.] Freilich glaube ich, daß gerade der starke Besuch meiner Vorlesungen und die Anhängerschar unter den Studenten mitschuld waren an dem Mißtrauen, das manche meiner Kollegen mir entgegenbrachten. Ich hoffe nunmehr in Mar-

---

[1] N. Söderblom's collection of letters, from foreigners, UUB, handwritten letter.

burg bleiben zu können, die noch bestehenden Reibungen lassen sich vielleicht im Laufe der Zeit noch vermindern.

Wie ich schon telegrafierte, habe ich mich nun zur Reise nach Schweden entschlossen. Die Lundenser Studenten haben mich bereits um Vorträge gebeten. Ich denke gleich nach Semesterschluß zu reisen, möchte zuerst nach Vadstena, dann nach Upsala, wo Billings im August sind, schließlich noch nach Ockelbo.

Hier bin ich viel mit der schwedischen Studentenkolonie zusammen. Vor 8 Tagen habe ich für sie in unserer Studentenkappelle schwedische högmässa[2] mit schwedischer Predigt gehalten. Das war für meine schwedischen Freunde wie für mich sehr erbaulich, eine schöne Erinnerung an die nordische Heimat.

Sehr dankbar bin ich Ihnen, wenn Sie meine telegrafisch übermittelte Bitte erfüllen und mir die Einreiseerlaubnis vermitteln. Grüßen Sie vielmals die ganze Familie. In inniger Fürbitte und tiefer Dankbarkeit und Verehrung bleibe ich

Ihr ergebenster
Fr. Heiler

171. To Friedrich Heiler[1]

Upsala 1.9.1920.

Käre vän!

Hjärtligt tack för brevet. Jag ville mycket gärna hava kunnat besöka Eder på vägen från Genève, men det var mig alldeles omöjligt. Över huvud skulle jag behövt mera tid för denna, den arbetsammaste resa, som jag någonsin företagit, men resultatet överträffade ju också efter stora svårigheter våra förväntningar och vi hava all anledning att prisa Gud för hans nåd. Eder kroppsliga klenhet inger mig oro. Skulle det icke vara möjligt för Eder att komma hit och få någon tids ordentlig vila? Respengar fram och tillbaka kan säkerligen anskaffas. Edra krafter äro dyrbara. Vi äro här många trogna vänner, som bedja för Eder och som gärna önska att troget stå vid Eder sida. Säg mig om Ni ser någon möjlighet att komma till Lund. Rörande var att mottaga Eder predikan i Christl. Welt, en svensk universitetsgudstjänst i ett tyskt universitet. Tack! Den 19 september skall E. Billing invigas till det heliga biskopsämbetet. Tänk om Ni då kunde komma och vara närvarande!

Tillgivne
N. S-m

---

[2] Literally: high mass; Lutheran worship service including the Lord's Supper.

[1] Fr. Heiler's papers (Ms. 999), Univ. Library Marburg, typewritten letter.

Uppsala, Sept. 1, 1920

Lieber Freund!
Herzlichen Dank für Ihren Brief. Ich wäre sehr gern in der Lage gewesen, Sie auf dem Weg von Genf[2] zu besuchen, aber es war mir völlig unmöglich. Überhaupt hätte ich mehr Zeit gebraucht für diese arbeitsreichste Reise, die ich jemals unternommen habe, aber das Resultat übertraf ja auch, nach großen Schwierigkeiten, unsere Erwartungen, und wir haben allen Anlass, Gott für seine Gnade zu loben. Ihre körperliche Schwäche macht mir Sorge. Wäre es Ihnen nicht möglich, hierher zu kommen und sich einige Zeit richtig auszuruhen? Reisekosten hin und zurück können sicherlich beschafft werden. Ihre Kräfte sind kostbar. Wir sind hier viele treue Freunde, die für Sie beten und die Ihnen gerne treu zur Seite stehen möchten. Sagen Sie mir, ob Sie eine Möglichkeit sehen, nach Lund zu kommen. Rührend war, Ihre Predigt in Christliche Welt[3] zu bekommen, ein schwedischer Universitätsgottesdienst an einer deutschen Universität. Danke! Am 19. September wird E. Billing zum heiligen Bischofsamt geweiht. Wenn Sie da kommen und dabei sein könnten!
Ihr
N. S-m

172. From FRIEDRICH HEILER[1]

München Wörthstr. 13, 3. Sept. 1920.
Hochverehrter Hochwürdigster Herr Erzbischof!
Leider war es nicht möglich Sie auf der Durchreise durch Deutschland zu treffen. Hätte ich den Zeitpunkt gewußt, an dem Sie durch Marburg kamen, so wäre ich auf den Bahnhof gekommen um Sie wenigstens zu begrüßen. Mein Gesundheitszustand hat sich nunmehr so weit gebessert, daß ich die Fahrt nach dem Norden hätte antreten können. Nunmehr mußte ich in die Heimat reisen um meinen Bruder noch einmal zu grüßen, der heute früh – nach monatelangem Siechtum – unerwartet rasch verschieden ist. Der Tod kam wohl als Erlöser, aber sein Hinscheiden ist doch ein schwerer Schlag für mich, der ich in ihm den hochsinnigen Philosophen bewunderte und den treuen Bruder und Mithelfer liebte. Sein philosophisches Erstlingswerk hat er noch vor seinem geistigen und körperlichen Zusammenbruch vollenden können, es wird in den nächsten Tagen erscheinen, leider hat er selbst nur die Korrekturbögen sehen dürfen.
Dieses Mal fühle ich mich in der Heimat als ein Fremdling, der offene Bruch mit der kath. Kirche hat mich dem heimatlichen Kreise entfremdet und ich bin eigentlich froh, daß mir Gott anderwärts eine wenn auch

---

[2] On the way home from no less than three big conferences: Life and Work August 9–12, Faith and Order Aug. 13–23 where Söderblom became Vice President; World Alliance Aug. 24–28 where Söderblom also became one of the vice-presidents. On the significance of these conferences, cf. Sundkler 239–247.
[3] CW 34/1920, 515–518: »Ut omnes unum sint. I Kor.12,2f; Joh. 17,20ff. (Predigt vom 1.7.1920).«

[1] N. Söderblom's collection of letters, from foreigners, UUB, handwritten letter.

274

schwierige Wirkungsstätte geschaffen hat. Ich denke so viel an die schönen Worte von der Heimatlosigkeit und Pilgerschaft, die Sie mir in einem Ihrer letzten Briefe schrieben. Sie sind mir ein besonderer Trost und Erquickung, wie mich überhaupt die Erinnerung an Ihre Persönlichkeit immer stärkt und aufrichtet, wenn ich von den traurigen Verhältnissen in den deutschen Landeskirchen niedergedrückt werde. Allmählich aber lerne ich auch diese Kirche in ihrer μορφὴ δούλου[2] lieben und mich in ihr heimischer zu fühlen.

... [Request to help a young lady find an opportunity for a stay in Sweden]

Grüßen Sie vielmals Ihre Familie, deren ich stets dankbar gedenke. Ich selbst verbleibe in tiefer Verehrung und aufrichtiger Fürbitte

Ihr dankbar ergebener

Friedrich Heiler.

173. To Adolf Deissmann[1]

Stockholm 29.10.1920

Hochverehrter, teurer Freund!

Herzlich danke ich für Ihren guten Brief. Mit heller Freude habe Ich soeben die Rede vom the Dean of St. Pauls in The Challenge gelesen, wo er Sie zustimmend citiert.

Ich sende Ihnen ein Exemplar vom Protokolle aus Genf und wir rechnen bestimmt damit, dass Sie mitmachen werden. Erst in März kann das Exekutivkommitté in Peterborough zusammentreten.

Ueber die polnische Frage habe ich eine große Reihe von bedeutsame Briefe und Dokumente bekommen. Wir haben verschiedene Pläne gehabt. Zunächst werde Ich dem Sekretär, Pastor Dibelius,[2] des Ausschusses für Auslandsarbeit die zunächst nötige Mittel hoffentlich überweisen können. Eine Skandinavischen Zusammenkunft in die Sache ist beantragt worden ... Ungemein wertvoll ist es mir daher 1) durch Sie Kenntnis vom neuen Staatsgesetz in Polen[3] zu bekommen, 2) Ihre Ansicht zu hören dass die Evangelischen Kirchen Polens sich schon jetzt federieren sollen. Das war mein frü-

---

[2] Nature of a slave, Philippians 2:7 on Christ.

[1] N. Söderblom's ecumenical collection, B 2, UUB, carbon copy.

[2] Otto Dibelius (1880–1967), at the time pastor in Berlin, Generalsuperintendent of the Kurmark 1925–1933. He had demanded complete independence of the church from the state in 1918 when the era of the state church ended with the abdication of the Kaiser. That made him *persona non grata* for the Nazis who forced him to early retirement. He then became a leading member of the Confessing Church, and after the liberation in 1945, bishop of Berlin-Brandenburg, which he remained until 1966. He was Chairman of the Council of the Evangelical (= Protestant) Church in Germany (EKD) 1949–1961 and one of the presidents of the World Council of Churches 1954–1961.

[3] The new constitution for Poland, which was independent since 1918, was enacted in 1921. It granted Roman Catholicism a leading position among the religious communities in the country.

herer Gedanke. Jetzt war Ich aber darauf gekommen zu bedenken ob es nicht vorsichtiger sei dass die Lutheraner und die Uniierten vorläufig getrennt auftreten dürfen, da ja, Gott sei dank, das nicht nur durch politische Gründe sondern auch durch konfessionelle Gründe angezeigt ist. Aber vielleicht haben Sie recht. Und die Massnahmen die polnische Staates erlauben vielleicht keine Verzögerung. Würden Sie es als klug betrachten dass eine Skandinavische Mission (nach Norwegischem Vorschlag) Vertreter von der Evangelischen in Posen und Warschau zur Beratung einladen. Bursche,[4] der schroff antideutsch gehandelt hat, der aber auch ein ernster Christ und hervorragender Kirchemman [Kirchenmann] ist, würde den einen senden. Wer in Posen könnte den uniierten Representanten senden? Soll in diesem Falle auch ein Reformierter eingeladen werden?

Mit herzliche Grüssen und mit Dankgebet an Gott dass Sie wieder arbeitsfähig sind, bin Ich

Ihr sehr ergebener

174. From FRIEDRICH HEILER[1]

Marburg/Lahn, Friedrichstr, 1 III, 14. November 1920.
Hochverehrter Hochwürdiger Herr Erzbischof!
… [On proofreading of the new edition of Söderblom/Tiele's *Kompendium der Religionsgeschichte* and on the Swedish translation of his own *Das Gebet*]
Meine Gesundheitsverhältnisse haben sich wieder etwas gebessert, so daß ich die volle Semesterarbeit aufgenommen habe. Ihr Vorschlag, auf ein Jahr nach Schweden zu kommen, hatte etwas sehr Verlockendes. Aber ich bin mit der Marburger Studentenschaft so eng verkettet, daß mir die Trennung schwer gefallen wäre. So schwierig für mich zuerst die Eingewöhnung in Marburg war, so lieb habe ich nun meine hiesige Tätigkeit gewonnen. Neben meiner akademischen Wirksamkeit verschafft mir die religiöse seelsorgerliche große Befriedigung; ich predige alle acht Tage. Unter den Studentenschaft weht ein frischer Geist, sie ist sehr empfänglich für neue Ideen. Sie hat ein richtiges Gefühl dafür, daß die deutsche Theologie auf einem toten Punkt angelangt ist und daß sie neue Bahnen einschlagen muß. Weder

---

[4] Juliusz Bursche (1862–1942), appointed General Superintendent of the Evangelical (= Protestant) Augsburg Church in Poland by Czar Nicholas II. in 1905, bishop in 1933. Bursche, whose church was half-Polish, half German (the other Protestant churches were all German) was convinced that the Protestant churches could only survive in the young Polish state if they adopted its language and culture. Because of this, he met with fierce opposition from much of the German-speaking minority of the country. One of his undisputed merits is the foundation of a Protestant theological faculty in Warsaw in 1921. In 1939, he courageously protested against the German occupation and was detained in Sachsenhausen concentration camp.

[1] N. Söderblom's collection of letters, from foreigners, UUB, handwritten letter.

der Ritschlianismus noch die einseitig historisch-kritische Theologie kann die Basis zu neuem Aufstieg bilden.

... [On a French review of his books]

Mit der Bitte Ihre verehrte Gemahlin und Ihre Kinder sowie Frl. Rodling herzlich zu grüßen bleibe ich in tiefer Dankbarkeit und Verehrung

Ihr ergebenster

Friedrich Heiler

175. To Friedrich Heiler[1]

Stockholm 20. 11. 1920.

Käre Professor och vän!

Tack för vänliga brevet och för allt värdefullt arbete med den nya upplagan av compendiet, som på detta sätt blir mycket användbarare.

Som Ni förstår skriver jag med största glädje ett förord till Eder bok om Bönen. Visserligen nödsakas jag oupphörligt avböja dylika förfrågningar om förord, men Eder bok är inom religionsforskningen och jag skulle vilja säga inom den levande fromhetens område en sådan källa till glädje och jag hoppas även till nytt liv och ny inspiration för såväl forskningen som själarna att jag betraktar det som en förmån att även genom ett förord introducera den i vår svenska litteratur. I England äro svårigheterna även stora att utgiva och trycka böcker. Däremot anser jag att en upplaga i Amerika mycket väl snart skulle kunna tänkas.

Vad Ni säger om teologiens döda punkt, är träffande. Så mycket mer böra vi tacka Gud för varje tecken till nyfödelse och nyskapelse.

Med hjärtligt tack för Edra hälsningar och med goda genhälsningar från oss alla

Eder tillgivne

N. S-m

Stockholm 20. 11. 1920

Lieber Professor und Freund!

Danke für den freundlichen Brief und für alle wertvolle Arbeit an der neuen Auflage des Kompendiums, das auf diese Weise viel brauchbarer wird.

Wie Sie sich denken können, schreibe ich mit größter Freude ein Vorwort zu Ihrem Buch über das Gebet. Gewiss bin ich andauernd genötigt, solche Anfragen wegen Vorworten abzulehnen, aber Ihr Buch ist auf dem Gebiet der Religionsforschung und ich würde sagen der lebendigen Frömmigkeit eine solche Quelle der Freude und wie ich hoffe auch neuen Lebens und neuer Inspiration sowohl für die Forschung als auch für die Seelen, dass ich es als ein Privileg betrachte, es auch durch ein Vorwort in unsere schwedische Literatur einzuführen. In England sind die Schwierigkeiten auch beim Herausbringen und Drucken von Büchern groß. Dagegen meine ich, dass eine Ausgabe in Amerika sehr wohl bald denkbar sein könnte.

---

[1] Fr. Heiler's papers (Ms. 999), Univ. Library Marburg, typewritten letter.

Was Sie über den toten Punkt der Theologie sagen, ist treffend. Umso mehr müssen wir Gott danken für jedes Zeichen von Wiedergeburt und Neuschöpfung.

Mit herzlichem Dank für Ihre Grüße und mit guten Gegengrüßen von uns allen Ihr Ihnen verbundener

N S-m

176. To Pope Benedict XV.[1]

[February 20, 1921]

Sanctitati suae
Pontifici Maximo Romano

Episcopi Havniensis, Oslovensis, Archiepiscopus Upsaliensis salutem in Domino nostro Jesu Christo summa cum reverentia dicimus.

Litteris nostris Upsaliae d. XI m. Martii a MCMXVIII datis, quibus de convocando universarum Ecclesiae partium concilio scribebamus, in quo et quaestiones quaedam communes ad officia vitae operasque caritatis pertinentes tractarentur et collegium delectorum ex singulis ecclesiis virorum constitueretur, quod, ubi communis ratio vel necessitas postularet, nomine totius corporis Christi loqueretur et ageret, Vestra Sanctitas per cardinalem Gasparri epistula d. XIX m. Junii a MCMXVIII data benigne rescribere dignata est. Iam res eo est perducta, ut in conventu Genevae mense Augusto proximi anni habito quindecim electi sunt, qui concilium illud universae Ecclesiae Christi de vita et opera in annum MCMXXII vel sequentem efficiendum curarent. Quorum e numero nobis mandatum est, ut Sanctitatem Vestram cum qua par est reverentia adiremus interrogantes, placeretne Vestrae Sanctitati ad illud concilium, quod quale futurum sit ex actis tabulisque adiunctis concludere licet, legatos mittere.

Aliis Ecclesiae gregisque sui partibus alia charismata Dominus distribuit. Neque ullo pacto confoederatio illa, quam constituere enitimur, pertinebit ad fidem, ritus, disciplinam ullius ecclesiae congregationisve temptanda. Hortamur vero omnes Christi discipulos, cuiuscumque sunt confessionis, ut uno animo unoque opere sequantur Magistrum in munere caritatis. Necessitas enim mundi Christi eget caritate, eget unito, quantum potest, opere Christianorum.

Die igitur XVIII mensis Aprilis proximi nos XV viri ex singulis communitatibus Christianis Europae, imperii Britannici, Americae ad id munus electi, Londonium ad rem praeparandam conveniemus; ubi si tunc nuntiare poterimus, Vestram Sanctitatem cum Romana Ecclesia concilium nostrum et

---

[1] Nathan Söderblom's ecumenical collection, UUB, typewritten letter (copy). The date at the end of the letter, 1920, is an error; it should read 1921; cf. the reply by Cardinal Gaspari, letter no. 179.

precibus et opera: legatis mittendis benigne se adiuturam annuisse, summam gratiam Vestrae Sanctitati habebimus.

Dabamus Christianiae, Havniae, Upsaliae
d. [XX] Februarii a MCMXX[I]

Archiepiscopus Upsaliensis

To His Holiness
The Roman Pontiff

we the bishops of Copenhagen, Oslo, the Archbishop of Uppsala, most reverently pay our respects in our Lord Jesus Christ.

To our letter set up in Uppsala on March 11, 1918, in which we wrote about a council of all the sections of the Church to be assembled, where also certain questions in common to us, pertaining to the duties of life and the works of love should be treated, and [for which] a board of men delegated by their respective churches should be constituted and which, whenever general agreement or necessity so demanded, should speak and act in the name of the whole body of Christ, Your Holiness has benevolently deigned to reply through Cardinal Gasparri by the letter written on June 19, 1918. The project has now been advanced to the point that at a conference held in Geneva in August of the next year, fifteen were elected to attend to that council of the universal Church of Christ on Life and Work being realized in 1922 or the following year. From their number, we received the mandate to approach Your Holiness with due reverence, inquiring if it pleases Your Holiness to send delegates to that council; what its character will be can be derived form the enclosed documents and protocols.

To different sections of his Church and flock the Lord has distributed different charismata. But by no means will the confederation we endeavor to establish take to analyzing the creed, ritual, discipline of any church or congregation. Rather, we are admonishing all disciples of Christ of whichever communion, that they follow the Master in the duty of love, united in mind, united in deed. For the need of the world requires the love of Christ, requires an effort of Christians as united as possible.

Therefore, we 15 men from our respective Christian communions of Europe, the British Empire, America, who have been elected for this task, will convene in London next April 18 in order to prepare the event. If there we can then announce that Your Holiness, together with the Roman Church has benevolently agreed to support our council in prayer as well as deed: by sending delegates, we shall be extremely grateful to Your Holiness.

Set up in Oslo, Copenhagen, Uppsala
on February [20], 1921

The Archbishop of Uppsala

177. From FRIEDRICH HEILER[1]

Marburg, 24. Februar 1921.

Hochverehrter Hochwürdigster Herr Erzbischof!

Nunmehr kann ich Ihnen und Ihrer verehrten Familie die freudige Mitteilung machen, daß ich mich verlobt habe, nicht mit einer Schwedin, sondern einer Westfalin, Anne Marie Ostermann, einer Pfarrerstochter, die hier Theologie studiert hat. Ich bin sehr froh, daß mir Gott eine Genossin geschenkt hat, mit der ich zusammen durchs Leben gehen kann, und daß die Zeit der Einsamkeit, unter der ich oft litt, vorüber ist. Im Monat April soll die Hochzeit sein.

Lange hatte ich geschwankt, ob ich nach alter mystischer Regel Zölibatär bleiben solle, zuletzt aber hat doch der Lutheraner über den Mystiker den Sieg davongetragen. So hoffe ich denn, daß Gott unsern Bund segnen wird. Meine Braut besitzt nicht nur eine reiche theologische Bildung, sondern vor allem ein frommes Herz. So soll denn unsere Ehe eine gute evangelische Theologenehe werden nach dem idealen Vorbild, das mir Ihre gottgesegnete Ehe darstellt. Meine Ehe wird sicher dazu beitragen, mich im ev. Christentum noch heimischer zu machen.

In diesen Tagen geht ein arbeitsreiches Semester zu Ende, das mir freilich auch viel Freude bereitet hat. In meinem religionsgeschichtlichen Seminar habe ich bei meinen Schülern recht gute Erfolge erzielt.

Mit verehrungsvollen Grüßen an Sie, hochwürdigster Herr Erzbischof, und Ihre verehrte Familie bleibe ich

Ihr dankbar ergebener
Friedrich Heiler.

178. From LUDWIG IHMELS[1]

Leipzig, Schillerstr. 8 II, den 31. März 1921.

Sehr geehrter Herr!

Es beschämt mich sehr, daß ich auf Ihre Aufforderung, in das Continuation Committee des Council of World Conference on Faith and Order einzutreten, noch nicht direkt geantwortet habe. Ein Übermaß an Arbeit ließ mich die wichtige Entscheidung immer wieder hinausschieben. Auch mußte ich mit den verschiedenen Freundeskreisen Fühlung zu nehmen versuchen. Eine Sitzung des Vorstandes, beziehungsweise des größeren Arbeitsausschusses unserer Allgemeinen Evangelisch-Lutherischen Konferenz, als deren Vor-

---

[1] Nathan Söderblom's collection of letters, from foreigners, UUB, handwritten letter.

[1] Ludwig Ihmels (1858–1933), professor of systematic theology in Erlangen 1898, in Leipzig 1902, bishop of the Lutheran church of Saxony 1922. He was well known as a preacher and as one of the heads of the so-called Erlangen school which was concerned with the certainty of faith as one of the chief problems posed to theology in modern times. – N. Söderblom's ecumenical collection, A 11, UUB, letter in the handwriting of Ihmels' secretary.

sitzender ich ja wohl berufen bin, ließ sich bei den gegenwärtigen Schwierigkeiten bisher nicht herbeiführen, sodaß ich erst zu Pfingsten, wo alljährlich unser Vorstand und Arbeitsausschuß hier tagt, die Angelegenheit vorlegen kann. Immerhin möchte ich Ihre wiederholten freundlichen Zusendungen doch nicht bis dahin ohne eine vorläufige Antwort lassen.

Das Resultat aller Erwägungen mußte dann leider immer wieder dies sein, daß meine Überbürdung mit anderer Arbeit mir persönlich den Eintritt in Ihren Ausschuß unmöglich macht. Ich darf ja nicht verschweigen, daß ich auch sachlich Bedenken habe. Zwar hoffe ich nicht erst aussprechen zu müssen, daß ich mit der Tendenz Ihrer Bestrebungen aufs lebhafteste sympathisiere. Auch in mir lodert die Sehnsucht nach dem: »Ut omnes unum.« Aber ich kann mir so schwer vorstellen, daß wir jetzt schon durch die von Ihnen so energisch betriebenen Bestrebungen zu einer äußeren Verwirklichung diese Zieles zu kommen vermöchten. Innerlich sind wir ja, gelobt sei Gott, schon heute, so viel unser Christum als unsern Herrn bekennen eins. Aber schließlich war immer das Entscheidende wieder das andere, daß wie man auch über jene Möglichkeit urteilen [mag], mir zurzeit eine ernstliche Mitarbeit in Ihrer Konferenz einfach unmöglich ist. Die Ausrichtung meiner bisherigen Arbeit bleibt schon so unvollkommen, daß es unrecht wäre noch neue Arbeitspläne zu unternehmen.

Immerhin bewegt mich die ganze Angelegenheit so ernstlich, daß ich mich gefragt habe, ob ich nicht versuchen sollte statt meiner einen Vertreter in Ihren Ausschuß zu entsenden. Auch in meinem Freundeskreise ist freilich das Urteil über jene Bestrebungen ein verschiedenes. Bei aller Sympathie für die Sache glaubt man zum Teil so wenig auf eine Durchführbarkeit zurzeit hoffen zu können, daß man für richtig hält, von vorn herein das auszusprechen und daher sich zurückzuhalten. Andere dagegen waren zu dem Urteil geneigt, daß wir jedenfalls erst einmal versuchen müßten mitzuarbeiten. Ich halte daher nicht für unmöglich, daß es gelingen möchte, einen Vertreter schon für die nächste in Amerika in Aussicht genommene Zusammenkunft zu entsenden. Freilich habe ich noch von keinem Herrn bisher eine bestimmte Zusage erhalten können, und leider sind auch die Mittel unserer Konferenz so überaus bescheiden, daß schon daraus der Entsendung eines Vertreters die ernstesten Schwierigkeiten erwachsen, wenn nicht der betreffende Herr vielleicht selbst wohlhabend ist. Immerhin hätte ich gern bis Pfingsten von Ihnen eine kurze Antwort, ob Sie eventuell auch mit der Entsendung eines Vertreters von mir einverstanden wären.

Was freilich die Anregung, die Sie in dem letzten in diesen Tagen hier eingegangenen Schreiben aufs neue gaben, um *Mittel* für die Konferenz zu werben, betrifft, so muß ich ja leider sagen, daß unsere Konferenz, wie ich schon andeutete, über so bescheidene Mittel verfügt, daß wir zu einer finanziellen Unterstützung in absehbarer Zeit schwerlich kommen werden. Sie wissen ja auch, wie schwierig gerade die kirchliche Lage in Deutschland gegenwärtig ist, und wie sehr wir dafür dankbar sein müssen, daß amerikanische lutherische Kreise unsere kirchliche Arbeit mit ihren Mitteln in der letzten Zeit unterstützen. Ich vermag mir daher nicht zu denken, daß unsere Konferenz zu Pfingsten eine finanzielle Unterstützung sollte beschließen können.

Indem ich unter allen Umständen Ihnen für den Ausdruck der Gemein-schaft des Glaubens herzlich dankbar bin und ihn von Herzen erwidere, bin ich
Ihr
ganz ergebener
Ihmels

179. From PIETRO CARDINAL GASPARRI[1]

Dal Vaticano, 13 Aprilis 1921.
Perillustres Viri,
Quas die 20 Februari huius anni ad Beatissimum Patrem Vos dedistis obse-quantes [sic; lege: obsequentes] litteras, eas una cum adjuncto libello rite Ipse accepit.

Nunc communicandum Vobiscum curo Sanctitatem Suam tum de huma-nissimis sensibus in enunciatis litteris expressis, tum de transmisso libello maximas Vobis agere gratias.

Ego vero ea qua par est observantia sum et permanere gaudeo Vobis addictissimus
P. C. Gasparri

Most illustrious men,
The polite letter you wrote to the Most Blessed Father on February 20 of the current year, together with the enclosed booklet, has been properly received by Him.

Now I am attending to communicate to you that His Holiness expresses [His] most sincere thanks both with regard to the most humane sentiments expressed in the said letter, and to the booklet dispatched.

As for myself, I am with due respect and glad to remain
Yours most faithfully,
P. C. Gasparri

---

[1] Nathan Söderblom's ecumenical collection, A 19, UUB, typewritten letter. Reply to letter no. 172. Note that this letter does not contain a single word about the request to nominate dele-gates for the planned ecumenical conference. This may be the reason why Pope Pius XI. (1857–1939, succeeded Benedict XV in 1922, known for his pursuit of world peace and for his social Encyclical Quadragesimo anno in 1931), under whom Cardinal Gasparri continued to serve as secretary of state, apparently did not receive another special invitation. Be that as it may, the new Pope unequivocally pronounced his rejection of the ecumenical movement, publicized in his Encyclical *Mortalium animos* of January 6, 1928 (AAS 20/1928, 5-16).

180. From Rudolf Otto[1]

Verehrter Herr Erzbischof.

... [On a call Otto received to succeed Julius Kaftan in Berlin; on sympathetic reactions to the idea of the »Religiöser Menschheitsbund« in Rome and in Buddhist circles in Japan] Die Arbeit dehnt sich aus. Wenn jetzt die führenden religiösen Kreise *der Neutralen* kräftig zugreifen würden, so würde eine Weltorganisation der R.M.B. möglich werden. Ich bitte herzlich, diese Angelegenheit in Erwägung zu ziehen. Bei jetziger Weltlage ist der gottgewollte Beruf der Neutralen ja so deutlich wie möglich: die Vermittlung und Ausgleichung der gespaltenen Welthälften, und die geistige *Führung*, die die getrennten Gegner sich nicht geben können.
...
Mit ergebenem Gruße Ihr
R. Otto, Prof.

181. From Friedrich Heiler[1]

Marburg/ Lahn, Friedrichstr.1, 5. Juni 1921.

Hochverehrter Hochwürdigster Herr Erzbischof!
Verzeihen Sie, daß ich erst heute Ihren Leipziger Brief beantworte. Ich wollte es nicht eher tun, als bis ich Klarheit in der Sache bekommen hatte. Ich war zuerst geneigt Ihrem Rate zu folgen, habe aber dann immer mehr Bedenken gefunden. Vor allem ist mir gesagt worden, daß das Leipziger Klima für meine schwache Lunge Gift sei, wie überhaupt für meinen Gesundheitszustand der Aufenthalt in einer großen Industriestadt nicht zuträglich ist. Ferner ist nach meinen Erkundigungen die Qualität der Leipziger Theologiestudenten mit der der Marburger nicht zu vergleichen. Leipzig ist »Examens«-Universität, die theol. Fakultät fast nur von Sachsen besucht. Unsere Fakultät zählt nur 1/3 hessische Studenten, alle anderen kommen aus den verschiedensten Teilen Deutschlands. Der wissenschaftliche Eifer unserer Studenten ist weit größer als an anderen Universitäten. Überdies hat das Ministerium nunmehr auf Antrag meiner Fakultät, die mich hier zu halten suchte, mir zugesichert 1) Umwandlung meiner Professur in eine etatsmäßige innerhalb dieses Jahres 2) Ernennung zum Ordinarius 3) Prüfungsrechte 4) Promotionsrechte in der theol. und phil. Fakultät. Es eröffnen sich mir dadurch hier viel größere Wirkungsmöglichkeiten als in Leipzig, wo ich als Extraordinarius neben Haas[2] doch nur wenig hätte ausrich-

---

[1] Nathan Söderblom's collection of letters, from foreigners, UUB, handwritten letter.

[1] Nathan Söderblom's collection of letters, from foreigners, UUB, handwritten letter.
[2] Hans Haas (1868–1934), Japanologist, Söderblom's successor on the chair of History of Religions in Leipzig in 1915. His approach to the field was predominantly historical; he was a liberal theologian for whom God revealed himself in all religions.

ten können. Da Haas prüft, müssen die Studenten eben zu ihm gehen. All diese Momente wiegen viel schwerer als die unleugbaren Vorteile, die mir Leipzig geboten hätte. Ich hoffe, daß Sie, hochverehrter Herr Erzbischof, diese Gründe würdigen und meinen Entschluß gutheißen werden.

Im Ehestand fühle ich mich ganz glücklich. Alle meine (aus meiner kath. Jugendzeit stammenden) Bedenken und Befürchtungen sind durch die wirklichen Erfahrungen widerlegt worden. Mir ist durch meine Ehe eine neue Seite am evangelischen Christentum aufgegangen. An meiner lieben Frau schaue ich täglich evangelische Frömmigkeit in ihrer feinsten Ausprägung. So trägt gerade die eheliche Gemeinschaft dazu bei mich im evangelischen Christentum heimisch zu machen und die Rudimente katholischer Askese und Mystik, die mir immer noch anhafteten, zu entwurzeln.

Für alle Ihre Bemühungen in Leipzig sage ich Ihnen herzlichen Dank. Grüßen Sie Ihre liebe Familie vielmals von mir. In Dankbarkeit und Verehrung bleibe ich

Ihr ergebenster

Friedrich Heiler

182. From TORSTEN BOHLIN[1]

Hille, Strömsbro 17/7 1921

H[ans] H[ögvördighet] Ärkebiskopen
D:r Nathan Söderblom.

Vördsamt tackar jag för det så hedrande anbudet. Glädjen att få vara med min syster i Paris och den plågsamma känslan att genom ett avböjande svar möjligen såra Ärkebiskopen ha samverkat att göra detta vänliga erbjudande till en svår frestelse för mig. När jag likväl ej *vågar* säga ja, så är det i grunden därför, att jag ej vågar prästviga mig. Mina svårigheter på denna punkt, vilka jag en gång fått framlägga för Ärkebiskopen, ha dessvärre ej lättat utan snarare motsatsen. Biskop Danells motion (om jag ännu en gång får tala om mig själv) öppnade en möjlighet; kyrkomötets behandling av den slog dörren till prästämbetet hårt till, och de friska intrycken av Biskop G. Billings skrift om innebörden av den pastorala förpliktelsen till Bekännelseskrifterna ha liksom skjutit regeln för. Är detta nu sjuklig överspändhet eller koketteri med samvetet? En min lärare har förebrått mig detta. Förmätet vore kanske påstå, att *intet* härav går in i betänksamheten. Och likväl: för en nycks skull korsar man nog inte sin kära dröm alltsen pojkåren: att

---

[1] Torsten Bohlin (1889–1950), lecturer in Uppsala in 1918, professor of systematic theology in Åbo in 1925 and in Uppsala in 1929, bishop in Härnösand in 1934. He was a renowned Kierkegaard scholar and as such critical of the so-called dialectical theology of Karl Barth and others (*Tro och uppenbarelse* Stockholm 1926, German transl. 1927). He published both an ethics (*Das Grundproblem der Ethik*, Stockholm 1923) and a dogmatics (*Evangelisk troslära*, 2nd ed. Stockholm 1938); and he was a leading churchman (chairman of the Swedish YMCA and vice-president of the World Student Christian Federation). – N. Söderblom's collection of letters, from Swedes, UUB, handwritten letter.

bli präst i Sveriges kyrka. Men, som det nu är för mig, skulle jag, fruktar jag, bli *sömnlös*, om jag toge detta steg, utan att ha samvetets gillande.

Vördsamt ville jag här fråga: Finns det ingen möjlighet i liturgin få klart uttryck för den *andliga frihet* i förhållande till Apostolikum och Bekännelseskrifterna, som kyrkans bästa män i verkligheten omfatta? Jag talar ju ej här blott om min egen svårighet. Blott för någon månad sedan bekände två unga allvarliga teologer, att de voro i samma nöd, och exemplen torde med lätthet kunna mångfaldigas.

I allt detta skulle det för mig vara en lisa veta, att mitt öppenhjärtiga svar icke alltför mycket frestat Ärkebiskopens tålamod och kostat mig en välvilja, som jag skattar som en av livets ljusa gåvor. Med vördsam tillgivenhet
Torsten Bohlin

Hille, Strömsbro, July 17, 1921

His Grace the Archbishop
Dr Nathan Söderblom

Reverent thanks for the so honorable offer.[2] The joy over the opportunity of being in Paris with my sister, and the agonizing sentiment of possibly hurting the Archbishop's feelings by a negative reply have jointly made this kind offer a strong temptation for me. Nonetheless, I do not *dare* to say yes, the reason being that I do not dare to be ordained. My difficulties in this respect that I once had the chance to explain to the Archbishop have unfortunely not eased, on the contrary. Bishop Danell's[3] move (if I may be allowed once more to talk about myself) opened up an opportunity; the church council's treatment of it slammed the door to the ministry shut, and the fresh impressions of Bishop Billing's book on the significance of the pastor's obligation of adhering to the Confessional Writings[4] have shot the bolt, as it were. Is this now morbid eccentricity or coquetry with conscience? One of my teachers reproached me with that. Asserting that *nothing* of the kind enters into my hesitation would perhaps be presumptuous. Be that as it may, one certainly does not thwart one's dream, cherished ever since boyhood, to become a pastor in Sweden's church, for the sake of a whim. However, as things now stand for me, I would have *sleepless nights*, I am afraid, if I took that step without having the approval of my conscience.

I should like to ask with due respect: Is there no way of finding in the liturgy a clear expression of the *spiritual freedom* with regard to the Apostles' Creed and the Confessional Writings, which in actual fact the best men of the church claim for themselves? I am talking not only about my own difficulty. Just a month or so ago, two serious young theologians confessed that they were in the same predicament, and examples could easily be multiplied.

In all of this it would be a relief for me to know that my candid reply has not

---

[2] Bohlin was offered to become pastor of the Swedish congregation in Paris, a post Söderblom had held from 1894 to 1901.

[3] Hjalmar Danell (1860–1938), bishop of Skara 1905–1935 (previously professor of dogmatics in Uppsala).

[4] It is not entirely clear which one of Gottfrid Billing's books Bohlin means; it may be *Lutherska bekännelseskrifter*, Lund 1895. The »fresh impressions« would then refer to a re-reading of the distinguished church leader's work.

overtaxed the Archbishop's patience and cost me a benevolence which I treasure as one of life's bright gifts.

Reverently yours,
Torsten Bohlin

183. To Henry A. Atkinson[1]

Upsala 16.11.1921

My dear Dr. Atkinson,
Your telegram told me that I should have the honour of receiving an explanatory letter. Please excuse me therefore that I have not anwered earlier.

As I told you in Järpan, it is very hard for me to leave my country and my episcopal duties for so long a time as two months. But, on the other hand, I beg You kindly to express my most respectful gratitude and appreciation to the Federal Council, the World Alliance, the Church Peace Union and the American Scandinavian Foundation. If God grants to me life and health, I have always considered a visit to the United States as a great opportunity for some of the ideals that inspire my prayer, thoughts and action. But i never dreamt of course of such a solemn patronage as that Your invitation implies. And indeed, if I do not consider my own great personal pleasure and profit from a visit to Your great nation, from which I keep such delightful and helpful remembrance since I was invited to represent the Scandinavian Universities thirty-one years ago at the New England Meeting[2], I see two chief tasks that would give me a kind of license to make such a long interruption in my regular and ordinary duties: I mean 1/ our sacred duty to promote United Life and Work of Christendom /on which subject I am writing a volume for Dr. Ainslie's collections[3]/ and 2: a most desirable platform for the scholarship, to which I have given what I must consider as the best of my force. Now Your most kind invitation offers to me both.[4]

My research has had two chief objects. 1: Comparative Religion and 2: The great genius of Religion who is called Martin Luther. Ever since Dr.

---

[1] Henry A. Atkinson (1877–1960) general secretary of the Church Peace Union, an organization founded by Andrew Carnegie in 1914 and closely connected with the Federal Council of Churches. – N. Söderblom's collection of letters, to Swedes and foreigners, UUB, typewritten letter (carbon copy).

[2] Söderblom spent the months from May to August, 1890, in the United States, on the occasion of the meeting of the Christian Student Movement in New Haven, CT.

[3] Nathan Söderblom, *Christian Fellowship or the United Life and Work of Christendom* (The Christian Unity Handbook Series, ed. by Peter Ainslie), New York/Chicago 1923.

[4] The journey did not come about until Sept.-Dec., 1923. In December 1922, Söderblom suffered a serious heart attack. Besides, as this letter indicates, he had accepted another invitation for about the same period of time by the Augustana Synod in America; so some sort of compromise had to be arranged. His biographer comments this as follows: »In making generous promises in both directions Söderblom had not perhaps fully realized that America was a vast country. He had never been fully content with the trivial limitation of unilocality ...« (Sundkler, op. cit. 302).

John Mott asked me, some twenty years ago, »Why do you not write something about Luther that will reveal to us something of his religious and human secret,« I have been looking forward to an occasion for presenting to the Anglo-Saxon public a literary work on Luther's psychology and on his position in the history of Religion. If the lectures You auggest at Harward (sic) would give me such an opportunity, I should consider them as a gift from the Almighty. I might call those lectures Humor and Melancholy in Luther, or something of that kind.[5]

I hope You have received my short and thankful letter. I must add three things:

1: I Had already given half a promise to another most honouring engagement for about the same epoch. I shall know in a few weeks if it will be possible to me to change it in order to be able to accept Your invitation.

2: I must ask you kindly not to crowd my program too much. What I want is, to have the opportunity of meeting You and some of the men that mean most for Christian life in the United States. If You want me to speak besides the intended lectures, I should prefer by far to be able to concentrate what I might have to say on a very few occasions. Overburdened with work I am sorry to say that my fysical forces are not any more what they used to be. May I ask You kindly to give me something of a short sketch of the intended program for my stay in America / with one day in Rock Island, the headquarter of our Swedish daughterchurch in America/

3: You most generously offers [read: offer] not only to myself, but also to Mrs Söderblom the great American hospitality that I know already from my former visit. You offer it from the day we leave Upsala to the day when we come back, and I am sorry to say that our actual conditions are such, to make me essentially dependent also of the economic side of this bald [read: bold] undertaking. The necessity, especially in my position, to share and help the dreadful needs of so many miseries in poor Europe has reduced my economic free action in a way that makes it necessary, alas, to me also to ask You kindly to give me a couple of lines on that side of the question.

... [Some details regarding the planned conference of Life and Work] I feel deeply that everything that can give to us a still nearer touch with American Christendom is necessary, yes, more necessary than anything else that we can do for the realization of our great venture.

Believe me, with our good respects to Mrs Atkinson, and with hearty greetings to mutual friends

affectionately Yours

---

[5] Söderblom had previously published a book in Swedish with this title: *Humor och melankoli och andra Lutherstudier* (Sveriges kristliga studentrörelsens skriftserie 100), Stockholm 1919.

184. To Henry A. Atkinson[1]

Upsala 26.11.1921

My dear Dr. Atkinson,

Now, I must tell You something that is really bad.

Riga, the capital of Latvia, has 185,137 inhabitants. Of those the very great majority are protestants /Evangelic Lutheran as we/ Only 16,000 are Roman Catholics. But the Roman Catholics have 4 churches, the Lutherans 14 in Riga. The population of the whole country amounts to 1.596,131 of which 924,106 are Evangelic, 375,227 Roman Catholic, 138,803 Greek Catholic and 73,310 »Altgläubige«.

You know that the Lett Galls in the East of Latvia number 496,226 of which about 292,000 are Roman Catholics. The actual Government in Riga is dependent of them,[2] /besides other political parties/. Now Rome, which is an accomplished and well known artist in all kind of political intrigues, has guaranteed to the Government of that protestant country the Roman Catholic votes, but on such conditions that might seem impossible to any other modern Evangelic state. ... The Latvian Church Government has protested and the members of the Consistory have all resigned. It is feared anyhow that the socialists and atheists will go with the Roman Catholics against the great bulk of the Protestant population in that matter. You see how unworthy it is for a modern state to offer to the tyrannical strivings of Rome such concessions as are here proposed.

Let me lay stress only on one chief thing. Although the Roman Catholics have comparatively more churches in Riga than the Lutherans, /the Romans one Church un [=on] 4.000 inhabitants, the Evangelic population one Church on 9.000 inhabitants/ they want now the Jacobi-Church, which is situated opposite to the Parliament and the Government building and where the Partliament used to open and end its work with Divine service. Besides a formerly Orthodox Church seems to have been given already to the Roman Catholics. Now think of that. The chief and most centrally situated church in that protestant town treacherously betrayed to Rome and that in this year, 300 years since Gustaf Adolf came to Latvia. This jubilee has been celebrated all over Latvia in the most spontaneous and enthusiastic way. At that epoch the Jacobi-church, which had been Evangelic ever since the Reformation, had been taken for some time by the Jesuits, but was restored to Evangelic Worship by Gustaf Adolf.[3]

---

[1] N. Söderblom's collection of letters, to Swedes and foreigners, UUB, typewritten letter (carbon copy).

[2] The east of Latvia known as Latgale remained under strong cultural and linguistic influence from Poland and Russia. The government felt obliged to its people, however, because they had courageously fought for the country's liberation. – The political development in the Baltic states was being watched very closely in Sweden because of its longstanding close ties to the region, and also because quite a few refugees had come to the country during the Russian occupation.

[3] Söderblom was a great admirer of Gustaf Adolf.

Now, what can be made against this attempt on our modern rule of respecting the rights and traditions and needs of the different confessions? Nothing can raise a more bitter and bad relation between the Evangelic and the Roman communions in Latvia.

Can the World Alliance or the Church Peace Union or any other representation in the United States send a telegram to the Government, Riga, Latvia, asking about the Jacobi-church and its fate, or do You see any mean[s] to raise an opinion in this matter in America? Leading Latvian Churchmen and christian laymen have told me, that nothing can be more helpful than publication in America and an American protest. But it must be made very soon in order to do its effect.

… It is too bad that the competition between our parts of Christendom should be carried out with such reckless political means instead of being of a purely spiritual kind.

Sincerely Yours

185. From Henry A. Atkinson[1]

December 6th, 1921.

Your Grace:

Your cordial letter of November 16th received. It was a great pleasure to hear from you, and I am delighted to know that you are coming to our country next autumn. I will arrange a tentative schedule of appointments for you, and submit it for your approval when I see you next. We will have a chance to talk this whole matter over when we meet at Copenhagen August 6–13th.

I have already taken up with Harvard University the question of your delivering the address on Luther before their body. No doubt this will be done. We will try to guard you from too many appointments, and at the same time will make every address that you deliver and every meeting that you attend count for the most possible.

We are going to announce your coming, and as soon as it is known that you are to be here you will be flooded with requests for addresses. In order that you may be spared from the annoyance occasioned by these many requests I suggest that you refer everything to me, and let your engagements be made through this office. This will protect you and at the same time will avoid mistakes in making arrangements.

I am enclosing herewith the Minutes of the meeting of the American Section of the Universal Conference on Life and Work. You will see by these minutes that we have finally put our organization upon a firm foundation. We are going still further and securing the cooperation of more churches. At present however we have strong bodies represented in our membership.

---

[1] N. Söderblom's collection of letters, from foreigners, UUB, typewritten letter.

... [On various conferences planned for the near future]

With all good wishes to yourself and family, in which Mrs. Atkinson joins, I am,

Cordially yours,

Henry A. Atkinson.

186. From Henry A. Atkinson[1]

December 23, 1921

Your Grace:

Your letter of November 26th relating to the bad situation in Riga was received in due time. Yesterday the Executive Committee of the World Alliance met here in New York and your letter was read. After thorough discussion it was,

VOTED to appoint a Committee of Three composed of the Secretary (Dr Atkinson), Dr Lynch and Dr Brown[2] to present this matter to the representative of the Latvian Government, Dr Seya,[3] in Washington and to protest against working this hardship upon the Lutheran groups in this new state.

In addition to sending this letter we propose to send the committee to Washington to interview Dr Seya and urge that he convey our feeling in this matter to the Premier of the Latvian Government.

It was also VOTED,

To co-operate with the American Committee on the Rights of Religious Minorities in sending another delegation to Poland, Upper Silesia and to Transylvania for a further study of the vexed situation in those countries.

Our attention has been called to the fact that the German churches are making a complaint of the treatment of their fellow workers by the French in Alsace-Lorraine. No attention has been paid to this complaint, for frankly it seemed to us that the motive back of all the charges made them unworthy of serious consideration.

As you know the Committee on Arrangements for the Conference of the Alliance, which is to be held in Copenhagen, August 6–13, is to meet in London on February 22nd. If you are to be in England at that time I wish that we might talk at length over some of these vexed problems.

With all good wishes, I am,

Yours cordially,

Henry A. Atkinson.

---

[1] N. Söderblom's collection of letters, from foreigners, UUB, typewritten letter.

[2] Frederick Lynch (1867–1934); Arthur Judson Brown (1856–1963), renowned Presbyterian clergyman and author, President of the World Alliance of Presbyterian and Reformed Churches 1933–1937.

[3] Louis Seya (I did not succeed in finding his biographical data. The Editor).

187. To Rudolf Otto[1]

Upsala 16.1.1922

Sehr geehrter Herr Professor!

Dass Ich das Heilige in der siebente Auflage nochmals gelesen habe[,] darf, neben den Seiten, die Ich Ihrem Buche in *När Stunderna växla och skrida*[2] gewidmet habe, als Beweis dafür dienen, wie hoch Ich Ihr Buch schätze. In dieser siebenten Auflage zitieren Sie mich auf Seite 91. Aber nicht in zutreffender Weise. Ein jeder Leser, der mein Werk nicht gelesen hat, muss irre geleitet werden. Der animistische Ursprung Jahves wird von mir gar nicht als eine Art primitiver Philosophie erklärt, wie Sie schreiben. Kap. 8 in Werden des Gottesglaubens[3] zeigt Die Gottheit als Wille und bezeichnet so ausdrücklich wie möglich Jahves Character als stürmischen gewaltigen Willen /ss 309–310/ Seite 320 schreibe Ich z. B. »Liegt auch im Animismus ein Ansatz dazu, sich die Gottheit als Willen zu denken, so kann doch nicht stark genug betont werden, dass keine Entwicklung der animistischen oder spiritualistischen Denkweise dazu führt, das Dasein einer einzigen göttlichen Willensmacht unterzuordnen. Nur durch das Geheimnis der prophetischen Erfahrung ist das möglich geworden.« Dass Jahve ursprünglich ein »Geist« und kein Urvater oder Urheber gewesen ist, ist meine Hypotese. Aber als Hauptsache wird bei mir sein Character als persönlicher Wille immer und immer betont.[4]

Dagegen enthält mein Buch für Ihre darstellung sehr nahe liegende Auskünfte, was die ruhenden grossen Götter oder, wie ich sie nenne Urheber betrifft, welche Ich vielleicht weniger dogmatisch als mein hochgeschätzter und gelehrter Freund Pater Schmidt[5] behandelt habe, und weiter was den Heiligkeitsbegriff selbst betrifft, den Ich in vielen Büchern und Abhandlungen als Wesen der Religion behandelt habe. Z. B. »Werden des Gottesglaubens« 112, wo gezeigt worden ist, dass das Heilige ausschlaggebend ist und Seite 211 ff., wo Ich auch zeige, dass sogar bei Kant heilig doch nicht gänzlich rationalisiert und moralisiert wurde. Ich habe immer meinen Studenten als Definition der Religion gesagt: »Fromm ist der Mensch, dem etwas heilig ist.«

---

[1] N. Söderblom's collection of letters, to Swedes and foreigners, UUB, typewritten letter (carbon copy).

[2] N. Söderblom, »Bönens historia,« in: *När stunderna växla och skrida*, 4. samling, Stockholm 1921(43–70), 68 f.

[3] N. Söderblom, *Das Werden des Gottesglaubens. Untersuchungen über die Anfänge der Religion* (deutsche Barbeitung von R. Stübe), Leipzig 1916.

[4] This misreading of Söderblom's book may be one of the reasons why Otto never fully recognized his deep indebtedness of his description of the Holy as *mysterium tremendum* and *fascinans* (*Das Heilige. Über das Irrationale in der Idee des Göttlichen und sein Verhältnis zum Rationalen* [1917], 10th ed. Breslau 1923, 13–27.39–53) to Söderblom's dialectic of *oundkomlig* and *oåtkomlig*, inescapable and inaccessible (*Naturlig religion och religionshistoria*, Stockholm 1914, 112, cf. German ed. *Natürliche Religion und Religionsgeschichte* [BRW 1], Stockholm 1913, 109), cf. Otto, op. cit. 17, note 1.

[5] Cf. Wilhelm Schmidt, *Der Ursprung der Gottesidee*, 12 vols., Münster 1912–1955.

Vielleicht wollen Sie daher die Güte haben, in einer folgenden Auflage entweder das Zitat s. 91 gütigst zu streichen, oder die Sache bei mir richtig anführen.

Mit Freude denke ich an die Richtung zum Centralen welche die Theologie in Deutschland in einigen Kreisen jetzt zeigt. Es würde mir Freude machen Sie einmal hier bei uns in Upsala zu sehen. Ich bin auch davon lebhaft überzeugt, dass wirklich fromme Menschen im allen höheren Religionen sich mehr und mehr finden werden — nach ihrem [=Ihrem] groszügigen Gedanken. Ich finde in einem Brief, den [=der] in dem »Congrès universel des Religions« des später unglücklichen Abbé Victor Charbonnel abgedruckt ist,[6] einige Worte, die ich damals schrieb, und die Sie interessieren werden: »A Paris en 1900, comme à Chicago en 1893, des croyants de l'univers entier, de l'Orient et de l'Occident, du temple, de l'église et de la synagogue, se rencontreront avec la mutuelle confiance des âmes qui cherchent Dieu. Ils montreront ainsi que la plus grande différence n'est pas entre Bouddha et le Christ, entre Laotsé et les prophètes de Yahveh, entre la foi grossière et naive de l'enfant de la nature et les idées des fils de la civilisation, mais seulement entre ceuz [=ceux] qui se laissent porter par la fatalité des choses, qui errent à la surface, flottant dans le soleil ou dans la tempête, et ceux qui cherchent un appui sûr[,] un appui éternel dans les profondeurs où est leur Dieu.«[7]

Mit guten Grüssen
Ihr sehr ergebener

188. From Rudolf Otto[1]

Marburg, Sybelstr. 8, 18.1.22

Verehrter Herr Erzbischof.
Ihr werter Brief kommt eben recht. Ich drucke grade die 8. Auflage meines Heiligen und werde meine Bemerkungen über Sie so gestalten, daß kein

---

[6] Victor Charbonnel, abbé (1860-1926), French freethinker who broke away from the Catholic church in 1897, became general secretary of the Associaton de libres penseurs in 1902, later was criticized as a former priest and left the freethinker movement. – The letter: »Lettre,« in: V. Charbonnel (ed.), *Congrès universel des religions en 1900. Histoire d'une idée*, Paris 1897, 217-222; the quote is to be found on p. 220.

[7] In Paris werden sich 1900, wie in Chicago 1893, Gläubige aus der ganzen Welt, aus dem Orient und dem Okzident, vom Tempel, der Kirche und der Synagoge, in dem gegenseitigen Vertrauen der Seelen treffen, die Gott suchen. Sie werden auf diese Weise zeigen, dass der größte Unterschied nicht der zwischen Buddha und Christus, zwischen Laotse und den Propheten Jahwes, zwischen dem rohen und naiven Glauben der Naturkinder und den Ideen der Söhne der Zivilisation ist, sondern allein zwischen denen, die sich von der Zwangsläufigkeit der Dinge tragen lassen, dahintreibend in der Sonne oder im Sturm, die auf der Oberfläche umherirren, und denen, die einen sicheren Halt, einen ewigen Halt in der Tiefe suchen, wo ihr Gott ist.

[1] N. Söderblom's ecumenical collection, A 19, UUB, typewritten letter.

Mißverständnis möglich sein wird. Ihre Verdienste um das Verständnis des Heiligen hatte ich schon auf S. 17 Anm. angedeutet und füge jetzt noch die Seitenzahlen hinzu. Auf S. 91 werde ich noch deutlicher, als das übrigens schon jetzt geschehen und gemeint war, bemerklich machen, daß Sie Jahveh grade als den Willensmächtigen auffassen, und daß für diese Auffassung die animistische Vorstellung nur »der Ansatz« gewesen ist, zu dem das prophetische Erleben hinzukommen mußte, um den eigentlichen Jahveh-Begriff zu gestalten.[2] Die Tendenz meiner Ausführung scheinen Sie aber doch mißdeutet zu haben. Ich behaupte ja garnicht, daß das Willensmäßige in Jahveh von Ihnen verkannt sei. Sondern daß Sie für den Unterschied von Jahveh und Elohim den Unterschied des *Ausganges* von *anima* oder *Urheber* von *Belang* sein lassen. *Diesen Belang* bestreite ich, weiter nichts. Und das muß ich auch nach Ihrem Briefe noch tun, da nach meiner Einsicht in die Dinge die ganze Konstruktion von Tylor[3] am eigentlichen religions-kundlich interessanten Problem vorbeigeht. Aber darüber mündlich, wenn ich einmal nach Schweden komme, oder Sie hierher, wie wir sehr wünschen und hoffen.

Wir hätten Ihrer hier sehr bedurft. Denn bei der Neugestaltung der »Christlichen Welt« haben wir fortwährend die Aufgaben eines neuzugestaltenden Protestantismus überhaupt erörtert. Ganz besonders auch hinsichtlich der Frage, was geschehen könne, um ihn in der Welt zusammenzuschließen und ihm für das sittlich-religiöse Leben im Gesammten der Menschheit seinen Platz und seine geschichtliche Mission zu wahren, die ihm zu entschwinden droht.

Ich verfolge dabei mit großem Anliegen Ihre Arbeiten für den Zusammenschluß für »life and work«, der mir viel lebensvoller und nötiger erscheint als die etwas seltsamen anglikanischen Bestrebungen nach Einer Einigung in »faith and order«. Das Zusammenarbeiten für große sittliche Gemeinschaftsaufgaben, besonders auf dem Gebiete des kollektiven Ethos, ist möglich und dringend nötig auch bei Bewahrung und vorläufigem Weitergelten der Unterschiede in Lehre, Bekenntnis und Aufbau. Und es ist wirklich allerhöchste Zeit, daß sich die christlichen Gemeinschaften darauf besinnen, daß sie Verpflichtungen haben gegenüber den großen sittlichen Gemeinaufgaben der menschlichen Gesellschaft. Wenn sie nicht endlich anfangen, in sozialer Frage, in Fragen internationaler Gerechtigkeit, und für Umstellung der gesellschaftlichen Verhältnisse aus den Formen des Wettbewerbes in die Formen der Cooperation wirklich etwas zu arbeiten und zu leisten, so werden sie allmählich sich überhaupt ausschalten, und diese größten sittlichen Aufgaben, gegen die die Aufgaben des privaten und Einzel-ethos immer erst die zweiten sind, werden übergleiten in die Kreise der

---

[2] Only the last one of these amendments has been realized. Neither have the page numbers been added (cf. 10th ed. of 1923, p. 17 note 1), nor has the assertion that Söderblom considered animism a kind of primitive philosophy been corrected (op.cit., p. 93).

[3] Edward Burnett Tylor, *The Origins of Culture* vol. II: *Religion in Primitive Culture*, London ²1873, 1–447 (= chapters XI-XVII: Animism).

ethischen Gesellschaften, der Idealisten außerhalb der Kirchen, und diese selber werden Licht und Salz verlieren. Schon der Trieb der Selbsterhaltung sollte sie treiben, endlich aus ihrer Wartestellung heraus zu gehen. Es ist beschämend, daß Japanische Buddhisten es sein mußten, die der Konferenz von Versailles auseinandersetzten, daß ein Bund der Völker nur möglich sei bei erwecktem Weltgewissen und bei religiöser Vertiefung der internationalen Arbeit.

Es ist für einen Protestanten ebenso trostlos, daß wol der Papst im Stande ist, im Rate der Völker seine Stimme zu erheben für moralische Forderungen aber daß der Protestantismus keinerlei gemeinsame Stimme hat, und leider noch viel weniger einen gemeinsamen Willen.

Zugleich erscheint mir ganz klar, und ich habe es Herrn Berggrav[4] bereits auseinandergesetzt, dass bei jedem Versuche, als Christen sich zu gemeinsamen praktischen Wirkungen zu vereinigen, wenn man wirklich auf Wirkungen in der *Welt* hinaus will, alle guten Willen der Welt mit aufzurufen und einzuladen sind. Denn es wäre doch wirklich ein etwas komisch erscheinender Versuch, wenn man etwa die Fragen gegenseitiger Gerechtigkeit im Verkehr der Völker, oder das Problem der Versittlichung der sozialen Frage, die doch alle große *kosmische* Aufgaben sind, und an denen die hunderte Millionen der Mohammedaner, Buddhisten, Hindu, Chinesen grade so lebendig interessiert sind, wie die Westhäl[f]te der Welt, glaubt, unter sich im nur christlichen und sogar im nur Nicht-römischen Teile der Menschheit mit Erfolg behandeln zu können. Sie schrieben mir schon früher, daß sich zu Ihrer geplanten Konferenz ein Türke, ein Perser und ein Inder gemeldet hätten. Und wie will man diese Kreise denn ernsthaft ausschließen, wenn es sich etwa um die Behandlung der Arbeiterfrage, die doch nur noch als Weltfrage lösbar ist, handelt. Oder um Fragen internationaler Gerechtigkeit und Versöhnung? Oder um eine kleinere Frage, wie etwa die Befreiung der Welt vom Fluche des Alkohol. In allen diesen Fragen arbeiten längst entschlossene Mohammedaner, Inder und Japaner so eifrig wie wir Christen, und zum Teil eifriger. Und wenn Ihr Conzil für Life and work zustande kommt, wie ich sehr wünsche, so wird man, sobald man wirklich zur Verhandlung des Programmes, das Sie aufstellen, schreitet, garnicht umhinkönnen, *mindestens als Gäste* jeden Guten Willen der Welt überhaupt mit aufzurufen. Ich erhalte soeben ein »manifesto« eines angesehenen Waishnava aus Indien, hatte gestern eine Unterredung mit einem Anhänger des Ārya-samāj, bekam neulich einen zustimmenden Brief des Japaners Nitche aus Genf,[5] und würde derlei wahrscheinlich schon hundertfach mehr haben, wenn mich meine lange Krankheit nicht fast ganz zur Ruhe gezwungen hätte[6]. Wir haben jetzt einen tüchtigen Generalsekretär gefunden,

---

[4] See letter no. 93, n. 1.
[5] Vaishnavism is a theistic Indian sect, *Arya-samaj* a 19th century Hindu reform movement. I have not been able to trace the Japanese Nitche, the ed.
[6] Otto had probably contracted malaria on his first journey to the orient in 1895; later, he suffered from severe bouts of depression which led to his early retirement in 1929.

der jetzt zum ersten Male auf Reisen gehen soll, um zunächst in Deutschland einen festeren Kern des R. M. B. zu sammeln. Aber meine Hoffnung ist, daß die Leitung einmal, und möglichst bald, von *neutralen* Gruppen übernommen wird. Denn alles was aus Deutschland kommt, ist in dieser Hinsicht immer noch mit Mißtrauen geschlagen.

Mit großer Freude habe ich im Herbste den jungen Birger Forell in seiner Tätigkeit in Rotterdam[7] besucht und gesehen. Es ist wundervoll, wie schnell und sicher er sich in seine Aufgaben hineinfindet. Ebensogroße Freude hat uns der Besuch der jungen Dozenten und Pastoren aus Upsala, Wästeroos [=Västerås] und anderswoher gemacht. Bohlin, Runestam, Nygren, Rosén[8] haben uns ihre Werke geschickt. Und ich bin erstaunt über das rege Schaffen in der schwedischen Theologie. – Aus Leipzig schreibt man mir, daß Ihre Schrift, die ich durch Peter Katz übersetzen ließ, dort mit großem Interesse gelesen wird.[9]

Ihre liebenswürdigen Grüße erwidere ich aufs beste und wünsche im neuen Jahre reichen Erfolg zu Ihrem erstaunlich weiten Wirken. Der Arzt verurteilt mich noch zu 3 Monaten völliger Ruhe. Aber dann soll ich wieder gesund werden. Und vielleicht werde ich dann einige Reisen machen. Was erwartet mich in Amerika, in England, bei meinen Quäkerfreunden, und in Peking, wohin mein Freund Dr. Wilhelm soeben als Dragoman der Botschaft wieder hinausgegangen ist.[10] Möglicher Weise auch in Japan, wo meine Freunde mich zu Vorträgen haben möchten. Wahrscheinlich aber werde ich diese Reisen alle »en pneúmati«[11] ausführen. Denn die Aufgaben hier bei uns sind so groß, daß man sich schwer von der Stelle trauen wird. Und außerdem sind wir durch unsere Währung so heilsam angebunden, daß die Tugend der Seßhaftigkeit uns leicht wird.

---

[7] Forell was a sailors' chaplain there from 1921 to 1926.

[8] Bohlin: cf. letter no. 182, n. 1; Arvid Runestam (1887–1962), lecturer in systematic theology in Uppsala 1917 and professor in 1922, bishop in Karlstad 1934–1956, known for his works on ethics and for his *Psykoanalys och kristendom*, Stockholm [3]1954 (German tr. Gütersloh 1928); Anders Nygren (1890–1978), professor of Christian ethics in Lund 1924–1948, then bishop there, central figure of the so-called Lund school which transformed systematic theology into the historical science of »motif research«, in Nygren's case combined with a purely formalistic Kantian philosophy and later with Anglo-Saxon philosophy of language; his most important works are *Den kristna kärlekstanken genom tiderna. Eros und Agape*, 2 vols., Stockholm 1930.1936 (German tr. *Eros und Agape* [SASW28.39], Gütersloh 1930.1937; English tr. *Agape and Eros*, London 1932.1939) and *Mening och metod*, Åbo 1973 (Engl. tr. *Meaning and Method*, London 1972; German tr. *Sinn und Methode*, Göttingen 1979); Hugo Rosén (1887–1963) became doctor of theology in 1919, taught as a lecturer at Lund university for a couple of years and then took over a teaching position as *lektor* at Lund's Cathedral School in 1923.

[9] *Gehen wir einer religiösen Erneuerung entgegen?* Leipzig 1921; for detailed bibliographical data, cf. letter no. 129, n. 8.

[10] Richard Wilhelm (1873–1930), missionary in Qingdao 1899–1920, adviser of the German ambassador in Beijing 1922–1924, then professor of sinology in Frankfurt/Main. A *Dragoman* (Arab. *Terjuman*) in the older Near East was an interpreter assisting foreign diplomats in communicating with state officials.

[11] Greek for »in the spirit«; here it means: in mind only.

Wir hoffen, etwa zu Pfingsten eine Zusammenkunft der Freunde eines Religiösen Weltbundes in Darmstadt zu halten. Wenn wir dazu wenigstens gastweise einige Schweden haben könnten, so würde uns das von großem Gewinne sein. – Mich Ihrer Frau Gemahlin empfehlend und meine Bekannten bestens grüßend

In aufrichtiger Ergebenheit Ihr

R. Otto.

Handwritten addition on back of last page: Ich behaupte nicht, daß der animistische Ursprung Jahveh's von Ihnen als primitive Filosofie erklärt werde, sondern daß die Theorie des Animismus *überhaupt*, und also auch Ihre Anschauung von Animismus (auf S. 10 ff.) religiös, d. h. für die Theorie der Religion, relativ irrelevant ist und viel eher die Wurzeln einer primitiven Filosofie abgiebt als zu eigentlich religiösen Bildern leitet. Seine Vorstellungs-erzeugnisse dienen der religiösen Entwicklung selber höchstens als Incitamente und Gestelle zum Daran-ranken.

189. To Ludwig Ihmels[1]

Upsala 11. 3. 1922

Sehr geehrter Herr College!

1: Sie wissen besser als ich, welche Schwierigkeiten unsere Glaubensgenossen in dem östlichen Gebiet durch die Zersplitterung haben. Wie oft habe ich brieflich und mündlich aus Ungarn und den durch den Versailles-frieden gewaltsam abgerissenen Gebieten die Aufforderung bekommen wenn möglich sogar eine besondere Konferenz für diese Fragen zu veranlassen oder wenigstens mit anderen Kirchenmännern des neutralen Auslandes Budapest und andere Gegenden zu besuchen. Wie die Amerikaner haben auch wir mehrmals urteilsfähige Männer dahin gesandt und es scheint mir, dass eine Tagung der Allgemeinen Evangelischen Konferenz dort im nächsten Jahre von grosser Bedeutung für die ganze Lage unserer dortigen Glaubensgenossen werden könnte. Entschuldigen Sie daher meine Zähe Rekommendation von Budapest.[2] Sicherlich hat Professor Morehead[3] viel Sinn für diesen Gesichtspunkt.

2: Kein gemeinsames Wort des Dankes wurde Ihnen gesagt für die weise Weise in welcher Sie die vertrauliche Sitzung Montag nachmittag leiteten. Ich bin fest überzeugt, dass daraus Segen kommen kann. Für das schöne Losungswort ὑπομονή danke ich besonders, da es nicht Geduld im Sinne von Warten sondern im Sinne von Ausharren heisst, wie es im Ebr. 12.1. heisst: δι᾽ ὑπομονῆς τρέχομεν τὸν ἀγῶνα. Auch in diesem Kampfe brauchen

---

[1] Landeskirchenarchiv Dresden, Best. 15, Nr. 1, typewritten letter.

[2] This insistence on Budapest as the location for the planned Lutheran world conference was part of Söderblom's strategy to strengthen the international outlook of Lutheranism. In the end, however, he agreed to Eisenach for 1923.

[3] John Alfred Morehead (1867–1936), Director, National Lutheran Council, New York.

wir ὑπομονή das Ausharren, das sich in der bei Martin Luther so gewaltigen Aktivität des Christen im Ertragen von Leiden und in unserer Arbeit zeigt.[4]

[3: request to send copies of a lecture on the Una Sancta]

Mit guten Grüssen an gemeinsame Freunde

Ihr sehr ergebener

Nathan Söderblom

190. To Arthur Headlam[1]

Upsala April 11th 1922

My dear Dr. Headlam,

Mrs Söderblom observed Your personal ressemblance to Erasmus[,] and indeed also spiritually the Erasmian part of the Church /the Anglican Communion/ has in our day, as far as I know, no more authentic and authoritative representative than You. Your review of Bishop Henson's[2] lectures in our University proves that once more. I thank You most heartily for Your kind letter. The copy of »The Times Literary Supplement« gives indeed, as far as I can see, an exact and characteristic notion of the very genious [sic] of Your section of the Church.

Already when the Olaus Petri Foundation of our University invited my old friend Dr. Henson, I was aware that he does not represent that genious in the central way in which You do. But the Church of England is here in Sweden and in Scandinavoa [sic] too often identified with ritualistic and sacramental anglo-catholicism in a way that is not only untrue, but also rather disastrous for our spiritual connection with Anglicanism. This is due partly to the sympathy of a very small group of clerics and laymen for High Church ideals, partly to the association of large groups of our Church people with English Nonconformism. I think that Dr. Henson's lectures also in their one-sidedness from an Anglican point of view have been not only captivating but also useful. One day our University will try to have an Anglican scholar, who would like to lecture on those four main types of non Roman

---

[4] Ihmels, a friend of Söderblom from his Leipzig years, was a cautious man. In view of all the problems besetting the ecumenical endeavors like the passionately debated issue of who was guilty of the World War, he had advocated ὑπομονή in his statement at the Wittenberg Lutheran conference a couple of days before in exactly the sense Söderblom here criticizes as a misapprehension of the verse from Hebrews. So Söderblom's comment betrays his chip on the shoulder. Ihmels later became one of Söderblom's most reliable collaborators.

[1] Arthur Headlam (1862-1947), Bishop of Gloucester. - N. Söderblom's collection of letters, to Swedes and foreigners, UUB, carbon copy of typed letter, with handwritten corrrections, so it is probably just a draft which, moreover, is incomplete.

[2] Herbert Hensley Henson (1863-1947), Canon of Westminster 1900-1912, Dean of Durham 1912-1918, Bishop of Hereford 1918-1920 and of Durham 1920-1939. He was an outspoken, even controversialist social conservative (he publicly opposed a miners' strike in 1920), a theological liberal (he did not believe, e.g., in the virgin birth), and a Latitudinarian in church affairs.

catholicism: 1: The Greek Orthodox and those who derive from 2: Erasmus, 3: Luther, 4: Calvin. Of course You would do that better than anybody else.

Finishing a manuscript that I promised an American editor more than two years ago on Church Unity, I have tried shortly to define Anglicanism as the only true continuation of Erasmian ideals in its comprehensiveness and in its sympathy for an older and wider type of the Church in difference to the violent differentiations operated by Luther /with Calvin/ and Loyola in the sixteenth century. This is not my domain of research, and I have regretted to be bound to take my few weeks for study from my special hobby, comparative Religion. An English translation of my book »On the Origins of the Idea of God« has been lying on my table for months for revision. I am eagerly longing for the possibility of taking up my particular study of eschatology which resulted in La Vie Future d'après le Mazdéisme, à la lumière des croyances parallèles dans les autres religions 22 years ago /Annales du Musée Guimet/ but which has since that given me new material and new insights that I would like to explain before selling my soul entirely to practical churchmanship or passing away.

... [a note on »1: the Swedish hymnbook question«[3]]

2: The Swedish Church has never been a state church in the German Danish, Norvegian and Anglican sense. Because our Church has always had a selfgovernment, founded on Parish councils: all communicants over 21 years, men and women, have vote to elect their pastors and take care of the Church. Chapters have power besides the bishops, who are choosen by the whole clergy and by the Crown which is bound to take one of the three, who have the majority of votes. Our Kyrkomöte, General Church Assembly, consisting of the bishops and laymen and clergymen choosen in a democratic way, has in all religious matters Veto against Parliament and Government, which is as far as we know, not the case with any other Church (except the Church in Finland). I do not know neither any communion with more democratic forms of election etc. But on the other hand, the Church is closely connected with the realm of Sweden according to the words of our great king Gustaf II Adolf, who spoke of the »realm of Sweden and God's church, which is in it«. The Church pretends to be the very soul of our nation.

The king has in Sweden never been Summus Episcopus. This is a fatal mistake by the writer in the Christian Patriot. That German idea has been spread during the last century in some circles in Sweden, but there is absolutely no official document stating it. On the contrary it is evident from the official documents of the Church of Sweden that it has had its own bishops and that the king is the Praecipium [= Praecipuum] Membrum Ecclesiae, being the first citizen of the country, but not Summus Episcopus.

---

[3] Probably a page is missing here as the change of subject is quite abrupt, and the numbering of the following passages 1–3 was not hitherto introduced.

3: The actual Archbishop, it is true, was only the third in number of the three bishops proposed by the election of the clergy, the chapters of Sweden and the University of Upsala.[4] The political reasons supposed in the article are a pure invention from the beginning to the end. But the actual archbishop Dr. N. S. is reported to have said more than once that the bishop of Skara, who had the majority of votes, and who visited India last year, is the best bishop amongst the Swedish bishops now living.[5]

Dr. N. S. has since 30 years given many contributions to theology and the history of religions. The leading thought in several of his more important books is to mark the difference between revealed religion and other religions. An originality in his investigations is the result that he tries to prove from a profound analysis of the history of religions, namely that an impartial investigator, who is not bound by reigning rationalistic ideas, must recognize that there is a decisive difference or contrast in all high religions between the revelation or the profetic and apostolic message on the one side, and all other creeds of mysticism and piety on the other side. Thus he advocates firmly the claim of Christian theology to have a special department and a task of its own besides the study of all other religions.

But on the other hand Dr. S. also with St. Paul believes in a general revelation to all mankind marred and deteriorated by the sin. Thus he thinks that it is a modern prejudice to laugh at animism and at all forms and beliefs in spirits and Gods as if it were an antiquatied [sic] folly to recognize a spiritual world, on the countrary [sic]. Dr. S. shows that all those heathen affirmations show a conception or an idea of the highest spiritual world although deteriorated. But in one single place the truth lying behind also the animistic idea of a supernatural will has been purified and found its full expression through God's revelation to Moses. Thus Jahve is in no wise an animistic God. But the fundamental although obscured idea of animism[,] that of a spiritual will behind the phenomena, has been fully revealed in the Bible where our God appears and acts as the souvereign holy and almighty will.

Those glimpses into Dr. Ss writings may prove that he is especially useful to missionaries if they have St. Pauls's method.[6] ... [here the fragment ends.]

---

[4] That depends on how you count: Since Hjalmar Danell and Johan Alfred Eklund shared the first place with an equal number of votes, Söderblom could also be counted fourth.

[5] Söderblom refers to Hjalmar Danell; cf. letter no. 182, n. 3.

[6] Cf. Acts 17:22–31.

191. From Friedrich Heiler[1]

Marburg/Lahn, Ockershäuser Allee 3, 14. Mai 1922.
Hochverehrter Hochwürdigster Herr Erzbischof!
Endlich darf ich Ihnen die freudige Mitteilung machen, dass uns Gott ein gesundes Töchterlein geschenkt hat, das wir Anna Elisabeth nennen. Es trägt so den Namen der großen Marburger Heiligen; im Schatten unserer Elisabethkirche und unter dem Geläute ihrer Glocken hat es das Licht der Welt erblickt. Das Wort aus dem letzten Sonntagsevangelium Joh. 16,21 hat sich auch an meiner Gattin voll bewahrheitet. Bange Tage und Stunden gingen voraus, in denen ich um das Leben von Mutter und Kind mich sorgte, und es bedurfte ärztlicher Hilfe um das Kind zur Welt zubringen. Nun aber ist die Freude doppelt. Sie, Hochwürdigster Herr Erzbischof, die Sie so oft diese Freude erfahren durften,[2] werden meine Freude ganz besonders verstehen.

Ihre freundliche Einladung zu späteren Olaus Petri Vorlesungen hat mich sehr gefreut. Ich danke Ihnen herzlich dafür. Schon lange grüble ich über ein Thema. Das mir von Ihnen vorgeschlagene ist sehr schön, aber auch sehr schwer. Ich dachte an eine Geschichte des Opfergedankens oder eine solche des Gnadengedankens. Letztere ist noch von niemand in Angriff genommen worden, erstere noch nicht vollständig bearbeitet. Loisy's Le sacrifice[3] hat mich trotz aller Reichhaltigkeit doch sehr enttäuscht. Er hat die sublimen Formen der Opferidee ignoriert und ihr innerstes Wesen verkannt. Ich hoffe über ihn hinaus Wichtiges und Neues bieten zu können.

In Bälde hoffe ich Ihnen ein neues großes Opus übersenden zu können, Der Katholizismus, seine Erscheinung und sein Ideal,[4] auch eine Schwergeburt. Ich habe zwei Jahre an ihm gearbeitet und suchte in ihm die »Skizze« meiner schwedischen Vorträge zu einem großen Gemälde zu machen. Diese Vorträge haben in Deutschland viel Staub aufgewirbelt und die katholische Literatur mehr beschäftigt und auch beeinflußt, als ich gedacht hatte.

Hier herrscht ein reges theologisches Leben. Die verschiedensten Richtungen stehen einander in unserer Fakultät gegenüber. Bultmann (Neues Testament) ist wohl der radikalste Exeget, den Deutschland bisher hervorbrachte.[5] In Niebergall haben wir nun einen feinsinnigen praktischen Theologen moderner Richtung gewonnen, ein gesundes Gegengewicht gegen Bornhäuser.[6] Leider ist Otto immer noch leidend.

---

[1] N. Söderblom's collection of letters, from foreigners, UUB, handwritten letter.

[2] Anna and Nathan Söderblom had 11 children.

[3] Alfred Loisy, *Essai historique sur le sacrifice*, Paris 1920.

[4] Published Munich 1923.

[5] Rudolf Bultmann (1884–1976), whose »demythologization« program after World War II caused passionate debates. As for his radicalism, Bruno Bauer (1809–1882) and Arthur Drews (1865–1935) who both denied the historical existence of Jesus seem to have been overlooked by Heiler in this remark.

[6] Friedrich Niebergall: cf. letter no. 137,7; Bornhäuser, Karl (1868–1947), his colleague in the same field (he also taught New Testament), 1902 professor in Greifswald, 1905 in Halle, and in 1907 in Marburg; a conservative »Biblicist«.

Grüßen Sie Ihre verehrte Gattin und Ihre liebe Familie und seien Sie selbst in tiefer Dankbarkeit und Verehrung gegrüßt von
Ihrem ergebenen
Friedrich Heiler

192. To Friedrich Heiler[1]

Upsala 23.5.1922

Käre vän!
Ni anar bäst själv vilken fröjd underrättelsen om Eder dotters födelse uppväckte här hos gamla och unga. Jag hade just predikat på den söndagen och tänkt på det sköna frälsarordet. Gud välsigne och skydde den kära lilla Anna Elisabeth, vilkens bekantskap jag hoppas i en snar framtid få göra.

Det är ingen brådska med Edra Olaus Petri föreläsningar. Jag hoppas vi få tillfälle att personligen tala om saken. Loisy's Le Sacrifice har jag verkligen icke läst.

Jag förvånar mig över Eder produktivitet och energi, som betyder mycket för den andliga och teologiska orientationen i vår tid.

Med hjärtliga lyckönskningar till Eder maka och dotter från oss alla, Eder alltid hjärtligt tillgivne
Nathan Söderblom

Upsala, 23.5.1922

Lieber Freund!
Sie ahnen selbst am besten, welche Freude die Nachricht von der Geburt Ihrer Tochter hier bei Alten und Jungen ausgelöst hat. Ich hatte gerade an diesem Sonntag gepredigt und an das schöne Wort des Erlösers gedacht. Gott segne und schütze die liebe kleine Anna Elisabeth, mit der ich in naher Zukunft hoffe Bekanntschaft machen zu können.

Mit Ihren Olaus Petri Vorlesungen hat es keine Eile. Ich hoffe, wir werden Gelegenheit haben, persönlich über die Sache zu sprechen. Loisys *Le sacrifice* habe ich tatsächlich nicht gelesen.

Ich bin erstaunt über Ihre Produktivität und Energie, die für die geistliche und theologische Orientierung in unserer Zeit viel bedeutet.

Mit herzlichen Glückwünschen für Ihre Frau und Tochter von uns allen, Ihr stets herzlich zugeneigter
Nathan Söderblom

---

[1] Fr. Heiler's papers (Ms. 999), Univ. Library Marburg, typewritten letter.

193. To Gustaf Aulén[1]

Schleiermacher glädas [sic] i sin himmel åt den sanningskära, självransa-kande [sic] polemiken i hans ande som Du givit i Evangel[iskt] o Ro-merskt.
Tack! Hälsa!
Tuus
N S-m
Bjuråker 3. eft[er Tref[aldighet]

Schleiermacher is rejoicing in his heaven about the truth-loving self-searching po-lemic in his spirit which you presented in Evangeliskt och Romerskt.[2]
Thanks! Greetings!
Yours
N S-m
Bjuråker 3rd Sunday after Trinity [= July 2; postal stamp is of July 3, 1922]

194. From Gottfrid Billing[1]

[Date at the end of letter]
Käre Broder,
I går fick jag ett bref från fröken Annie Wall, i hvilket hon hemställer, »huruvida icke de svenska prästerna skulle kunna sätta sig i förbindelse med prästerna i de andra neutrala länderna och i England och Amerika för att utöfva ett starkt moraliskt tryck på Frankrike« i fråga om de färgade truppernas användning i Tyskland.
Själf har jag länge känt en önskan, att från de neutrala länderna kunde komma protest mot skändligheter, och skulle gärna underskrifva en sådan. Men jag har ej kunnat se, huru en sådan skulle kunna åstadkommas. Och icke borde den afgifvas endast af präster.
Som du vet, har jag ingen som helst beröring med utlandet, och därför kunde fröken W. i fråga om internationel åtgärd icke vända sig till någon mera inkompetent än mig.
Jag har dock ansett mig böra gifva dig del af fröken W's önskan och för-slag.
...
Vördsam och hjärtlig hälsning till ärkebiskopinnan,
Din vän
Gottfrid Billing
Lund 22/9 1922.

---

[1] Collection Aulén. G., Lund University Library, handwritten postcard.
[2] Gustaf Aulén, *Evangeliskt och Romerskt* (Sveriges kristliga studentrörelsens skriftserie 139), Stockholm 1922.

[1] N. Söderblom's collection of letters, from Swedes, UUB, handwritten letter.

Dear Brother,

Yesterday I received a letter from Miss Annie Wall,[2] in which she is submitting to consideration »whether Swedish pastors could not get in contact with pastors in other neutral countries and in England and America in order to exert strong moral pressure on France« with regard to the use of colored troops in Germany.[3]

As for myself, I have long been sensing the desire that a protest be issued from the neutral countries against atrocities and would be willing to sign some such. I have not been able to see, however, how this could be achieved. And under no circumstances should it be issued only by pastors.

As you know, I do not have any connections abroad whatsoever; therefore, Miss W. could not have addressed anyone more incompetent concerning international undertakings than me.

[On Billing's notes from the bishops' meeting]
Respectful and kind regards to Mrs. Söderblom.
Your friend
Gottfrid Billing
Lund, Sept. 22, 1922

195. To Gottfrid Billing[1]

Upsala 25.9.1922

Högt vördade Broder!

Även till mig skriver Annie Wall då och då mycket ivriga skrivelser. Min erfarenhet säger att hon, med all sin välmening och iver, icke har det säkra omdöme som kräves i så viktiga ting.

De svarta trupperna utgöra endast en del, kanske icke ens den värsta, av hela den franska besättningen vid Rhen, som utgör en draksådd liksom enkom inrättad för att leda till ett kommande krig. Underrättelserna därifrån komma hjärtat att sjuda av harm. För två år sedan sände vi en mycket vederhäftig kommission dit, som lämnade ingående upplysningar, och jag försökte i fjol våras i London få betydande krafter i rörelse i England, där man också är upprörd, men vanmäktig gentemot den franska politiken. I mitt föredrag vid Allmänkyrkliga Förbundets stora möte i Köpenhamn uttalade jag att besättningen vid Rhen är en ohygglig förberedelse för ett kommande förödande europeiskt krig, och påpekade hur mycket bättre pengarna kunde användas för återuppbyggande. Icke ens de närvarande fransmännen uttalade någon gensaga. Som Du kanske minns, hade Branting och undertecknad yttranden i samma riktning på Auditorium i Stockholm. Vad kan göras för att uttrycka opinionen i detta stycke? Skall något ske, måste det vara imponerande och värdigt. Hur skulle det vara att för

---

[2] Annie Wall (1863-?), Swedish writer.
[3] This refers to the occupation of a section of the Rhineland around Düsseldorf and Duisburg by the French since March 8, 1921, a measure which was meant to punish Germany for what was conceived to be her sole guilt in triggering the war.

[1] Collection Billing. G., Lund University Library, typewritten letter.

ändamålet söka mobilisera alla de nordiska biskoparna? Då jag så ofta är ute, hemställer jag huruvida Du icke skulle vilja fråga Ostenfeld i Köpenhamn om saken, som från Dig kommer med stor auktoritet, så skall jag gärna höra mig för i Finland och Norge. Jag undrar om Du skulle vilja sammanskriva några rader i saken för eventuellt upprop.
...

Med vördsam hälsning
tillgivne
Nathan Söderblom

Highly esteemed Brother,
Also to me Annie Wall writes very fervent letters every now and then. My experience tells me that she, for all her goodwill and eagerness, does not possess the sure judgment required in such important matters.

The black troops constitute only part, perhaps not even the worst, of the whole French occupation in the Rhineland which amounts to sowing dragons' teeth, as if designed purposefully to lead to a future war. The news about it makes your heart seethe with resentment. Two years ago, we sent a very reliable commission there which submitted detailed information, and I tried in London last spring to set in motion important leaders in England, where they are also upset but powerless against French politics. In my speech at the great meeting of the World Alliance of Churches in Copenhagen,[2] I remarked that the Rhine occupation is an appalling preparation for a future devastating European war and pointed out ways in which the money could be much better spent for reconstruction. Not even the Frenchmen present protested. As you perhaps remember, Branting[3] and this writer had signed statements in the same vein at Stockholm's Auditorium. What can be done in order to speak one's mind in this matter? If something is to happen, it must be impressive and dignified. How about trying to mobilize all Northern bishops to this end? As I am so often away, I leave it to you if you would be willing to consult Ostenfeld in Copenhagen on the subject, which would carry great authority coming from you; so I am prepared to inquire in Finland and Norway. I wonder if you would be willing to write up a few lines in this affair for a conceivable appeal.

[On Billing's notes of a bishops' meeting]
With respectful regards
yours sincerely,
Nathan Söderblom

---

[2] August 7–10, 1922. As for the World Alliance, cf. letter no. 110, n. 4.

[3] Hjalmar Branting, labor leader and first Social Democratic prime minister in Sweden (1920, 1921–1923, 1924–1925), introduced welfare legislation and supported the League of Nations. Nobel Peace Prize 1921.

196. From Gottfrid Billing[1]

Käre Broder,
Tack för ditt bref.
Naturligtvis skulle jag ej vilja undandraga mig att skrifve till Ostenfeld, om jag ansåge därmed något kunna vinnas. Men jag delar fullt din uppfattning, att »skall något ske, måste det vara imponerande och värdigt«. En opinionsyttring af allenest Nordens biskopar blefve säkert ej detta. Jag kan därför ej tillråda en sådan. Den borde bedömas endast såsom uttryck för biskoparnas alltför höga uppskattning af sin ställning.
Din vän
Gottfrid Billing
Lund 28/9 1922.

Dear Brother,
Thanks for your letter.
It goes without saying that I would not want to shirk from writing to Ostenfeld if I thought that something could be gained thereby. But I completely share your view that »if something is to happen, it must be impressive and dignified.« An opinion expressed only by the bishops of the North would certainly not be that. I can therefore not advise something like that. It would certainly be considered only as an expression of the bishops' all too high valuation of their position.
Your friend,
Gottfrid Billing
Lund, Sept. 28, 1922.

197. To Gottfrid Billing[1]

Upsala 31.10.1922

Vördade Broder!
Mycken tack för Ditt brev, som påvisar åtskilliga oklarheter i förslaget, vilka allra först måste avlägsnas för att saken över huvud skall kunna tänkas vara möjlig. Själva förslaget är uppgjort i Stockholm efter samtal med mig. Jag har icke tänkt mig möjligheten av att kyrkostämma skulle kunna besluta en sådan utgift. Man riskerar överklagande. Däremot hava så många präster både från detta stift och från andra stift vänt sig till mig med förfrågningar om icke en samlad aktion kunde göras, att jag tror att många ämbetsbröder i landet skulle i ett förslag sådant som detta se en betryggande utväg att i någon större omfattning utföra det som deras samvete i varje fall

---

[1] N. Söderblom's collection, from Swedes, UUB, handwritten letter.

[1] Collection Billing. G., Lund University Library, typewritten letter.

bjuder dem. En myckenhet enskilda människor komma ju också ständigt med yrkande, och jag tror att man gjorde hela saken en tjänst genom att söka finna en organisation. Emellertid måste ju i förslaget tydligen utsättas att kyrkostämmorna icke avses. ... Kanske kan det gå på det sätt som i bilagda förslag är antytt?

Vad undertecknare angår, hade jag tänkt mig att där skulle stå endast Biskopsmötets Delegation. Danell har telegrafiskt lämnat sitt bifall. Orsaken varför jag tänkte mig denna enklare utväg i stället för att tillskriva samtliga biskopar är den stora apparaten med en mängd avskrifter och med det långa posthållet till Luleå etc. Det förefaller mig som om biskoparna skulle vara tacksamma för att delegationen eventuellt sköter om saken.

Det längre cirkuläret, som jag icke medsände, talar om fördelningen. Den skulle ske genom centralnämnden eventuellt efter uttalade önskningar, och meningen är, att vi därvidlag skulle anlita ingen mindre än den av Deutscher Evangelischer Kirchenbund tillsatta fyra-mans-nämnden för internationella förbindelser, samt att den närmare fördelningen skulle ske dels genom rent kyrkliga, dels genom den tyska inre missionens och diakoniverksamhetens organ.

Orsaken till att endast Tyskland är föreslaget är helt enkelt nödig koncentration. I Ryssland lider man naturligtvis allra värst, och vi hava ju gjort de yttersta anträngningar för att komma till hjälp. I Österrike är läget lika svårt eller kanske svårare än i Tyskland. Men lejonparten av vår verksamhet har ju hittils gått till Österrike, och går allt fortfarande dit. Vi trodde också att reformationens moderland skulle sätta givare i rörelse på ett särskilt sätt. Min erfarenhet under dessa år, då så många även oändligt rörande gåvor gått genom våra händer, är, att ju konkretare föremålet är, dess hellre giver man. Gärna vill jag tillfoga Österrike, om Du så tycker. Men jag tror att vi förfela målet om vi utbreda oss alltför mycket. Därtill kommer att hela den evangeliska kristendomens ställning i Tyskland är utsatt för en högst betänklig fara, därigenom att dess kärleksverksamhet delvis dör av svält, och därigenom att dess lidande präster i stor utsträckning måste övergå till kroppsarbetarnas klass. [Handskrivet tillägg: De romerska få hjälp från Italien o Sydamerika.] Kanske vore det allra enklast att i början av uppropet göra ett tillägg om att hjälp förmedlas även till andra lidande folk och länder.

Jag bör i förtroende tillägga, att Röda Korset, som hos oss ju är allt igenom kristet och kyrkovänligt, däremot i Tyskland behärskas av judar, så att klagomål redan för flera år sedan kommo hit att det tyska Röda Korsets förmedling icke låter det tyska folket känna att det är trosförvanter som äro givare. Därtill kommer att hela apparaten enligt vad Svenska Kyrkans Offervecka visade, på det föreslagna sättet blir så billig som möjligt.

...

Genom frånvaron av sommarvila har tyvärr mitt hjärta befunnits vara överansträngt, så att jag nu lever mycket försiktigt. Avsaknaden är störst efter promenader. Jag kan nämligen icke gå långt förrän hjärtat säger till. Men allt är på ett mycket tidigt stadium. Ingen utvidgning eller förändring

306

av hjärtmuskeln har skett, och läkarna ge mig förhoppning att efter nödig
kur återvinna fulla kroppskrafter, som ja så väl behöver.
    Din vördnadsfullt tillgivne
    Nathan Söderblom

                                                            Upsala, Oct. 31, 1922
Esteemed Brother,
Many thanks for your letter that points to a lack of clarity in several aspects of the
proposal[2] which must be eliminated first of all so the plan can even begin to look
feasible. The proposal itself was conceived in Stockholm after a conversation with
me. I have not thought of the possibility that church elders decide on such an expen-
diture. There is the risk of an appeal. On the other hand, so many pastors from this
diocese as well as from other dioceses have approached me, inquiring whether or
not a concerted action could be undertaken, that I believe many fellow clergymen in
the country would recognize in a proposal such as this one a reassuring expedient
for carrying out on a wider scale what their conscience bids them to do anyway. A
great many individuals also keep coming all the time with demands, of course, so I
believe one would facilitate the whole procedure by trying to find some sort of organizational framework. However, it should be clearly stated in the proposal that we
are not addressing the church elders. Perhaps it can be done in the way it is hinted
at in the enclosed proposal?[3]
    As for signers, I had thought that only the deputies of the bishops's meeting
should appear. Danell[4] let his approval be known by cable. The reason why I have
thought of this simpler expedient instead of writing to all bishops is the huge appa-
ratus with lots of copies and with long distance mail to Luleå etc. It seems to me as
though the bishops would be grateful that the deputies may take care of the matter.
    The longer circular I did not enclose talks about distribution. That should be ta-
ken care of by the central committee, perhaps after requests have been made, the
idea being that in this matter we should draw upon no less an agency than the four-
men-committee for international relations set up by *Deutscher Evangelischer Kirchentag*,[5] and in addition that the distribution on the ground should be performed
partly by purely church-related agencies, partly by those of the German *Innere Mission* and *Diakonisches Werk*[6].
    The reason why only Germany has been proposed is quite simply the need for
concentration. Of course, in Russia suffering is at its very worst, and we did make
the greatest efforts to come to the rescue. In Austria the situation is just as grave, or
even more so, as in Germany. But the lion's share of our activities has thus far been
directed towards Austria and still continues to do so. We also felt that the Reforma-

---

    [2] As will become clearer from the second paragraph onwards, the subject of this letter is a
new stage in the large-scale relief work Söderblom had started in 1918. It was aimed in particular at undernourished Austrian and German children who were invited to Sweden for several
weeks. It is an effort similar in scope to the one also initiated by Söderblom for prisoners of
war during World War I. Like that previous effort, this new one also inspired the Swedish Red
Cross to join ranks. Cf. Sundkler 219.
    [3] The document referred to was not to be found among Söderblom's papers.
    [4] Bishop of Skara; cf. letter no. 182, n. 3.
    [5] Representative body of the Evangelical (= Protestant) Church of Germany set up in
1919, after its separation from the state.
    [6] The main agencies for social work in the Evangelical (= Protestant) Church of Germany.

tion's country of origin would inspire donors in a special way. It has been my experience during these years when so many deeply moving donations changed hands among us, that the more concrete the purpose is, the more willing one is to give. I shall be glad to add Austria if you think I should. However, I think that we miss the mark if we spread too widely. Moreover, the whole position of Protestant Christianity in Germany is exposed to very serious jeopardy because of the fact that its charitable work in part is dying from starvation, and that its suffering clergy to a large extent must join the manual laborer's class. [Handwritten insertion: The Romans receive aid from Italy and South America.] Perhaps the simplest thing would be to make an addition at the beginning of the appeal to the effect that aid is also being supplied to other suffering peoples and countries.

I must add confidentially that the Red Cross which, of course, with us is thoroughly Christian and friendly towards the church, in Germany is dominated by Jews, so that complaints arrived here already several years ago that mediation by the German Red Cross does not let the German people recognize that it is fellow believers who are the donors. In addition, according to the evidence of the Swedish church's Week of Sacrifice, the whole organizational mechanism is the cheapest possible with the procedure suggested.

... [Further details concerning the next steps to be taken]

Unfortunately, my heart has turned out to be severely strained as a result of the lacking summer recess; so I am living very cautiously now. What I am missing most is taking walks. For I cannot walk long before my heart makes itself felt. But everything is at a very early stage. No enlargement or alteration of the heart muscle has occurred, and the doctors let me hope that after the required curative measures I can regain full physical strength which I need so much.

Respectfully yours,
Nathan Söderblom

198. From Gustaf Aulén[1]

Lund d. 23 XII 22

Käre Ärkebiskop

På det hjärtligaste tackar jag för det senaste vänliga brevet. ...

Så kanske jag får och bör skriva några rader om en fråga, som jag vet intresserar Dig – nämligen successionen efter Pfannenstill. Det har försports här att Du skulle anse att Lindskog borde kallas hit. Konkurrensen i Uppsala synes ju ock giva vid handen, att detta lätt skulle kunna ske. Jag har här haft långa overläggningar med fakultetsmedlemmarna, särskildt med Lehmann och Rodhe. Men alla (utom Herner) äro fullkomligt övertygade om att en kallelse för närvarande är alldeles omöjlig. Kallelsen strander på att vi här ha en docent, Nygren, som vid specimenstidens slut kommer att lägga fram åtminstone 4 större arbeten jämte diverse smått. Fakulteten gav honom redan på hans docentavhandling det högsta betyg, som den överhuvud utdelat (a), och hans mycket flitiga senare produktion kan icke sägas ha svikit de löften han då gav. Icke minst Lehmann var absolut mot kallelse

---

[1] N. Söderblom's collection of letters, from Swedes, UUB, handwritten letter.

och ansåg att det skulle vara orätt att förhindra Nygren att söka och speci-
minera. [fotnot: Lehmann sätter Nygren synnerligen högt.] Jag varken vill
eller kan nu jämföra Lindskog och Nygren – men säkert är att N. har åtm.
tvänne goda kvalifikationer: stor beläsenhet och stor skärpa. Det är många
här som vänta sig mycket av honom. ... Därtill kommer att L. ju börjar på
att vara väl till åren – det är nog icke så lätt att *begynna* en akademisk verksamhet så pass sent. Huru det skall gå med tillsättningen om det nu blir ansökan är ju en annan fråga. Förlåt att jag besvärat med denna redogörelse,
men jag tänkte att kanske några ord till förklaring skulle kunna vara på sin
plats.

Men framför allt vilja nu min maka och jag förena oss i önskningar om
en god jul för eder alla samt i förhoppningar att det nya året skall komma
med hälsa och glädje till ärkebiskopshuset – vi få vara med i den stora
skara, som hoppas därpå och bedja därom.

Din vördsamt och tacksamt tillgivne Gustaf Aulén

P. S. Jag har fått hem min kära hustru till julen, men hon är bra klen, och
det är icke uteslutet att ett ingrepp kommer att ske, när hon bättre orkar
med det.

Lund, Dec. 23, 1922

Dear Archbishop,
Thank you ever so much for your latest kind letter. ... [On an article Aulén was
asked to write for *Constructive Quarterly*]

Well, perhaps I can and should write a few lines on a subject which I know is of
interest for you – namely the succession of Pfannenstill[2]. You have been reported to
think that Lindskog[3] should be called here. The competition in Uppsala does indeed
seem to make appear obvious that such a move could easily happen. I have had long
deliberations with the faculty members, especially with Lehmann and Rodhe[4]. But
all of them (except Herner[5]) are completely convinced that a call is at present entirely impossible. The call would run aground because of the fact that we have a lecturer here, Nygren[6], who at the time of submission of academic specimens will hand
in at least four larger works as well as various smaller things. The faculty already
gave him the highest credit it ever granted for his doctoral thesis (A), and his very
assiduous later production cannot be said to have disappointed the expectations he
then raised. Particularly Lehmann was absolutely opposed to a call and thought it
would be utterly wrong to prevent Nygren's application and submission of speci-

---

[2] Cf. letter no. 21, n. 1.
[3] Erik Lindskog (1867–1923), lecturer in systematic theology in Uppsala, who apparently
had thus far not succeeded in climbing the academic ladder.
[4] Johannes Edvard Lehmann (1862–1930), lecturer in the history of religions in Copenhagen 1900, was called to the first German chair in the field at Berlin university in 1910, in Lund
1913, one of the most important representatives of the phenomenology of religion, beside Söderblom, R. Otto, G. van der Leeuw, F. Heiler. – Edvard Magnus Rodhe (1878–1954), 1905
lecturer in church history in Lund, 1912 professor of practical theology in Uppsala, continued
to publish in both fields, 1925–1948 bishop of Lund.
[5] Sven Herner (1863–1949), professor of »exegetisk teologi« (exegetical theology).
[6] Cf. letter no. 188, n. 8.

mens. [Footnote: Lehmann holds Nygren in particularly high esteem] I neither want nor am I able to compare Lindskog and Nygren – but it is for sure that N. has at least two good qualifications: he is a man of wide reading and a very sharp mind. There are many here who expect a lot from him ... In addition, L. is beginning to be well advanced in years – it is certainly not so easy to *start* an academic activity so late. – How filling the chair will come about if there are to be applications is of course a different question. Forgive me for troubling you with this account, but I thought that perhaps some words in explanation would be in order.

But above all, my wife and I unite in our best wishes for Christmas to all of you, and in our hopes that the new year will bring good health and joy to the Archbishop's mansion – we are among the host of people hoping and praying for that.

Reverently and gratefully yours,   Gustaf Aulén

P.S. I have got my dear wife back home for Christmas, but she is quite weak, and it cannot be excluded that surgery will be performed when she is better able to endure it.

199. To Friedrich Heiler[1]

Upsala 23. 1. 1923

Käre vän!

Diger är boken, men jag läste den såsom ett brev på posten från början till slut, icke lika fängslad utan för varje sida och kapitel i en starkare spänning. För någon tid sedan klagade en Berlintidning över att man i det evangeliska Tyskland kände så lite till katolicismen. Nu har katolicismen fått en skildring, vars like, så vitt jag vet, intet århundrade kan uppvisa. Tankarna strömma över mig. De starkaste äro först tacksamhet mot Gud för den pietet som boken andas och som utesluter tanken på renegat. I stället skulle jag vilja säga en medlem av och en tjänare åt den katolicism som är idealet även för Rom, men som Roms världsliga maktbegär och pactum turpe med vidskepelsen ömöjliggör. Vidare svindlar blicken inför de utsikter och de ytterst ömtåliga problem som här upprulla sig för en evangelisk katolicitet. Därom hoppas jag at få yttra mig utförligare. Münchens universitet inbjöd mig i somras att där hålla en serie föreläsningar, så mycket märkligare som Magnificus nu är katolsk kyrkohistoriker. Jag såg ingen möjlighet. Men jag känner nu trots mitt överansträngda hjärta däri en bestämd kallelse, dels i enhetstankens tjänst, dels och framför allt för att på en sådan plattform med all hänsyn till den romerska katolicismen och dess fromhet ändå med all önskvärd klarhet och skärpa uttala min tanke om evangelisk katolicitet som redan nu i den djupa evangeliska fromheten i våra av reformationen förvandlade folklynnen i själva verket är mer vidhjärtad än Roms världsfamnande och neråt toleranta metod. Det var Eder bok som klargjorde för mig nödvändigheten att om möjligt svara ja till München. Om Edert nya storverk hoppas jag få utförligare uttala mig i brev eller tryck så snart tid och krafter medgiva.

---

[1] Fr. Heiler's papers (Ms. 999), Univ. Library Marburg, typewritten letter.

Mitt hjärta är överansträngd, men har icke undergått någon organisk förändring.

Dag och natt ligger tanken på Frankrikes våldsdåd som en mara över mig.

Gud välsigne Eder i Eder maktpåliggande kallelse i fromhetens och vetenskapens och kyrkans tjänst!

Med vördnad till Eder fru och hälsning från oss alla

tillgivne

Nathan Söderblom

Uppsala 23. 1. 1923

Lieber Freund!

Dick ist das Buch[2], aber ich las es wie einen Brief im Postamt vom Anfang bis zum Schluss, nicht genauso gefesselt, sondern mit jeder Seite und jedem Kapitel mit größerer Spannung. Vor einiger Zeit klagte eine Berliner Zeitung darüber, dass man im evangelischen Deutschland den Katholizismus so wenig kenne. Jetzt ist dem Katholizismus eine Schilderung zuteil geworden, dergleichen soweit ich weiß kein Jahrhundert aufzuweisen hat. Die Gedanken überströmen mich. Die stärksten sind zuerst Dankbarkeit gegenüber Gott für die Pietät, die das Buch atmet und die den Gedanken an einen Renegaten ausschließt. Stattdessen möchte ich sagen: ein Glied und ein Diener desjenigen Katholizismus, der das Ideal auch für Rom ist, den jedoch Roms weltliche Machtbegier und sein pactum turpe [schändlicher Pakt] mit dem Aberglauben unmöglich machen. Ferner: Es schwindelt den Blick vor der Aussicht und den äußerst verwickelten Problemen, die sich hier für eine evangelische Katholizität auftun. Darüber hoffe ich mich ausführlicher äußern zu können. Die Münchner Universität lud mich letzten Sommer ein, dort eine Reihe von Vorlesungen zu halten – um so bemerkenswerter, als Magnificus [der Rektor] jetzt ein katholischer Kirchenhistoriker ist. Ich sah keine Möglichkeit [der Einladung zu folgen]. Aber ich erkenne darin jetzt trotz meines überanstrengten Herzens einen deutlichen Aufruf, teils im Dienst des Einheitsgedankens, teils und vor allem auf einer solchen Plattform, bei aller Achtung vor dem römischen Katholizismus und seiner Frömmigkeit doch mit aller wünschenswerten Klarheit und Schärfe meine Gedanken über evangelische Katholizität vorzutragen, die schon jetzt in der tiefen evangelischen Frömmigkeit in unseren von der Reformation verwandelten Volkscharakteren tatsächlich weiterziger ist als Roms weltumfassende und nach unten hin tolerante Methode. Ihr Buch war es, das mir die Notwendigkeit klar machte, wenn möglich in München zuzusagen. Über Ihr neues Großwerk hoffe ich mich in Brief oder Druck ausführlicher äußern zu können, sobald Zeit und Kräfte es zulassen.

Mein Herz ist überanstrengt, hat aber keine organischen Veränderungen erlitten.

Tag und Nacht liegt der Gedanke an Frankreichs Gewaltaktion wie ein Albtraum auf mir.[3]

---

[2] Friedrich Heiler, *Der Katholizismus. Seine Idee und seine Erscheinung*, München 1923 (completely revised and considerably enlarged version of *Das Wesen des Katholizismus*, 1920).

[3] Söderblom refers to the French occupation of the Ruhr area on Jan. 11, 1923 which was to enforce the delivery of coal accorded to France in the Versailles peace treaty.

Gott segne Sie und Ihre verantwortungsvolle Aufgabe im Dienst der Frömmigkeit, der Wissenschaft und der Kirche!
Mit Ehrerbietung für Ihre Frau und Gruß von uns allen
Ihr Ihnen verbundener
Nathan Söderblom

200. To Gottfrid Billing[1]

Upsala 27.1.1923

Högt vördade Broder!
Jag kan icke sova på nätterna för den mara som består i våldets fräcka ogärningar vid Rhen, och jag kan icke säga hur glad jag blev när jag nyss mottog Ditt brev. Kunna vi båda gemensamt uppmana biskoparna, så gå de nog med. Jag har grubblat mycket över saken och funderat på, om det icke skulle vara bäst att giva vårt korta, lugna, men i sak för samvetet uttrycksfulla uttalande formen av en hänvändelse till våra medkristna i skilda länder. Bäst är väl att vi taga fasta på två moment, 1: Dels vår kristna medkänsla, som också yttrar sig i Samariterhjälpen mot de uthungrade, pinade och förödmjukade, dels 2: vår insikt om att det förbannelsens utsäde, som nu utsås, måste leda Europa in i ännu värre förödande krig. Således skulle vi yttra oss i barmhärtighetens och fredsviljans namn. Gillar Du i princip detta, vågar jag vördnadsfullt hos Dig anhålla om två ting.
1: Skulle Du godhetsfullt vilja sätta ihop några rader om saken. Jag skall icke undandraga mig någon möda för att få vår vädjan undertecknad och effektiv. Men det vore ovärderligt att från Din hand få en formulering som sätter prägel på det hela.
2: Vidare vågar jag liksom i höstas åter hemställa, att Du godhetsfullt ville med några rader hänvända Dig till Biskop Ostenfeld i Köpenhamn för att uppmana honom att själv med sina danska kolleger deltaga i vår vädjan. Jag har ju ofta att göra med Ostenfeld och har fått honom med på en hel del företag och uttalanden, som han efteråt är mycket belåten med att hava deltagit i, men som det mer än en gång kostat mycken möda att få honom med på av förklarliga orsaker. Nu vet jag att en hänvändelse från Dig skulle mycket underlätta hans och hans kollegers deltagande. Jag sätter mig i förbindelse med övriga svenska biskopar och med biskoparna i Norge, Finland, Estland och Lettland.
3: Eller tycker Du att vi skola inskränka oss till de svenska biskoparna? Det skulle förenkla saken, förkorta proceduren, men naturligtvis ute i världen förminska räckvidden av får [läs: vår] åtgärd. I Sverige skulle vi få massanslutning.
Din vördnadsfullt tillgivne
Nathan Söderblom

---

[1] Collection Billing. G., Lund University Library, typewritten letter.

Uppsala, January 27, 1923

Highly esteemed Brother,

I cannot sleep by night because of the nightmare consisting of the outrageous misdeeds of violence on the Rhine, and I cannot say how glad I was when I recently received your letter. If the two of us together can summon the bishops, they may well comply. I have pondered a great deal on the matter and wondered whether it would not be best to lend to our pronouncement – which is to be short, calm, but, with regard to the issue significant for the conscience – the form of an appeal to our fellow Christians in various countries. It is probably best to concentrate on two points: 1° our Christian sympathy which is also expressed in Samaritan aid to the starving, tormented, and humiliated, 2° our insight that the seed of plague now being sown must lead Europe into even more devastating wars. In this way we would speak out in the name of mercy and the will to peace. If you agree to this in principle, I venture respectfully to request two things from you.

1° Would you be so kind as to write up a few lines on the subject? I shall not shirk from taking any trouble to get our appeal signed and [make it] effective. It would be invaluable, however, to receive a formulation from your hand which leaves its impress on the whole thing.

2° Moreover, I venture to suggest once again, as I did last fall, that you be so kind as to address Bishop Ostenfeld in Copenhagen with a line or two, inviting him to join our appeal, together with his Danish colleagues. I do have to deal with Ostenfeld often, and I had him go along with a whole range of enterprises and pronouncements that he afterwards was quite content with having been a part of, but which more than once, for understandable reasons, had cost a great deal of effort to have him go along with. Now I know that an appeal from you would considerably facilitate his and his colleagues' participation. I shall contact the other Swedish bishops and the bishops in Norway, Finland, Estonia, and Lithuania.

3° Or do you think that we should limit ourselves to the Swedish bishops? That would simplify things, shorten the procedure, but of course reduce the range of our enterprise in the outside world. In Sweden, we should get massive support.

Respectfully yours,
Nathan Söderblom

201. To Gustaf Johansson[1]

Upsala 2 februari 1923

Broder!

Hosföljande vädjan från Sveriges samtliga biskopar till våra medkristna i

---

[1] Gustaf Johansson (1844–1930), Finnish archbishop in Åbo 1899–1930. Previous to his tenure as bishop, he was a systematic theologian at Helsinki. His theological views were strongly influenced by the German Johann Tobias Beck (1804–1878). Central to his system of thought was the strictly otherworldly concept of the Kingdom of God, the eschatological fulfillment of which could only be awaited in patience of faith and hope. J. therefore vehemently opposed all kinds of church activism, be it of the Social Gospel or the pietistic type, that claimed to further the Kingdom of God. Cf. Geert Sentzke, *Die Theologie Johann Tobias Becks und ihr Einfluss auf Finnland*, vol. 2 (SLAG 9), Helsinki 1957, 117–147. – N. Söderblom's collection of letters, to Swedes and foreigners, UUB, typewritten letter. The enclosed document is the one discussed in the previous letter.

alla länder och till de ansvariga statsmännen, särskilt till Förenta Staternas president sändes härmed på Svenska Biskopsmötets vägnar med hjärtlig fridshälsning till våra kära trosfränder i Finland genom
vördnadsfullt och broderligt tillgivne
Nathan Söderblom

Bilaga

Ingen kan räkna de många, som över allt i världen uppröras i sitt innersta av vad som nu sker. Vi hoppades på fredens välsignelser efter kriget, men folkens sammanlevnad har ytterligare förvärrats. Hunger, bitterhetens gift i kränkta själar och kroppslig och sedlig smitta förhärjar ädla delar av Centraleuropas mänsklighet. Och nu skär fulländad vapenmakt under fredens täckmantel stora stycken ur den avväpnade grannens land, därmed förvärrande ett redan himmelsskriande nödtillstånd. Förbannelsen som utsås skall bära frukt i nya, ännu fruktansvärdare krig. Ty vad människan sår, det skall hon ock skörda. Det har världskriget nogsamt besannat.

Grunden till Europas olycka är uppenbar. Man låter makt och kortsynt egennytta vara högsta lag stället för att lyssna till Kristi bud. Vi döma ingen, ty människan ser endels, men vi fördöma våldets metoder.

Samveten och hjärtan brännas överallt av frågan: Vad kan göras? Vi, Kyrkans tjänare i Sverige, uppmana våra medkristna i Frankrike och alla länder, särskilt i Norden och i Amerika[2] att med oss anropa Gud om klarhet och kraft till behjärtad handling. Hela frågan om fred och nödvändigt skadestånd måste lyftas ur dess nuvarande försumpning i krigshot och vedergällning till den högre ståndpunkten av inbördes förtroende och god vilja. Människor måste förlåta varandra så visst som de själva hoppas förlåtelse. Vi hemställa vördsamt till de ansvariga statsmännen och särskilt till Förenta Staternas president, att ofördröjligen genom möte och ärlig uppgörelse mellan makternas representanter åstadkomma en utjämning av spänningen som blir allt olidligare och olycksdigrare för varje dag.

Nathan Söderblom, J.W. Personne, Hjalmar Danell, U.L. Ullman, V.E. Rundgren, Einar Billing, K.L. Lindberg, Gottfrid Billing, E.H. Rodhe, J.A. Eklund, E.F. Lönegren, O. Bergqvist, Nils Widner.

Upsala, February 2, 1923

Brother,

The enclosed appeal from all of Sweden's bishops to our fellow Christians in all countries and to the responsible statesmen, in particular to the President of the United States, is hereby sent with cordial greetings of peace to our dear brethren in the faith in Finland through
yours respectfully and brotherly,
Nathan Söderblom

---

[2] The words »särskilt i Norden och i Amerika« were left out in the printed version, »Till våra medkristna i Frankrike och alla länder och till de ansvarige statsmännen, särskilt till Förenta Staternas president«, (dated Febr. 1, 1923), Uppsala 1923.

No one can count the numbers of those in all parts of the world who are moved in their innermost by the present events. We hoped for the blessings of peace after the horrors of war. But disunity in the European commonwealth grows worse. Starvation, the poison of bitterness in outraged souls, physical contamination and moral degradation are ravaging noble groups of the human family in Central Europe. During so-called peace skilled armies are cutting big parts away from the country of their disarmed neighbour, thus aggravating atrocious miseries. The course [sic; read: curse] now being sown will bear fruit in new and more frightful wars. For whatsoever a man soweth, that shall he also reap,[4] as the world war proved abundantly.

Europe's distress evidently comes from making brutal power and short-sighted selfishness the highest law, instead of listening to Christ's voice. We judge nobody, because man sees in part.[5] But we condemn the methods of violence.

Earnest hearts everywhere burn with the question: What can be done?

We servants of the Church in Sweden urge our fellow Christians in France and all lands to implore with us from God vision and power for wholehearted action. The whole problem of peace and necessary reparation must be lifted from the present level of reprisals and threats to the higher plane of mutual trust and good-will. Men must forgive as they hope for forgiveness.

We humble [sic; l.: humbly] appeal to the responsible statesmen, and especially to the President of the United States, with all possible speed to relieve by a straightforward agreement between the representatives of the powers the tension which grows daily more unbearable and baleful.

The Archbishop in Uppsala, the Bishop in Linköping, the Bishop in Skara, the Bishop in Strängnäs, the Bishop in Västerås, the Bishop in Växjö, the Bishop in Lund, the Bishop in Göteborg, the Bishop in Karlstad, the Bishop in Härnösand, the Bishop in Luleå, the Bishop in Visby.

Pastor Primarius in Stockholm

202. To Erik Rinman[1]
PRIVAT

[Febr. 1923]

Broder!

Bilagda citat är ordagrannt hämtat ur Docenten Wetters slutpåminnelser sådana de avtryckts i Dagens Nyher och Upsala Nya Tidning.

---

[3] The following translation which can be found in Söderblom's ecumenical collection, box 11, at the UUB, underwent only minor changes to become the official English version. The names of the signatories are here replaced by their church positions (Swedish even in the English original, here translated), with Viktor Rundgren, bishop of Visby, being moved from fifth place to the first from the last.

[4] Gal. 6:7.

[5] An allusion to I Cor. 13:12b: »No I know in part.«

[1] N. Söderblom's collection of letters, to Swedes and foreigners, UUB, undated typewritten letter. It was answered on Febr. 15, 1923.

Vi hava blivit förbluffade många med mig. Satsen är ju meningslös, helt enkelt en groda. Varje bibelläsare vet att Jesus och Paulus hade judisk härkomst, att Nya Testamentet är fullt av gammaltestamentliga citat och att de första kristna församlingarna i Jerusalem och annorstädes framgingo ur judendomen, betraktade sig som arvtagare till Gamla Testamentet och av utomstående betraktades såsom en riktning inom judendomen. Att sätta frågetecken efter detta är ju ren fantasi. Vad skulle fariseer, sadduceer, templet, synagogan, lagen, profeterna och så vidare vara om icke judiska? En annan sak är det inflytande som från hellenismen och andra håll redan starkt påverkat judendomen och åstadkommit en hellenistisk riktning, av vilken jag endast behöver nämna Filo. En annan fråga är också det inflytande från den omgivande religionsblandningen som gjorde sig gällande redan vid kristendomens uppkomst, än mer längre fram i kyrkan. Reitzenstein [interlineärt, handskrivet tillägg: Wetter's läromästare], Norden, Bousset och andra hava förtjänsten att hava uttagit Nya Testamentet från isoleringen och behandlat det i samband med hela den samtida religiösa situationen. Men alla tre betona åter och åter igen, att judendomen naturligtvis är kristendomens modersköte och hur vådligt det är att lösrycka den därifrån. Wetter har råkat ut för epigoners öde att, såsom man väl känner från vetenskapens historia, driva en berättigad reaktion in absurdum och därmed påskynda dess beriktigande. Men det ligger någonting groteskt i att tänka sig en professor i Nya Testamentet som förnekar eller betvivlar dess judiska ursprung, som kanslersämbetet såvitt jag förstår på ett fullkomligt exakt och omotsägligt sätt uttryckt.

Jag har noga avhållit mig från att söka påverka någon enda som röstat i denna strid mellan Lindblom och Wetter, och får även förebråelser därför. Jag vill därför heller icke nu gärna framträda. Vore icke satsen ironiskt tillspetsad, skulle man tänka sig ett missöde, en dumhet som den mänskliga ofullkomligheten då och då har rätt till. Men som det nu står synes det mig vara orättfärdigt, att satsen, som i D.N. och annorstädes får gälla såsom själva dödsstöten åt den hederlige, vid detta ärendes behandling säkert ytterst samvetsgranne kanslern, skall stå offentligen omotsagd såsom sista ordet i ärendet innan K.M. avgör. Därför hemställer jag till Dig om Du anser det vara riktigt och nödvändigt att på något sätt låta saken komma fram. Jag skulle gärna taga till orda, om inte min ställning som prokansler i den nuvarande situationen förhindrade det.

Din tillgivne
Nathan Söderblom

[February, 1923]
Dear friend,
The enclosed quotation[2] has been taken literally from lecturer Wetter's final remarks as they were printed in D[agens] N[yheter] and Upsala Nya Tidning.[3]

---

[2] The newspaper clip referred to is missing in Söderblom's papers.
[3] In an article concerning Wetter's and Lindblom's credentials for promotion to professor

316

We were perplexed, many [others] with me. The proposition is meaningless, a blunder, quite simply. Each reader of the Bible knows that Jesus and Paul were of Jewish descent, that the New Testament is full of Old Testament quotations, and that the first Christian congregations in Jerusalem and elsewhere originated in Judaism, considered themselves heirs of the Old Testament and by outsiders were considered a school within Judaism. Putting a question mark after this is, of course, pure fancy. What should Pharisees, Sadducees, the temple, the synagogue, the law, the prophets, and so forth be other than Jewish? A different matter is the influence from Hellenism and other directions that had already strongly affected Judaism and resulted in a Hellenistic school of thought, of which I only have to name Philo. A different question, too, is the influence of the surrounding amalgam of religions which was holding sway already at the beginning of Christianity, and more so later on in the church. Reitzenstein [interlinear, handwritten addition: Wetter's teacher], Norden, Bousset[4] and others have the merit of having taken the New Testament out of its isolation and treating it in connection with the whole contemporary religious situation. But all three emphasize time and again that Judaism is, of course, Christianity's womb, and how perilous it is to detach it from there. Wetter has fallen victim to the fate of the epigone, well known from the history of learning, of carrying a legitimate reaction to absurdity and thereby hastening its correction. But there is something grotesque about imagining a professor of New Testament who denies or doubts its Jewish origin, as the chancellor's office, as I understand, expressed in a completely exact and irrefutable way.

I have been careful to abstain from trying to influence any single person who voted in this conflict between Lindblom and Wetter, and I am even being reproached for that. Therefore, I am reluctant to step forward now, too. Had the proposition not been pointed in an ironic way, one could think of a mishap, [the kind of] stupidity human imperfection is entitled to every now and then. But as it now stands, it seems to me to be unjustified that the proposition, which in *Dagens Nyheter* and elsewhere is bound to pass for the very deathblow to the upright chancellor [of the university], who in treating this matter certainly is most conscientious, should remain publicly undisputed as the last word on the matter, before His Majesty decides. Therefore I submit to you if you consider it right and necessary to let the matter come to the fore some way or other. I would have liked to speak out, if my position as vice-chancellor[5] did not prevent me from doing so in the present situation.

Sincerely yours,
Nathan Söderblom

---

of New Testament. Gillis Albert Petersson Wetter (1887-1926), was at the time lecturer in the history of religions in Stockholm. He was actually appointed. The other contender, Johannes Lindblom (1882-1974), became professor of exegesis in Lund in 1930.

[4] Richard Reitzenstein (1861-1931), professor of classical languages and the history of religions, in Göttingen since 1914. One of his famous books is *Die hellenistischen Mysterienreligionen nach ihren Grundgedanken und Wirkungen*, Leipzig 1910, 3rd ed. 1927. Eduard Norden (1868-1941), of Jewish descent but converted to Protestantism, professor of classical languages, in Berlin since 1906 (forced to early retirement and emigration by the Nazi regime). His best known book is *Agnostos Theos. Untersuchungen zur Formengeschichte religiöser Rede*, Leipzig 1913, 5th ed. 1923. Both of them strongly influenced Rudolf Bultmann, among others. For Wilhelm Bousset, cf. letter no. 39, note 1.

[5] As archbishop, Söderblom automatically held that post.

203. From Friedrich Heiler[1]

Marburg/Lahn, Ockershäuser Allee 5, 15. Februar 1923

Hochverehrter Hochwürdigster Herr Erzbischof!

Für Ihren lieben Brief sage ich Ihnen vielen herzlichen Dank. Ich habe mich so sehr über ihn gefreut. Daß Sie auch dieses Buch, das zu schreiben mir sehr schwer war, so liebevoll und verständnisinnig aufnahmen, ist mir eine besondere Ermunterung. Ich hatte es mit viel Liebe und Herzeleid geschrieben, es ist darum trotz alles Strebens nach Sachlichkeit und Objektivität ein recht persönliches Buch geworden, und das ist ein Vorteil und Nachteil zugleich. Von »modernistischen« Katholiken habe ich begeisterte Zustimmung erhalten. Auch dies ist mir eine Freude, daß ich diesen unter dem Druck Roms schwer seufzenden und nach Freiheit, Wahrheit und Liebe sehnsüchtig verlangenden Theologen etwas Trost, Stärkung und Ermunterung bringen durfte. Dagegen wird das Buch von den Vertretern des juristisch-dogmatisch-hierarchischen Kirchentums sehr scharf abgelehnt, weil sehr unbequem empfunden. Diese Kreise hätten es viel lieber gesehen, wenn ich mit Renegateneifer gegen die römische Kirche angekämpft hätte; eine aus Liebe und Schmerz geborene Kritik fürchten sie viel mehr als eine radikale Polemik. Aber ich bin fest überzeugt, der Gedanke einer evangelischen Katholizität wird auch in den bisher streng exklusiven Kreisen Raum gewinnen, und die Liebe zu Christus und den Brüdern wird, wenn auch langsam, das harte und kalte Recht erweichen und erwärmen. Als ich das Buch schrieb, war ich in Gedanken so oft bei Ihnen, und als ich den Traum vom »Papa Angelico« niederschrieb,[2] mußte ich so viel an Sie denken und Ihren schönen Hirtenbrief, als dessen Leitworte Sie die Worte Ihres sterbenden Vaters gebrauchten.[3] Wann wird wohl ein solcher Hirtenbrief von der Cathedra Petri in Rom kommen?

An Weihnachten bekam ich von einer lieben Freundin in Skara ein Geschenk, das mich besonders freute, ein Bild, auf dem Sie zusammen neben dem Sâdhu[4] in Ihrem Arbeitszimmer stehen. Es hängt jetzt in meinem Studierzimmer und ich freue mich so oft an ihm; sehe ich doch auf ihm die

---

[1] N. Söderblom's collection of letters, from foreigners, UUB, handwritten letter.

[2] This refers to the chapter »Die Sehnsuchtsträume vom Pastor angelicus« (on the ideal pope) in Heilers book *Der Katholizismus* (cf. letter no. 199, note 2), pp. 334–340.

[3] Nathan Söderblom, *Herdabref till prästerskapet och församlingarna i Upsala ärkestift* [Episcopal Charge], Uppsala 1914. It was based on II Cor. 1:24: »Not that we lord it over your faith; we work with you for your joy« [Revised Standard Version], words his father entrusted to him on his deathbed.

[4] The Indian autodidactic theologian Sadhu (migrant monk), Sundar Singh, 1888–1928 (?), independent missionary who preached an indigenous Gospel, based on reading of the Bible and mystical, even ecstatic experience. Nominally Anglican, he was considered Protestant in a wider sense. In 1920, he lectured in the UK and the US, and in 1922, in several European countries, also in Sweden. After that, he concentrated his missionary efforts on the Indian subcontinent. He strongly influenced the Ashram movement. – Söderblom dedicated to him the first chapter of his *Tre livsformer. Mystik – förtröstan – vetenskap*, Stockholm 1922, as well as the book *Sundar Singhs budskap utgivet och belyst*, 2nd ed. Stockholm 1923.

318

zwei Männer, die ein wahrhaft ökumenisches Christentum vertreten, beide frei von den engen Banden eines exklusiven Konfessionschristentums.

Mit Bedauern hörte ich schon von schwedischen Freunden über Ihr Herzübel und Ihre geschwächte körperliche Kraft. Möge Ihnen Gott bald wieder die volle Frische schenken! Ich selbst war im Sommer und Herbst auch viel krank, lag auch kurze Zeit in der Klinik; es war die Folge der äußeren und inneren Anstrengung bei der Abfassung des Buches. Jetzt geht es mir wieder sehr gut.

Wir hatten beabsichtigt im März nach Vesterås zu fahren. Aber die politische Unsicherheit macht die Ausführung unseres Planes unsicher. Die Zeiten sind ja unsagbar traurig. Die Gewalttaten der Franzosen, vor allem ihre Grausamkeiten gegenüber wehrlosen Menschen haben eine unsagbare Erbitterung allenthalben hervorgerufen und eine neue Atmosphäre des Krieges geschaffen. Es ist so furchtbar und für das Christentum des Abendlandes so beschämend, nach den vierjährigen Schrecken des Weltkrieges einen neuen noch schrecklicheren Krieg heraufziehen zu sehen, der den »Untergang des Abendlandes«[5] herbeizuführen droht. Rußland steht gewappnet im Osten und man sagt, es wolle im Frühjahr zum großen Schlag wider die Westmächte ausholen. Wollte Gott, daß alle diese Gerüchte, Befürchtungen und Mutmaßungen unzutreffend seien.

Eine große Freude war mir das mannhafte Wort der schwedischen Bischöfe an die Staatsmänner.[6] Es sind ja ganz wenige im Ausland, die offen für Recht und Wahrheit eintreten. Um so größer ist unsere dankbare Freude gegenüber diesen wenigen.

Vielen herzlichen Dank sage ich Ihnen auch für die Zusendung des schönen Aufsatzes über Friedrich von Hügel.[7] Ich verehre und liebe ihn sosehr. Nur eines kann ich ihm nicht verzeihen, daß er gar kein tieferes Verständnis für Luther aufbringt. Es ist ganz merkwürdig, wie sein beispielloser Weitsinn hier plötzlich Schranken aufrichtet und sich mit Scheuklappen umgibt.

Grüßen Sie bitte Ihre verehrte Frau und Ihre lieben Kinder. Mit herzlichen Wünschen und verehrungsvollen Grüßen bleibe ich

Ihr dankbar ergebener
Friedrich Heiler
Auch meine Frau grüßt Sie verehrungsvoll.

---

[5] Allusion to Oswald Spengler's book *Der Untergang des Abendlandes. Umrisse einer Morphologie der Weltgeschichte*, 2 vols., München 1918, I 33rd to 47th, compeletely revised ed. 1923, II 16th to 30th ed. 1922.

[6] Cf. letter no. 201.

[7] Friedrich Freiherr von Hügel (1852–1925), autodidactic Roman Catholic philosopher of religion who pleaded for the exegetical ideas of modernist Alfred Loisy. The article is: »Baron Friedrich von Hügels andliga självdeklaration. En studie i evangelisk och katolsk etik,« FS M. Pfannenstill, Lund 1923, 168–183.

204. From Raymond Poincaré[1]

Paris, 15/2 1923

J'ai bien reçu l'appel des évêques de Suède transmis par votre télégramme du 2 février. Trop de grands souvenirs communs unissent la Suède et la France pour que je ne tienne pas à donner aux plus hauts représentants de l'église suédoise des explications franches et sincères. La France, attaquée sans provocation en 1914, alors que tous les efforts de son gouvernement tendaient à faciliter le maintien de la paix, a vu une partie de son territoire envahie et systématiquement saccagée par les armées allemandes. Son moral n'a pas faibli. Contrainte de repousser la force par la force, elle a tenu bon contre l'envahisseur et avec l'appui et le concours des ses alliés, unis avec elle pour la défense du droit cyniquement violé dans la personne de la Belgique, elle a triomphé. Dans les négociations de la paix, les alliés ont tenu à montrer leurs sentiments d'humanité et leur modération en renonçant à exiger des vaincus, comme il était jusque là d'usage dans les traités de paix, le remboursement des frais de la guerre. Ils ne pouvaient toutefois, sans porter à la loi morale les plus graves atteintes, renoncer à exiger la réparation des dommages causés volontairement par les envahisseurs. Bien que la responsabilité de l'Allemagne à cet égard ne puisse faire de doute, les gouvernements qui se sont succédés dans ce pays depuis l'armistice se sont ingéniés à éluder leurs obligations. Loin de hâter par une loyale exécution du traité la fin de mesures d'occupation que les alliés avaient dû prescrire, ils semblent n'avoir eu d'autre souci que de ruiner leur état, de pratiquer une politique de prodigalités et d'avilir leur monnaie, n'ayant aucun égard aux souffrances qu'ils imposaient à la grande masse de la population au seul profit de quelques uns. Ils ont poursuivi cette politique de désastre dans le dessein d'éviter de réparer les maux que leurs prédécesseurs avaient causés à la France et à la Belgique. Après avoir attendu pendant trois longues années un changement de conduite des coupables, après avoir même dans le vain espoir de faciliter ce changement consenti des atténuations à leurs droits, la France et la Belgique se sont vu forcées, devant les manquements volontaires dûment constatés de l'Allemagne, de recourir à des sanctions d'ailleurs par le traité, fermement résolues à faire valoir leurs droits et conscients qu'elles agissent dans la limite de ces droits. La France et la Belgique ne se sentent pas atteintes par les calomnies qui les représentent comme animées d'un esprit de violence et de haine. Elles sont résolues à user de leur droit avec modération,

---

[1] Raymond Poincaré (1860-1934), French President 1913-1920, Prime Minister and Foreign Secretary 1922-1924. He pursued a policy of uncompromising enforcement of the Versailles peace treaty. However, the occupation of the Ruhr area in 1923 increasingly isolated France internationally. So he had to make concessions, thus facilitating the Dawes Plan of 1924 which reduced the burden of reparations for Germany and rejected the French measure. France's troops began to vacate the occupied territory in 1925. – Nathan Söderblom's ecumenical collection A 20, UUB, Telegram. Accents and punctuation in the French text added, spelling errors eliminated.

sans recourir aux brutalités ni aux violences, surtout envers les ouvriers et les populations allemandes trompés par de mauvais derniers. La France souhaite ardemment qu'un jour vienne où elle pourra pardonner le crime commis par l'Allemagne en déchaînant la plus terrible des guerres. Elle sait que la condition première du pardon est que le coupable se répente et change de conduite. Elle ne veut donc pas douter que les sages conseils des évêques de Suède inclineront les coeurs des dirigeants de l'Allemagne vers cette répentance et hâteront ainsi le jour du pardon.
Poincaré

Paris, February 15, 1923
I was pleased to receive the appeal by the bishops of Sweden, transmitted by your cable of February 2.[2] Too many great common memories unite Sweden and France for me to hesitate giving frank and sincere comments to the highest representatives of the Swedish church. France, attacked without provocation in 1914, while all efforts of its government aimed at facilitating the maintenance of peace, saw a portion of its territory invaded and systematically looted by the German armies. Its morale did not falter. Constrained to push back force by force, it resisted the invader and with the support and cooperation of its allies, united with it in the defense of the law that was cynically violated in the person of Belgium,[3] it obtained victory. In the peace negotiations, the allies set great store by showing their sentiments of humanity and their moderation in that they waived demanding from the defeated, as was customary until now in peace treaties, the reimbursement for the cost of war. They could not, however, without inflicting the most serious impairment on the moral law, waive demanding reparations for the damage purposefully caused by the invaders. Although Germany's responsibility in this regard is beyond doubt, the governments which succeeded each other in that country since the armistice have been deliberating how to elude their obligations. Far from hastening, by loyal compliance to the treaty, the end of the occupation measures the allies had to prescribe, they do not seem to have had any concern other than ruining their state, practicing a policy of prodigality and devaluating their currency, having no regard for the suffering they imposed on the bulk of the population, for the sole profit of a few. They have pursued this disastrous policy with the intention of avoiding making atonement for the evils that their predecessors have caused to France and Belgium. Having awaited a change of the culprits' behavior for three long years, having even agreed to a weakening of their rights, in the vain hope of facilitating that change, France and Belgium, confronted with Germany's duly confirmed purposeful failures, felt compelled to recur to the sanctions which after all were provided for by the treaty, firmly resolved to assert their rights and consciously acting within the limits of these rights. France and Belgium do not feel disturbed by the calumnies which depict them as being motivated by a spirit of violence and hatred. They are resolved to make use of their right with moderation, without having recourse either to brutality or to violence, particularly against the German workers and population who have been deceived by evil villains. France ardently desires that a day may come when it

---

[2] Cf. the enclosure added to letter no. 201.
[3] Belgium, *la Belgique* in French, is metaphorically depicted as a person here.

will be able to forgive the crime committed by Germany in unleashing the most terrible of wars. It knows that the primary condition of forgiveness is that the culprit repents and changes his behavior. It therefore does not want to doubt that the sage counsel of Sweden's bishops will incline the hearts of Germany's leaders towards that repentance and thereby hasten the day of forgiveness.

Poincaré

205. To Gustaf Aulén[1]

Upsala 16.2.1923

Broder!

Jag kommer till Dig och andra vänner i Lund med ett dubbelt bekymmer:

1: Den alltmer kännbara prästbristen här uppe är icke enda anledningen till att jag nu frågar: Finns det en ung präst med goda studier, helst licentiat, framstående intelligens och tillräcklig prästerlig vana, som kunde i vår förordnas till Paris för att sedan där bli ordinarie? Där behövs en man som kan draga nytta av teologiska fakulteten och övriga utomordentliga studiemöjligheter, och som samtidigt värdigt företräder den svenska kristenheten. Men framför allt skall han ha ett tjänstvilligt och offervilligt herdesinne mot alla skandinaver han behöver uppsöka och hjälpa.

2: Inför de omständigheter som komma studenter att flykta från vår fakultet, är det en mycket stor lycka för kyrkan i vårt land, att Lunda-fakulteten finns, att den har en vetenskaplig storhetstid och äger förtroende även i sådana kretsar som sky Upsala. Men följden blir att vår prästbrist ökas här uppe. Finns det icke bland Edra unga män några som äga förutsättning och vilja för att tjänstgöra i Stockholm och Ärkestiftet? Det gäller icke endast nu, utan även under den närmaste framtiden.

Du kan icke tro hur tacksamma och glada min maka och jag hava varit över att höra ljusningen i Din frus hälsa. Vi hålla så innerligt av Eder, att vi känna med Eder som med nära anhöriga.

Din tillgivne

Nathan Söderblom

Upsala, February 16, 1923

Brother,

I am approaching you and other friends in Lund with a twofold concern.

1° The ever more serious lack of ministers up here is not the only reason for my asking you now: Is there a young minister to be found with a good academic record, preferably licentiate[2], outstanding intelligence and sufficient pastoral practice, who in the spring could be appointed for Paris in order to become a regular pastor there later on? A man is needed there who can benefit from the theological faculty and [the] other excellent facilities for study, and who at the same time is a worthy repre-

---

[1] Collection Aulén. G., Lund University Library, typewritten letter.
[2] Roughly equivalent to today's doctorate in theology in most countries.

sentative of Swedish Christianity. Above all, however, he shall have a pastoral mind eager for service and for sacrifice on behalf of all the Scandinavians he needs to visit and support.

2° In view of the circumstances which cause students to vanish from our faculty, it is a very good fortune for the church in our country that there is Lund's faculty, that it is having a period of academic brilliance and is being trusted even in such quarters that shun Uppsala. But the consequence is that our lack of ministers is increasing up here. Aren't there among your young men some who meet the requirements and are willing to serve in Stockholm and the archdiocese? This concerns not only the present but also the immediate future.

You cannot believe how grateful and glad my wife and I are to learn about the improvement in your wife's health. We esteem you so highly that we feel with you as with close family relations.

Sincerely yours,
Nathan Söderblom

206. From Otto Braun[1]

Berlin W. 8, den 17. Februar 1923

Der Deutsche Evangelische Kirchenausschuß in Berlin hat mir Mitteilung gemacht von dem hochbedeutsamen Aufruf, der, von Ihnen, Hochwürdigster Herr Erzbischof, und sämtlichen Bischöfen Schwedens unterzeichnet, im Namen des Kongresses der Schwedischen Bischöfe aus Anlaß des Einbruchs ins Ruhrgebiet zur notwendigen Völkerversöhnung mahnt und die Methoden der Gewalt und Machtgier, wie sie von Frankreich und Belgien mitten im Frieden gegen ein wehrloses Land angewandt werden, als untaugliche Mittel zur Behebung der ständig steigenden Not Europas kennzeichnet. Durch die Tageszeitungen war mir der Aufruf schon bekannt geworden. Er hat mich mit herzlichster Genugtuung erfüllt. Seine menschenfreundlichen Worte sind uns Deutschen in den gegenwärtigen Schicksalstagen, die für weite Kreise unserer Bevölkerung von Hunger und Elend begleitet sind, hoffnungsfrohe Lichtblicke in eine hellere Zukunft! Beweisen sie doch, in welchem Maße man auch außerhalb Deutschlands noch ein Verständnis dafür hat, daß Vorgänge, wie sie sich jetzt täglich am Rhein und an der Ruhr abspielen, eine Versündigung an dem großen Gedanken der europäischen Kulturgemeinschaft bedeuten. Es ist mir daher aufrichtigstes Bedürfnis, Eurer Erzbischöflichen Gnaden und dem gesamten Kongreß der Bischöfe Schwedens für die mutige, das Weltgewissen aufrüttelnde und uns Trost spendende Kundgebung meinen und der Preußischen Staatsregierung tiefempfundenen Dank zu sagen.

Braun

---

[1] Otto Braun (1872–1955), Prussian prime minister. Nathan Söderblom's ecumenical collection, A 3, UUB, calligraphic letter (secretary's handwriting).

207. From Édouard Gruner[1]

Paris, le 28 Mars 1923

Monsieur et très honoré frère,

J'ai l'honneur de vous accuser réception de votre lettre du 3 Mars dernier, que je me suis empressé de transmettre au Conseil de la FEDERATION PROTESTANTE de France. Vous avez bien vu que notre effort essentiel a été d'établir les faits dans leur réalité et de collaborer, dans l'intérêt supérieur de la justice et de la vérité, avec des chrétiens de bonne volonté. Vous pensez avec nous que la communion spirituelle ne peut être complète que dans une atmosphère de confiance et de sincérité, et que cette atmosphère ne peut être créée que par des échanges fraternels d'explications loyales. Nous vous savons gré d'avoir communiqué notre message à la presse de votre pays.

Il nous plait d'apprendre que l'omission d'une phrase essentielle dans le texte français de votre Appel n'a été, comme vous nous écrivez, que le résultat d'un accident malheureux. Mais vous sentez comme nous combien il eût été déplorable que, par suite de cet accident, nous eussions l'air de n'avoir rien à opposer à une accusation portée par ce document dans le monde entier. Vous nous envoyez le texte français que vous avez publié dans les journaux suédois. Permettez-nous de vous faire remarquer qu'il n'est, en plusieurs de ses parties, et non les moins importantes, qu'une traduction singulièrement édulcorée de la rédaction anglaise, allemande ou suédoise du même document. Tout cela ne montre-t-il pas, chez les traducteurs sinon chez les rédacteurs de ce message, une mentalité sourdement hostile à la France?

Nous vous remercions de ce que vous nous dites de votre attitude personnelle devant la violation de la neutralité belge. Nous voudrions qu'elle ait été celle de tous les signataires de l'appel qui nous a si douloureusement émus. Nous ne pouvions pas deviner tout le sens que vous donniez à cette phrase: »Ce qu'un homme aura semé, il le moissonnera aussi. Voilà ce que la guerre mondiale a pleinement prouvé«. Nous pouvions difficilement soupçonner que vous visiez l'attentat commis en 1914 par celui qui s'intitulait le »Seigneur de la guerre«. Il est clair que l'occupation actuelle de la Ruhr n'est qu'une conséquence directe de cet attentat. Le message des Evêques suédois ne le disait pas clairement.

Vous nous assurez que vous ne perdez pas une occasion de rappeler à vos compatriotes les souffrances des provinces dévastées de la France. Nous apprécions votre intention. Mais nous vous demandons de ne pas admettre trop vite l'équivalence que la propagande allemande s'applique à établir entre des dévastations qui avaient pour but de tuer économiquement notre pays, et dont les effets se feront sentir pendant des longues générations, et le gêne momentanée des populations allemandes dont l'industrie et le commerce n'ont été atteints dans aucun de leurs organes vitaux ...

Ne croyez pas que nous soyons insensibles à certaines souffrances que les

---

[1] Nathan Söderblom's ecumenical collection A 9, UUB, typewritten letter.

évènements actuels peuvent entraîner. Mais vous nous permettrez de dire qu'il n y a aucune comparaison à tenter entre ce que la France fait dans la Ruhr pour avoir raison d'une mauvaise volonté qui est la violation de la paix signée, et ce que les Allemands ont commis dans toutes nos villes occupées pour extorquer des sommes formidables aux populations opprimées ou terroriseées. Nous sommes prêts, si vous le jugez utile, à vous communiquer des documents qu'il serait bon de faire connaître à vos compatriotes. A la verité, nous souhaitons que la situation actuelle prenne fin le plus tôt possible. Mais nous n'admettons pas qu'on en rende responsable une prétendue cruauté de la France, alors que la vraie cause en est l'egoïsme des magnats de l'industrie allemande qui aiment mieux risquer d'affamer leur peuple (afin de le mieux exciter) que de consentir eux mêmes des sacrifices nécessaires ...

Si nos amis de Suède n'y prennent garde, ils sont exposés, sous la pression de reseignements inexacts, à se ranger à coté des riches de ce monde qui exploitent la misère de leurs compatriotes pour ne pas payer les dévastations dont ils avaient attendu tant de profits.

Nous tenons, en finissant, à vous dire avec quelle peine nous avons constaté que vous vous êtes laissé égarer par la propagande allemande au point de prononcer, devant une assemblée solennelle des Eglises de Suède, trois jours après nous avoir écrit votre lettre, le violent et offensant réquisitoire contre la France, dont nous avons la traduction sous les yeux. Notre étonnement est grand. Nous attendions mieux des sentiments dont vous parlez et des fruits de la méditation de l'Evangile. Espérant que vous arriverez à pénétrer ce qui est au fond de nos coeurs et de nos pensées, nous comptons qu'un jour viendra où vous contribuerez, à votre tour, à dissiper les malentendues et les erreurs qui entretiennent trop longtemps des antagonismes dangereux et où vous travaillerez avec nous, dans une intimité confiante et fraternelle, à hâter la venue des temps nouveaux que les disciples du Christ doivent attendre et préparer.

Veuillez, Monsieur et honoré Frère, agréer l'assurance de nos sentiments respectueux et dévoués.

Le Président

E. Gruner.

Paris, March 28, 1923

Sir and highly esteemed Brother,

I have the honor of confirming to you the receipt of your letter of March 3 which I speedily dispatched to the Council of the Protestant Federation of France. You will have been aware that our effort has essentially been to establish the facts in their reality and to collaborate, in the superior interest of justice and truth, with the Christians of good will. You think as we do that spiritual communion can only be complete in an atmosphere of trust and sincerity, and that this atmosphere can only be created through brotherly exchanges of straightforward accounts. We are grateful to you for having communicated our message to the press of your country.

We are pleased to learn that the omission of an essential phrase in the French text of your appeal[2] only was the result, as you are writing us, of an unfortunate accident.[3] But you feel as we do how very deplorable it has been that because of that accident, we appeared to have nothing to oppose to an accusation carried into the whole world by that document. Your are sending us the French text that you published in the Swedish papers. Permit us to remark to you that it is, in several of its parts and not the least important ones, only a singularly dulcified translation of the English, German, or Swedish version of the said document. Does all this not show, with regard to the translators if not the editors of that message, a veiled hostile mentality toward France?

We thank you for what you are telling us about your personal attitude toward the violation of Belgian neutrality. We wish that it had been the one of all the signatories of the appeal which so painfully affected us. We were not able to divine the whole meaning you lent to the following phrase: »Whatsoever a man soweth, that shall he also reap, as the world war proved abundantly.« With difficulty we could surmise that you had in mind the assault committed in 1914 by the one who called himself the »Lord of the War«.[4] It is obvious that the occupation of the Ruhr area is only a direct consequence of that assault. The message of the Swedish bishops did not say that clearly.

You are assuring us that you do not leave out an opportunity of reminding your compatriots of the sufferings of France's devastated provinces. We appreciate your intention. But we ask you not to accept too quickly the equivalence that the German propaganda endeavors to establish between the devastations that were aimed at putting our country to death economically and whose effects will make themselves felt for long generations, and the momentary distress of the German population whose industry and commerce have not been affected in any of its vital organs ... [Gruner goes on to quote a lengthy passage from a report about a visit to the Ruhr area by four Scottish members of the Labor Party who say that prices may be higher and wages lower there than in Scottish mining areas, but that both the people and their houses are in much better shape.]

Do not believe that we are insensitive to certain sufferings that current events can entail. But you will permit us to say that one cannot attempt any comparison between what France is doing in the Ruhr area in order to come to terms with an ill-will which is the violation of the signed peace, and what the Germans committed in all our occupied towns for extorting formidable sums from the oppressed or terrorized population. We are ready, if you consider it useful, to make accessible to you some documents which it would be good to bring to the knowledge of your compa-

---

[2] Cf. the enclosure added to letter no. 201.

[3] The statements that the occupation had entailed »sexual degradation« and that the troops had »torn large pieces of territory from their unarmed neighbours« had been left out in the French telegram version of the appeal. The mistake went through several corrections undetected. When it finally caught the attention of Yngve Brilioth, a new edition of the French text was immediately printed and sent to France. According to the complete story as unfolded by Söderblom at a bishops' meeting on March 7, 1924, the correct version must have been in Gruner's hands when he wrote this letter. Whether the omissions were committed on purpose by the person who gave up the telegram – certainly someone other than the Archbishop – is open for speculation. It should be emphasized, however, that they did not change the gist of the appeal. – I owe this detailed account to inquiries by Staffan Runestam. The material in question can be found in Nathan Söderblom's ecumenical collection, box 11, at the UUB.

[4] Allusion to the German phraseology of the time, calling the Kaiser the *Oberster Kriegsherr*.

triots. Actually, we wish that the present situation come to an end as soon as possible. But we do not tolerate that one makes an alleged cruelty of France responsible for it, while its true cause is the egoism of the magnates of German industry who prefer to run the risk of starving their people (in order to instigate them more easily) than agree to make the necessary sacrifices themselves. ... [Another reference to the report by the Scotsmen mentioned above.]

If our friends in Sweden do not watch out, they will be exposed, under the pressure of inexact information, as siding with the wealthy of this world who exploit the misery of their compatriots in order not to pay for the devastation from which they had expected such great profit.

In concluding, we put much store by telling you with what grief we have noticed that you allowed yourself to be led astray by the German propaganda to the point of pronouncing, before a solemn assembly of the churches of Sweden, three days after having written your letter to us, the violent and offensive reproach against France, the translation of which we have before us.[5] Our astonishment is great. We had expected something better from the sentiments of which you speak and of the fruits of the meditation of the Gospel. Hoping that you will arrive at penetrating what is at the bottom of our hearts and minds, we trust that a day will come when you will contribute, in your turn, to dissipating the misunderstandings and the errors that all too long have nourished dangerous antagonisms, and when you will work with us, in confidential and brotherly intimacy, to hasten the arrival of the new times which the disciples of Christ must await and prepare.

We request you, Sir and esteemed Brother, to accept the assurance of our respectful and devoted sentiments.

The President
E. Gruner.

208. To Édouard Gruner[1]

Upsala, le 4 avril 1923

Monsieur et très honoré Frère,
J'ai l'honneur de vous accuser réception de votre lettre du 28 mars dernier.
Quant aux traductions de notre appel, je regrette de ne pas pouvoir les

---

[5] Söderblom had addressed the 12th general church meeting in Stockholm under the heading *Tidens tecken* on March 4, 1923 (printed in *Kirke og kultur* 30/1923, 193–209, and in an enlarged version in *För tanke och tro. Skrifter tillägnade Oscar Ekman*, Uppsala 1923, 1–43, from which the following page numbers). In it, he criticized the violation of Belgian neutrality in 1914 and the destruction of large parts of Northern France by the Germans, and the continuation of the blockade by the Allies and the French occupation of the Ruhr, with equal candor (6–9), just like the bishops' appeal had done, and also repeated that he did not intend to judge the French nation, but only condemned the methods of violence (14–16. 25). The address also included a passage on Söderblom's gratefulness to France and his admiration for its contributions to the history of Western thought, for the spirit and self-discipline of its people and for its beautiful language (18 f.). How this address could be construed as a rehash of »German propaganda« and as a »violent and offensive reproach against France«, is hard to grasp. It should be added that Gruner's view was not shared by all French Protestants. Cf. Staffan Runestam, *Söderblomsstudier*, Uppsala 2004, 133–135.

[1] Nathan Söderblom's ecumenical collection B 3, UUB, typewritten letter (carbon copy).

discuter. Je sais que la traduction française a été faite et soigneusement révisée par un homme très distingué dont je puis dire en toute sincérité que je ne connais dans sa position aucun suédois qui soit plus nettement anti-allemand et francophile.

Osé-je (sic; lis: Ose-je) vous poser deux questions?

La plus puissante organisation libre en Suède, la Fédération des associations ouvrières socialistes /anti-allemandes pendant la guerre/, étant la grande majorité du parti socialiste, auquel appartient notre excellent gouvernement actuel, a publié le 10 février dernier une protestation unanime au nom des ouvriers organisés: – »Representantskapet vet sig tala i alla de fackligt organiserade arbetarnas namn, då det ger uttryck för sin avsky inför det oerhörda brott Frankrike med Belgiens bistånd nu begår genom den militära ockupationen av Ruhr. Sveriges arbetare ha känt med de franska och belgiska folken under kriget och erkänna det berättigade i deras krav på hjälp till de av kriget ödelagda områdenas återuppbyggande. Det är en bitter missräkning för de svenska arbetarna att nu finna, att de belgiska och franska fackorganisationerna ännu icke ansett sig kunna vidtaga behövliga åtgärder i syfte att förhindra det ärelösa militära överfallet på det avväpnade Tyskland och den hårt pressade industribefolkningen i Ruhr. Representantskapet uttalar det svenska fackföreningsfolkets varma sympati för de tyska fackorganisationernas sega kamp mot den militära ockupationen och förväntar att de belgiska och franska fackorganisationerna snarast skola träda till för att omintetgöra den franska militarist- och våldspolitiken.« – J'ai donné le texte suédois. Car traduction est une chose risquée. Et on est vraiment tenté d'édulcorer les expressions de la protestation la plus forte, comme fait remarquer l'organe des pacifistes suédois, parmi toutes celles publiées dans notre pays. Des déclarations pareilles ont été dictées par la conscience de la classe ouvrière dans la plupart des pays civilisées comme par tant d'autres groupes d'hommes et de femmes.

Croyez-vous que de telles déclarations ont été faites en faveur des »riches de ce monde qui exploitent la misère de leurs compatriotes«? Croyez-vous que de telles déclarations faites dans presque tous les pays par des hommes qui connaissent ce qu'ils disent, auraient paru si la situation dans ces régions occupées était si excellente que vous le supposez?

Les serviteurs de la Charité scandinave et d'autres témoins oculaires /entre autres une personne membre d'une commission envoyée là bas pour une sérieuse étude, qui s'était prononcée pendant la guerre d'une façon enthousiaste pour la France et contre l'Allemagne/ nous racontent à l'unanimité ce qui a forcé les Évêques de Suède *non pas à protester*, car nous ne sommes pas des juges, mais à publier un appel aux hommes de bonne volonté. Quand vous appelez mon discours un »violent et offensant réquisitoire contre la France«, cela ne peut avoir qu'une des deux raisons suivantes: votre traduction est fausse; ou bien vous concevez l'amour et l'admiration pour la France d'une manière qui est incompatible avec le libre examen, et qui doit attrister les véritables propagateurs du Génie français et de l'Idéal français dans le monde. J'ai de mon mieux tâché de faire comprendre le point de vue

français. Et j'ai tâché d'approfondir notre sens de responsabilité et d'humi-
lité devant Dieu. Je n'ai jugé personne, j'ai dit au contraire: ne jugez pas la
France comme on le fait à présent! Devant votre grave jugement je reste
donc muet.

Agréez, Monsieur et très honoré Frère, l'assurance de mes sentiments
respectueux et dévoués

Archevêque d'Upsala, Suède.

Sir and highly esteemed Brother,

I have the honor of confirming to you the receipt of your letter of March 28.

As regards the translations of our appeal, I regret not to be able to discuss them.
I know that the French translation was made and carefully revised by a very distinguished man of whom I can say in all sincerity that I do not know any Swede in his
position who would be just as clearly anti-German and Francophile.

May I dare to ask you two questions?

The most powerful free organization in Sweden, the Federation of socialist
workers' associations (anti-German during the war), being the great majority of the
socialist party to which our excellent present government belongs,[2] on February 10
published a unanimous protestation in the name of all the organized workers:[3] —
»The body of representatives knows itself to be speaking in the name of all union-
ized workers as it gives expression to its abhorrence with regard to the exorbitant
crime that France, with the support of Belgium, is now committing through the military occupation of the Ruhr area. Sweden's workers have been in sympathy with the
French and Belgian nations during the war and recognize the legitimacy of their demand for aid for the reconstruction of the regions devastated by the war. It is a bitter disappointment for the Swedish workers now to find that the Belgian and French
unions have not yet deemed themselves able to take necessary measures aimed at
preventing the dishonorable military assault on the disarmed Germany and the
hard-pressed industrial population in the Ruhr area. The body of representatives
declares the warm sympathy of the Swedish union people for the German unions' te-
nacious struggle against the military occupation and expects that the Belgian and
French unions step forward as soon as possible to thwart the French policy of militarism and violence.« — I have given the Swedish text. For translation is a risky
business. And one is really tempted to dulcify the expressions of, as the organ of the
Swedish pacifists points out, the strongest of all the protestations published in our
country. Similar declarations have been dictated by the conscience of the working
class in the majority of civilized countries, as well as by so many other groups of
men and women.

Do you believe that such declarations were made in favor of »the wealthy of this
world who exploit the misery of their compatriots«? Do you believe that such declarations made in almost all countries by men who know what they are saying,

---

[2] The Swedish government of the time was headed by Hjalmar Branting (1860–1925), the
first social democratic prime minister who led cabinets in 1920, 1921–1923, and 1924–1925.
He received the Nobel Peace Prize in 1921.

[3] The following quote is rendered by Söderblom in the original Swedish.

would have appeared if the situation in those occupied regions were as excellent as you suppose it to be?

The servants of the Scandinavian Charity and other eyewitnesses (among others one person, a member of a commission sent down there for a serious study, who during the war pronounced in an enthusiastic way for France and against Germany) unanimously tell us what forced Sweden's bishops *not to protest*, for we are not judges, but to publish an appeal to men of good will. When you call my speech a »fierce offensive accusation against France«, that can only have one of the following two reasons: your translation is wrong; or else you conceive of the love and admiration for France in a way which is incompatible with free examination, and which must sadden the true propagators of the French Genius and the French Ideal in the world. I tried to do my best to make the French point of view understood. And I tried to deepen our sense of responsibility and of humility before God. I did not judge anyone, on the contrary, I said: Do not judge France as it is being done today! Before your grave judgment, I therefore remain silent.

Accept, Sir and esteemed Brother, the assurance of our respectful and devoted sentiments.

Archbishop of Uppsala, Sweden.

209. From ADOLF VON HARNACK[1]

[30.4.1923]

Hochverehrter Herr Erzbischof!
Im Laufe dieses Sommers wird der 6. Band meiner »Reden und Aufsätze« unter dem Titel »Erforschtes u. Erlebtes« erscheinen. Ich bitte um die Erlaubniss, den Band Ihnen widmen zu dürfen; denn ich möchte die gegebene Gelegenheit ergreifen, um ohne viele Worte zum Ausdruck zu bringen, wie hoch ich Ihr kräftiges Wirken für die »Una Sancta«, Ihre religionsgeschichtliche Arbeit und vor allem Ihre persönliche Eigenart als protestantischen Charakter schätze und verehre.[2]

Die sechs Bände meiner »Reden und Aufsätze« bilden ungesucht eine Art von biographischen Rechenschaftsbericht in Bezug auf Umfang und Inhalt meiner Arbeit. Die Vielseitigkeit derselben ist mir vom Leben aufgezwungen worden. So werden Sie auch im 6. Bande neben der Theologie sehr viel anderes finden, was gesagt u. geschrieben werden musste, obschon es Andere besser hätten sagen können; aber ich hoffe, Sie werden in dem Vielen eine letzte Einheitlichkeit nicht vermissen; sie stammt aus dem evangelischen Geiste, den auch Sie als das höchste Gut u. die höchste Weisheit schätzen u. so kraftvoll bezeugen. Eben desshalb möchte ich Ihren Namen

---

[1] N. Söderblom's collection of letters, from foreigners, UUB, handwritten postcard.
[2] The volume did appear in 1923, with the dedication to Söderblom.

auf mein Buch setzen dürfen. Dazu kommt die persönliche herzliche Verehrung, in der ich bleibe
Ihr
ergebenster
v. Harnack
NS: Haben Sie noch besten Dank für den schönen Vortrag über die
»Christl. Lebens- u. Arbeitsgemeinschaft.«[3]

210. To Adolf von Harnack[1]

z. Zt. Bad Nauheim, Hotel Kaiserhof. 2.5.1923
Hochgeehrter Herr Professor!
Als ich als junger Student von der ersten Auflage Ihrer Dogmengeschichte[2]
nicht nur begeistert, sondern, ich möchte wohl sagen, berauscht wurde und
die Eigenart des freien wissenschaftlichen Forschens zum ersten Male voll
genossen habe, hatte ich nie träumen können, dass ich einmal Ihre persönliche Bekanntschaft machen würde,[3] noch weniger, dass ich Sie einmal in
meinem Hause, wie ich jetzt hoffe, wenigstens für ein paar Wochen aufnehmen darf. S[a]muel Fries war mein nächster theologischer Freund, daher
habe ich gegen ihn nie ein Gefühl von Neid hegen können. Aber wie oft hat
er mir nicht von Ihrem Besuche in Stockholm erzählt!
   Aber was Sie jetzt vorschlagen, ist doch zu viel. Ich würde eine derartig
wirklich unverdiente Ehre gewiss und entschieden ablehnen, wenn nicht alles Gute, das wir im Leben erfahren, unverdient wäre. Ich bin ein dankbarer
Leser von Ihren »Reden und Gesetzen«[4] und ich kenne keinen zweiten
Theologen, der ein solches Zeugnis von Vielseitigkeit und gründlichem Ein-
dringen auf so weiten, wichtigen Gebieten ablegen könnte. – Aber das
Merkwürdigste bleibt doch die strenge, unreflektierte[5], unmittelbare Einheitlichkeit Ihres gesamten Wirkens, welche ich jetzt, nachdem ich sie mehr
als früher persönlich sehen durfte, noch tiefer empfinde, und diese Einheitlichkeit ist mir um so reizender und sympathischer als sie nichts von Schul-
meisterei und Schema in sich hat sondern den verschiedenen das Auge be-
glückenden Farben ähnlich ist, welche ein edler Schmuck in verschiedenen
Momenten zeigt.

---

[3] Nathan Söderblom, *Christliche Lebens- und Arbeitsgemeinschaft. Kircheneinheit im Sinne Luthers, Vortrag*, Wittenberg 1922.

[1] Harnack's papers – letters, Staatsbibliothek zu Berlin, Preußischer Kulturbesitz, typed letter.
[2] Adolf Harnack, *Lehrbuch der Dogmengeschichte*, 3 vols., Freiburg 1886–1890.
[3] This must have been before he had visited Harnack in his home in 1894 (cf. letter no. 5).
[4] Sic! Söderblom meant: *Reden und Aufsätzen.*
[5] This word here means: spontaneous.

Gott gebe Ihnen Kraft und Gesundheit, uns alle noch viele Jahre durch neue Schöpfungen zu bereichern.

Ich bin, hochverehrtester Meister der Geisteswissenschaft,

Ihr ehrerbietig und dankbar ergebenster

Nathan Söderblom

211. To Adolf von Harnack[1]

Upsala 18.7.1923

Excellenz,

Für Ihren gütigen Brief herzlichen Dank.

Meine Tochter Yvonne weilt gegenwärtig in Oxford und Worcester, ist es doch von Ihnen, der grössten Theologe unserer Zeit, mehr als rührend an das Kind zu denken. Meine Tochter Lucie hat sich soeben mit dem jungen Ordinarius Professor Dr. Runestam[2] verlobt.

Gott erhalte Sie! Sie wissen nicht was für eine Geistesfrische Sie uns aus dem unmenschlich behandelten deutschen Vaterlande und aus den bedrückten Leben Ihrer Hauptstadt gebracht haben.[3]

Soeben komme ich von London, Oxford und Glasgow, wo ich wiederholt mit meinen englischen Freunden von Ihnen gesprochen habe. Man schämt sich dort, wo man die herrlichen Früchte Ihres Geistes und anderer Deutschen Gelehrten geniesst, zu denken wie das Leben in Deutschland sich jetzt gestaltet. Lord Parmoor[4] sagte mit, der jetzige Ministerpräsident Baldwin und der stärkste Mann seiner Regierung, der Markis von Salisbury,[5] sind Christen und Gewissensmenschen, die das Möglichste tun werden.

Ihr verehrungsvoll ergebenster

Nathan Söderblom

---

[1] Harnack's papers – letters, Staatsbibliothek zu Berlin, Preußischer Kulturbesitz, typed letter.

[2] Arvid Runestam, cf. letter no. 188, n. 8.

[3] Harnack had lectured on Marcion, int. al., in Sweden in March, 1923; he had been in Upsala on March 13. Cf. A. v. Harnack, *Marcion. Der moderne Gläubige, der erste Reformator. Die Dorpater Preisschrift (1870)*, hg. v. F. Steck, TU 149, Berlin 2003, XLIV. The notes Harnack had prepared for his lecture in Sweden are printed in that volume as »Beilage 3«, pp. 394–400.

[4] Cf. letter no. 129, n. 4.

[5] [Earl] Stanley Baldwin [of Bewdley, 1937] (1867–1947), conservative prime minister 1923–1924, 1924–1929 and 1935- 1937. (He pursued an appeasement policy towards Nazi Germany which was continued by his successor, Neville Chamberlain.) The second person must be James Edward Hubert Gascoyne-Cecil, 4th Marquess of Salisbury (1861–1947), not a member of the cabinet but Tory leader in the House of Lords.

212. To Gottfrid Billing[1]

Upsala 11.8.1923

Vördade Broder!

I anledning av inneliggande brev från Personne, vill jag nämna, att Pastor Jonzon i Diakonistyrelsen verkligen först föreslog att biskoparna skulle göra ett uttalande i anledning av våldsdådet i Riga. Men då initiativet till en opinionsyttring utgått från lekmannahåll, och då jag är så illa anskriven på romerskt håll, så tyckte jag att opinionsyttringen kunde ha sin gång för sig.

Nu vill jag emellertid fråga Dig om Du tycker att de svenska biskoparna böra taga till orda. Själva saken är otrolig. Rom har utnyttjat situationen till det yttersta och skaffat sig ett konkordat gynnsammare än i ärkekatolska länder. Vill Du med ett ord säga, huruvida Du vill vara med på en opinions-yttring av biskoparna, som ju då kan få formen av en deltagande och be-klagande skrivelse till biskop Irbe i Riga. Jag inväntar Ditt svar, innan jag skriver till övriga biskopar.

Jag har nu fått K.M:s uppdrag till Augustanasynoden och dess högskola och det visar sig, att om jag nu skall våga mig på en dylik färd, så kan jag icke gärna vara åter förrän i december månad.

Det vore ju bra att kunna hålla ett biskopsmöte rörande de två nämnda ärendena, kvinnliga präster och jordfästning, och kan detta lämpligen sät-tas till 10 eller 12 november. Då måste jag besvära Dig med att godhetsfullt hålla detta möte. I annat fall skulle biskopsmötet uppskjutas till nästa år. Möjligen kunna även andra frågor i november påkalla uppmärksamhet.

Vill Du godhetsfullt med ett par ord säga Din mening även om denna sak.

Vördnadsfullt tillgivne
Nathan Söderblom

Uppsala, August 11, 1923

Esteemed Brother,

Occasioned by the enclosed letter by Personne,[2] I would like to mention that Pastor Jonzon of Diakonistyrelsen[3] indeed at first suggested that the bishops issue a state-ment on the occasion of the outrage in Riga.[4] But since the initiative came from the part of laymen, and since I am in such disrepute in Rome,[5] I thought that statement could be left alone.

---

[1] Collection Billing. G., Lund University Library, typewritten letter.

[2] Bishop John Personne: cf. letter no. 12, n. 5.

[3] Bengt Jonzon (1888-1967), later bishop. *Diakonistyrelsen* is the social work agency of the Swedish church.

[4] The *Jakobikirche* (St. James's church) in central Riga, a church building that had belonged to the Lutherans for 300 years, had been sealed by police, because the government of newly in-dependent Latvia was going to turn it over to the Roman Catholic church as its cathedral. This was done on the basis of the concordat which was concluded with the Vatican on July 22, 1922, in view of the small Catholic minority in the northern part of the country. The deal could not be prevented. Cf. letter no. 184.

[5] This was due to Söderblom's cordial relations to the Catholic modernists, notably Loisy

Now, however, I want to ask you whether you feel that the Swedish bishops should speak up. The affair itself is unbelievable. Rome took utmost advantage of the situation and obtained a concordat more favorable than in arch-catholic countries. Would you say in one word whether you will go along with a statement by the bishops, which can of course then take the form of a sympathizing and regretful address to Bishop Irbe in Riga.[6] I shall wait for your reply before I write to the other bishops.

I have now received His Majesty's mandate for the Augustana Synod and its college,[7] and it turns out that if I now venture on such a journey, I can hardly be back before the month of December.

It would of course be good to be able to convene a bishops' meeting concerning the two stated subjects, female pastors[8] and funeral services, and is it appropriate to let it take place on the 10th or 12th of November? In that case, I must bother you kindly to hold that meeting. Otherwise the bishops' meeting would have to be put off until next year. Possibly other issues may call for attention too in November.

Would you please be so kind as to let me know your opinion on this matter in a word or two?

Respectfully yours,
Nathan Söderblom

213. From Gustaf Aulén[1]

Lund den 29 augusti 1923

Käre Ärkebiskop!
När jag ber Dig mottaga medföljande bok om Den allmänneliga kristna tron, känner jag ett djupt behov att samtidigt få säga ett varmt tack för all den hjälp, som jag fått av Dig både under min studietid i Uppsala och därefter. Det skulle glädja mig ofantligt, om Du i denna bok kunde finna något som står i samklang med Dina egna intentioner och så kunde konstatera att

---

in Paris, as well as to his book *Religionsproblemet inom katolicism och protestantism*, Stockholm 1910, which draws a differentiated picture of Roman catholism, is sympathetic to the modernists, and quite outspoken in its criticism of Rome's official policy. Cf. also *Svenska kyrkans kropp och själ*, Stockholm 1916, 74, where Söderblom states that making the relationship of faith to Christ dependent on the relation to the church, as Jesuit doctrine does, is anti-Christian; for Protestantism, the relation to the church conversely is dependent on one's relationship to Christ (a radicalization of Schleiermacher's famous definition of Protestantism and Catholicsm in his *The Christian Faith*, 2nd ed., § 24).

[6] Karlis Irbe (1861–1934) was consecrated as bishop for the Latvian majority, together with Harald Poelchau for the German minority, by Söderblom in 1922. He resigned in 1931.

[7] Söderblom spent the months of September through December in the United States. Augustana Synod was the Swedish Lutheran church in America which was on its way toward full integration into American society. Söderblom encouraged it in this during his visit, including its plan to switch to the English language in its publications. Cf. Sundkler, op. cit., 302 f. Augustana College is still in existence; its location is Rock Island, IL.

[8] In spite of this remarkably early beginning of this debate, the first female pastor of the Church of Sweden was ordained only in 1960.

[1] N. Söderblom's collection of letters, from Swedes, UUB, typewritten letter.

jag icke varit en alldeles oläraktig lärjunge. I varje fall känner jag mig stå i
stor tacksamhetsskuld för vidgade vyer och livgivande impulser.

... Hjärtligaste hälsning
från Din
tacksamt tillgivne
Gustaf Aulén

Lund, August 29, 1923

Dear Archbishop,

As I ask you to accept the enclosed book on *Den allmänneliga kristna tron*[2], I am
moved by a deeply felt need to express my sincere gratitude for all the support I received from you, both during my academic study in Uppsala and afterwards. I
would be hugely pleased if you were able to detect in this book something that is
consonant with your own intentions, and thus confirm that I have not been an altogether unteachable disciple. In any case, I am aware of owing a great debt of gratitude for widened views and invigorating, stimulating impulses.

... [On technical problems concerning Söderblom's planned journey to the United States]

Kindest regards
from your grateful
Gustaf Aulén

214. To ADOLF VON HARNACK[1]

Upsala 12.9.1923

Meister und hochgeehrter Herr Professor!

Richesse oblige. Wenn Gott irgend jemand einen Reichtum verliehen hat,
wird vom Verwalter eines solchen geistigen oder materiellen Vermögens erwartet, dass er seine gewaltigen Mitteln zum Wohl seiner armen Mitmenschen und der gesammten Menschlichen Gesellschaft anwendet. Seitdem
ich Ihre Schriften lese und mit Begeisterung verehre, d. h. seit meiner Stu-
dentenzeit habe ich Sie als den eigentlichen Milliardaire[2] der Theologie
und der Geistes Wissenschaft unserer Zeit betrachtet, und seitdem ich Sie
persönlich kennen gelernt habe, ist jene mehr als menschliche Frische und
Ueberfülle des Geistes mir noch grösser geworden.

---

[2] Gustaf Aulén, *Den allmänneliga kristna tron*, Stockholm 1923, 6th ed. 1965; English
transl. from 4th ed.: *The Faith of the Christian Church*, tr. by E. H. Wahlstrom and G. E. Arden,
London 1954. The book was translated into five languages and became a standard work in
Scandinavian theological teaching. – Aulén had been primarily a student of Einar Billing to
whom he owed his »dramatic« view of the history of revelation. But Söderblom had considerable influence on him too, as for instance the mere title of this book shows: it implies the same
view of the essence of Protestantism and its position among the Christian churches. Cf. letters
no. 97 and 137, n. 6.

[1] Harnack's papers – letters, Staatsbibliothek zu Berlin, Preußischer Kulturbesitz, typewritten letter.
[2] Billionaire: no allusion to Germany's galloping inflation of the time.

Freigiebig, mit der stolzen und freien Grossmütigkeit des echten Edel-
mannes haben Sie die Früchte und Ergebnisse Ihres Geistes und Ihres Wissens während eines halben Jahrhundert der Kirche, der Menschheit und der
Welt ausgestreut. Hier braucht man ja nicht zu teilen. Sondern einjeder
kann sich von jenem Reichtum aneignen, so viel er überhaupt zu fassen vermag. Ich bin einer der unzähligen dankbaren Empfänger. Aber dass Sie
mich zum Beisitzer des Verwaltungsrates Ihres für ungezählte künftige Generationen hinreichenden Reichtums gewissermaßen ernannt haben, das ist
eine Ehre die ich mir nie träumen konnte und die wirklich sehr unverdient
ist.[3] Wie ungemein gross meine Freude und Dankbarkeit dafür ist, dass Sie
meinen guten Willen würdig gerechnet haben, in dieser Weise mit Erzeug-
nissen Ihrer geistigen Schöpfung verbunden zu werden, kann ich Ihnen
nicht sagen. Sie werden es aber mit den zarten Instrumenten Ihrer instinkti-
ven Wahrnehmung sicher nachempfinden.

In der Hoffnung Sie im nächsten Jahre empfangen und hören zu dürfen,
und mit verehrungsvollen Grüssen an Ihre Frau Gemahlin und mit guten
Wünschen an Ihre gesammte Familie bin ich, hochgeehrter lieber Meister,
    Ihr ehrerbietig ergebener
    Nathan Söderblom

215. To Adolf Deissmann[1]

Upsala 12.9.1923

Lieber Freund!

Wie Sie wohl wissen, beschäftigt mich seit mehr als 20 Jahren der Unterschied in der höheren Religion zwischen dem mystischen asketischen Typus
der durch besondere Vorbereitungen und Uebungen nach den Kosten der
Gottheit gelangen will, und dem prophetischen evangelischen Typus, man
könnte sagen den Offenbahrungstypus, der von der Gottheit überweltigt
ist.[2] Zutreffend ist [scil. an dieser Stelle] nicht mein Unterschied zwischen
Persönlichkeit, Mystik und Unendlichkeitsmystik,[3] da ja der psykologisch
methodische Typus gar nicht eine panteistische Auffassung immer hat. In
meinen Vorlesungen in München im Mai dieses Jahres, habe ich versucht
mit Beispielen den Unterschied als Uebungsmystik und sich offenbahrende
Gottheit zu beschreiben. Sie können selbst meine angenehme Ueberra-
schung beurteilen, wenn ich jetzt in Die Expository Times über Ihre Dis-

---

[3] Söderblom had meanwhile received the volume of collected papers Harnack dedicated to
him; cf. letters no. 209 and 210.

[1] N. Söderblom's collection of letters, to Swedes and foreigners, UUB, typewritten letter
(carbon copy).
[2] Clearest exposition in: N. Söderblom, *Tre livsformer*, 2nd ed. Stockholm 1922, 79–94.
[3] Cf. N. Söderblom, *Uppenbarelsereligion* (1903), 2nd ed. Stockholm 1930, 70.75.112–
114.133.

kussion über acting Mysticism und reacting Mysticism[4] lese, welche ich jetzt in meinen Vorlesungen in Harvard im November erwähnen werde als Bekräftigung meiner eigenen Wahrnehmung. Ich freue mich an diese Ihre Vorlesungen in England und grüsse Sie herzlich mit Ihrer lieben Familie.

Ihr sehr ergebener

216. To Charles Macfarland[1]

The Vanderbilt Hotel, New York, September 27th, 1923

My dear Dr. Macfarland,

Already in 1919 I had the honour of being invited by the Federal Council of the Churches of Christ to visit American Evangelic Christendom, which constitutes the mightiest bulwark of Evangelic Christendom as a whole to day. Two years earlier the Swedish Church in America, the Augustana Synod, and the Reformation Committee had invited me to come.[2]

It seems to me like a dream, that it has been permitted to me after several delays to visit your great country. And I regret very much indeed that the detailed program, fixed after long pourparlers before my arrival, takes me to San Francisco, starting early Wednesday morning, thus excluding every possibility to be present at your meeting October 5th.[3]

And I am a believer in the federalist principles, say 1. that each community has to preserve its entire independence, 2. that the deep concordance in faith and love and aim makes it possible and necessary to unite in common action, strengthening thereby also the life of each religious body, which joins hands with Christian brethren for greater and smaller common purposes. It is not possible to me to tell in these lines, what the existence of your Federal Council has meant and still means for Evangelic Christendom in Europe. It will be possible to me to indicate at least one single point in that respect at the luncheon to which I have the privilege of being invited for monday.

Hoping that you will present my brotherly and hearty greetings to the revered brethren of the Federal Council I am cordially yours

Nathan Söderblom

---

[4] A note by W.E. Wilson on lectures given by Deißmann in Birmingham: »Mysticism: A New Distinction,« in: ET 34/1922–23, 476. The lectures were published later that year as: The Religion of Jesus and the Faith of Paul, London 1923.

[1] Nathan Söderblom's collection of letters, to Swedes and foreigners, UUB, typewritten letter.

[2] Söderblom had been invited to the United States for the months from September to December, 1923, to visit, and preach in, congregations of the Augustana Synod and to conduct a lecture tour to several renowned American universities. One result of this journey is his book Från Upsala till Rock Island. En predikofärd i nya världen, Stockholm, 2nd ed. 1924, a collection of sermons and contemplations on his visit.

[3] As this was also the time of preparations for the Stockholm conference of 1925, there seems to have been a certain lack of coordination between the Augustana Synod and the Federal Council in planning Söderblom's schedule for this journey.

217. To Gustaf Johansson[1]

Upsala 30.1.1924

Vördade käre Ämbetsbroder!

Tyvärr kände jag icke på förhand när 80-årsdagen skulle inträffa. Eljest hade jag gärna velat vara en bland de många som på den dagen uppvaktade med hjärtliga och vördnadsfulla tacksägelser och lyckönskningar.

Jag skattar det som en hög förmån att ha fått personligen lära känna Finlands Ärkebiskop. Intrycket av den oförfalskade friskheten och av djupet i hans väsen lever i min själ och åstadkommer en känsla av samhörighet som är starkt personligt betonad, ehuru vi så kort råkat varandra.

Jag återkommer till en sak, som med hänsyn till Ärkebiskopen i Åbo för mig är ett praeterea censeo. Under vandringen på Auras is, föll talet på den oklarhet som råder om Kristi lära och kristenhetens uppgifter i fråga om samfundens sociala och ekonomiska problem. En evangelisk luthersk frihet från allt lagväsen måste därvid göras gällande. Jag förstod att Du ägnat just detta problem särskild uppmärksamhet, och nu frågar jag: Skulle icke det internationella kyrkomöte, som otroligt nog (jag vågar icke tro det förrän jag ser det, ehuru Gud ju vill att vi skola vara djärva i vår tro) är avsett att upptaga större delen av augusti månad 1925 i Stockholm, kunna få räkna på ett uttalande från Dig av principiell art i nyss nämnda spörsmål? Jag vet att vi alla skulle vara tacksamma därför, och genom att bli till vägledning för the Universal Christian Conference on Life and Work eller som tyskar och fransmän säga, Mötet för Praktisk Kristendom, kunde också Din erfarenhet och Din tanke i detta hänseende bli till gagn för kyrkan i större utsträckning.

Med min vördnadsfulla hälsning är jag
Din tillgivne
Nathan Söderblom

Uppsala, January 30, 1924

Esteemed dear fellow Bishop,

Unfortunately I did not know in advance when your 80th birthday would occur. Otherwise I would have wanted to be one among the many who on that day offered their heartfelt and respectful thanks and wellwishing.

I consider it a great privilege to have met Finland's archbishop in person. The impression of unalloyed freshness and of the profundity of his character is alive in my soul and brings about a feeling of solidarity which has a strongly personal accent, even though we had met for such a short time.

I return to a subject which, as regards the archbishop in Åbo, is a praeterea censeo[2] for me. During our walk on Aura's ice[3], the conversation turned to the prevail-

---

[1] N. Söderblom's ecumenical collection A 11, UUB, typewritten letter.

[2] Latin for: besides, I am of the opinion; stands for any tenaciously repeated utterance. The original version is: »ceterum censeo Carthaginem esse delendam«, besides, I am of the opinion that Carthage must be destroyed. It is attributed to the elder Cato (234–149 B.C.) who is re-

ing obscurity concerning Christ's teaching and Christianity's obligations concerning society's social and economic problems. A Protestant-Lutheran freedom from all legalism must be brought to bear on this matter. I understand that you have paid special attention to this very problem, so I now ask: Shouldn't the international church meeting which unlikely enough (I dare not believe it before I have seen it, though God indeed wants us to be bold in our faith) will take up the better part of the month of August, 1925, in Stockholm, be able to count on a statement of a fundamental nature from you on the issue just mentioned? I know that all of us would be grateful for that, and by way of serving as guidance for the Universal Christian Conference on Life and Work, or, as Germans and Frenchmen put it, the Conference on Practical Christendom, your experience and your thinking on this matter could be useful for the church at large.

With my respectful regards I am
sincerely yours,
Nathan Söderblom

218. From RANDALL DAVIDSON[1]

Lambeth Palace S. E., 25th March 1924

My dear Brother and Friend,
I am a little uneasy by the circulation of notions about the Conference on Life and Work, on the papers of which it appears that my name stands at the head of the Presidents of the whole, and I am thus made really responsible for what is being done. I think you know that while I have always wished well to the endeavour and heartily pray Godspeed to yourself and those who work with you I have never been able to satisfy myself that this particular Conference is likely to be very effective. Nor have I taken any real part in its organisation. I suppose the statement that I am a Joint President with yourself is derived from what passed in a conversation which we had during a walk in St. James' Park, for I do not remember ever having written to say that I was prepared to be its President or Joint President. You are the very last person to wish to represent me as doing anything other than I have done and I have confidence in your wisdom in such matters, but I am anxious that my name should be as little prominent as possible in connexion with it. For to tell the honest truth when people ask me about it I am compelled to show some less enthusiasm than you and some others would desire and this may harm work which I have no wish to harm if only I could be allowed to be obtrusively [sic; read: unobtrusively] connected with it. If I have put the matter unfairly please pardon me, but I have wanted to relieve my mind by telling you how it strikes me.

---

ported to have concluded each of his speeches concerning the third Punic war with this sentence.

[3] The Aura river flows through Åbo/Turku, Finland.

[1] Nathan Söderblom's ecumenical collection A 5, UUB, typewritten letter.

I am just starting with my wife to try to obtain a few weeks' rest in Italy, but any letters written to Lambeth will reach me in due course.

I am my dear brother
Your faithful friend
Randall Cantuar

219. INVITATION TO THE STOCKHOLM CONFERENCE[1]

ΣΥΝΕΡΓΟΙ ΕΙΣ ΤΗΝ ΒΑΣΙΛΕΙΑΝ ΤΟΥ ΘΕΟΥ[2]
UNIVERSAL CHRISTIAN CONFERENCE ON LIFE AND WORK[3]

Dear Brothers in Christ,
You have doubtleß heard that as a result of Conferences held at the Hague in 1919, and in Geneva in 1920, arrangements have now been made for holding a Universal Conference of Christian Communions at Stockholm during the month of August, 1925.

We believe that there is a longing on the part, not merely of the trusted servants of the church, but of all followers of our Lord and Master, to see Christendom so far united as to be able to work together in applying the principles taught by Him to the problems which confront us both in national and international life. These problems bewilder and baffle us so long as we are content to seek solutions which rely upon motives lower than the highest that we can discern for them. No Christian can doubt that the world's greatest need is the Christian way of Life not merely in personal and social behaviour but in public opinion and its outcome in public action. The responsibility for helping to meet this need which rests upon all who name the Name of Christ cannot be exaggerated.

The common purpose of our Conference therefore will be to discover lines along which we may all unite in endeavouring to meet this grave responsibility.

In our deliberations we do not propose to deal with matters of Faith and Order, although we are not unmindful of their importance. Our prayer and our hope is that through this Conference a new impetus will be given to the various movements and strivings for reunion, but the world's need is so urgent and the demand for common action on the part of all Christians so insistent at this juncture, that we cannot afford to await the fulfilment of that great hope of a reunited Christendom before putting our hearts and our

---

[1] Harnack's papers – letters, Staatsbibliothek zu Berlin, Preußischer Kulturbesitz, in Old English Gothic print. Also printed in Adolf Deißmann, *Die Stockholmer Weltkirchenkonferenz 1925*, Berlin 1926, 11–14.
[2] Col 4:11.
[3] In five languages: English, German, French, Latin, and Greek.

hands into a united effort that God's will may be done on earth as it is in heaven. To this end we will consider such concrete questions as that of industry and property, in relation to the Kingdom of God; what the Church should teach and do to help to create right relations between the different and at times warring claßes and groups in the community; how to promote friendship between the nations and thus lay the only sure foundation upon which permanent international peace can be built. In short, we hope that under the guidance of the Spirit of God, through the counsel of all, to be able to formulate programmes and devise means for making them effective, whereby the fatherhood of God and the brotherhood of all peoples will become more completely realized through the Church of Christ.

The following subjects have been decided upon, after very careful consideration, as best expreßing these ideas, and they will therefore form the basis of our studies preliminary to the conference, and upon them will be based all actions and resolutions:

1. The Church's Obligation in view of God's Purpose for the World.
2. The Church and Economic and Industrial Problems.
3. The Church and Social and Moral Problems.
4. The Church and International Relations.
5. The Church and Christian Education
6. Methods of Co-operative and Federative Efforts by the Christian Communions

Much work has already been done on these subjects, in particular in connection with the reports of the Conference on Christian Politics, Economics and Citizenship held at Birmingham, England. Careful preparation is also going forward in the countries of continental Europe and in the United States of America.

It is distinctly understood that the Resolutions passed will not be in any way binding on the Christian Communions represented at the Conference, unleß and until they are presented by the authorities of each Communion.

The Conference will meet in Stockholm from August nineteenth to August thirtieth of next year (August 19–30, 1925) and during that time its members will enjoy the hospitality of the Swedish people, whose King and leading men are taking a keen interest in the enterprize. Indeed a high and widespread appreciation for the Conference is being manifested throughout the whole Church in the North.

Therefore at the request of the International Executive Committee of the Universal Christian Conference on Life and work, we who are its officers have the honor and very great pleasure of inviting your Communion to be represented by members appointed for this purpose, who will add their prayer and counsel to our common deliberations.

This letter goes forward to you as the official invitation and call for the Conference. For purposes of administration and in order that all Communions may be adequately and justly represented, the Conference has been organized in four sections, one for Europe, one for the British Empire, one for America, and one for the Eastern Orthodox Church. From the section

341

of which your Nation and Communion is a part, a statement of the number of your apportioned delegates is being sent.

The Conference, we believe, will afford a unique opportunity for stirring the mind and conscience of Christendom and for acquiring a clearer common vision on our Christian duties in the world today, and we therefore confidently trust that your Communion will not only appoint its full number of delegates, but will do all in its power to secure for the Conference the interest, sympathy and prayers of its members.

We depend for succeß from first to last upon the guidance of the Holy Spirit.

Accepting this letter as a message from your fellow workers, will you kindly send your formal reply to the General Secretary Henry A. Atkinson, 4 Avenue Calas, Geneva, Switzerland, to whom or to the Bureau on Life and Work, Sancta Clara, Stockholm, Sweden, requests for additional information may be addressed.

Signed on behalf of the International Committee.

Theodore Winton: [Theodore Woods, Bishop of Winchester, England]

Nathan Söderblom

Arthur J. Brown [Gen. Secretary, Board of Foreign Missions, Presbyterian Church in the U. S. A.]

+ Ὁ Κωνσταντινωπόλεως Γρηγόριος [Ho Konstantinopoleos Gregorios; Gregorios VII., Ecumenical Patriarch of Constantinople]

Moeller [Reinhardt Moeller, President of the Deutscher Evangelischer Kirchenausschuss, German Protestant Church Executive Committee, Germany]

J. A. McClymont [The Very Rev. James A. McClymont, Edinburgh, ex-moderator of the Church of Scotland]

+ Germanos Thyateira [Strenopoulos Germanos, Metropolitan of Thyateira]

Charles S. Macfarland [General Secretary, Federal Council of Churches, USA]

Henry A. Atkinson [General Secretary, Church Peace Union]

J. E. Choisy [Jacques Eugène Choisy, professor of church history in Geneva and president of the Schweizerischer evangelischer Kirchenbund, Swiss Protestant Church Federation]

Tho. Nightingale [Thomas Nightingale, President of the National Council of Evangelical Free Churches of England]

Adolf Keller [Secretary of the German language section of the Swiss Protestant Church Federation]

Stockholm the Bureau on Life and Work April 1924.

220. To Adolf von Harnack[1]

Upsala May 5th 1924

Excellency,

The plans for this Universal Christian Conference on Life and Work are progressing in a very gratifying way. The Christian Communions of Europe are manifesting deep interest. They are looking forward to the Conference with hope and prayer. In America twentytwo denominations are represented on the Committee of Arrangements and others will join later. The COPEC Conference at Birmingham[2] gave a new impetus to our work, and has clarified our thinking and made concrete the methods, by which we hope to get results from this meeting which will be held in Stockholm August 19–30, 1925.

At the meeting held in Birmingham, when a large number of the International Committee was present, it was voted to commit to our hands the pleasant task of writing to such leaders in the Church as were suggested, asking them to be prepared to take some part in the Conference.

In our judgment you are the man, who from the history of the Church and from your own experience can give to our Conference the vision of the way that Christendom ought to go in order to fulfill its sacred vocation. Therefore we would like to have you consider this as your subject and we have the honour to offer you this place on the program. We can assure you of a very wide hearing.

Every section of the Church has been invited or is being invited. There will be approximately six hundred official delegates representing all the Christian Communions in the world with the exception of the Roman Catholics, and in addition to the accredited delegates there will be a large number of visitors. We hope and think that the opportunity will be a unique one. [Here the Berlin copy ends.]

Upsala May 8th

We are writing you at this early date, because we know how many things are constantly demanding your time.

Trusting that you may be able to accept this invitation and with all good wishes we are in hearty Christian fellowship

Sincerely yours

Chairman of the International Committee   General Secretary
Archbishop of Upsala   New York

---

[1] Harnack's papers – letters, Staatsbibliothek zu Berlin, Preußischer Kulturbesitz, typed letter. As it is an official letter, signed by both Söderblom and Charles MacFarland, General Secretary of the Federal Council of the Churches of Christ in the United States, it was originally written in English. The postscript and greetings are missing in Harnack's papers in Berlin; they are here being taken from the carbon copy extant in N. Söderblom's collection of letters, to Swedes and foreigners, UUB.

[2] Conference on Christian Politics, Economics, and Citizenship, the first such conference of the Church of England. It was organized by William Temple (1881–1944), at the time member of the Labour Party (1918–1921) bishop of Manchester 1921, archbishop of York 1929, archbishop of Canterbury 1942.

221. From Friedrich Heiler[1]

Marburg/Lahn, Moltkestr. 19, 9. Juli 1924

Hochverehrter, Hochwürdigster Herr Erzbischof,

Für Ihre freundliche Einladung zu Pastor Gustavssen sage ich Ihnen meinen herzlichsten Dank. Meine Frau und ich wären so gerne heuer nach Schweden gereist, wohin wir uns beide sehnen. Leider muss ich aber in Deutschland bleiben, weil mein lieber Vater hoffnungslos krank an Magenkrebs darniederliegt. Ich habe ihn an Pfingsten besucht und will nach Schluss des Semesters wieder dorthin fahren. Möge Gott seinem schmerzvollen Leiden wenigstens Linderung schenken!

Herzlichen Dank sage ich Ihnen für die freundliche Zusendung Ihrer schönen Uebersetzung des neuen Buches Sundar Singhs.[2] Ich wollte es ursprünglich ins Deutsche übersetzen, hatte auch vom Sadhu die Erlaubnis dazu; Aber es stellte sich heraus, dass der gute Sadhu ausser mir noch zwei anderen Deutschen das Uebersetzungsrecht übertragen hatte, woraufhin ich verzichtete. Mein Buch über ihn werden Sie in der zweiten Auflage erhalten haben.[3] Ich legte Ihnen zwei Aufsätze katholischer Mönche über ihn bei, die Sie interessieren werden.[4] Mein Buch hat nämlich in den Kreisen der römischen Kirche große Unruhe, ja geradezu Bestürzung hervorgerufen. Dass ausserhalb der allein seligmachenden Kirche ein Heiliger auftritt, ist den meisten römischen Katholiken ein Ding der Unmöglichkeit. Uebrigens hat auch in Indien von Seite der römischen Mission, vor allem von Seiten der Jesuiten, eine Polemik gegen den Sadhu eingesetzt. Sundar Singh schrieb mir selbst, dass seine Vorträge in Indien auch von römischen Katholiken stark besucht würden und dass die römischen Priester den Abfall vieler Bekehrter befürchteten, wenn sie nicht gegen ihn aufträten.

Die junge deutsche Theologenwelt ist augenblicklich in einem Fieberzustand. Barth, Gogarten, Emil Brunner in Zürich und mein hiesiger Kollege Bultmann propagieren mit Leidenschaft ihren seltsamen dialektischen Gnostizismus, den sie als genuines Luthertum ansehen.[5] Ich bin sehr besorgt um

[1] N. Söderblom's collection of letters, from foreigners, UUB, typewritten letter.
[2] Sadhu Sundar Singh, *Verklighet och religion. Betraktelser om Gud, människan och naturen*, Stockholm 1924. Cf. letter no. 203, n. 4.
[3] Friedrich Heiler, *Sadhu Sundar Singh, ein Apostel des Ostens und Westens*, München 1924 (4th ed. 1926).
[4] The huge amount of literature on this case does not allow with any degree of certainty to identify these two articles. Cf. the literature listed by Michael Biehl, *Der Fall Sadhu Sundar Singh. Theologie zwischen den Kulturen* (Diss.Kiel), SIGC 66, Frankfurt u. a. 1990.
[5] Karl Barth (1886–1968), 1911 pastor in Safenwil/Aargau, Switzerland, 1921 professor in Göttingen, 1925 in Münster and 1930 in Bonn; after his dismissal by the Nazi government in 1935, he continued in Basel. At the time, his fame was based on the 2nd ed. of his *Der Römerbrief*, Munich 1922, later on his monumental *Kirchliche Dogmatik*, Zollikon 1932–1970. – Friedrich Gogarten (1887–1967), pastor in Stelzendorf, Thuringia 1914, professor in Breslau/Wroclaw 1931 and in Göttingen 1935 (s. also letter no. 283, n. 4). – Emil Brunner (1889–1966), professor in Zürich 1924. Emil Brunner (1889–1966), was influenced by Swiss religious socialism (Hermann Kutter) and personalist philosophy (Martin Buber, Ferdinand Ebner). He saw human responsibility as a point of contact for God's revelation. This evoked Barth's wrath,

die Zukunft der deutschen Theologie in der nächsten Zeit. Ich beobachte hier beständig die verheerenden Wirkungen, welche diese »neue Theologie« anrichtet. Unser alter Senior Karl Budde[6] hat mit Recht gesagt, diese Theologie sei eine Verkehrung des εὐαγγέλιον in ein δυσαγγέλιον. Glücklicherweise hat jetzt der junge Althaus von Rostock energisch seine Stimme erhoben.[7] Ich wollte, unser Freund Einar Billing schriebe einmal etwas gegen dieses »Neuluthertum«, das von der Gottfreudigkeit des alten Luthertums gar nichts geerbt hat, sondern geradezu die Heils*un*gewissheit und *Un*erlöstheit predigt. Aber es gibt eben auch in der Theologie Psychosen, die schwer heilbar sind.

Nun danke ich Ihnen nochmals von Herzen für Ihre große Freundlichkeit und grüsse zusammen mit meiner Frau Sie und Ihre verehrte Familie. In aufrichtiger Verehrung und Dankbarkeit verbleibe ich

Ihr ergebenster
Friedrich Heiler.

222. TO FRIEDRICH HEILER[1]

Upsala 17.7.1924

Käre vän!

Hjärtligt tack för det vänskapliga och synnerligen märkliga brevet. Det skulle vara viktigt att höra något om denne Barths riktning. När kunna vi träffas, så att jag får besked därom? Kan Ni inte skriva eller för Eder maka diktera en kort uppsats om denna »Neue Theologie«. Var har Althaus höjt sin stämma till opposition? Jag skulle gärna vilja läsa hans artikel. Pessimis-

---

who accused him of »natural theology« (*Nein. Antwort an Emil Brunner*, TEH 14, München 1934) and (falsely) lumped him together with the Nazi German Christians. This contributed to limiting Brunner's influence primarily to non-German speaking countries, such as the United States. – These systematic theologians were joined by the New Testament scholar Rudolf Bultmann (1884-1976, professor in Marburg since 1921) who after World War II became known for his radical program of »demythologization« (*Neues Testament und Mythologie*, BevTh 7, München 1941). As a group, they were called »dialectical theologians«. What they had in common was their protest against the predominant theological liberalism. Their public mouthpiece was the periodical *Zwischen den Zeiten* – until 1933 when the group broke up because of differences both in theology and in politics, differences which in part had been smoldering all along. Nonetheless, their influence on 20th century theology came to be paramount.

[6] Karl Budde (1850-1935), professor of Old Testament in Marburg 1900, retired 1921.

[7] Paul Althaus, *Theologie und Geschichte. Zur Auseinandersetzung mit der dialektischen Theologie*, in: ZSTh 1/1923, 741-786. – Althaus (1888-1966), professor of systematic theology and New Testament in Rostock 1919-1925 and in Erlangen until 1956, is known particularly for his research on Luther. He was one of the most outspoken critics of the Dialectical theology, advocating an »original revelation« (*Uroffenbarung*) of God as a precondition for understanding human sin, and in social ethics a theology of the orders of creation (*Schöpfungsordnungen*) as God's way of providing orientation in social life. Althaus agreed to the initial measures of the Nazi dictatorship but later tried to be a mediator in church politics as best he could. In theology too, his work can best be decribed as mediating between the extremes.

[1] Fr. Heiler's papers (Ms. 999), Univ. Library Marburg, typewritten letter.

men är bitterljuv och dispenserar från den bekvämare [sic! läs: obekvämare] plikten att handla.

Tack för de nya bokgåvorna. Underbart är vilken vitalitet som ligger i Edra böcker, och som ger dem sådan spridning. Även Gandhi är ett helgon utan romersk sanktion. Jag läser med intresse den romerska oron.

Men med smärta erfar jag att Eder älsklige fader, som hade den stora godheten att i Mürren uppsöka mig och låta mig göra bekantskap med den käre Friedrich Heilers Fader, nu ligger i en plågsam och dödlig sjukdom. Gud välsigne honom för hans trogna livsverk och för de frön av gudsvänskap som han nedlagt i Edert hjärta!

...

I trofast vänskap Eder tillgivne
Nathan Söderblom

Uppsala, den 17. Juli 1924

Lieber Freund!

Herzlichen Dank für den freundschaftlichen und besonders bemerkenswerten Brief. Es wäre wichtig, etwas über die Richtung dieses Barth zu erfahren. Wann können wir uns treffen, damit ich Aufschluss darüber bekomme? Können Sie nicht einen kurzen Aufsatz über diese »Neue Theologie« schreiben oder Ihrer Frau diktieren? Wo hat Althaus seine Stimme in Opposition erhoben? Ich möchte gerne seinen Artikel lesen. Pessimismus ist bittersüß und dispensiert von der [un]bequemeren Pflicht zu handeln.

Danke für die neuen Buchgeschenke. Es ist wunderbar, welche Vitalität in Ihren Büchern steckt und ihnen eine solche Ausbreitung verschafft. Auch Gandhi ist ein Heiliger ohne römische Sanktionierung. Ich lese mit Interesse über die römische Aufregung.

Aber mit Schmerz erfahre ich, dass Ihr liebenswürdiger Vater, der die große Güte hatte, mich in Mürren[2] aufzusuchen und mich die Bekanntschaft mit dem Vater des lieben Friedrich Heiler machen zu lassen, jetzt mit einer qualvollen und tödlichen Krankheit darniederliegt. Gott segne ihn für sein treues Lebenswerk und für den Samen der Gottesliebe, den er in Ihr Herz gelegt hat!

... [A couple of remarks on various plans for the near future, e.g. on an invitation to lecture in Prague]

In treuer Freundschaft Ihr
Nathan Söderblom

---

[2] Mürren is a small town in the Bernese Alps, Switzerland. Söderblom took part in a conference there, organized by Sir Henry Lunn (1859-1939), at the time a wealthy Methodist layman, owner of several ski hotels in the Bernese Alps and formerly a physician and missionary in India. The conference was held in preparation of the great Life and Work Conference to be held in Stockholm in 1925. – Probably, however, Söderblom here mixed up Mürren with München, cf. letter no. 226. Heiler's father may have come to listen to Söderblom's guest lectures at Munich University in May, 1923, cf. letter no. 215.

223. To Charles Macfarland[1]

Upsala August the 15th 1924

My dear Friend,

I thank you most heartily for the very important document on the position and role of the Federal Council.

It was a great loss, that I could not meet your Federal Council, when I was i [sic] U.S.A. But my program, in which already before I started every day was occupied, prevented me. For me the Federal Council of the Churches of Christ in U.S.A. means the first really important step towards a federal effort in Evangelic Christendom in all Church matters.

By the way I wonder, if you have a photograph of the members of the Council for publishing here and especially for our Universal Christian Conference on Life and Work.

I was told many times in different communions in U.S.A. that I had over-rated the situation of the Federal Council. It might be that I have gone too far, because we joined in our pronouncement to Universal Christendom November 1914.[2] I have praised God for the existence of such an admirable instrument for the Evangelic conscience and I see that I might have been mistaken in some informations that I gave publicity before as to the position of your federation vis à vis all the Evangelic Christendom in U.S.A. But I am glad to see from your letter that I am regarding the Federal Council as a real representation of Evangelic Christendom.

... [Thanks for documents and a book]

You are happily the man of one great idea, which God has committed to you and which you have realized to a wonderful extent with your friends.

Believe me, with good greetings,

Sincerely yours
Nathan Söderblom

224. From Alfred Loisy[1]

Ceffonds, le 26 août 1924

Révérend et Cher Archevêque,

Si je vous ai envoyé mon livre de *La Morale humaine*, c'était dans la pensée qu'il ne vous déplairait pas. Je suis heureux de recevoir de vous-même l'assurance que je ne me suis pas trompé. [...]

Mais quelle tâche que la nôtre! J'ai commencé seulement de lire votre *Christian Fellowship*, que vous avez bien voulu m'envoyer et dont je vous re-

---

[1] Nathan Söderblom's collection of letters, to Swedes and foreigners, UUB, typewritten letter.
[2] The document referred to is printed as no.75 in the present selection.

[1] N. Söderblom's collection of letters, from foreigners, UUB, handwritten letter.

mercie bien sincèrement. Ce que j'en ai lu me montre que vous construisez votre programme d'union chrétienne sur des principes très larges, comme il fallait le construire pour qu'il eût un sens. Je me demande seulement si vous manoeuvrerez plus facilement vos théologiens que je ne réussis à me faire entendre de nos rationalistes. Inutile de vous dire que ces derniers, pour la plupart, sinon tous, s'expliquent mal ce qu'ils appellent mon *mysticisme*, et croient volontiers que c'est un vieux reste d'éducation catholique. Ma persuasion intime est que la théologie scolastique a enfanté le pur rationalisme et que mon prétendu mysticisme est le fruit de mon expérience. C'est une expérience aussi que vous faites valoir. Réussirez vous à convaincre tous les chrétiens que le christianisme est avant tout un esprit, comme le dit assez clairement le quatrième Evangile? Je le souhaite. Quoiqu'il advienne vous travaillez à l'union de l'humanité, à la société des nations.

Si, d'aventure, j'avais été pape, nous aurions pu nous entendre. Mais l'occupant de la *Cathedra Petri* ne renoncera pas de sitôt à imposer son formulaire. Et pourtant, c'est son formulaire qui le perdra ..... Malheureusement il ne compromet pas que son propre avenir, et les peuples qui lui échappent ne savent encore où aller.

J'ai écrit à mon éditeur de vous envoyer un exemplaire de *La Religion*, 2e édition. Vous m'excuserez si l'exemplaire vous arrive sans un mot de ma main. Je n'ai moi-même ici qu'un exemplaire en épreuves. J'ai changé presque entièrement l'introduction, qui était de circonstance, et j'ai substitué aux considérations sur la guerre mondiale une modeste étude sur le sens mystique. [...]

Les années passent, et nous avons vu de terribles choses. Je me souviens encore de votre visite à Ceffonds, et de ce que vous m'avez dit pour me consoler de ce que l'herbe poussait dans les allées de mon jardin. Elle y pousse de plus en plus. Je n'ai plus de poules, depuis la bataille de la Marne; même mon poulailler a été en 1917–1918 une prison militaire. Je suis absorbé par mes travaux d'exégèse et mon enseignement. On m'a, cette année, obligé à prendre un enseignement à l'Ecole des Hautes Etudes en plus de celui du Collège de France. Je suis comme le bon Saint Martin: Non recuso laborem. Mais les forces commencent à me trahir.

Veuillez me croire, Révérend et cher Archevêque, très respectueusement et sincèrement à vous

Alfred Loisy

Ceffonds, August 26, 1924

Your Grace and dear Archbishop,

If I sent you my book *La morale humaine*,[2] this was done with the idea that it might not displease you. I am glad to receive from yourself the assurance that I have not been mistaken. [...]

But what kind of a task [is] ours! I have only begun to read your *Christian Fel-*

---

[2] Alfred Loisy, *La morale humaine*, Paris 1923 (²1928).

lowship,[3] which you were kind enough to send me and for which I most sincerely thank you. What I have read of it shows that you are building your program on very generous principles, as it must be if it is to make sense. I am only asking myself whether you are going to maneuver your theologians more easily than I have succeeded in making myself understood by our rationalists. Needless to tell you that the latter, the majority if not all of them, [content themselves with] a poor explanation of what they consider my mysticism; they like to believe that this is an old remnant of a catholic upbringing. It is my innermost conviction that scholastic theology generated pure rationalism, and that my alleged mysticism is the fruit of my experience. It is also an experience which you are bringing to bear. Will you succeed in convincing all Christians that Christianity is above all a spiritual attitude, as the fourth Gospel states clearly enough? I hope so. Whatever happens, you are working for the unity of humankind, for the association of the nations.

If, by chance, I had been pope, we would have been able to reach an agreement. But the occupant of the Cathedra Petri will not so soon renounce imposing his formulary. Nonetheless, it is his formulary that will be his undoing ..... Unfortunately, he does not jeopardize anything but his own future, and the nations that escape him do not know yet where to go.

I have written to my publisher, asking him to send you a copy of *La religion*, 2nd edition.[4] You will excuse me if the copy reaches you without a word from my hand. I do not have but one copy in proof sheets here myself. I have changed almost completely the introduction that was conditioned by the circumstances, and I have substituted the considerations on the world war by a modest study of the mystical sense. [...]

The years are passing by, and we have seen horrible things. I still remember your visit at Ceffonds, and what you said to me in order to comfort me regarding the grass growing on the walkways in my garden. It is growing there more and more. I have not had hens any more since the battle of the Marne;[5] even my hennery was a military prison in 1917–1918. I am being absorbed by my exegetical work and my teaching. This year, they have obliged me to accept a teaching assignment at the Ecole des Hautes Etudes, over and above that at the Collège de France. I am like good Saint Martin: Non recuso laborem[6] [I do not refuse work]. But vigor is beginning to fail me.[7]

Believe me, Your Grace and dear Archbishop, yours very respectfully and sincerely,
Alfred Loisy

---

[3] Nathan Söderblom, *Christian Fellowship and the United Life and Work of Christendom* (The Christian Unity Handbook Series), New York/Chicago 1923.

[4] Alfred Loisy, *La religion*, 2nd ed., Paris 1924 (1st ed. 1917).

[5] Ceffonds is situated in the Département Haute-Marne, it was not directly touched by the war.

[6] »Domine, si adhuc populo tuo sum necessarius, non recuso subire propter eos laborem,« (Lord, if am still needed by your people, I shall not refuse to take work upon me for their sake), a prayer ascribed to St. Martin, bishop of Tours (316/317–397), which he is supposed to have spoken in very old age.

[7] As a matter of fact, Loisy continued to work assiduously for another 16 years.

225. From FRIEDRICH HEILER[1]

Marburg, den 19. September 1924

Hochverehrter, Hochwürdiger Herr Erzbischof,
in den nächsten Tagen wird Ihnen auf meine Veranlassung eine Nummer
der jesuitischen »Stimmen der Zeit« zugehen, welche den schärfsten Angriff
gegen den Sadhu enthält, der mir je zu Gesicht gekommen ist.[2] Sundar
Singh wird hier als raffinierter Schwindler hingestellt, der höchstens als
Psychopath zu entschuldigen sei. Diese ungeheuren Behauptungen beruhen
angeblich auf jahrelangen systematischen Nachforschungen, welche die indischen Jesuitenmissionare angestellt haben. Beifügen muss ich, dass mir
schon vor mehreren Monaten ein katholischer Benediktinermönch erzählte,
dass die Jesuiten »scharf hinter dem Sadhu her seien und an seiner Entlar-
vung arbeiteten«. Es handelt sich also um einen längst vorbereiteten, plan-
mässigen Feldzug gegen Sundar Singh. In dem betreffenden Aufsatz werden
auch Sie mit angegriffen, weil Sie auf diesen »Schwindel« hereingefallen sei-
en. Letzten Endes ist die evangelische Christenheit überhaupt getroffen, die
dem Sadhu ihr Vertrauen geschenkt und ihn begeistert angehört habe.

Das Material, auf das sich die Jesuiten stützen, kann ich nur zum geringsten Teil nachprüfen, das kann nur an Ort und Stelle geschehen. Ich möchte
Ihnen darum den Vorschlag machen, dass Sie den betreffenden Aufsatz der
schwedischen Mission in Indien schicken und sie veranlassen, die Behauptungen der Jesuiten einer Nachprüfung zu unterziehen. Vor allem müsste
der Jesuit Hosten in Darjeeling, der zuerst im Catholic Herald of India
diese Anschuldigungen gegen den Sadhu erhoben hat, aufgefordert werden,
sein Material zur Einsichtnahme einer unparteiischen Kommission vorzule-
gen.[3] Ich bin überzeugt, dass die Jesuiten nicht mit einwandfreien Mitteln
gearbeitet haben. Wer die Geschichte der Jesuitenmission in Indien kennt,
wird diesen Leuten mit grösstem Misstrauen begegnen müssen. Vielleicht
nehmen Sie die Angelegenheit in die Hand, die im Interesse der gesamten
evangelischen Christenheit liegt.

... [On a visit by a Marburg colleague to Söderblom]

Ich grüsse Sie mit meiner Frau, Sie und alle die Ihrigen, in Verehrung
und dankbarer Ergebenheit.

Ihr ergebenster
Friedrich Heiler.

---

[1] Nathan Söderblom's collection of letters, from foreigners, UUB, typewritten letter.
[2] The article is by Heinrich Sierp S.J., »Sadhu Sundar Singh,« in: StZ 107/1924, 415–425.
Heiler wrote two rejoinders: »Sierp and Sundar. Eine Antwort,« in: Münchner Neueste Nachrichten, Febr. 5, 1925; and: »Nochmals Sierp und Sundar,« ib., March 5, 1925.
[3] H. Hosten, S.J., wrote a whole series of 31 articles on the subject in the periodical mentioned above, from July 1923 till March 1924; cf. M. Biehl, op. cit. (letter no. 216, n. 4). Sierp
heavily relies on Hosten.

226. To FRIEDRICH HEILER[1]

Upsala 18.11.1924

Käre Vän!

Meddelandet med svarta kanter kommer ju icke oväntat efter vad vi förut erfarit från Eder själv och från andra. Men det gör ändå lika starkt intryck. Ingen kan känna vännen Friedrich Heiler utan att tänka på hans fader och moder. Även om jag icke hade hört Eder rörande sonliga pietet och förstått vad en oskrymtad gudsfruktan och innerlighet hos Edra föräldrar betytt för Eder stora livsgärning, skulle mitt korta möte med Eder fader i München hava givit åt detta dödsfall för mig en personlig prägel. Gud förläne honom i sin barmhärtighet ro och glädje efter arbetsdagens mödor och trohet, och Gud hjälpe oss alla att rätt leva och rätt dö.

Jag ber The Review of the Churches sända Eder sitt sista nummer för oktober 1924, och hoppas att Ni icke ogillar vad jag skrivit sidan 464 och 465 om Eder själv. Jag borde uttryckligen hava begärt ännu ett bemyndigande, men därtill var icke tid, och Alpernas majestät skärpte min blick för det höga och väsentliga.

Med många goda hälsningar till Eder fru och alla Edra kära
Eder hjärtligt tillgivne
Nathan Söderblom

Uppsala, November 18, 1924

Lieber Freund,

Die Nachricht mit schwarzem Rand kommt natürlich nicht unerwartet, nach dem, was wir zuvor von Ihnen selbst und von anderen erfahren hatten. Aber sie hinterlässt gleichwohl einen ebenso starken Eindruck. Niemand kann den Freund Friedrich Heiler kennen, ohne an seinen Vater und seine Mutter zu denken. Selbst wenn ich nicht von Ihrer rührenden Sohnes-Pietät gehört und nicht verstanden hätte, was die ungeheuchelte Gottesfurcht und Innerlichkeit bei Ihren Eltern für Ihre großes Lebenswerk bedeutet hat, hätte meine kurze Zusammenkunft mit Ihrem Vater in München diesem Todesfall für mich ein persönliches Gepräge gegeben. Gott verleihe ihm in seiner Barmherzigkeit Ruhe und Freude nach den Mühen und der Treue des Arbeitstages, und Gott verhelfe uns allen dazu, recht zu leben und recht zu sterben.

Ich bitte The Review of the Churches, Ihnen seine letzte Nummer von Oktober 1924 zu schicken, und hoffe, dass Sie nicht missbilligen, was ich auf Seite 464 und 465 über Sie geschrieben habe.[2] Ich hätte ausdrücklich noch um eine Ermächtigung

---

[1] Fr. Heiler's papers (Ms. 999), Univ. Library Marburg, typewritten letter.

[2] N. Söderblom, »Why Rome Makes Converts. A discussion of A. Lunn's new book ›Roman Converts‹,« in: *The Review of the Churches*, N.S., vol. 1/1924, 463-470. The passage referred to above is a eulogy on Heiler's *Das Gebet* and some reflections on his conversion, used as an example for the superior importance of a personal relationship to Christ over against membership in the church as an institution, as well as the question of Catholic elements remaining in Heiler's thinking. – Söderblom seems to have written the article in a hurry during his stay in Mürren, Switzerland, in July, 1924; see the following sentence.

351

nachsuchen sollen, aber dazu war keine Zeit, und die Majestät der Alpen schärfte meinen Blick für das Hohe und Wesentliche.

Mit vielen guten Grüßen an Ihre Frau und alle Ihre Lieben
Ihr Ihnen herzlich zugetaner
Nathan Söderblom

227. From GustAF Johansson[1]

Åbo den 24. XI. 24.

Högtärade Broder!

Inbjudningen till den finska kyrkan har jag emottagit, men jag kan ej god-känna den allmänna världskonferensens programm. Christi sinnelag och vilja beträffande de sociala, ekonomiska och politiska förhållandena äro nog kända från evangelierna. Han inlåter sig ej på dessa frågor, emedan Hans rike ej är af denna världen. Vi hafva nu att bygga upp Andens tempel. Vid Cristi återkomst blifva dessa förhållanden förnyade. Det kristligt sedli-ga kan ej omedelbart införas i nuvarande sociala förhållanden, emedan Cristi Ande ej beherrskar folken. Men det gagnar ej att här orda härom. Våra lifsåskådningar äro väsendtligen olika. Världskonferensens programm lederar flera af Christendomens grundsatser. Det som Gud allena kan om-besörja intresserar nu mången, men det som människor har att göra, för-summas. Denna världskonferens är den första i sitt slag, och den skall bringa stor skada åt protestantismen. Jag kan blott inlägga min protest emot dess sammankallande. Detta smärtar mig djupt. Från den finska kyr-kan kunna ej officiella representanter väljas, ty sådana kan blott kyrkomö-tet välja, hvilket ej kan sammankallas för ett sådant ändamål. Det är ej rätt, om enskilda prestkretsar välja delegerade till ett sådant möte. Tidsläget motiverar ej på något sätt denna världskonferens sammankallande. Detta är ett stort steg nedåt. Bevare Gud vår kristenhet för de faror, som omgifva den! önskar

med högaktning
Gustaf Johansson.

Åbo, November 24, 24.

Highly esteemed Brother,

I have received the invitation to the Finnish church, but I cannot approve of the pro-gram of the world conference. Christ's disposition and will regarding the social, economic, and political conditions are surely known from the Gospels. He does not tackle these issues because His kingdom is not of this world.[2] We now have to build the temple of the Spirit.[3] At Christ's second coming, those conditions will be trans-formed. Christian morality cannot immediately be introduced into present social conditions, since Christ's Spirit does not govern the nations. But discussing this is to

---

[1] Nathan Söderblom's ecumenical collection, A 11, UUB, handwritten letter.
[2] John 18:36.
[3] Eph 2:21.

no avail here. Our views of life are essentially different. The program of the world conference violates several of Christianity's basic tenets. What God alone can attend to interests many a person now, but what humans have to do is being neglected. This world conference is the first of its kind, and it will inflict great harm on Protestantism. I can only lodge my protest against its being convened. I am deeply aggrieved by this. Official delegates from the Finnish church cannot be elected, because only the synod can elect such, and it cannot be convened for such a purpose. It is not right that individual groups of pastors choose delegates for such a meeting. The state of affairs in no way warrants convening this world conference. This is a big step downwards. May God protect Christianity from the dangers which surround it! Wishing [this]

in high regard

Gustaf Johansson.

228. From Friedrich Heiler[1]

Marburg, den 25. November 1924

Hochverehrter, Hochwürdigster Herr Erzbischof,

für Ihre freundliche Teilnahme beim Tode meines Vaters sage ich Ihnen meinen herzlichsten Dank. Monate lang ertrug er sein schweres Leiden in Geduld und Gottergebenheit. Ich hatte den grössten Teil des Oktober bei ihm verbracht und war Anfang November zu den Vorlesungen hierher zurückgekehrt. Trotzdem sein Tod längst vorauszusehen war, kam er überraschend, sodass ich nicht rechtzeitig in München eintraf. Er ging ganz bewusst in den Tod, in voller Gewissheit seines Heils. »Ich glaube an Jesus Christus; Herr Jesus, komm, und hole mich« diese Worte wiederholte er immer wieder, ehe die Bewusstlosigkeit eintrat. Der römisch-katholische Priester, der ihm die Sakramente gebracht hatte und der ihn öfters besuchte, schrieb nach dem Tode meiner Mutter, wie sehr er sich an dem Glauben meines Vaters erbaut habe. Und der Arzt, welcher anwesend war, als mein Vater von den Meinen Abschied nahm, erklärte ihnen, er habe nie in den 18 Jahren seiner Tätigkeit jemanden so bewusst und gewiss in den Tod gehen sehen. Obgleich frommer Katholik (der in seinen gesunden Tagen täglich in die Messe ging), ist mein Vater als evangelischer Christ im Glauben an die Gewissheit des Heils in Christus gestorben. Ich hatte ihm in den letzten Wochen seines Lebens viel aus der Bibel und aus den Reden und Schriften des Sadhu vorgelesen, was ihn sehr erbaute und tröstete. Ich bin Gott so dankbar dafür, dass durch meine innere Entwicklung mein Verhältnis zu meinem Vater nie getrübt wurde. Als er mich einmal hier in Marburg besuchte, spielte er die Orgel, als ich Gottesdienst hielt. Er war ein eifriger und leibevoller [l.: liebevoller] Leser meiner Schriften, und noch auf dem Sterbebette sagte er, er freue sich darüber, dass durch meine Schriften viele Menschen zum religiösen Leben geführt worden seien. Meinem Vater und

---

[1] N. Söderblom's collection of letters, from foreigners, UUB, typewritten letter.

seiner Erziehung verdanke ich den Sinn für das Religiöse, aber nicht nur das, ihm verdanke ich auch die weitherzige Liebe zu allen christlichen Konfessionen. Trotzdem mein Vater immer am Glauben und Kult seiner Kirche hing, war er nie ultramontaner Katholik und verabscheute alle römische Intoleranz und Gewaltpolitik und hatte hohe Achtung vor evangelischer Frömmigkeit, und zwar längst bevor er durch meine Schriften tiefer in evangelischen Geist eingeführt wurde. Nun ruht er im ewigen Frieden. Ich habe nie ein solches Bild des stillen und frohen Friedens gesehen wie meinen Vater auf der Totenbahre. Als ich dieses Bild sah, da *sah* ich auch, dass er in der Gewissheit seines Heils entschlafen war.

... [Thanks for an article by Söderblom on Sundar Singh, without a comment on its contents]

Herzlichen Dank sage ich Ihnen auch für die freundliche Zusendung Ihres Buches.[2] Ihre Vorträge zu lesen ist mir eine grosse Freude und Erquikkung; denn sie sind eine Theologie, die mit dem Herzen geschrieben ist. Unsere deutsche Theologie wird immer kälter und verstandesmässiger; ich wollte, sie könnte etwas von Ihrer Wärme und Liebe empfangen. Denn wenn es so weiter geht, wie es jetzt den Anschein hat, dann wird die deutsche Theologie noch zu einer Eiswüste.

Nun möchte ich noch zwei Bitten aussprechen: 1. Verschiedene deutsche Evangelische haben mich gebeten, mich an Sie zu wenden wegen des immer stärkeren Anwachsens eines hässlichen Nationalismus und Chauvinismus innerhalb des deutschen Protestantismus. Ich selbst habe an der Tagung des Evangelischen Bundes in München teilgenommen, mit Scham und Zorn über manches, was hier geboten wurde. Diese Tagung ist, wie einer meiner hiesigen Freunde gesagt hat ›ein Nagel für den Sarg des deutschen Protestantismus‹ gewesen. Der Evangelische Bund hat sich hier in seinem nationalistisch-politischen Charakter entpuppt und seinem Namen Unehre gemacht.[3] Evangelisch wurde da einfach mit deutsch-völkisch gleichgesetzt. Ich war entrüstet, in einer Festpredigt von der Kanzel zu hören: Gott hat in der Geschichte nur zwei Völker »auserwählt«, das israelitische und das deutsche, – sowie das lieblose Urteil: »Die deutschen sind ein frommes Volk, ganz anders als die stumpfen Russen und die kalten, herzlosen Eng-

    [2] This probably refers to the collection of sermons: *Från Upsala till Rock Island. En predikofärd i Nya Världen*, Stockholm 1924 (3rd ed. 1925).
    [3] The *Evangelischer Bund* was founded in 1886 in order to promote Protestant unity, with a strongly anti-Catholic stance. During World War I, it urged perseverance in the war effort. Nationalist tendencies were still prevalent during the years following the war; the Wartburg program of 1921 declared the Gospel the highest spiritual good and German nationhood (*Volkstum*) the highest mundane good. But the *Ev. Bund* kept its distance to the far-right *Alldeutscher Verband*; it held a leading position within international Protestantism since 1923. The rise of the Nazi regime in 1933 brought internal strife, but efforts at bringing the organization in line failed. Since 1945, the *Ev. Bund* has been dedicated to mutual understanding between the Christian churches. Cf. the article by Heiner Grote, »Evangelischer Bund,« in *TRE* 10, 683–686.

länder«. Das sagte der mecklenburgische Landesbischof Tolzien.[4] Ich möchte Sie darum im Namen von vielen anderen bitten, einmal Ihre Stimme gegen diese unheilvolle und unchristliche Politisierung des evangelischen Christentums in Deutschland zu erheben, die nur Wasser auf die Mühlen der Ultramontanen ist. Vielleicht wäre es Ihnen möglich, etwa um Neujahr oder an Weihnachten eine Botschaft an die deutschen evangelischen Kirchen zu senden, in der Sie sich über diese Dinge aussprechen.[5]

2. Ferner haben mich die Reformkatholiken und katholischen Modernisten gebeten, mich an Sie zu wenden. Vor dem Krieg hatten diese ein eigenes Organ ›Das Neue Jahrhundert‹, das von vielen katholischen Geistlichen gelesen wurde. Diese Zeitschrift ist auch ein Opfer der Zeitverhältnisse geworden. Nun denken diese Kreis wieder daran, ihr altes Organ aufleben zu lassen, haben aber nicht die nötigen Mittel für die Anfangszeit. Wäre es nicht möglich, dass etwa der schwedische Gustaf Adolf-Verein sie unterstützte, bis sie sich auf eigene Füsse stellen könnten? Ich glaube, die Unterstützung dieser Kreise wäre eine wirksamere Abwehr der unheimlichen ultramontanen Welle und ein besserer Schutz gegen ihr Anwachsen als alle direkte Polemik und bewusste ›Los von Rom Bewegung‹. Auf diese Weise kann allein der Zugang zu den römischen Laien und vor allem zu den römischen Priestern gefunden werden, die sonst ganz im Banne ihrer Hierarchie stehen. Vielleicht wäre es Ihnen möglich, mir eine Korrespondenz mit den Leuten des schwedischen Gustaf Adolf-Vereins zu vermitteln.[6] Im Voraus danke ich Ihnen für alle Freundlichkeit.

Nun grüsse ich Sie, hochverehrter Herr Erzbischof, und die Ihrigen zusammen mit meiner Frau und bleibe in steter Dankbarkeit und Verehrung
Ihr ergebenster
Friedrich Heiler.

---

[4] Gerhard Tolzien (1870–1946), bishop of Mecklenburg 1921–1933. He had become renowned for his war sermons (*Kriegspredigten*, 6 vols., Schwerin 1915–1918) that show him as the typical German Protestant nationalist of his time. However, he did not sympathize with the Nazis. He was forced from his see in 1933 and continued as a simple pastor in the village of Basedow until his death.

[5] Among Heiler's papers, I have found no written reply to this letter. The next time Heiler himself wrote, on Dec. 19, 1924, he did not mention a reply either. Nor does Söderblom's bibliography contain a trace of a reaction to Heiler's request. It is quite likely that preparations for the Stockholm conference which had already gone into high gear had left no time for that.

[6] Söderblom does not seem to have fulfilled this second request either. Here the explanation probably is not just a lack of time but a lack of enthusiasm for meddling in internal Catholic affairs.

229. To Gustaf Johansson[1]

Upsala 1 december 1924

Högt vördade Broder!

Tvärtom. Finlands vördnadsvärde och andekraftige Ärkebiskop måste själv trots sin ålder komma över till Stockholm och predika för konferensen söndagen den 23 augusti 1925. Och än mer, Du måste, såsom Du yttrade då vi vandrade på Auras is, säga kristenheten ett ord just om den så kallade sociala frågans religiösa och kristliga sedliga innebörd och förpliktelser.

När de kristna på olika tider sökt i lydnad mot sin Herre uträtta Hans vilja i denna onda värld, så hava de ej sällan mött Gudsförnekarnas hån som säga:»Om det finns en Gud, så borde väl han utföra saken själv. Vad haven I att skaffa därmed«? Men så få vi icke säga. Guds vilja sker väl vår bön förutan, men vi bedja i denna bön att den må ske hos oss, i våra hjärtan, i våra liv, men även i våra samfund och folk. Hur detta skall ske, därom finnas även hos evangeliska kristna olika tankar. Ja, det råder i viss mån en olidlig anarki som måste botas.

Protestantismens splittring är ett brott inför Gud och en skam inför människor. Vår Frälsare beder att lärjungarna må vara ett,»för att världen skall förstå att Du har sänt mig«. Men världen kan icke se alla sannt troendes andliga osynliga eviga enhet i Kristus och Gud, utan Frälsaren avser här uppenbarligen en gemenskap, ett samförstånd som världen kan se för att den må bringas till tro på Kristi utgående från Fadren. Vi kunna icke jämka på det som hör till vår tro och bekännelse. Men kunna vi icke ens så långt ena oss, att vi gemensamt söka efterfölja Mästaren i Hans kärlek och rättfärdighet, då är den evangeliska kristenheten dömd, till stor glädje för den triumferande otron och för den hätska hädelsen som har sin påve i Moskva, och även för Rom, som nu utför en metodisk kontrareformation liksom för trehundra år sedan. Var och en vill vandra sin egen väg, fastän samme Frälsare är utgiven i döden för oss alla. Det är så att hjärtat svider. Hur har icke redan Martin Luther att kämpa emot denna söndringens ande? Mötet i Stockholm är ingenting annat än en sen uppfyllelse av vad han skriver i företalet till de Schmalkaldiska Artiklarna, då han påyrkar ett möte för fred och kristen förbättring:

»Förutom detta, som angår religionen och den kristna kyrkan, vore ock stora saker att ändra och rätta i det världsliga ståndet, såsom furstars och ständers oenighet; ocker och girighet hava uppstigit såsom en syndaflod och försvaras under sken av rätt; självsvåld, otukt, högmod, överflöd och högfärd i kläder, dryckenskap, spel, prål tillika med allehanda synder och laster, arghet, undersåtars ohörsamhet. − Om dessa huvudsaker, som i andliga och världsliga stånden emot Gud förövas, skulle i ett möte avhandlas, så finge man för mycket att göra och skulle icke behöva att hålla narraktiga samtal.–«

Vad nu särskilt den sociala frågan angår, kan man hysa olika meningar

---

[1] Nathan Söderblom's ecumenical collection, B 4, UUB, typewritten letter (carbon copy).

om vad som är vår kristna plikt och kyrkans plikt. Just därför behöva vi bedja, betrakta Ordet och rådgöra med varandra. Men enligt mitt Nya Testamente har Jesus talat mycket om Mamon, vilket ju betyder helt enkelt egendom, ägodelar och pengar. Skulle då hans kyrka och församling ingenting alls ha att säga om den saken i våra dagar? Det är för mig ofattligt. Kunna vi läsa profeter, Frälsaren och apostlarna och sedan påstå att kristendomen i vår tid ingenting har att säga och göra inför våldet och Mamons dyrkan och orättfärdigheten och kärlekslösheten i folklivet och mellan nationerna?

En så erfaren och vördad patriark i församlingens tjänst som Finlands Ärkebiskop menar ingalunda detta.

Domsöndagen firade vi i söndags. Jesus säger där fruktansvärda ord om våra försummelser, om vad vi hava underlåtit att göra. Världsklokheten säger: Det är bekvämare och lättare att hålla sig utan för. Och vad särskilt detta företag angår, har jag ofta känt samma frestelse. Men stillar jag min själ inför min Gud, så kommer kravet åter igen lika obönhörligt. Detsamma gäller många medkristna. Ett möte som framgått ur en dylik samvetsnöd och en dylik ingalunda lockande men oundkomlig känsla av Guds fordran, skall säkerligen präglas av mänsklig ofullkomlighet som allt annat mänskligt och försvagas i den mån erfarna kristna män vägra sin förbön och sin medverkan. Men se vi på Kristi kyrkas historia, så tycks efteråt mycket vara ganska självklart, som när det på sin tid genomdrevs till välsignelse för församlingen i Kristi namn förbereddes och utfördes i mycken ängslan under motstånd från många håll och med uppbjudande av den allra yttersta kraften, i ständig bönekamp för förtröstan på den Gud som är mäktig i de svaga.

Ondskan rustar sig, är enig och snar. Skola Kristi bekännare dröja och genom onödig splittring bevisa sin vanmakt? Rom sysselsätter sig mycket med vårt möte och gör allt för att misskreditera och förhindra det. Rom har alltid känt glädje över den evangeliska kristenhetens oförmåga till samförstånd och samarbete.

Vi må icke göra oss någon illusion om vad ett sådant möte kan uträtta. Rom fruktar det. Från Sovjetlandet lär icke tillåtelse kunna utverkas /detta sagt i förtroende/ att deltaga i ett dylikt fritt möte av dem som nitälska för Kristi sak. Skola den svarte och den röde påven få rätt?

För mig står det också såsom en oundkomlig uppgift för Lutherdomen att i den evangeliska kristenheten och särskilt vid detta möte göra sin särskilda djupare inblick i kristendomens väsen gällande.

Jag förstår såsom lutheran en del av min högt vördade Broders betänkligheter. Men det är för oss en ytterligare anledning att hävda vår evangelisk lutherska åskådning vid mötet.

Uppriktigt sagt har jag i min ringa mån därför gjort allt för att mötet skall hållas i ett lutherskt land, icke i ett reformert eller anglosaxiskt land, hur stor respekt jag än äger för dessa våra medkristna och deras arbete. Lutherdomen har i dessa saker sitt särskilda ord att säga och därför räkna vi också särskilt på Din närvaro och på Ditt uttalande.

Kom över hit och hjälp oss!
Med sann vördnad och god hälsning
tillgivne

Uppsala, December 1, 1924

Highly esteemed Brother,
On the contrary. Finland's venerable and spiritually powerful Archbishop must come to Stockholm in spite of his age and preach to the conference on Sunday, August 23, 1925. And more still, you must, as you remarked when we were walking on Aura's ice, say a word to Christianity exactly on the meaning of the so-called social question in terms of religious and Christian morals and its obligations.

When the Christians in various times in obedience to their Lord tried to do His will in this evil world, they often encountered the scorn of the atheists who say: »If there is a God, he should pretty well take care of things himself. What do you have to do with that?« But we must not talk that way. God's will is done even without our prayer, to be sure, but we ask in that prayer that it may be done among us, in our hearts, in our lives, but also in our society and nation. There are different opinions even among Protestant Christians as to how this is to happen. Yea, to a certain degree even an intolerable anarchy prevails which must be remedied.

The disunity of Protestantism is a sacrilege before God and a shame before humans. Our Redeemer prays that the disciples may be one, »that the world may believe that thou didst send me.«[2] But the world cannot see the spiritual, invisible, eternal unity of all true believers in Christ and God; yet the Redeemer here obviously has in mind a communion, a concord the world can see, so that it may be induced to believe in Christ's proceeding from the Father. We cannot budge concerning what belongs to our faith and confession. But if we cannot even agree to the extent of together trying to follow the Master in his love and righteousness, then Protestant Christianity is doomed, to the great joy of triumphant unbelief and of the rancorous blasphemy which has its pope in Moscow, and also of Rome which is now conducting a methodical Counter Reformation, just like three hundred years ago. Each and everyone wants to go his own way, even though the same Redeemer was given up to death for all of us.[3] That makes the heart ache. How hard did not already Martin Luther have to struggle with that spirit of discord? The Stockholm meeting is nothing but a late fulfillment of what he writes in his preface to the Schmalkalden Articles, where he is demanding a council for peace and Christian betterment:[4]

»Apart from that[5] which concerns [religion and] the [Christian] church, there are also great things that would have to be [changed and] set right in the worldly estate, such as discord among princes and estates; usury and greed have risen like a deluge and are being defended under the guise of legality; recklessness, depravity, haughtiness, luxury and vanity in clothing, drunkenness, gambling, ostentatiousness along with all kinds of sins and vices, maliciousness, and disobedience of sub-

---

[2] John 17:21.
[3] Rom 4:25.
[4] BSLK 412f. The Swedish translation by Gottfrid Billing, *Lutherska Kyrkans Bekännelseskrifter*, Lund 1914, p.250 that Söderblom uses, follows partly the German, partly the Latin text. The words in [] are Swedish additions to both versions. I shall here translate the Swedish version into English so the reader has before himself the same wording Johansson did.
[5] The following word in the original is »urgent«, omitted in the Swedish text.

jects. ... If these principal offences which are committed against God by spiritual and worldly estates were to be treated at a council, one would have too much to do and would have no need for foolish chatter ...«

As for the social question in particular now, one can cherish different opinions as to what our Christian duty and the duty of the church is. Just for that reason we need to pray, contemplate the Word and deliberate with one another. However, according to my New Testament, Jesus spoke a lot about Mammon, which of course simply means property, possessions, and money. Should then his church and congregation have nothing to say at all on this matter in our day and age? That is inconceivable for me. Can we read prophets, the Redeemer, and the apostles, and then assert that Christianity in our time had nothing to say and to do in the face of violence and worship of Mammon and injustice and lovelessness in the life and manners of the people and between the nations?

A patriarch as revered and experienced in the service of the church as Finland's archbishop cannot possibly mean that.

It was Judgment Sunday that we celebrated last Sunday.[6] Jesus speaks shocking words there about our shortcomings, about what we failed to do. Worldly prudence says: It is more convenient and easier to stay aloof. And as far as this particular undertaking [the planned ecumenical conference] is concerned, I often felt the same temptation. But when I let my soul become quiet before God, the demand comes back again just as inexorably. The same is true for many fellow Christians. A conference born out of such a constraint of conscience and such a perception – by no means enticing but inescapable – of God's demand will certainly bear the imprint of human imperfection, like everything else that is human, and be weakened to the extent experienced Christian men refuse to offer their prayers and their cooperation. But if we look at the history of Christ's church, much seems to be quite self-evident afterwards which, when being followed through at its time to the benefit of the church in the name of Christ, was prepared and carried out with quite a bit of anxiety, against resistance from many quarters, and summoning the utmost exertion, in constantly struggling prayer for trust in the God whose power is strong in the weak.[7]

Evil is mobilizing, is united and quick. Should Christ's confessors hesitate and demonstrate their helplessness by unnecessary divisions? Rome is paying great attention to our conference, trying everything to discredit and prevent it. Rome has always felt joy over Protestant Christianity's inability to achieve unanimity and cooperation.

We must not indulge in any illusion about what such a conference can accomplish. It seems that from the Soviet country permission cannot be obtained (this being said confidentially) for participation in such a free conference by those who are eager to promote Christ's cause. Shall the black and the red popes be proved right?

For me it also stands out as an inescapable obligation for Lutheranism to bring to bear its particular, more profound insight into the essence of Christianity within Protestant Christendom, especially at this meeting.

As a Lutheran, I understand part of my highly esteemed Brother's scruples. How-

---

[6] *Domsöndag*, Swedish name of the Sunday before Advent Sunday, which is devoted to the subject of the Last Judgment. The sermon is to be held on the Gospel reading from Matth 25:31–46; cf. the following sentence.

[7] II Cor 12:9.

ever, that is for us yet another reason for asserting our evangelic Lutheran view at the conference.

Quite frankly, I have therefore done everything in my humble powers to have the conference held in a Lutheran country, not in a Reformed or Anglo-Saxon country, however much I respect these fellow Christians and their work. Lutheranism has its particular word to say on these matters, and therefore we also particularly count on your presence and on your statement.

Come over here and help us!

With true respect and good wishes

Sincerely

230. From GUSTAF JOHANSSON[1]

Åbo 10 december 1924.

Vördade Broder.

Hjärtligt tackar jag för den vänliga skrivelsen av den 1 december, vilken dock icke kunnat ändra min övertygelse. I mer än tio år har jag såsom professor i Helsingfors haft att vårda den systematiska teologin och under denna tid har det intrycket blivit outplånligt, att de sociala, ekonomiska och politiska frågorna icke tillhöra kyrkans uppgiftsområde. Då en kyrklig världskonferens sammankallas, som blott handlägger sociala, ekonomiska och politiska frågor, innebär detta, att dessa frågor skulle tillhöra kyrkans uppgift och därmed skulle kyrkan övertaga ett oerhört ansvar. Politiken har länge tjänat egoistiska intressen. Varje folk söker sin egen fördel. Klasshatet och partistriderna hava splittrat det medborgerliga samhället och gjort ett samförstånd omöjligt. Vi hava fått det stela egendomsbegreppet från den romerska rätten. Det gamla förbundets lag gav den fattige mycket skydd. Vart sjunde år fick han söka sig näring på den förmögnes åkerfält. Under jubelåret skulle han återfå sin egendom, om den gått i gäld o.s.v. De humanitära principerna hade bort få inträde hos kristenhetens jurister, men de älskade mera den romerska rättens principer. Och arbetsgivaren behandlade ofta arbetstagaren på ett sätt, som kränkte hans människovärde. Här finnes frön till det klasshat, som härjar folkens hemfrid. Och på det ekonomiska området härskar egennyttan i handel och vandel. Dessa djupa missförhållanden kunna icke under denna världstid övervinnas, ty det onda är en växande makt. Skulle kyrkorna nu värkligen övertaga dessa sociala, ekonomiska och politiska frågor, vilka icke tillhöra henne, men som nu befinna sig i ett läge, där statsmannen icke ser någon utsikt till räddning? Om världskonferensen i Stockholm värkligen ägnar sitt arbete åt lösningen av dessa frågor, framkallar den hos kristenheten den tanken, att de kristna värkligen på fullt allvar böra taga ihop med dessa missförhållanden, men då är det också slut med kristenhetens egentliga uppgift. Den skall varken hava tid, krafter eller stillhet för den andliga tempelbyggnad, som är dess

---

[1] Nathan Söderblom's ecumenical collection, A 11, UUB, typewritten letter.

egentliga uppgift; och då har mänskligheten förlorat hundrafalt mera än den vunnit. Kristus har inte inlåtit sig på dessa sociala, ekonomiska och politiska frågor, ty de tillhöra det gamla, som skall förgås. Såsom bifrågor kunna de ju alltid behandlas på ett kyrkligt möte, men de kunna icke bliva grundfrågor, som uteslutande sysselsätta en allmän kyrklig världskonferens. Den bildstod Nebukadnezar såg, förskingrades såsom agnarna för vinden, och stenen, som krossade den, blev det rike, där allting är nytt. Nöden är stor i världen, och den kristne arbetar såsom medborgare på förbättrandet av det sociala läget, men vid ondskans ständiga tillväxt äger han intet hopp om att dessa skola förnyas, och hans samfund är i det nya Jerusalem.

I företalet till de Schmalkaldiska Artiklarna tänker ju Luther icke på en allmän kristlig och kyrklig världskonferens, och själv hade han helt visst icke infunnit sig till världskonferensen i Stockholm, vars program han ej skulle godkänna. Det är för mig gåtfullt, huru man vid betraktande av det närvarande tidsläget och det ondas stigande tillväxt kan vänta sig någon nytta av en kristlig världskonferens med hänsyn till dessa frågor. Kristus allena kan nyskapa allt. Och den gudomliga lagen lyder: »Om du skiljer det goda från det onda, så skall du vara såsom min mun« (Jer. 15,19). Gud åtskiljer, men människorna sammanblanda. Dessa världskonferenser, som tro sig kunna bringa hjälp åt mänskligheten, äro icke enligt Kristi sinne. I de stora konferenserna plägar icke Gud vara med och detta är dock det första, att Gud är med oss. Protestantismen är splittrad och ett mäktigt strömdrag, som vill göra kristendomen till något av denna världen, rör sig inom den. Denna riktning är den antikristliga, som fräter omkring sig såsom giftet, men Kristi rike är icke av denna världen, och av dess överjordiska kraft beror folkens räddning. Då världskonferensen i Stockholm icke upptager trons frågor[2], kringgår den den djupaste fråga, som borde vid en sådan världskonferens behandlas. Det går icke an att sammanblanda rationalism och kristendom. Och av denna orsak är mitt deltagande i Stockholms världskonferens fullkomligt omöjligt. Jag kan icke arbeta tillsammans med sådana, som förneka Kristi gudom, ty sådana skola också säkert deltaga i mötet. Rationalismen står lägre än katolicismen med all dess vantro, och en världskonferens, i vilken rationalister deltaga med protestanter, befinner sig kraftlös gentemot katolicismen, vilken dock alltid fasthåller det överjordiska i kristendomen. Därför är det fullkomligt fåfängt att vänta mig till predikant vid mötet. Våra livsåskådningar äro i mycket avvikande från varandra. Detta framgår av motiveringen i broschyren »Världskonferens för praktisk kristendom«. Kristi sinnelag och tankar äro nog klara i Skriften. Han vill icke omedelbart införa det väsentligt kristliga i sociala förhållanden. Och det är mig ofattligt, huru alla kristna kyrkor nu borde samman-

---

[2] The last three words are underlined in pencil and the whole sentence is marked by a big exclamation mark on the margin, probably by Söderblom.

komma för att utgrunda, vilka föreskrifter borde givas de kristna med avseende å sociala frågor.

Samvetet är grundkraften i människans ande, men dess odling är alldeles försummad. Det är samvetsgranhet, som framför allt erfordras för våra sociala forhållandens förbättrande. Då den allmänna religiositeten och sedligheten äro gemensamma för kyrkan och staten, har kyrkan försökt uppfostra folken, men dess verksamhet har blivit allt mera tillbakaträngd. På skolans område betonas nu det mångsidiga kunskapsmåttet och metoden. Eleverna äro marionettdockor i lärarens hand. Karaktärsbildningen är skjuten åt sidan, och dessa skolor hava också kommunisterna i sitt program. Principerna äro på så många områden ensidiga, men av världskonferensen kan man icke hoppas någon förbättring i detta hänseende.

En upplösning av det gamla går hastigt framåt och vi kunna icke hejda den, men Kristus gör allting nytt, då Han kommer. Jag har icke velat störa förberedelserna för världskonferensen, men då även den finska kyrkan skulle utse officiella ombud till den, har det varit min plikt att uttala mig. Synbarligen är det aktningen för Sveas vördade ärkebiskop, som föranlett en så talrik anslutning till mötesprogrammet, men då mötet misslyckas, vilka följder skall det hava för kyrkorna? Mycket kan ske till augusti i nästa år och bäst vore det, om ingen världskonferens skulle hållas med detta program. Det smärtar mig att vara av annan åsikt i denna fråga, men jag har bemödat mig att som biskop handla med gott samvete och kan därför icke nu handla annorlunda. Hjärtligt önskar jag min vördade Broder välgång och krafter.

Med högaktning och vänskap
Gustaf Johansson.

Åbo, December 10, 1924.

Esteemed Brother,

I sincerely thank you for your kind letter of Dec. 1, which, however, has not been able to change my conviction. In more than ten years as a professor in Helsinki, I had to take care of systematic theology, and during that time the impression has become ineradicable that social, economic, and political issues do not fall within the scope of the church's mission. If a world conference of churches is convened that only deals with social, economic, and political issues, that implies that these issues should be part of the church's mission, and thereby the church would assume a tremendous responsibility. Politics has long served egoistic interests. Each nation seeks its own advantage. Class hatred and party strife have split civil society and made mutual understanding impossible. We have received the rigid concept of property from Roman law. The law of the old covenant provided great protection to the poor man. Each seventh year he was allowed to look for food on the rich man's field. During the year of jubilee, he was to have his property restored to him, if it had been encumbered, etc.[3] Humanitarian principles should have been allowed access by Christendom's jurists, but they liked the principles of Roman law better. And the employer often treated the employee in a way that violated his human dignity. Here

---

[3] Lev 25.

is the seed of the class hatred which works havoc with the domestic peace of the nations. And in the field of economics, selfishness dominates each and every trade. These profound grievances cannot be overcome in this age, since evil is a growing power. Should the churches now really take on these social, economic, and political issues which do not belong to them but are now in a state in which the statesman sees no chance of salvation? If the world conference in Stockholm really devotes its work to the solution of these problems, it evokes in Christianity the notion that Christians really in all seriousness should cope with these grievances, but that is then also the end of Christianity's original purpose. It will neither have time, strength nor peace of mind for building the spiritual temple[4] which is its proper purpose; and then mankind will have lost a hundred times more than it gained. Christ did not tackle these social, economic, and political issues, for they belong to the old order which is to perish.[5] They can of course always be treated as side issues at a church meeting, but they cannot become basic issues which exclusively occupy a general church world conference. The statue Nebuchadnezzar saw, was swept away like chaff before the wind, and the stone which shattered it became the kingdom where everything is new.[6] Misery is great in the world, and the Christian as a citizen works for the improvement of the social situation, but in view of the continual growth of evil he cherishes no hope that these things will be made new, and his communion is in the new Jerusalem.

In the preface to the Schmalkalden Articles, Luther is of course not thinking of a general Christian and church world conference, and he himself quite certainly would not have attended the world conference in Stockholm, the program of which he would not approve of. It is a mystery to me how one can expect any benefit from a Christian world conference concerning these issues, when contemplating the present state of affairs and the increasing growth of evil. Christ alone can create everything anew. And the divine law runs: »If you distinguish good from evil, you shall serve as my mouthpiece« (Jer 15:19).[7] God distinguishes, but men mix [things] up. These world conferences which believe they can bring relief to mankind are not in accordance with the mind of Christ. At the great conferences God usually is not present; and that God is with us is after all of primary importance. Protestantism is divided, and a powerful undertow aiming to render Christendom something of this world is seething within it. This school of thought is the anti-Christian one which is eroding [everything] around itself like poison, but the kingdom of Christ does not belong to this world,[8] and on its supernatural power the salvation of the peoples depends. Since the world conference in Stockholm does not take up the concerns of faith[9], it dodges the most profound concern that should be treated at such a conference. There is no way of mixing up rationalism and Christianity. And for that reason my participation in Stockholm's world conference is utterly impossible. I cannot collaborate with such people who deny the divinity of Christ, for such people will certainly also participate in the meeting. Rationalism is inferior to Catholicism with all its superstition, and a world conference in which rationalists take part along with Protestants is in a powerless condition over against Catholicism which after all re-

---

[4] Eph 2:21.
[5] Cf. II Cor 5:17.
[6] Nebuchadnezzars dream, Dan 2:31-45.
[7] Free rendering from memory.
[8] John 18:36.
[9] Cf. note 2.

tains the supernatural in Christianity. That is why expecting me to be a preacher at the meeting is completely in vain. Our views of life diverge from each other in many respects. That is evident from the brochure »The World Conference for Practical Christianity«. The mind and thoughts of Christ are surely clear in Scripture. He does not intend to introduce immediately what is essentially Christian into social affairs. It is beyond my comprehension how all Christian churches should now convene in order to fathom which directions should be given to Christians with regard to social issues.

Conscience is the primary force in man's soul, but its cultivation is being totally neglected. It is conscientiousness that is required first of all for the improvement of our social conditions. Since church and state have general religiosity and morality in common, the church has tried to educate the nations, but its activities have been more and more repelled. In school affairs, the emphasis is now on a many-sided range of knowledge and on method. The students are puppets in the teacher's hand. Character formation is being pushed aside, and the communists also have these schools in their program. The principles are one-sided in so many fields, but from the world conference one cannot expect an improvement in this regard.

Dissolution of the old order is rapidly progressing, and we cannot hinder it, but Christ makes everything new when He comes. I did not intend to disturb preparations for the world conference,[10] but since the Finnish church too is supposed to appoint official delegates to it, it was my duty to speak out. Apparently it has been the respect for Svea's[11] revered archbishop which has occasioned such a numerous following for the program of the conference; but in case the meeting turns out a failure, which consequences is that to have for the churches? Much can happen until August of next year, and it would be best if no world conference were held with that program. I deplore being of a different opinion on this matter, but as bishop I have tried to act with a clear conscience, and therefore I cannot act differently now. I sincerely wish my revered Brother well-being and strength.

Respectfully and in friendship,
Gustaf Johansson.

231. To Gustaf Johansson[1]

Upsala 13.12.1924

Högt vördade Ämbetsbroder!
I mitt brev kom jag icke att beröra en viktig sak i min högt vördade Broders meddelande. Jag menar Finlands Biskopskonferens' bristande befogenhet att utse ombud till Stockholms-mötet. Förmodligen föreligger här en rest från den ryska tiden, då väl statsmakten var angelägen om att icke heller Finlands Biskopsko[n]ferens skulle äga alltför stor befogenhet.

[...]

---

[10] Johansson nonetheless agitated vehemently against Söderblom's ecumenical plans in general and the Stockholm conference in particular; cf. Staffan Runestam, *Söderblomsstudier*, Uppsala 2004, 151.

[11] Sweden's.

[1] Nathan Söderblom's ecumenical collection, B 4, UUB, typewritten letter (carbon copy).

Jag vågar antaga att min högt vördade Ämbetsbroder i Åbo och jag äro ense om den utomordentliga vikten av att vid detta möte den evangelisk lutherska kyrkans charisma gör sig fullt ut gällande. Tro vi på sanningen och värdet i vår bekännelse, måste det också för oss vara en helig plikt att göra den gällande i den evangeliska kristenhetens gemenskap.

Detta sker dels kvantitativt, dels kvalitativt. Vad omfånget angår, veta vi redan att lutherdomen i Europa blir åtminstone i det allra närmaste fullständigt företrädd. Vi hava nämligen ännu icke underrättelse från alla, men väl från de allra flesta evangelisk-lutherska kyrkosamfund. Så t.ex. bli samtliga tyska evangelisk lutherska kyrkor företrädda, vidare våra trosfränder i Frankrike, Elsass Lothringen, Jugo-Slavien, Rumänien, Ungern, Tjecko-Slovakiet, Polen, Lettland, Estland, Norge, Danmark, Island, säkerligen även Holland, fastän underrättelse ännu icke föreligger. Vad Ryssland angår, är man ännu oviss om de kunna komma på grund av passvårigheter, men vi hoppas att saken kan ordnas.

[...]

Vad angår representationens kvalitet, så återkommer jag med min djärva, men ingalunda hopplösa inbjudan till kyrkans Primas i Finland att själv personligen komma och tala till Konferensen. Jag erinrar mig livligt hurusom min högt vördade Broder vid det besök jag hade förmånen göra i Åbo för några år tillbaka, talade om sin avsikt att en gång göra ett uttalande rörande det som vi kalla det sociala problemet och kristendomens ställning därtill. Detta tillfälle skulle ju vara det bästa möjliga.

Med de bästa önskningar för Jul och Nyår och med vördnadsfulla hälsningar

Upsala 16.12.1924[2]

Högt vördade Broder!

Jag hade just skrivit inneliggande, då jag erhåller min vördade Broders vänliga brev av 10 december, som jag läst med levande intresse både för auktors och för innehållets skull. Icke skulle jag ytterligare besvära med mitt skriveri, om icke här tydligen förelåge ett missförstånd. I bilagda urkund säges t. ex. så tydligt som möjligt ifrån, att kristendomens tillämpning på dessa sociala och mellanfolkliga förhållanden, som naturligtvis enligt Ditt eget brev äro i mångt och mycket hedniska, ingalunda är huvudsaken i kristendomen. Det ena nödvändiga framhålles så starkt som möjligt. Men här gäller väl om någonsin att det ena göra och det andra icke låta. För min del vågar jag icke inför min Herre och Mästare lägga armarna i kors och beskåda världens gång. Ty Frälsaren talar om surdegen, och alla hans vittnen, som icke konsekvent tillämpa munkidealet i den ena eller den andra formen, hava också hävdat sanningens och kärlekens rätt i alla mänskliga förhållanden. Särskilt gäller detta Martin Luther. Min vördade Broder nämner

[2] Continuation of previous letter. In this case, it is the (typewritten) original the UUB has obtained.

365

företalet till de Schmalkaldiska Artiklarna. Han önskar ju »ein recht christliches Concilium«[3] och han tillägger ju uttryckligen att »Da ist Uneinigkeit der Fürsten und Stände, Wucher und Geiz sind wie eine Sündfluth eingerissen und eitel Recht worden, Mutwill, Unzucht, Uebermuth mit Kleidern, Fressen, Spielen, Prangen mit allerlei Untugend und Bosheit, Ungehorsam der Unterthanen, Gesinde und Erbeiter etz.«

Sådana ting ville han behandla »im Concilio« i stället för vissa ecklesiastiska småsaker, och så tillägger han med sin oförlikneliga korthet ackurat vad som är program för Stockholmsmötet: »Wenn wir zuvor hätten Gottes Gebot und Befehl ausgericht im geistlichen und weltlischen [sic] Stande...« Således skulle Luther säkerligen icke hålla sig undan, utan komma till Stockholm och säga ett ord som hördes över hela världen. Om någonsin behöver världen nu ett oförfärat kristet vittnesmål sådant profeterna och Frälsaren avlade för sin tid. Vad något dylikt kan uträtta, det veta vi ej. Men jag kan åtminstone icke lugna mitt samvete med att ställa mig utanför ansvaret. Och när jag läser inledningen till min vördade Broders sista brev med den för honom egendomliga förmågan att kärnfullt formulera klara tankar, så beklagar jag med svidande saknad att en dylik röst icke i ord eller skrift blir hörd på vårt möte, ty där omordas just de frågor det gäller. Om Kristi sinnelag och tankar råder en bedrövlig oklarhet inom den kyrka som kallar sig med hans namn. Och när skulle världen bättre än nu behöva påminnas om det andliga och eviga och allas vårt ansvar inför Guds dom. Man tror sig ju om att kunna leva och ordna sakerna utan Gud och andligt sinne.

Att mötet icke upptager trosfrågor betyder intet kringgående, utan en klart och medvetet uttalad abetsfördelning. Om huset brinner måste man hjälpas åt att släcka, även om den som hjälper mig med ämbaret skulle i ett och annat tänka olika mot mig, bara vi båda besjälas av den i Kristi efterföljelse självklara plikten att hjälpa.

För min del har jag alltid framhållit vari den djupaste frågan för kristendomen och kyrkan består, och det blir vid Konferensen sörjt för att detta åter och åter inpräglas. Men i mina ögon [sic; läs: öron!] ljuda den gamle utmärglade ungerske prästens ord i Genève 1920 inför dylik tvekan: »Ondskan väntar icke. Skola vi kristna vänta och se på?«

Ja, tillgiv mig detta envishet. Vi hava icke råd att avvara Ärkebiskopen i Åbo. *Besvära Dig icke nu med ett svar*, men låt oss se hur Du känner Dina möjligheter längre fram på våren.

Kanske kommer tilldragelser som ännu brutalare än nu tvinga hopen av kristna till samdräkt och samarbete.

I varje fall känner jag det som en oavvislig plikt att inom denna rörelse i min ringa mån bidraga till att *lutherdomens egendomliga charisma* icke blir oanvänd och obekant utan om möjligt kommer till sin rätt.

---

[3] This and the following sentences are quoted here in the original German by Söderblom; BSLK 411–413. Luther himself says »ein recht frei Concilium« (408) or »ein recht Concilium« (412).

Med uppriktig vördnad och varma välönskningar för den store glädjefes-
ten och det nya året, samt vördsamma hälsningar till de Dina är jag med
oförbätterlig känsla av situationens fruktansvärda allvar
Din tillgivne
Nathan Söderblom

Uppsala, December 13, 1924
Highly esteemed fellow bishop,
In my letter I forgot to mention an important point in my highly esteemed Brother's
message. I mean the lacking authority of Finland's conference of bishops to appoint
delegates to the Stockholm meeting. Presumably this is a relic from the Russian
times when the executive of the state apparently was anxious that Finland's conference of bishops should not have too much authority either.
    ... [A lengthy passage on the procedure of selecting delegates observed in Swe-
den]
    I dare assume that my highly esteemed fellow Bishop in Åbo and I are in agree-
ment on the extraordinary importance of bringing fully to bear the charisma of the
evangelic Lutheran church at this conference. If we do believe in the truth and value
of our confession, then it must also be a sacred duty for us to bring it to bear in the
communion of Protestant Christianity.
    This is coming about partly in terms of quantity, partly in terms of quality. As
for the size, we already know that Lutheranism in Europe will be at least very nearly
completely represented. For we have reports not from all, but nearly every single
evangelic Lutheran church body. Thus e.g. all of the German evangelic Lutheran
churches will be represented, furthermore our fellow believers in France, Alsace-
Lorraine, Yugo-Slavia, Romania, Hungary, Czecho-Slovakia, Poland, Lithuania,
Estonia, Norway, Denmark, Iceland, certainly also the Netherlands, though reports are not yet available. As for Russia, it is as yet uncertain whether they can
come, because of passport complications, but we hope that this can be settled.
    ... [On other delegations]
    As for the quality of representation, I come again with my bold but by no means
hopeless invitation to the Primate of the church in Finland to come himself in person and to speak to the conference. I vividly recall my highly respected Brother, at a
visit to Åbo I had the privilege to pay a couple of years ago, talking about his intention some time to deliver a statement concerning what we call the social problem
and Christianity's position towards it. Well, this should be the best conceivable occasion to do so.
    With best wishes for Christmas and the New Year and with repectful regards

Uppsala, December 16, 1924
Highly esteemed Brother,
I had just written the enclosed when I received my esteemed Brother's kind letter of
December 10, which I have read with vivid interest, both on account of its author
and of its content. Never would I further bother you with my letter-writing, had
there not occurred an obvious misunderstanding. In the attached document for example, it is being affirmed in the clearest possible terms that Christianity's application to these social and international conditions, which are of course, according to
your own letter, pagan in many respects, is by no means the main point in Christian-

367

ity. The one thing that is necessary[4] is pointed out as forcefully as possible. Here indeed though, if ever, it is a matter of having to do the one and not omit the other. For my part, facing my Lord and Master, I dare not fold my arms and gaze at the course of the world. For the Redeemer speaks about the leaven,[5] and all his witnesses who do not consistently follow the monastic ideal in one form or another, also asserted the right of truth and love in all human affairs. This is particularly true of Martin Luther. My esteemed Brother mentions the preface to the Schmalkalden Articles. He [Luther] is indeed pleading for »a real Christian Council«, and he expressly adds that »There is discord of princes and estates; usury and greed have spread like a deluge and have become completely legal; recklessness, fornication, luxury, and haughtiness in clothing, gluttony, gambling, ostentatiousness along with all kinds of vices and maliciousness, disobedience of subjects, servants, and workers etc.«[6]

Such things he wants to treat »at the Council«, instead of certain ecclesiastical paraphernalia, and then he adds in his incomparable terseness precisely what the program is for the Stockholm conference: »If we had first fulfilled God's commandment and order in the spiritual and the worldly estates...« Hence, Luther would certainly not stay aloof but come to Stockholm and say a word that would be heard across the whole world. If ever, the world now needs an undaunted Christian witness such as the prophets and the Redeemer bore for their time. What something like that can achieve, we do not know. Anyway though, I cannot calm my conscience by taking my position apart from responsibility. And when I read the introduction to my respected Brother's last letter with his characteristic capacity for vigorously formulating clear thoughts, I deplore with deep regret that such a voice will not be heard at our meeting either in speech or in writing, as precisely the decisive issues are being discussed there. As for the mind and thought of Christ, there is a distressing lack of clarity in the church called by His name. And when would the world more than now need to be reminded of the spiritual and eternal responsibility of us all before God's judgment? For people believe they can live and arrange things without God and a spiritual mind.

The fact that the conference does not take up questions of faith implies no dodging but a clear and deliberately announced division of labor. When the house is burning, one must be helped in extinguishing the flames, even if the person helping me with the bucket may oppose me in his thinking in one respect or another, if only both of us are inspired by the duty of helping which is a matter of course in Christ's discipleship.

For my part, I always pointed out what constitutes the most profound quest for Christianity and the church, and it will be seen to it at the Conference that this point be driven home time and again. But in my ears, the words of the old emaciated Hungarian pastor in Geneva in 1920 are ringing over against such hesitation: »Evil does not wait. Shall we Christians wait and look on?«

Well, forgive me that stubbornness. We cannot afford to do without the Archbishop in Åbo. *Do not bother with a reply now*, but let us see how you will view your options later on in the spring.[7]

---

[4] Luke 10:42.

[5] Matth 13:33.

[6] These quotes and the next one are rendered in the original German. *BSLK* 411-413.

[7] Söderblom was in the end unsuccessful in his effort to win Johansson for his conference. Jaakko Gummerus (1870-1933), bishop of Porvoo 1920, of Tampere since 1923, did take part,

Perhaps events are going to occur that will force the Christian flock even more brutally towards unanimity and cooperation.

In any case, I consider it an irrefutable duty in my humble measure to make a contribution in this movement to the effect that *Lutheranism's peculiar charisma* be not unused and unknown but if possible receive due recognition.

With sincere respect and very best wishes for the great festival of joy and the New Year, and with respectful regards to your loved ones, I am with an incorrigible sense of the situation's formidable seriousness

Yours truly,

Nathan Söderblom

232. From FRIEDRICH HEILER[1]

Marburg, den 19. Dezember 1924

Hochverehrter, hochwürdigster Herr Erzbischof,

für die freundlichen Worte, welche Sie mir in The Review of the Churches gewidmet haben, sage ich Ihnen herzlichen Dank.[2] Sie haben mich um so mehr gefreut, als ich solch liebevolle und verständnisinnige Aeusserungen selten zu hören bekomme. Ich stehe vielmehr ständig im heftigsten Kreuzfeuer römischer und protestantischer Kritik und habe äusserlich und innerlich viel unter den menschlich so betrübenswerten Anfeindungen zu leiden. Es ist sehr tragisch, dass nahezu alle meine früheren »modernistischen« Gesinnungsgenossen und engen Freunde gegen mich geschrieben haben und zwar teilweise in höchst ungerechter und kränkender Weise: Philipp Funk, der ehemalige Herausgeber des »Neuen Jahrhunderts«, mein eigener Vetter Prof. J. N. Brunner, Dr. Jos. Bernhart und mein früherer Lieblingslehrer an der Münchener Universität und intimer Freund Karl Adam, jetzt Professor in Tübingen. Letzterer hat gegen mich – und zwar auf höheren hierarchischen Wink – ein grosses Buch über »Das Wesen des Katholizismus« geschrieben,[3] für das jetzt in der gesamten katholischen Presse eine kolossale Propaganda gemacht wird. Dazu der systematische Feldzug der Jesuiten gegen mich. Auf der andern Seite die immer wiederkehrenden Verdächtigungen meiner »kryptokatholischen« Tendenzen. Ich habe mir schon oft überlegt, ob es nicht besser wäre, mich diesem unruhigen Getriebe zu ent-

---

along with a number of others, but not as an official Finnish delegation, because of their archbishop's relentless resistance. Gummerus became one of the most faithful advocates of Söderblom's cause in Finland. Cf. Sundkler, op. cit. 358.

[1] Nathan Söderblom's collection of letters, from foreigners, UUB, typewritten letter.

[2] Cf. letter no. 226.

[3] Karl Adam, *Das Wesen des Katholizismus*, Düsseldorf 1924 (12th ed. 1949). Adam (1876–1966) was a lecturer in Munich from 1908–1917 and from 1919–1949 professor of dogmatics in Tübingen. Philipp Funk (1884–1937), studied in Munich 1903–1907, professor of history in Freiburg 1929–1937; Joseph Bernhart (1881–1969), studied theology in Munich 1900–1904, married in 1913 which meant automatic excommunication, prolific writer, rehabilitated by his church in 1942. I have been unable to verify either the personal data of J. N. Brunner or the articles of the three.

ziehen und aus Deutschland fortzugehen. Wenn es nicht wegen meiner bei-
den Kinder so schwierig wäre, so würde ich mich wohl entschliessen, als
Missionar nach Indien zu gehen (vielleicht im Dienst einer anglikanischen
Missionsgesellschaft).

Ich bin eben dabei, mit Hilfe des Materials, das mir Frau Parker geliefert
hat, einen Artikel gegen die Jesuiten zu schreiben, in dem ich vieles aufdek-
ken werde. Wenn Sie es wünschen, so kann ich Ihnen für eine schwedische
Veröffentlichung einen Durchschlag zusenden.

Ich wäre Ihnen nun ausserordentlich dankbar, wenn Sie mich umgehend
wissen liessen, welche Schritte Sie selbst in dieser Angelegenheit unternommen haben, wen Sie mit einer Untersuchung an Ort und Stelle beauftragt
haben und wann etwa Sie Antwort aus Indien zu erhalten hoffen. Vielleicht
haben Sie sich ebenfalls an Frau Parker gewandt. Jedenfalls wäre ich Ihnen
für sachdienliche Mitteilungen sehr dankbar.

Nun wünsche ich Ihnen und Ihrer werten Familie ein frohes und friedvol-
les Christfest und verbleibe mit verehrungsvollen Grüssen von meiner Frau
und mir
Ihr ergebenster
Friedrich Heiler.

233. To Friedrich Heiler[1]

Upsala den 23 december 1924
Min käre vän,
Hjärtligt tack för brevet. Pilgrimskapet kan vara tungt i världen för en Fräl-
sarens lärjunge, som haft den smärtsamma ehuru för sina medkristna oänd-
ligen värdefulla lotten att i sin person nedbryta skiljemuren och ena det
bästa i evangelisk och romersk mystik. Jag har själv brukat säga, då jag blivit och blir häftigt angripen från båda sidor, att den som blir knuffad från
både höger och vänster, bör komma att gå vägen rakt fram. Men det är
ganska bittert ibland, och där en rätt evangelisk ande råder blir hjärtats gemenskap härigenom innerligare.

Vi ha icke råd att mista Eder till Indien, huru väl jag än förstår den känsla, som drager Eder dit. Eder mission här hemma är större än någonsin.

Tack för »Das Suchen nach Gott«. Jag har just nedskrivit en principiell
studie om den jesuitiska polemiken och vore tacksam erhålla avskrift av
Eder artikel.

Jag skriver genast till vår ledande missionär i Indien Herman Sandegren,
som, om han fått mitt brev litet tidigare[,] skulle ha kunnat göra en undersökning på ort och ställe, men nu har satt i gång med en undersökning med
hjälp av andra missionärer i närheten av de trakter där tilldragelserna skola
ha ägt rum.

---

[1] Fr. Heiler's papers (Ms. 999), Univ. Library Marburg, typewritten letter.

Med varma önskningar om en god jul och ett gott nytt år är jag Eder tillgivne
i innerlig gemenskap i kärlek, hopp och tro[2]
Nathan Söderblom

Uppsala, den 23. Dezember 1924

Mein lieber Freund,
herzlichen Dank für Ihren Brief. Die Pilgerschaft kann in der Welt schwer sein für
einen Jünger des Erlösers, dem das schmerzhafte, aber für seine Mitchristen unendlich wertvolle Los zuteil geworden ist, in seiner Person die Scheidewand niederzu-
reißen und das Beste von evangelischer und römischer Mystik zu vereinigen. Ich
pflegte selbst zu sagen, wenn ich von beiden Seiten heftig angegriffen wurde und
werde, dass derjenige, der von der rechten wie von der linken Seite angerempelt
wird, schon seinen Weg geradeaus gehen wird. Das ist freilich manchmal ziemlich
bitter, und wo ein rechter evangelischer Geist herrscht, wird die Gemeinschaft der
Herzen dadurch umso inniger.

Wir können es uns nicht erlauben, Sie an Indien zu verlieren, so gut ich auch das
Gefühl verstehe, das Sie dorthin zieht. Ihre Mission hier zu Hause ist wichtiger als
je.

Danke für »Das Suchen nach Gott«[3]. Ich habe gerade eine prinzipielle Studie
über die jesuitische Polemik niedergeschrieben und wäre dankbar, eine Abschrift
Ihres Artikels zu erhalten.[4]

Ich schreibe sofort an unseren leitenden Missionar in Indien Herman Sandegren,[5] der, wenn er meinen Brief etwas früher bekommen hätte, eine Untersuchung
an Ort und Stelle hätte durchführen können, aber jetzt eine Untersuchung in Gang
gesetzt hat mit Hilfe anderer Missionare in der Nähe der Gegend, wo die Ereignisse
sich zugetragen haben sollen.[6]

Mit herzlichen Wünschen für frohe Weihnachten und ein gutes Neues Jahr bin
ich Ihnen verbunden
in enger Gemeinschaft in Liebe, Hoffnung und Glaube[7], Ihr
Nathan Söderblom

---

[2] This line is added in handwriting.

[3] Sadhu Sundar Singh, *Das Suchen nach Gott. Gedanken über Hinduismus, Buddhismus, Islam und Christentum*, tr. by Fr. Heiler, München 1925.

[4] The Swedish version of Heiler's article appeared in the newspaper *Svenska Dagbladet* on
May 3, 1925 under the heading »Jesuiternas förföljelse av Sundar Singh« [The persecution of
Sundar Singh by the Jesuits].The German original is »Der Streit um Sundar Singh. 3. Der Feldzug der Jesuiten gegen den Sadhu,« in: *ChW* 39/1925, 78-84.118-127.155-164. Söderblom's
article either is: »Ett försvar för Sundar Singh av vår ärkebiskop. Systematisk jesuitisk förföljelse,« in: *Svenska Dagbladet* of Nov. 2, 1924 – though it was not »just written down« – or perhaps more likely »Striden om den kristne Sadhun« (The Debate on the Christian Sadhu),
Stockholms-Tidningen of April 29, 1925, in which he made use of the material requested from
Heiler. In either case, there is a remaining uncertainty, caused by the predicate »fundamental
study« as applied to a newspaper article.

[5] Herman Sandegren (1881-1938), director of missions in India.

[6] This refers to healings, among other things, that Sundar Singh was reported to have performed.

[7] See note 2.

234. From FRIEDRICH HEILER[1]

Marburg/Lahn, den 10.März 1925.

Hochverehrter, Hochwürdigster Herr Erzbischof,
haben Sie vielen herzlichen Dank für die große Freundlichkeit, in der Sie
mir von der Olaus Petri-Stiftung einen so hohen Beitrag für meine Nachforschungen in Indien vermittelt haben. Ich habe mittlerweile viel neues Be-
weismaterial aus Indien erhalten, das ich in einer eigenen Broschüre heraus-
gebe.[2]

... [Details on this material]

Ich übersandte Ihnen bereits je 5 Exemplare der »Christlichen Welt« wie
der »Münchener Neuesten Nachrichten«,[3] in denen meine bisherige Auseinandersetzung mit den Jesuiten erschienen ist, und werde Ihnen auch von
allen weiteren Veröffentlichungen die gleiche Zahl zugehen lassen.

Eben weilt in meinem Hause ein sehr tüchtiger römisch-katholischer
Modernist, Dr. Joh. Hessen, Dozent der Philosophie an der Universität
Köln. Er ist Priester und wird von den kirchlichen Behörden sehr verfolgt;
die Oberen des Jesuitenordens haben ihn bereits für ihre Ordensmitglieder
als vitandus[4] erklärt. Sein Büchlein »Gotteskindschaft« ist von seinem Bischof der Indexkongregation übersandt worden.[5] Da er die Katastrophe für
unvermeidlich hält, erklärte er mir, dass er sich nicht scheuen würde, an
der Stockholmer ökumenischen Konferenz teilzunehmen. Da wohl wenige
römisch-katholische Priester, wenn überhaupt einer, kommen werden,
möchte ich Sie fragen, ob es Ihnen nicht erwünscht wäre, dass Dr. Hessen
als römischer Katholik daran teilnähme. Er ist freilich arm und könnte
nicht für die ganzen Reisekosten aufkommen. Aber vielleicht läge es in Ihrer Hand, ihm die Teilnahme zu ermöglichen. Ich habe ihm gesagt, er
möchte verschiedene seiner Schriften Ihnen senden. Schon vor Jahren ist
eine seiner philosophischen Arbeiten von der Kantgesellschaft preisgekrönt
worden. Er wirkt heute in Deutschland sehr für die Verbreitung Tyrrell'-
scher[6] Gedanken.

Nochmals sage ich Ihnen herzlichen Dank für alle Ihre Freundlichkeit
und grüsse Sie und Ihre verehrte Familie vielmals.

Ihr dankbar ergebener

Friedrich Heiler

---

[1] Nathan Söderblom's collection of letters, from foreigners, UUB, typewritten letter.
[2] Friedrich Heiler, *Apostel oder Betrüger? Dokumente zum Sadhustreit*, München 1925. With
XV + 191 pages, it is not exactly a brochure.
[3] Cf. letter no. 225, n. 2, and previous letter, n. 4.
[4] Latin: to be avoided.
[5] Johannes Hessen (1889–1971), professor of philosophy in Cologne. Because of his critical
view of official Catholic doctrine, he never became full professor, although he was an excellent
representative of his field and the author of many widely read books. He was forbidden by the
Nazis to speak in public and to write. On his 80th birthday, he was named honorary prelate by
the Vatican. His book *Gotteskindschaft* (Bücher der Wiedergeburt 10) was published in Breslau, 1924 (2nd ed. 1924).
[6] Cf. letter no. 46, n. 3.

[Handwritten postscript concerning the Sundar Singh affair]

235. From Selma Lagerlöf[1]

Mårbacka Sunne 25.3.1925.

Min käre Ärkebiskop!
Tack för brevet. Det var roligt att få höra litet om kandidaterna.
...
Jag är glad, att nu samtidigt få tillfälle att tacka för din bok. När vi rå-
kades i julas visste jag inte om att jag hade fått den, den låg här på Mårbacka då. Jag tror, att jag kan intet bättre säga än att jag önskar, att du
måtte få styrka och medgång till att genomföra ditt kall som försonare och
förenare. Jag har ofta under läsningen känt mig rörd och tacksam över denna din verksamhet. Du skall få se, att du i sommar kommer ett gott stycke
väg. Det låter visst förfärligt dumt, men när jag läste boken, så tänkte jag
som Överstelöjtnant Duwa i Fänrik Stål: »Gud skydde den ädle gossen, han
för arméer en gång.« Du är nog också kallad att föra arméer, men det for-
dras så otroliga krafter därtill i våra dagar[,] ett arbete utan rast och ro, så
att jag frågar mig hur du skall stå ut.
Med de bästa hälsningar till din hustru
Din tillgivna
Selma Lagerlöf.

Mårbacka Sunne, March 25, 1925.

My dear Archbishop,
Thank you for your letter. It was nice to hear a bit about the candidates.[2]
... [on the candidates for the Academy]
I am glad that I now simultaneously have the opportunity to thank you for your
book.[3] When we met at Christmas time, I did not know that I had received it; it was
lying here at Mårbacka then. I guess I cannot say anything better than that I wish
you may have strength and success in fulfilling your calling as a reconciler and unit-
er. When reading [your book], I often felt moved and grateful for that activity of
yours. You will see that you shall advance a good deal in the summer. It certainly
sounds terribly stupid, but when I was reading your book, I thought like Lieutenant
Colonel Duwa i Fänrik Stål: »May God protect the magnanimous boy, he will lead
armies some time.«[4] You have also been called to lead armies, but such unbelievable

---

[1] Selma Lagerlöf (1858-1940), renowned Swedish author, Nobel Prize for literature 1903,
member of the Swedish Academy as first woman 1914. – Nathan Söderblom's ecumenical collection, UUB, handwritten letter.
[2] There was a vacancy in the Swedish Academy after the death of bishop Gottfrid Billing.
Söderblom had characterized the candidates in his letter of March 20.
[3] This is probably Från Upsala to Rock Island. En predikofärd i Nya Världen [From Uppsala
to Rock Island. A sermon itinerary in the New World], Stockhom 1924.
[4] Fänrik Ståls Sägner (Cadet Stål's Tales) is a humorous epic by the Swedish-writing Finnish
author Johan Ludvig Runeberg (1804-1877), glorifying the Finnish victories over Russia in the
war of 1808/1809. It was published in two parts, in 1848 and 1860: Samlade skrifter 5, Hel-

energies are required for that these days, work without rest and repose, that I ask myself how you will endure.

With best regards to your wife,

yours sincerely,

Selma Lagerlöf.

236. To Selma Lagerlöf[1]

Upsala 3 april 1925

Kära ädla Selma!

Du skriver till mig som en själasörjare, Din hjärtlighet fyller själen med ljus och värme, väl behövliga, då främst den egna otillräckligheten, därnäst levnadens trångmål, därnäst det ofattligt djärva företaget over Evne, därnäst övriga kallelsens svårigheter förmörka utsikten åtminstone om morgnarna, innan man hunnit bedja, läsa, arbeta och erfara luftens och jordens härlighet. –

[…]

Med sann vördnad

Din tillgivne

Nathan Söderblom

Uppsala, April 3, 1925

Dear magnanimous Selma,

You write to me like a pastoral counselor, your cordiality fills the soul with light and warmth, well needed, when first and foremost one's own inadequacy, then the hardships of life, then the incredibly audacious undertaking beyond [one's] capability,[2] then the other difficulties of [one's] calling darken the view at least in the mornings, before one has had time to pray, read, work, and experience the glory of the air and the earth.

[On the chances of the candidates for membership in the Academy]

With true respect

yours sincerely,

Nathan Söderblom

---

singfors 1974. The quote is from Part II, p.77, verses 71 f., where the young Count of Schwerin is lauded by Lt. Colonel Drufva for his heroism. (Selma Lagerlöf obviously did not have in mind that according to the poem, the young soldier dies in action shortly afterwards, cf. pp.78f., verses 89–136.)

[1] Nathan Söderblom's ecumenical collection, UUB, handwritten letter.

[2] Beyond capability: An allusion to the drama Over Ævne (1883.1895) by the Norwegian playwright Bjørnstjerne Bjørnson (1832–1910), a popular contemporary of Hendrik Ibsen and Nobel Prize winner in 1903 (here in Danish spelling, »over Evne«). The central personage of the drama's first part is a pious pastor and perpetrator of miracles, Adolf Sang, whose faith lets him appear beyond reach for human capabilities and makes him a formidable challenge to his family and colleagues. (B. Bjørnsons Samlede Værker 8, 5–49 and 11, 5–90, Oslo 1932).

237. To Eivind Berggrav[1]

Upsala 8.4.1925
Broder!
[...]
Religionens terskel är ju en av de böcker som man läser som ett brev, i sanning ett innehållsrikt brev. Tanken kraftig och originell. Särskilt beundrar jag självbehärskningen att icke medtaga något av det som ligger mycket nära till hands, särskilt för teologer, men som icke är nödvändigt för tankegångens genomförande. Boken ger tankar och väcker tankar och är högst nödvändig för vår tid. Tag till exempel sidan 65 om andelivets primat även när det gäller naturvetenskapens upptäckter. Min vana trogen har jag illustrerat boken med understrykningar, och det är en sådan bok, till vilken man gärna återvänder för att friska upp sin tanke och sin själ. Sidan 240 tänker jag på Luthers ord om Heiligtümer, reliker, i utläggningen av fjärde budet. Han säger att relikerna hava en dubbel egenskap /likaså föräldrarna/ att dels väcka bävan och fruktan, dels draga till sig. Sådan är ju det heligas egenart, och jag förstår inte varför inte Otto i stället för de konstiga namnen nöjer sig helt enkelt med begreppet »det heliga«. Aldrig har jag tänkt på härledningen av »sublim«, sidan 169. Den säger ju hela saken.

Detta är ett mycket ofullständigt tack, överlupen som jag är med allehanda sysslor. Det är uppfriskande och välgörande att läsa ett arbete som bryter sig fram med möda och kraft på en egen bana i stället för att köra med snabbare eller långsammare takt på sönderkörda och nödtorftigt reparerade vägar. En friskhet erhåller boken också genom de egna iakttagelserna till exempel om hästens psykologi. Vi hava ju så oändligt mycket att lära av det som vi ständigt se och som ingen därför märker.

Med hjärtligt tack och välönskan
Din tillgivne
Nathan Söderblom

Uppsala, April 8, 1925
Brother!
... [On a Norwegian hymn Söderblom wanted to include in his planned ecumenical hymnbook for the Stockholm conference]
Religionens terskel [The Threshold to Religion][2] certainly is one of the books one reads like a letter, a letter truly rich in content. Strong and original thinking. I admire in particular the self-restraint of not taking up any of the things that are so close at hand, especially for theologians, but are not necessary for pursuing your line of thought. The book offers thought and provokes thought and is urgently needed in our time. Take for instance p.65 on the primacy of spiritual life even when

---

[1] Riksarkivet, Oslo, Pa-0320: Berggrav, Eivind, Del 1 – avlevering 1975–1986, korrespondanse, eske nr. 5; typewritten letters.
[2] Eivind Berggrav, *Religionens terskel. Ett bidrag til granskningen av religionens sjelelige frambrudd*, Kristiania [Oslo] 1924 (German transl. by V. H. Günther: *Der Durchbruch der Religion im menschlichen Seelenleben*, Göttingen 1929).

it comes to the discoveries of natural science. True to my habit, I illustrated the book with underlinings; it is a book of the kind one likes to return to in order to reinvigorate one's mind and one's soul. On p. 240 I think of Luther's words on *Heiligtümer*, relics, in his interpretation of the fourth commandment. He is saying that relics have a twofold quality (just as parents do): they arouse trembling and fear on the one hand and allure on the other.[3] Such is, of course, the character of the Holy, and I do not understand why Otto does not quite simply content himself with the notion of »the Holy«, instead of those odd terms.[4] Never did I think of your derivation of »sublime«, p. 169; it really says it all.[5]

This is a very incomplete way of saying thanks, overrun as I am by all kinds of activities. It is refreshing and beneficial to read a work which is laboriously and forcefully pioneering on a track of its own instead of running more quickly or more slowly on run-down and barely repaired roads. The book receives freshness also from your own observations, e. g. on horse psychology. We do have to learn such an infinite amount from what we are seeing all the time and which therefore no one is taking note of.

With many thanks and best wishes,
yours sincerely,
Nathan Söderblom

238. From RUDOLF OTTO[1]

Marburg, Sybelstr. 8.   1 5 25

Verehrter und lieber Herr Erzbischof.

Wir bedauern hier in Marburg außerordentlich die Auswahl von Abgesandten, die der Kirchentag zur Stockholmer Konferenz senden wird. Grade die Kreise, die den Gedanken dieser Konferenz am meisten vertreten, der Kreis um Rade, Hermelink,[2] ich selber, und die uns nahe Stehenden, sind gänzlich ausgeschaltet. Und die Auswahl selber ist in vielen Hinsichten zu bemängeln. Wir möchten Sie bitten, als Vertreter unseres Kreises unserm Kollegen Hermelink irgendwie die Möglichkeit zu verschaffen, in irgend einer

---

[3] Cf. Martin Luther, *Von den guten Werken* (1520), WA 6 (202–276), 251,5–12: »Gleich als wir heyligthum ehren mit furcht, und doch nit flihen davor als vor einer straff, sondern mehr hyntzu dringen«, just as we revere a relic with anxiety, yet do not flee from it as from a punishment. Later on, Luther reinterpreted the medieval term *Heiligtum*, cf. *Großer Katechismus* (Larger Catechism, 1529), BSLK 590, 31f, identifying it with the Word of God.

[4] The »odd terms« are *mysterium tremendum* and *fascinans*, cf. Rudolf Otto, *Das Heilige. Über das Irrationale in der Idee des Göttlichen und sein Verhältnis zum Rationalen*, 10th ed. Breslau 1923, 13–27. 39–53.

[5] Berggrav interprets »sublime« as »exalted« in the sense of beyond the limits of human understanding, both enchanting and repelling. This reminds one of Söderblom's own interpretation of the holy as both inaccessible and inescapable: *Natürliche Religion und Religionsgeschichte* (BRW I/1), Stockholm 1913, 109 (published before Otto's book).

[1] Nathan Söderblom's ecumenical collection, A 19, UUB, typewritten letter.

[2] For Martin Rade, cf. letter no. 88, n. 3; Heinrich Hermelink, (1877–1958), professor of church history in Marburg 1916–1935 (ousted by the Nazis), then pastor in Württemberg. He is known, inter al., for his studies on Christian denominations.

376

Form an den Sitzungen der Konferenz teilzunehmen und ihm in Stockholm bei Freunden ein Unterkommen zukommen zu lassen. Wir hoffen, daß er als Berichterstatter für die Frankfurter Zeitung, die Vossische Zeitung und die Christliche Welt nach Stockholm kommen wird. Aber das genügt nicht. Er müßte auch Gelegenheit haben, enger mit den Arbeiten der Konferenz vertraut zu werden, als das ein Berichterstatter kann.

Unsere Meinung ist, daß die Konferenz erst dann eine sichere Grundlage hat, wenn neben der griechischen und der anglikanischen Gruppe die protestantische Gruppe von Lutheranern, Reformierten und Unierten[3] und der aus der deutschen und calvinischen Reformation hervorgegangenen Protestanten sich als fester zusammengeschlossene Untergruppe der Konferenz einfügt, und wir wünschen, einen solchen Zusammenschluß des Protestantismus in der Welt im angegebenen Sinne herbeizuführen, nicht um die weiter greifenden Ziele Ihrer Konferenz zu stören, sondern grade, um sie sicherer zu unterbauen.[4] Und wir hoffen dabei sehr auf Ihre Hilfe. Unser ›Marburger Plan‹, im Jubeljahre des Marburger Religionsgespräches hier eine Tagung des Weltprotestantismus zu haben, um das zu stande zu bringen, was damals mißlang, nämlich eine Einigung des Protestantismus in engerer Fühlungnahme seiner zerstreuten Gruppen, wird Ihnen bereits bekannt sein.[5] Auf meiner Amerikareise im letzten Herbste habe ich auch die Vertreter des Federal council dafür zu interessieren versucht. Und ich hoffe, daß dieselben nach der Stockholmer Konferenz uns besuchen werden. Besonders würden wir uns freuen, wenn daran dann auch Schweden teilnehmen würden.

Inzwischen grüßen wir Sie herzlich und wünschen der Tagung den besten Erfolg.

Ihr aufrichtig ergebener
R. Otto.

239. To Paul Althaus[1]

7/5 1925

Sehr geehrter lieber Herr Professor.
Während meiner Reise durch das Sachsenland, stand das geistige und kör-

---

[3] The church of the *Altpreußische Union* united the Lutheran majority and the Calvinist minority in Prussia into a single church body in 1817.

[4] This intention could be read as an institutional implementation of Söderblom's idea of evangelic catholicity; cf. letter no. 97, n. 3.

[5] This conference did not come about, possibly because Otto retired for health reasons in 1929. The earlier event he refers to here, is the failed *Marburger Religionsgespräch*, Marburg dialogue on religion, between Luther, Zwingli and others, in 1529, which was intended to bridge the gap between the differing interpretations of the Lord's Supper.

[1] For Paul Althaus, cf. letter no. 221, n. 7. – Nathan Söderblom's collection of letters, to Swedes and foreigners, UUB, typewritten final draft with handwritten corrections.

perliche Bild Ihres liebevollen und geliebten Vaters immer vor meiner Augen, weil ich in Dresden von seiner Heimberufung zu meinem Schmerzen erfahren hatte. Ich empfand seine Nähe wie nie, seit den Jahren wo ich die Reinheit seines feinen, innigen Wesens geniessen konnte in Leipzig, in der Mozartstrasse und sonst.[2] Nirgendwo habe ich ein innigeres Familienverhältniss gespürt. Daher sind wir von der Härte der Prüfungen der letzten Jahre doppelt und schmerzlich berührt worden.

Nach meiner Heimkehr bekam ich Ihren schönen Brief und danke Ihnen für diesen Beweis Ihrer Freundschaft, die ich hoffe mit Ihnen auch persönlich in der Zukunft pflegen zu dürfen.

Mit Dr. Kapler[3] und anderen Vertretern der Deutsch-evangelischen Christenheit in der Konferenz für Praktisches Christentum, die in Stockholm 19–30 August stattfinden wird, habe ich die Möglichkeit und unsere sehnliche Hoffnung ausgesprochen, Sie, Herr Professor, in der Deutschen Delegation rechnen zu dürfen, und zwar Sie bei der Konferenz als Verkünder des Evangeliums in Anspruch nehmen zu können.

Wir senden Ihnen unsere ehrerbietige und herzliche Grüssen und an Ihrer Frau Mutter. Gott führt seine Freunde sonderbar[.] Und seien Sie, mit allen Ihren Lieben herzlichst begrüsst von Ihrem treu ergebener

240. To Rudolf Otto[1]

Upsala den 6. Mai 1925

Sehr verehrter Professor und Freund!

Schon längst habe ich nach der Wahl über die deutsche Delegation mit Herrn Dr. Kapler vertraulich gesprochen. Er scheint mir als ein sehr objektiver und gerechter Mensch, und selbstverständlich habe ich ja gar kein Recht die Wahl zu beeinflussen. Eine jede Kirchengemeinschaft wählt selbst und ich glaube, dass die deutsche Delegation in einer gewissenhaften Weise gewählt worden ist. Aber ich kenne das ungemein wertvolle und kenntnisreiche Interesse [,das] der grossen Sache von Seiten der Marburger entgegengebracht wird. Leider waren schon bei meinem Gespräch mit Herrn Dr. Kapler die Ersatzmänner zum grossen Teile gewählt worden. Ich brauche Ihnen aber nicht zu sagen wie gern wir Sie, Dr. Rade und Professor Hermelink bei uns in Stockholm empfangen möchten. Aber wir müssen die Sache loyal nach den längst festgestellten Regeln behandeln.

Ich werde noch einmal mit Dr. Kapler die Sache besprechen und unter al-

---

[2] Paul Althaus sen. (1861–1925) was professor of systematic and practical theology in Göttingen 1899–1912 and of systematic theology and New Testament Leipzig from 1912 onwards, and thus a colleague of Söderblom when he taught history of religions there from 1912–1914.
[3] Hermann Kapler (1867–1941), president of the *Deutscher evangelischer Kirchenausschuss* (German Protestant Church Executive Committee) from 1925–1933.

[1] Nathan Söderblom's ecumenical collection, B 7, UUB, typewritten letter (carbon copy). This letter is missing in Otto's papers in Marburg.

len Umständen einen Form finden um Professor Hermelink als Teilnehmer der Konferenz rechnen zu dürfen. Immer habe ich gedacht bei dieser Gelegenheit meinen hochzuverehrenden und um die Einheit und Liebe so hochverdienten Freund Martin Rade hier zu sehen.

Eine Gesamtorganization der evangelischen Welt ist eine notwendige aber ungemein schwierige und empfindliche Sache, welche nur durch Anziehung und Organizierung aller lebendigen Zellen der evangelischen Welt möglich wird. Die Zentralstelle in Zürich hat einen beträchtlichen Beginn gemacht.[2] Es freut mich, dass die Marburger Fakultät die Sache am Herzen trägt, und ich hoffe, dass ich einmal Gelegenheit finden möchte mit Ihnen eingehend zu sprechen über die verschiedenen Wege eine Gesamtorganization zu schaffen. Mich selbst hat die Sache seit Jahren in Gebet und Handeln beschäftigt, und ungemein sympathisch ist es Marburg als Einheitspunkt nicht nur als Scheidelinie betrachten zu dürfen.

Mit guten Grüssen bin ich, verehrter Herr Professor und Freund,
Ihr sehr ergebener

241. From SELMA LAGERLÖF[1]

Mårbacka Sunne 14.5.1925.

Käre Ärkebiskop!
Förlåt mig om jag frågar dumt, men jag har hört något talas om ett stort ekumeniskt möte, som skall avhållas i Stockholm i Augusti, och jag ville bra gärna vara med, oaktat jag inte har några kvalifikationer utan bara är en nyfiken och intresserad individ.

Du behöver inte svara själv på detta. Det finns väl någon mötesbyrå, som kan upplysa om jag och min vän Fröken Valborg Olander förut Seminarieadjunkt i Falun få komma med som åhörare av förhandlingarna och var vi skola få inträdeskort och dylikt, om vi nu få lov att komma. Det pinar mig att besvära dig med brevet, men jag visste inte till vem annars jag skulle vända mig. Men låt för all del någon annan svara.

[...]
Med de bästa hälsningar
Din tillgivna
Selma Lagerlöf.

---

[2] Zentralstelle für kirchliche Hilfsaktionen, European Central Office for Inter-Church Aid, founded in Zürich in 1922. Adolf Keller (1872–1963), one of the most prominent ecumenical co-workers of Söderblom, had become its director in 1924. Keller later taught ecumenics in Zürich (1926) and Geneva (1929) and became one of the founders of the World Council of Churches. His seminars in Geneva included such luminaries as Karl Barth, Emil Brunner, and Paul Tillich.

[1] Nathan Söderblom's ecumenical collection, UUB, handwritten letter.

Mårbacka Sunne, May 14, 1925.

Dear Archbishop,

Forgive me if I ask a stupid question, but I have heard some talk about a great ecumenical conference to be held in Stockholm in August, and I should very much like to attend, notwithstanding my not having any qualifications but just being a curious and interested individual.

You do not have to reply yourself to this. There certainly is some conference office which can provide information whether I and my friend, Miss Valborg Olander,[2] former teacher at Teacher's College in Falun, may come along to listen to the debates, and where we shall get entrance tickets and the like, in case we do get permission to come. It is embarrassing for me to trouble you with this letter, but I did not know to whom else I should turn. But by all means, let someone else reply.

[On the result of the election for membership in the Academy]

With best regards,
yours sincerely,
Selma Lagerlöf.

242. From Adolf von Harnack[1]

Berlin-Grunewald 18.5.1925

Hochgeehrter Herr!

Zu *meinem grossen Bedauern* sehe ich mich aus Gesundheitsrücksichten gezwungen, auf den Besuch der »Universal Christian Conference on Life and Work« zu verzichten. Meine besten Wünsche werden die Tagung begleiten.

In vorzüglicher Hochachtung
ergebenst
Prof. D. v. Harnack[2]

243. To Adolf von Harnack[1]

Upsala den 25. Mai 1925

Hochverehrter Professor und Meister!

Zu meinem tiefen Bedauern erfahre ich, dass Sie aus Gesundheitsrücksichten der Stockholmkonferenz nicht beiwohnen können.

Aber würde es doch nicht möglich sein uns einen Vortrag über die Einheitsbestrebungen in der Kirche zu geben? Die Reise und den Aufenthalt wollen wir in solcher Weise zu gestalten versuchen, dass sie nicht ermüdend

---

[2] Valborg Henrika Christina Olander (1861–1943), teacher and town councillor in Falun, author of several textbooks. For a time, she was Selma Lagerlöf's life-companion.

[1] Nathan Söderblom's ecumenical collection, A 9, UUB, handwritten postcard.
[2] The extremely formal style of this message is explained by the fact that it is not directed to Söderblom personally but to the Bureau on Life and Work in Stockholm.

[1] Harnack's papers – letters, Staatsbibliothek zu Berlin, Preußischer Kulturbesitz, typewritten letter.

werden. Dürften wir nicht für Sie und Ihre Familie einen ruhigen Aufenthalt in Schweden anordnen?[2]

Ihr verehrungsvoll ergebener
Nathan Söderblom

244. From ADOLF VON HARNACK[1]

[Date at the end of the letter]

Hochwürdiger und Hochverehrter Herr Bischof!

Es ist sehr gütig, daß Sie sich bei Ihrer unsäglichen Arbeitslast die Mühe gemacht haben, an mich zu schreiben. Wie gerne käme ich! Aber ich muß im August in die Höhe d.h. in die Berge u. werde froh sein, wenn meine Stimme im Juni und Juli noch für die Vorlesungen u. das Seminar ausreicht. Einen Aufsatz über die Frage, ob der Consensus quinquesaecularis eine Basis für die Vereinigung der christlichen Kirchen sein kann, habe ich verfaßt u. D. Siegmund-Schultze übergeben.[2]

Meine tiefsten Segenswünsche werden die Konferenz begleiten.

In Verehrung
stets Ihr
ergebenster
D.v. Harnack
Berlin-Grunewald
28.5.25.

245. To TORSTEN BOHLIN[1]

Uppsala den 28 maj 1925.

Käre vän!

Vad tänker Du på? För inte längesedan fick jag Ditt stora vetenskapliga

---

[2] The word is used here in the sense of the Swedish *ordna*, to arrange.

[1] Nathan Söderblom's ecumenical collection, A 9, UUB, handwritten letter.

[2] Adolf v. Harnack, »Über den sogenannten ›Consensus quinquesaecularis‹ als Grundlage der Wiedervereinigung der Kirchen,« in: *Die Eiche* 13/1925, *Sonderheft*, 287–299 (also in: A. v. Harnack, *Reden und Aufsätze N. F. 5. Aus der Werkstatt des Vollendeten*, hg. v. Axel v. Harnack, Gießen 1930, 65–83). That such a consensus on the dogmas promulgated during the first five centuries of church history could be the basis of a reunion of the churches, was an idea Georg Calixt promoted in his *Prooemium to the Commonitorium of Vincentius of Lerinum*, Helmstedt 1629; abridged reprint of 2nd. ed. (1655) in: G. Calixt, *Ausgewählte Werke* vol. 1, ed. by I. Mager, Göttingen 1978, 369–418, esp. 393.396–400. Harnack argued that neither did such a common basis exist, nor could it, if it did, serve such a purpose, because that would lead to a reunion under purely Catholic auspices. Instead, he pleaded for practical cooperation between the churches in the common service of mankind and thus implicitly recommended the Stockholm conference as an alternative.

[1] Nathan Söderblom's collection of letters, to Swedes and foreigners, UUB, typewritten letter (carbon copy).

verk, som kräver ett grundligare och mer samlat studium än jag hittils fått ägna detsamma men till vilket jag av hjärtat lyckönskar Dig, då jag väl förstår vilket intensivt och strängt tankearbete, som en dylik väldig studie av ett bland de svåraste problem, som kan sysselsätta människotanken och den religiösa och etiska erfarenheten, måste kräva.

Och nu vad ligger på mitt bord? En bok om Kirkegaards teologi, som att döma av de inblickar jag mellan slagen smugit mig till att genast göra i densamma, äger goda förutsättningar för att på fullt allvar och med organiskt klart fattat sammanhang införa det ostyriga skrivarsnillet i den andliga värld, dit han trots allt hör, och som har sin största representant i ingen mindre än Martin Luther.

Jag går till läsningen av denna bok under det friska intrycket av Din nyttiga utredning i den nya kvartalskriften om den med all respekt sagt mer rafflande än innehållsrika nya tyska teologien och av Din historik härom dagen av »15 år i Kristliga Studentförbundet«. [...]

Det finnes i Ditt intellekt och i Din andliga utrustning vissa drag, för vilka jag kanske äger en partisk svaghet. Innerligheten förbjuder ingalunda en glansfullhet som blixtrar i solskenet från ovan.

Detta kan jag ha rätt att säga, då Du nu snart reser ifrån oss, särskilt om jag därtill fogar mitt praeterea censeo: Du som varit med om att se hur Gud i vår tid hos oss har upphöjt det föraktade och ringa och låtit det tända hänförelse och målmedvetna livsgärningar, borde också ha modet att draga på Dig det plagget, som kanske icke alltid är så roligt att bära, men som ändå, när allt kommer till allt, är en uniform i vår Herres Armé.

Säkerligen har Du många gånger sagt till Din maka, att hon är en oändligt stor Guds gåva, som Du oförtjänt fått. Om Du nu upprepar det från mig, är det sålunda för henne ingen nyhet, men hon kanske ställer sig mindre avvisande till en dylik betraktelse, om jag stryker ordet oförtjänt.

Gud välsigne Eder båda och Eder framtid.

Din gamle vän

Uppsala, May 28, 1925

Dear friend,

What do you know? Not long ago I received your great scholarly work which requires a more thorough and concentrated study than I have thus far been able to devote to it, but on which I heartily congratulate you, as I readily understand what an intense and strenuous intellectual labor such a huge study of one of the most difficult problems which can engage the human mind and religious and moral experience, must require.[2]

---

[2] It would seem from the wording of the preceding sentences that Bohlin had sent his book *Das Grundproblem der Ethik*, Uppsala 1923. – Later on, *Tro och uppenbarelse. En studie till teologiens kris och »krisens teologi«*, Stockholm 1926, became important for Söderblom (German transl.: *Glaube und Offenbarung*, Berlin 1928). In this book, Bohlin criticizes Barth and Gogarten for their abstract metaphysical conception of God as the »Wholly Other« (German ed., 68 f.) which failed to do justice to the idea of creation (74) and blurred the distinction between man's finitude and his sin (76), thus reducing the revelation of grace to a mere postulate (86).

And now, what is lying on my desk? A book on Kierkegaard's theology[3] which, judging form the furtive glances I managed to take right away between duties, is well suited to introducing seriously and in a clear, organic, and coherent way that unruly writer's genius into the spiritual world to which he belongs after all and which has its greatest representative in no one less than Martin Luther.

I set about reading this book under the fresh impression of your recent useful analysis of – this being said in all due respect – the more thrilling than substantial new German theology in the new quarterly[4] and of your recent history of »15 years in the Student Christian Federation«.[5] [...]

There are in your intellect and in your spiritual endowment certain traits for which I perhaps have a partial foible. Ardency by no means prohibits brilliance sparkling in the sunshine from above.

I may be entitled to say this, since you are soon going to leave us, especially if I add to this my *praeterea censeo*: You who has shared the experience of how God has exalted in our midst that which is despised and humble[6] and let it incite enthusiasm and purposeful activities in life, you should also have the courage to put on that garment which is perhaps not always pleasant to wear, but which is, when all is said and done, a uniform in the Lord's Army.[7]

Surely you told your wife many times that she is an immensely great gift of God which you received undeservedly. If you now repeat it on my behalf, it is therefore no news for her, but perhaps she will be less objecting to such a view if I delete the word undeservedly.

May God bless the two of you and your future.

Your old friend

246. To Adolf von Harnack[1]

Upsala, den 14. Juli 1925.

Genius, Gottesgelahrter und Freund:
Soeben komme ich von der letzten Sitzung des Internationalen Comités für die Welt Konferenz für Praktisches Christentum aus England zurück, und ich hoffe, dass Sie es mir nicht verdenken, dass ich Sie noch mit einem Worte plage. Diese Konferenz ist auch insofern einzigartig, dass viele erwähn-

---

He attributes that, in part, to a one-sided interpretation of Kierkegaard which neglects the latter's emphasis on religious experience (72. 96. 129–134).

[3] Torsten Bohlin, *Sören Kierkegaards dogmatiska åskådning i dess historiska sammanhang*, Stockholm 1925 (German tr. by I. Meyer-Lüne: *Kierkegaards dogmatische Anschauung in ihrem geschichtlichen Zusammenhang*, Gütersloh 1927).

[4] Torsten Bohlin, »Trosbegreppet och den dialektiska teologien,« and: »Den historiska uppenbarelsen och den dialektiska teologien,« in: *STK* 1/1925, 156–176. 219–232.

[5] »15 år i Kristliga Studentförbundet. Idéer och strömningar inom Studentförbundet 1908–1925,« in: *Uppsala kristliga studentförbund 1901–1926*, Stockholm 1926, 159–167.

[6] Luke 1:52.

[7] As for Bohlin's hesitation to be ordained, cf. letter no. 182.

[1] Harnack's papers – letters, Staatsbibliothek zu Berlin, Preußischer Kulturbesitz, typwritten letter.

ten Theologen, Kirchenmänner und Leihen [sic; lies: Laien] in vornähmlicher Stellung aus verschiedenen Ländern Gelegenheit haben werden, einmal im Leben einen persönlichen Eindruck zu bekommen von Erscheinungen, die sie sonst nur literarisch kennen. Ich erfahre ja immer wieder, wie ungemein lebhaft man sich in der Anglo-Säksischen Welt, wie auch sonst, für Adolf von Harnack interessiert, und wie gerne man ihn bei dieser Gelegenheit sehen und hören möchte.

Ich will nichts tun um die kluge Anwendung Ihrer Lebenskraft zu stören, aber könnte es nicht etwas von Ruhe sein, eine bequeme Reise nach und von Stockholm zwischen 19. und 30. August zu machen, keine Vorträge und Verhandlungen zu hören, was ja, wenn man nicht besonders verantwortlich in der Sache ist, wie ich stehe, und auch dann, zum Teil Strafarbeit heisst. Aber nur während einer halben Stunde Abends in einer der Sitzungen der Konferenz zwischen 5-7 und 9-10 im grössten Lokale in Stockholm, Blasieholms Kyrkan, kurz über die Hauptlinien des Einheitsgedankens in der kirchlichen Geschichte zu erzählen. Wir würden Ihnen und Ihrer Begleiterin das Leben so bequem wie möglich gestalten während des Aufenthaltes in Stockholm.

Aber leider muss ich fragen ob es Ihnen nicht möglich wäre uns einen Leitfaden [Exposé] so bald wie möglich im Voraus zu senden, um das Manuskript zu übersetzen in zwei andere Sprachen, drucken, und unter den zuhörenden zu verteilen, um eine mündliche Uebersetzung zu vermeiden.

Fürchterlich bin ich, das weiss ich schon, aber ich hege für die Konferenz das Desiderium Perfectionis.[2] Sollte man umsonst fragen: »aber wo ist Harnack? - - - Wir haben ihn immer wieder gelesen, er hat uns belehrt und angefeuert, wir hofften ihn einmal auch persönlich hören zu dürfen.«

Mit guten und ehrerbietigen Grüssen von meiner Frau und mir und der ganzen Familie, bin ich,

Ihr verehrungsvoll ergebenster,
Nathan Söderblom

247. From Selma Lagerlöf[1]

Mårbacka Sunne 16.7.1925.

Min käre Ärkebiskop!

I dag äntligen skickar jag det tal, som jag skulle hålla vid ekumeniska mötet. Jag är visst inte nöjd med det, jag har inga talareanlag, men jag tror inte, att jag nu i sommarhetta och med de många störande turisterna kan åstadkomma något bättre. Jag skulle dock vara bra tacksam, om du kunde

---

[2] Latin for: desire for perfection.

[1] Nathan Söderblom's collection of letters, from Swedes, UUB, handwritten letter.

ge dig tid, att titta igenom det och tillse om det är lämpligt alls, eller om något bör strykas och något kan bibehållas.

Ännu en sak vore jag så tacksam för. Om du tycker, att jag kan hålla talet vill du då låta mig bli den första i raden av den svenska aftonens talare. Jag är rädd för att bli för trött om jag skall sitta och först höra på de andra.

Nej, nu skall jag inte längre upptaga din tid utan slutar med en varm lyckönskan för det stora företaget.

Din tillgivna
Selma Lagerlöf.

Mårbacka Sunne, July 16, 1925.

My dear Archbishop,
Today at last I am sending the address I am to deliver at the ecumenical conference. I am certainly not content with it, I do not possess any rhetorical skills, but I do not think that I can now, in the summer heat and with those many distracting tourists, accomplish anything better. However, I would be quite grateful if you could find some time to go through it and see if it is at all appropriate, or if something must be discarded or something can be kept.

There is yet another thing I would be so grateful for. If you think that I can deliver the address, will you let me be first in the succession of the Swedish evening's speakers. I am afraid of getting too tired should I be seated and first listen to the others.[2]

No, now I shall no longer take your time but conclude with warm congratulations on the great undertaking.

Yours sincerely,
Selma Lagerlöf.

248. To René H. Wallau[1]

Upsala den 16 Juli 1925

Sehr geehrter Herr Pfarrer! Sie haben mir durch die Widmung Ihres Buches[2] eine allzu große Ehre erwiesen, wofür ich Ihnen herzlichst danke.

Meine Münchenervorträge werden Sie interessieren, wenn sie einmal erscheinen werden.

Die Evangelische Katholicität definiere ich dort in drei Punkten:

1: Eine geschichtliche Tatsache. Die Evangelische Kirche stellt eine ebenso autentische Fortsetzung der Kirche mehr als die Römische, die nach Tri-

---

[2] Selma Lagerlöf suffered from a congenital hip ailment.

[1] René Heinrich Wallau, Protestant minister in Frankfurt/Main, member of the Una-Sancta-Movement which worked for the renewal and visible unity of the Christian church. – Nathan Söderblom's collection of letters, to Swedes and foreigners, UUB, typewritten letter (carbon copy).

[2] René Wallau, *Die Einigung der christlichen Kirche vom evangelischen Glauben aus*, Berlin 1925, 306–315.

dentinum und durch den Einfluss der Jesuiten auch eine Neuerung, aber nicht auf Grund des Evangeliums ist.

2: Eine Lehre. Die Evangelische Christenheit lehrt grundsätzlich die Universalität des Glaubens und der Kirche, wenigstens ebenso principiell klar, ja klarer, als die zwei anderen Hauptabteilungen der katholischen Kirche, die Römische und die Orthodoxe. Siehe Luthers Erklärung zum Dritten Artikel im Kleinen Katechismus! Die gesamte Christenheit auf Erden.[3]

3: Evangelische Katholicität bedeutet drittens eine Methode der Einheit. Auch wenn man sich keinen Urteil über den Wert der verschiedenen Auffassungen erlaubt, ist es logisch vollständig klar, dass eine Einheit in Vielheit und überhaupt eine wirklich organische Einheit der Kirche dadurch erschwert wird, dass [= wenn?] die Religion nomistisch ist, Gesetzesreligion. Denn wenn äussere Sachen, Hierarchie, Dekrete u.s.w. das ganze äussere System der Heilsanstalt für die Einheit notwendig ist, wird die Verwirkligung der Einheit und Universalität unvergleichlich schwieriger als wenn die Religion geistig ist und nicht äussere Einrichtungen als notwendig für die Einheit auffasst. Die Evangelische Kirche kann somit die Einheit ohne Vergewaltigung anderer Kirchen verwirklichen. Für die heilige Sache dieser Einheit bedeutet Ihr Buch eine sehr wertvolle Orientation zu der ich Sie und uns und die Kirche beglückwünsche.

Mit den besten Wünschen Ihr dankbar ergebener

249. From Adolf von Harnack[1]

Berlin-Grunewald 19. 7. 25.

Hochverehrter und hochwürdiger Herr Erzbischof!

Ihre freundlichen und dringenden Zeilen haben mir das Herz schwer gemacht – zumal da ich mir immer wieder sagen mußte: »auf diesem Kongreß zu sein, den Sie gestalten werden, ist Pflicht u. Freude.« Aber ich darf nach Rücksprache mit den Autoritäten den einzigen Ferienmonat, den ich habe, nicht unterbrechen. Wenn ich in Berlin wäre, ginge es vielleicht noch; aber ich werde tief in den Alpen sein und müßte 48 Stunden reisen, um nach Stockholm zu kommen und 48 Stunden wieder zurück. Das kann ich nicht leisten.

Einen Artikel für die Konferenz habe ich geschrieben; er ist in der »Eiche« erschienen und wird ins Englische u. Französische übersetzt.

Haben Sie vielen Dank für Ihren Brief – von der Konferenz erwarte ich das Beste; denn sie will nicht zuviel und nicht zuwenig und wird eben deßhalb das Mögliche durchsetzen. Aber selbst wenn nicht alles, was möglich ist, erreicht wird, soll uns das nicht verdrießen. Erst auf dem Constantino-

---

[3] Literally: die ganze Christenheit auf Erden.

[1] Nathan Söderblom's ecumenical collection, B 3, UUB, handwritten letter.

politanum im J[ahre] 381 wurde das Nicänum für den Orient perfekt. Ich
bin gewiß, daß wir nicht noch 56 Jahre warten müssen[2].
In herzlicher Verehrung
bleibe ich Ew. Hochwürden
ergebenster
v. Harnack

250. To Selma Lagerlöf[1]

Upsala, den 20 juli 1925

Ärade kära Selma!

Nog visste jag att Du skulle ge oss en berättelse, dubbelt välbehövlig, svalk-
ande och vederkvickande under allt diskuterande, övervägande och före-
dragande under Allmänkyrkliga Världskonferensen, och jag har gått i en
spänd förväntan på att få läsa och höra den historien.

Men inte drömde jag om att Du hade något i Ditt till synes outtömliga
förråd så näraliggande, med en sådan anknytning till heliga känslor och
minnen och med en tillämpning så direkt och oundkomlig.

Eftersom Du vill ändra ett och annat, skickar jag enligt önskan tillbaka
manuskriptet, fastän jag inte kan begripa att någon ändring behövs. När vi
sedan få manuskriptet tillbaka, översättes det till de främmande språken
och delas ut, så att alla kunna stilla lyssna till Ditt svenska språk och se på
sina blad och förstå utan att någon muntlig tolkning stör stämningen.

Naturligtvis kan Du gärna tala först. Orsaken till att vi hava satt Dig,
liksom en och annan huvudtalare i övrigt sist, är dels den, att de föregående, som vi nog inskränka till två, skulle yttra sig mera inledningsvis
och kortfattat, dels därför att vi tro att efter Ditt anförande publikum icke
gärna vill höra mera talare. I så fall skulle vi bedja Dig anlända till exempel
en halvtimme efter början, just då de två föregående talarna slutat. Men om
Du föredrager, så skall Du naturligtvis tala först. Vi hade annars tänkt oss
de övriga mera såsom inledning till Selma, ett par portaler, genom vilka
man vandrar till högtidsssalen. Men, som sagt, det provisoriska program-
met kan i det fallet mycket lätt ändras.

Med sann vördnad tillgivne
Nathan Söderblom

---

[2] Wait for 56 years: as did the ancient church for the final acceptance of the Nicene Creed,
from the Council in Nicaea 325 until the one in Constantinople mentioned above.

[1] Nathan Söderblom's collection of letters, to Swedes and foreigners, UUB, typewritten
letter.

Uppsala, July 20, 1925

Honorable, dear Selma,

Surely did I know that you would give us a narrative[2], twice necessary, cooling and reinvigorating in all the debating, deliberating, and lecturing during the Universal Church World Conference, and I took to reading and hearing that story, excited with expectation.

Never did I dream, however, that you had in your apparently inexhaustible store something so obvious, with such a connection to holy feelings and reminiscences and with so direct and inescapable an application.

Since you want to change something or other, I am returning the manuscript according to your request, even though I cannot conceive of anything that needed change. When we then get the manuscript back, it will be translated into the foreign languages and distributed, so that everybody can quietly listen to your Swedish language and look at their sheets and understand, with no oral translation disturbing the impression.

Of course you can speak first. The reason why we have placed you last, just like some other keynote speakers beside you, is partly that the preceding ones, whom we will certainly limit to two, should talk in a more introductory and brief fashion, partly because we believe that after your speech, the public would not like to hear another speaker. In that case we would like to ask you to arrive, for example, half an hour after the beginning, just when the two preceding speakers have finished. But if you so prefer, you shall of course speak first. We had otherwise imagined the two others more like an introduction to Selma, a couple of portals, through which one walks into the festive hall. But as I said, the preliminary program can in that case quite easily be changed.

With true respect,
sincerely,
Nathan Söderblom

251. To Adolf von Harnack[1]

Upsala den 20. Juli 1925.

Excellenz!

Es it nicht zu wundern, dass man an der Konferenz für Leben und Wirken den Mann gern sehen und hören möchte, der um nicht viele unvergleichlich wichtigere Dinge zu erwähnen, das schöne Bild von dem Garten entwarf, mit dem Wunsche: »Möge die gemeinsame Arbeit in Luft und Licht die Arbeitenden immer enger verbinden! Möge vor allem eine jede Kirche ihren

---

[2] Selma Lagerlöf's address made use of historical material from her novel *Jerusalem* (1901/1902): a group of evangelical Swedish peasants emigrating to Jerusalem in 1896 and joining a group of Americans there whose leader, a lady, had narrowly escaped a shipwreck. All of them united in doing charitable work for the local poor. This story served her as a parable for international reconciliation and unanimity of the churches and the nations after the war. The address was published in: Nathan Söderblom, *Kristenhetens möte i Stockholm augusti 1925. Historik, aktstycken, grundtankar, personligheter, eftermäle, skärskådade och återgivna*, 1926, 579–588.

[1] Harnack's papers – letters, Staatsbibliothek zu Berlin, Preußischer Kulturbesitz, typewritten letter.

Gläubigen die volle Freiheit zu Betätigung und Schaffen geben und in der Religion nur die Religion gelten lassen. Dann wird die Annäherung und Gemeinschaft im höheren Sinne nicht ausbleiben, und einzig eine solche Gemeinschaft können wir erhoffen und wünschen«. Und mit dem Grundsatze: »So paradox das Wort scheinen mag – die Frage der Annäherung der Kirchen fällt mit der Frage der Verinnerlichung und Freiheit in jeder einzelnen Kirche zusammen«.[2]

In verehrungsvoller Ergebenheit

Nathan Söderblom

252. To ADOLF VON HARNACK[1]

Upsala den 22 Juli 1925.

Excellenz!

Ach, jetzt haben Sie sich doch mit noch einem Briefe Mühe machen müssen. Freilich hat mir den Brief große Freude gemacht und Sie werden mir erlauben das tröstende Beispiel v. 325–381 bei unserer Konferenz anzuwenden.[2]

Möge die höchst nötige Ruhe Ihnen die Geistesfrische behalten mit welcher Sie Menschen intellektuell und geistig bereichern und erfrischen.

In wahrer Verehrung

Ihr ergebenster

Nathan Söderblom

---

[2] The quote is from Harnack's speech at Emperor Wilhelm's II. birthday on Jan. 27, 1907, on »Protestantismus und Katholizismus in Deutschland« (*Aus Wissenschaft und Leben* vol. 1, Gießen 1911, [225–250], 234). In this context, he uses the image Söderblom refers to: Catholics and Protestants live in a garden, in an old fortified castle and in various modern houses, respectively. They each retreat to their lodgings for the night, but are required during the day to cooperate in the common garden. Harnack further argues, to the dismay of many contemporaries, that cooperation calls for serious talks among the churches, not for glossing over their differences, but for discovering areas of honest agreement. Only then could one hope to bring to bear the faith against the quicksands of secularism. This image appears to have been one of the main inspirations for Söderblom's own concept of the three kinds of catholicity, cf. letter no. 97, n. 3.

[1] Harnack's papers – letters, Staatsbibliothek zu Berlin, Preußischer Kulturbesitz, typewritten letter.

[2] Cf. letter no. 249, n. 2. The emphasis in the parallel between Nicaea and Stockholm here is on comfort in times of slow progress. At the conference itself, however, as well as in Söderblom's own account of it, the parallel played a more substantial role. In the face of Catholic and conservative Protestant criticism that the conference had neglected Christ as the focus of Christian faith, it was stressed that just as the Nicene creed spoken at the conference referred to Christ as both the voice of God and a real human being, faith in Christ was at the starting point from which the ethical deliberations flowed. Besides, Söderblom had called for an ethical confession, though not in the sense of dogmatization or uniformity. For these reasons, the Stockholm conference later came to be called the Nicaea of Christian ethics. Cf. Söderblom, *Kristenhetens möte ...* (cf. letter no. 250, n. 2), 232–324, esp. 247 f.; 335 f. 629–636. 696. 698 f. 900.

253. From PAUL ALTHAUS[1]

Rostock, den 26. Juli 1925

Hochverehrter Herr Erzbischof!
Auf Ihren gütigen Brief vom 14. Juli kann ich eine Absage *nicht* schreiben. Ich nehme also Ihre freundliche Einladung dankbar und gerne an, am Sonntag, den 23. August eine Predigt zu halten. Gerne bleibe ich auch einige Tage auf der Konferenz. Da ich etwa am 6. September in Riga sein muß, könnte ich vielleicht inzwischen mir Schweden noch ein wenig ansehen. Wollen Sie nur die Güte haben, mich wissen zu lassen, wie lang etwa die Predigt sein soll und ob ein bestimmter Gegenstand für sie gewünscht ist; auch ob ich einen Talar mitbringen soll. Ich würde dann vielleicht am 19. oder 20. August eintreffen dürfen? Meine Frau kann mich leider nicht begleiten, da sie durch unser jüngstes Kind gebunden ist.
    Mit verehrungsvoller Begrüßung
    Ihr
    ergebenster
    D. P. Althaus.

254. From THEODOR KAFTAN[1]

Baden-Baden, 18. 8. 25

Verehrter und lieber Herr Erzbischof!
Sie trugen und tragen z[ur] Z[eit] eine große Last. Ich bitte Gott, daß er Sie nicht darunter gesundheitlich zusammenbrechen lasse, daß er Ihr großes Werk segne.
    Sie haben jetzt nicht Zeit lange Briefe zu lesen. Daher ein kurzes Wort.
    Daß Sie mich recht verstehen, dieses woraus Sie wissen, daß Ihr Werk unter den Lutheranern mit viel Widerstand zu kämpfen hat, vielleicht auch, daß ich unter jenen nach Kräften für dasselbe eingetreten bin. Die Gegner fürchten den weltlichen Begriff von Gottes Reich bei den Anglikanern gegenüber der lutherischen Fassung dieses Reichs als einer überweltlichen Größe. M. E. ist der biblisch richtige der von meinem Bruder vertretene Begriff: das Reich Gottes eine überweltliche Größe, deren (innerlich notwendiges) innerweltliches Korrelat das Reich des Sittlichen ist.[2] Den Lutherischen habe ich gesagt: seid Ihr nicht Manns genug gegenüber den Anglikanern?

---

[1] Nathan Söderblom's collection of letters, from foreigners, UUB, handwritten letter.

[1] Theodor Kaftan (1847–1932), Generalsuperintendent for Schleswig, after his retirement in 1917 pastor in Baden-Baden. As a theologian he was »modern-positiv«, a mediator between the conservative and the critical wings. He supported the ecumenical movement, and he advocated protection of the Danish minority in pre-war Schleswig Holstein. However, the minorities he refers to at the end of the current letter are most likely German populations in territories under Polish rule after World War I. – Nathan Söderblom's collection of letters, from foreigners, UUB, handwritten letter.
[2] Vgl. Julius Kaftan, *Dogmatik* (GThW V/1), 5th and 6th ed., Tübingen 1909, 148 f.

Allerneuestens ist mir aber entgegengetreten, was mir Sorge macht: es heißt, die Anglikaner erstrebten in Stockholm *einen religiösen Unterbau des* »*Völkerbunds*«. Das wäre tötlich (sic) für Ihr Werk, wenigstens in dem miß-handelten Deutschland, aber, ich glaube auch darüber hinaus. Ich müßte sehr bitter werden, wollte ich den heutigen sog. Völkerbund in seiner Wirk-lichkeit charakterisieren. Diesen Bestand kann auch Deutschland nicht überwinden, wenn es aus bitterer Notwendigkeit in diesen Bund hinein müßte.[3] Wer aber sagt, die gegenwärtige Karikatur eines Völkerbunds sei nun einmal das Gegebene, das ausgebaut und verbessert werden müsse, der sagt nicht, wie viel Lüge und Brutalität heute in diesem Bunde regiert – trotz einzelner trefflicher Mitglieder desselben. Aber genug davon.

Sie durchschauen die Lage viel besser als ich. Wollen die Anglikaner wirklich im Interesse ihrer Weltherrschaft die werdende Einigung der Chri-stenheit als religiösen Unterbau des gegenwärtigen »Völkerbunds« miß-brauchen, dann schützen Sie Ihr Werk davor! Sie sind der einzige, der es kann.[4] Die werdende Einigung der Christenheit mit diesem Völkerbund verknüpfen hieße ein großes, so Gott will, zukunftreiches Werk an ein un-lauteres Werk der momentanen Zeitpolitik verkaufen.

Wie die Dinge heute liegen, ist es gewiß geboten, die heutigen politischen Fragen tunlichst draußenan [?] zu halten. Wir leben auch in politischem Nebel. Nur eins! Der mißhandelten Minoritäten *muß* eine christliche Welt-konferenz sich annehmen.

Gott helfe zu Ihm wohlgefälliger Frucht!

Ihr

Th Kaftan

255. From Adolf von Harnack[1]

Elmau bei Klaib (Oberbayern) den 20. 8. 1925.

Hochwürdiger Herr Erzbischof!

Hochverehrter Herr!

Gestern haben Ew. Hochwürden den großen kirchlichen Kongreß für prak-tisches Christentum eröffnet: meine Gedanken und tiefsten Wünsche und Segenswünsche werden in diesen Tagen stetig bei der Versammlung sein, der persönlich beizuwohnen mir zu meinem Schmerze nicht vergönnt ist.

Angesichts dieser großen Versammlung drängen sich mir alle meine kir-

---

[3] Germany did not become a member of the League of Nations until Sept. 8, 1926.

[4] Kaftan probably was not aware of Söderblom's own political analogy to the League of Nations as a means of achieving reconciliation and peace. He had argued that the League needed a Christian soul for fulfilling its political mission. Of course, in Söderblom's mind this implies neither an instumentalization of the Stockholm conference for political ends nor a con-cept of the Kingdom of God as an essentially mundane idea. Cf. letter no.134; Sundkler, op. cit., 232.236.332.379.

[1] Nathan Söderblom's ecumenical collection, A 9, UUB, handwritten letter.

chengeschichtlichen Erinnerungen zusammen; sie erscheinen mir alle wie eine Vorgeschichte dieses Kongreßes, dessen Herbeiführung die Christenheit Ihnen, hochverehrter Herr Erzbischof, verdankt. Tausende empfinden so, Hunderte werden es Ihnen aussprechen: nehmen Sie am heutigen Tage auch meinen ehrerbietigen und wärmsten Dank entgegen!

Was der Kongreß erreichen wird, kann noch Niemand voraussagen; aber gewiß ist er nicht zu früh gekommen und gewiß kann er kein Fehlschlag sein; denn hier gilt »Gott will es, und das christliche Gewissen verlangt es, und die Not der Zeit fordert es.« Und sollte sich selbst nichts anderes ergeben als eine Orientierung über die Not und eine brüderliche Aussprache, so wäre doch ein Anfang gemacht, der nicht vergeblich sein kann. Aber ich hoffe bestimmt, daß schon dieser Kongreß, sei es auch in losester Form, eine Organisation schaffen wird, durch welche der große Gedanke Form und Dauer erhält. An Geduld wollen wir es nicht fehlen lassen, wenn nur das Samenkorn nicht im Winde verweht, sondern Wurzel schlägt.

Möge Gottes Gnade im brüderlichen Sinn der Beteiligten zum Ausdruck kommen, und möge Sein Geist die Verhandlungen beherrschen!

In herzlicher Verehrung
Ew. Hochwürden
ergebenster
D. v. Harnack

256. From Selma Lagerlöf[1]

Mårbacka, Sunne 8.9.1925.

Min käre Ärkebiskop!

Först i går kom jag hem till Mårbacka och nu skyndar jag att tacka för att jag fick vara med och se hur det stora verket sattes i gång, och framför allt för att lyckönska till den underbara framgången. Jag är övertygad att mångfaldig välsignelse och god utveckling skall följa ur det påbegynta verket, om du bara får fortsätta att leda det efter dina vittskådande, människoälskande idéer.

Jag blev gripen av Patriarkens död, jag som alla andra. Men vilken lycka, att han inte dog i Stockholm under mötesdagarna.

Vill du säga ett varmt tack till din hustru för hennes vänlighet mot mig under mötesdagarna. Jag tycker att hon skall vara lycklig att hon har dig hel och sund åter i Uppsala.

Och nu skall jag inte skriva längre, jag tänker, att du är rent uttråkad av tacksamhet och beundran från världens alla hörn. Ingen tror jag dock bättre förstår hur stor den insats är, som du har gjort än

din tacksamt tillgivna
Selma Lagerlöf.

---

[1] Nathan Söderblom's collection of letters, from Swedes, UUB, handwritten letter.

Mårbacka, Sunne 8.9.1925.

My dear Archbishop,

Only yesterday did I come home to Mårbacka, and now I hurry to thank you for letting me participate and watch this great enterprise being set in motion, and above all to congratulate you on the wonderful success. I am convinced that manifold blessing and good development will result from the enterprise [thus] initiated, if only you will be able to guide it in accordance with your farsighted, philanthropic ideas.

I was moved by the Patriarch's death,[2] I like everybody else. But how lucky that he did not die in Stockholm during the conference days.

Would you please say warm thanks to your wife for her kindness towards me during the conference days. I guess that she will be happy to have you back in Uppsala in good health.

And now I shall write no more; I think you will be really tired of gratitude and admiration from all corners of the world. I think, however, that no one better understands how great the contribution is that you have made than

yours gratefully,
Selma Lagerlöf.

257. From Otto Dibelius[1]

Berlin M 30, am 17. September 1925

Hochverehrter Herr Erzbischof!

Es ist mir ein Bedürfnis, nach meiner Rückkehr in die Heimat Ihnen ein Wort des Dankes und der Bewunderung für das in Stockholm geleistete Werk zu sagen. Es scheint mir sehr billig, an einer solchen Sache Kritik zu üben, weil Hoffnungen nicht in Erfüllung gegangen und überstiegene Erwartungen enttäuscht worden sind. Wichtiger und notwendiger scheint es mir, die Ansätze zu positiven, neuen, zukunftskräftigen Entwicklungen zu erkennen, die sich auf der Weltkonferenz ausgewirkt haben, diese Ansätze zu bejahen und an ihrer weiteren Entfaltung mitzuarbeiten. Die eigenartige und schwierige Stellung der deutschen Delegation, verursacht durch den Druck unserer gesamten äusseren Lage, hat vielleicht hin und her den Anschein erweckt, als überwöge in unsern Reihen ein fruchtloser Pessimismus, der die Entschlusskraft nicht aufbringe, sich dem Bösen in der Welt kraftvoll entgegenzuwerfen. Ich glaube sagen zu dürfen, dass dem nicht so ist. Auch unter denen, die sich, wie ich selbst, auf der Weltkonferenz aus bestimmten Gründen diesmal zurückgehalten haben, lebt ein fester Wille, im Namen Jesu Christi für den Sieg des Gottesreiches über die sündige Welt zu kämpfen. In diesem Willen hat uns das große Erlebnis der Stockholmer Ta-

---

[2] Photios I. Peroglou (1853–1925), Patriarch of Alexandria 1900–1925, had died in Zürich on his journey back home on Sept. 5, 1925.

[1] Nathan Söderblom's ecumenical collection, UUB, typewritten letter.

gung gefestigt. Das danken wir Ihnen. Sie dürfen weiterer Mitarbeit von unserer Seite auch bei der Fortsetzung des grossen Werkes gewiss sein!
Ich bin in aufrichtiger Verehrung
Ihr ganz ergebenster
Dibelius

258. To Selma Lagerlöf[1]

Upsala 20 sept 1925

Selma optima!
Av livet har Du lärt Dig att när Du tänker vänliga tankar inte låta dem stanna hos Dig utan sända dem vidare till den som därav kan hugsvalas och styrkas. Tack många gånger tack för breven. Du erhöll kallet att sända slika goda tankar även till mångtusende okända hjärtan.

En tysk präst skriver och frågar oss om han inte kan få 70,000 exemplar av Ditt tal till Kristenhetens möte, ty han vet inte bättre sätt att bibringa människor något av det som mötet ville.

De två patriarkernas bortgång omedelbart efter mötet – den 77 årige prof. Clutz var nestor i amerikanska delegationen – verkade på mig som om den Evige själv underströk Mötets vikt och de efterlevandes ansvar. »Herre, nu låter Du Din tjänare fara i frid, ty mina ögon hava sett« en enad kristenhet. –

[...]
Min hustru tackar särskildt för Dina goda ord. När få vi mottaga Dig i vårt hem? Det finns ett rum.
Tuus
Nathan Söderblom

Uppsala, Sept. 20, 1925

Selma optima,[2]
From life you have learned, when you think friendly thoughts, not to let them remain with you but to send them out to those who can be comforted and strengthened by them. Thank you many times, thanks for your letters. You have received the calling also to send such good thoughts to many thousands of unknown hearts.

A German pastor writes, asking us if he could get 70,000 copies of your address to the meeting of Christianity. For he knows of no better way of teaching people something of what the Conference intended.

The passing away of the two patriarchs immediately after the conference – the 77-year old professor Clutz[3] was the nestor of the American delegation – made an impression on me as if the Eternal himself underlined the weight of the conference

---

[1] Nathan Söderblom's collection of letters, from Swedes, UUB, handwritten letter.

[2] Latin: Best Selma.

[3] Jacob Abraham Clutz (1848–1925), at the age of 16 a participant in the American Civil War under Lincoln, Lutheran theologian, Secretary of the Board of Foreign Missions 1883–1889, Lutheran professor at Western Theological Seminary, Atchison KS 1894–1904 and at

and the survivors' responsibility. »Lord, now lettest thou thy servant depart in peace, for mine eyes have seen« a united Christendom.[4] –

[On the upcoming election for membership in the Swedish Academy]

My wife especially thanks you for your good words. When may we welcome you in our home? There is a room.

Yours,
Nathan Söderblom

259. To OTTO DIBELIUS[1]

Upsala, den 26 September 1925

Sehr geehrter Herr Generalsuperintendent!

Für Ihren Brief herzlich dankend, möchte ich Ihnen sagen, was ich immer wieder den Anglosaxen, Franzosen und Anderen gesagt habe. Die Deutsche Evangelische Christenheit hat die Weltkonferenz am ernstesten genommen. Denn die Delegation bestand nicht aus Männer und Frauen die grundsätzlich oder zufällig für die Sache von vornerein [sic; l. vornherein] interessiert waren, sondern von den Vertrauensmännern der Kirche selbst. Das bedeutete selbstverständlich, neben den von Ihnen angedeuteten allbekannten komplizierten Schwierigkeiten Deutschlands, eine unvergleichlich schwieriger Aufgabe für die deutsche Delegation als für die aller meisten Anderen. Aber es ist auch eine tiefe und zukunftsreiche Beteiligung an der Sache. Soweit ich weiss, hat sich der evangelisch Lutherische Geist nie so kräftig mit dem Anglosaxismus aus einander gesetzt wie in Stockholm. Wir haben selbstverständlich von einander zu lernen, aber es ist vor allen Dingen notwendig, dass das evangelisch Lutherische Wesen in Gross-Britannien und Amerika besser bekannt wird.

In brüderlicher Gemeinschaft
Ihr sehr ergebener

260. To FRIEDRICH HEILER[1]

Upsala den 6 oktober 1925.

Käre Vän!

För några dagar sedan träffade jag Ärkebiskop Germanos, som just var på återväg från en visitationsresa i de ortodoxa församlingarna i Finland. Han stannade någon dag i Stockholm och talade bland annat om för mig

---

Gettysburg Seminary 1909–1925, active in the formation of UCLA. He died as a result of a Stockholm traffic accident when traveling home on Sept. 7, 1925.

[4] According to Luke 2:29, Simeon said these words upon seeing Jesus who had been brought to the temple for circumcision: »... for mine eyes have seen thy salvation«.

[1] Nathan Söderblom's ecumenical collection, UUB, typewritten letter (carbon copy).

[1] Fr. Heiler's papers (Ms. 999), Univ. Library Marburg, typewritten letter.

om Edert föredrag på den gammalkatolska kongressen i Bern. Han gjorde också det förslaget, att Bern skulle bliva en central för Life and Work rörelsens framtida arbete.

Jag skriver för att fråga om Eder åsikt i frågan. Ur många synpunkter kanske Bern skulle vara lämpligt. Svårigheten är blott, att Schweiz endast har reformert gudstjänstform, som ju anglikanerna och lutheranerna icke äro fullt tillfredsställda med. Men med Bern är ju förhållandet något annorlunda då det ju är huvudsätet för gammalkatolicismen i Schweiz. Ha gammalkatolikerna i Bern en stor och vacker kyrka och är deras liturgi värdig och vad synes Eder i övrigt om förslaget?

Med goda hälsningar förblir jag
Eder tillgivne
Nathan Söderblom

Uppsala, den 6. Oktober 1925

Lieber Freund,

vor einigen Tagen traf ich Erzbischof Germanos,[2] der gerade auf dem Rückweg von einer Visitationsreise bei den orthodoxen Gemeinden in Finnland war. Er blieb einige Tage in Stockholm und sprach mit mir unter anderem über Ihren Vortrag auf dem altkatholischen Kongress in Bern.[3] Er machte auch den Vorschlag, dass Bern eine Zentrale für die zukünftige Arbeit der Life und Work-Bewegung werden solle.

Ich schreibe, um nach Ihrer Ansicht in der Sache zu fragen. Unter vielen Gesichtspunkten wäre Bern vielleicht geeignet. Die Schwierigkeit ist bloß, dass die Schweiz nur die reformierte Gottesdienstform hat, mit der ja die Anglikaner und die Lutheraner nicht völlig zufrieden sind. Aber mit Bern verhält sich die Sache ja etwas anders, weil es ja der Hauptsitz des Altkatholizismus in der Schweiz ist. Haben die Altkatholiken in Bern eine große und schöne Kirche, und ist ihre Liturgie würdig, und was halten Sie im Übrigen von dem Vorschlag?

Mit guten Grüßen verbleibe ich
Ihr Ihnen verbundener
Nathan Söderblom

---

[2] Strenopoulos Germanos (1872–1951), Metropolitan of Thyateira. Söderblom had first met Germanos at a Christian students' conference in Constantinople; he was rector of the theological academy of Chalkis at that time. Cf. N. Söderblom, *Kristenhetens möte* (letter no. 250, n. 2), 841 f.
[3] The Old Catholic Church is a group of Catholics that split off from Rome because they rejected the dogma of papal infallibility promulgated in 1870. – Heiler's lecture is not contained in his bibliography (*Inter confessiones. Fr. Heiler zum Gedächtnis*, ed. A.M. Heiler, MThSt 10, 154–196).

261. From FRIEDRICH HEILER[1]

Marburg/Lahn, Moltkestr. 19, 9.10.25.

Hochverehrter, Hochwürdigster Herr Erzbischof,

Meine letzte Sendung, enthaltend meinen Stockholmartikel[2] und einen solchen meiner Frau hat sich mit Ihrem freundlichen Briefe gekreuzt. Sie werden aus ihm sehen, wie ich mit ganzem Herzen an der Konferenz teilnahm und wie viel ich von ihr empfangen habe, aber ebenso wie wenig die Haltung der Deutschen mir entspricht. Meine Frau, der gegenüber sich viele Deutsche noch offener ausgesprochen haben als mir, hat noch mehr unter ihnen gelitten. Nach reiflicher Ueberlegung und nach Rücksprache mit Siegmund-Schultze habe ich mit meiner Kritik an den Deutschen nicht zurückgehalten, aber ihr ganz den Charakter eines persönlichen Bekenntnisses gegeben. Ich glaube, dass ein offenes Wort in unserer überhitzten nationalistischen Atmosphäre manche zur Besinnung bringt. Die Verwechslung von evangelischer Verkündigung und völkischer Propaganda hat allmählich in Deutschland Dimensionen angenommen, dass man nicht schweigen darf.

Um Ihre Frage zu beantworten, so möchte ich sagen, dass ich eine Verlegung der Life and Work-Zentrale nach Bern sehr glücklich finde. Einmal ist Bern eine ruhige Stadt im Vergleich zu Genf. Ferner findet sich dort neben einer evangelischen Fakultät eine altkatholische, die offiziell den Charakter einer internationalen Fakultät hat, trotzdem mangels an Geldmitteln sie nicht international ausgebaut werden konnte. Die altkatholische Kirche ist schön und geräumig. Der altkatholische Gottesdienst ist sehr würdig, schlicht und feierlich zugleich. Der Inhalt der Liturgie ist durchaus evangelisch, alles Römische in dogmatischer Hinsicht ist ausgemerzt, sodass ein Lutheraner an ihr ebenso teilnehmen kann wie an der schwedischen Högmässa.[3] Uebrigens sind die allermeisten Lieder des altkatholischen Gesangbuchs dem deutschen lutherischen Liederschatz entnommen. Die religiöse Einstellung der Altkatholiken ist durchaus evangelisch. Der verstorbene Bischof Herzog,[4] der durch sein fast fünfzigjähriges Hirtenamt der Schweizer altkatholischen Kirche seinen Geist eingepflanzt hat, war eine rein evangelische Persönlichkeit. Die katholischen Formen in Kult und Verfassung ziehen naturgemäss die Anglikaner und Orientalen an. Aus all diesen Gründen wäre Bern der reformierten Stadt Genf mit ihren einseitig calvini-

---

[1] Nathan Söderblom's collection of letters, from foreigners, UUB, typewritten letter.

[2] Friedrich Heiler, »Die religiöse Einheit der Stockholmer Weltkonferenz,« in: *ChW* 39/1925, 865–875, and/or: »Die Stockholmer Weltkonferenz. Ein kritischer Bericht,« in: *Una sancta* 1/1925, 153–157. A summary of all of Heiler's reports on the conference can be found in the chapter Die Weltkonferenz von Stockholm, in his book *Evangelische Katholizität*, München 1926, 56–150.

[3] High Mass, Swedish Lutheran worship service including the celebration of the Lord's Supper.

[4] Eduard Herzog (1841–1924), Old Catholic Bishop.

schen Traditionen vorzuziehen. Ich kenne den jetzigen altkatholischen Bischof Dr. Adolf Küry gut.[5]

Das große Sammelwerk »Religion in Geschichte und Gegenwart« soll nun ganz neu herausgegeben werden.[6] Die Religionsgeschichte soll bei der neuen Auflage besonders berücksichtigt werden. Ich bin ersucht worden, als Beirat Prof. Gunkel[7] in religionsgeschichtlichen Dingen bei der Redaktion zu beraten. Es läge mir viel daran, dass auch Sie einige Artikel über solche Dinge, die Ihnen von Ihren früheren Arbeiten her vertraut sind, schrieben. Da die Herausgabe sechs bis sieben Jahre umfassen wird, ist die Zeitfrage ja sekundär. Auch wäre ich Ihnen sehr dankbar, wenn ich Ihnen meinen Vorschlag für die Nomenklatur (Titel der Artikel) samt Mitarbeitervorschlag zur Durchsicht senden dürfte, da Sie mit Ihrer grossen Sach- und Personenkenntnis alles noch viel besser überschauen als ich.

Ich sende Ihnen beiliegend einen Artikel über Sie, den ich vor der Konferenz geschrieben und der während derselben erschienen ist.[8] Ich habe ihn erst heute zugesandt bekommen. Nehmen Sie ihn als Zeichen meiner aufrichtigen Dankbarkeit für alles, was ich in vielen Jahren von Ihnen empfangen habe. Auf besondern Wunsch von Siegmund Schultze werde ich in der »Eiche« auf die Ae[u]sserungen von Wallau und Katz über die angeblichen Differenzen zwischen Ihrer und meiner evangelischen Katholizität antworten.[9] Ich finde die Ausführungen von beiden wenig glücklich.

Es tut mir leid, dass Laible in der Allg. Ev-luth. Kirchenzeitung seinen hässlichen Kampf gegen das Werk der Konferenz fortsetzt und direkt unwahre Berichte gibt.[10] Seine Artikel werden mit grosser Schadenfreude von den römischen Katholiken ausgeschlachtet.

---

[5] Adolf Küry (1870-1956), Herzog's successor.

[6] *Die Religion in Geschichte und Gegenwart*, 6 vols., 2nd edition Tübingen 1927-1932.

[7] Hermann Gunkel (1862-1932), professor of Old Testament in Berlin 1894-1907, Gießen 1907-1920, Halle 1920-1927; prominent member of the so-called *Religionsgeschichtliche Schule* (History of religions school) which interpreted the books of the Bible in the context of the religions surrounding them.

[8] Friedrich Heiler, »Erzbischof Söderbloms Lebenswerk,« in: *Münchner Neueste Nachrichten* Aug. 28, 1925.

[9] Fr. Heiler, »Der Streit um die evangelische Katholizität. Meine Stellung zu Erzbischof Söderblom,« in: *Die Eiche* 14/1926, 20-26; also in: Fr. Heiler, *Evangelische Katholizität*, München 1926, 179-198. Heiler's opponents were Peter Katz, *Erzbischof Söderblom. Ein Führer zu kirchlicher Einheit*, Halle 1925 (Engl. tr. N. S., *A Prophet of Christian Unity*, London 1949), and René Wallau, *Die Einigung der christlichen Kirche vom evangelischen Glauben aus*, Berlin 1925, 306-315, esp. 312-314. They argued that while Heiler pleaded for a transformation of the Roman Catholic ideal of the church, Söderblom's concept of evangelic catholicity (cf. letter no. 97, no. 3) had its basis in the *sola fide* of the Reformation.

[10] Wilhelm Laible (editor) in *AELKZ* 58/1925, 663-666. 685-689. 707-714. 724-727. Heiler wrote a rejoinder: »Ein Zerrbild von Stockholm,« in: *ChW* 39/1925, 991-997, pointing to a series of factual errors and, more particularly, to Laible's one-sided nationalistic and narrowly dogmatic view. Laible had stressed the rift between the view of many members of the German delegation (shared by him) that the German role in the war had been solely that of peace-loving victims, and the representatives from the victorious nations. This overshadowed the real theological differences between Lutheran and Anglo-Saxon interpretations of the Kingdom of God; cf. Fr. Heiler, »Die religiöse Einheit ...« (cf. letter no. 261, n. 2, 873). - The

Die römischen Katholiken Deutschlands sind zur Zeit tief beunruhigt durch die Indizierung von fünf Werken des Breslauer Professors und Volksschriftstellers Josef Wittig. Seine stark evangelisch geprägten Werke haben eine weite Verbreitung in ganz Deutschland. Wittig ist auch einer [sic] der führenden Persönlichkeiten der katholischen Jugendbewegung, die mit ihm getroffen ist und werden sollte. Ich hoffe über ihn schreiben zu können.[11]

Nun grüsse ich Sie und Ihre verehrte Familie zusammen mit meiner Frau und bleibe in steter Verehrung

Ihr dankbar ergebener
Friedrich Heiler

262. From GUSTAF JOHANSSON[1]

Åbo, Finnland, den 19. X. 25.

Ärade Broder!

Våra vägar hafva gått så långt från hvarandra att de ej mera här kunna förenas. Det smärtar mig, att Konferensen i Stockholm vid en sådan tidpunkt spränger kyrkorna. Världssituationen är en annan än man i Stockholm tänkte sig. Det lönar sig ej att tala härom, då våra världsåskådningar äro alldeles olika.

Jag måste inlägga min reservation däremot, att Stockholms världskonferens gör sig permanent och bildar en fortsättningskomité, som får fullmakt att sätta i verket dess planer. Detta beslut är ej motiveradt. Den finska kyrkan vill ej blifva ett föremål för dessa åtgöranden, ehuru en biskop är invald i komitén.

Katolicismen och rationalismen skola fröjda sig.

Mina ögon äro lidande.

Måtte Gud leda våra kyrkor efter sin vilja! önskar med högaktning

Gustaf Johansson

Åbo, Finland, October 19, 1925

Revered Brother,

Our paths have parted so widely from each other that they can no longer be rejoined here. I deplore that the conference in Stockholm blows the churches apart at such a juncture. The world situation is not what one thought it was in Stockholm. This is

---

speeches are printed in: Adolf Deißmann, *Die Stockholmer Weltkirchenkonferenz. Vorgeschichte, Dienst und Arbeit der Weltkirchenkonferenz für Praktisches Christentum 19.–30. August 1925, Amtlicher deutscher Bericht*, Berlin 1926.

[11] Joseph Wittig (1879-1949), professor of church history in Wroclaw (then German: Breslau) 1915-1925 and popular religious writer. His article »Die Erlösten,« in *Hochland* 19/II, 1922, 1-26, was the cause of his excommunication and compulsory retirement in 1925. Heiler's bibliography contains nothing on Wittig.

[1] Nathan Söderblom's collection of letters, from Swedes, UUB, handwritten letter.

not worth talking about, since our world views are completely different form each other.

I must lodge my reservation against the world conference in Stockholm rendering itself permanent and forming a continuation Committee[2] which is given authority to implement its plans. That decision is unwarranted. The Finnish church does not want to become an object of these activities, even though a bishop has been elected into the committee.

Catholicism and rationalism will rejoice.

My eyes are suffering.[3]

May God guide our churches according to his will! wishes with respect

Gustaf Johansson

263. To Élie Gounelle[1]

Upsala, le 24 Octobre 1925

Cher Frère et Ami,

Vous me demandez mes impressions dominantes de la Conférence Universelle du Christianisme Pratique. Il ne m'est pas possible de les concentrer et de les dire comme je voudrais. Elles commencent seulement à se détacher et se distinguer les unes des autres. Je suis aussi occupé à présent par l'Assemblée nationale de l'Eglise en Suède qui se reunit tous les cinq ans et dont je suis le Président.

Les difficultés semblaient insurmontables. Il est vrai, il ne vaut pas la peine de donner ses forces à des choses faciles. Mais ici il fallait un peu de la folie chrétienne pour entreprendre une telle oeuvre. Quand nous avons refléchi, elle nous paraissait impossible. Quand nous avons prié, elle nous paraissait, je ne dis pas possible, mais nécéssaire. Et nous avons vu encore une fois que Dieu peut faire ce qui est impossible.

Il y avait trois espèces de grandes difficultés.

1: Les contrastes politiques accidentels ou approfondis par une longue tradition historique.

2: Il y avait les deux mondes spirituels de l'Ouest et de l'Est. La Sainte Eglise Catholique et Apostolique que nous confessons, a trois grandes sections, celle qui s'appelle Orthodoxe, celle qui s'appelle Romaine, celle qui s'appelle Evangélique. La première et la troisième avaient accepté l'invita-

---

[2] The decision of the Stockholm conference to form this committee was the first step on the long way towards a World Council of Churches that Söderblom had advocated from 1919 onwards. (The foundation of the Council of Life and Work in 1930 preceded that.) As for possible political implications, cf. letter no. 254, n. 4.

[3] The Swedish word could refer both to the events Johansson's eyes see and to an ailment.

[1] Elie Gounelle (1865–1950), French Methodist minister, one of the leaders of the Christian Socialist movement in France, active in missionary efforts among the working class, member of the Socialist Party. – Nathan Söderblom's collection of letters, to Swedes and foreigners, UUB, typewritten letter (carbon copy).

tion. Elles ne se sont jamais rencontrées d'une façon si solennelle et si complète auparavant. Ce rencontre historique et la connaissance et la confiance et le sentiment d'unité qui en decoulent, furent scellées d'une manière majestueuse entre toutes par le déces du vénérable Patriarche d'Alexandrie à Zürich, appelé par son Seigneur en voyant comme Moise du sommet de Nebo le pays de la promesse et de l'esperance: l'Unité des Chrétiens pour laquelle il avait prié et travaillé pendant une longue vie. Les travaux et l'importance de la Conférence semblent avoir été sous-ligné par Dieu Lui même aussi par la mort du Patriarche de la grande délégation Americaine, M.J. A. Clutz, D. Th. professeur à la Faculté de Théologie de Gettysburg, le plus vieux séminaire de Théologie de l'Eglise luthérienne aux Etats Unis.

3: Il y avait aussi les différences des dénominations évangeliques et, ce qui veut dire peut être d'avantage, les directions différentes au sein de la même Eglise. Des Leaders des plus autorisés de la Théologie et de la piété conservatrice et d'une conception soi-disante moderne ont collaboré à Stockholm. Car tous sentaient l'urgence de l'appel du Maître à Le suivre dans un service devoué et desintéressé.

Il se sont détachées deux conceptions fondamentales du Royaume /ou plutôt du Règne/ de Dieu, comme Vous avez signalé déjà et comme je lis dans les reçits publiés ici dans le Nord, en Allemagne, dans la prèsse Française, en Angleterre, en Amerique et d'autres parts. Le Regne de Dieu, est-il une force immanente de l'humanité, un programme pour notre activité energique et enthousiaste? Ou bien le Regne de Dieu, est-il le jugement et le salut operé par Dieu d'une manière inscrutable au cours de l'histoire et dans son achevement, une activité divine devant laquelle il faut s'incliner et adorer même quand notre pauvre intelligence n'y comprend rien? La difference est encore celle ci. Le Regne de Dieu peut-il opérer une conversion et une amélioration de la société humaine et de ses conditions; ou implique-t-il seulement la régénération de l'individu?

Ces tempéraments differents ne se sont pas revelés à Stockholm d'une manière si crude et simple comme j'ai indiqué ici. On peut parler de activisme, calviniste et de quietisme luthérien. On peut aussi parler de optimisme Anglosaxon et d'une conception plus compliquée, plus lourde et plus sombre du Christianisme du Vieux Monde.

Ces deux conceptions ne se sont jamais rencontrées autant que je sache, comme à Stockholm. Ils ont beaucoup à apprendre l'une de l'autre. Car elles sont necéssaires toutes les deux. Il y a une synthèse. Vous Vous rappelez comment, à la fin de la discussion sur un nombre considérable de problèmes sociaux et de tâches particulières, M. Garvie de Londre a ramené tous ces détails et tous ces oeuvres pratiques au seul principe de notre foi et de notre vie, l'amour divin. Il a fini par montrer avec une ferveur toute évangelique comme notre religion n'est pas une loi, mais un don divin, un pardon, une miséricorde paradoxale, qui implique pour nous la volonté de servir et les actes du service.

Ce que l'Evêque de la Saxonie Dr. L. Ihmels as dit le dernier jour à Stockholm, le 29 Août, est vrai de toutes ces différences: »Nous nous sommes regardés dans l'oeil et dans le coeur. Et desormais il ne peut jamais devenir comme il était auparavant«.

Mes impressions dominantes?

1: Nous avons prié avec S:ta Birgitta: »Seigneur! Montre nous la route et rend nous prêts à la marcher«.

J'ai l'impression très forte que les préparations multiples dans les commissions des sections et du Comité International et puis le travail assidu du Congrès lui même nous a fait voir un peu plus claire dans les problèmes sociaux et internationaux qui constituent le programme du Life and Work.

Nous avons une grande promesse dans l'Institut international du Christianisme social proposé par Vous, par mon frère l'Evêque de Västerås et par d'autres, et acceptée en principe par la Conférence Universelle.

En tous cas la responsabilité a été sentie d'une manière plus universelle qu'auparavant. L'Eglise Chrétienne comme telle ne peut pas se dérober de cette responsabilité et de cette solidarité dans la repentence proclamée par notre Conférence et dans le travail de coeur, de pensée, de vie et d'activité claire et commune guidés par l'Esprit. A ce point de vu il est d'une importance particulière, que toute une série de délégations, comme celle de l'Allemagne, de la France, de la Finlande, de la Suède etc. n'ont pas été choisies parmi les hommes gagnés auparavant pour cette cause, mais qu'elle representent d'une façon plenière l'Eglise Chrétienne comme telle, c'est à dire tous ceux, qui constituent le noyau des croyants sincères.

2: J'ai déjà sous-ligné combien nous avons à apprendre chacun des autres sans abandonner notre propre caractère spirituel et l'héritage sacré confié à chacun de nous. Des membres nombreux et éminents de l'Eglise Orthodoxe et de l'Eglise Evangelique m'ont dis [sic; lis: dit] oralement et par écrit que notre assemblée à Stockholm leur a été une revelation. Les uns disent: »Nous n'avions aucune idée de ce que nos Frères Orthodoxes ont quelque chose à nous donner dont nous avons besoin.« Les autres disent: »Nous Orthodoxes Orientaux avons vu comme jamais auparavant comment l'Evangile nous unit à nos Frères de l'Eglise Evangelique, et combien ils peuvent nous donner, tout en respectant le caractère propre de nos Eglises.«

Cela me rappelle les paroles du Régent de l'Etiopie, le Prince Impérial Ras Tafari dans la Cathédrale d'Upsala l'année dernière, lorsqu'il a loué les missionaires évangeliques, qui ne tâchent pas de detourner les Etiopiens de leur ancienne église, mais de leurs donner l'instruction et une connaissance plus intime de l'Evangile. Desormais les Eglises du Vieux Monde ne doivent jamais être regardées par d'autres Eglises comme un champ de mission, mais comme des soeurs.

3: Mon impression la plus intime et la plus forte a été l'Unité spirituelle révelée pous moi de la façon la plus sacrée et la plus monumentale dans la Sainte Cène dans Engelbrektskyrkan le Dimanche le 23, quand des hommes appartenants à des tendences et des confessions diverses s'agenouillaient autour de cette table du Seigneur qui devait être le point de ralliement entre tous pour tous les chrétiens sincèrs mais qui est devenue par un zèle cruel une division, qui crucifie le Seigneur de nouveau.

Nous avons prié, invoqué et adoré ensemble: »Communion in adorando et serviendo oecumenica«. Si l'Unité s'est manifestée malgré et dans toutes ces différences profondes, cela tient en premier lieu bien entendu à

l'Esprit de Dieu

dont nous avons senti la puissante présence dans cette discipline qui a régné pendant toute la Conférence. Il a été utile que la Conférence a été occupé jusqu'au dernier degré avec un travail surchargeant et sérieux. Mais surtout nous devons le revélation de notre Unité surtout à la place préponderante donné aux services réligieux et la dévotion commune.

Ces souvenirs resteront dans nos âmes et exerceront, prions-le, un influence bienfaisante partout dans nos Eglises.

4: Mais nous devons la réalisation de notre profonde Unité spirituelle avant tout aux personnalités dont la présence et vie spirituelle a été une force purificatrice et conciliatrice. Ici mon regret est aussi grand que ma gratidude envers Dieu. J'ai vu ces chers visages et j'ai regardé pour la première fois des personnes dont je bénie depuis longtemps l'oeuvre, sans pouvoir /avec deux ou trois exceptions/ avoir une conversation et une communion proche de l'âme à l'âme avec eux pendant ces jours si remplis. Mais je sens d'avantage qu'elles existent dans le monde. J'en remercie Dieu et je me sens lié avec elles pour le temps et l'éternité.

5: Est-il un rêve ou un exaucement de prières que nous avons déjà le commencement d'une cooperation organisée des Eglises Evangeliques et Orthodoxes?

Si Dieu nous a accordé dans cette Conférence si surchargée, si difficile, beaucoup plus que nous ne pouvions songer et esperer, notre responsabilité à nous est devenue pour cela d'autant plus grande. Nous avons surtout besoin de l'union de nos prières, qui n'ont probablement jamais monté jusqu'à Dieu si unies comme après le rencontre de la Chrétienté de toute part de notre planet.

Je ne peux pas finir ces lignes trop incomplètes sans mentionner la contribution essentielle de la Délégation Française si hautement qualifiée pour une telle grande tâche et dont des membres ont été les instruments de Dieu pour élever nos coeurs et pour éclaircir notre intelligence sur les problèmes qui nous occupont [sic].

Sachez moi, cher et honoré Frère, Votre de tout coeur devoué

Uppsala, October 24, 1925

Dear Brother and friend,

You ask me about my dominant impressions of the Universal Conference of Practical Christianity. It is not possible for me to concentrate them and to name them to you as I would like to. They are just beginning to take shape and to become distinct from one another. I am also occupied right now by the national Assembly of the Church in Sweden which meets every five years and whose President I am.

The difficulties seemed insurmountable. It is true, easy matters are not worth applying your energy to. But here a bit of the Christian folly was needed for undertaking such an enterprise. When we pondered, it seemed impossible to us. When we prayed, it seemed to us, I do not say possible, but necessary. And we have seen once more that God can do what is impossible.

There were three kinds of great difficulties.

1° The political contrasts, accidental or deepened by a long historical tradition.

2° There were the two spiritual worlds of the West and the East. The Holy Catholic and Apostolic Church which we confess has three great sections, the one that calls itself Orthodox, the one that calls itself Roman, the one that calls itself Protestant. The first and the third [of these] had accepted the invitation. They have never encountered each other in such a solemn and complete fashion before. This historic meeting and the knowledge and the confidence and the sense of unity which it entails, were sealed in a majestic fashion more than anything else by the decease of the venerable Patriarch of Alexandria in Zürich, called by his Lord as he saw, like Moses from the summit of Nebo, the land of promise and hope: the Unity of Christians for which he had prayed and worked during a long life. The endeavors and the importance of the Conference seem to have been underlined by God Himself also by means of the death of the Patriarch of the large American delegation, Mr. J.A. Clutz, Th. D., professor at the Faculty of Theology of Gettysburg, the oldest theological seminary of the Lutheran Church in the United States.

3° There were also the differences of the Protestant denominations and, what is perhaps even more telling, the different schools of thought within the same Church. Some of the most authorized Leaders of conservative theology and allegiance and of a self-avowed modern concept collaborated in Stockholm. For everybody felt the urgency of the Master's appeal to follow Him in devout and disinterested service.

Two basic concepts of the Kingdom (or rather the Lordship) of God have taken shape, as you already pointed out and as I read it in the reports published here in the North, in Germany, in the French press, in England, in America and in other parts [of the world]. Is the Lordship of God an immanent force of humanity, a program for our energetic and enthusiastic activity? Or is the Lordship of God rather the judgment and the salvation wrought by God in an inscrutable way in the course of history and in its consummation, a divine activity in view of which one must bow and worship, even if our poor reason does not understand anything? The difference is still that. Can the Lordship of God effect a transformation and an amelioration of human society and its conditions, or does it only imply a rebirth of the individual?

These different stamps did not become manifest in Stockholm in a way as crude and simple as I have indicated here. One can speak of Calvinist activism and Lutheran quietism. One can also speak of Anglo-Saxon optimism and of a more complicated, graver, and more sombre concept of Christianity of the Old World.

These two concepts have never encountered each other, as far as I know, in such a way as in Stockholm. They have much to learn from each other. For they are both necessary. There is a synthesis. You will remember how Mr. Garvie from London,[2] at the end of a discussion about a considerable number of social problems and specific tasks, reduced all these details and all these practical activities to the sole principle of our faith and our life, divine love. He concluded by demonstrating, with an entirely evangelic fervor, how our religion is not a law but a divine gift, a forgiveness, a paradoxical mercy, which implies for us the will to serve, and the activities of service.

---

[2] Alfred Ernest Garvie (1861–1945), Principal of New College, London, leading Congregationalist churchman, participant in the COPEC conference in 1924 (cf. letter no. 220, n. 2).

What the bishop of Saxony, Dr. L. Ihmels, said on the last day in Stockholm, August 29, is true of all these differences: »We have looked into each other's eyes and hearts. And from now on things can never become as they were before.«

My dominant impressions?

1° We prayed with St. Birgitta:[3] »Oh Lord! Show us the way and make us ready to walk it.«

I have the very strong impression that the multiple preparations in the committees of the sections and of the International Committee, and then the assiduous endeavor of the Conference itself made us see a little more clearly with regard to the social and international problems which constitute the program of Life and Work.

We have a great promise in the form of the International Institute of Social Christianity proposed by you, by my Brother, the bishop of Västerås,[4] and by others, and accepted in principle by the Universal Conference.

In any case, the responsibility has been felt in a more universal way than before. The Christian Church as such cannot divest itself of that responsibility and that solidarity in repentance proclaimed by our Conference and in the endeavor of heart, mind, life and the clear and common activity guided by the Spirit. From this point of view it is of particular importance that a whole series of delegations, like that of Germany, France, Finland, Sweden etc., have not been selected from people won for that cause before, but that they represent in a comprehensive way the Christian Church as such, that is, all those who constitute the nucleus of sincere believers.

2° I have already underlined how much we have to learn from each other, without abandoning our own spiritual character and the sacred heritage entrusted to each of us. Numerous and eminent members of the Orthodox Church and of the Protestant Church have told me in both oral and written form that our assembly in Stockholm has been a revelation for them. The ones say: »We had no idea that our orthodox Brothers had something to give to us that we need.« The others say: »We orthodox Orientals have seen like never before how the Gospel unites us with our Brothers of the Protestant Church, and how much they can give to us, while respecting the particular character of our Churches.«

That reminds me of the words of the Regent of Ethiopia, the Imperial Prince Ras Tafari,[5] in Uppsala Cathedral last year, when he lauded the Protestant missionaries who did not strive to avert the Ethiopians from their ancient Church, but to give them instruction and a more intimate consciousness of the Gospel. From now on the Churches of the Old World must never be regarded by the other Churches as a field of missions, but as sisters.

3° My most intimate and strong impression has been the spiritual Unity revealed for me in the most sacred and most monumental form in the Lord's Supper in Engelbrekt Church on Sunday the 23rd, when people belonging to different schools of thought and demominations knelt around that table of the Lord which more than anything else should become the rallying point for all sincere Christians but which by a cruel zeal has become a division which crucifies the Lord once again.

We prayed, invoked and worshiped together: »Communio in adorando et ser-

---

[3] The Swedish national saint, founder of a nuns' order in Vadstena in 1346, known for her deep piety, works of charity and her influence on the great and powerful in church and state towards a spiritual and moral renewal. Canonized in 1391.

[4] Einar Billing; cf. letters no. 20 n. 3; 167, n. 7; and 265.

[5] Ras Tafari (1892–1975) became regent in 1916, Negus (king) in 1928, and Emperor by the name of Haile Selassie I. in 1930. He was removed from power by a coup in 1974.

viendo oecumenica.«[6] If the Unity has manifested itself despite, and in the midst of, all those profound differences, that derives of course in the first place from
the Spirit of God
whose powerful presence we have felt in that discipline which has been prevailing throughout the Conference. It was useful that the Conference was occupied to the utmost by exorbitant and serious work. But above all we owe the revelation of our Unity to the crucial role accorded to our religious services and common devotion.

These memories shall remain in our souls and exert, let us pray, a beneficent influence everywhere in our Churches.

4° But we owe the realization of our profound spiritual Unity above all to the personalities whose presence and spiritual life have been a purifying and conciliatory force. Here my regret is as great as my gratitude towards God. I saw these cherished faces and for the first time looked at persons whose work I have been praising for a long time, without being able (with two or three exceptions) to have a conversation and a close communion from soul to soul with them during these crowded days. But I am more aware that they exist in the world. I thank God for that and I feel being bound to them in time and eternity.

5° Is it a dream or an answer to prayers, that we already have the beginning of an organized cooperation of the Protestant and Orthodox Churches?

If God has accorded to us at this so overburdened, so difficult Conference much more than we could have dreamed of and expected, our responsibility has become all the greater for us. We need above all the union of our prayers, which have probably never risen to God so united as after the meeting of Christendom from every part of our planet.

I cannot conclude these all too incomplete lines without mentioning the essential contribution of the French delegation so highly qualified for such a great task, whose members have been the instruments of God for elevating our hearts and for clarifying our understanding of the problems occupying us.

Believe me, dear and respected Brother, yours with all his heart dedicated

264. To Gustaf Johansson[1]

Upsala den 28 oktober 1925

Högt vördade Broder!

Brevet har djupt smärtat mig. Ingen av oss, icke ens Finlands högst vördade och av mig med uppriktig beundran och aktning omfattade Ärkebiskop har makt att genom någon slags påvlig bannbulla förhindra det verk som Guds Ande verkar i människornas hjärtan. Förvisso hade Stockholmsmötet sin uppkomst däri, at kristna i skilda länder, bedjande och uppriktiga själar, kände samvetets nöd och Mästarens ovillkorliga bud och därför med något av trons dåraktighet gentemot mycken klokskap, förhånande, ja även fördömande från personer och grupper i kyrka och stat, sökte åstadkomma ett vittnesbörd om att det, trots alla verkliga åtskillnader, som icke få utsud-

---

[6] Latin for: Ecumenical communion in worshiping and serving.

[1] Nathan Söderblom's collection of letters, to Swedes and foreigners, UUB, typewritten letter.

das, dock finns något redan här på jorden som uppenbarar den Ena Heliga Katolska och Apostoliska kyrkan. Jag vill icke utlåta mig om sanningen i det omdöme som en fransk tidning angav, at endast den gammaldags äkta lutherdomen var i stånd att bilda en dylik samlingspunkt. Se vi på kyrkans historia, så har Andens mäktiga rörelser alltid mötts av något av samma motstånd och protester som nu från vissa håll riktats mot Stockholms-mötet. Jag är fullt medveten om dess brister och fel. Men jag är i likhet med många, många andra, icke minst inom den äkta verkligt renläriga lutherdomen, (i motsats emot en mera lagisk eller svärmisk religionsuppfattning) djupt och ofrånkomligt medveten om att Guds helige Ande trots allt drivit oss och gjort sig mäktigt märkbar under Stockholmsmötet.

Från början till slut har med största skärpa betonats, att Mötet självt och dess Fortsättningskomitté icke har någon som helst myndighet över något kyrkosamfund. Kan Mötet och dess fortsättning uträtta något, så sker det enligt Apostelns regel i II.Kor.4.2 på ett andligt sätt genom Sanningens uppenbarande inför mänskliga samveten.

Hur mycket än min högt vördade Ämbetsbroders fördömande av denna strävan smärtar mig, så skall ett dylikt fördömande aldrig kunna förhindra mig att känna tacksamhet för den välvilja, varmed jag blivit av Finlands Ärkebiskop omfattad, och för värdefulla intryck och lärdomar jag erhållit av honom i hans litterära alstring och särskilt under vandringen i Åbo, icke minst rörande just det sociala problem, som tillhörde Stockholmsmötets viktigaste uppgift.

I djup och oföränderlig vördnad tillgivne
Nathan Söderblom

Uppsala, October 28, 1925

Highly esteemed Brother,
your letter has deeply saddened me. None of us, not even Finland's highly esteemed Archbishop who is being held in sincere admiration and respect by me, has the power to prevent the work the Spirit of God effects in human hearts by some kind of papal bull of excommunication. Quite certainly, the origin of the Stockholm conference was: Christians in various countries, prayerful and upright souls, perceived the constraint of their consciences and the Master's unconditional commandment, and therefore they tried, with a measure of the folly of faith,[2] in the face of much shrewdness, derision, and even condemnation by individuals and groups in church and state, to bear witness to there being something already here on earth which, in spite of all those real differences which must not be blotted out, reveals the One Holy, Catholic, and Apostolic church. I do not want to pronounce on the truth in the opinion of a French newspaper that only old-fashioned, genuine Lutheranism was capable of becoming such a rallying point. If we look at the history of the church, the mighty works of the Spirit have always met with something of the same resistance and protest that are now being aimed against the Stockholm meeting from certain quarters. I am fully aware of its shortcomings and faults. But I am, in conformity with many, many others, not least within genuine, really doctrinally pure

---

[2] I Cor 1:18-31.

Lutheranism (as opposed to a more legalistic or visionary view of religion), profoundly and inescapably aware that in spite of it all God's Holy Spirit was compel-
ling us and made himself strongly felt during the Stockholm conference.

From beginning to end it has been stressed with the utmost of poignancy that the
Conference itself and the Continuation Committee have no authority whatsoever
over any church body. If the Conference and its continuation achieve something,
this happens, in accordance with the Apostle's rule in II Cor 4:2, in a spiritual way
by means of the revelation of Truth to human consciences.

However much the condemnation of this endeavor by my highly esteemed fellow
Archbishop saddens me, such a condemnation shall never be able to prevent me
feeling gratitude for the benevolence I have been conferred upon, and for the valuable impressions and instruction I received from him through his literary production
and particularly when walking in Åbo, not least concerning precisely the social problem which was part of the Stockholm conference's most important purpose.

In deep and unalterable respect
yours sincerely,
Nathan Söderblom

265. To Arthur Titius[1]

Stockholm den 31 Oktober 1925

Sehr geehrter Herr Professor und Kollege!
Es ist in hohem Masse dankenswert, dass Sie sofort die große Aufgabe ins
Auge gefasst haben, welche Ihnen, dem Unterzeichneten[,] Billing[2] und
Anderen von der Weltkonferenz anvertraut wurde.

Wir haben auch von Professor William Adams Brown[3] ein sehr wertvolles Gutachten bekommen mit einer Klarlegung der beiden vor der Weltkonferenz gemachten und vor der Konferenz gutgeheissenen Aufgaben in dieser Hinsicht. Es ist selbstverständlich sehr wichtig, diese beiden ungemein
wichtigen Aufgaben von Beginn an klar zu unterscheiden.

1: Das von der schwedischen Kommission, Gounelle, Ihnen, Dr. Spiek-
ker[4] und vielen Anderen angeregte und von der Weltkonferenz förmlich be-
schlossene Forschungsinstitut[5] für rein wissenschaftliche Behandlung vom

---

[1] Nathan Söderblom's collection of letters, to Swedes and foreigners, UUB, typed copy.
The Humboldt University Library in Berlin has Titius' papers, but they are not ordered.

[2] Einar Billing, cf. letter no. 263.

[3] William A. Brown (1865-1943), 1898-1936 professor of systematic and applied theology
at Union Seminary, New York. Harnack and Troeltsch were his foremost teachers. He was a
leading figure in the activities leading to the formation of the World Council of Churches
which was founded in Edinburgh in 1937, but officially inaugurated only in Amsterdam in
1948.

[4] Friedrich Albert Spiecker (1854-1936), director of the Siemens & Halske corporation in
Berlin, an active promotor of social and ecumenical concerns.

[5] Einar Billing, professor of Christian ethics in Uppsala, was the driving force behind this
idea, which was conceived in analogy to the International Labor Office, founded in 1919. Cf.
his Stockholm speech, in: Deißmann, op. cit. (cf. letter no. 261, n. 10), 225-229. The international institute of social science was actually founded at the conference of the Continuation

Standpunkte der christlichen Ethik von der bei uns so genannten Sozialen Frage die von den Anglosachsen Das Industrielle und Ekonomische Problem genannt wird.

2: Ein Centralbureau für Grundfragen der Erziehung, besonders auf solchen Gebieten, welche für den socialen und internationalen Frieden von Bedeutung sind.[6]

Wo soll man beginnen? Professor W.A. Brown schlägt vor, dass das Fortsetzungskomitté die allgemeineren Aufgabe II zuerst zu verwirklichen versuchen soll, um sodann, wenn weitere Klarheit gewonnen wird, die speziellere Aufgabe des socialen Forschungsinstituts aufzunehmen. Für die Unterzeichneten scheint es ebenso angezeigt zu sein, alle beide Sachen anzugreifen und zwar sobald wie möglich unter dem frischen Eindrucke der Weltkonferenz.

Wir sprechen hier zunächst von der von Ihnen besprochenen Socialen Kommission.

Mit Recht bezeichnen Sie das Ziel unserer Bemühungen als ein in geeigneter Stätte festgelegtes Institut mit einer Reihe von befähigten Persönlichkeiten, die für diesen Zweck besoldet sind, und sich der Aufgabe gänzlich widmen können. Aber selbstverständlich kann, wie Sie schreiben, eine solche Akademie nicht sofort eingerichtet werden.

Einstweilen kann die Arbeit doch begonnen werden durch die Schon gewählte Kommission, die sich mit geeigneten Persönlichkeiten vervollständigen kann. Wir meinen, dass die Mitglieder der gewählten Kommission und andere Sachkündigen wichtige Beiträge zu der Aufgabe des socialen Institutes geben können, indem Sie in ihren verschiedenen Berufen bleiben. Freilich stimmen wir Ihrer Ansicht völlig bei, dass in dieser Kommission an erster Stelle Akademiker, Ethiker, Nationalekonomen etc., aber auch berufene Vertreter der Diakonia, der karitativen und social-pedagogischen Tätigkeit der Kirche, welche Tätigkeit zu ernser Befassung mit der socialen Frage zwingt, und weiter, denkende Repräsentanten der Arbeiterbewegung, der Arbeitsleitung und der Arbeitgeber herangezogen werden müssen.

Das Erste und Wichtigste scheint es uns zu sein, für diese Sache einen geeigneten Sekretär zu finden.

Das Fortsetzungskomitté hat ja schon ein sehr hervorragendes Sekretariat, aber Niemanden der sich der Fortsetzung der Weltkonferenz wesentlich widmen. kann. Einen solchen müssen wir haben. Es scheint uns praktisch und richtig, dass dieser zu schaffende Sekretär jetzt an erster Stelle als Centralpunkt der permanenten socialen Kommission angestellt werden soll. Dann [sic; lies: Denn] seine Tätigkeit und die Fortsetzung der Weltkonferenz überhaupt kann wohl am besten dadurch beginnen, dass der Beginn des zu beschaffenden Centralbureaus mit einer sehr genau bestimmten Auf-

---

Committee in Bern 1926. It was located in Zürich, Adolf Keller (cf. letter no. 240, n. 3) became its director.

[6] One of the most important practical ideas was the revision of history books in the schools.

gabe gemacht wird. Nach unserer Meinung wäre es somit gut, zunächst die nötigen Mittel, über die das Kommitté leider nicht verfügt, aufzubringen, um einen geeigneten Sekretär an einem geeigneten Orte fest anzustellen, der Informationen über die socialen, ekonomischen und industriellen Fragen anschaffen und Bearbeitung jener Fragen von den Mitgliedern der permanenten Kommission ermitteln soll, dabei selbstverständlich die schon vorhandenen Institutionen praktisch ausnutzend.

Die zweite nicht unwichtige Frage scheint uns zu sein, wo der Beginn des Centralbureaus für Leben und Wirken eingerichtet werden soll. Heut zu Tage muss man noch an ein ex-neutrales Land denken. Die skandinavischen Ländern sind zu entfernt und haben ihre eigenen Sprachen. Holland ist sehr central belegen. Und wir haben in Professor Slotemaker de Bruine,[7] den Sie kennen, eine ganzherzige und ungemein töchtige [lies: tüchtige] Person für diese Aufgabe, obwohl er selbstverständlich nicht seine Stellung als Akademiker und Kirchenmann verlassen kann, aber daneben wie bisher wertvolle und unermüdliche Arbeit für die sociale Aufgabe der Kirche leisten kann. Aber eine gewisse Schwierigkeit besteht darin, dass unsere evangelischen Schwesterkirchen in Holland, mit seiner heroischen Geschichte und Christentumsform keine gemeinsame Organisation besitzen, und durch ihre Verfassung auch wenige Kontinuität in der Kirchenleitung. Obwohl die Holländer bewundernswerte Sprachkenntnisse besitzen, wäre es auch von einem gewissen Wert wenigstens eine der drei grossen abendländischen Sprachen im Landes des Centralbureaus zu haben.

In der Schweiz haben wir ohne weiteres, was wir in der Person unseren ausgezeichneten Dolmetschers Pastor Koochlin [sic][8] bewundert haben, zwei der drei Sprachen, eine gemeinsame Organisation der dortigen Evangelischen Christenheit und eine für praktische Zwecke und internationale Arbeit längst bewährte Kirchenleitung. Dazu kommt, dass die Nähe des internationalen Bureaus des Völkerbundes selbstverständlich für die Arbeit des socialen Institutes ungemein bequem ist. Wir haben nach vieler Erwägung und Beratung gegenwärtig die Ueberzeugung bekommen, dass Bern sich in mehreren Hinsichten als Sitz des Instituts und des Bureaus eignen würde. Das ist selbstverständlich gründlich zu erwägen.

Mit Recht haben Sie auch andere Mittel vorgeschlagen. Errichtung socialer Bibliotheken, Studiereisen, Kongresse u.s.w. Aber wir wollen hier an dritter Stelle die von Ihnen angeregte Frage von einer Zeitschrift besprechen. Selbstverständlich muss das Institut, oder sagen wir die Kommission, ehe das förmliche Institut zustandekommt, einen Organ, eine Zeitschrift[9]

---

[7] Jan Rudolph Slotemaker de Bruine (1869–1941), Dutch Reformed theologian and politician, pastor 1894, professor of systematic and practical theology in Utrecht 1916, Secretary of Labor 1926 and Secretary of Education in 1935.

[8] Alphons Koechlin (1885–1965), Basel, chief interpreter at the conference, president of the Swiss Church Federation 1933–1954, active in leading postions of the ecumenical movement.

[9] Keller's Institute (cf. note 6) launched the periodical *Stockholm. International Review for*

oder eine Reihe von sonstigen Publikationen herausgeben. Aber es scheint uns ungemein wichtig zu sein, dass diese Zeitschrift oder diese Publikation nicht beginnt, ehe die Linien völlig klar geworden sind, da ja das, wie wir hoffen, zukunftschwere Unternehmen der Weltkonferenz eine Forschungs-anstalt zu beschaffen, von vielen Seiten mit lebhaftem Interesse oder mit wacher Kritik beobachtet wird und da diese Publikation sofort in den Au-gen der Christenheit dem ganzen Unternehmen seinen Karaktär geben wird. So scheint uns daher notwendig das Material und die Aufgabe näher zu bestimmen, ehe die Zeitschrift beginnt. Wir warten noch von Dr. Henry Atkinson[10] das Protokoll der Weltkonferenz. Sobald es kommt, möchten wir Sie auffordern, die Mitglieder der von dem Fortsetzungskommitté ge-wählten socialen Kommission zu einer Sitzung in Berlin oder irgendwo sonst zu berufen, um die ganze Sache gründlich mit einander zu durchdis-kutieren, und sehen ob nicht schon dem Arbeitausschusse des Fortsetzungs-kommitté der wahrscheinlich in Juni tagen kann, ein bestimmter Vorschlag eingereicht werden kann, so dass das gesamte Fortsetzungskommitté in Au-gust oder September die organisierte Arbeit der socialen Kommission förm-lich feststellen und einleiten kann.

Hierbei möchten wir einen besonderen Punkt erwähnen. Wir wissen was für eine bedeutsame Rolle die christlich sociale Tätigkeit und die christli-chen Gewerkschaften spielen, besonders für die Verbreitung und Anwen-dung der christlichen Weltanschauung unter den Arbeitern. Aber bei uns ist die Situation anders. Innerhalb der Social-Demokratie haben wir ausge-zeichnete christlich wirksame und Verantwortungsfühlende und tragende Männer und Frauen in immer wachsender Menge. Tausende von Socialde-mokraten sind Vertrauensmänner in der kirchlichen Arbeit. Ausgezeichnete Pastoren gehören seit einem Menschenalter der Socialdemokratischen Par-tei und leisten zum Teil im Reichstag eine wertvolle Wirksamkeit für Chri-stentum und Kirche. Unter solchen Umständen ist es nicht bei uns möglich die Sache der Kirche und des Christentums in der Arbeiterschaft an einer gegen die Socialdemokratie gerichteten Gewerkschaftlichen Organisation zu binden, obwohl wir genau wissen was für eine Bedeutung solche Organi-sation in anderen Ländern haben.

Solche Probleme müssen genau diskutiert werden, ehe eine Publikation die Orientierung der socialen Kommission und des socialen Instituts aller Welt angiebt.

Was viertens die Mittel betrifft, glauben wir, dass es zunächst notwendig sein wird, die Mittel durch Gaben aufzubringen. In einer baldigen Zukunft wird der schon vorhandenen Beginn einer Gesammtkirchlichen Organisati-on die Mittel leisten können. Aber noch nicht. Die vom Fortsetzungskom-mitté eventuell aufzubringenden Mittel sind für die Publikation der Akten

---

the Social Activities of the Churches, 1928–1931, published in English, French, and German in Göttingen, London, and Chicago.

[10] Henry Atkinson, cf. letter no. 183, n. 1.

bestimmt. Daher müssen wir in unseren verschiedenen Ländern alles tun um von interessierten Seiten die nötigen Mittel zu bekommen.

Wir fragen Sie somit zunächst, ob Sie unsere Meinung teilen, dass der nächste Schritt die Anstellung eines geeigneten Sekretärs sein soll. Aber ehe etwas darüber bestimmt werden kann, schlagen wir Ihnen vor, die Mitglieder der sozialen Kommissions sobald wie möglich zu einer Zusammenkunft zusammenzurufen. Vielleicht schon im Februar des nächsten Jahres.

Bis dahin würden wir es als sehr wertvoll betrachten, wenn die gegenseitige Beratung durch Briefe fortgesetzt werden kann.

In der Ueberzeugung dass der von so vielen Seiten angeregte und von der Weltkonferenz ohne Widerspruch angenommenen Plan eines socialen Instituts (bzw. Kommission) eine bedeutsame Aufgabe und Zukunft haben wird, sind wir Ihre, in dankbarer Hochachtung sehr ergebene

. . . .

266. To Eivind Berggrav[1]

Upsala den 1 december 1925

Käre Vän!

Tack för besöket och Dina rader!

Jag hör av Runestam att Du frågat om Fortsättningsnämnden. Dess sammanträden här i Konstistorierummet och i Första Kammarens Plenisal i Riksdagshuset i Stockholm på måndagen hade ju en mängd ärenden att behandla, och det hela försiggick i den allra bästa anda. [...] Det enda som jag beklagar är, att biskop Ammundsen, som från början var enhälligt uppsatt för Arbetsutskottet, av nobel hänsyn till att Öst-Europa där skulle företrädas, avsade sig till förmån för en ungrare. Vi borde hava haft både. Ingen är viktigare än Ammundsen. Vid nästa sammanträde bör han därför inväljas i utskottet.

Biskop Ihmels' närvaro och visserligen efter hans lynne betänksamma, men allt igenom lojala sätt att deltaga i Liv och Arbete kan till sin betydelse icke överskattas. Min dotter som är i Dresden skriver att hon hört ett föredrag av Ihmels därstädes som hette »Von Stockholm bis Oslo och var alldeles utmärkt. Jag satt förstås med spända öron för att upptäcka något ord emot konferensen, men han sade inte ett ord för mycket – en del kritiserade han ju, men drog då samtidigt fram andras åsikter. Han talade så att man till slut tyckte man varit med om en gudstjänst.«

[...]

Tillgivne

Nathan Söderblom

_____

[1] Nathan Söderblom's collection of letters, to Swedes and foreigners, UUB, typewritten letter (carbon copy).

Uppsala, December 1, 1925

Dear friend,
Thank you for the visit and your lines!
I hear from Runestam[2] that you asked about the continuation commission. Its meeting here in the Senate room [of the University] and in the plenary hall of the Upper House in the Diet building in Stockholm had of course a lot of issues to treat, and the whole thing proceeded in the very best spirit. ... [On an inconsequential disturbance] The only thing I deplore is that Bishop Ammundsen, who from the beginning was unanimously nominated for the working committee, out of the noble consideration that Eastern Europe should be represented there, declined in favor of a Hungarian. We should have had both of them. No one is more important than Ammundsen. At the next meeting, he must therefore be elected into the committee.

Bishop Ihmels' presence and, in accordance to his temperament, cautious but on the whole loyal way of participating in Life and Work cannot be overestimated in its significance. My daughter who is in Dresden writes that she heard a speech of Ihmels there which was entitled »Von Stockholm bis Oslo [From Stockholm to Oslo][3] and was quite excellent. I was sitting there with wide-open ears, of course, in order to detect some word against the conference, but he did not say one word too many – part of it he did criticize, of course, but along with that, he cited opinions of others. He talked in such a way that in the end one felt like having participated in a worship service.«

... [On a newspaper article Söderblom had sent to Berggrav]
Sincerely yours,
Nathan Söderblom

267. From Eivind Berggrav[1]

Oslo 8/12 25

Kjære Erkebiskop.
Jeg er meget teknemelig for alt hvad jeg har mottatt. Det er nu blevet til en större »Ekumenisk kringsjå« (Rundschau) i desember heftet. Av Professor Hromádka (tsjekken) har jeg laget en större redaksjonel leder: »Gjorde reformasjonen arvelös?« Det er ingen sak å være redaktör når man har slike kilder!

---

[2] Cf. letters no. 184, n. 8, and 208.

[3] The title refers to the General Evangelical (= Protestant) Lutheran Conference which took place under the auspices of the theological faculty of Oslo University immediately after Stockholm, Sept. 2–5, 1925. It stood pretty much in the shade of Uppsala, and further complications arose out of the tensions between the Norwegian university theologians and those of the conservative *Menighetsfakultet*. Söderblom was not present. Participants were mainly Germans, many of whom were critical of him and the Life and Work movement. Cf. Heinrich Hermelink, »Oslo und Stockholm,« in: *CW* 40/41, 1925, 884–892, esp. 884 f. Ihmels fulfilled a mediating function there, just as he had done in Stockholm. Cf. Hanns Kerner, *Luthertum und ökumenische Bewegung für Praktisches Christentum 1919–1926* (LKGG 5), Gütersloh 1983, 268–270.

[1] Nathan Söderblom's collection of letters, from foreigners, UUB, handwritten letter.

[...] ...hvor jeg også har havt nytte av din dotters korrespondanse. Jeg har stillet *Ihmels* sterkt frem. Din tanke om ham har jeg overveiet meget og er kommet til det resultat at det var overmøde heldig om han blev sektionsformann. Han tåles ju også av den liberale fløj. Selvsagt har jeg ikke nevnt noget om dette. [...]
Din ærbødig hengivne
Eivind Berggrav

Oslo, December 8, 1925
Dear Archbishop,
I am very grateful for all that I have received. It has now become a wider »Ecumenical panorama« in the December issue.[2] Of Professor Hromádka (the Czech),[3] I have produced a lengthy editorial: »Did the reformation leave us bereft of heritage?« It is no feat being an editor if one has such sources!
[On newspaper clips Söderblom had sent to Berggrav] ... where I also profited from your daughter's correspondence. I presented *Ihmels* very strongly. I have pondered quite a bit on your thoughts on him and have come to the conclusion that it would be more than great if he became section chairman. For he is also being tolerated by the liberal wing. It goes without saying that I did not mention any of this.
[On a planned visit of Söderblom to Oslo]
Respectfully yours,
Eivind Berggrav

268. From FRIEDRICH HEILER[1]

Marburg / Lahn 12. Jänner 1926.
Hochverehrter Hochwürdigster Herr Erzbischof,
Zu Ihrem 60. Geburtstage bringe ich Ihnen die herzlichsten Glückwünsche von mir und meiner Frau dar. Wir beide nehmen herzlichen Anteil an der Freude Ihrer ganzen Familie, die mit Ihnen diesen schönen Tag feiert. Mein innigster Gebetswunsch an diesem Tage ist, daß Gott Ihr großes Lebenswerk, die Einigung der Christenheit, bald der Vollendung entgegenführe. Mein zweiter Wunsch an diesem Tage ist, daß, wenn das große Einheitswerk befestigt ist, Gott Ihnen noch volle Kraft gebe, uns aus der Fülle Ihres religionsgeschichtlichen Wissens noch manch schönes Werk zu schenken.
In tiefer Dankbarkeit gedenke ich an diesem Tage alles dessen, was ich

---

[2] Berggrav refers to the periodical *Kirke og kultur* of which he was the editor.
[3] Josef Lukl Hromádka (1889–1969), professor of systematic theology at the Hus Theological Faculty in Prague 1920–1939 and 1947–1969, in between as an emigrant in Princeton. His theological position was centered around the concept of revelation. In social ethics, he was a socialist, engaged in dialogue with reform-minded Marxists in his country. He was one of the founders of the Christian Peace Conference; he resigned as its president after Soviet troops had invaded Czechoslovakia in 1968.

[1] Nathan Söderblom's collection of letters, from foreigners, UUB, handwritten letter.

im Laufe von vielen Jahren von Ihnen empfangen habe, Wissen, Freude, Liebe, Trost und Erquickung. Worte vermögen das nicht auszudrücken. Als bescheidenes Zeichen meiner Dankbarkeit sende ich Ihnen eine Schrift, die ich Ihnen zu diesem Gedenktage widmete. Leider ist sie im Druck nicht fertig geworden; so bitte ich, einstweilen die Revisionsbogen entgegennehmen zu wollen (in denen noch einige Druckfehler stehen). In 10 Tagen hoffe ich Ihnen das Werk fertig übersenden zu können. Ich lege ferner einen Artikel bei, den ich für eine Münchener Zeitung geschrieben habe, und der in diesen Tagen erscheinen soll – δόσις ὀλίγη τε φίλη τε.[2] Mehr noch als dieser Aufsatz und ähnliche legen alle meine Bücher Zeugnis ab von dem, was ich Ihnen verdanke. Ohne Ihre Einwirkung wäre alles in meinem Leben anders gegangen. Ich weiß, daß niemand für mein inneres Leben soviel bedeutet hat als Sie. Aber das Wunderbarste ist, daß Sie auch mir das geworden sind, was Sie Ihren Schutzbefohlenen werden wollten und geworden sind. »Mithelfer zur Freude.«[3]

Mit innigen Segenswünschen begrüße ich Sie und Ihre ganze verehrte Familie zusammen mit meiner Frau und bleibe Ihr stets dankbar ergebener

Friedrich Heiler

269. CIRCULAR LETTER[1]

Välgörare och vän!

Siffrorna som beteckna vår ålder, gå uppåt. Men har man hunnit till nian, så ramlar man strax ohjälpligt ner i nollan, intighetens och den mänskliga ynkedomens bomärke.

När man nått de högre tiotalen, begås också emellanåt en högtid med blommor och tal enligt regeln: De mortuis nihil nisi bene.

Kanske är denna sed ej en tillfällighet. Vårt lynne är stelt. Ej sällan hålla vi inne med de vänliga orden, tills det är för sent. Men när årtalet med nollan uppträder i en äldre, ja numera även i en medelålders persons levnad, öppna vi våra hjärtan. –

Vem vågar tänka på möda och kostnad som människor gjort sig för ens skull? Det är förödmjukande att mottaga mycken oförtjänt godhet. Men – »om jag icke gör dig en tjänst, så har du ingen del med mig.« Den över-

---

[2] δόσις δ' ὀλίγη τε φίλη τε, a small yet friendly gift, quotation from Homer's *Odyssey*, 6,208 and 14,58 where it refers to hospitality granted to Odysseus. The booklet is *Christlicher Glaube und indisches Geistesleben. Rabindranath Tagore, Mahatma Gandhi, Brahmabandav Upadhyaya, Sadhu Sundar Singh* (CFR 3), München 1926; the newspaper article »Ein nordischer Kirchenfürst« [this formulation is not Heiler's], *Münchner Neueste Nachrichten* January 15, 1926.

[3] Allusion to one of Söderblom's favorite texts from Scripture: »Not that we lord it over your faith; we work with you for your joy«, II Cor 1:24 (RSV).

[1] Nathan Söderblom's collection of letters, to Swedes and foreigners, UUB, handwritten (photocopied) letter to wellwishers on the occasion of his 60th birthday (January 15).

strömmande välviljan vittnar om att vi höra tillsammans och bero av varandra.

Vänskapens överseende och kärleksfullt förstorande ord bliva gärna en konturteckning av ett oupphunnet ideal. Vi nödgas besinna vad Skaparen ansåg med oss och vad våra bästa stunder velat.

»När I haven gjort allt som har blivit eder befallt, då skolen I säga: Vi äro blott ringa tjänare. Vi hava endast gjort vad vi voro pliktiga att göra.« Ingen har gjort vad han borde göra utom den Ende. Låt mig därför ändra texten: »Har någon gjort något av det han borde göra, så må han hugsvala själen med att säga: Jag är blott en onyttig tjänare. Jag har icke ens gjort vad jag var pliktig att göra.«

Hur vi skrapa ihop våra säkra – äro de så säkra? – och osäkra tillgångar, så blir ändå överskottet förkrossande, när vi draga det vi givit, ifrån skuldsumman av vad vi fått av Guds och människors godhet. Mästaren avvisar barskt slik uträkning. »Skall du med onda ögon se på, att jag är så god«?

Enda utvägen är att ödmjukt hugnas av kärleken som tillgiver och understödjer. »Om vi älska varandra, så förbliver Gud i oss, och hans kärlek är fullkomnad i oss.«

Med stor tacksamhet
tilgivne
Nathan Söderblom
Upsala januari 1926

Benefactor and friend,

The numerals indicating our age move upwards. But once one has reached the nine, one irretrievably plunges to the zero, the earmark of vanity and human misery.

When one has reached the higher number of decades, a feast will at times be celebrated with flowers and speeches, according to the rule: *De mortuis nihil nisi bene.*[2]

Perhaps this custom is no coincidence. Our temper is rigid. Not infrequently we keep kind words to ourselves until it is too late. But when the number of years with a zero appears in the lifetime of an older, or nowadays even of a middle-aged person, we open our hearts. –

Who dares to think of the toil and expenses people have taken upon themselves for one's own sake? It is humiliating to receive much undeserved kindness. But – »if I do not do you a favor, you do not share anything with me.« The overflowing benevolence bears witness to our belonging together and our depending upon each other.

Friendship's leniency and lovingly enhancing words easily become the outline of an unobtained ideal. We are being compelled to reflect upon what the Creator had in mind with us and what our best moments aspired to.

»When you have done all that is commanded you, you shall say: We are un-

---

[2] Latin: [Say] only good things about the dead. Probably a translation of a saying ascribed to an ancient Spartan official called Chilon, in: Diogenes Laertius, *Lives and Opinions of Eminent Philosophers*, I 70.

worthy servants; we have only done what was our duty.«[3] No one has done what he ought to have done except for the Only One. Let me therefore change the text: »When someone has done what he ought to have done, he may comfort his soul by saying: I am only a useless servant. I have not even done what was my duty.«

However much we scrape together our secure – are they so secure? – and insecure assets, the surplus still remains overwhelming when we subtract what we have given from the amount of debt we owe to what we have received from divine and human benevolence. The Master sternly rebukes such calculation. »Are you going to observe with sore eyes that I am so kind?«[4]

The only way out is to be comforted humbly by the love which forgives and relieves. »If we love one another God abides in us and his love is perfected in us.«[5]

Full of gratitude
sincerely,
Nathan Söderblom
Uppsala, January 1926

270. To Adolf von Harnack[1]

Upsala 26. 1. 1926

Excellenz!

Ihr Name unter dem allzu gütigen Gruss zu meinem Geburtstag erwecht [lies: erweckt] in mir ein Heer von geistigen Errungenschaften, Genüssen und Besitzen, die ich Ihnen seit bald vierzig Jahren verdanke. Wann wird Gott wieder einen Mann kommen lassen, der wie Sie die Welt der Religion in ihren Höhen und Tiefen, in ihrer Geschichte und ihren mannigfachigen Verbindungen in Einzelkeiten und in Grossen kennen und schildern kann? Thörichte Frage. Gott segne Sie und alles was ihr freigiebiger und leuchtender Geist gegeben hat! Es ist stärkend an Sie zu denken.

In Verehrung und dankbarer Freundschaft
bin ich Ihr sehr ergebener
Nathan Söderblom

271. To Friedrich Heiler[1]

Upsala 2. 2. 1926

Käre Vän!

Vänskapen förstorar. Men hjärtligt tackar jag Gud för all den rikedom jag mottagit genom Eder. Under krigets svartaste mörker lyste för mig från det

---

[3] Luke 17:10, Söderblom's motto for his life which is also engraved on his tombstone.
[4] Matth 20:15, here in a literal translation from the Swedish.
[5] I John 4:12.

[1] Harnack's papers – letters, Staatsbibliothek zu Berlin, Preußischer Kulturbesitz, typewritten letter.

[1] Friedrich Heiler's papers (Ms. 999), Univ. Library Marburg, typewritten letter.

innestängda Tyskland två var och en i sitt slag strålande stjärnor av snille och hängivenhet. Från båda var det mig också särskilt kärt att på 60-årsdagen erhålla goda önskningar från Friedrich Heiler och Wilhelm Kempff. Med vemod höra vi om sjukdomen i Eder familj och hoppas att det snart skall ljusna. Min hustru har lyckligt genomgått en lindrig operation. Vår son Bror Carl däremot är fortfarande mycket allvarligt sjuk i sin njuråkomma. Vemodigt höra om Sadhuns lidanden.

Den sköna bok jag oförtjänt fick /jämte ett Te Deum från Wilhelm Kempff/ ger en samlad bild av kristendomens makt i Indiens högsta människoliv. Jag har naturligtvis läst åtskilligt om och av Banerjee, men aldrig uppfattat att han var så betydande.

Eder evärderligt tacksamme och tillgivne
Nathan Söderblom

Uppsala, February 2, 1926

Lieber Freund,

Freundschaft vergrößert. Aber herzlich danke ich Gott für all den Reichtum, den ich von Ihnen empfangen habe. Während des schwärzesten Dunkels des Krieges leuchteten für mich aus dem eingeschlossenen Deutschland zwei jeder auf seine Weise strahlende Sterne von Genie und Hingabe. Von beiden war es mir auch besonders lieb, zum 60. Geburtstag gute Wünsche zu bekommen, von Friedrich Heiler und Wilhelm Kempff.[2]

Mit Wehmut hören wir von der Krankheit in Ihrer Familie und hoffen, dass die Lage sich bald wieder aufhellen wird. Meine Frau hat eine leichte Operation glücklich überstanden. Unser Sohn Bror Carl dagegen ist weiterhin sehr ernstlich krank mit seinem Nierenleiden.

Traurig, von Sadhus Leiden zu hören.

Das schöne Buch, das ich unverdient bekam[3] (zusammen mit einem Te Deum von Wilhelm Kempff) gibt ein einheitliches Bild von der Macht des Christentums in Indiens bedeutendstem Menschenleben. Ich habe natürlich viel über und von Benarjee[4] gelesen, aber niemals begriffen, dass er so bedeutend war.

Ihr stets dankbarer und Ihnen verbundener
Nathan Söderblom

---

[2] Wilhelm Kempff (1895-1991), renowned German pianist, organist, and composer. International concert tours, and a great many recordings from 1920 onwards (see the last paragraph of this letter). On a tour in Sweden in 1918, he appeared primarily as an organist.

[3] Cf. letter no. 268, n. 2.

[4] Bhavani Charan Banerji (Brahmabandav Upadhyaya, 1861- ca. 1907), Indian mystic who tried to reconcile Hinduism with the Roman Catholicism he had adopted in 1892. These efforts were rejected by Rome. He was arrested by the British colonial power in 1907 for alleged sedition. – Söderblom refers to Heiler's book, p. 51, where Banerji ranks above the other two »Christian Hindus«.

272. From Gustaf Aulén[1]
SVENSK TEOLOGISK KVARTALSKRIFT

LUND påskdagen 1926.

Högtärade Broder!
Jag övervinner min tvekan och dristar mig att göra en förfrågan å tidskriftens, egna och ännu en tredje parts vägnar. Min förfrågan eller rättare sagt bön gäller detta: skulle det finnas någon möjlighet för att Du godhetsfullt skulle vilja skriva en eller ett par sidor om Berggravs bok Religionens terskel till vår tidskrift?

Berggrav är här i Lund och skriver en avhandling i ett etiskt-religionspsykologiskt ämne. Det finnes möjlighet för att professuren efter Ording kan bli anslagen ledig i etik och religionspsykologi. Och B. skulle i så fall söka. Saken är emellertid högst komplicerad, såsom kanske Lyder Brun meddelade då han nyligen var i Uppsala. Andra röster, icke hans, höjas för att den skall återgå till att bli en professur i Novum: i så fall skulle Fak:n få 4 professurer i exegetik och endast en i systematisk teologi – den som innehas av Ihlen, vilken visst hälst vill vara ensam herre på täppan. Blir det – såsom icke osannolikt är – delade meningar i Fak:n, är det ganska troligt, att stortinget drar in professuren.

I själva verket befinner sig Fak:n i Oslo i ett ytterst prekärt läge. Menighetsfak:n vinner stadigt flera studenter och universitetsfak:n går tillbaka. Kan Fak:n icke få en ung och frisk systematiker vid Ihlens sida, kommer den med säkerhet att få en ytterst blygsam tillvaro. Nu har förmodligen Lyder Brun talat om allt detta och mera därtill. Som saken ligger vore det ovärderligt om vi i vår tidskrift skulle kunna få några rader från Dig om Berggravs bok, som sade vilka dess förtjänster äro och gärna naturligtvis också vilka dess brister äro. I går kom en recension i Kristendomen och vår tid av en liten viktig filosofie docent här, A. Nyman, som överhuvud icke har något förstånd på religion och som f. ö. anlade en mycket hög ton vid sitt bedömande – alldeles omotiverat. B., som håller på att arbeta som bäst, blev ganska nedstämd och fruktade att denna recension skulle komma att utnyttjas till hans skada i Norge – där ju alla vapen gärna tillgripas. Jag vet ingen mer än Du som jag kan vända mig till för att få ett verkligt sakligt och vägande uttalande om boken. Det behövde ej vara någon ingående recension blott ett återgivande av Ditt huvudintryck vid läsningen /jag har hört att Du läst boken/. Att ett omdöme om boken från detta håll ofantligt skulle glädja vännen Berggrav behöver jag ju icke säga. Ett häfte skall gå i press i mitten av denna månad – kunde jag få något dessförinnan vore det storartat. Förlåt min bön – jag har varit tveksam med tanke på den ärkebiskopliga arbetsbördan, men har dock icke kunnat låta bli att skriva om saken.

...

Hjärtlig, vördsam hälsning
från Din tillgivne   Gustaf Aulén

---

[1] Nathan Söderblom's collection of letters, from Swedes, UUB, typewritten letter.

SVENSK TEOLOGISK KVARTALSKRIFT

Lund, Easter Sunday [= April 4], 1926

Highly revered Brother,

I am overcoming my hesitation, being bold enough to put forth an inquiry on behalf of the periodical, of myself, and also of a third party. My inquiry or, put more correctly, my entreaty concerns this: Is there any chance at all of your kindly writing a page or two on Berggrav's book *Religionens terskel* for our periodical?[2]

Berggrav is here in Lund, writing a thesis in the field of ethics/psychology of religion.[3] There is a possibility of Ording's chair[4] being declared vacant in ethics and psychology of religion. And B. would in that case apply. The matter is highly complicated, however, as perhaps Lyder Brun told [you] when he was in Uppsala recently.[5] Other voices, not his, are being raised in favor of transforming it into a chair of New [Testament]; in that case, the faculty would have 4 chairs in exegesis and only one in systematic theology – the one occupied by Ihlen[6] who certainly would like best to rule the roost all by himself. If – as is not unlikely – opinions are divided in the faculty, it is quite probable that parliament will sack the chair.

The faculty in Oslo is indeed in a very precarious situation. The *Menighetsfakultet*[7] is attracting ever more students, and the university's faculty is waning. Unless the faculty can get a young and stimulating systematic theologian beside Ihlen, it will surely be reduced to an extremely modest subsistence. Now Lyder Brun presumably talked about all this and more. As things are, it would be invaluable if we could get a few lines from you on B.'s book in our periodical, saying what its merits and, of course, also what its deficiencies are, if you like. Yesterday a review appeared in *Kristendomen och vår tid* by an important little lecturer in philosophy here, A. Nyman[8], who does not have the slightest understanding of religion and, in addition, struck quite an overbearing tone in his critique – entirely unwarranted. B. who is in the process of doing great work was quite downcast and afraid that this review might be utilized to his disadvantage in Norway – where as you know one likes to take up all kinds of weapons. I do not know of anyone but you whom I can turn to in order to get a truly pertinent and measured account of the book. It would not have to be a thorough review, just a rendering of your principal reading impression (I heard that you have read the book). That a critique of the book from this source would tremendously gladden [our] friend Berggrav, I do not of course need to tell you. The next issue shall go to the press in the middle of this month – if I could get something before that, it would be great. Forgive me for my request – I have been

---

[2] As for Berggrav's book, see Söderblom's enthusiastic comments in letter no. 237. The periodical *Svensk teologisk kvartalskrift* had been founded in 1925; Aulén was its first editor.

[3] Eivind Berggrav, *Den religiøse følelse i sundt sjeleliv. En analyse av stemning og sinnelag i kristendommen*, Oslo 1927.

[4] Johannes Ording (1869–1929), liberal professor of systematic theology in Oslo 1906–1926. His accession to the chair caused great turmoil which resulted in the founding of the independent *Menighetsfakultet*, literally: Congregation's faculty, which was – and is – decidedly conservative in outlook. Cf. the following text.

[5] Johan Lyder Brun (1870–1950), professor of church history in Oslo 1897–1940.

[6] Christian Ihlen (1868–1958), professor of systematic theology in Oslo 1906–1938. He called himself neo-conservative. Active in the Norwegian mission to Israel from 1907 onwards.

[7] See note 4.

[8] Alf Nyman (1884–1968), physiologist and philosopher, lecturer in theoretical philosophy in 1918.

420

hesitant in view of the archbishop's workload, but nonetheless simply could not abstain from writing about the matter.[9]

... [On a planned journey to England]
Cordial and respectful regards,
yours sincerely,   Gustaf Aulén

273. To Strenopoulos Germanos[1]

Upsala 27th of April 1926.

Your Grace, my dear Friend,

I hope that we can count upon you for the session of the Continuation Committee 26th – 31st August in Berne, also for the Executive Committee 24th – 25th and for Faith and Order 23rd, also in Berne. An invitation has been sent to the Ecumenical Patriarchy Constantinople. Shall I write once more to His Holiness about this important session?

We have been awaiting for months in order to know well, if His Grace of Thyateira will come to the Continuation Committee as His Holiness of Alexandria, succeeding to the late Photios[2], whose image will for ever live in the memory of the Church also in the West. Our Minister in Cairo has sent me information and papers from time to time, but as yet I have not seen any telegram about the final election.[3]

I am sorry that I cannot come and meet you in Amsterdam May 7th – 8th. But I expect in any case to see you in Berne in August.

May I ask you kindly to keep the evening of 27th August free for a dinner with me and the whole committee in Hotel Bellevue, Berne.

I have had two kind letters from His Holiness the Patriarch of Constantinople lately. I understand that the Ecumenical council will be held during Pentecost on Mount Athos. It has been said that Western communions, keeping the Nicene Creed, can send churchmen to be present as fraternal visitors, of course not as members of that Council.

Please tell me frankly if I can send the Reverend Dr. Herman Neander for that purpose?[4] You know how great importance I attach to a free mutual respect and cooperation of the venerable Orthodox Church and Evangelic Christendom. In that respect I hope that Stockholm meant the beginning of a new epoch.

I know how complicated and difficult your historic task is in Orthodox

---

[9] Söderblom did write the requested review. But this did not lead to the desired result of a call to a professorship for Berggrav.

[1] Nathan Söderblom's collection of letters, to Swedes and foreigners, UUB, typewritten letter (carbon copy).

[2] For Photios, cf. letter no. 256, n. 2.

[3] The successor to Photios was Meletios II., elected in May 1926.

[4] Herman Neander (cf. Letter no. 100, n. 2) was Söderblom's intermediary with the Orthodox church leaders and is credited with having achieved their consent to participate in the Stockholm conference of 1925.

as well as in Western Christendom. Do you see any way of settling the difficulties between the Patriarchal throne in Constantinople and the Church in
Bulgaria?[5] I have just heard about the most aggressive propaganda made by
the Roman Church in Bulgaria, and I pray for the unity and strength of the
Orthodox Faith of our Orthodox brethren, who have still such a great calling in the world.

Believe me most sincerely and brotherly yours,
in common service of our Lord Jesus Christ,

Archbishop of Upsala.
Prochancellor of the University of Upsala.

274. From Strenopoulos Germanos[1]

London, May 11th, 1926.

Your Grace, My dear Brother in Christ,
I express my heartfelt thanks for your letter of the 27th April.

Dr Atkinson[2] whom I met at the beginning of March at Geneva told me
about the time when our Continuation Committee will be called at Berne;
from another place likewise I was informed about the gathering at the same
time of the Committee of Faith and Order. Your proceeding to send an invitation to the Oecumenical Patriarchate for this purpose meets with my full
approval, but I think it would not be superfluous to write onde more to His
Holiness later on, at the beginning of July. Inasmuch as the Metropolitan
of Thyateira has such benevolent friends as Your Grace and His Grace the
Lord Archbishop of Canterbury, he thinks it most advisable not to leave
Western Europe and also the immediate and frequent contact with the Sister Churches here, even if it were for the succession of the Patriarch Photius of Alexandria. I hope that we shall not have to wait long before hearing
the name of the Patriarch elected, but I am afraid that our friend the Metropolitan of Noubia, despite the support given to him by the Greek community in Egypt will not be elected. Perhaps the Metropolitan of Trebizond
Chrysanthos or the Archbishop of Athens, Chrysostomos, will be chosen.
Both are distinguished and very esteemed prelates of our Church.[3]

---

[5] In the course of rising national consciousness after the Ottoman occupation, part of the
Bulgarian orthodox church opted for union with Rome in 1861 and became the Bulgarian
Catholic Church, but returned to the orthodox fold in 1870 when the orthodox church of Bulgaria as a whole was established as an independent exarchate. This church body was excommunicated by Constantinople, however, a rift that was not healed until 1945. Meanwhile, the Bulgarian Catholic Church had reemerged and reorganized itself in 1926; it became a new Apostolic Exarchate.

[1] Nathan Söderblom's collection of letters, from foreigners, UUB, typewritten letter.
[2] Henry Atkinson, cf. letter no. 183, n. 1.
[3] Chrysanthos, metropolitan of Trabzon, Turkey, supported the revolutionary Pontus organization, a group of revolutionary young Greeks who wanted to »re-Grecify« part of Turkey. Chrysostomos I. (1868–1938) was archbishop of Athens 1923–1938.

The General Strike made my journey to Amsterdam impossible and I am sorry to say that neither the Bureau in London nor my English colleagues informed me of anything, whether this meeting had taken place or not.

While expecting news from Constantinople, all I can say is that according to my information from Athens with regard to the forthcoming Council at Mount Athos, the meeting of the Oecumenical Council for the present time has been postponed owing to the desire expressed by some of the autocephalous Churches. I now hear that the Oecumenical Patriarch intends to call a Prosynod i.e. a Body of Representatives of all the Orthodox Churches to prepare the work of a future Oecumenical Synod. It was certain that in the event of a meeting of the Oecumenical Synod, an invitation should be sent to all the Churches standing on the basis of the Nicene Creed to send representatives. But I cannot say if this be the case in the event of only a Prosynod being called. Up to the present moment I have not received any informal news from Constantinople about this Prosynod.

I do not think that any great difficulties will be met with in the removal of the Bulgarian Schism, if, on the part of the Bulgarians[,] there exists the same good-will as there is on the part of the Oecumenical Patriarchate. Few men perhaps can realise, as I do, the need of an intimate relationship between the various autocephalous Churches in order to face the Roman propaganda. They (the Romans) are very much disturbed about our friendly relations with the Western Churches and are doing their utmost to prevent a closer tie between the Orthodox Church and the Anglican Church. I thought it was my duty to reply to this attempt by publishing some articles in an Athens newspaper.

I pray for the good health of your Grace and remain your Grace's beloved Brother in Christ,

+ Germanos Thyat.

275. To ADOLF VON HARNACK[1]

Upsala den 12 Mai 1926

Hochverehrter Herr Professor!

Es bestand die Absicht bei der Sitzung des Ausschusses den das Fortsetzungskomité der Weltkonferenz in Stockholm in August gewählt hatte, in Amsterdam am Freitag siebente[2] eine gemeinsame Huldigung an den angesichts seiner riesenhaften schöpferischen Tätigkeit ungewöhnlich jungen, und für seine Geistesfrische und Vitalität ungewöhnlich alten Fünf-und-siebzig-jährigen zu telegraphieren. Es wäre eine erwünschte Gelegenheit

---

[1] Harnack's papers – letters, Staatsbibliothek zu Berlin, Preußischer Kulturbesitz, typewritten letter.

[2] Friday, May 7, 1926, was the date of Harnack's 75th birthday.

gewesen unsere tiefe Dankbarkeit auch für den an die Weltkonferenz in Stockholm gesandten wuchtigen Gruss auszudrücken. Aber es wurde anders. Der Ausschuss hat getagt und tüchtige Arbeit geleistet. Aber der Bischof von Winchester konnte wegen des Streiks nicht England verlassen. Und ich wurde von unumgänglichen Amtspflichten in meiner Diözese verhindert dabei zu sein. Soeben nach Upsala zurückgekehrt, sende ich daher diesen verspäteten Gruss an einen Mann, dem die Christenheit wohl noch mehr als sie weiss schuldig ist, und der mir wie ungezählten Anderen seitdem ein theologischer Gedanke bei mir wirklich wach wurde, für Herz, Forschung, Orientierung in der geistigen Welt, für Intellekt und Leben ungeheuer viel gegeben hat. Mit einer stolzen oder vielmehr demütigen Freigiebigkeit haben Sie Ihre Gaben und Ihre in mühevoller, zielbewusster, nie ruhender Arbeit gewonnenen Errungenschaften der Welt ausgeschüttet. Besonders lieb und unvergesslich war es meiner Frau und mir und uns Allen in diesem Hause einen unmittelbaren unvergesslichen Hauch von Ihrer Persönlichkeit bekommen zu dürfen.

Es ist in den Schwierigkeiten und Kummern des Lebens stärkend und erhebend an Ihren freien, hohen Geist zu denken. Gott segne Sie!

Ihr verehrungsvoll dankbarer

Nathan Söderblom

276. From Adolf von Harnack[1]

[middle of May, 1926]

Prof. D. von Harnack

spricht seinen wärmsten Dank aus für die ihm zu seinem 75. Geburtstage freundlichst übersandten Glückwünsche und Gaben, die ihn hoch erfreut haben;

zugleich meinen verehrungsvollen Gruß! Ihre gütige Anerkennung meiner Arbeit ist mir fort und fort ein Sporn, etwas davon zu erreichen, was noch nicht erreicht zu haben ich mir wohl bewußt bin.

Aufblickend zu Ihrer kraftvollen Tätigkeit, bleibe ich, hochverehrter Herr Erzbischof, Ihr treu ergebener

v. Harnack

Berlin-Grunewald

im Mai 1926

---

[1] Nathan Söderblom's collection of letters, from foreigners, UUB, printed card, with a handwritten addition after the colon. Reply to belated congratulation of May 12, cf. previous letter.

277. From Rudolf Otto[1]

Marburg, 15 5 26

Verehrter Herr Erzbischof.

Der 28–30. September würde mir sehr gut passen. Mein Thema:
›Die Bhakti-Religion Indiens im Vergleich mit dem Christentum.‹[2]
Wenn Sie es etwas anders formulieren wollen, so tun Sie es bitte. Diese Fassung wird es mir ermöglichen, nicht nur religionsgeschichtlich zu verfahren, sondern auch theologisch, nämlich durch Vergleich von Ähnlichkeit und Verschiedenheit zugleich das Besondere, und wie ich glaube, das völlig Überlegene christlichen Heilsglaubens darzustellen.

Ich werde etwa am 20. September in Stockholm eintreffen, dort einige Tage bleiben und dann mit Ihrer freundlichen Erlaubnis am 24. oder 25. zu Ihnen kommen. Vielleicht könnte mir Birger Forell[3] angeben, wo ich in Stockholm wohnen kann, und mir einige Männer nennen, die ich besuchen könnte und die mir helfen würden, Schweden und schwedische Eigenart kennen zu lernen. Ich freue mich herzlich auf den Besuch.

Etwa am 9. Oktober müßte ich wieder zurück sein, um in der Nähe von Kiel an einer theologischen Konferenz teilzunehmen.

Inzwischen mit ergebenem Gruße in Verehrung
Ihr R. Otto.

278. To Adolf Deissmann[1]

Upsala den 7 Juni 1926

Sehr geehrter Professor und Freund!

Um nicht länger zu zögern, sandte ich Ihnen vor einigen Tagen die Dokumente. Es wird vielleicht die Leser interessieren etwas über die wirklich ungemein komplizierte Arbeit mit der Statistik und der Verteilung der Delegierten zu erfahren. Die Statistik ist während 3–4 Jahren von Pastor Folke Palmgren[2] und mir hergestellt worden. Sie ist sicherlich in vielen Hinsichten unrichtig. Ich gab mir nicht Zeit um die [sic; lies: im] Manuskript einige seitdem durch weitere Auskünfte geänderte Zahlen zu verbessern, da Sie doch wohl die Zahlen nicht angeben werden. Wenn Sie wollen, kann ich ein korrigiertes Exemplar senden lassen.

---

[1] Nathan Söderblom's collection of letters, from foreigners, UUB, typewritten letter.

[2] This lecture was delivered in Kassel in 1924, in Uppsala and Oslo in 1926, and published in enlarged form as *Die Gnadenreligion Indiens und das Christentum. Vergleich und Unterscheidung*, München 1930 (English transl.: *India's Religion of Grace and Christianity Compared and Contrasted*, London 1930).

[3] For Forell, cf. letter no. 155, n. 4.

[1] Nathan Söderblom's collection of letters, to Swedes and foreigners, UUB, typewritten letter (carbon copy).

[2] Folke Palmgren (1897–1977), pastor of the Swedish church in Helsinki.

Wie eigentümlich mit Dr. Karl Holl, der seine tiefe und große Bedeutung als Forscher erst spät im Leben beoffenbart hat, und dann bald danach abberufen worden ist. Bitte bezeugen Sie seiner Familie meine tief empfundene Teilnahme.[3]

Ihre Ausgabe dem Andenken von Patriarken von Alexandria zu widmen[4] ist ein genialer Idée, in aller Hinsicht nützlich.

Ihr sehr ergebener

279. From RUDOLF OTTO[1]

[Date at the end of the letter]

Verehrter Herr Erzbischof.

Besten Dank für Ihren Brief vom 9. Juni. Ich schrieb schon früher, daß ich am Donnerstag, dem 8. Oktober in Kremsmühlen bei Lübeck[2] an einer theologischen Konferenz teilnehmen muß. Ich bitte darum, die vier Vorlesungen so zu legen, daß ich etwa am Freitag, dem 1. Oktober oder am Sonnabend, dem 2. Okt., damit zu Ende bin. Auch bitte ich, daß wir an unserer früheren Verabredung festhalten, und daß ich schon am 23. September zu Ihnen nach Upsala komme. Vom 23. September bis zum 2. Oktober werden sich die vier Vorlesungen gewiß gut verteilen lassen. Auch könnte ich, wenn Sie wollen zwei Vorlesungen an einem Tage halten. Doch empfiehlt sich das für die Hörer nicht.

[A short survey of the practical conditions.]

Zu diesen Punkten darf ich den persönlichen Wunsch fügen, daß mir Gelegenheit gegeben sein möge, ausgiebig mit Ihnen selber über die uns gemeinsam interessierenden Fragen zu reden. Daß es mir persönlich ein großes Anliegen, und ein Hauptanreiz zur Reise ist, Sie wiederzusehen und abgesehen von großen und wichtigen allgemeinen Interessen mit Ihnen zusammen zu sein, das brauche ich nicht zu wiederholen. Ich gestehe, daß dieses egoistische Interesse bei mir fast so stark ist wie das sachliche.

Da auch sonst die Olaus Petri Vorlesungen, wie ich annehme, gelegentlich schwedisch erscheinen, so besitzt die Stiftung vermutlich Mittel, um den jeweiligen Übersetzer für seine Arbeit zu honorieren. Wenn dieses der

---

[3] For Holl, cf. letter no. 105, n. 1. Söderblom's books on Luther were written before Holl's pioneering works (*Den lutherska reformationens grundtankar*, Stockholm 1893; *Humor och melankoli och andra Lutherstudier*, Stockholm 1919: even here, the material was conceived before Holl's great work »Was verstand Luther unter Religion?« [1917], in: *GAufs zur Kirchengeschichte I, Luther*, 6th ed. Tübingen 1932, 1–110). The somewhat cool distance to be perceived in the current letter is probably due to Holl's nationalist tendencies which Söderblom must have strongly rejected.

[4] Adolf Deißmann, *Die Stockholmer Weltkirchenkonferenz* ... (cf. letter no. 261, n. 10). For Photios, cf. letter no. 256, n. 2.

[1] Nathan Söderblom's collection of letters, from foreigners, UUB, typewritten letter.

[2] Otto means Gremsmühlen, today part of the town of Malente, which is situated about halfway between Kiel (cf. letter no. 277) and Lübeck. October 8, 1926, was a Friday.

Fall ist, so würde ich bitten, daß man auch Herrn B. Forell für seine Übersetzer-mühe ein angemessenes Honorar aus den Mitteln der Stiftung bewilligt.[3]

[...]

Mit großer Freude verfolge ich die Arbeit von H.Bohlin.[4] Seine tiefe theologische Bildung und seine gesunde Denkart wäre in unserer hiesigen, durch die Bahrtschen [lies: Barthschen] sterien[5] und durch die Bultmannsche Skepsis verwirrten Jugend eine wahre Heilkraft. Und ich habe mich schon bemüht, ihn für einen Lehrstuhl vorzuschlagen, werde auch, wenn ich zu Ende Juni nach Berlin reise, ihn dem Minister dringend empfehlen. Gewiß ist er auch in Åbo an rechtem Orte. Aber an einer unserer Fakultäten würde er doch ein weiteres und vielleicht noch wichtigeres Feld der Wirksamkeit haben. Ich weiß, daß er schon jetzt des Deutschen mächtig ist. Aber vielleicht täte er gut, sich in dieser Hinsicht noch sicherer auszubilden. Es ist für mich etwas penibel, ihm direkt mit Ratschlägen nahezukommen, da mein Verhältnis zu ihm in dieser Hinsicht mich nicht berechtigt. Sollten Sie aber mein Urteil über ihn billigen, so würden Sie vielleicht von sich aus ihm etwa den Rat erteilen, seine Ferien zu einem längeren Aufenthalte in Deutschland zu benützen, damit er das Deutsche völlig zu beherrschen lernt. Ich würde mich ganz besonders freuen, wenn er zu uns kommen wollte. Die Übersetzung seines bedeutenden Werkes über Kierkeggard [Kierkegaard][6] wird ihn bald bei uns bekannt machen. Wäre sie ein Jahr eher erschienen, so wäre es mir vielleicht doch gelungen ihn bei der Besetzung der systematischen Stelle in Halle mit auf den Vorschlag zu bringen.

Mich Ihnen und Frau Söderblom empfehlend, in herzlicher Verehrung

Ihr

R. Otto

Marburg, 16 6 26.

Buonaiuti in Rom übersetzt eben mein Heiliges ins Italienische. In unserm Briefwechsel erfahre ich tiefe Einblicke in die geistigen Nöte dieser Entheimateten. Er scheint jetzt eine eigene ›Schule für Religionswissenschaft‹ eröffnet zu haben.[7]

---

[3] The translation appeared in print as: *Indiens nådesreligion och kristendomen*, Stockholm 1927.

[4] Sic. Otto means Torsten Bohlin, and in particular his critical stance concerning the dialectical theology, cf. the following text, and letter no.182, n.1.

[5] The word is incomplete. The »i« is my conjecture (Otto's typewriter ribbon obviously needed replacement), and in the beginning, two letters seem to be missing. My guess is: Mysterien. This would make sense in the context. The editor.

[6] Cf. letter no.245n.3.

[7] Ernesto Buonaiuti (1881-1946), church historian, 1905 deposed as a modernist, 1915 professor of history in Rome. He was excommunicated 1926 and, on the basis of the Italian concordate, deposed even from his new position: An excommunicated person was not allowed to teach at a state university. He earned his living by doing research until he was denied that because of his refusal to swear a fascist oath in 1931. Subsequently, he served as a guest professor at various universities, among others, in Lausanne, Switzerland. – The translation mentioned above appeared as *Il sacro* in Bologna, 1926.

280. To Friedrich Heiler[1]

Upsala den 4 augusti 1926

Käre vän!

Före mina föreläsningar i Dublin och min vistelse i England, där mig bevisad heder blivit föremål för en mycket hätsk artikel i The Catholic Herold, skrev jag några sidor till festskriften för Deissmann om Evangelisk Katolicitet. Hade jag haft Eder bok, skulle jag hava skrivit mycket utförligare.

Till min stora glädje hörde jag i England, att Ni kommer dit. Det är icke en dag för tidigt. Bland Anglo Catholics finnas hängivna kristna och även goda huvuden, men också ett snobberi med vaxljus, rökelse, nygjorda mässdräkter och så vidare, som verkar tillgjort och luktar sakristia, men är mycket främmande för Kristi evangelium. Jag har själv utmärkta vänner bland Anglo Catholics. Biskopen av Bombay är en härlig man, som höjer sig över mängden. Men många av dem äro sekteriskt småsinta, och det känns som en befrielse att i England råka en av dem som besjälas av en stark och fri evangelisk katolicitet såsom ärkebiskopen av Canterbury, domprosten Bell, biskopen av Manchester, biskopen av Lichfield, biskopen av Winchester, biskopen av Plymouth, Chelmsford, ärkebiskopen av York, en härlig människa, som först smittades av sträng högkyrklighet i Oxford, och icke kunde gå med på aftonandakten i det presbyterianska prästhem i Scotland där han var född, men som under levnadens, det är under Guds lärdom har utvecklats till en fri evangelisk människa, en kyrkoman i stor stil. Jag längtar att åter få råka Eder!

När kommer Ni hit? Vi måste få ett långt och grundligt samtal tillsammans. Jag tänker på våra timmar på järnvägen och i München i fjol. De voro ljuvliga och andaktsfulla. När reser Ni till England? Den 21–31 augusti är jag i Bern, Villa Favorite, Diakonissenhaus, och sedan predikar jag den 5 september i Genève i St. Pierre. Tänk om vi skulle stämma möte där? Jag bor hos professor Choisy, som säkert gärna också skaffar Eder rum.

Eder bok kommer i grevens tid — om jag nu äntligen skulle kunna bli färdig med det stora arbete om Ekumeniska Mötet som jag arbetat på under lediga stunder. Man lär sig mycket i Eder bok, och man blir varm om hjärtat. Jag genomlever återigen de oförgätliga dagarna i augusti i fjol, vilkas like vi nog aldrig här på jorden få uppleva, vi som voro med i Adoratio.

Vad Ni säger s. 237 om de stängda kyrkorna är som talat ur mitt hjärta. Tyvärr har det icke lyckats mig att öppna kyrkorna i sådan utsträckning som jag ville här i Sverige.

Läs sidan 135 i Eder bok. Den är himmelsk.

Vad Ni s. 215 säger om Augustana är alldeles sannt. Däremot vill jag påpeka vad jag tror professor Rawlinson i Oxford icke längesedan har understrukit, att när *protestant* användes 1529 var det ingalunda i meningen av opposition eller protest, huru nödvändig än en sådan i evigheten är gentemot vidskepelse, världslig och ogudlig kyrkomakt och fariseism i alla for-

---

[1] Friedrich Heiler's papers (Ms. 999), Univ. Library Marburg, typewritten letter.

mer likaväl som vår Frälsare kraftigt protesterade. Utan protestant betyder till sin uppkomst protestati sumus, det är, wir behaupten mit aller Kraft, nämlich die Rechtfertigung durch Glauben.

S. 234. Jag delar Eder mening om den formulerade bönens välsignelse. Uppenbart är nu för alla att Life and Work måste föregå Faith and Order.

Jag kan heller icke med /234/ den liturgiska dilettantismen hos mina vänner Otto och Linderholm och andra. När jag ser huru Ni helt naturligt på grund av barndomens och ungdomens intryck hyser en förkärlek för fromhetsformer som äro mig alldeles främmande, och så vitt jag kan se, icke sakna sin betänklighet, jag skall strax tala därom, så fröjdar det mig i själen, att Ni har liksom jag uppbyggelse av det äkta evangeliska patos hos en så tvättäkta protestant som Wilfred Monod. /s. 229./

Nu citerar jag alldeles härs och tvärs. Men jag får icke glömma att påpeka ett par små misstag, som kunna ändras i den nya upplaga som säkert snart kommer.

S. 125: För Message har Monod gjort det mesta, därnäst Garvie, Deissmann och Ammundsen, men även bidragen från *Ihmels* och *Conrad* äga betydelse. Dock, vad jag egentligen ville påpeka är raden om Roms uteblivande i början av Message, som Winchester och jag hade satt dit såsom ett historiskt faktum, men som av oss alla enhälligt ströks på yrkande av Kapler. Han sade:»Den romersk katolska pressen i Tyskland har behandlat vårt möte med aktning. Vi vilja icke på något sätt störa det goda förhållandet till våra romersk katolska bröder. Ett ord om at Rom ej deltagit kan lätt tolkas som ett klander, en polemik. Därför låt oss icke säga någonting.« Därför skall ordet Verneinung ersättas av *Polemik eller Tadel.* /»Dabei wurde der Abschnitt, der sich an die römische Kirche richtete, gestrichen, *weil man die Befürchtung hegte, ein Ausdruck des Bedauerns über die Nicht-teilnahme der päpstlichen Kirche könne als Polemik oder Tadel gedeutet werden.«* / Detta faktum är ett nytt bevis på hur allt igenom positivt allt försiggick i Stockholm. Jag skulle kunna berätta interiörer härom när vi råkas. Karakteristiskt är, att det var tyska delegationens ordförande, Kapler, som ville undvika ens varje sken av tadel eller klander gentemot Rom.

S. 140. Gustaf Jensen är Norweger, icke Däne.

Klart är att i evangelisch katholisch jag mer betonar evangelisch, Ni mer katholisch. För mig betyder evangelische Katholicität att endast den evangeliska frälsningsläran, som icke binder i stadgar, utan befriar till obetingad tjänst hos den Allsmäktige Guden kan åstadkomma en verklig Katholicität. Därom skola vi nästa gång tala länge med varandra.

I en enda punkt har jag verklig betänklighet. Det är sakramentets bevarande, preservatio. Själva bevarandet kan väl försvaras dels som en akt av skyldig pietet, dels för sjukas räkning. Men Kristi hemlighetsfulla närvaro är icke betingad av någon formel och förvandlar således icke hostian till en gudom som kan tillbedjas, utan den betingas av Kristi löfte, den gudomliga naturens ubiquitet och av tron. Det är för mig mycket naturligt att ett krucifix eller en annan bild eller ett ljus samlar tillbedjan på en bestämd punkt i helgedomen eller i rummet. Det är ett naturligt psykologiskt behov. Men att den konsekrerade hostian i sitt sakramentshus tjänstgör såsom en kroppslig gudom synes mig vara mycket betänkligt, en analogi till Soma, Haoma, utan någon egentlig förbindelseled med Nya Testamentet och Uppenbarelsen.

Därför har den eucharistiska kongressen, vilken Påven hälsade med gudsmoderns ord om henne själv, gjort på mig ett ytterst nedslående intryck. Visst är att den gagnar propagandan och imponerar där borta på många själar, särskilt gentemot den stupida antiklerikalismen i Mexiko. Men med all vidhjärtenhet kan jag icke undgå att känna avsmak inför en sådan dyrkan av ett föremål.

Två religiösa moment hava uppfyllt tidningarna i U. S. A. Ett verkar genom kvantiteten, kongressen i Chicago, ett genom kvaliteten, den rättframme svenske kronprinsen.

Hade professor Heiler varit med från början, hade väl Una sancta aldrig fått det olämpliga tillägget »hochkirchlich.« Det räcker väl med kirchlich. Jag behöver också råka Eder för att höra närmare om denna rörelse i Tyskland.

Jag förstår Eder oro inför de teologiska skolornas andliga kamp. Men egentligen är den ett livstecken och nödvändig i Kristi kyrka. Ty Kyrkan är stark nog att smälta även den dialektiska teologien, även den kommer att lära oss något. Endast i frihetens luft kan Kristi sak segra, och jag vet och ser med vilken övertygelse Ni, käre professor och vän, hävdar och utövar forskningens frihet. Jag har ofta frågat mig varför Gud sände mig under jordelivet en så oförtjänt och oändligt stor välsignelse som bekantskapen med Eder och allt vad den medfört. Vi vilja både leva under himmelen och icke låta oss instoppas i de fållor som vänner eller motståndare anvisa åt oss, och intet bevisar bättre una sancta än det faktum att vi två från så olika urspsrung och omgivningar och andra med oss, en Monod, en Garvie, en Bombay, en Sundar Singh, en Glubokowsky förstå varandra så innerligt väl utan föregående överenskommelse. Denna katolicitet tillhör livets och evighetens gudomliga hemlighet.

Med hjärtliga hälsningar Eder tillgivne
Nathan Söderblom

Uppsala, den 4. August 1926

Lieber Freund,
vor meinen Vorlesungen in Dublin und meinem Besuch in England, wo mir erwiesene Ehre zum Gegenstand eines sehr gehässigen Artikels in The Catholic Herald[2] wurde, schrieb ich einige Seiten für die Festschrift für Deißmann über Evangelische Katholizität.[3] Hätte ich Ihr Buch gehabt, hätte ich viel ausführlicher geschrieben.

---

[2] The *Catholic Herald* 33/1926; I have not been able to get hold of this volume in order to secure the bibilographical data. The Donellan Lectures were delivered in Dublin in June, 1926.

[3] Nathan Söderblom, »Evangelische Katholizität,« in: *FS Deißmann*, Tübingen 1927, 327–334.

Zu meiner großen Freude hörte ich in England, dass Sie dorthin kommen. Das ist keinen Tag zu früh. Unter Anglo-Catholics finden sich hingebungsvolle Christen und auch gute Köpfe, aber ebenso ein Snobismus mit Kerzen, Räucherwerk, Messgewänder nach neuer Manier und so weiter, die maniert wirkt und nach Sakristei riecht, aber dem Evangelium Christi sehr fremd ist. Ich habe selbst ausgezeichnete Freunde unter Anglo-Catholics. Der Bischof von Bombay ist ein herrlicher Mann, der die Menge überragt.[4] Aber viele von ihnen sind sektiererisch engstirnig, und man fühlt sich wie befreit, wenn man in England einen von denen trifft, die von einer starken und freien evangelischen Katholizität beseelt sind, wie der Erzbischof von Canterbury, der Dekan Bell, der Bischof von Manchester, der Bischof von Lichfield, der Bischof von Winchester, der Bischof von Plymouth, Chelmsford, der Erzbischof von York, ein herrlicher Mensch, der anfangs in Oxford von strenger Hochkirchlichkeit angesteckt wurde und nicht mit zur Abendandacht in dem presbyterianischen Pfarrhaus in Schottland gehen konnte, wo er geboren war, aber in der Schule des Lebens, das heißt Gottes, sich zu einem freien evangelischen Menschen entwickelt hat, ein Kirchenmann in großem Stil.[5] Ich sehne mich danach, Sie wieder zu treffen!

Wann kommen Sie hierher? Wir müssen ein langes und gründliches Gespräch miteinander haben. Ich denke an unsere Stunden auf der Eisenbahn und in München im vorigen Jahr.[6] Die waren wundervoll und erbaulich. Wann reisen Sie nach England? Vom 21.-31. August bin ich in Bern, Villa Favorite, Diakonissenhaus, und dann predige ich am 5. September in Genf in St. Pierre.[7] Was halten Sie davon, dort ein Treffen zu vereinbaren? Ich wohne bei Professor Choisy,[8] der Ihnen sicher gern auch ein Zimmer besorgt.

Ihr Buch kommt fünf Minuten vor zwölf – wenn ich nur endlich mit der großen Arbeit über die ökumenische Konferenz fertig werden könnte, an der ich in freien Stunden gearbeitet habe.[9] Man lernt viel in Ihrem Buch, und es wird einem warm ums Herz. Ich durchlebe noch einmal die unvergesslichen Tage im August des vorigen Jahres, deren gleichen wir wohl niemals hier auf Erden erleben können, wir, die in Adoratio [Anbetung] dabei waren.

Was Sie S. 237 über die geschlossenen Kirchen sagen, ist mir aus dem Herzen gesprochen. Leider ist es mir nicht gelungen, die Kirchen hier in Schweden in dem Ausmaß zu öffnen, wie ich es wollte.

---

[4] Edwin James Palmer (1869-1954), located in London.

[5] Randall Davidson, Archbishop of Canterbury; cf. letter no. 85, n. 1; George Bell, Dean of Canterbury, cf. letter no. 141, no. 2; Willliam Temple, bishop of Manchester, cf. letter no. 220, n. 2; John Augustine Kempthorne (1864-1946), bishop of Lichfield 1913-1937; Frank Theodore Woods (1874-1932), bishop of Winchester, one of the signers of the invitation to the Stockholm conference (letter no. 219); John H. B. Masterman, bishop of Plymouth, cf. letter no. 134, n. 4; F. S. Guy Warman (1872-1953), bishop of Chelmsford 1923-1929 (1929-1947 Manchester); Cosmo Gordon Lang (1864-1945), Archbishop of York 1908-1928 (Canterbury 1928-1942; previously a pastor in London slums).

[6] Söderblom had traveled to the Zürich meeting of the European section of Life and Work in April 1925, and interrupted his journey in München for a walk with Heiler, who then on the return trip accompanied Söderblom; cf. Misner, op. cit., 249, n. 10.

[7] In Bern, Söderblom attended a conference of the Continuation Committee, and in Geneva, he preached for the League of Nations.

[8] Jacques Eugène Choisy, one of those signing the invitation to the Stockholm conference, cf. letter no. 208.

[9] Friedrich Heiler, *Evangelische Katholizität. GAufs u. Vorträge* I, München 1926, pp. 37-150.292-302 are on the Stockholm conference.

Man lese Seite 135 in Ihrem Buch. Die ist himmlisch.[10]

Was Sie S. 215 über die Augustana sagen, ist völlig wahr.[11] Dagegen will ich auf etwas hinweisen, was, glaube ich, Professor Rawlinson in Oxford vor nicht langer Zeit unterstrichen hat, dass, als man »Protestant« 1529 benutzte, dies keinesfalls im Sinn von Opposition oder Protest geschah, so notwendig auch ein solcher in Ewigkeit ist gegen Aberglauben, weltliche und ungöttliche Kirchenmacht und Pharisäismus in allen Formen, so wie auch unser Erlöser kräftig protestiert hat. Sondern Protestant bedeutet seiner Herkunft nach protestati sumus, das heißt, wir behaupten mit aller Kraft, nämlich die Rechtfertigung durch Glauben.[12]

S. 234. Ich teile Ihre Meinung über den Segen des formulierten Gebets. Offensichtlich ist jetzt für alle, dass [die Konferenz von] Life and Work [einer solchen von] Faith and Order vorausgehen musste.

Auch ich kann (234) mit dem liturgischen Dilettantismus bei meinen Freunden Otto und Linderholm und anderen nicht mitgehen.[13] Wenn ich sehe, wie Sie ganz natürlich auf Grund der Eindrücke von Kindheit und Jugend eine Vorliebe für Frömmigkeitsformen hegen, die mir gänzlich fremd sind und, soweit ich sehen kann, nicht unbedenklich sind, ich werde gleich davon sprechen, so freut es mich in der Seele, dass Sie ebenso wie ich Erbauung finden an dem echten evangelischen Pathos bei einem so waschechten Protestanten wie Wilfred Monod. (S. 229.)[14]

Jetzt zitiere ich ganz kreuz und quer. Aber ich darf nicht vergessen, auf ein paar kleine Versehen hinzuweisen, die in der neuen Auflage geändert werden können, die sicher bald kommt.

S. 125: Für *Message*[15] hat Monod das Meiste getan, nächst ihm Garvie, Deißmann und Ammundsen, aber auch die Beiträge von *Ihmels* und *Conrad* sind von Be-

---

[10] Heiler is emphasizing there the crucial role of the confession to Christ at the conference. This is important for Söderblom inasmuch as a great deal of the criticism leveled was directed against the alleged marginalization of Christology in favor of the ethical concerns.

[11] That is, that the *CA* is »die Bekenntnisschrift der Evangelischen Katholizität«, (the Confessional Writing of evangelic catholicity), but that as such it belongs to one particular church and therefore cannot be placed on an equal level with the ecumenical symbols. Even as the doctrinal basis of Lutheranism, it is not exhaustive (215 f.).

[12] The words after »das heißt« are in German in the original. They are not a quotation but Söderblom's own formulation. The passage refers to the *Protestatio* of Lutheran princes at the second Imperial Diet at Speyer 1529. Cf. also Söderblom's article, mentioned in note 3, p. 328. Actually, the *Protestatio* was both: a confession of faith and a protest – not against the Catholic church, but against the breach of the resolution of the first Imperial Diet of Speyer in 1526 that had granted religious freedom to the »Protestant« territories until a future General Council. Cf. *Die Appellation und Protestation der evangelischen Stände auf dem Reichstage zu Speyer* 1529, ed. J. Ney (QGS 5), Leipzig 1906, 74 f., where the princes »protestirn und bezeugen« (protest and bear witness) that they consider that move against the Word of God and the earlier Diet as null and void. Cf. Heinrich Bornkamm, *Das Jahrhundert der Reformation* (1961), insel-tb 713, Frankfurt a. M. 1983, 160. – As for Alfred Edwin John Rawlinson, I have not been able to verify the above interpretation of *protestati sumus* in his works. He does state that »Protestantism, historically considered, was not primarily a revolt against the idea of authority in religion as such«, but aimed at substituting the authority of God for that of men, as a »guarantee« of salvation: *Authority and Freedom*, London 1924, 54. 56. But this is not meant as an explanation of the term Protestantism.

[13] Otto and his disciples had celebrated liturgically free services in Marburg; for Linderholm cf. letter no. 167, n. 7.

[14] Wilfred Monod, Reformed theologian, professor of practical theology at the *Faculté Libre* in Paris. He was acquainted with Söderblom since 1888.

[15] The short *Message* of the conference to the Christians and the world at large had been

deutung.[16] Aber worauf ich eigentlich hinweisen wollte, ist die Zeile über Roms Fernbleiben am Anfang von *Message*, die [der Bischof von] Winchester und ich dort hingesetzt hatten als ein historisches Faktum, die aber auf Vorschlag von Kapler[17] von uns allen einmütig gestrichen wurde. Er sagte:»Die römisch-katholische Presse in Deutschland hat unsere Konferenz mit Achtung behandelt. Wir wollen nicht auf irgendeine Weise das gute Verhältnis zu unseren römisch-katholischen Brüdern stören. Ein Wort darüber, dass Rom nicht teilgenommen hat, kann leicht als ein Tadel, als eine Polemik gedeutet werden. Deshalb lassen Sie uns nichts [dazu] sagen.« Deshalb sollte das Wort Verneinung durch *Polemik oder Tadel* ersetzt werden.[18] (»Dabei wurde der Abschnitt, der sich an die römische Kirche richtete, gestrichen, *weil man die Befürchtung hegte, ein Ausdruck des Bedauerns über die Nichtteilnahme der päpstlichen Kirche könne als Polemik oder Tadel gedeutet werden.«*) Dieses Faktum ist ein neuer Beweis dafür, wie durchweg positiv alles in Stockholm vor sich ging. Ich könnte Interna darüber erzählen, wenn wir uns treffen. Charakteristisch ist, dass es der Sprecher der deutschen Delegation, Kapler, war, der selbst jeden Anschein von Tadel oder Rüge Rom gegenüber vermeiden wollte.

S. 140. Gustaf Jensen ist Norweger, nicht Däne.[19]

Klar ist, dass in evangelisch-katholisch ich mehr evangelisch, Sie mehr katholisch betonen.[20] Für mich bedeutet evangelische Katholizität, dass allein die evangelische Erlösungslehre, die nicht an Vorschriften bindet, sondern zum unbedingten Dienst für den Allmächtigen Gott befreit, eine wirkliche Katholizität zustande bringen kann. Darüber müssen wir das nächste Mal lange miteinander reden.

In einem einzigen Punkt habe ich wirklich Bedenken. Das ist die Aufbewahrung des Sakraments, reservatio.[21] Die Aufbewahrung selbst kann man zwar einerseits als Akt schuldiger Pietät, andererseits um der Kranken willen verteidigen. Aber Christi geheimnisvolle Gegenwart ist nicht durch irgendeine Formel bedingt und verwandelt folglich nicht die Hostie in etwas Göttliches, das man anbeten kann, sondern sie ist durch Christi Verheißung, die Ubiquität der göttlichen Natur und durch den Glauben bedingt. Es ist für mich sehr natürlich, dass ein Kruzifix oder ein anderes Bild oder eine Kerze die Anbetung auf einen bestimmten Punkt im Gotteshaus oder im Raum hin sammelt. Das ist ein natürliches psychologisches Bedürfnis. Aber dass die konsekrierte Hostie in ihrem Sakramentshäuschen als eine leibliche Gottheit fungiert, scheint mir sehr bedenklich zu sein, eine Analogie zu Soma,

---

published on August 29, 1925; cf. Söderblom, *Kristenhetens möte* … (cf. letter no. 250, n. 2), 675–693.

[16] Paul Conrad (1865–1927) was theological vice-president of the Evangelischer Oberkirchenrat in Berlin, the head office of the Prussian Union Church (*Altpreußische Union*, the union of the Lutheran and Reformed churches in Prussia, founded in 1817).

[17] For Hermann Kapler, cf. letter no. 240, n. 2.

[18] *Verneinung* is either a reading error or a typing error; the end of Heiler's sentence the correction of which Söderblom suggests is the following: »… könnte als Verneigung vor ihr verstanden werden.«

[19] Gustav Jensen (1848–1895), Norwegian author of hymns.

[20] Söderblom thus disagrees with Heiler on this point with regard to the ~~article~~ by René ⊢ book Wallau mentioned in letter no. 261, n. 9. Misner, op. cit. 235, n. 8, asserts that Söderblom in his reply to Heiler of Oct. 24, 1925, had assured Heiler that he had asked Wallau to modify the rendering of his, Söderblom's, concept of evangelic catholicity. However, Söderblom does not even touch on the subject in the letter cited by Misner. The latter may have mixed it up with Söderblom's letter to Wallau of July 16, 1925 (cf. no. 248 of the current edition). But even there, no explicit request for changes is made.

[21] The original has *preservatio*.

Haoma,[22] ohne eigentliches Verbindungsglied zum Neuen Testament und zur Offenbarung.

Deshalb hat der eucharistische Kongress, den der Papst mit Worten der Gottesmutter über sich selbst begrüßt hat, auf mich einen äußerst deprimierenden Eindruck gemacht.[23] Sicher ist, dass er der Propaganda zugute kommt und dort drüben vielen Seelen imponiert, besonders gegenüber dem stupiden Antiklerikalismus in Mexiko. Aber bei aller Weitherzigkeit kann ich nicht umhin, angesichts einer solchen Anbetung eines Dinges Abscheu zu empfinden.

Zwei religiöse Punkte haben die Zeitungen in den U.S.A. gefüllt, der eine durch die Quantität, der Kongress in Chicago, einer durch die Qualität, der aufrichtige schwedische Kronprinz.[24]

Wäre Professor Heiler von Anfang an dabei gewesen, hätte wohl Una sancta nicht den unpassenden Zusatz »hochkirchlich« bekommen.[25] Kirchlich reicht doch wohl. Ich muss Sie auch treffen, um Näheres über diese Bewegung in Deutschland zu hören.

Ich verstehe Ihre Unruhe angesichts des geistigen Kampfes der theologischen Schulen. Aber im Grunde ist er ein Lebenszeichen und notwendig in Christi Kirche. Denn die Kirche ist stark genug, um selbst die dialektische Theologie zu verdauen, auch sie wird uns etwas lehren. Nur in der Luft der Freiheit kann die Sache Christi siegen, und ich weiß und sehe, mit welcher Überzeugung Sie, lieber Professor und Freund, für die Freiheit der Forschung eintreten und sie ausüben. Ich habe mich oft gefragt, warum Gott mir während des Erdenlebens einen so unverdienten und unendlich großen Segen hat zuteil werden lassen wie die Bekanntschaft mit Ihnen und alles, was sie mit sich gebracht hat. Wir wollen beide unter dem Himmel leben und uns nicht in die Pferche stopfen lassen, die Freunde oder Gegner uns zuweisen, und nichts beweist besser una sancta als das Faktum, dass wir zwei von so ungleicher Herkunft und Umgebung, und andere mit uns, ein Monod, ein Garvie, ein [Bischof von] Bombay, ein Sundar Singh, ein Glubokowsky[26] einander ohne vorhergehende Vereinbarung so herzlich gut verstehen. Diese Katholizität gehört zum göttlichen Geheimnis des Lebens und der Ewigkeit.

Mit herzlichen Grüßen Ihr Ihnen verbundener
Nathan Söderblom

---

[22] Libation in Vedic India and ancient Iran.

[23] 28th International Eucharistic Congress in Chicago, April 20–26, 1926.

[24] Gustaf VI Adolf (1882–1973), king in 1950. As a crown-prince, he often traveled abroad in representative missions.

[25] *Una Sancta. Zeitschrift des Hochkirchlich-Oekumenischen Bundes*, Stuttgart 1/1921–4/1927. Heiler was a contributor from 1925 onwards. He does not seem to have been averse to the epithet »high church«, contrary to Söderblom's intimation. Heiler's article »Evangelisches Hochkirchentum« (a lecture of Dec. 1, 1925), in: op. cit. (n. 8), 198–250, marks the beginning of his work for the Protestant high church movement in Germany.

[26] Cf. letter no. 124, n. 3.

281. To Sven Hedin[1]

Upsala den 4 augusti 1926

En av De Aderton
Doktor Sven Hedin
Stockholm

Käre Broder!
Mitt brev har förorsakat Dig en lång skrivelse och jag beklagar detta. Men samtidigt är jag glad över att jag skrev till Dig. Ty 1: har jag fått ett nytt bevis på Din vänskap, 2: har jag fått fullkomligt överraskande underrättelser om kejsarens ekonomi, 3: får jag läsa ett par av hans predikningar, som jag sedan skall återsända.

För min del har jag liksom hela allmänheten här och i Tyskland varit övertygad om att kejsaren av sina possessioner erhåller en mycket stor årlig inkomst och dessutom har högst omfattande räntemedel. Jag tror att det skulle vara en stor tjänst, icke bara åt kejsaren, utan även åt tyska riket om i någon lämplig form genom interview med kejsarens närmaste man eller på annat sätt de förhållanden bleve allmänt kända, om vilka Du talar. Många av de bästa tyskarna som jag känner, nobla och rakryggade män, tala icke gärna om kejsaren. Ty de tycka visserligen att han har blivit orätt uppfattad och mycket smädad, men att han ändå räddat sig i tid, medan de ha stått och burit nöd och smälek och ansvar. Ingen är mer beundransvärd härutinnan än den gamle Hindenburg. Jag tror att det skulle vara en Entlassung [sic; läs: Entlastung] både för honom och för många av tyska rikets bästa ansvarskännande män och kvinnor om från kejsaren kunde, icke i ord, utan i handling komma något som visade hans redobogenhet att för sin del bära med på den försakelse och de svårigheter som drabbat riket. Nu ser jag av Ditt brev att en sådan tjänst skulle göras bara genom en underrättelse om hur livet föres på Doorn och särskilt att kejsaren använder sitt kapital för sin årliga existens.

Din trofasthet har Du sannerligen bevisat honom.

Min tanke var naturligtvis också att om det hade varit möjligt, kejsaren naturligtvis icke skulle hava gjort någon som helst eftergift för krav och påtryckningar, utan i stället att han skulle hava tagit ett initiativ. Vi hava i vår historia ett magnifikt föredöme, nämligen när Gustaf II Adolf skänkte just sina ärvda gods till Upsala Universitet. Han avhände kungafamiljen en oerhört stor förmögenhet. Men han gagnade landet och välsignas i alla århundraden. Jag tror icke att hans föredöme är lämpligt att framhålla till kejsar Wilhelm, ty kejsar Wilhelm förbjöd i Berlin en församling som ville det, att uppkalla sin kyrka efter Gustaf Adolf. Som Du minns, måste Gustaf Adolf ta i med hårdhandskarna för att få sin brandenburgske svåger att taga reson.

---

[1] Sven Anders Hedin (1865–1952), Swedish geographer and explorer of central Asia. – Nathan Söderblom's collection of letters, to Swedes and foreigners, UUB, typewritten letter (carbon copy).

Ett annat exempel är Karl Johans stora personliga gåvor fär byggandet av Carolina och dåvarande katedralskolan i Upsala, andra många svenska kungliga mecenater att förtiga. Jag tänkte mig att om kejsar Wilhelm gjorde något liknande och bestämde att — jag sätter icke ifråga en så stor frikostighet som Gustaf Adolfs, men dock att en väsentlig del av hans gods i Preussen skulle gå som gåva till universitetet i Berlin eller Preussiska Vetenskapsakademien som kejsaren ju så intresserade sig för och gynnade, eller till andra högskolor, så skulle detta vara icke blott en storstilad handling, utan även en akt av statsmannavisdom.

Själv har jag naturligtvis icke någon tanke på att göra en dylik hemställan till kejsaren. Jag tror knappast någon annan i världen än Du kan göra det. Förmodligen skulle det också innebära att inkomsten från hans återstående gods skulle komma honom mycket säkrare och redobognare till del. Allt under förutsättning att hans ekonomiska existens tillåter något sådant. Jag förutsätter att den knapphet som Du bevittnat och berättar, beror på att han icke erhåller för närvarande inkomsten från godsen.

Med min vördnad for Dina systrar är jag
Din tacksamt tillgivne gamle vän

Uppsala, August 4, 1926

One of the Eighteen[2]
Doctor Sven Hedin
Stockholm

Dear friend!
My letter has caused you to write a long reply, and I am sorry for that. However, at the same time I am glad that I wrote to you. For 1° I received a new proof of your friendship, 2° I received utterly surprising information about the Kaiser's economic circumstances,[3] 3° I shall be able to read some of his sermons which I shall return afterwards.

As far as I am concerned, I had been convinced, like the general public here and in Germany, that the Kaiser receives a very large annual income from his possessions and besides has quite a large amount of money coming from interests. I believe it would be a great service, not only to the Kaiser but also to the German nation, if the circumstances you are talking about became generally known, in some appropriate way, by means of an interview with his closest man [adviser] or in some other way. Many of the best Germans I know, noble and upright men, do not like to talk about the Kaiser. For they certainly think that he has been wrongly interpreted and much reviled, but that notwithstanding, that he saved himself in time, while they have stayed on and borne misery and disgrace and responsibility. No one is more admirable in this respect than old Hindenburg[4]. I believe it would be an *Entlastung*

---

[2] One of the eighteen members of the Swedish Academy. This is the institution which awards the Nobel prizes for literature. Söderblom too belonged to this exclusive group; he had been elected in 1921.

[3] Emperor Wilhelm II. went into exile in the Netherlands on November 9, 1918, where he lived in the palace Huis te Doorn, in the province of Utrecht, until his death in 1940.

[4] Paul von Beneckendorff und von Hindenburg (1847–1934), field marshal in World War I.

[exoneration] both for him and for many of the German nation's best responsible men and women if there could come from the Kaiser something, not in words but in deed, which would show his willingness, for his part to join in bearing the privation and the hardships affecting the nation. Now I see from your letter that such a service could only be rendered by information on how life is being lived at Doorn, and in particular that the Kaiser is using his capital funds for his annual subsistence.

You have certainly proved your faithfulness to him.

What I had in mind was of course also that, if it had been possible, the Kaiser should of course not have made any concession to demands and pressure, but rather that he should have taken the initiative. We have in our history a magnificent example, namely when Gustaf II Adolf donated his inherited property to Uppsala University.[5] He deprived the royal family of a tremendously great wealth. But he benefitted the country and has been praised all through the centuries. I do not believe that his example can suitably be held up to Kaiser Wilhelm, for Kaiser Wilhelm prohibited a congregation in Berlin that had wanted to name its church after Gustaf Adolf from doing so. As you will recall, Gustaf Adolf had to play hardball with his Brandenburg brother-in-law to bring him to his senses.[6]

Another example are Karl Johan's large personal donations for building Carolina and the erstwhile cathedral's school in Uppsala,[7] let alone many other Swedish royal Maecenases. I imagined that if Kaiser Wilhelm did something of that kind and decided – I am not suggesting a generosity as great as that of Gustaf Adolf, but still that a substantial part of his property should go as a donation to the university in Berlin or to the Prussian Academy of Sciences that the Kaiser was so interested in and which he patronized, or to other schools of higher learning, then that would not only be a noble deed but also an act of statesmanlike wisdom.

I am not of course planning to make such a suggestion to the Kaiser. I believe that hardly anyone in the world could do that but you.[8] Presumably that would also entail that income from his remaining property would fall to his lot more securely and readily. All of this on the supposition that his economic situation permits something of the kind. I assume that the scarcity you witnessed and are reporting on is due to the fact that at present he does not receive income from his properties.

With my reverence for your sisters I am

your grateful old friend

Through his victory over the Russian army in 1914, he was extremely popular and subsequently was able, together with his chief of staff, General Erich von Ludendorf, to wield considerable power even in domestic politics. As the figurehead of the German right, he became German President in 1925 which he remained until his death. In 1933, he allowed himself to be egged into appointing Hitler as Chancellor.

[5] Gustaf II Adolf (1594–1632), became king of Sweden 1611. He donated more than 300 farms in 1624 for the enlargement of Uppsala University. Cf. Sten Carlsson / Jerker Rosén, *Svensk historia*, vol. 1, 1962, 496 f.

[6] Elector Georg Wilhelm of Brandenburg (1595–1640), reigned from 1619–1640. He had tried to remain neutral when Gustaf Adolf had decided to take an active part in the 30-years' war. The Swedish king then moved his troops towards Brandenburg in 1631 and thereby forced the Elector to side with him. After Gustaf Adolf's death in 1632, Georg Wilhelm once again sided with the Emperor. Cf. Carlsson / Rosén, op. cit., vol. 1, 506.

[7] Karl XIV Johan (1763–1844), king of Sweden since 1810. Carolina is the University library in Uppsala, finished in 1887.

[8] Because of Hedin's good relations to the Kaiser, but also his rightist views which Söderblom opposed.

Stockholm, den 8 aug. 1926

Käre Broder

Tack för Ditt så vänliga och innehållsrika brev.

[...] Kejsaren *har* redan förlorat de slott, domäner och jordegendomar han som Konung af Preussen och tysk kejsare ägde. ... Han var ägare av hela Tiergarten! Hade denna centrala stadsdel sålts till tomter, så hade den representerat ett fullkomligt fantasibelopp. Men Tiergarten har nu övergått i statens ägo. Kejsaren ägde även slottet i Berlin, Neues Palais och en mängd andra slott, vilka alla nu äro statsegendom. Under årens lopp hade han ur eget schatull genom köp ökat slottssamlingen – otaliga gånger. Även detta är för honom förlorat. Av allt vad han ägde gick han genom revolutionen förlustig 83%. Då man avgjorde hvilka slott han skulle få behålla, valde man sådana som endast kostade dyra pengar i underhåll, t. ex. Bellevue. De 17% han fick behålla innesluta sålunda i väsentlig mån egendomar och slott, som icke giva en pfennig i inkomst. Under kriget offrade han, enligt vad hon mindes, femtio millioner guldmark till einheimische Kriegsanleihe. Det belopp i pengar, varöver han nu förfogar, är, enligt vad även grevinnan visste, mycket för smått för att räcka till honom själv och hans närmaste. På sina inkomster måste han nämligen underhålla 21 tyska furstar, som uteslutande leva på honom. Därför är hans ekonomiska ställning ytterst prekär. [...]

Jag vet att otaliga tyskar klandra kejsaren att han for till Holland, och Gud skall veta att detta steg var beklagansvärt. Men jag *kan* icke döma honom. Han var uppsliten, hopplös, nervös och förlorade besinningen i det avgörande ögonblicket, då den ohängde Gröner i kommandoton ropade: »Majestät, die Autos sind da, los!« Och hela generalitetet med *Hindenburg* i spetsen instämde. Den sistnämnde har helt nyligen skriftligen erkänt att han rådde kejsaren att resa till Holland, *endast* till Holland.

[...] Jag frågade Mewes varför kejsaren inte red såsom förr. »Vi har inte *råd* att hålla något stall, kejsaren måste helt enkelt avstå från ridten.«

Haus Doorn har 14 rum (jag o mina systrar har 17). Måltiderna under de tre dagar jag gästade Doorn voro *mycket* enkla. Våra grevar och baroner och våra godsägare leva högre än invånarna på Doorn, där livet var anspråkslöst, enkelt och allvarligt.

Att under sådana förhållanden giva kejsaren ett om också aldrig så välment råd, vore att såra honom och att tillfoga honom ännu en förödmjukelse till alla de andra bördor »ödet på hans skuldra lagt.«

Om nya indragningar bleve absolut nödvändiga på Doorn, vet jag sannerligen inte *vad* som skulle offras. Man behöver dock en köksmästare, ett par köksbiträden, ett par lakejer, tjänstekvinnor som städar rummen, chaufför, trädgårdsmästare, några arbetare som hålla parken i ordning, etc. Allt som allt finnas 21 tjänare, av vilka de manliga ha sina familjer boende i Doorn.

---

[1] Nathan Söderblom's collection of letters, from Swedes, UUB, handwritten letter.

Allt detta kostar, och kapitalet sjunker från år till år.

Jag kommer därför icke att ge kejsaren några finansiella råd och om någon av mina vänner skulle känna sig kallad at göra det, skulle jag på det livligaste avråda därifrån.

Varje morgon håller kejsaren husandakt, då alla tjänare också äro med. Vanligen läser han blott en predikan, en psalm, Fader vår och Välsignelsen. Men ibland, såsom en av de dagar jag tillbringade i Doorn, predikar han med egna ord. Han talar med kraft och övertygelse. Då jag tackade honom frågade han om jag ville behålla ett par av hans predikningar. Ja, naturligtvis. Vid lunchen hade han dem med sig, räckte mig dem och sade: »Sie können sie auch Söderblom zeigen«, vilket jag lovade. Att det icke skett förr är mycket slarvigt av mig, men jag hade tänkt att vid tillfälle i Akademien fråga om Du ville se dem.

Det skulle glädja honom om Du skrev och delgav honom Din tanke om hans ord. Sannolikt skulle Du få svar.

Men rör icke vid hans ekonomi, utan säg honom något stärkande, upplyftande och hoppgivande, ty han är mycket ensam, mycket smädad och hårt prövad av ödet. Han är också missförstådd av hela världen och orättvist bedömd.

Min vördnad till Ärkebiskopinnan och de hjärtligaste hälsningar från Alma och övriga systrar från Din mycket tillgivne vän

Sven Hedin

Stockholm, August 8, 1926

Dear friend,

thank you for your so kind and comprehensive letter.

[On Countess Scheel-Plessen who belonged to the Kaiser's inner circle, as his source of information]

The Kaiser *has* already lost the palaces, domains, and landed property that he owned as king of Prussia and German emperor. .... He was the owner of the whole of Tiergarten! Had this central part of the city been sold as real estate, it would have represented an absolutely fantastic amount of money. But Tiergarten has now been turned into state property. The Kaiser also owned the palace in Berlin, Neues Palais and a lot of other palaces, all of which are now state property. In the course of years, he had increased the palace collection by purchases from his own privy purse – countless times. That too is lost for him. Of all that he owned, he incurred a loss of 83% through the revolution. When it was decided which palaces he should be allowed to keep, such were selected which only cost lots of money for maintenance, e. g. Bellevue. The 17% he was allowed to keep thus essentially include properties and palaces which do not yield a pfennig in revenue. During the war, according to what she [the Countess] recalled, he sacrificed fifty million gold marks to einheimische *Kriegsanleihe* [domestic war loan]. The amount of money he is now disposing of is again, according to what the Countess knew, far too small to be adequate for himself and those nearest to him. For out of his revenues, he must support 21 German princes who live exclusively at his expense. Therefore his financial situation is extremely precarious. ...

I know that countless Germans find fault with the Kaiser because he went to the Netherlands, and God knows that this step was deplorable. But I *cannot* condemn him. He was worn out, hopeless, nervous, and he lost his self-control in the decisive moment when the brazen Groener[2] yelled in a commanding voice: »Majestät, die Autos sind da, los!« [Your Majesty, the cars are here, go ahead], and all the generals, *Hindenburg* at the top, joined in. The last-named quite recently conceded that he advised the Kaiser to travel to the Netherlands, *only* to the Netherlands.

... [Another example for the Kaiser's economic condition]

I asked Mewes[3] why the Kaiser did not ride as he used to. »We cannot *afford* to keep up a stable; the Kaiser must simply give up riding.«

Haus Doorn has 14 rooms (I and my sisters have 17). The meals during the days when I was a guest at Doorn were *very* simple. Our counts and barons and our landowners live a better life than the inhabitants at Doorn, where life was unpretentious, simple, and serious.

In such circumstances, giving advice to the Kaiser, be it as well-meaning as it may, would mean to hurt him and to inflict on him yet another humiliation, in addition to all the other burdens »fate has put on his shoulders«.[4]

If new reductions became absolutely necessary at Doorn, I really do not know *what* should be sacrificed. For one surely needs a chef, a couple of kitchen hands, a couple of footmen, charwomen who clean the rooms, driver, gardener, some workers who keep the park in order, etc. In all, there are 21 servants, of which the male ones live at Doorn with their families.

All of this is costly, and the capital is diminishing from year to year.

I shall therefore not give the Kaiser any financial advice, and if one of my friends felt called upon to do that, I would most vigorously dissuade him.

Each morning, the Kaiser conducts a family prayer service in which all servants also participate. Normally he only reads a sermon, a psalm, Our Father, and the blessing. Sometimes, however, as on one of the days I spent at Doorn, he preaches in his own words. He speaks with firmness and conviction. When I thanked him, he asked if I wanted to keep some of his sermons. Yes, of course. At lunch, he had them with him, gave them to me and said: »Sie können sie auch Söderblom zeigen« [You can also show them to Söderblom], which I promised to do. That this did not happen earlier has been very sloppy of me, but I had thought of asking you when I had the chance at the Academy to ask if you wanted to see them.

He would be pleased if you wrote and conveyed your comments on his words. Probably you would get a reply.

But do not touch on his economics, rather say to him something supportive, uplifting and hope-inspiring, for he is very lonely, much reviled and severely tried by his fate. He is also being misunderstood by the whole world and unjustly judged.

---

[2] Wilhelm Groener (1867–1939), general, organizer of railroad transportation for the armies in World War I. He was also responsible for the organization of the retreat in 1918, and he pleaded for the Kaiser's abdication and for cooperation with Chancellor Friedrich Ebert. Under him, he became secretary of the *Reichswehr* (army) from 1920 till 1923 and 1928–1928, in 1931 also secretary of the interior. He prohibited the SS in 1932 and subsequently was forced to resign.

[3] Friedrich Wilhelm Mewes, Lieutenant Colonel, the Kaiser's last aide-de-camp.

[4] Quotation from Elias Tegnér, *Försonligheten* [Conciliatoriness], 1808, in: *Samlade dikter* [Collected Poems] vol. 1, Lund 1990, p. 212f., lines 18–20: »Döm ej den vilseförde,/ stolte Vise, med förakt./ Icke vägde du den börda,/ ödet på hans skuldra lagt.« Prose transl.: Do not condemn him who was led astray, proud wise man, with contempt. You did not weigh the burden fate has put on his shoulder.

My respect to Mrs. Söderblom, and most sincere regards from Alma and the other sisters, from your very dedicated friend
Sven Hedin

283. From FRIEDRICH HEILER[1]

Marburg, den 10. August 1926

Hochverehrter, hochwürdigster Herr Erzbischof,

haben Sie sehr herzlichen Dank für Ihren lieben Brief, der mir eine aufrichtige Freude und ein erquickender Trost ist in allen Anfechtungen, die ich in der letzten Zeit zu erleiden hatte. Ihre verständnisinnige Liebe ist mir ein wahres Gottesgeschenk, für das ich nicht genug dankbar sein kann inmitten von Missverständnissen und Anfeindungen. Die Angriffe kommen von beiden Seiten. Der hiesige römisch-katholische Pfarrer, ein sehr frommer, aber engherziger Priester, hat kürzlich auf der Kanzel beim Gottesdienst in zornigen Worten vor mir gewarnt (weil zahlreiche römische Studenten meine Vorlesungen besuchten). Auf der anderen Seite werde ich sogar von ernsten Leuten als »Kryptojesuit« verdächtigt, der mit raffinierter Technik die deutschen Protestanten in den Schafstall des heiligen Vaters zu locken versucht. Der hessische Zweigverein des Evangelischen Bundes suchte das Konsistorium in Cassel gegen mich scharf zu machen, um so meine Entfernung aus der theologischen Fakultät herbeizuführen. Das Konsistorium hat jedoch keine Schritte unternommen. So geht es hin und her und immer wieder schaffen sich hüben und drüben Angst und Misstrauen einen bildhaften Ausdruck in Märchen und Legenden über meine Person. Augenblicklich habe ich freilich mehr von protestantischer als von römischer Seite zu leiden.

... [On Söderblom's corrections]

Ihre Bemerkungen betreffend die Reservation der Eucharistie, besser gesagt, die Andacht zur aufbewahrten Eucharistie, verstehe ich sehr wohl. Ich selber möchte niemals daraus ein Gesetz machen und jenen, die diese Sitte nicht annehmen, eine geringere Schätzung des Abendmahls zum Vorwurf machen. Ich selber habe ja seiner Zeit im »Gebet« den sehr späten Ursprung dieser Devotion aufgedeckt.[2] Die ganze alte Kirche und alle heutigen Kirchen des Ostens kennen wohl eine Aufbewahrung der Eucharistie für die Kranken, aber nicht zum Zweck der privaten oder öffentlichen Andacht. Und doch wird niemand auf den Gedanken kommen, ihnen eine geringere Schätzung der Eucharistie zuzuschreiben. Dennoch glaube ich mit vielen römischen und anglikanischen Katholiken an die besondere Segenskraft dieser Sitte; ich denke dabei nicht nur an Franz von Assisi und Thomas von Aquino, sondern auch an unsern unvergesslichen Freund Friedrich von Hügel, der sie selber so eifrig übte. Natürlich können sich an die Aufbewahrung der Eucharistie schwere Missbräuche und abergläubische Vorstellun-

---

[1] Nathan Söderblom's collection of letters, from foreigners, UUB, typewritten letter.
[2] *Das Gebet*, 4th ed. München 1921, 325–331.

gen knüpfen, wie die mittelalterliche Frömmigkeitsgeschichte und die heutige Praxis der römischen Kirche zeigt. Ich selber verabscheue von ganzer Seele den pomphaften und aufdringlichen Eucharistiekult, wie er vor allem in den eucharistischen Kongressen zu Tage tritt. Ich sehe darin geradezu eine Entwürdigung des Mysteriums. Aber ich glaube nicht, dass all diese Auswüchse die notwendigen Konsequenzen des altchristlichen Eucharistieglaubens sind, sondern bin überzeugt, dass gerade eine reinere und zartere Auffassung der Eucharistie im Stande ist, dies Missbräuche zu entwurzeln. Ich glaube auch keineswegs, dass die Gegenwart Christi an die Abendmahlselemente gebunden sei; den[n] Christus ist in erster Linie in den Herzen der von ihm gerechtfertigten und geheiligten Gläubigen, der Χριστόφοροι,[3] und darum ist er allzeit mit ihnen. Aber die Andacht vor der aufbewahrten Eucharistie ist ein ausgezeichnetes Mittel, um sich auf Christus und seine unmittelbare Gegenwart im eigenen Herzen zu konzentrieren. Die Seele denkt vor dem Altar nicht an die Hostie, sondern nur an Christus, dessen Zeichen sie ist und auf den sie hinweist. Der Anblick des Tabernakels ist nur ein erster Anreiz für den Glauben; dann aber tritt das äussere Zeichen zurück und Christus allein tritt vor die Seele. Die sinnenfällige Erscheinung weist so über sich hinaus und ruft uns ein stetes ›quaerere super nos‹[4] entgegen. Natürlich kann dieselbe Wirkung auch von einem Crucifix oder einem Altarbilde ausgehen; aber ich gebe der aufbewahrten Eucharistie deshalb den Vorzug, weil sie eine Verbindung herstellt mit dem zentralen christlichen Gottesdienst und gerade dadurch einen intimen Kontakt des Privatgebets mit dem gottesdienstlichen Gemeindegebet ermöglicht. Ich kann in dieser Auffassung nichts Bedenkliches finden; ich habe einmal darüber Sundar Singh gefragt, und er antwortete mir, er habe »nicht einmal einen Einwand gegen die Verehrung von Idolen, wenn sie sich als ein Mittel erweise, die Menschen zu Christus zu bringen, und als eine Hilfe zur Sammlung des Geistes und zum Gebet.« Ich habe dieses Mittel oft genug erprobt und verdanke ihm viele glückliche Stunden meines Lebens. Dennoch würde ich es nie anderen aufdrängen. Ein jeder möge in seinem Umgang mit Christus den Weg gehen und die Mittel gebrauchen, die ihm nützlich und heilsam sind. Ich glaube, die Kirchenchristen sollten in dieser Frage wie in anderen einander volle Freiheit einräumen. Es scheint mir gleich verfehlt, wenn solche, die diese Sitte üben, ihr irgend welche Exklusivität und Gesetzlichkeit zuschreiben, wie wenn jene, die sie nicht gutheissen, den anderen ein Abweichen vom neutestamentlichen Geist vorwerfen.

Von Herzen stimme ich Ihnen darin bei, dass das Wesen des Christentums im unmittelbaren, persönlichen Leben, in der Gemeinschaft des Herzens mit Christus zu suchen ist, und nicht in einer Institution, sei sie auch noch so altehrwürdig; eine Institution ohne Leben und Liebe ist nur tönendes Erz.[5] Die Institution ist auch für mich nur Mittel im Dienste jenes Hö-

---

[3] Bearers of Christ.
[4] Latin: searching beyond ourselves.
[5] I Cor 13:1.

heren und Reicheren. Wenn die Institution für einen Menschen oder eine Gruppe den Weg zum persönlichen Leben versperrt, so erkenne ich ihnen durchaus das Recht zu, sich über die Institution hinwegzusetzen. Aber andererseits glaube ich, dass die schon im Leben der urchristlichen Gemeinde wurzelnden Institutionen der alten Kirche für die grössere Zahl der Christen die besten Hilfsmittel für das persönliche Glaubensleben sind. Ich sehe darum das christliche Ideal in der Harmonie eines starken persönlichen Lebens mit den christlichen Institutionen; die grösste christliche Freiheit scheint mir nicht die Freiheit *von* den Institutionen, sondern *in* den Institutionen zu sein: οὐκ ἄνομος ἀλλ᾽ ἔννομος Χριστοῦ.⁶

Für die Anglokatholiken hege ich große Sympathie, aber nur für Männer vom Typ eines Pusey, Keble, Stones, Gore, Palmer, nicht für jene, die nur den römischen Ritualismus recht und schlecht imitieren und die z. T. päpstlicher sind als der Papst; Tyrrell hat einmal gesagt, diese Leute würden ihn noch schlechter behandeln als die römische Kirche.⁷ Ich werde das auch, wenn ich nach England komme, sagen. Ich werde in Oxford, wahrscheinlich auch in London und Canterbury einen Vortrag über Luthers Bedeutung halten.⁸

Meine Unruhe hinsichtlich der Lage der deutschen Theologie ist tatsächlich sehr gross. Weniger wegen der neuesten theologischen Theorien, als vielmehr wegen ihrer verheerenden praktischen Wirkungen. Ich finde bei den jungen Leuten, welche die dialektische Theologie eingesogen haben, allenthalben Intellektualismus und Skeptizismus, Aufgeblasenheit, Lieblosigkeit und geistige Armut, aber keinen lebendigen, frohen und sieghaften Glauben. Ich will hier nur eine Begebenheit erzählen, welche die Situation beleuchtet. Gogarten, einer der Führer der Dialektiker⁹, ging mit der Dichterin der »Hymnen an die Kirche« (dem grössten religiösen Dichtwerk der

---

⁶ I Cor 9:21: »not being without law … but under the law of Christ,« there referring to the Jewish law.

⁷ Edward Bouverie Pusey (1800–1882), after John Henry Newman's (1801–1890) conversion to Roman Catholicism (1845) leading figure of the Oxford Movement, which tried to revive the High Church ideal of the 17th century by focussing on the Eucharist and the apostolic origin of the episcopacy; John Keble's (1792–1866), sermon *On National Apostasy* (1833), in which he critized the state's meddling in church affairs, initiated the Oxford movement; Darwell Stone (1859–1941), principal of Pusey House in Oxford; Charles Gore (1853–1932) at first belonged to the liberal wing of the Anglo-Catholic movement but turned conservative around 1891, bishop of Worcester 1902, Birmingham 1905, and Oxford 1911–1919, lecturer in theology, Dean of the theological faculty of London University 1924–1928; for Edwin James Palmer, cf. letter no. 280, n. 4.

⁸ The lecture was delivered in different forms from 1921–1928 under the heading »Luthers Bedeutung für die christliche Kirche;« the latest version is printed in: *Im Ringen um die Kirche. GAufs u. Vorträge II*, München 1931, 198–259 as »Luther und die katholische Kirche.«

⁹ Friedrich Gogarten: see letter no. 221, n. 5. Initially a disciple of Ernst Troeltsch, he rebuked liberal theology under the impression of both his Luther studies (since 1917) and World War I and joined the »dialectical« theologians, editors of the periodical *Zwischen den Zeiten*. His political conservatism (member of the German Christians for a short time, who sympathized with the Nazis) estranged him from Karl Barth, however. After World War II, he became known for his theory of the secular world, which he interpreted as a legitimate conse-

letzten Jahre in Deutschland)[10] in der Nähe von München an der Isar spazieren und entwickelte ihr seine negativistische Theologie. Schliesslich sagte ihm seine Begleiterin: »Hören Sie auf, Herr Gogarten, denn wenn das so ist, wie Sie sagen, dann springe ich sofort in die Isar.« Das ist eben die Theologie der Verzweiflung, doch nicht der salubris desperatio, von der Luther redet.[11]

Sehr gern würde ich mit Ihnen zusammentreffen. Ich werde erst Ende September nach England reisen. Vom 17. August bis 17. September werde ich in Bayern, zumeist in München sein. Wäre es nicht möglich, dass ich Sie dort auf Ihrer Reise in die Schweiz treffen könnte, sei es nun auf der Hin- oder auf der Rückreise? Der Weg über Berlin – München – Lindau in die Schweiz ist ja nicht wesentlich weiter als der über Berlin – Frankfurt – Basel. Eine Reise nach Genf ist für mich doch mit einigen Schwierigkeiten verbunden. Meine Adresse ist von nächster Woche an: München, Breisacherstrasse 2/III.

Ich habe eben mit meiner Frau die »Visionen« des Sadhu übersetzt, ein wunderbar nüchternes Buch von ausgesprochen ethischem Pathos, das mir viel Freude gemacht hat, ebenso wie das andere von den Meditationen, das ebenfalls sehr feine Gedanken enthält.[12]

Mit den herzlichsten Grüßen an Sie und Ihre verehrte Gattin von meiner Frau und mir verbleibe ich in der Freude auf ein baldiges Wiedersehen

Ihr stets dankbar ergebener
Friedrich Heiler

284. To Sven Hedin[1]

Uppsala den 12 augusti 1926

Käre Broder!

Jag är Dig mycket tacksam för dessa upplysningar, och jag tror att det verkligen skall bli till stort gagn särskilt för många av de bästa människorna i Tyskland, om kejsarens ekonomiska situation kan komma till offentligheten.

De vänner, vilkas omdöme jag antydde i mitt förra brev, höra nog till dem, som allra bittrast harmas över Wilsons och de andras grova löftes-

quence of the Reformation (secularization) on the one hand, and anti-Christian (secularism) on the other.

[10] Gertrud Freiin von le Fort, *Hymnen an die Kirche*, München 1924 (5th ed. 1948). The author (1876-1971) was, like Gogarten, originally a disciple of Troeltsch. She converted to Roman Catholicism in 1925, a decision presaged by her book.

[11] *Salutaris desperatio*, i.e. despair that is converted into the certitude of faith by the Gospel of Christ; in: *De servo arbitrio* (1525), WA 18 (600–787), 719,11 f.

[12] *Visions of the Spiritual Life*, London 1926, German transl.: *Gesichte aus der jenseitigen Welt*, Aarau 1926; *Meditations on Various Aspects of the Spiritual Life*, London 1926.

[1] Nathan Söderblom's collection of letters, to Swedes and foreigners, UUB, typewritten letter (carbon copy).

brott. Men hur mycket jag än beklagar kejsaren och hur väl jag förstår svårigheten, ja olösligheten av den situation, från vilken han reste till Holland, så kan jag också begripa de tyskar, som helst bli tysta, då talet faller på kejsaren. Detta sammanhänger naturligtvis också därmed, att jag under mina år i Leipzig före kriget i Professoren Zimmer från åtskilliga av universitetets ypperste män hörde en sorg, som kunde bli till bitterhet och sjudande harm över vad de ansågo vara hos kejsaren med hela hans begåvning och alla hans goda egenskaper och hans ärliga vilja en obetänksamhet och en förhävelse, så skarpt stridande mot vad de lärt sig vörda och beundra hos Bismarck och hos Preussens stora härskare. Nu är han en olycklig man och skulle kunna vara en tragisk personlighet. Hans omgifte har emellertid tagit bort denna tragik. Jag unnar honom av hjärtat en god kvinnas huldhet i ensamheten, men fastän jag aldrig råkat den gamla riktiga kejsarinnan, så är mitt intryck av henne sådant, att det är svårt att förlika sig med tanken på att hon fått en efterträderska.

Nå, detta tyckes knappast höra till ämnet. Men jag måste uppriktigt säga, att jag har sökt i min tanke efter en möjlighet för kejsaren att med en ädelmodig handling, som kanske till och med kunde ha karaktären utav uppoffring och medkänsla med tyska riket, skriva ett ytterligare kapitel i sin levnads saga. Snart är den slut för honom liksom för oss alla. Han har säkert velat det bästa.

Din tillgivne tacksamme vän

Uppsala, August 12, 1926

Dear friend,

I am very grateful to you for these facts, and I believe it will really be very useful, particularly for many of the best people in Germany, if the Kaiser's economic circumstances could be made public.

The friends whose judgment I hinted at in my last letter, certainly belong to those who are most indignant at the rude breach of promise by Wilson and the others.[2] But as much as I pity the Kaiser and as much as I understand the hardship, yea intractability of the situation from which he went to the Netherlands, I can also understand those Germans who prefer to become silent when the conversation turns on the Kaiser. This is, of course, also bound up with the fact that during my Leipzig years before the war, I heard from several of the foremost men of the university in the *Professoren Zimmer* [the professors' room] a sadness which could turn to bitterness and boiling indignation at what they considered in the Kaiser, for all his giftedness and good points of character and his honest will, a rashness and an arrogance

---

[2] President Woodrow Wilson in his speech of Jan. 22, 1917, promised a »Peace without Victory«, not revenge but justice among equals, instututionalized by the League of Nations. And in his famous 14 points of January 18, 1918, all of which stress the self-determination of nations, he spoke of »open covenants of peace, openly arrived at« (# 1), and of »a general association of nations … for the purpose of affording mutual guarantees of political independence and territorial integrity to great and small states alike« (# 14). The breach of promise Söderblom refers to is both the Versailles peace treaty of 1919 which crippled the German economy, and the French occupation of the Rhineland in 1923. Cf. letters no.136, n.2; 194, n.3; 195; 199, n.3.

so sharply contrasting with what they had learned to appreciate and admire in Bismarck and in Prussia's great rulers. Now he is an unlucky man, and he might be a tragic personality. His remarriage[3] has removed that tragedy, however. I do not at all grudge him a good woman's kindliness in his solitude; but even though I never met the old real empress, my impression of her is such that it is hard to become reconciled with the idea that she has got a successor.

Well, this hardly seems to belong to the subject. But I must honestly say that in my thoughts I have been searching for an opportunity for the Kaiser to write a further chapter in his life's tale by a magnanimous action which might even have the character of sacrifice and sympathy with the German nation. Soon it will be over for him as for all of us. He has certainly had the best intentions.

   Your grateful friend

285. From RUDOLF OTTO[1]

                                        vor Karlskrona. Mittwoch. 6. 10. 26.
Verehrter Herr u. Frau Erzbischof.
Die lange Fahrt durch die Schären von Stockholm liegt hinter uns. Öland ist eben verschwunden, ich wandle im schönsten Sonnenscheine und lasse still die Bilder der vergangenen Tage an mir vorüber gleiten. Ich weiß noch nicht was stärker ist: der Eindruck dieser farbenleuchtenden Landschaft oder der dieser kraftvoll aufsteigenden Nationalkultur oder dieser bedeutenden und eigenartigen Geistigkeit Ihres unverbrauchten jugendkräftigen Volkes. Jedenfalls bin ich der »Eroberte« und gehe heim mit einem reichen Schatze neuer und starker Erfahrung.

   Bischof Billing interessierte sich für die Idee eines protestantischen Zusammenschlusses. Er betonte seine enge Verbindung mit der lutherischen Weltgemeinschaft, aber er fühlte wohl auch ihre gewissen Einseitigkeiten und Engigkeiten. Er will aber, wenn die lutherische Weltkonferenz für unsere Pläne zu gewinnen ist, gern mit arbeiten. So gehe ich auch in dieser Hinsicht mit großen Hoffnungen von Schweden heim. Mein Wunsch ist, daß wir ein protestantisches Weltblatt gründen in 3 Sprachen. Und ich möchte dafür Dr. Berggrav als Herausgeber gewinnen. Er hat dafür glänzende Talente.

   Eine sehr interessante Stunde hatte ich mit Dr. Beskow.[2] Ich werde versuchen meinen jungen Freund und Schüler Dr. Küssner,[3] zu ihm und nach Sigtuna zu schicken, damit er das schwedische Volks-bildungs-wesen stu-

---

[3] The Kaiser's first wife, nee Princess Auguste Viktoria of Schleswig-Holstein-Sonderburg-Augustenburg (1858–1921), with whom he had seven children, died in April, 1921. On November 5, 1922, he married Hermine Princess of Reuß (elder line), widowed Princess Schönaich-Carolath (1887–1947) who thus became Princess of Prussia.

[1] Nathan Söderblom's collection of letters, from foreigners, UUB, handwritten letter.
[2] Natanael Beskow (1865–1953), schoolman, hymnwriter, social reformer, diplomat, theologian and pacifist.
[3] Karl Küssner, author of Gespräche mit Rudolf Otto, Stuttgart 1941.

diere. Durch ihn hoffe ich eine Form zu finden, um unsere geistig und religiös verarmten Proletarier-Kreise zu erreichen: eine Aufgabe, an der ich seit Jahren interessiert bin.

Dr. Hedin empfing mich äußerst freundlich. Vielleicht sehe ich ihn demnächst wieder bei meiner Freundin, der Gräfin Siersdorpff.[4] Er will im Oktober nach Wiesbaden kommen und ist dann ganz in unserer Nähe.

In Berlin treffe ich einen japanischen Freund und Schüler von mir: Professor Yamashita.[5] Ich werde ihn beauftragen, den Gedanken einer interreligiösen Arbeitsgemeinschaft mit nach Japan zu nehmen und die Fäden neu zu knüpfen, die sich dorthin bereits früher gesponnen haben. Mr. Atkinson hoffe ich in Marburg zu sehen.

Von Herzen hoffe ich, meinen jungen Freund B. Forell einmal wieder in Deutschland zu haben. Ich habe mich aufs neue von der Begabung und dem sicheren Takte dieses jungen Mannes überzeugt und erhoffe noch viel von ihm.

Und nun sage ich Ihnen und Schweden noch einmal Lebewohl und auf Wiedersehen. Und dieses besonders auch Ihnen, Frau Erzbischof. Ihre innige Güte ging mir so warm zu Herzen, daß ich den herzlichsten Wunsch hege, Sie einmal in unserem Marburg begrüßen zu können. Auch an Frl. Yvonne[6] die besten Grüße und an Ihre Söhne. Leid war es mir, daß ich dem Fröken[7], das so trefflich für mich gesorgt hat, in der Eile der Abfahrt nicht Lebewohl gesagt habe. Tun Sie es für mich. – Dieses Schiff ist das niedlichste der Welt. Es fährt so still wie ein Schwan. Man hat Raum zu spazieren, und in einem langen behaglichen Saale sind zur Zeit ich selber und eine rote blühende Aster die einzigen Gäste. Auch die Aster schickt einen ergebenen Gruß mit Ihrem
R. Otto.

286. To Alfred Loisy[1]

Upsala le 18 Déc. 1926

Chèr Monsieur,

Les fêtes avec lesquelles nous espérons célébrer une date dans Votre vie de savant, de théologien et de personnalité mondiale pour les recherches réligieuses et morales seraient pour moi une excellente occasion de revenir à Paris pour satisfaire à ma nostalgie de continuer cet entretien pour moi in-

---

[4] Gräfin Franken-Siersdorf, according to the list of Otto's correspondence at the Univ.-Library in Marburg. She might be identical with Berta Gräfin Sierdorf who founded a recreation home for mothers and children in Neunkirchen, Saar, in 1927.

[5] This being a frequent Japanese name, I have not been able to find out who he was.

[6] Daughter of Söderblom.

[7] Swedish for Miss; Otto probably refers to a servant.

[1] Papers of Alfred Loisy, letters, Bibliothèque nationale de France, n.a.f. 15661, fol. 431–432, typewritten letter.

oubliable et sacré, que Vous m'avez accordé si amicalement dans le recueillement du sanctuaire de Vos pensées, de Votre vie intérieure et de Vos travaux. J'ai deviné peut être plus exactement qu'auparavant l'unité quand même de Votre histoire personnelle si mouvementée vis à vis de l'Eglise — comme j'admire aujourd'hui comme toujours l'énergie chercheuse, la droiture sérieuse de Votre conscience sans réserve, Votre grande envergure de vue, de savoir et de pensée, Votre pénétration exégétique et Votre sens profond et salutaire du rôle de l'irrationel et de l'impératif dans la morale.

J'ai été heureux de vous trouver en si bonne santé, et je vous vois encore devant ce depositum fidei et cordis qui était devant vous sur la table en forme de Votre correspondence avec le feu évêque laique du modernisme. J'aurais voulu entendre de vous encore beaucoup de choses sur les hommes d'aujourd'hui et de jadis et sur l'Eglise et la vie et la pensée quelque fois si tordue qui devrait refléter la lumière éternelle, mais qui quelques fois dans l'action et les hommes de l'Eglise ressemble plutôt à un feu de Bengale ou à une incendie d'intrigues et de passions qu'à la force pénétrante des rayons X.

Rien n'est plus délicat et plus difficile que de parler de l'Etre surhumain et sur-rational qui est au fond de toutes les choses et dont la présence mystérieuse et insondable dans nos coeurs, dans l'Univers et dans l'histoire donnent cependent à notre vie un sens. Aucune réalité me parait être plus réelle, ni plus proche de nous. En lisant Vos livres, surtout celui de la Morale, je sens cette présence divine.

Mais, hélas, il ne me sera pas possible de revenir si tôt à Paris. Je garde notre entretien avec d'autant plus de reconnaissance.

Savez-Vous ce que la concierge a dit quand Madame Söderblom est venue me chercher? Madame Söderblom a demandé: Où demeure Monsieur Loisy? La concierge a répété, en corrigeant absolument justement: »Père Loisy demeure« etc. Vous Vous rapellez-Vous ce que le bon homme à Ceffonds m'a dit à moi quand j'ai voulu trouver la maison de Monsieur Loisy? »Ah, Monsieur, Vous voulez dire Monsieur l'Abbé Loisy«.

J'ai été particulièrement heureux d'entendre Vos plans pour le travail qui Vous occupe à présent. J'espère que Vous écrivez aussi une continuation de Votre biographie personnelle en continuant Autour d'un petit Livre jusqu'à nos jours. Il est bien néçessaire de corriger des opinions superficielles, erronnées sur Votre relation avec von Hügel et d'autres personnes de la vie contemporaine intellectuelle et religieuse.

Madame Söderblom Vous prie de recevoir ses hommages. Croyez moi, chèr Monsieur et frère, Votre avec les meilleurs voeux de tout coeur dévoué
Nathan Söderblom
(handwritten addition:) Mille remerciments de L'Eglise et la France – lecture captivante.
P. s. Vous ai'je envoyé mon livre »Das Werden des Gottesglaubens« dans la seconde édition, raccourcie et révisée et parue à Leipzig?

Uppsala, December 18, 1926

Dear Sir,

The festivities with which we hope to celebrate a date in your life[2] as a scholar, theologian and personality of world-wide renown in religious and moral research, would be an excellent occasion for me to return to Paris in order to satisfy my nostalgia for continuing that conversation, unforgettable and sacred for me, which you so kindly granted me in the meditative mood of the sanctuary of your thought, your inner life and your works.[3] I have divined, perhaps more exactly than before, the unity of your so turbulent personal history over against the Church, in spite of it all – as I admire today as always the investigative energy, the serious and unreserved judgment of your conscience, your wide range of view, knowledge, and thought, your exegetical acumen and your deep and salutary sense of the role of the irrational and of the moral imperative.

I was glad to find you in such good health, and I am still seeing you in front of that depositium fidei et cordis[4] which was on the table in front of you, in the form of your correspondence with the late lay bishop of modernism.[5] I would have liked to hear from you many more things about the people of today and the past and about the Church and life and the sometimes so twisted thinking that should reflect the eternal light, but which at times in the actions and the men of the Church bears more resemblance to a Bengal light or a blaze of intrigues and passions than to the penetrating force of X-rays.

Nothing is more delicate and more difficult than speaking about the superhuman and suprarational Being that is at the bottom of all things, and whose mysterious and inscrutable presence in our hearts, in the Universe, and in history nevertheless gives meaning to our life. No reality seems more real to me, nor closer to us. When reading your books, particularly the one on Morals[6], I sense that divine presence.

But alas, it will not be possible for me to return to Paris so soon. I cherish our conversation with all the more gratitude.

Do you know what the doorkeeper said when Mrs. Söderblom came to look for me? Mrs. Söderblom asked: Where does Mr. Loisy live? The doorkeeper replied, correcting her absolutely right: »Father Loisy lives« etc. Do you remember what the good man at Ceffonds said to me when I wanted to find Mr. Loisy's house? »Oh, you mean to say Reverend Loisy.«

I was particularly glad to hear about your plans for the work currently occupying you. I hope you will also write a continuation of your personal biography by continuing *Autour d'un petit livre*[7] until the present day. It is quite necessary to correct the superficial, erroneous opinions about your relation to von Hügel and to other personalities of contemporary intellectual and religious life.

Mrs Söderblom asks you to accept her respect. Believe me, dear Sir and Brother, yours with best wishes and devoted with all my heart,

Nathan Söderblom

---

[2] Loisy's 70th birthday (February 28, 1927) was to be celebrated by the Congrès d'histoire du christianisme in April, 1927; Söderblom was part of the initiative.

[3] Söderblom had visited Loisy on December 11, 1926.

[4] Latin, deposit of faith and the heart. *Depositum fidei* is the Roman Catholic term for the body of revealed truth administrated by the Church.

[5] Friedrich Freiherr von Hügel (1852–1925), autodidactic theological scholar, leading Catholic modernist.

[6] *La morale humaine*, Paris 1903.

[7] Söderblom must have meant Loisy's autobiography *Choses passées*, Paris 1913.

(handwritten addition:) Thank you so much for *L'Eglise et la France*[8] – captivating reading.

P.S.: Did I send you my book *Das Werden des Gottesglaubens* in its second edition, abridged and revised and published at Leipzig?

287. From ADOLF VON HARNACK[1]

Berlin-Grunewald, 26.12.26.

Hochverehrter Herr Erzbischof!

Für die freundliche Übersendung Ihres Werks über die »Weltkonferenz der Kirchen«[2] sage ich Ihnen meinen besten Dank. Niemand war berufener als Sie, dieses Werk zu schreiben. Achilles fand seinen Homer, Perikles seinen Thukydides – in diesem Falle haben das der Domprobst von Canterbury u. Deißmann besorgt[3] –; aber Cäsar hat De bello Gallico selbst geschrieben, und wir freuen uns, daß sich das – De pace et unitate ecclesiastica[4] – wiederholt hat.

Mit herzlichen Wünschen z. neuen Jahr verehrungsvoll   v. Harnack

288. From ALFRED LOISY[1]

Paris, le 30 décembre 1926

Très Révérend et cher Archevêque

J'ai été, comme je vous l'ai dit, très touché de votre visite; je suis très touché de votre bonne lettre. Il doit être vrai que, nonobstant les ruptures apparentes, j'ai toujours suivi à peu près la même ligne. Je me suis tiré le moins mal que j'ai pu des situations, extérieures et intérieures, assez difficiles. Même maintenant je prends un rôle assez ingrat en prêchant à notre laïcisme la nécessité d'une morale religieusement comprise. Quelques-uns, – dont je ne garantis pas la finesse psychologique, – se sont demandé si je ne m'orientais pas vers Rome. Mais le temps de mon service est près de finir, et je puis dire, avec le saint homme Job, que j'attends la relève.

Hier, pour m'instruire des choses de l'Eglise romaine, j'ai acheté un *Almanach catholique* qui se publie sous le patronage de Mgr Baudrillart, et au-

---

[8] Alfred Loisy, *L'Eglise et la France*, Paris 1925.

[1] Nathan Söderblom's collection of letters, from foreigners, UUB, handwritten letter.
[2] Nathan Söderblom, *Kristenhetens möte* ·, cf. letter no. 250, n. 2.
[3] George K. A. Bell, *The Stockholm Conference 1925. The Official Report of the Universal Christian Conference on Life and Work held in Stockholm, 19–30 August, 1925*, London 1926; Adolf Deißmann, *Die Stockholmer Weltkirchenkonferenz 1925. Vorgeschichte, Dienst und Arbeit der Weltkonferenz für Praktisches Christentum 19.–30. August 1925. Amtlicher Deutscher Bericht*, Berlin 1926.
[4] Latin: On church peace and unity; parallel to Caesar's *On the Gallic War*.

[1] Nathan Söderblom's collection of letters, from foreigners, UUB, handwritten letter.

450

quel collaborent de notables personnalités. Je n'ai perdu mon argent; car, en l'ouvrant, je suis tombé sur un article signé Pierre *Batiffol*, où est exposée *l'Evolution du mouvement pour l'union des Eglises.* Deux paragraphes vous concernent: *La Conférence de Stockholm*, et *Le mot des Allemands à Stockholm.* Cela peut se resumer dans la phrase: »Bien évidemment *l'Essence du christianisme* était le Nouveau Testament des congressistes.« Rien à attendre de vous pour le rapprochement des Eglises. Du reste, »l'archevêque lutherien d'Upsal« est »bien connu pour sa germanophilie et son modernisme«. On veut espérer davantage de l'épiscopat anglican, et l'on rappelle discrètement les »conversations« de Malines par une image de l'archevêché et une photographie de Lord Halifax. Tout cela est fort habilement tourné, mais ce n'est que de l'habileté. Je vous raconte cette petite histoire pour vous amuser. Vous n'avez pas besoin d'être encouragé dans votre oeuvre, mais vous pouvez la continuer sans crainte, bien que le concours de Batiffol ne vous soit pas assuré.

Les catholiques de ce pays sont toujours occupés de la condamnation que Pie XI a portée contre *l'Action française.* Ce journal monarchiste, qui a été le bras droit de Pie X au temps de la Séparation et contre le modernisme, ne s'attendait pas à tant d'ingratitude. Certains évêques semblent assez déconcertés. Il paraît que le pape a été vraiment scandalisé de l'incrédulité foncière que Maurras a toujours étalée dans ses livres. Mais, en reprenant la politique de Léon XIII contre le parti réactionnaire, il garde celle de Pie X et veut mobiliser les catholiques pour faire régner le Christ dans nos lois. S'il s'agissait de l'Evangile, moyennant une exégèse un peu souple, on pourrait s'entendre; mais le droit du Christ est celui du pape, un droit qui ne connaît pas de limites. Il en résulte que le pape, avec ses bonnes intentions pourra tourner contre lui les hommes de réaction et les hommes de progrès ... A lui d'y voir.

Je n'ai pas la seconde édition de *Das Werden des Gottesglaubens.* Si vous voulez bien me l'envoyer, je vous en serai très reconnaissant, et d'avance je vous en remercie.

Veuillez présenter mon respectueux souvenir à Madame Söderblom.

Respectueusement et cordialement à vous.

A. Loisy

Paris, December 30, 1926

Highly revered and dear Archbishop,

I was, as I told you, very moved by your visit; I am very moved by your good letter. It must be true that, notwithstanding the apparent ruptures, I have always been following just about the same line. I have drawn as little adversity as I could from quite difficult situations, both interior and exterior. Even now I am assuming quite a thankless role, preaching the necessity of religiously based morals to our secularized society. Some [people] – whose psychological discernment I do not vouch for – have asked themselves whether I was orienting myself towards Rome. But the time of my service is about to end, and I can say, with the saintly man Job, that I am awaiting the relief.

Yesterday, in order to ascertain information about the affairs of the Roman Church, I bought an *Almanach catholique* which is published under the aegis of Mgr. Baudrillart, with renowned personalities collaborating.[2] I did not waste my money, for when I opened it, I stumbled over an article signed [by] Pierre Batiffol, where *The Development of the Movement for the Union of the Churches* is being expounded.[3] Two paragraphs concern you: *The Conference in Stockholm* and *The Word of the Germans at Stockholm.* That can be summed up in the sentence: »Quite obviously, *The Essence of Christianity*[4] was the New Testament of the participants.« Nothing to be expected from you for the rapprochement of the Churches. Besides, »the Lutheran archbishop of Uppsala is well known for his Germanophilia and his modernism.« One is willing to expect more from the Anglican episcopate, and one discreetly reminds of the Malines [Mecheln] »conversations« by a picture of the archbishop's mansion and a photograph of Lord Halifax.[5] All this quite adroitly done, but it is nothing but adroitness. I am telling you that little story in order to amuse you. You have no need to be encouraged in your work, but can continue without fear, even though you may not be assured of the concurrence of Batiffol.

The Catholics in this country are still being occupied by the condemnation which Pius XI. has directed against the *Action française.*[6] This monarchist journal which had been the right arm of Pius X. at the time of the Separation[7] and modernism, did not reckon with such ingratitude. Certain bishops seem to be quite disconcerted. It

---

[2] *Almanach catholique français pour 1927*, 85–88; this volume actually was published under the aegis of Mgr. Beaupin; Mgr. Baudrillart was responsible for the previous volume.

[3] Pierre Batiffol (1861–1929), like Loisy a disciple of Louis Marie Olivier Duchesne, was an old adversary of Loisy, though he too was a critical exegete (founder of the periodical *Revue biblique* in 1892) and had been deposed from his teaching position at the Institut catholique in Toulouse because of that.

[4] This is an allusion to Adolf von Harnack's famous book *Das Wesen des Christentums*, Leipzig 1900, and to Söderblom's great respect for Harnack. The conclusion as to a liberal character of the whole Stockholm conference is of course a completely unwarranted generalization, in view of the wide variety of Protestants represented, let alone the Anglican and the Orthodox churches,. Besides, the Catholic author in his polemic presents a very one-sided image of Söderblom himself, picturing him as a kind of liberal anti-pope who advocates a vague, impoverished version of Christianity. Neither is it true that the Germans had dominated the conference, as Batiffol asserts, though the unabashed nationalism in some of their speeches was indeed embarrassing.

[5] The Malines conversations (1921–1926), conducted in the Archbishop's, Désiré Cardinal Mercier's mansion with the tacit toleration of Pope Benedict XV., were four more or less secretive talks of 3–5 representatives of the Roman and Anglican churches on a possible church union. The chief initiators were Charles Lindsey Wood Viscount Lord Halifax (1839–1934), a representative of the Anglo-Catholic wing of his church, and Étienne Fernand Portal. The talks were doomed to failure, however, for two reasons: The Anglican church was deeply divided over the issue, and the succeeding pope Pius XI., reigning from 1922–1939, was strictly opposed to any kind of rapprochement between the Catholic church and the emerging ecumenical communion. Cf. Owen Chadwick, »The Church of England and the Church of Rome, from the beginning to the present day,« in: St. Runciman et al., *Anglican Initiatives in Christian Unity*, London 1967, 73–107, esp. 91–94.

[6] The news that Action Française had been put on the Index was published in *L'Osservatore Romano* of Dec. 26, 1926, and the official condemnation followed three days later: *AASW* XVIII/1926, 529 f.

[7] The law of Dec. 9, 1905, concerning the separation of the state and the churches.

appears that the pope had really been offended by the fundamental unbelief that Maurras always displayed in his books.[8] However, in recanting the politics of Leo XIII. against the reactionary party, he both preserves that of Pius X. and wants to mobilize the Catholics for making Christ rule in our laws. If the Gospel were concerned, then by means of a somewhat supple exegesis one could reach agreement; but the law of Christ is that of the pope, a law which knows of no limits. The result is that the pope, for all his good intentions, will be able to turn against him both the men of reaction and the men of progress... His worry.

I do not have the second edition of *Das Werden des Gottesglaubens*. If you would be so kind as to send it to me, I would be very grateful, and I thank you in advance for it.

Please express my respectful remembrance to Mrs. Söderblom.

Respectfully and cordially yours,

A. Loisy

289. From Friedrich Heiler[1]

Marburg/Lahn, Moltkestr. 19, 4.1.27.

Hochverehrter Hochwürdigster Herr Erzbischof,

Endlich komme ich dazu, Ihnen den längst versprochenen Brief zu schreiben. Ich habe so ausgefüllte schwere Wochen hinter mir, dass ich erst jetzt die Ruhe finde.

Allererst danke ich Ihnen vielmals für das wundervolle Standard Work über die Stockholmer Konferenz, das Sie mir auf den Weihnachtstisch gelegt haben.[2] Ich freue mich so sehr darüber, dass Sie selbst uns nochmals dieses ganze wunderbare Einheitswerk von Stockholm vor Augen führen, und nicht nur das, was dort geschah, sondern auch die vielfältigen Wirkungen, die die Konferenz auslöste. Es ist erfrischend und lehrreich, das vielstimmige Echo von Stockholm durch das Medium Ihres Buches zu vernehmen. Dass auch meine schwache Stimme in diesem Chor der dankbaren

---

[8] Charles Marie Photius Maurras (1868–1952), agnostic journalist, writer, politician. In connection with the Dreyfus affair, he founded the Action française in 1899, and a newspaper of the same name in 1908. Its political stance was royalist, anti-democratic, nationalist, xenophobic, anti-semitic, and anti-protestant. The Catholic church was considered politically indispensable and defended since 1905. The organization became quite militant from 1923 onwards, condoning even illegal violence in pursuing its goals. It showed sympathies for fascism and for the Nazi collaborator Pétain (though not for Hitler). The journal was put on the index of forbidden literature, and the organization condemned, by Pope Pius XI. in December, 1926.

[1] Nathan Söderblom's collection of letters, from foreigners, UUB, typewritten letter. In the original, this letter bears the date of January 4, 1926. However, Söderblom's book mentioned in the beginning was not published before late 1926, and the journey to England referred to in hindsight later on took place in September, 1926, cf. letter no. 273. It is thus once again an early January error, cf. letter no. 149, n. 1.

[2] *Kristenhetens möte* ... (cf. letter no. 250, n. 2).

Verkünder des Stockholmer Pfingstwunders mitsingen durfte, ist mir eine besondere Freude. Schade nur, dass Ihr Buch nur schwedisch erschien. Wäre es nicht möglich, dass es in gekürzter Form (unter Weglassung der Abschnitte, die in extenso im offiziellen Deissmann'schen Bericht erschienen sind) ins Deutsche übersetzt würde?

Aus England bin ich voll Enthusiasmus zurückgekommen. Vom Anglokatholizismus habe ich nicht durchweg, aber doch zum grossen Teil sehr tiefe Eindrücke bekommen. Vieles hat mir natürlich nicht gefallen. Ist mir schon ein römisches Pontifikalamt etwas Unerträgliches, so erst recht eine anglikanische Kopie desselben. Das kritiklose Kopieren römischer Observanzen ist für mich etwas sehr Unkatholisches. Was mir am meisten fremd ist, (und was natürlich wiederum römische Kopie ist), das ist jene sektiererische Enge, die allem wirklich Oekumenischen sich verschliesst. Wenn man, wie ich es in meine eigene [sic] Ohren gehört habe, Sie wegen Ihres Einigungswerkes als »dangerous man« verketzert, so ist dies für mich nicht einladend. Aber allen diesen unerfreulichen Eindrücken stehn doch sehr tiefe gegenüber. Ich denke dabei nicht zuerst an die würdigen und erbaulichen Gottesdienste, sondern an den persönlichen Heiligungseifer, wie er sich in einem Leben des Gebets und der Askese und Liebesarbeit auswirkt. Ich habe eine Reihe heiligmässiger Menschen getroffen, die das traktarianische Heiligkeitsideal in ihrem Leben verwirklicht haben. ... [Several examples] Diese Gestalten sind mir die schönste Apologie des Anglokatholizismus, eine Offenbarung der wunderbaren heiligenden Kraft des sakramentalen Lebens, das im Anglokatholizismus seine Heimstätte hat. Dass ich den Pulsschlag dieses Lebens täglich von neuem in den anglikanischen Kirchen spüren durfte, war mir eine wahre Erquickung nach der Oede unseres deutschen Gottesdienstlebens. Auf Schritt und Tritt gewahrt man die einzigartige Kraft der Oxford-Bewegung, von der keineswegs nur die anglokatholische Partei, sondern die gesamte ecclesia anglicana (mit Ausnahme einiger modernistischer und streitbar-protestantischer Kreise) zehrt. Ich habe wirklich das Beste meiner römischen Mutterkirche (was ich im deutschen Protestantismus so vermisse) in der anglikanischen Kirche, und vor allem bei den »moderate Anglocatholics« wiedergefunden. Und so wurde mir in England klar, dass die Oxford-Bewegung eine universale Mission für die Kirche Christi hat genau so wie das Luthertum. Davon bin ich überzeugt, trotzdem ich in der Frage der Heilsgewissheit ganz anders als die Traktarianer, nämlich rein lutherisch denke. Und ich bin nach Deutschland zurückgekommen mit dem Bewusstsein, dass der deutsche Protestantismus eine Oxford-Bewegung braucht.

Das ist es, was ich in England vor allem lernte. Dass ich viel Schönes auch bei den Nonkonformisten gesehen habe, erwähne ich nur nebenbei. Die Kapelle des Mansfield College in Oxford ist ein wunderbares Symbol des ökumenischen Geistes. Was ich den Anglikanern zu bringen mich getrieben fühlte, war ein besseres Verständnis von Luther. Es ist merkwürdig, wie geringschätzig die Anglikaner über Luther urteilen, der Erzbischof von York genau so wie der Bischof von Gloucester, Dean Inge wie Dean Mat-

thews.[3] Ich habe darum in London wie in Oxford über Luther gelesen.[4] ...
[On the echo to his lectures] So glaube ich doch, dass ich etwas für Luther
in England ausrichten konnte. Und wenn wir nur die rechten Missionare
Luthers in England hätten, so würden nicht nur die Nonkonformisten, sondern auch die Anglikaner mehr von Luther annehmen. Wenn man den Anglikanern klar macht, dass lutherische Heilsgewissheit sich sehr wohl ver-
trägt mit Traditionstreue und sakramentalem Leben, dann sind sie eher geneigt in Luthers Schule zu gehen. Ich hoffe, dass meine Vorträge englisch
gedruckt werden können.
... [On polemics against him and against Sadhu Sundar Singh)
Anfang Dezember hatten wir eine sehr interessante Tagung des »Hoch-
kirchlich-ökumenischen Bundes« in Berlin. Wir haben freilich recht große
Schwierigkeiten im Bunde. Einmal, weil ein Teil sich ganz nach Rom hin
orientiert und in erster Linie auf die Gunst römischer Kreise bedacht ist.
Ich habe diesen gegenüber einen schweren Stand. Die andere Schwierigkeit
liegt darin, dass ein Teil unserer Geistlichen sich in ihrer Amtstätigkeit beunruhigt fühlt in dem Gedanken, dass sie keine episkopale Ordination besitzen. Dazu kommt, dass von anglikanischer Seite uns immer gesagt wird:
The first thing you need is valid orders. Ich selber denke ja in diesen Dingen nicht so enge, trotzdem ich natürlich ein Vorkämpfer für ein Bischofsamt mit apostolischer Sukzession bin. [...] Ich möchte deshalb an Sie die
Frage richten, ob Sie nicht um törichte Schritte unserer hochkirchlichen
Freunde hintanzuhalten, bereit wären, solchen deutschen Geistlichen, die
sich wegen des Mangels episkopaler Weihe im Gewissen bedrängt fühlen,
durch Ihre Handauflegung die Gewissheit zu geben, dass ihr Amt völlig le-
gitim ist. Ich weiss wohl, dass die schwedische Kirche in Unterschied der
anglikanischen Kirche die nichtepiskopalen Ordinationen anerkennt. Aber
da Sie auch bereits evangelischen Bischöfen nachträglich die bischöfliche
Handauflegung gespendet haben, würden Sie vielleicht doch in Erwägung
ziehen, dasselbe bei Geistlichen zu tun. Jedenfalls würde ich dies für eine
glücklichere Lösung halten, als wenn ein anglikanischer Bischof es täte, da
dann auch der Anstoss bei einem grossen Teil unserer deutschen Protestanten wegfällt.
Nun muss ich für heute schließen. Ich danke Ihnen nochmals für die große Freude, die Sie mir mit Ihrem grossen Werke bereitet haben und verbleibe mit verehrungsvollen Grüssen von meiner Frau und mir an Sie und Ihre
Familie und Fräulein Rodling
Ihr dankbar ergebener
Friedrich Heiler

[3] William Ralph Inge (1860-1954), professor of Divinity in Cambridge 1907-1934, Dean
of St Paul's Cathedral in London 1911-1934; Walter Robert Matthews (1881-1973), professor
of philosophy of religion and Dean of King's College, London, 1918-1932; Dean of St. Paul's
as Inge's successor 1934-1967.
[4] Cf. letter no. 283, n. 5.

290. To Friedrich Heiler[1]

Uppsala, den 14. Januari 1927.

Min käre Vän!

Det var mig en stor glädje att höra närmare om Edra intryck från England. Jag förstår så väl allt, vad Ni säger. Den utomordentligt rika och mångsidiga anglikanismen har en fattigdom, i det att den i allmänhet icke har tillägnat sig Martin Luther. Det mest glädjande tecknet är att den nyare anglokatolicismen förstår, att evangelium måste vara kärnan. Och irländaren Gore förvånar mig alltid med sin andes friskhet och sin blick för det väsentliga.

Men jag kan icke dela Eder önskan om att vid det kommande mötet i Lausanne eller eljest företaga en uppdelning av katolska och protestantiska medlemmar och samfund. Min huvudanmärkning gentemot ett sådant förslag är, att det blir osant och oklart, och jag får just nu ett brev från Wilfred Monod, som nästan ord för ord uttrycker mina tankar och mina farhågor. Nödvändigt är ju, att vi röra oss med realiteter och icke med namn och lätt missförstådda uttryck, och det gemensamma för de orthodoxa och oss är ju, att vi sätta evangelium över allt annat. Sedan finns en oändlig nyansering med hänsyn till den mer eller mindre nödvändiga anknytning och förbindelse, som evangeliet äger med kyrkans inrättningar. Egentligen skulle ju hela tillvaron, den materiella lika väl som den personliga och samhälleliga, renad från synd och ondska, vara ett sakrament, ett uttryck för andens rena liv, eller, om man så vill, genomträngd av Kristi mandomsanammelse eller av den uppståndnes herravälde. Men härvidlag röra sig tankarna i så många banor, att det enligt min mening skulle vara ödesdigert att göra upp en gräns. Det är ju underbart att finna det kanske sublimaste uttryck i nutiden för sakramentets mystik hos en sådan ärkeprotestant och modern människa som Wilfred Monod, under det att man bakom den tjockaste sakramentalism här och var finner ett tunnt rationalistiskt minimum av religion. Ni har här i denna sak en mission i nutiden såsom ingen annan, jag menar att icke stänga dörrarna, utan tvärtom låta den gudomliga kärlekens ljus lysa ut över stängslen och genom dem.

...

Tag bort ordet »Hoch« i förbundets namn. Kalla det för Kirchlich-Ekumenisch och säg till Edra vänner, att de liksom överallt i kyrkohistorien måste taga frågan om den episkopala ordinationen varsamt och grundligt. I kyrkan får man icke hava bråttom. Saken kommer nog med nödvändighet. Ni vet också av Headlams bok, att successia [successio] apostolica icke betyder handpåläggningens oavbrutenhet utan att en biskopsstol icke har varit vakant. Alldeles galet och dilettantiskt vore det att anlita någon episcopus vagans såsom Herford. Det vore bedrövligt. Vi måste få tala närmare om saken. Jag vill gärna stå till tjänst, men denna sak fordrar mycken försiktighet, särdeles då det gäller präster utanför min egen biskopliga jurisdiktion. Enklaste lösningen vore väl, att om de så önska anlita den av mig vigde

---

[1] Friedrich Heiler's papers, Ms 999, University Library Marburg, typewritten letter.

tysk-baltiske biskopen D:r Poelchau från Riga, en vidsynt och intelligent man, som Ni fritt och uppriktigt kan vända Eder till. Ingen engelsk biskop skulle låna sig till en sådan akt utan ärkebiskopens av Canterbury medgivande, och han tänker evangeliskt.

Än en gång tack för Edert märkliga brev. Gud styrke och uppehålle Eder i Eder viktiga tjänst.

Jag borde have betonat att den rörelse, som kallar sig Hochkirchlich-Ekumenisch och som borde kalla sig helt enkelt Kirchlich-Ekumenisch, enligt min mening hävdar tre viktiga och omistliga ting.

1) Mysteriet och tillbedjan i religionen, som icke får bliva en mer eller mindre tråkig skola eller en förening. Här är orientalernas, lika med de ortodoxas, gemenskap med oss av utomordentlig vikt. Ty hos dem finns mer känsla för mysteriet och tillbedjan än hos det officiella Rom.

2) Vidare, vi behöva medvetandet om kyrkan såsom en på samma gång historisk och överhistorisk gemenskap över alla gränser av folk och länder.

3) Vidare behöva vi i vårt fromhetsliv mera tukt och ordning och övning.

Allt detta står i den bästa överensstämmelse med den evangeliska kristendomens bekännelse och ideal.

Eder mycket tillgivne
N S-m

Uppsala, den 14. Januar 1927.

Mein lieber Freund!

Es war mir eine große Freude, Näheres über Ihre Eindrücke aus England zu hören. Ich verstehe so gut alles, was Sie sagen. Der außerordentlich reiche und vielseitige Anglikanismus hat eine Armut, insofern er sich im Allgemeinen nicht Martin Luther angeeignet hat. Das erfreulichste Zeichen ist, dass der neuere Anglokatholizismus versteht, dass das Evangelium der Kern sein muss. Und der Ire Gore[2] erstaunt mich immer wieder mit der Frische seines Geistes und seinem Blick für das Wesentliche.

Aber ich kann Ihren Wunsch nicht teilen, auf der kommenden Konferenz in Lausanne oder sonst irgendwann eine Aufteilung von katholischen und protestantischen Mitgliedern und Gemeinschaften vorzunehmen. Mein Hauptbedenken gegenüber einem solchen Vorschlag ist, dass er unwahr und unklar wird, und ich bekomme gerade einen Brief von Wilfred Monod, der fast Wort für Wort meine Gedanken und meine Befürchtungen zum Ausdruck bringt. Notwendig ist ja, dass wir uns mit Realitäten befassen und nicht mit Namen und leicht missverständlichen Ausdrücken, und das Gemeinsame für die Orthodoxen und uns ist ja, dass wir das Evangelium über alles andere stellen. Sodann gibt es eine unendliche Nuancierung im Blick auf die mehr oder weniger notwendige Anknüpfung und Verbindung, die das Evangelium mit den Institutionen der Kirche hat. Eigentlich sollte ja das ganze Dasein, das materielle ebenso wie das persönliche und gesellschaftliche, von Sünde und Bösem gereinigt, ein Sakrament sein, ein Ausdruck für das reine Leben des Geistes, oder wenn man so will, durchdrungen von Christi Annahme der Menschheit oder der Herrschaft des Auferstandenen. Aber diesbezüglich bewegen sich die Gedanken auf so vielen Bahnen, dass es meiner Meinung nach verhängnisvoll wäre, eine Grenze

---

[2] Cf. letter no. 283, n. 5.

festzulegen. Es ist ja wunderbar, den vielleicht sublimsten Ausdruck für das Geheimnis des Sakraments in der Gegenwart bei einem solchen Erzprotestanten wie Wilfred Monod zu finden, während man hinter dem massivsten Sakramentalismus hier und da ein dünnes rationalistisches Minimum von Religion findet. Sie haben in dieser Sache eine Mission in der Gegenwart wie kein anderer, ich meine die Türen nicht zu schließen, sondern umgekehrt das Licht der göttlichen Liebe über die Zäune und durch sie hindurch leuchten zu lassen.

... [A couple of short remarks on a variety of issues, among others on Heiler's continued research on Sadhu Sundar Singh.]

Nehmen Sie das Wort »Hoch« aus dem Namen des Bundes[3] heraus. Nennen Sie ihn Kirchlich-Ökumenisch und sagen Sie Ihren Freunden, dass sie wie überall in der Kirchengeschichte die Frage der bischöflichen Ordination behutsam und gründlich anfassen müssen. In der Kirche darf man es nicht eilig haben. Die Sache wird schon kommen, wenn es notwendig ist. Sie wissen auch aus Headlams Buch, dass die successio apostolica nicht ununterbrochene Handauflegung bedeutet, sondern dass ein Bischofsstuhl nicht vakant gewesen ist.[4] Völlig verkehrt und dilettantisch wäre es, einen episcopus vagans wie Herford in Anspruch zu nehmen.[5] Das wäre kläglich. Wir müssen des Näheren über die Sache reden. Ich will gerne zu Diensten sein, aber diese Sache erfordert große Vorsicht, zumal es sich um Pfarrer außerhalb meiner eigenen bischöflichen Jurisdiktion handelt. Die einfachste Lösung wäre wohl, dass sie, wenn sie es wünschen, den von mir ordinierten deutsch-baltischen Bischof Dr. Poelchau in Riga,[6] einen weitblickenden und intelligenten Mann, in Anspruch nehmen, an den Sie sich frei und offen wenden können. Kein englischer Bischof würde sich für einen solchen Akt hergeben ohne Erlaubnis des Erzbischofs von Canterbury, und der denkt evangelisch.

Noch einmal Dank für Ihren bemerkenswerten Brief. Gott stärke und erhalte Sie in Ihrem wichtigen Dienst.

Ich hätte betonen sollen, dass die Bewegung, die sich Hochkirchlich-Ökumenisch nennt und die sich ganz einfach Kirchlich-Ökumenisch nennen sollte, sich nach meiner Auffassung für drei wichtige und unentbehrliche Dinge einsetzt:

---

[3] *Hochkirchlich-Ökumenischer Bund* was the name of the organization Heiler was active in; cf. letter no. 280, n. 25. Cf. also Söderblom's comments in the letter itself.

[4] Arthur Headlam, *The Doctrine of the Church and Christian Reunion*, 2nd ed. London 1920. The actual thesis of this book differs somewhat from what Söderblom here cites from memory. Headlam maintains that what is essential for apostolic succession is not the uninterrupted repetition of the rite of laying on of hands (even though this should be the rule), but the appointment of a bishop by the Church for performing the functions of the apostles. Even though he considers an episcopal constitution as necessary for a reunited church in the future, its order must be sufficiently elastic to accommodate Presbyterians, Methodists, etc.; cf. op. cit., pp. 261–269. 307.

[5] Ulric Vernon Herford, called Mar Jacobus, broke away from Anglicanism and was consecrated by Mar Basilius (Luis Mariano Soares) of the Syro-Chaldean church in India, as titular bishop of Mercia (a diocese that had ceased to exist in 669) and Middlesex in 1902. He was an *episcopus vagans* (itinerant bishop) for mission in the West. Such bishops originally were χωρεπίσκοποι, delegates of city bishops to remote rural areas with limited episcopal authority. They took part in the councils of the 4th century. Later the church curtailed their rights in order to preserve its unity. But they never quite disappeared. The line of bishops consecrated by Herford was transferred to the U. S. and became the basis of the Evangelical Apostolic Church of North America (incorporated as Autocephalous Syro-Chaldean Church in 1976, present name 1992; source: www.eacna.org).

[6] Peter Poelchau (1870–1945), bishop of Riga.

1) Das Mysterium und die Anbetung in der Religion, die nicht zu einer mehr oder minder langweiligen Schule oder zu einem Verein werden darf. Hier ist die Gemeinschaft der Orientalen, das heißt der Orthodoxen, mit uns von außerordentlichem Gewicht. Denn bei ihnen gibt es mehr Gefühl für das Mysterium und die Anbetung als beim offiziellen Rom.

2) Ferner, wir brauchen das Bewusstsein von der Kirche als einer zugleich geschichtlichen und übergeschichtlichen Gemeinschaft über alle Grenzen von Völkern und Ländern hinweg.

3) Ferner brauchen wir in unserem geistlichen Leben mehr Zucht und Ordnung und Übung.

All dies steht in bester Übereinstimmung mir dem Bekenntnis und Ideal des evangelischen Christentums.

Ihr Ihnen sehr verbundener

N S-m

291. To Alfred Loisy[1]

Upsala, le 18 Janvier 1927.

Très honoré et cher Monsieur,

Votre lettre m'a fait une grande joie. Quel dommage de ne pas pouvoir continuer la conversation avec vous en personne. J'ai demandé à l'éditeur à Leipzig de vous envoyer la seconde édition de DAS WERDEN DES GOTTESGLAUBENS. Si ce livre parvient, vous n'avez pas besoin de m'écrire. Mais je serais reconnaissant de savoir s'il ne vous arrive pas.

La condamnation de »L'Action Française« est cependant à l'honneur de Pius XI. Ces gens qui croyent très fortement au pape mais pas du tout en Dieu, sont des hybrides. Vos remarques me semblent bien justifiées.

J'ai été très amusé de ce que vous racontez de Mgr. Batiffol, et j'ai demandé à la librairie de me faire venir cet Almanach Catholique. – Après la guerre un membre du gouvernement anglais a été assez intelligent pour dire dans un discours publique, que quiconque sait quelque chose de la Suède, comprends que l'ennemi de la Russie est toujours l'ami politique de la Suède. Car la Russie a conquis systématiquement l'Esthonie, la Finlande etc.[,] plus d'une troisième [partie] du territoire du Royaume de Suède, et la Russie a constitué le seule [sic] véritable danger de notre indépendance nationale. Les journaux Russes de St. Petersbourg parlaient avant la guerre ouvertement de la nécessité pour la Russie d'avoir les mines de fer dans le Nord de la Suède actuelle. La Russie a construit trois chemins de fer militaires à travers la Finlande. Voilà pourquoi la situation pour la Suède a été radicalement changée par la révolution Russe. Voilà aussi, pourquoi la délivrance de la Finlande, de l'Esthonie, de la Lettonie et de la Lithuanie et la résurrection miraculeuse de la Pologne constituent pour la Suède non seulement une satisfaction de la Justice mais aussi un suprème intérêt national. Le point de vue national n'est pas le suprème. Je pourrais en parler très lon-

---

[1] Alfred Loisy's papers, letters, Bibliothèque nationale de France, n. a. f. 15661, fol. 433.

guement. Les Russes nous sont très sympathiques. Nous avons une tâche particulière dans la Russie, fondée entrefois [sic; lis: autrefois] par les Väringar Suédois, les »Ros« de Roslagen (pays de mon diocèse) qui ont créé les principautés de Moscou, Novgorod, Kieff, et qui ont donné le nom à la Russie. Aucun pays n'a sacrifié rélativement autant que la Suède pour la Russie pendant la famine après la guerre. Voilà aussi, pourquoi il me semble peu chrétien d'utiliser, comme on le fait, les difficultés atroces de l'Eglise Orthodoxe Russe et la haine sovjetique contre elle pour la propagande romaine ou pour n'importe quelle autre propagande.

Ainsi je suis arrivé loin de Mgr. Batiffol, qui était très charmant lorsque je l'ai rencontré à Paris dans une famille qui l'avait invité pour me rencontrer. [...]

Sachez-moi, votre respectueusement et cordialement dévoué
Nathan Söderblom

Uppsala, January 18, 1927

Highly respected and dear Sir,
Your letter has been a great joy to me. What a pity not to be able to continue the conversation with you in person. I asked the publisher in Leipzig to send you the second edition of *Das Werden des Gottesglaubens.* If that book arrives, you need not write to me. But I would be grateful to know if it does not reach you.

The condemnation of »L'Action Française« is after all to Pius' XI. credit. These people who very strongly believe in the Pope but not at all in God are hybrids. Your remarks seem to me quite justified.

I was very much amused by what you told about Mgr. Batiffol, and I asked the library to procure for me that *Almanach Catholique.* – After the war a member of the British government was intelligent enough to say in a public speech that whoever knows something about Sweden will understand that Russia's foe is always Sweden's political friend. For Russia has systematically conquered Estonia, Finland, etc.[,] more than a third of the territory of the kingdom of Sweden,[2] and Russia has constituted the sole veritable danger to our national independence. The Russian newspapers of St. Petersburg spoke openly before the war about the need for Russia to have the ore mines in the North of contemporary Sweden. Russia has built three military railroads across Finland. That is why the situation for Sweden has radically changed through the Russian revolution. That is also why the liberation of Finland, Estonia, Latvia, and Lithuania and the miraculous resurrection of Poland constitute for Sweden not only a satisfaction of justice but also a supreme national interest. The national point of view is not the supreme one. I could talk on this at great length. We like the Russians quite well. We have a special obligation in Russia, which was once founded by the Swedish Varangians,[3] the »Russ« of Roslagen (region in my diocese) who created the principalities of Moscow, Novgorod, Kiev, and who gave Russia its name. No country has by comparison sacrificed as much for

---

[2] This refers to the Swedish empire before 1709 when King Karl XII. had to surrender to the Russians.

[3] Varangians, or Vikings, began colonizing large territories in Eastern Europe in the 9th century.

Russia during the famine after the war as Sweden. That is also why it does not seem to me very Christian to utilize, as is being done, the heinous difficulties of the Orthodox Russian Church and the Soviet hatred against it for Roman propaganda or any other propaganda whatever.

So I have come a long way from Mgr. Batiffol, who was quite charming when I met him in Paris with a family that had invited him to meet me. [...]

Recognize me, yours respectfully and cordially dedicated,

Nathan Söderblom

292. To Arthur Titius[1]

Upsala den 16 März 1927

Sehr geehrter Herr Professor!

Vor einigen Tagen habe ich ein ungemein interessantes Gespräch mit Bischof Billing gehabt, der mir von seinem sehr wichtigen Gespräch mit Ihnen erzählt hat. Was den Namen der Zeitschrift betrifft, ist es sicherlich nicht schlimm ein pregnantes Wort zu haben neben dem Untertitel »Organ des von dem Stockholmer Weltkirchenkonferenz gestifteten sozialethischen Instituts«. Er erwähnte dass Sie dabei auch den Namen »Stockholm« genannt haben.[2] Für uns in Schweden scheint ja dieser Name eigentümlich, aber so weit ich verstehen kann, hat man schon den Namen in anderen Ländern wie in der Schweiz, Frankreich, England, Amerika ebenso adoptiert wie die Namen Versailles, Locarno, etz., die freilich einen sehr verschiedenen Klang haben. Vielleicht wäre es doch am Ende nicht geradezu unpraktisch den Namen »Stockholm« zu verwenden. Ich lese ja von »the spirit of Stockholm«, »Les idées de Stockholm«, »Die Stockholmer Grundsätze«.

Aber eigentlich schreibe ich um Sie zu bitten vor der Sitzung des Exekutivkomités im Juli in Winchester, eine Liste von Artikeln die in den zwei oder drei ersten Hefte dieser Quartalschrift erscheinen werden, mit Angabe der Verfasser. Wertvoll wäre auch zu wissen, wie viele von diesen Artikeln schon bei Ihnen fertig da liegen. Nach meiner Erfahrung wird ein solches grosses Zeitschriftunternehmen ungemein viel Arbeit erheischen, und es ist notwendig von Vornherein ein ganzes Jahr oder beinahe ein ganzes Jahr fertig zu haben. Es müssen ja selbstverständlich auch die Artikeln verkürzt oder vervollständigt oder sonst umgestaltet werden. Die Informationsabteilung muss ja feste Proportionen haben u.s.w. Es ist ungemein wichtig, dass Sie, Herr Professor und Doktor, für diese ekumänische Aufgabe solche einzigartige Voraussetzungen haben.

[On a possible cooperation with *The Review of Churches* and *Le Christianisme Social*, summaries in English and French, etc.]

---

[1] Nathan Söderblom's collection of letters, to Swedes and foreigners, UUB, typewritten letter (carbon copy).

[2] For the quarterly which did appear under that name, cf. letter no. 265, n. 9.

Mit Freude erfahre ich, dass Dr. Wünsch aus Marburg[3] für das Institut
zu haben sein wird.
Mit den besten Wünschen und Grüssen
Ihr sehr ergebener

293. From ADOLF DEISSMANN[1]

Berlin-Wilmersdorf, den 5.April 1927.
Hochverehrter, teuerer Freund!
Unsere Altpreussische Generalsynode wird nach Ostern Stellung nehmen
zu der Amtsbezeichnung »Bischof«.[2] Die Gegner arbeiten in der Presse sehr
stark mit unsinnigen Gerüchten. So wird jetzt behauptet, Sie hätten in
Stockholm im Privatgespräch zu Mitgliedern der deutschen Delegation gesagt, Sie freuten sich schon darauf, die Berliner bezw. Preussischen Bischöfe zu weihen. Ich halte dieses Gerücht für ebenso unglaubhaft wie ein anderes, dass bereits zwei Preussische Generalsuperintendenten sich bei Ihnen
eine heimliche Weihe geholt hätten. Da solche einfältigen Gerüchte oft sehr
wirksam sind, möchte ich sie aus der Welt schaffen. Das letztere habe ich
bereits dementiert, das erste über Ihre angebliche Vorfreude möchte ich
aber auch noch dementieren und wäre Ihnen dankbar für eine gütigst baldi-
ge Mitteilung, da die Sache hier sehr eilig ist.
Mit den herzlichsten Grüssen
Ihr stets treu ergebener
Adolf Deißmann

---

[3] Georg Wünsch (1887–1964), originally a religious socialist, known by the time of this letter by his *Religion und Wirtschaft*, Tübingen 1925. He was a lecturer in systematic theology
and social ethics in Marburg and became full professor in 1931. Because of his political position during the Nazi era (*Ethik des Politischen*, Tübingen 1936), he was dismissed in 1945. He
once again became a social democrat and was readmitted to his teaching position in 1950 until
regular retirement in 1955.

[1] Nathan Söderblom's collection of letters, from foreigners, UUB, typewritten letter.

[2] As the German Protestant Church had ceased to be a state church in 1918, it had to draw
up a new constitution. This is the context of the above issue. Deißmann had suggested a »syno-
dical episcopacy« providing for a bishop elected by, and answerable to, the synod, which eventually became the basic idea of a Protestant bishop. The influence of foreign models of church
constitution on the one hand and anti-hierarchical resentment on the other made for passionate debates. The actual term bishop was not yet commonly used in the 1920s.

294. To Adolf Deissmann[1]

Uppsala den 8. April 1927.

Hochverehrter Professor und Freund!

Zu meinem Erstaunen erfahre ich, dass bei Ihnen sogar in der Presse unsinnige und unglaubliche Gerüchte verbreitet werden, wo ich in geradezu komischer Weise mit der Bischofsfrage der grossen preussischen Kirche in Verbindung gesetzt werde. Unfassbar ist mir, dass irgendjemand glauben kann, dass irgend ein preussischer Generalsuperintendent eine Art von »Weihe« bei uns bekommen habe. Das ist erstens absolut lügenhaft ohne irgend eine Begründung in der Wirklichkeit, aber dazu kommt, dass eine solche Behauptung nach meiner Meinung eine verworrene, unevangelische, d.h. ketzerische Auffassung von »Weihe« und »Bischof« offenbart.

Niemals ist der Gedanke durch meinen Kompf [=Kopf] gegangen, dass ich eingeladen werden sollte, an der Installation von preussischen Bischöfen teilzunehmen. Somit habe ich auch niemals ein Wort darüber geäussert. Am aller wenigsten hätte ich die Taktlosigkeit gehabt, mit verehrten Mitgliedern der deutschen Delegation in Stockholm darüber zu sprechen. Finden Sie es der Sache wert, bitte ich Sie solche Albernheiten gründlich zu vernichten.

Man fragt sich: Ist der biblische Name Episkopos wirklich heutzutage in der evangelischen Christenheit zu gefährlich, dass man allerlei geradezu lächerliche Erfindungen machen muss um Stimmung dagegen zu schaffen?

Mit herzlichen Segenswünschen und Grüssen

Ihr sehr Ergebener

295. From Rudolf Otto[1]

(Date at the end of the letter: May 7, 1927)

Verehrter Herr Erzbischof.

Meinen herzlichsten Dank für Ihren freundlichen Brief und für Ihre Empfehlungen. Sie sind mir von sehr großem Werte. Ich kann zugleich zwei gute Meldungen machen:

1. Der preußische Landtag hat jetzt die erbetenen M. 40000 für unsere »Marburger Sammlung« bewilligt.[2] Das ist eine große Sache und zeugt von dem Idealismus unserer Volksvertretung, in der Zeit jetziger Knappheit für eine rein ideale Sache große Mittel zu geben. Damit ist die eine Hälfte mei-

---

[1] Nathan Söderblom's collection of letters, to Swedes and foreigners, UUB, typewritten letter (carbon copy).

[1] Nathan Söderblom's collection of letters, from foreigners, UUB, typewritten letter. Neither Söderblom's letter mentioned above nor his reply of May 17 (according to a handwritten note on top of this letter) is extant in Otto's papers.

[2] Today: *Religionskundliche Sammlung*, collection of exhibits in the field of the history of religion.

ner Arbeit in Indien und Kl[ein] Asien gesichert: der Einkauf für unser Religionsmuseum.

2. Zugleich wird mir von der Notgemeinschaft der deutschen Wissenschaft mitgeteilt, daß die erbetenen Mittel zur Bestreitung der Unkosten meiner Studienreise mir in fast sicherer Aussicht stehen. ...

Nach menschlichem Ermessen ist damit meine Reise sicher gestellt, und ich setze meine Vorbereitungen dafür kräftig fort.

Pastor Birger Forell schreibt mir, daß er Ihnen seinen Wunsch vorgetragen hat, mich auf dieser Reise zu begleiten. Ich erlaube mir dazu einiges zu bemerken.

Forell hat früher bei mir und Heiler Religionsgeschichte studiert. Er ist auf dem Gebiete der Sprachen, wie ich in Holland und Italien bemerkt habe, sehr begabt, faßt leicht und sicher auf und findet sich mit Leichtigkeit in dem fremdesten Milieu zurecht. Er nimmt sich als Studiengegenstand etwas, das für unsere Theologie sehr wichtig ist: nämlich die bedeutsamen Versuche der östlichen Religionen, sich zu regenerieren und zu reformieren, die besonders in den großen theistischen Gruppen Indiens sichtbar sind. Die Kenntnis solcher innerer Erneuerungsbewegungen, in denen auch das Problem steckt, ob diese Religionen auf die Dauer sich gegenüber dem Christentume behaupten können oder nicht, halte ich für sehr notwendig. Wir wissen in unseren theologischen Kreisen davon fast nichts, unterschätzen die fremden Kräfte und machen uns und unsern Schülern von der religiösen Lage in der Welt ein sehr schiefes Bild. (Besonders gilt das auch vom Islam.) Wenn sich nun ein begabter junger Mensch findet, der für einen solchen Gegenstand Vorbereitungen, Interessen und Veranlag[ung]en besitzt, so liegt nach meiner Meinung Grund dazu vor, ihm behilflich zu sein. ... [Lengthy reflections on the possibility of financial support for Forell by the Swedish government, and a recommendation of a postgraduate student who plans to spend a year on a scholarship in Sweden]

Wegen der Besetzung der sozialen Stelle an dem ökumenischen Fortsetzungs-ausschusse in Zürich erfahre ich soeben, daß unser Dr. Wünsch nur einen einzigen ernsten Konkurrenten hat. Dieser wird besonders von Herrn Philips und Mumm[3] bevorzugt, die gegen Wünsch's theologische und politische Stellung Verdacht haben. Der Konkurrent ist ›Nationalökonom‹, worin man einen Vorteil zu sehen glaubt. Ich widerhole [sic], daß diese Lösung der Sache mir fast katastrofal erscheinen würde. Sie würde nämlich sofort den Anschein erwecken, als ob es sich im Grunde eben nicht um eine gemein *christliche* Unternehmung handelt, die von Theologen und Geistlichen getragen ist, sondern um eine christlich nur verkappte humanitäre Un-

---

[3] I have not been able to find out who Mr. Philips is, even allowing for Otto's penchant for misspelling names. The other man is Reinhard Mumm (1873–1932), first a member of Adolf Stoecker's Christlich-Soziale Arbeiterpartei (Christian Social Worker's Party), later of the far right Deutsch-Nationale Volkspartei (German National People's Party), a member of parliament from 1912–1932. He also held many influential church positions and was a delegate to the Stockholm conference of Life and Work in 1925.

ternehmung im Allgemeinen. Und die Meinung, daß die christlichen Kirchen heute nur noch Sinn haben als ›humanitäre Anstalten‹ würde dadurch auf eine fatale Weise unterstrichen werden. Zugleich wäre diese Lösung eine unsagbare Blamage für die deutsche Theologie, die damit vor aller Welt erweisen würde, daß sie aus ihrem eigenem Kreise nicht einen tüchtigen Vertreter für die Fragen des christlich-sozialen Ethos aufbringen kann. Wünsch druckt soeben seine sehr umfassende ›Christliche Sozialethik‹.[4] Ich wünsche sehr, dass die Entscheidung über die Stelle in Zürich jedenfalls solange hinausgeschoben werden möchte, bis dieses Werk vorliegt. Ich zweifele nicht daß dieses Buch die Angst vor Wünsch's ›Radikalismen‹ vertreiben wird, und daß es andererseits seine Geeignetheit für den Platz zeigen wird. Übrigens ist Wünsch soeben vom Minister zum Professor ernannt worden.[5]

Endlich ist nun die Ausgabe meines neuen Perikopenbuches im Druck.[6] Sie geht Ihnen zu, sobald sie gebunden sein wird. Linderholms Grundlage habe ich in wesentlichen Stücken beibehalten. Aber meiner eigenen dogmatischen Einstellung gemäß habe ich das Buch sehr wesentlich erweitert und umgestaltet. Ich hoffe, dass es auf diese Weise seinen Dienst leisten wird.

Empfehlen Sie mich, verehrter Herr Erzbischof, den Ihrigen und meinen Freunden. Mit nochmaligem Danke und ergebenen Grüßen

Ihr
R. Otto.
Marburg 7. 5. 27

296. From Rudolf Otto[1]

Anuradhapura, den 10. November 1927.

Verehrter Herr Erzbischof.

Wir sind hier an der heiligen Stätte des singhalesischen Buddhismus beim herrlichsten Wetter und bei guter Gesundheit. Die naive Frömmigkeit des schlichten Volkes hier macht uns einen tiefen Eindruck. In Colombo haben wir den angesehenen Führer der Neubuddhisten Herrn de Silva[2] getroffen. Ich habe dort einen Vortrag gehalten über das Zusammenwirken der religiösen Gemeinschaften des Ostens und des Westens in sittlichen Fragen. Der Vortrag erschien darnach in der Zeitung, wo Sie verwandelt wurden in den »Archbishop of Zwitzerland« Dr. Blom. Der Vortrag wurde sehr gut aufgenommen. Wir werden diese Arbeit auch in Indien fortsetzen. Atkinson schrieb mir, dass er mich in Indien treffen wird. Er hat für Herrn Pastor Forell Dollar 500 als Beihilfe zu seiner Reise und für seine fleissige Mitwir-

---

[4] Otto means Georg Wünsch, *Evangelische Wirtschaftsethik*, Tübingen 1927).
[5] Otto' intervention was in the end not successful.
[6] Rudolf Otto, *Das Jahr der Kirche*, 2nd ed. Gotha 1927.

[1] Nathan Söderblom's collection of letters, from foreigners, UUB, typewritten letter.
[2] It has not been possible to find out which person of this name Otto is referring to.

kung in Aussicht gestellt. ... [A listing of the further destinations of his trip.]

Ich kaufe gleichzeitig allerhand Gegenstände für unsere Marburger religionswissenschaftliche Sammlung. Herr Forell und ich machen gleichzeitig nach Möglichkeit Studien hinsichtlich der Erneuerung der hiesigen Religionen. Die Erneuerung des Buddhismus hier ist wirklich bemerkenswert. Man gründet in Dörfern und Städten Schulen, die unseren Sonntagsschulen auffallend ähnlich sind. Die Missionare selber geben zu, dass dadurch der Mission eine bedeutsame Konkurrenz erwächst. Allerdings ist deutlich, dass der Nationalismus, der auch hier erstarkt, das hauptsächlich treibende Motiv ist. So wird es wohl auch in Indien sein. ...

Herzliche Grüsse von Ihren beiden Wanderern.

In Verehrung
Ihr ergebener
R. Otto

297. To Gustaf Aulén[1]

Upsala den 1 december 1927

Broder!

Just nu i detta ögonblick erhåller jag Heilers uppsatser om Lausanne i Die Hochkirche. Interessant är att han också i Lausanne framhäver lutherdomens avgörande betydelse. Då han därvidlag ägnar flera rader åt undertecknad, kan jag icke gärna återgiva hans ord. Men jag sänder en avskrift för den händelse Redaktioen skulle ha utrymme och tycka det vore intressant att såsom en ytterligare upplysning återge vad han har att säga i saken. Hade jag fått uppsatsen tidigare, skulle jag i min uppsats have infogat endast den första satsen: »Näst anglikanismen utövade ingen kristen grupp ett så djupgående, ja avgörande inflytande på konferensens gång som lutherdomen.«

Din tillgivne
Nathan Söderblom

Uppsala, December 1, 1927

Dear Brother,

Just now in this moment I receive Heiler's articles on Lausanne in *Die Hochkirche*.[2] What is interesting is that he emphasizes the decisive significance of Lutheranism also in Lausanne. As he is dedicating several lines to the undersigned in this connection, I cannot very well render his words.[3] But I am sending a copy in case the Edi-

---

[1] Collection Aulén. G., University Library Lund, typewritten letter.

[2] The World Conference on Faith and Order took place in Lausanne August 2-21, 1927. Heiler's article »Die Lausanner Konferenz für Glaube und Kirchenverfassung« appeared in two installments in *Die Hochkirche* 9/1927, 297-301. 323-341.

[3] Heiler's words reflect his admiration for Söderblom in very strong terms. In particular, he

tor[4] has space left and thinks it might be interesting to render what he has to say on the subject, as an additional piece of information. Had I received the article earlier I would have included just the first sentence in my own article: »Next to Anglicanism, no Christian group exerted such a profound, even decisive influence on the course of the conference as Lutheranism.«[5]
Sincerely yours,
Nathan Söderblom

298. From GUSTAF JOHANSSON[1]

Åbo den 18 januari 1928.

Herr Ärkebiskop.
Då Ni senast besökte mig i Åbo, visste jag icke, att Sveriges Ärkebiskop var en frimurare. Detta vet jag nu, och derföre måste jag nu fatta i pennan för att taga avsked av Eder. Mellan en ärkebiskop, som är frimurare, och en luthersk biskop har varje föreningsband brustit. Ärlig skall en kristen framför allt vara.

Varje förfalskning av Bibelns Kristus-bild medför en förbannelse. Ehuru Eder vistelse i Finland varit så kort, förspörjes dock bittra klagomål över de dåliga frukter Eder verksamhet här framkallat. Hurudana skola de väl då vara i Sverige? Eder vandring är ju den vilsegångnes, som finner en glädje i att vilseföra. Jag hyser ingen förhoppning om att kunna utöva något inflytande på Eder, utan vill i min levnads sena kväll säga Eder farväl. Vi borde ju dock med allvar betänka, vilket ansvar vårt viktiga ämbete medför. Farväl!
Med smärta
Gustaf Johansson.

Åbo, January 18, 1928.

Lord Archbishop.
When you last visited me in Åbo, I did not know that Sweden's Archbishop was a Freemason. I do know that now, and therefore I must take up my pen and take leave of you. Between an archbishop who is a Freemason and a Lutheran bishop every bond of communion has broken. Honest is what a Christian must be above all.

---

stresses Söderblom's unequivocal advocacy of the central Lutheran tenet, the Gospel as liberation from the Law, over against »the Erasmian legalistic spirit of Anglicanism,« his fluency in the conference's three languages English, German, and French, and not least his charismatic personality.
[4] Aulén was the editor of the periodical *Svensk teologisk kvartalskrift*.
[5] Söderblom's report on the conference had appeared as »Randanmärkningar till Lausanne« [Marginalia on Lausanne] in: *STK* 3/1927, 336–381 (German tr. in: *ZSTh* 6/1929, 538–598).

[1] Nathan Söderblom's collection of letters, from Swedes [and Swedish-speaking Finns], UUB, typewritten letter.

Every adulteration of the Bible's image of Christ entails a curse. Even though your visit to Finland was so short, bitter complaints are heard of the evil fruits your activities have borne here. What will they then be like in Sweden? Your pilgrimage is of course that of one gone astray who finds his joy in leading astray. I cherish no hope of being able to exert any influence on you, but will in my life's late evening say farewell to you. We should in any case seriously consider what [great] responsibility our important ministry involves. Farewell!

Woefully,

Gustaf Johansson.

299. To Gustaf Johansson[1]

Upsala den 21 jan. 1928

Vördade Broder!

I anledning av det egendomliga och för mig ytterst smärtsamma brevet, får jag upplysa om att jag aldrig någonsin varit frimurare, icke är det och heller aldrig kommer att bli det. Jag har aldrig haft den avlägsnaste tanke på att gå in i Frimurareorden. Visserligen känner jag mycket hedervärda människor, allt ifrån Sveriges Konung, som tillhöra Frimurareorden, men för mig skulle det vara omöjligt att sluta mig till detta sällskap av många orsaker, som jag här icke behöver utveckla. Vem som påstått att jag är frimurare, vet jag ej. En bland Sveriges biskopar, en bland de allra bästa, tillhör Frimurareorden. Jag förmodar att också någon av mina företrädare på ärkestolen möjligen varit frimurare. Det vet jag ej. Ett vet jag, att jag som sagt varken har varit, är, eller kommer att bli frimurare.

Hur min vördade Broder kan förena det, jag säger icke med ett kristligt sinnelag och biskoplig värdighet, men helt enkelt med vanlig mänsklig ansvarskänsla att skriva till mig på detta sätt, och detta på grund av en falsk hörsägen utan att ens fråga mig om saken, är för mig ofattligt.

Vördsamt tillgivne

Nathan Söderblom

Uppsala, January 21, 1928

Esteemed Brother,

Occasioned by the strange and for me extremely hurtful letter, I must inform you that I have never ever been a Freemason, that I am not, nor shall ever be one. I have never had the least thought of joining the society of Freemasons. To be sure, I know very honorable people, Sweden's King to begin with, who belong to the society of Freemasons, but for myself it would be impossible to join that association for many reasons which I do not have to to expound here. Who it was that asserted that I was a Freemason, I do not know. One of Sweden's bishops, one of the very best, belongs to the society of Freemasons. I presume that also some predecessor of mine at the

---

[1] Nathan Söderblom's collection of letters, to Swedes and foreigners, UUB, typewritten letter.

archbishop's see possibly was a Freemason.[2] I do not know about that. One thing I do know, is that, as I said, I neither was, am, nor will be a Freemason.

How my esteemed Brother can reconcile writing to me in this fashion, I do not say with a Christian mind and episcopal dignity, but quite simply with a ordinary human sense of responsibility, and that on the basis of false hearsay, without so much as asking me about the matter, is incomprehensible to me.

Respectfully yours,
Nathan Söderblom

300. From GUSTAF JOHANSSON[1]

Åbo den 26 januari 1928.

Högt ärade Herr Ärkebiskop.

Vördade Broder.

Hjärtligt tackar jag för meddelandet. Här pågår en livlig propaganda för frimurareorden och såsom agitationsmedel begagnas bland annat det påståendet, att Sveriges Ärkebiskop tillhör denna orden. I det svenska stiftet äro också tvenne präster frimurare. Då sannfärdigheten vill vara en av frimurarens huvuddygder och tvenne frimurare här påstodo, att Bror också var frimurare, kunde jag ej annat än sätta tro därtill, helst mångt och mycket tycktes giva stöd åt detta påstående, och då var det min plikt att skriva. Emellertid har jag utkastat en falsk beskyllning mot Bror och ber därföre om förlåtelse. Detta intermezzo har dock här givit klarhet i denna punkt.

Kristus och Kristi rike äro icke av denna världen. Det överjordiska utgör kristendomens väsende, och dess neddragande till något, som vore av denna världen, är en principiell förfalskning av kristendomen. Stockholmer världskonferens' största missgrepp är, att den neddrager kristentdomen till något, som är av denna världen. Brors skrifter röra sig över huvud inom detta område. Och Kristus är icke, vad Han enligt Bibeln bör vara. Uti en i Amerika hållen predikan säger Bror till exempel, att det icke är farligt, om Kristus har synd, då Han älskar. I en annan predikan säger Bror, att »Jesus ger sina lärjungar en uppmaning, som synes skäligen onödig, för att icke säga lättsinnig«. I Åbo höll Bror ett föredrag om helgonen. Därvid nämndes också Sadhu Sundar Singh. Och Bror sade, att Jesus, då Han utdrev dem, som sålde och köpte i tempelförgården, visade brist på självbehärskning. Det är ovärdigt en luthersk ärkebiskop att uttala sig på detta sätt om Honom, som var i Faderns härlighet, förrän världen var till, och som var i Faderns sköte, då Han var på jorden. Sådan är icke Kristus i Guds evangelium. Och om Han hade synd, vore Han icke världsförsonare. Syndens

---

[2] The contemporary bishop was Olof Bergquist (1862–1940), bishop of Luleå; there were two predecessors of Söderblom as archbishop who also were Freemasons: Carl von Rosenstein (1766–1836) and Henrik Reuterdahl (1795–1870). Kind information by Staffan Runestam.

[1] Nathan Söderblom's collection of letters, from Swedes [and Swedish-speaking Finns], UUB, typewritten letter.

värklighet och det djupa behovet av en världsförsoning framträder icke tillräckligt i Brors förkunnelse.

En av det svenska stiftes främsta präster, som nitälskar för Guds rikes sak och ofta bereser sitt stift, uttalade nyligen sitt bittra beklagande över det fördärvliga inflytandet, som Bror utövat på stiftet. Detta inflytande framgår självfallet av en förkunnelse med de principer, vilka jag ovan antytt. Tidningarna hava omnämnt, att omkring 300 unga präster i Sverige icke tro på Symbolum Apostolicum. Detta tyder på djupa missförhållanden.

I den internationella kyrkliga tidskrift, vars första nummer nyligen utkommit och vari bland annat A. Harnack är en medarbetare, säger Bror i en artikel bland annat, att den evangeliska principens användning på våra förhållanden »endast kan lösas med förenade krafter, med den bästa förhandenvarande sakkunskap och den grundligaste erfarenhet hos skarpa och klara huvuden«. Och sedan kommer Guds rike. I hela naturen härskar den grundlag, att vägen till livet går genom döden, och samma lag härskar i andens värld. Kristendomen vilar också på denna grundsanning, men den ekumeniska tro, som Stockholms världskonferens vill dana, vet intet härav, och denna tro är icke heller kristendomens.

Bibelns uppfattning om de yttersta tiderna synes besannas av det närvarande tidsläget, men Brors uppfattning i den nämnda artikeln är en annan. Guds rike kommer icke med mänskliga krafter. Give Gud, att de kristne bland våra folk skulle rätt kämpa trons goda kamp, fullända loppet och slutligen få rättfärdighetens krona.

Högaktningsfullt
Gustaf Johansson

Åbo, January 26, 1928

Most honorable Archbishop.
Esteemed Brother.
Sincere thanks for the information. Here a lively propaganda for the Freemason society is going on, and as a means of agitation the assertion is being used, among others, that Sweden's Archbishop belongs to that society. In the Swedish diocese[2] two pastors are also Freemasons. Since truthfulness is supposed to be one of the Freemasons' main virtues, and two Freemasons here asserted that Brother[3] also was a Freemason, I could not but give credence to it, all the more so since so much seemed to lend support to that assertion, and therefore it was my duty to write. However, I drew up a false incrimination against Brother and ask for forgiveness for that. But this intermezzo has nonetheless provided clarity here on this point.

Christ and the Kingdom of Christ are not of this world. The otherworldly constitutes the essence of Christianity, and its degradation to something which is of this world is a principal falsification of Christianity. The biggest blunder of the Stock-

---

[2] The diocese in that area of SW Finland where most of the Swedish-speaking minority lives.

[3] In very formal Swedish usage, the third person singular is used for addressing a person, here combined with »Brother«. Johansson uses this combination of both distancing himself from Söderblom and preserving the form of episcopal collegiality for getting his point across.

holm world conference is that it degrades Christianity to something that is of this world. Brother's writings altogether belong in this sphere. And Christ is not what He must be according to the Bible. In a sermon preached in America Brother says, for example, that it is not a serious matter if Christ has sin, for He is loving. In another sermon Brother says that »Jesus made a demand to his disciples which seems fairly unnecessary, not to say rash.«[4] In Åbo Bror gave a lecture on saints. In this connection also Sadhu Sundar Singh was mentioned. And Brother said that Jesus, when He drove out all who were buying and selling in the temple precincts,[5] he showed a lack of self-control. It is unworthy of a Lutheran archbishop to make such utterances about Him, who was in the glory of the Father before the world existed, and who was in the bosom of the Father while He was on earth.[6] Such is not the Christ in God's Gospel. And if He had sin, He would not be the world's conciliator. The reality of sin and the profound need of a reconciliation of the world does not come out sufficiently in Brother's preaching.

One of the most excellent pastors of the Swedish diocese, who eagerly works for the kingdom of God and often travels through his diocese, recently uttered his bitter complaint about the detrimental influence Brother has exerted on the diocese. That influence derives as a natural consequence from a preaching on the basis of the principles I have indicated above. The newspapers reported that about 300 young pastors in Sweden do not believe in *Symbolum Apostolicum* [the Apostles' Creed]. This points to a profound disarray.

In the new international church periodical, the first issue of which recently appeared and of which A. Harnack, among others, is a contributor, Brother is saying in an article, among other things, that the application of the Protestant principle to our circumstances [is a problem which] »can only be solved by unified endeavors, with the best available expertise and the most thorough experience of sharp and clear minds.« And then the kingdom of God will come.[7] In all of nature the fundamental law prevails that the way towards life leads through death, and the same law also prevails in the spiritual world. Christianity also rests on that basic truth; but

---

[4] Both references are to the same sermon »Helgon« (Saints), in: *Från Upsala to Rock Island. En predikofärd i nya världen*, 2nd ed. Stockholm 1924, 72–83. In the former case (p. 82), Johansson ignores the context which criticizes the moralistic interpretations of sin as exhibited in pietistic and rationalistic interpretations. Söderblom then continues: »Vad hade det gagnat oss, om Jesus varit fri från allehanda mänskliga fel och synder? Vad som gagnat oss är hans kärlek, som gav sig ut hel och hållen. Jesu Kristi fullkomlighet består i kärlekens och rättfärdighetens högspänning i hans själ och liv.« (What would it have helped us if Jesus had been free from all kinds of human shortcomings and [so-called] sins? What has helped us is his love which wholly gave itself away. The perfection of Jesus Christ consists in the high intensity of love and righteousness in his soul and life.) His being totally informed by God's love is his *perfection*, i.e. his sinlessness! – In the second case (p. 81), Johansson apparently ignores the all-important qualification by the verb »seems«.

[5] Matth 21:12.

[6] John 1:14. 18.

[7] This is an account of Söderblom's »Geleitwort« [preface] to the journal *Stockholm*'s first issue (1/1928, 4–6). Söderblom does say there that for solving contemporary social problems, it is not sufficient to consult the Bible and the church's classics. Rather, appropriate transformation of Christian principles into concrete action requires mediation by human responsibility. That is conceived, however, to be obedience to the Kingdom of God (»Gehorsam gegen Gottes Herrschaft«) which has entered the world through Jesus Christ – and not, as Johansson seems to suggest, its establishment by means of human activity.

the ecumenical faith the Stockholm conference wants to shape knows nothing about that, and that faith is not the faith of Christianity, either.

The Bible's view of the final age seems to be vindicated by the present situation, but Brother's view in the article mentioned is a different one. The kingdom of God does not come by human endeavor. God grant that the Christians among our nations truly fight the good fight of the faith, finish the race and finally receive the crown of righteousness.[8]

Yours truly,
Gustaf Johansson[9]

301. From EIVIND BERGGRAV[1]

Oslo 11/2 28.

Kjære Erkebiskop!

Med stor glede og med dyp takk for trofast ihukommelse mottok jeg igår artikkelen om Encyklikan. ...

– En tilföielse[2] av rent annen art: nettop nu fikk jeg i telefonen et nytt bevis på din ubiquitet, ikke minst i vennskapsgodhet. Det blev ringt op fra universitetet, at kollegiet (konsistoriet) nettop hadde vedtatt å foreslå professorat i etik og religionspsykologi – istedet for i nytest. eksegese nu da Friedrichsen »gjör svenske av sig.« I den anledning hadde rektor, juristen Fredrik Stang, spurt om man nu hadde nogen kvalificeret mann til dette? Da så navnet blev nevnt, sa han: »Aa ja, det skal være en dyktig mann. Jeg hadde slett ikke vært opmerksom på ham; men så nevnte Söderblom ham for mig og siden har jeg fulgt ham.« – Der har du *ett* bevis for hvad du kan bety for utviklingen av ens liv!

Jeg nevner det, fordi det akkurat kom i dette öieblikk!

...

Hjertelig hilset i ærbödighet
Din
Eivind Berggrav

Oslo, February 11, 1928.

Dear Archbishop,

With great joy and with most hearty thanks for loyal remembrance I received the article on the Encyclical yesterday.[3] ... [On details about printing the article.]

---

[8] I Tim 6:12; II Tim 4:7f. (*RSV*); cf. also I Tim 4:1; II Tim 3:1.

[9] The rift between the two men was never healed. Johansson did not even invite Söderblom at the occasion of Åbo Cathedral's 700-year anniversary in 1929, a clear violation of ordinary politeness. Nonetheless, at Johansson's death in 1930 Söderblom sent a noble telegram of condolences to the Finnish church. Cf. S. Runestam, op. cit., 157f.

[1] Nathan Söderblom's collection of letters, from foreigners, UUB, handwritten letter.

[2] Berggrav often writes ö instead of ø, sometimes even ä instead of æ. Likewise, he uses aa and å interchangeably.

[3] »Påvestolen och kyrkans enhet. Den påvliga encyklikan mot ekumenerna. 1–4,« in: *Kirke*

A postscript of a totally different kind: Just now on the phone I received new proof of your ubiquity, not least in terms of a friend's kindness. A call came from the university, saying that the board had just decided to propose a chair in ethics and psychology of religion – instead of one in New Testament exegesis now that Fridrichsen »makes a Swede of himself.«[4] In this affair the rector,[5] the jurist Fredrik Stang, had inquired whether there now was a man available who was qualified for the job. When the name was mentioned then, he said: »Oh yes, that should be a capable man. I had simply not paid attention to him, but then Söderblom mentioned him to me, and then I followed his advice.« – There you have *one* proof of what you can mean for the development of one's life!

I mentioned this, because it has happened just in this moment!

... [About remaining uncertainties of the matter.][6]

Cordially greeting in reverence,

yours,

Eivind Berggrav

302. To Strenopoulos Germanos[1]

Upsala May 14th 1928

My dear and reveared Brother,

I have four important things to write.

1: It seems to me to have been providential that you should be President of our Ecumenical Commission the year of the anti-catholic and anti-evangelic Encyclica[l] of the Pope, and I thank you most heartily.

2: In reading the different documents after Stockholm in Lausanne and after Mortalium Animos, one question comes on me again and again. The really ecumenical initiative for a new epoch of cooperation and unity in the Church and in Christendom came from the Ecumenical Patriarchate in Constantinople 1920, that is certainly from you. Would not time be ripe now for you to propose such a federation or league of Churches?[2] You have the kernel in the Continuation Committee which you preside yourself. Besides we have the World Alliance, the International Missionary Council,

---

og kultur 35/1928, 134–156. Berggrav was the editor of that periodical. The Encyclical is *Mortalium animos* of January 6; cf. letter no. 179, n. 1.

[4] Anton Fridrichsen (1888–1953) exchanged his Oslo chair for one in Uppsala in 1928. »Making a Swede of oneself« is a Norwegian idiomatic gibe at Swedes, which means »taking to one's heels.«

[5] »Rektor« in the original; president in more common American usage.

[6] In fact, Berggrav was not nominated for the chair after all, cf. letter no. 91, n. 1.

[1] Nathan Söderblom's collection of letters, to Swedes and foreigners, UUB, typewritten letter (carbon copy).

[2] As for the invitation to an ecumenical conference referred to above, cf. letter no. 141, n. 4. The idea behind this initiative was to form a League of Churches, a kind of Eastern ecclesiastical parallel to the Western political League of Nations. The official report on the respective decision by the Holy Synod was mainly written by Germanos, then dean of the theological school of Halkis. As for Söderblom's own thinking which began to develop in a similar direction at about the same time, cf. Sundkler, op. cit., 219. 248.

which has become, I am glad to say, eager to have also the Orthodox Church represented. Further there is the Continuation Committee on Faith and Order. Can you not propose to the Executive Committee on Life and Work to invite a few men to come together and propose lines and rules for such a federation? In several cases, as with regard to yourself, the same man represents his Church in two or three or even in some cases in all four of those strivings and organisations for cooperation and unity. Such a federation would of course be most clearly distinguished from a real Church Unity, a reunited Church, an organic Unity, but as you said at Lausanne, and as you have explained on different occasions, federation is the first step and a necessary step. If such a committee could be trusted in Prague[3] with proposing and unlining [=outlining] the scheme of an Ecumenical Church Federation, it is not excluded that the Ecumenical Patriarchate of Constantinople and Christendom can celebrate 1930 the pastoral letter of 1920 on a league of Churches with the formation of such a Koinonia.

3. Would it be wise to have, besides the representative or representatives of each Nation in our Continuation Committee on Life and Work[,] a Committee in each country, and in each denomination or national section of a denomination for studying and advancing the sacred cause of Life and Work? We are contemplating here in Sweden the plan of enlarging the existing Swedish Committee of the World Alliance for the promotion of the program of Life and Work. Would it not be wise to recommend the creation of such commissions and to recommend to them the propagation and the study of the Message of Stockholm?[4] It is a pity that that message was not in the hands of the members of the Jerusalem Conference, since the Jerusalem Conference was also fully aware of the necessity for the Christian Church to take up seriously the religious and moral problems involved in the industrial and social situation.

4. The International Missionary Council and its congress in Jerusalem in April, where I was announced for a paper, but prevented from coming, made nothing more important than the proposal to create an Institute for Industrial and Social Research, especially for non Christian lands. This is a corroboration of our decision in Stockholm. But it would be a too Protestant overlapping to have two such social institutes. The question came up late in Jerusalem and Dr. Atkinson and Mr. Sandegren[5] and other members mentioned of course our Institute in Geneva. It is of course absolutely necessary to combine both, which will make both stronger. ... [Suggestions as to persons to be invited to the Prague conference.]

Besides those, of course Mr. Oldham and the Bishop of Manchester,[6]

---

[3] At the World Alliance conference planned for August of that year.

[4] Cf. letter no. 280, n. 15.

[5] Paul Sandegren (1887–1972), former missionary in Southern India, spokesman of Section V of Life and Work for the Younger Churches (Sundkler, op. cit. 399).

[6] Joseph Houldsworth Oldham (1874–1969), since 1921 Secretary of the International Board of Missions; Later one of the chief promoters of the idea of a World Council of

vice President in Jerusalem, would be most valuable. Would it not be wise to contemplate a joint Committee from Life and Work and the International Missionary Council for an enlarged Institute? Because the social industrial problems are just about the same everywhere in the world, and can not be divided upon two Christian social institutes.[7]

Rejoicing in the hope of meeting you in Prague and praying God that He will give us wisdom, strength and self-forgetting clearness in our joint work for the Kingdom of God /I.Cor.3.9/, I am brotherly and most sincerely yours

P. s. The creation of such a social Institute is now referred to the Executive Committee of Jerusalem, and it is of course important to come into touch with them as soon as possible.

303. From RUDOLF OTTO[1]

Marburg, i3 8 28

Verehrter Herr Erzbischof
Herzlich willkommen in Deutschland. Ich bedaure sehr, dass ich durch eine schwere Überreizung der Nerven nicht nach Eisenach kommen kann, um Sie zu begrüssen.[2] Würde es Ihnen vielleicht möglich sein, uns hier in Marburg zu besuchen auf Ihrer Durchreise nach Köln,[3] von der mir Hermelink soeben schreibt? Wir würden gern mit Ihnen den Plan unserer Fakultät und unserer hessischen Landeskirche besprechen, im nächsten Jahre

---

Churches, together with William Temple, at this time the bishop of Manchester mentioned above; for him cf. letter no. 220, n. 2. Today, Oldham is best known for the concept of »middle axiom«, a seminal idea in modern social ethics (cf. A. Visser't Hooft and J. H. Oldham, *Die Kirche und ihr Dienst in der Welt*, Berlin 1937, 200).

[7] Bengt Sundkler, op. cit., p. 415, comments on the gist of this letter: »In its broad outlines this plan of Söderblom's, foreshadowing as early as 1928 an integrated World Council was a great document, a testament bequeathed by the ailing leader to the whole of the ecumenical movement.«

[1] Nathan Söderblom's ecumenical collection, A 19, UUB, typewritten letter.

[2] Otto repeatedly suffered from bouts of depression. – In Eisenach, Söderblom attended the meeting of a small but high-ranking group of British and German theologians, Aug. 11–17, 1928. One of his well-documented comments at this conference was, by the way: »If the Wartburg comes to Canterbury and Canterbury to the Wartburg, then a new era of church history and theological thinking has begun,« i.e., both parties have much to learn from each other, justification by faith alone on the one hand and a more thorough reflection on the church in the other.

[3] Handwritten footnote by Otto: oder auf der Fahrt von Köln nach Prag? This is an indication of the grueling schedule Söderblom maintained in spite of his declining health: From Eisenach (previous note) he traveled to the Protestant Day of the Press in Cologne (it met Aug. 16–21) where he also gave a speech, from there, he went to the Conference of the World Alliance in Prague (Aug. 24–30) and then to Eisenach again for the last day or two of yet another conference (Aug. 29–31).

die vierhundert-jährige Wiederkehr des Marburger Religionsgespräches[4] zu feiern und dazu Vertreter des gesamten historischen Protestantismus einzuladen. Es handelt sich um den Plan, den ich in Ihrem Hause schon vortragen durfte.

Noch mehrere andere wichtige Anliegen möchte ich Ihnen vortragen, z. B. den Plan, ein morgenländisch-orthodoxes Studienhaus zu schaffen, in dem Priester der östlichen Kirchen Gelegenheit haben sollen, westliche Theologie zu studieren, und wo sie doch zugleich in ihrem eigenen Milieu bleiben können. Ich habe diesen Plan führenden Männern in Konstantinopel und auch dem Bischofe Irenäus von Novisad[5] vorgetragen, die beide dafür interessiert waren.

Ich würde mich freuen, wenn Sie dann hier mein Gast sein möchten.
Mit den ergebensten Grüssen in Verehrung
Ihr
R. Otto.

304. To Rudolf Otto[1]

Eisenach, den 15. August 1928.

Verehrter Herr Professor!

Für Ihren inhaltsreichen Brief herzlichsten Dank. Mit Prof. Frick[2] habe ich soeben ein interessantes Gespräch gehabt über Ihre Sammlung für Religionsgeschichte und über Ihre sonstigen Pläne. Leider habe ich eine Predigt für die Tausendjahrfeier in Dinkelsbühl in Bayern versprochen, sodass jede Stunde in Anspruch genommen wird. Ich werde daher leider nicht die Freude haben, Sie in Marburg zu besuchen. Aber es freut mich zu hören, dass Sie den Plan einer Feier des Marburger-Religionsgespräches festhalten. Von besonderem Interesse und Wert für die Einheitsarbeit wäre es, die damaligen Unterschiede in ihrem geistigen Inhalte zu untersuchen und zu besprechen. Dadurch dient man am Besten der Einheit.

Ich habe eben hier die Frage von einem orthodox-lutherischen Kolloquium angeregt. Ich hoffe, eine solche Institution zustande bringen zu können mit einer kleinen Zahl von Theologen auf beiden Seiten. Noch wichtiger wäre selbstverständlich ein solches Studienhaus zu schaffen, von dem Sie sprachen. Wie Sie wissen, studieren schon mehrere rumänische Orthodox-Priester an der evangelischen Fakultät in Paris. Sehr verlockend ist es

---

[4] The debate between Luther, Zwingli and others on the doctrine of the Lord's Supper in 1529, which in the end did not succeed in settling the differences and thereby preserving the unity of Protestantism.

[5] Irinej, bishop of Novi Sad and Bachka. I have not been able to find his biographical dates.

[1] Nathan Söderblom's ecumenical collection, B 7, UUB, typewritten letter (carbon copy).

[2] Heinrich Frick (1893–1952), professor of practical theology in Gießen(1924) and the history of religion (1926), in Marburg for systematic theology and the history of religion in 1929.

nochmals, Ihr Gast sein zu dürfen nach 30 Jahren. Aber leider ist es diesmal nicht möglich.

Ihr herzlich ergebenster

305. To Torsten Bohlin[1]

Upsala den 24 okt. 1928

Broder!

Nu kan jag av två anledningar inte nöja mig med de korta raderna som försenade renskrivits. Jag har läst Din bok med ett levande intresse och med behållning, och jag tackar Dig alldeles särskilt för det bibelställe Du i noten sid. 413 anfört ur Andra Mosebok om det alltför tunga arbetets för det andliga och sedliga livet menliga verkan.

Jag tackar Dig också för den enligt min tanke självklara, men mycket sällan ihågkomna riktiga kritik som Du sid. 444 riktat mot Althaus, men därmed till alla dem som ur tävlingens oundkomlighet på denna jord sluter sig till krigets oundviklighet.

Varje tid har sina gudar. Så även inom teologin. Du må tro att det har rört och fröjdat mitt hjärta att här möta mina egna svenska och utländska lärare och vänner, som Du har ägnat en ärlig pietetens och kärlekens möda. Du förstår också att det för en man av min generation måste hava sitt särskilda intresse att i denna tid, då frågeställningarna förändrats, och då det näst föregående enligt släktenas lag är nästan mest ringaktat och bortglömt, läsa den ingående behandlingen av Beck, Ritschl med flera.

Den andra anledningen är sorgebudet om Eder käre lille gosses bortgång. Det berör oss ömt. Vi miste för 29 år sedan i dessa dagar en liten flicka i samma ålder – ett svidande sår. Men barnen voro till hjälp. Den sjuka syster hade lagts ner i graven. Men den friska, som sprungit och sjungit, hon var uppe hos Gud. [...] Livet är ovisst och hårt. Jesus såg i barnen inte bara en början och förhoppning, utan hela varelser i sitt slag. Den lille Sverker drar Eder uppåt. Det är liksom en del av Eder själva, som flyttat över. I ären i färd att fullborda flyttningen. Eja, vore vi där!

Jag lever i förhoppningen att Upsala skall återbörda Eder, om än Åbo då på en gång lider åderlåtning.

Hjärtat blir varmt, glädjen ren vid tanken på Er.

Din tillgivne

Nathan S-m

---

[1] Nathan Söderblom's collection of letters, to Swedes and foreigners, UUB, typewritten letter (copy).

Uppsala, October 24, 1928

Dear Brother,

Now for two reasons I cannot content myself with the short lines a fair copy of which was late in being made. I have read your book[2] with a lively interest and with benefit, and I thank you quite particularly for the Biblical quotation from the second book of Moses in the footnote on p. 413, concerning the detrimental effects of an all too heavy workload on the spiritual and moral life.[3]

I also thank you for the appropriate criticism on p. 444 – in my opinion self-evident but very rarely remembered – that you are directing against Althaus, but by the same token also addressing all those who from the inescapability of contest in this world derive the inevitability of war.[4]

Each time has its gods. Thus also in theology. You may believe that it moved and gladdened my heart to meet my own Swedish and foreign teachers and friends here, to whom you devoted a sincere effort of both piety and love. You will also understand that for a man of my generation, it must be of particular interest at this time, when issues have changed and, according to the law of generations, the immediately preceding one is about the most depreciated and forgotten one, to read the penetrating treatment of Beck,[5] Ritschl, and others.

The other reason is the mournful news of your dear little boy's passing away. This is touching us sorely. 29 years ago these days, we lost a little girl of the same age – a burning wound. But the children helped. The sick sister had been laid down into the grave. But the healthy one who had been running and singing, she was up there with God. ...[References to the Swedish hymnbook] Life is precarious and hard. Jesus saw in children not only a beginning and hope, but whole beings in their own way. Little Sverker is pulling you upwards. It is like a part of yourselves which has moved across. You are on your way towards consummating your pilgrimage. Eia, if only we were there![6]

---

[2] Torsten Bohlin, *Den kristna gudsrikestanken under 1800-talet och i nutiden*, Lund 1928 (German tr.: Die Reich-Gottes-Idee im letzten halben Jahrhundert, Tübingen 1929).

[3] Ex 6:9.

[4] Cf. Paul Althaus, *Das Problem des Krieges*, originally published in 1925, reprinted as Chapter 2 of the 3rd ed. of his booklet *Staatsgedanke und Reich Gottes*, Langensalza 1926 (in the 4th ed. of 1931: pp. 61–114). This view, tinged by social Darwinism, that war was part and parcel of the natural order of history, was shared by many German Lutherans at the time. – Althaus later published, along with Emanuel Hirsch, a polemic decrying ecumenical endeavors for the reconciliation of formerly belligerent nations as long as Germany suffered from the excessive reparations demanded by the Versailles peace treaty: *ThBl* 10/1931, 117 f. The editor of the periodical, Karl Ludwig Schmidt, attached a note of poignant rebuke (178 f.). The appeal aroused passionate debate, cf. the note on p. 213 in the same volume. The contrast to Althaus' active part in the Stockholm conference of 1925 is striking, cf. letter no. 253.

[5] Johann Tobias Beck (1804–1878), professor of systematic theology in Basel, since 1843 in Tübingen, advocated a strictly Biblical »system« of theology in the wake of the Swabian »church fathers« Albrecht Bengel and Christoph Oetinger. His central notion was the coming of the Kingdom of God. Beck's influence was very strong during his lifetime, both nationally and internationally, particularly in Finland; cf. letter no. 201, n. 1. Cf. Michael Beintker, »Johann Tobias Beck und die neuere evangelische Theologie,« in: *ZThK* 102/2005, 226–245.

[6] Cf. *Den svenska psalmboken*, Stockholm 1986, no. 433 *In dulci jubilo*, last line of stanzas 3 and 4, referring to life eternal. The English version of this Christmas Carol is »Good Christian men [for gender reasons today: friends] rejoice«, e.g., Presbyterian Hymnal, Louisville KY 1990, no. 28; however, this is a free rendering of the ancient text in which the words in question do not occur.

I am living in the hope that Uppsala will bring you back,[7] even though Åbo will then at once suffer a severe bloodletting.

My heart is warm and my gladness pure when I think of you.

Yours sincerely,

Nathan S-m

306. From TORSTEN BOHLIN[1]

Åbo den 26. X. 1928

Hr. Ärkebiskop!

Min Anna har av Ärkebiskopinnan fått ett hugsvalande, moderligt brev, för vilket hon ber att själv få tacka, så snart hennes krafter medgiva att skriva. Själv kan jag inte dröja med att säga, huru djupt Ärkebiskopens brev har rört och tröstat mitt hjärta.

En händelse som denna skakar ens väsen i dess grundvalar. Och vilken allvarsam affär är det ändå inte att dö. Ack, inte ens en av feber utmattad liten tvååring förskonas alldeles från dödskamp.

Ändå var hans bortgång stillhet och – ljus. Anna förmådde till det sista nynna en liten vaggvisa för den älskade lille. Och det allra sista han förnam av denna världen var Mors ljusa, goda leende. »Tårarna få komma efteråt,« viskade hon tappert. Så flög den oskuldsfulla barnasjälen till de eviga ängarna.

Det är stort få erfara, att trons brygga håller, även om vi stundom måste gå den med bävande steg. Och Gud har varit så god, som också låtit oss få *förnimma* något av Guds frid mitt i det tunga.

Med starkt deltagande hörde vi av Brita (hon har varit Anna till sådan hjälp och tröst!) om orostecknen ifråga om Ärkebiskopens hälsa. Det är ju något man icke talar om, men misstyck icke när jag bekänner, att också i min svaga förbön frambäres ofta den vördade och kära människa, till vilken jag nu skriver, med bön om välsignelse över det stora verket, om kraft och hälsa.

Med vördsam tillgivenhet

Torsten Bohlin

Åbo, October 26, 1928

Lord Archbishop,

My Anna has received from the Archbishop's wife a consoling, motherly letter which she would like to say thanks for herself as soon as her strength permits her to write. As for myself, I cannot wait to say how profoundly the Archbishop's letter has moved and consoled my heart.

An event like this shakes one's being in its foundations. And what a serious affair

---

[7] Bohlin did indeed receive a call to the chair of dogmatics in Uppsala in 1929 which he accepted.

[1] Nathan Söderblom's collection of letters, from Swedes, UUB, handwritten letter.

it really is to die. Alas, not even a little two-year old, exhausted by fever, is completely spared the death struggle.

Nonetheless, his passing away was calmness and – light. Anna was able until the end to hum a little lullaby for the beloved little one. And the very last thing he perceived of this world was his mother's bright, good smile. »Tears may come later,« she bravely whispered. So the innocent infant soul flew to the eternal pastures.[2]

It is grand to have the experience that the bridge of faith is holding, even if we sometimes must walk it with wavering steps. And God has been so good, who let us *perceive* something of God's peace in the midst of hardship

With great sympathy we heard from Brita[3] (she was of such help and consolation to Anna!) about the disturbing signs concerning the Archbishop's health. It is actually something one does not talk about, but do not disapprove of me when I confess that also in my feeble intercession the revered and dear person I am just writing to is often mentioned, praying for blessing for the great work, for strength and health.

Reverently yours,
Torsten Bohlin

307. From Eivind Berggrav[1]

Tromsø 16. Januar 1929.

Kjære Erkebiskop.

Det første personlige brev fra min »bispestol« skal være til dig. (A pro po bispestol, vet du hvad denne stol realiter utgjøres av i øieblikket? Jo, av en av fru Størens efterlatte kjøkkenkrakker! Annet sitteinventar finnes ikke i verdens nordligste bispekontor).

Som du kan tenke dig, har jeg lenge ønsket aa finne en god stund til aa skrive. Men jeg er blitt avskrekket ved at det var ganske umulig for mig aa faa det gjort paa maskin, og jeg vet at du lider ved aa faa breve som er haandgjort med daarlige hieroglyfer. Sammen med den utrolige travelhet den siste tid i Oslo har dette bevirket en likefrem uhøflighet mot din hustru og dig, – de siste mennesker i verden jeg hadde tenkt mig aa begaa denslags mot. Jeg har jo nemlig ikke engang sagt takk for sist!

At det for mig var uforglemmelig, vil I nok forstaa. Først dette aa møte dig personlig nu efter min utnevnelse for første gang. Kjære erkebiskop, du er saa vanskelig aa faa sagt *takk* til. Du blender vaar takk med din sol av älskværdighet, – vi blir staaende der og kan ingenting faa frem om det *egentlige* vi vilde ha sagt dig. Kjenner du Tategalleriets billede: Love locked out? Det er en gutt som staar nøken utenfor en stengt dør med en rose i

---

[2] Cf. Ps. 23,2.
[3] Brita Brilioth, nee Söderblom.

[1] Nathan Söderblom's collection of letters, from foreigners, UUB, typewritten letter. Söderblom's reply to this letter – if there ever was a written one – is not to be found among either Berggrav's papers in *Riksarkivet* in Oslo or among Söderblom's papers in Uppsala. So I surmise that the two men met in person some time after this letter and talked things over.

haanden. Jeg tror ikke bare det er mig som ofte har kjendt sig som denne gutten overfor dig, – bare at døren ikke er *stengt* hos dig, tvertimot, men du gik altid selv ut av den, henimot oss, saa vi fik aldrig komme oss *inn* med det hjerteblad vi lengtat efter aa rekke dig. Vet du, en gang imellem maa vi mennesker faa lov aa si hverandre rett ut at vi *holder av hverandre*.

Jeg mener ikke dermed bare at vi er takknemlige mot hverandre. Jeg mener helt barnlig, enfoldig at vi kjenner oss innerst inne livsavhengige av et menneske. Det fornemmes som noget i retning av at »hvis *han* ikke var, saa hadde ikke jeg hatt det liv som jeg nu har.«[2]

Engang imellem kjenner man sig da næsten ulykkelig ved aldri aa kunne faa vise noget, [there obviously is a gap here.]

Der gaar mange omkring som har denne kjensle overfor dig. Mon du vet det? Min første takk til dig er alltid fra et barn i mig, som kjenner sig velsignet og rikt hvergang tanken gaar til dig personlig. Alt hvar jeg *ellers* har aa takke dig for, blir som gnister i forhold til dette baal. Og derfor kjentes det som en dyp lengsel i mig, da jeg nu skulde bære en biskops navn, at jeg kunne faa møte dig personlig. Det var som en styrkelse og en vigsel for mig, og dette er noget *blivende*, jeg eier det like saa sterkt nu som da jeg var i Upsala.

Men saa ogsaa Ärentuna og den oplevelse det gav mig. De billeder derfra som du i din utrolige omtanke sendte mig, er som tittelen paa en rik bok. Du vet, *første gang* har en særskilt rang. Og det er første gang jeg som en biskop staar foran et alter. At dette skulde være sammen med dig, ja, jeg synes næsten der maatte være en styrelse i det.

Og saa siden: du har jo latt det regne med godhet over mig, alterbøkene, visitasjonsprotokollen, fotografiene og nu finner jeg her i Tromsø ogsaa Bøndagsplakaten. Det var det første domprosten møtte mig med her: der ligger en stor konvolutt til dig fra Søderblom. Ja, jeg kunde tenke det! Jeg som ikke engang hadde gjort den simple høflighets plikt mot dig, skulde opleve din omtanke straks jeg steg iland paa min nye strand!

Og saa sitter jeg da her. Du kan tro Ishavet tok imot mig. Et mörke som jeg ikke hadde tenkt mig muligheten av, hersket her den hele første dag. Naar jeg saa ut i luften og tenkte paa at solen var overhoved *forsvunnet*, saa kunde der gaa en kold gysen gjennem en: forlatt av solen, verdens undergang. Men da jeg kom i kirken søndag morgen i en snøstorm som om natten hadde tatt menneskeliv i flere 10=tall her like omkring øen, da var der lys. Vi hadde en fest saa sterk og dyp at all avstand og alt mørke blev borte. Her er storm og mørke og kulde, men *menneskene* er derav blitt lune, lyse og varme. Jeg tror jeg skal trives her!

Og en underlig oplevelse har ogsaa ordinasjonen været. Det er virkelig den første mai-dag i vaar norske kirke i denne vaar vintergenerasjon. Ikke paa grunn av Lunde bare, endnu mindre paa grunn av mig, men paa grunn av den aand som utløstes i hele vort presteskap, ja hos store dele av lægfol-

---

[2] This does not seem to be a quotation.

ket ogsaa. De vidnesbyrd som er kommet offentlig frem om dette og de jeg har mottat privat, er ganske overveldende sterke. Hvis du engang har tid, saa kik igjennem de »Ordinasjonsdokumenter« som jeg lar avtrykke i første hefte av »Kirke og Kultur«.

Men trots dette sitter jeg her og har aldri kjent mig saa dvergaktig som nu. Det er saa knugende, men jeg merker at innerst inne skaper det en aapenhet for naaden, som gjør at jeg paa *bunden* er frimodig og trygg.

Og saa hilser jeg dig fra »de høge logers land«, hvor flammeskæret ikke kommer fra menneskers rikdom, men lyser inn i vaar natt fra stjernens hjem.

Din innerlig hengivne
Eivind Berggrav.

Tromsø, January 16, 1929
Dear Archbishop,
The first personal letter from my »bishop's chair« shall be directed to you. (Apropos bishop's chair: do you know what this chair *realiter* consists of at the moment? Oh yes, one of the kitchen stools that Mrs. Støre left behind! Other than that, there is no seating furniture at the world's northernmost bishop's see).

Believe me that I had long wanted to find a good opportunity for writing. But I have been deterred by the outright impossibility of getting it done by way of typewriter, and I know that you suffer from getting letters which are written by hand in bad hieroglyphics.[3] Along with that unbelievably busy time in Oslo lately, this has entailed a downright discourtesy towards your wife and yourself – the last persons in the world to whom I would have meant to commit something like that. For I have not even said thanks for last [time].[4]

You will certainly understand that it was unforgettable for me. First of all, meeting you now in person for the first time since my appointment. Dear Archbishop, you are such a difficult person to give *thanks* to. You blind our thanks with your sun of amiability, – we remain standing there and cannot get across the *actual* thing we wanted to say to you. Do you know the painting at Tate Gallery, Love locked out? It is a boy standing there naked outside a closed door with a rose in his hand.[5] I think it is not only me who often felt over against you like that boy – except that the door is not *closed* in your case, on the contrary, but you always went out through it yourself, towards us, so we never succeeded in coming *forward* with that budding

---

[3] This is bound to be laden with subtle irony, as Berggrav's handwriting was beautiful, if at times indeed difficult to read, but recipients of Söderblom's letters must have »suffered« significantly more. Söderblom knew it and spoke of his »crow's feet« (kråkfötter), the Swedish idiom for a hardly legible handwriting, cf. letter to Gottfrid Billing of Sept. 7, 1920, Collection Billing. G., Lund University Library (not in the present edition).

[4] It is a custom observed throughout Scandinavia to thank a person for an invitation once again on the day afterwards, and even as the first thing to say when one is invited again.

[5] »Love locked out« was painted in oil by the American artist Anna Lea Merritt (1844–1930) in 1889. The rose in the boy's hand is Berggrav's addition; on the painting, a rose bush grows up the column to the boy's right. Also a burnt out lantern lies on the floor, symbolizing his desperation from having tried all night to get in.

blossom[6] we had desired to hand to you. You know, every once in a while we humans must be allowed to say to each other straightforwardly that we *hold each other in high esteem.*

I do not only mean by this that we are grateful to each other. I mean in quite a childlike, simple way that we feel in our innermost that our lives depend on a person. It is perceived as something like »Had *he* not been, I would not have the life I am having now.«

Every once in a while one then feels almost unhappy for never being able to demonstrate something, [Berggrav left the sentence unfinished after a comma].

There are many people around who have that feeling towards you. Maybe you know it? My first thanks to you always comes from a child within myself who considers himself blessed and rich each time his thinking turns towards you personally. Anything I have to thank you for *apart from this,* is like [mere] sparks in relation to that balefire. And that is why it was like a profound desire within myself, as I now was to bear a bishop's name, to get to meet you in person. It was like a strengthening and a blessing for me, and that is something *lasting*; I am cherishing it just as much now as I did when I was in Uppsala.

But then also Ärentuna and the experience it gave me. The pictures of it which you in your unbelievable thoughtfulness sent to me are like the title of an opulent book. You know, the *first time* has a special significance. And it is for the first time that I stand in front of an altar as a bishop. That this should happen together with you, well, it almost seems to me that there must be divine guidance behind it.

And thus [ever] since: you have been showering kindness on me, the altar books, the inspection protocols, the photographs, and now I find the Repentance Day placards too here in Tromsø. That was the first thing the Dean encountered me with here: There is a large envelope from Söderblom waiting for you. Oh yes, I thought as much! I who not even fulfilled the simple obligation of courtesy towards you, should experience your thoughtfulness the very moment I went ashore on my new coast!

So I am sitting here now. You may believe that the polar sea received me. A darkness I had not deemed possible was holding sway here all through the first day. When I looked out into the open air and thought that the sun had *disappeared* altogether, a cold shiver could pervade one: abandoned by the sun, the world's extermination. But when I came into the church on Sunday morning in a blizzard which during the night had taken the lives of several tens of people right here around the island, there was light there. We had a foothold so strong and deep that all the distance and all the darkness had gone. Here there is storm and darkness and cold, but the *people* have thereby become full of humor, light, and warmth. I think I will like it here!

Ordination too was a strange experience. That is truly the first May Day in our Norwegian church in our winter generation. Not only because of Lunde,[7] still less because of myself, but because of the spirit aroused in our whole clergy, even in large parts of lay folks. The testimonies on this which were uttered in public and which I received privately are quite overwhelmingly strong. When you have time one of these days, browse through the »Documents of Ordination« which I shall have printed in the first issue of *Kirke og Kultur.*

---

[6] In Norwegian: *hjerteblad,* which means both bud, innermost leaf of a blossom, and darling.

[7] Johan Lunde (1866-1938), the Oslo bishop who consecrated Berggrav.

But in spite of this I am sitting here, never having felt as dwarfed as I am doing now. It is so depressing, but I notice that deep inside this creates an openness for grace which at *bottom* makes me undaunted and confident.

So I am greeting you from »the land of high flames«[8] where the glare of fire originates not from human wealth but shines into our night from the home of the stars.

Sincerely yours,

Eivind Berggrav.

308. From Rudolf Otto[1]

Marburg 27 2 29

Verehrter Herr Erzbischof.

Wir drucken soeben den Bericht über unsere Genfer Tagung, betreffend die interreligiöse Weltkonferenz, den ich mir erlauben werde Ihnen zuzusenden.[2] Ich weiss, das Sie sich für diese Angelegenheit interessieren. Es kann aus ihr Gutes entstehen, wenn es gelingt, den allzustark pragmatistischen Einfluss der Amerikaner zu mässigen und gegenüber dem westlich-amerikanischen Prestige den Ostländern die Zuversicht zu geben, dass unsere Arbeit nicht im westlichen »business-interesse« geführt wird. Ich freue mich, dass die beiden schwedischen Vertreter, Neander[3] und Forel[l], in dieser Hinsicht ganz auf meiner Seite sind. Mein lebhafter Wunsch ist, dass beide einen möglichst starken Einfluss gewinnen, den sie als Vertreter des Neutralen Schweden im allgemeinen Interesse am besten ausüben können.

Von H[errn] Forel[l] höre ich, dass er mit auf der Vorschlagsliste steht für die Berliner Gesandtschafts=Prediger=stelle. Ich würde mich nicht nur persönlich sehr freuen, wenn er diesen Platz erhalten könnte, sondern ich würde es für ausserordentlich wichtig halten. Forel[l] ist ja gradezu ein lebendiger Vertreter der geistigen Beziehungen unserer beiden Länder und Kirchen, und zugleich ein so die Herzen gewinnender Vertreter des Schwedentumes, dass er wie berufen erscheint für einen solchen Platz. Sollte mein Urteil über ihn Ihnen irgendwie von Belang sein, so stelle ich es Ihnen gern zur etwaigen Verwendung zur Verfügung. Auch bin ich gern bereit, wenn das erwünscht sein sollte, aus meiner langjährigen Kenntnis ein mehr ins einzelne gehendes Urteil abzugeben. Ich möchte noch auf etwas anderes hinweisen: das ist das *Klima* von Berlin. Berlin hat infolge seines märkischen Sandbodens eine ganz ausserordentliche Heilkraft für alle katarrhalischen Zustände, die sich bei Forel[l] im feuchten Klima von Rotterdam, wie ich beobachtet habe, bedenklich gesteigert haben. Ich selber, und

---

[8] »De høge logers land«, same as Hålagoland, i.e., Northern Norway, Berggravs diocese.

[1] Nathan Söderblom's collection of letters, from foreigners, UUB, typewritten letter.

[2] There were two preparatory meetings for such a conference in Geneva (1928, 1930). An actual conference did not take place during Otto's lifetime, however. One such conference was convened in Chicago in 1958 by the International Association for Liberal Christianity and Religious Freedom, concerning the role of religion for solving urgent world problems.

[3] For Herman Neander, cf. letter no. 274, n. 4.

484

Schücking[4] und andere meiner Freunde haben die Heilkraft von Berlin in dieser Hinsicht erfahren. Ich bin sicher, dass Forel[l], der an jenen Zuständen bisweilen sehr schwer zu leiden hatte, in Berlin in einigen Jahren ein völlig gesunder Mensch werden würde und dann wegen seiner grossen Begabung für seine Kirche und sein Land vielleicht noch einmal Bedeutendes leisten könnte. Und mir scheint, dass es sehr berechtigt sein würde, unter höheren und allgemeineren Gesichtspunkten diesen Umstand bei einer derartigen Gelegenheit mit zu berücksichtigen.

Ich habe inzwischen den Minister gebeten, mich von meinen Amtspflichten zu entbinden. Mein Nachfolger wird Frick aus Giessen.[5] Ich hoffe, dass unser sehr tüchtiger Wünsch[6] Fricks Nachfolger werden wird. Natürlich hoffe ich sehr, meine Lehrtätigkeit noch einige Jahre fortzusetzen, und daneben mich dem Ausbau unserer »Marburger religionskundlichen Sammlung« zu widmen.

Wann werden wir Sie einmal wieder bei uns in Deutschland begrüssen? Unsere Vorbereitungen für die Feier des Marburger Religionsgespräches sind im Gange. Hoffentlich gelingt uns dann die Einigung des Weltprotestantismus, die dann für die Stockholmer Konferenz zugleich die sichernde Basis werden wird.

Jetzt, wo der Papst einen neuen ungeheuern Zuschuss seiner Macht gefunden hat, ist der Zusammenschluss des Protestantismus wichtiger denn je geworden.

In aufrichtiger Verehrung, und mit den besten Grüssen auch an Frau Erzbischof Ihr ergebener

R. Otto, Marburg

Ich bemerke noch, dass H. Forel[l] von meinem Schreiben nichts weiss: er hat mich nie gebeten, mich bei Ihnen für ihn zu verwenden. Aber ich tue es mit Freude, da ich zugleich überzeugt bin, dass er einen ausgezeichneten Pfarrer und Seelsorger darstellen wird.

309. To Erik Rinman[1]

Upsala den 4 april 1929

Broder!

Ditt kärkomna brev av Påskdagen vittnar om hur noga Du följer de andliga företeelserna. Att Karl Barth och hans teologi blivit särskilt uppmärksammad i Danmark har en väsentlig grund däri, att han och hela hans riktning är en direkt epigon till Sören Kierkegaard, vilken således har rent av bildat

---

[4] Walter Schücking (1875–1935), professor of international law in Berlin.
[5] Cf. letter no. 305, n. 2.
[6] Cf. letter no. 292, n. 3.

[1] Nathan Söderblom's collection of letters, to Swedes and foreigners, UUB, typewritten letter.

skola i teologin så många årtionden efter sin död. Han [handskrivet tillägg: Kierkegaard] hör till kyrkans evärdeliga personligheter. Det skulle ligga mig nära att skriva om denna sak, och jag tackar Dig för förtroendet. Men jag har icke tillräckligt satt mig in i denna nya riktning. Jag börjar nu bli gammal. Den ojämförligt bäste och förnämste inom denna teologiska riktning är Brunner i Zürich, som jag hade tänkt vid tillfälle få hit till Sverige. Även här hos oss är bland prästerna och naturligtvis i fakulteterna Barths teologi livligt omdebatterad. Bäst hemma i saken torde nog professor T. Bohlin i Åbo vara. Därnäst anbefaller jag docenten S. v. Engeström i Upsala, båda goda skribenter.

För egen del vill jag gärna snart få skriva något för Din tidning. Just nu får jag från jesuitpatern Max Pribilla en stor bok om »Kirchliche Einheit. Stockholm, Lausanne, Rom,« som jag måste ingående befatta mig med. Visserligen finner jag att konvertiten Bodström har försett honom med alla möjliga mer eller mindre lömska utdrag och uttalanden av undertecknad ur pressen i Stockholm och Sverige. Men det är en allvarlig bok, och jag måste allvarligt behandla den. Men jag får nog inte tid att läsa boken förrän under de veckor i slutet av april, då professor Thorling dömer mig till vila.

Din tillgivne
Nathan Söderblom

Uppsala, April 4, 1929
Dear friend,
Your welcome letter of Easter Sunday is witness of how closely you are keeping abreast with intellectual events. The special attention Karl Barth and his theology have received in Denmark is largely due to the fact that he with his whole school of thought is a direct epigone of Sören Kierkegaard, who has thus founded a veritable school in theology so many decades after his death. He [handwritten addition: Kierkegaard] belongs to the immortal personalities of the church. It would seem the obvious thing for me to write something on this subject, and I thank you for your trust. But I have not sufficiently got into that new school. I am beginning to get old now. The incomparably best and noble one within this theological school is Brunner in Zürich,[2] whom I have been thinking of inviting to Sweden when I have a chance. Here with us too, among pastors and of course in the faculties, Barth's theology is being eagerly discussed. The one who is best acquainted with the subject should certainly be Professor T. Bohlin in Åbo. Next to him I recommend lecturer S. v. Engeström in Uppsala[3] – both of them good writers.

As for myself, I shall be glad to write something for your paper soon. Just now I have received a large book by the Jesuit Father Max Pribilla on *Kirchliche Einheit. Stockholm, Lausanne, Rom*,[4] which I must thoroughly address myself to. I certainly find that the convert Bodström[5] provided him with all kinds of more or less disin-

---

[2] Cf. letter no. 221, n. 5.
[3] Sigfrid von Engeström (1889–1984), professor of Christian ethics in Uppsala 1939.
[4] Max Pribilla, *Um kirchliche Einheit. Stockholm, Lausanne, Rom*, Freiburg i. Br. 1929. Söderblom wrote a rather lengthy review of this book: »Pater Max Pribilla und die ökumenische Erweckung. Einige Randbemerkungen,« in: *KHÅ* 31/1931, 1–99.
[5] I have not been successful in tracking down this person. The ed.

genuous extracts and statements by the undersigned from the press in Stockholm and Sweden. But it is a serious book, and I have to treat is seriously. However, I shall not have time to read the book before those weeks at the end of April for which Professor Thorlin[6] condemns me to rest.

Yours sincerely,
Nathan Söderblom

310. From Otto Dibelius[1]

Berlin-Steglitz, am, 29. Mai 1929

Hochverehrter Herr Erzbischof!

Es sind jetzt gerade hundert Jahre her, dass Friedrich Wilhelm III.[2] das Amt des Generalsuperintendenten im damaligen preussischen Staat neu geordnet hat. Während bis dahin die Generalsuperintendenten lediglich hervorragendere Superintendenten mit einem beschränkten Visitationsrecht waren, hat er sie in organische Verbindung mit den Konsistorien gebracht und damit den Anfang zu einer Wiederherstellung eines wirklichen bischöflichen Amtes in unserer Kirche gemacht, wie wir es nach jahrzehntelangem Widerstand der Bürokratie seit unserer neuen Kirchenverfassung haben – wenn auch der Name »Bischof« noch nicht wieder eingeführt ist. (Dass die neue Kirchenverfassung für Posen die Amtsbezeichnung »Bischof« vorsieht, haben Sie vielleicht bemerkt. Wenn die staatliche Genehmigung dort erreicht ist, wird wenigstens vor aller Welt dokumentiert sein, dass das Amt des Generalsuperintendenten bei uns wieder das bischöfliche Amt ist, wie es die lutherischen Kirchen der Welt auch sonst besitzen.)

Aus dem jetzigen Anlass möchte ich der demnächst zusammentretenden Konferenz der preussischen Generalsuperintendenten ein kleines Referat über die Entwicklung des Generalsuperintendenten-Amtes von 1829 bis 1929 halten. Ich habe die Akten durchsehen lassen, die hier auf dem Ministerium und bei den Kirchenbehörden sich befinden. Das Bild steht mir jetzt fertig vor der Seele.

Nun aber erzählte mir vor einiger Zeit in zufälligem Gespräch Geheimrat von Dryander, der in den letzten Zeiten der Monarchie vortragender Rat im Zivilkabinett des Kaisers war, dass Sie, sehr verehrter Herr Erzbischof, im Jahre 1914 an den Kaiser geschrieben und die Wiederherstellung des bischöflichen Amtes in Preussen angeregt hätten. Er habe damals die Antwort selbst entworfen, die trotz des dringenden Widerstrebens des Kultusministers nicht ablehnend gewesen sei, sondern lediglich gesagt habe, dass eine solche Massnahme nicht während des Krieges vorgenommen werden könne.[3]

---

[6] Ivar Thorlin (1878–1963), Söderblom's physician.

[1] For Otto Dibelius, cf. letter no. 173, n. 2. – Nathan Söderblom's collection of letters, from foreigners, UUB, typewritten letter.
[2] Friedrich Wilhelm III. (1770–1840), Prussian king since 1797.

Geheimrat von Dryander fügte hinzu, dass er sich bemüht habe, dieses Briefwechsels in den Akten des Staatsministeriums habhaft zu werden. Es sei ihm das aber nicht gelungen.

Nun ist dieser Briefwechsel zwischen Ihnen und dem Kaiser bei uns völlig unbekannt. Wieweit der Oberkirchenrat im Jahre 1914 davon Kenntnis erhalten hat, weiss ich nicht. Jedenfalls ist nie ein Sterbenswort darüber verlautet, auch in den Jahren nicht, in denen ich selbst zum Oberkirchenrat gehörte. Für meine Kollegen aber würde es überaus interessant sein, diesen Schriftwechsel kennen zu lernen. Unter Umständen könnte es auch für die Debatte über die Wiedereinführung des Bischofstitels, die auch bei uns sicherlich einmal fortgeführt werden wird, von Nutzen sein, wenn man im geeigneten Moment darauf zurückgreifen könnte. Eine Veröffentlichung im Augenblick würde ich nicht für ratsam halten.

Meine Frage geht nun dahin, ob Sie vielleicht in der Lage wären, mir eine Abschrift Ihres damaligen Briefes an den Kaiser und eine Abschrift von der Antwort des Kaisers zur Verfügung zu stellen. Ich wiederhole: Ich würde sie nicht veröffentlichen, würde nur in dem geschlossenen Kreise der Generalsuperintendenten selbst bei Gelegenheit unserer Jubiläums-Tagung davon Gebrauch machen.

Ich bin in alter Verehrung und Ergebenheit
Ihr getreuer
Dibelius

311. To Otto Dibelius[1]

Upsala den 5 Juni 1929

Hochverehrter Herr Generalsuperintendent und Bruder!

Richtig! Aber ist es wirklich angezeigt, diese Sache wieder aufzunehmen? Könnte es nicht im Gegenteil der von Ihnen mit solcher Kraft und Klarheit betriebenen Angelegenheit schädlich sein, wenn es herauskommt, dass der Kaiser damals nicht ganz ähnliche, aber doch auch nicht ganz unähnliche Absichten gehabt hat? Solche Fragen können Sie selbst am Besten beantworten. Unter allen Umständen ist es vielleicht doch unrichtig, dass mein Namen auch in kleinen Kreisen genannt wird. Ich bin ja nämlich Ausländer.

---

[3] Söderblom had written to the Kaiser in October, 1917 (letter no. 108). The Kaiser's reply, (letter no. 111), written by Gottfried von Dryander (same letter, n. 1), said that he was favorable to the title of bishop, but to the title only, as for him, the summepiscopate was here to stay because it had proved a blessing for the church. Geheimrat von Dryander either had forgotten this, or he did not want to mention it to Dibelius since he was aware that the latter had advocated strict independence of the church from the state early on; cf. letter no. 173, n. 2. Furthermore, the Kaiser's reply had not referred to the war as the reason for not introducing the title of bishop.

[1] Nathan Söderblom's collection of letters, to Swedes and foreigners, UUB, typewritten letter (carbon copy).

Die Ursache meines Unternehmens war einfach dass ich von sehr sicherer Stelle erfuhr, dass der Kaiser die Absicht hatte, einige Kirchendiener, oder, was dasselbe ist, Kirchenfürsten im Schleiermachers Sinne[2] mit dem Bischofstitel auszuzeichnen. Es erschien mir nicht glücklich, wenn der Bischofsname in der evangelischen Kirche Deutschlands nach Jahrzehnten nur als eine Art von Dekoration oder persönlicher Auszeichnung wieder aufkommen sollte. Ich habe daher einen Brief an den Kaiser geschrieben, (Ich habe den Kaiser nie getroffen), selbstverständlich ohne jede art von Kritik, da es sich ja nur um ein Gerücht handelte, aber mit der positiven Voraussetzung dass nicht einzelne von dem Kaiser geschätzte Persönlichkeiten, sondern gewisse Ämter den Bischofsnamen haben sollten. Das war der einzige Grund, warum ich überhaupt in dieser Sache gewagt habe, eine Initiative zu nehmen. Die drei Beilagen zeigen Ihnen die Peripathie der Sache. Vor allen Dingen. Lassen Sie unter allen Umständen meine Person ausserhalb der Sache und, wäre es nicht das klügste, diese ganze Angelegenheit der künftigen Geschichte zu überlassen, bis die jetzt tatsächlich das bischöfliche Amt verwaltenden Generalsuperintendenten auch mit dem biblischen und griekischen Namen genannt werden?

Ihr sehr herzlich und brüderlich ergebenster

312. From Rudolf Otto[1]

Marburg, 22 6 29

Verehrter Herr Erzbischof.

Für Ihre freundlichen Grüsse durch Herrn cand. Karlström[2] meinen besten Dank. Ich höre von ihm, dass Sie zu Beginn des September nach Eisenach kommen werden und dann nach Nauheim gehen wollen. So haben wir um so mehr Hoffnung, dass Sie auf unserer Feier des Marburger Religionsgespräches bei uns sein werden. Und ich bitte um die Erlaubnis, Ihnen sagen zu dürfen, wie sehr wir uns darüber freuen würden und wie sehr wir auf Ihre Mithilfe hoffen, dass diese Feier nicht nur eine geschichtliche Erinnerung sein wird, sondern der Anfang einer anzubahnenden Gemeinschaft protestantischer Kirchen zu verbundener Arbeit, die so dringend nötig ist. Sie erlaubten mir seinerzeit, Ihnen unsere Pläne und Gründe auseinander zu setzen. In der Zwischenzeit habe ich mich noch mehr mit der Überzeugung durchdrungen, dass wir auf diese Weise zugleich der »Stockholmer« Sache

---

[2] Cf. Friedrich Schleiermacher, *Kurze Darstellung des theologischen Studiums zum Behuf einleitender Vorlesungen*, 2nd ed., critical ed. by H. Scholz, (QGP 10) Leipzig 1910, § 9.

[1] Nathan Söderblom's collection of letters, from foreigners, UUB, typewritten letter.

[2] Nils Karlström (1902–1976), later Dean.

am besten dienen werden. Ich halte an meiner »Drei-Pfeiler-theorie« fest, die das tragfähige Gerüst abgeben wird für den allgemeinen Oberbau der Stockholmer concordia zwischen Protestantismus, Anglikanismus und östlichem Kirchentum.[3]

Mir und meiner Schwester würde es eine Freude sein, wenn wir Sie dann bei uns beherbergen dürften. Wir können Ihnen ein Arbeitszimmer und ein Schlafzimmer zur Verfügung stellen – schlicht genug, aber wie ich hoffe, hinreichend bequem, und ruhig gelegen.

... [On a translation of a Sanskrit text he is working on, and on the Swedish translation of a collection of his articles.]

Herr Präsident Kappler [sic; lies: Kapler] und eine ganze Anzahl Vertreter der verschiedenen in- und ausländischen Gruppen haben ihr Erscheinen zugesagt [i. e. at the anniversary referred to above], und es treffen täglich neue Zusagen ein. Rev. Cadman hat eine Ansprache übernommen.[4] Auch von dänischen und norwegischen Bischöfen haben wir Zusagen erhalten. Und unsere hessische Kirchenregierung arbeitet mit unserer Fakultät in dieser Sache in erfreulichster und regster Gemeinschaft.

Ich empfehle mich Ihnen und Frau Erzbischof und füge die Grüsse meiner Schwester für Sie beide bei.

In aufrichtiger Verehrung

Ihr ergebener

R. Otto

Mit aufrichtiger Freude erfahre ich von meinem jungen Freunde, H. Pastor B. Forel[l,] dass er Pfarrer in Berlin werden wird. Seine gediegene und verbindliche Art, sein tüchtiger Charakter und seine treffliche Begabung werden ihm sicher bald die Herzen seiner Gemeinde gewinnen, und nicht minder das Vertrauen seiner neuen Umwelt. Ich habe mir erlaubt, ihn Bekannten in Berlin und auch dem Auswärtigen Amte warm zu empfehlen. Sollte hinsichtlich seiner sonst eine Vermittlung erwünscht sein, die in meinem Vermögen steht, so stehe ich dafür ganz zur Verfügung.

Wenn Sie bei uns sein werden, werde ich Ihnen die Anfänge unserer »Marburger religionskundlichen Sammlung« zeigen, bei der er mir auf mei-

---

[3] For the »theory of the three pillars«, cf. the lecture »Gemeinsame Aufgaben des Protestantismus und die Form ihrer Erfüllung« (Common Tasks of Protestantism and the Way of their Fulfillment) Otto gave at the above-mentioned meeting in Marburg on Sept. 14. The lecture was printed in Rudolf Otto, *Sünde und Urschuld*, München 1932, 239–247. The three pillars Protestantism, Anglicanism, and Orthodoxy (245 f.) were supposed to bear the ecumenical »roof«and thus consolidate the Life and Work movement. To fulfill its function in such a setup, Protestantism would have to speak with one voice. For this purpose, Otto thought of founding an *Allgemeiner Evangelischer Weltrat zur Wahrung protestantischer Gesamtinteressen* (General Protestant World Council for Safeguarding All-Protestant Interests, 241), supported by a church-owned institute for research on the various Christian denominations, »perhaps here in Marburg« (242 f.).

[4] Samuel Parkes Cadman (1864–1936), British-born Methodist minister of a Congregational Church in Brooklyn 1901 until his death; and early radio preacher, president of the Federal Council of Churches of Christ 1924–1928.

ner Reise so ausgezeichnet und so geschickt geholfen hat. Wir planen, aus derselben und aus Beständen deutscher Missionen hier im Oktober eine Ausstellung für Missionskunde und Kunde fremder Religionen zu gestalten.

313. From EIVIND BERGGRAV[1]

Kjære Erkebiskop!
Først en liten notis i Svensk kyrkotidning om at du var i god bedring, og så idag en Stockholmstidning sendt fra ditt kontor, men hvori jag opdaget din egen hånd i det lille blyantord »Tromsø« i marginen, har satt mitt hjerte i ny sving. Du kan ellers prise din lykke att du ikke får brev fra Tromsø hver gang jeg er fyllt av trang til å skrive. Men idag hat du gitt mig en direkte foranledning, og nu kan du ikke slippe.

...

Et intenst halvår har jeg bak mig. Jeg visste at Nord-Norge var en individuallitet for sig selv, men jeg visste ikke *hvor* stor og hvor særpreget den var. Nu har jeg favnet disse veldige nye inntrykk, har reist disse asiatiske avstande og drukket inn både natur og folkelynde, så jeg snart er inntrykks-sløv. Nu trengte jeg et øieblikks avstand for at billedet kunde få sette sig.

Alt i alt er det gledelig hvad jeg har sett. Nord-Norge er en kampplass, hvor livselementene tumler for åpen scene. Såvel slagg som gull i folkelivet ligger mer fremme i dagen enn i de mer »civiliserte«, tettere strøk. Her nord er der en primitiv åpenhet i godt som i ondt.

Og så er jeg kommet like op i kirkelig utenrikspolitikk! Vårt forhold til Finnland er jo blitt så merkelig i det siste. Der er på et par år skjedd en tydelig forandring. Ikke lenger nogen politiske spørsmål er på ferde. Nei, der er snarere tale om en *psykologisk* affære. Finnland lokker, Finnland optrer som Gosen; på finsk side av grensen, der får folket kommunikasjoner, kirker, kunnskapsanstalter! På disse tre k'ers område står der for tiden en dragkamp som gjelder sinnelag, sympati, ønsker, velbehag. Bare en slik liten detalj: de finske menigheters felles råd ønsket å utdele en del finske opbyggelseslitteratur gjennem Hålagoland biskop til de finsktalende menighetslemmer her oppe. Vi svarte ja. Der kom en overdådig sending, deriblandt en stor del bibler. Men disse var i stort utstyr, digre skinnbøker med metalspenner, rene bryllupsgaver, en hel vognladning. Og inne i hver, på finsk: gave fra Finnland. Timeo danaos -.

Her åpner sig en situasjon som interesserer mig sterkt, men jeg er ikke

---

[1] Nathan Söderblom's collection of letters, from foreigners, UUB, typewritten letters. Undated; written about July, 1929. Again, there exists no reply from Söderblom; cf. letter no. 307, n. 1.

diplomat nok til snakke med Helsinki om slike emner. Foreløbig vil jeg prø-
ve å komme en tur til søster Svea og høre hvordan hun fornemmer disse
problemer.

Ellers er her ensomt, endnu. Jeg er en miljø-sjel, jeg gror i venners sol-
skin, jeg inspireres av opgaver og samtaler. Og her oppe er det litet av det.
Endnu iallfall. Jeg merker også at dette med »biskopen« gir en avstand, en
smule vacuum. Kanskje også fra min side. Ved venner forstår jeg først og
fremst en forståelse, i hvis favn jeg selv kan gjøre og si dumheter, fordi de i
godt lag og i venners ozonluft kan bli vandt til sannheter. Men en biskop
tør vel ikke si dumheter?

Det indre liv har også sine vanskeligheter. Jeg lever for meget på reserve-
ne. Jeg får ikke vegetere nok. Jeg mangler »ørken« i paulinsk forstand. Ellers oplever jeg nok at jeg blir satt avsides av Chefen, voldsomt også. Og
må slite med uværdigheten. Da lenges jeg efter Eder som er mine »bærere«
(Lc.5.18).

Og stundom blir det hele samlet i dette ene: gjør alt hvad du er blitt satt
til uten tanke på hvad du ellers synes du duger til og hvad der kommer ut av
det; det er vel den gamle kallstanke. Og der er alltid ny velsignelse i den.

Men nu omfavner jeg dig tilslutt og ber dig ikke bli trett om jeg nu og ellers kommer ubeleilig som min egen lille 4 årige kommer til mig på kontoret
midt i travlheten og vil »klemme far.«

Din hengivne
Eivind Berggrav.
En særskildt hilsen til Erkebiskopinnan, som *ofta* er i mina tanker.

Dear Archbishop,
First a little note in *Svensk kyrkotidning* [Swedish Church Journal], saying you are
in the process of recovery, and then today a [copy of] *Stockholmstidning* sent from
your office, in which, however, I detected your own hand in the little penciled word
»Tromsø« on the margin, have encouraged my heart anew. You can otherwise praise
your good luck that you do not get letters from Tromsø each time I feel the impulse
to write. Today, however, you have given me a direct inducement, so now you cannot escape.
    ... [Some general remarks about his liking for Söderblom's articles]
    I have an intense half year behind myself. I knew that northern Norway has an
individuality all of its own, but I did not know *how* great and how special it was.
Now I have taken in these tremendous new impressions, traveled these Asiatic distances and imbibed both nature and the people's mood, so I shall soon be blunted
for impressions. Now I felt compelled to distance myself for a moment, so the picture may settle.
    On the whole, what I have seen has been pleasing. Northern Norway is a battle-
ground where the elements of life are struggling on an open stage. Both slag and
gold in the life and manners of the people lie more openly on the surface than in the
more »civilized«, more densely populated areas. Up north here, there is a primitive
openness, in good and bad.
    Also, I have become involved in church foreign policy right away! Our relation-
ship to Finland has become so odd recently, you know. In the course of a few years

a distinct change has occurred. No longer is there a political problem brewing.[2] No, it is rather about a *psychological* affair. Finland allures, Finland presents itself as Goshen;[3] on the Finnish side of the border, people find communications, churches, institutions of learning! In the field of these three,[4] a tug-of-war is taking place at present which concerns mentality, sympathy, desires, well-being. Just this little detail: The Council of Finnish Congregations wanted to distribute edifying literature to Finnish-speaking church members up here through the bishop of Hålagoland. We agreed. Then an extravagant shipment arrived, among other things a great deal of Bibles. But these were decked out elegantly, thick leatherbound books with metal clasps, downright wedding gifts, a whole truckload of them. And inside each one, in Finnish: gift from Finland. Timeo Danaos -.[5]

A situation is arising here which I am very much interested in, but I am not enough of a diplomat to talk with Helsinki about such matters. For the time being, I shall try to make a trip to sister Svea [Sweden] and hear about the way she perceives these problems.

Otherwise, it feels lonely here, thus far. I am a sociable soul, I thrive in the sunshine of friends, I am inspired by tasks and conversations. And there is little of that up here. Thus far at least. I also notice that the »bishop« business makes for a distance, a bit of a vacuum. Perhaps also from my side. By friends, I mean above all a mutual understanding, in the embrace of which I myself can do and say foolish things, because these can in good humor and in the ozone air of friends be turned into truths. But a bishop is perhaps not supposed to say foolish things?

The inner life also has its difficulties. I am living too much on my reserves. I cannot loaf sufficiently. I lack »the desert« in the Pauline sense.[6] Besides, I certainly experience being set aside by the Chief, and forcibly at that. And I have to struggle with unworthiness. Then I long for you who are my »bearers« (Luke 5:18).

And sometimes all of this is brought together in this single sentence: Do all of what you have been assigned to do without thinking of what you may otherwise believe to be capable of and what will come of it; that is, of course, the old idea of calling. And there is always a new blessing in it.

But now I embrace you and ask you not to become weary if I now or at some other time come at an inopportune moment, like my own little four-year-old comes to my office in the midst of all the hustle and bustle, wanting to »hug Dad.«

Yours sincerely,
Eivind Berggrav.
Regards in particular to Mrs. Söderblom who *often* is on my mind.

---

[2] Since the late 19th century, Norway had been pursuing a rigid »Norwegianizing« policy towards the Finnish speaking (»Kven«) minority in its part of Lapland. Berggrav seems to have viewed support to the Kvens by the Finnish government as a latent threat to the Norwegian nation. (Information by Johann Christian Põder).

[3] Allusion to the OT story on the region of pastures which had been spared the Egyptian plagues and which was granted to the Israelites by the Pharaoh, Gen. 47:1-6.

[4] »Three k's« in the original, as the words rendered here by communications, churches, institutions of learning, all start with a »k« in Norwegian.

[5] Cf. Vergil, Aeneis 2,49: »Quidquid id est, timeo Danaos, et dona ferentes«, (whatever it is, I fear the Greeks, even if they bring gifts), the Trojan priest Laocoon said when he had seen the wooden horse that Odysseus had surreptitiously smuggled into the city.

[6] 2. Cor. 11:26? Probably rather Gal. 1:17, even though the word there is »Arabia«, not desert.

314. To Strenopoulos Germanos[1]

Upsala July 28th, 1929

Your Grace and dear Friend,
... [On a committee meeting where Germanos had been absent]
    Now I write these lines in order to ask you if you would kindly gather the Coordination Committee at Eisenach.[2] I have asked Dr. Kapler for a suitable hour. As soon as I receive his answer I shall write to you again. ... [A listing of the members appointed by Faith and Order and by Life and Work]
    When I proposed that the two movements [named a moment ago] should keep distinct from each other still some years, I hope I was in full agreement with the Encyclical Letter of your Ecumenical Patriarchate, and with the Orthodox delegation at Lausanne and thus with you. But Prof. Deissmann had a practical proposal about our future meetings, and it would be useful to have a fuller session of that Coordination Committee in Eisenach.[3]
    I do not know whether the Doctor will allow me to go to Eisenach. My heart is not well. I must have a rather explicit cure and rest in order to get full strength again and ability for work. If I am sent to Nauheim in September, I shall certainly come to see you in Eisenach.[4]
    With good and hearty wishes and respectful greetings from my whole house, I am
    brotherly yours

315. To Birger Forell[1]

Upsala den 26 aug. 1929

Käre vän!
Från Neander har jag mottagit Ottos föredrag vid Marburger-jubileet om »Gemeinsame Aufgaben des Protestantismus«. Som Ni ser av bilagda yttrande, finner jag hans förslag ytterst betänkligt, och jag hoppas att Ni kraftigt hävdar detsamma i Marburg. Att ett sådant förslag kan framkomma, måste bero på Ottos obekantskap med våra mångåriga strävanden.
    Med goda önskningar för Marburger-jubileet
    Eder tillgivne
    Nathan Söderblom
    P. S. – Tyvärr blir jag av min sjukdom förhindrad att förrätta Eder in-

---

[1] Nathan Söderblom's collection of letters, to Swedes and foreigners, UUB, typewritten letter (carbon copy).
[2] Cf. letter no. 304, n. 3.
[3] The comittee designed to coordinate Life and Work with Faith and Order.
[4] As it turned out, Söderblom was not able to attend the conference, for the health reasons mentioned.

[1] For Forell, cf. letter no. 155, n. 4. – MS. 797/563 UB Marburg, typewritten letter.

vigning, hur gärna jag än ville komma. Bäst vore om Biskopen eller någon annan i Lund kunde göra det. Jag skall höra mig för.

D. S.

med anledning av Prof. Ottos uppsats »Gemeinsame Aufgaben des Protestantismus
und die Form ihrer Erfüllung«[2]

Professor Ottos idé om en »Weltprotestantismus« synes mig ganska betänklig, särskilt att han skiljer mellan protestantism och anglikanism. Lutherdomen åtminstone här i Norden och även i Amerika och flerstädes känner sig i sina gudstjänstformer och i sin organisation mer befryndad med anglikanismen än med en formlös protestantism och dess gudstjänst. Jag har själv varit i tillfälle att iaktta hur svenska arbetare och bildade reagera inför olika konfessioner och gudstjänstformer. Vi har ju våra bönhus, som nära förbinder oss med den icke-liturgiska och icke-episkopala protestantismen, men våra kyrkor förbinda oss mycket närmare med anglikanismen.

Betänklig är Professor Ottos åtskillnad även därför, att anglikanismen är reformationens barn likaväl som den evangeliska kristenheten i övrigt. Anglikanismen är som bekant mångfaldig, och det vore principiellt och kyrkohistoriskt oriktigt att karakterisera hela anglikanismen utifrån den extrema och tillfälliga anglokatolicismen. Skall anglikanismen på detta sätt isoleras, blir det nödvändigt att på samma sätt särskilja lutherdomen från protestantismen. Vi ha ju en nattvardslära, som kommer den medeltida och romerska mystiken närmare, än fallet är även med anglikanismen, och även vår gudstjänstordning är i väsentliga stycken mer konservativ än den anglikanska. Lutherdomens närmaste trosfränder äro givetvis presbyterianerna.

Inom anglikanismen finnas olika riktningar. Vid en sådan tredelning, som den av Prof. Otto förslagna, skulle säkerligen majoriteten sluta sig till protestantismen. En liten minoritet skulle betona sin frändskap med Rom. Den äkta erasmiska anglikanismen kvarstode då, men kan inte betraktas som en enhet för sig. Både historiskt och principiellt är det enligt min mening viktigt att både lutherdomen och anglikanismen inräknas i den evangeliska delen av den katolska kyrkan.

Jag kan alltså inte biträda förslaget om »die Gründung eines ›protestantischen Allgemeinen Senates zur Wahrung protestantischer Gesamtinteressen‹«, detta av följande skäl:

1. anglikanismen skulle på ett oriktigt sätt bli isolerad;

2. En stor del av lutherdomen skulle vara med om en dylik organisation men se sig förhindrad genom anglikanismens uteslutande;

3. I allmänkulturella frågor likaväl som rörande minoritetsproblemen finnes redan ett betydelsefullt samarbete mellan anglikanismen och den evangeliska kristenheten i övrigt. Så t.ex. sände undertecknad för några år

---

[2] MS 797/707 UB Marburg, typescript with Söderblom's corrections and signature.

sedan tillsammans med Ärkebiskopen av Canterbury en prästerlig delegation till det besatta Saar-området. Att sönderbryta en betydelsefull och
verksam enhet vore ett steg tillbaka. Betänk World Alliance. För de sociala
frågornas vidkommande gäller detsamma om Life and Work-rörelsen;

4. för tillvaratagande av protestantismens intressen ha vi redan en verksam och dugande organisation i »Internationaler Verband zur Verteidigung
und Förderung des Protestantismus« med dess trespråkiga tidskrift »Protestantische Rundschau« – »Protestant Review« – »Revue Protestante«. Jag
vill inte vara med om något beslut, som skulle innebära ett direkt eller indirekt underkännande av deras verksamhet.

Eder
Nathan Söderblom

Uppsala, August 26, 1929
Dear friend,
From Neander[3] I received Otto's lecture at the Marburg anniversary on »Common
Tasks of Protestantism«.[4] As you will see from the enclosed statement, I find his
proposal extremely questionable, and I hope that you will strongly affirm the same
in Marburg.[5] That such a proposal can come to the fore must be due to Otto's unfa-
miliarity with our endeavors of many years.

With good wishes for the Marburg anniversary,
yours sincerely,
Nathan Söderblom
P. S. Unfortunately I am prevented by my illlness to perform your installation, much
as I would like to come. It would be best if the Bishop or someone else in Lund
could do it. I shall make inquiries about it.

D. S. [The same]

Statement
occasioned by Prof. Otto's article »Gemeinsame Aufgaben des Protestantismus
und die Form ihrer Erfüllung«
Professor Otto's idea of a »Weltprotestantismus« [World Protestantism] appears to
me to be quite questionable, particularly that he distinguishes between Protestantism and Anglicanism. At least here in the North and also in America, Lutheranism
feels much more akin to Anglicanism, with regard to its forms of worship and its organization, than to an informal Protestantism and its worship services. I have myself had the opportunity to observe how Swedish workers and educated people react
to various denominations and their forms of worship. We do have our meeting-
houses[6] which closely link us to non-liturgical and non-episcopal Protestantism, but
our churches link us much more closely to Anglicanism.

Professor Otto's distinction is questionable also for the reason that Anglicanism

---

[3] Cf. letter no. 279, n. 4.

[4] Cf. letter no. 312, n. 3.

[5] The statement was, of course, also sent to Otto, cf. letter no. 320. Söderblom was not able
to attend.

[6] Reference to Swedish Baptists and Pentecostals with whom contacts had been intensified
in those years.

is the Reformation's offspring, just like the rest of Protestant Christendom. As is well known, Anglicanism is diverse, and it would be incorrect on principle and in terms of church history to characterize Anglicanism as a whole on the basis of the extreme and ephemeral Anglo-Catholicism. If Anglicanism is isolated in this fashion, then it becomes necessary likewise to distinguish Lutheranism from Protestantism. For we have a doctrine of the Lord's Supper which is closer to medieval and Roman mysticism than is the case even with Anglicanism; also, our order of worship is in essential respects more conservative than the Anglican one. Lutheranism's closest brethren in the faith are, of course, the Presbyterians.

Within Anglicanism there are different schools of thought. Under a tripartition such as that proposed by Prof. Otto, the majority certainly would side with Protestantism. A small minority would emphasize its kinship with Rome. Genuine Erasmian[7] Anglicanism would then persist but cannot be regarded as a unit of its own. Both historically and on principle, it is important in my view that both Lutheranism and Anglicanism be reckoned among the Protestant part of the catholic church.[8]

I therefore cannot support the proposal concerning »die Gründung eines ›protestantischen Allgemeinen Senates zur Wahrung protestantischer Gesamtinteressen‹« [the foundation of a Protestant General Senate for Safeguarding All-Protestant Interests[9]], and that for the following reasons:

1° Anglicanism would wrongly be isolated;

2° a large part of Lutheranism would belong to such an organization but find itself impeded by the exclusion of Anglicanism;

3° With regard to general cultural issues as well as concerning minority problems, there already exists a significant cooperation between Anglicanism and the rest of Protestant Christendom. Thus, for example, the undersigned, together with the Archbishop of Canterbury, sent a delegation of clergy to the occupied Saar area a couple of years ago.[10] Breaking up a significant and efficient unity would be a step backwards. Consider the World Alliance.[11] As concerns social issues, the same holds true for the Life and Work movement.

4° For safeguarding Protestantism's interests, we already have an efficient and useful organization in the »Internationaler Verband zur Verteidigung und Förderung des Protestantismus« [International League for the Defence and Development of Protestantism] with its three-language journal *Protestantische Rundschau - Protestant Review - Revue Protestante.*[12] I do not want to be part of a resolution which would imply a direct or indirect disapproval of their activities.

Yours,

Nathan Söderblom

---

[7] Reference to the great humanist Erasmus of Rotterdam (1466/69–1536) who inspired much of Anglican thought.

[8] The term »catholic« is here to be taken in its original meaning as »general, comprehensive«. For Söderblom's theory of the three forms of catholicity (Orthodox, Roman, Protestant), cf. letter no. 97, n. 3.

[9] Otto's own terminology was »allgemeiner evangelischer Weltrat«, General Protestant World Council.

[10] The Saar area was occupied by France after World War I.

[11] Söderblom may be thinking here of the foundation of the International Fellowship of Reconciliation in 1919 as having contributed, in his view, to rendering the World Alliance for Promoting International Friendship through the Churches (cf. letter no. 11, n. 5) inefficient.

[12] The League was founded in 1923 at an instigation from the Netherlands and lasted almost until the end of World War II; the journal appeared from 1924 to 1944.

316. From STRENOPOULOS GERMANOS[1]

London, August 7th 1929

Your Grace and Dear Friend

I received Your letter of 28th last by my return from the Continent and I am very sorry to learn that Your health laisse beaucoup à desirer.[2] I express my heartfelt wishes for Your recovery and I pray God may give You full strength for the great work You are doing to the glory of His name.

Dr Keller has sent me the Minutes of the Coordination Committee met in London May 22nd and I answered his letter from Vichy, where I passed a cure after my pastoral tour on the Continent. I gladly accept Your proposal to gather the Coordination Committee at Eisenach when Dr Kapler fixes the hour.

Hoping to see Your Grace next month at Eisenach
I remain
Yours sincerely
+Germanos of Thyateira

317. To TORSTEN BOHLIN[1]

Upsala 27. VIII. 29

Käre vän och landsman,

Glädjen är stor i Upsala hos alla dem, som veta vad Din utnämning innebär. Jag undrar, om Du liksom Rodhe vill installeras redan denna termin utan hinder av Din tjänstledighet. Jag har tidigare hört från ett par olika håll, att Du under alla omständigheter hade tänkt Dig prästvigning i höst. Om så är, borde vi så fort som möjligt bestämma dagen. Hur skulle det vara med söndagen den 6 oktober? Du skulle då kunna eventuellt installeras den 5 eller 7 oktober, om Rektor har tillfälle därtill.

Två andra hälsingar Wahlström och Bergvik skulle då förmodligen vilja samtidigt prästvigas. Och mest för min egen skull[2] hade jag tänkt mig att prästvigningen skulle äga rum i Samariterhemmet. Jag är själv prästvigd i Ersta.

Vi längta efter Dig och Eder. Jag fröjdar mig över denna fakultet. [...]
Gud välsigne Dig i hjärta, hem och gärning!
Tillgivne gamle vännen
Nathan Söderbom

---

[1] Nathan Söderblom's collection of letters, from foreigners, UUB, handwritten letter.
[2] French for: leaves much to be desired.

[1] Nathan Söderblom's collection of letters, to Swedes and foreigners, UUB, copy.
[2] The text has *skulle* here, but that must be an error.

Dear friend and compatriot,[3]

Joy is great in Uppsala with all those who know what your appointment implies.[4] I wonder if you want, like Rodhe,[5] to be inaugurated already this semester, without impediments because of your leave. I heard earlier from various sources that you under any circumstances had thought of being ordained in the fall. If that is so, we should set the date as soon as possible. How about Sunday, October 6? You could then possibly be inaugurated on October 5 or 7, in case the Rector has the time to do it.

Two others from Hälsingland, Wahlström and Bergvik,[6] would probably want to be ordained at the same time. And mostly for my own sake I had thought that the ordination should take place at the Samariterhem. I was myself ordained in Ersta.[7]

We are longing for you and your family. I am happy about this faculty. ... [A couple of casual remarks of a personal nature.]

May God bless you in heart, home, and activities!

Your old friend,

Nathan Söderblom

318. From Torsten Bohlin[1]

Åbo den 28. VIII. 29

Vördade och käre Herr Ärkebiskop!

Tack för det så vänliga brevet, som nådde mig nyss!

Ja, det är sant: huru utgången än blivit, hade jag ämnat vända mig till Ärkebiskopen i denna angelägenhet. Min principiella ställning till Apostolicum har ju ej förändrats. Men numera kan jag ej känna samma betänkligheter för egen del som tidigare tyngt mig och hindrat detta steg. Så starkt känner jag samband med andelivet i Sveriges kyrka, att jag nu känner det som en förmån att få varda en dess vigde tjänare. Men låt mig här få tala öppet som till en Far! Vår älskade lille gosses bortgång skakade mitt innersta. Men denna natt, då jag tyckte mig uppleva hela livets fasa, lärde mig något oförgätligt: att trons brygga håller, även om vi stundom måste vandra den med skälvande steg. Jag har alltid fruktat, att min tro tilläventyrs satt utanpå, ej längst inne. Svagt, splittrat är alltfort mitt stackars trosliv. Men ändå tror jag att jag vågar bekänna: »Herre, Du vet allting, Du vet, att jag

---

[3] Bohlin, like Söderblom, hailed from the province of Hälsingland.

[4] Bohlin was appointed professor of dogmatics in Uppsala.

[5] Edvard M. Rodhe (cf. letter no. 198, n. 4), bishop of Lund and former Uppsala professor, apparently wanted to participate in the ceremony.

[6] I have not been able to identify these two men.

[7] »Samaritan's home«, a Swedish Church's school for nurses, Samaritergränd 2, Uppsala. Bohlin's reply (see following letter) proves Söderblom's sure touch in his choice of locality. – Ersta is a part of the city of Stockholm where a church-run center with hospital, home for the elderly, and school for nurses is located. Söderblom became chaplain at an Uppsala hospital after his ordination there (cf. letter no. 2).

[1] Nathan Söderblom's collection of letters, from Swedes, UUB, handwritten letter.

älskar dig.« Guds outsägliga nåd i vår Herre Kristus är mitt enda hopp i liv och i död, det enda – men tillräckliga.

Angående själva prästvigningen skulle jag önska, at den ej sattes i samband med installationen. Den senare önskar jag först efter min överflyttning. Men gärna den 6. oktober ur min synpunkt. Alldeles särskilt tacksam är jag, om akten får ske i Samariterhemmet. Jag ber riktigt därom. Har länge i tankarna bävat för alla skådelystna i Domkyrkan!

Ang. assistenter kanske jag får skriva senare. Min Far har längtat efter denna stund. Min bror kyrkoherden i Karesuando kan nog tyvärr ej göra den långa resan. Men jag har kära vänner, som nog gärna ville vara med.

Med vördnad och tillgivenhet
Torsten Bohlin

Åbo, August 28,1929

Esteemed and dear Lord Archbishop,
Thank you for your so kind letter which has just reached me!

Yes, it is true: Whatever the outcome would have been,[2] I had intended to turn to the Archbishop in this matter. My fundamental position concerning the Apostles' Creed has not changed, to be sure. But henceforth I cannot feel the same scruples for my part which had weighed me down earlier and prevented that step. So strongly do I feel connected to the spiritual life of Sweden's church that I now consider it a privilege to become one of its ordained servants. But let me speak frankly here as to a Father! Our beloved little boy's passing away shook me in the innermost. But that night when I thought I was experiencing all of life's horror, taught me something unforgettable: that the bridge of faith holds, even if we must sometimes walk it with wavering steps. I had always feared that my faith might perchance sit on the surface, not in my innermost. Weak, scattered, is what my poor spiritual life still is. Nonetheless, I believe I dare to confess: »Lord, you know everything; you know that I love you.«[3] God's inexpressible grace in our Lord Jesus Christ is my only hope in life and in death, the only – but the sufficient one.

As for ordination itself, I would wish that it not be connected with my inauguration. I wish to have the latter only after my removal. But October 6 would be fine as far as I am concerned. I am particularly grateful if the ceremony can be performed in the *Samariterhem*. I actually request it. Have long been shivering in my mind for all those gazers in the Cathedral!

As regards assistants, I may perhaps write later on. My Father has been longing for this moment. My brother, pastor in Karesuando,[4] will probably not be able to make the long journey, unfortunately. But I have dear friends who certainly will be delighted to take part.

Reverently and sincerely yours,
Torsten Bohlin

---

[2] I.e., of Bohlin's application for the chair in dogmatics.
[3] According to John 21:17, Peter's words to the risen Christ.
[4] Small village in the northernmost part of Swedish Lapland, near the Finnish border.

319. To Torsten Bohlin[1]

Upsala den 31 aug. 1929

Käre Broder!

Hjärtligt tack för Dina brev, som berett mig stor glädje. Den livssanning, som Du med så enkelt och hjärtegripande allvar uttalar, är den enda bärande för oss alla.

Sålunda anordnas prästvigningen i Samariterhemmet den 6 okt., då vi, om vi leva och ha hälsan, bli fyra landsmän av Gästrike-Hälsinge nation: utom undertecknad och Dig, Wahlström och Bergvik. Var välkommen att bo här hos oss under Din vistelse i Upsala.

Din tillgivne
Nathan Söderblom

Uppsala, August 31, 1929

Dear Brother,

Many thanks for your letters[2] which gave me great pleasure. The vital truth which you pronounced in such simple and heartwarming seriousness is the only sustaining one for all of us.

So ordination is arranged in the *Samariterhem* on October 6, when we, if we are alive and are in good health, shall be four compatriots from the Gästrike-Hälsinge fraternity:[3] besides the undersigned and yourself, Wahlström and Bergvik. You are welcome to stay with us during your visit to Uppsala.

Sincerely yours,
Nathan Söderblom

320. To Friedrich Heiler[1]

Upsala den 31 aug. 1929

Ärade och käre Vän!

Hjärtligt tack för Edert brev. För Olaus Petri-föreläsningarna kan Ni välja vilketdera av ämnena Ni helst önskar; vi ta lika gärna »Die Absolutheit etc.« som det andra ämnet.

Tyvärr är det mig omöjligt att komma till Marburger-jubileet. Jag närsluter ett yttrande med anledning av professor Ottos föredrag om »Gemeinsame Aufgaben des Protestantismus«, vilket yttrande jag tillställt de svenska representanterna vid jubileet och professor Otto. Skulle jag få be Eder att göra en tysk översättning och lämna till landesoberpfarrer D. Möller

---

[1] Nathan Söderblom's collection of letters, to Swedes and foreigners, UUB, copy.

[2] Bohlin had probably in the meantime notified Söderblom whom he wanted to assist in the ceremony.

[3] A fraternity in Swedish universities is formed by students from a particular province, or, as in this case, two provinces, Gästrikland and Hälsingland.

[1] Friedrich Heiler's papers, Ms 999, University Library Marburg, typewritten letter.

och professor Hermelink. Som Ni ser, finner jag Ottos förslag om en
»Weltprotestantismus« ganska betänkligt.

Med de bästa hälsningar till Eder maka och Eder själv
Eder tillgivne
Nathan Söderblom

Uppsala, den 31. August 1929

Verehrter und lieber Freund!
Herzlichen Dank für Ihren Brief. Für die Olaus-Petri-Vorlesungen können Sie wäh-
len welches von den Themen Sie am liebsten wollen; wir nehmen ebenso gern »Die
Absolutheit etc.« wie die anderen Themen.

Leider ist es mir unmöglich, zum Marburger Jubiläum zu kommen. Ich füge eine
Erklärung bei aus Anlass von Professor Ottos Vortrag »Gemeinsame Aufgaben des
Protestantismus«,[2] eine Erklärung die ich den schwedischen Repräsentanten beim
Jubiläum und Professor Otto zugestellt habe. Darf ich Sie bitten, eine deutsche
Übersetzung anzufertigen und Landesoberpfarrer D. Möller und Professor Herme-
link[3] zu übergeben? Wie Sie sehen, finde ich Professor Ottos Vorschlag betr. einen
»Weltprotestantismus« ziemlich bedenklich.

Mit den besten Wünschen für Ihre Frau und für Sie selbst
Ihr ergebener
Nathan Söderblom

321. From Strenopoulos Germanos[1]

Eisenach den 9ten Sept./29

Lieber Freund!
Ein griechisches Sprichwort sagt dass es kein Frühling ohne Rosen gibt.
Wir haben alle das Gefühl dass Sie uns fehlten dass es unsere Freude an
dem gesengneten [gesegneten] Werke woll [voll] sei. Wünsche Ich vom
Herzen volle Genesung und ein fröhliches Wiedersehen
Ergebenst
+Germanos of Thyat.

---

[2] Cf. letter no. 315, enclosure (under the heading »Yttrande«, resp. »Statement«).

[3] For Heinrich Hermelink, cf. letter no. 304, n. 4. – Heinrich Möller (1864–1939) was
Landesoberpfarrer, the equivalent to church president, of the church of Hessen-Kassel from
1924–1933. Marburg belonged to his diocese. Söderblom had met him at the Stockholm conference as a member of the German delegation. Söderblom certainly did not share Möller's
conservative views (he was an old-style monarchist and court chaplain until 1918; he had to resign in 1933, ostensibly because of old age but in fact because he was helpless over against the
Nazi regime). But Möller had to be informed, being the relevant church leader.

[1] Nathan Söderblom's collection of letters, from foreigners, UUB, handwritten postcard.

502

322. To Rudolf Otto[1]

Upsala den 12 okt. 1929

Ärade, käre Herr Professor!

Jag trodde att jag hade antecknat sextioårsdagen i min almanacka, och nu finner jag, att den har passerat, utan att Ni, ärade Vän och store forskare och religionskännare, mottagit ett synligt intyg om att mina tankar då voro hos Eder. Ett sådant årtal är en kärkommen anledning för att säga vad hjärtat alltid känner och hjärnan alltid tänker. Under många år har jag samlat en stor tacksamhetsskuld till Eder. Jag har ännu ett livligt minne av hur Ni firade hundraårsminnet av Schleiermachers Reden genom att sätta in denna märkliga bok i dess plats i religionens utveckling. Föga anade Ni då, att Ni själv skulle på ett sätt, som erbjuder en tydlig analogi till Schleiermachers Reden och dess betydelse, med koncentrerad kraft uppsamla, genomtänka och framställa och med originalitet och en, enligt den mänskliga tankeutvecklingens lagar just genom vad jag skulle våga kalla en viss ensidighet eller överdrivet verksam, [och][2] för ändamålet gagnelig, framställning av helighetsbegreppets innebörd och betydelse, sätta ett märke i religionsvetenskapens utveckling jämförligt med det, som betecknas av Schleiermachers Reden. Jag skall här icke söka tala om vad som ligger däremellan och min uppskattning av det, som det även efter Das Heilige har förunnats Eder att åstadkomma. Särskilt vill jag dock nämna den korta, men betydelsefulla och djupt ingripande framställning som Ni skänkte oss här vid Upsala Universitet.

Ni har öppnat för oss dörren till den trosrättfärdighet och Gudskärlek som i Fjärran Östern äger största frändskapen med uppenbarelsereligionens gudsgemenskap. Och Ni har alltiftrån början förbundit Eder forskning med ett levande och verksamt intresse för kyrkans liv och historia här i vår gamla kristenhet.

Låt mig också uttala en särskild erkänsla för att min unge vän kyrkoherde Forell fick följa Eder till Indien. Jag har just fått hans livfulla och upplysande skildring av denna färd.

Jag beder Gud uppehålla Edra krafter, välsigna Eder under många år av fortsatt verksamhet i hjärta, gärning och hem.

Eder tillgivne gamle vän
Nathan Söderblom

Uppsala, October 12, 1929

Verehrter, lieber Herr Professor!

Ich glaubte, ich hätte Ihren 60. Geburtstag in meinem Kalender vermerkt, und jetzt bemerke ich, dass er vorüber gegangen ist, ohne dass Sie, verehrter Freund und großer Forscher und Religionskenner, ein sichtbares Zeugnis dafür empfangen hätten,

---

[1] MS 797/857 UB Marburg, typewritten letter.
[2] This overloaded sentence becomes comprehensible only if the Swedish »och«, or German »und«, is eliminated.

dass meine Gedanken da bei Ihnen waren. Eine solche Jahreszahl ist ein willkomme-
ner Anlass, um auszusprechen, was das Herz allezeit fühlt und das Hirn allezeit
denkt. Im Lauf vieler Jahre habe ich eine große Dankesschuld Ihnen gegenüber an-
gesammelt. Ich habe noch eine lebhafte Erinnerung daran, wie Sie das hundertjähri-
ge Gedenken von Schleiermachers Reden dadurch feierten, dass Sie dieses bemer-
kenswerte Buch an seinen Platz in der religionsgeschichtlichen Entwicklung stellten.
Kaum ahnten Sie damals, dass Sie selbst auf eine Weise, die eine deutliche Analogie
zu Schleiermachers Reden und deren Bedeutung bietet, mit konzentrierter Kraft
sammeln, durchdenken und darstellen und mit Originalität und einer – nach den
Gesetzen der Entwicklung des menschlichen Geistes gerade durch das, was ich eine
gewisse Einseitigkeit oder übertrieben wirkungsvoll zu nennen wagen möchte, für
den Zweck gewinnbringenden – Darstellung des Gehaltes und Sinnes des Heilig-
keitsbegriffes, eine Markierung in der Entwicklung der Religionswissenschaft setzen würden, vergleichbar mit derjenigen, die durch Schleiermachers Reden bezeichnet ist. Ich will hier nicht versuchen, über das zu reden, was zwischen dieser Leistung und meiner Hochschätzung für das liegt, was Ihnen auch nach *Das Heilige*
zustande zu bringen vergönnt war. Doch will ich besonders die kurze, aber bedeutsame und tiefschürfende Darstellung nennen, die Sie uns hier an der Universität
Uppsala schenkten.[3]
 Sie haben uns die Tür zu der Glaubensgerechtigkeit und Gottesliebe geöffnet,
die im fernen Osten die größte Verwandtschaft mit der Gottesgemeinschaft der Of-
fenbarungsreligion besitzt. Und Sie haben von Anfang an Ihre Forschung mit einem
lebendigen und wirksamen Interesse für Leben und Geschichte der Kirche in unserer
alten Christenheit verbunden.
 Lassen Sie mich auch eine besondere Erkenntlichkeit dafür aussprechen, dass
mein junger Freund Pastor Forell Sie nach Indien begleiten durfte. Ich habe gerade
seine lebensvolle und erhellende Schilderung von dieser Reise bekommen.
 Ich bitte Gott, Ihre Kräfte zu erhalten, Sie für viele Jahre weiterer Wirksamkeit
im Herzen, in Arbeit und Heim zu segnen.
 Ihr ergebener alter Freund
 Nathan Söderblom

323. From Strenopoulos Germanos[1]

 Park Hotel München den 19ten November 1929
Sehr geehrter und Hochwürdiger Erzbischof, lieber Freund,
während meiner Visitationsreise in Deutschland habe Ich den beigefügten
Friedensbrief Seiner Allheiligkeit des Oecum[enischen] Patriarchen erhalten.[2] Seine Allheiligkeit aus Anlass ihrer Besteigung des Thrones[3] sendet
seinen brüderlichen Gruss Euerer Eminenz und spricht den herzlichen

[3] For Otto's Olaus-Petri-lectures in 1926, cf. letter no. 277, n. 2, as well as the following
paragraph.

[1] Nathan Söderblom's collection of letters, from foreigners, UUB, handwritten letter.
[2] Not found in Söderblom's collection.
[3] By »inthronization«, Germanos refers to the accession of Patriarch Photios II. (1878–
1935) to the See of Constantinople. He served from 1929–1935.

Wunsch aus die bestehenden freundlichen Beziehungen zwischen unseren Kirchen weiter zu fördern.

Aus [?] dieser Gelegenheit S. H. teilt Ihnen mit dass Er gnädigst geruht hat meine Wenigkeit als ständigen Vertreter des Oecum. Patriarchates bei Ihnen und bei Ihrer Ehrwürdigen Schwedischen Kirche zu ernennen mit der Bitte dass Ihre Eminenz mich als solchen anerkennen wolle und die Gunst Ihrer Liebe und Vertrauens zeige.

In dieser meinen neuen Eigenschaf[t] grüsse Ich herzlich Ihre Eminenz und sende Ich Ihnen zusammen mit dem obengenannten Briefe auch eine Übersetzung desselben.

Mit den besten Wünschen und Gebeten für Sie und für Ihre gesamte Kirche verbleibe Ich
ergebenst
Ihr geliebter Bruder in Christo
+Germanos von Thyateira

324. From Rudolf Otto[1]

Marburg, 13 1 30

Verehrter Herr Erzbischof,
Die herzlichsten Glückwünsche zu Ihrem frohen Familienereignisse![2] Und zugleich die besten Wünsche zum neuen Jahre. Möge es Ihnen die alte Frische vollkommen wiederbringen, und wolle Ihnen Gott noch lange die Kraft verleihen, Ihr hohes Amt, an dem sovieles gelegen ist weit über den Rahmen der Schwedischen Kirche hinaus, noch lange im Segen zu verwalten. Ich habe Ihnen noch besonders zu danken, für Ihre gütigen Wünsche zu meinem 60 ten Geburtstage, die mir eine so tiefe Freude bereitet haben. Ich wollte meine Antwort darauf gern begleiten mit einer kleinen Gabe, die ich fertig gestellt habe, deren Druck sich aber immer noch hinausgeschoben hat durch die gehemmten Umstände unserer Verleger. Es ist die deutsche Ausgabe meiner Upsala-vorlesungen.[3] Ich habe sie erweitert und einige der mir besonders am Herzen liegenden Gesichtspunkte und Grundsätze meiner eigenen »Glaubenslehre« etwas weiter ausgeführt als das im Rahmen jener 4 Vorlesungen möglich war. Das Heftchen nähert sich nun endlich seiner Vollendung und soll Ihnen dann umgehend zugehen.

Birger Forell ist eben bei mir. Wir hatten hier unter dem Vorsitze von Dr. S. Schultze[4] eine Konferenz betreffend die interreligiöse Arbeitsgemeinschaft, die von der Church Peace Union gestiftet worden ist. Wir sind einmütig darin, dass die amerikanische Behandlung dieser Aufgabe große

---

[1] Nathan Söderblom's collection of letters, from foreigners, UUB, typewritten letter.
[2] The marriage of Söderblom's daughter Yvonne.
[3] Cf. letter no. 277, n. 2.
[4] Friedrich Siegmund-Schultze, cf. letter no. 167, n. 3.

Mängel hat und dass die erste Konferenz in Genf[5] nicht eben glücklich zusammengesetzt war. Ich hatte nach Der Frankfurter Tagung fast den Mut verloren, gegenüber diesem allzu pragmatistischen Verfahren noch weiter mit zu arbeiten. Aber da nun S. Schultze eingetreten ist, so hoffen wir, dass doch vielleicht auch Gedeihliches daraus entspringen kann. Und so bin ich dabei geblieben, wenn auch nicht in irgend einer führenden Stellung. Ob es bei der Leitung durch Mr. Atkinson und Shailer Matthews[6] gelingen wird, das Vertrauen der »churches« zu gewinnen, ist mir persönlich noch zweifelhaft. Eigentlich waren nur die Kongre[ga]tionalisten Englands wirklich dabei vertreten. Die Anglikaner, und die schottischen Presbyterianer sowie auch die englischen Freikirchen hielten[7] ... eine wie ich glaube, indertat sehr frühe und echte Form von »Gottesglaube«, die zwar nicht, wie Schmidt meint, ein allgemeiner »Urmonotheismus« gewesen ist,[8] aber doch ein »uralter Gottesglaube«, und die zugleich entsprechend dem kollektiven Milieu primitiver Menschheit ganz andere Züge trägt als der von Schmidt angenommene »Urmonotheismus«. Es wird mir sehr wertvoll sein, Ihre Meinung darüber zu hören.

Unser junger Frueund [Freund] Forell scheint seine Aufgabe in Berlin mit prachtvollem Eifer anzupacken. Eine Nichte von mir, die jetzt in Berlin lebt, schrieb den beiliegenden Brief – verzeihen Sie seine unparlamentarische Form – der Sie vielleicht interessieren wird. Ihr Urteil über Menschen ist gut und sie pflegt im allgemeinen in ihrer Kritik scharf zu sein. Um so mehr freute mich ihre gute Aussage.

Wir werden nun den tüchtigen Missionar Johannsen hierher bekommen für Missionswissenschaft, durch den wir dann einen regelmäßigen Verkehr mit den Missionen hinsichtlich unserer »Religionskundlichen Sammlung« zu erlangen hoffen.[9] Wir wollen auch zu unsern deutschen katholischen Missionen feste Beziehungen gewinnen und auf diese Weise versuchen, für den Norden das zu schaffen, wenn auch in sehr viel bescheideneren Verhältnissen, was Pater Schmidt in seiner Lateranischen Sammlung geschaffen hat. Ein Schüler von ihm hat uns sein Interesse bereits zugesagt.

Ich erlaube mir, einen Entwurf für den Gebetsteil im Gottesdienste, nach der Predigt, beizulegen. Vielleicht hat er für Ihre liturgischen Reformideen ein Interesse. Er soll der kirchlichen Feier einen Höhepunkt im Gebet geben, der ihm in unsern Liturgien fehlt. Vielleicht wird Forell ihn für Vår Lösen übersetzen.

---

[5] Cf. letter no. 308, n. 2.

[6] For Henry Atkinson, cf. letter no. 183, n. 1. Shailer Mathews (one »t«! 1863–1941), Baptist theologian at Chicago University (1894–1933), influential proponent of the Social Gospel.

[7] A page is missing here.

[8] Cf. Wilhelm Schmidt, *Der Ursprung der Gottesidee*, 12 vols., Münster 1912–1955.

[9] As far as I have been able to find out, this must be Hinrich Johannsen (1873–1950), since 1927 Director of the *Gesamtverband Deutscher Missionskonferenzen*, 1934–1946 responsible for the Department on Africa at the *Rheinische Missionsgesellschaft*. Apparently, he had been given a teaching assignment in Marburg.

Heute waren wir zusammen auf dem »Frauenberge«, auf dem Sie einmal geweilt haben: seit längerer Zeit der erste Ausflug, den mir mein sehr angegriffenes Herz wieder erlaubt hat. Es war still und erfreuend auf der einsamen Höhe dort.

Mit herzlichen Grüssen
in alter Verehrung Ihr ergebener
Rudolf Otto

325. To Strenopoulos Germanos[1]

Upsala February 6th 1930

My dear Brother,

My deep and warm thanks for your kind letter of November last year from Munich with the most important message from His Holiness the new Patriarch, which reached me in due time. But the answer has been delayed partly because of reasons expressed in my letter to the Ecumenical Throne, of which I add a copy,[2] partly because of manifold occupations and the fact that my health does not as yet allow me full work.

We shall rejoice heartily when you come next time to Sweden.

What is to be done against the horrible persecutions in Russia?

I thought of you when you met on that subject and other subjects in London.

Eisenach markes [sic] a new step in our strivings for Unity, because I hope that our Continuation Committee will accept the excellent proposition of creating, according to the wish in Lausanne, out of it a permanent thing: the Universal Council on Life and Work.

With most respectful and hearty greetings from this house, especially from my daughter Yvonne, who has lately married the Archpriest of the Cathedral and who can never forget the high privilege she had to follow S:t Chrysostom's liturgy at your advice in Lausanne, I am in affectionate, brotherly communion

sincerely yours

---

[1] Nathan Söderblom's collection of letters, to Swedes and foreigners, UUB, typewritten letter (carbon copy).

[2] Not found in Söderblom's collection.

326. To Hermann Kapler[1]

Uppsala, 15. Februar 1930.

Mein lieber Freund!

Darf ich Ihnen einen ganz vorläufigen Vorschlag in schlechtem Englisch senden. Ich meine, dass eine Erklärung von den Präsidenten und Generalsekretären von Life and Work sehr nützlich, ja ich möchte sagen, sehr notwendig sein würde. Ich meine es würde sehr nützlich sein, wenn Sie diesen Appell sobald wie möglich schreiben würden. Könnten Sie nicht die Unterschriften von Cadman und Atkinson telegrafisch sich verschaffen und Ihren Appell in London und durch die Telegrafenagenturen dort veröffentlichen. Wir haben Gebete für die Verfolgten in Russland in allen unseren Kirchen für den 2. März, Quinquagesima, Esto Mihi, Fastensonntag, Beginn der Fastenzeit, Passion in Aussicht genommen. Könnten Sie nicht alle Kirchen auffordern, das Gleiche zu tun? Ich bin sicher, dass Sie, wie ich auch, mit Briefen und Aufrufen in dieser Sache überschüttet werden.[2]

Es ist ganz einleuchtend, dass die Sowjet-Regierung die Absicht hat, nicht nur den orthodoxen Glauben, die nationale Religion Russland, sondern auch alle Formen des Christentums, ja nicht nur die christliche Kirche, sondern jede Religion zu vertilgen. Eine solche Absicht entspringt dem Gedanken, dass die Menschheit ohne Religion glücklicher sein würde. Diese Idee ist ja schon früher aufgetreten, aber es hat sich erwiesen, dass sie gegen die tiefsten und erhabensten Empfindungen des menschlichen Herzens verstößt, und dass es unmöglich ist, sie durchzuführen.

In jedem Fall gehört es zu den besten und wertvollsten Errungenschaften der menschlichen Zivilisation, dem Menschen das heilige Recht auf Gedanken, -Glaubens- und Kultusfreiheit insoweit zu gewähren, als es nicht mit der Gesellschaftsordnung in Konflikt gerät. Wer kann leugnen, dass frühere Religionsverfolgungen zu den bedauerlichsten und beschämendsten Kapiteln der menschlichen Geschichte gehören? Aber die Verfolgung, die augenblicklich mit solch' konzentrierter Energie inmitten Europas vonstatten geht, steht in der Geschichte einzigartig da, weil sie nicht nur vorübergehend gegen einen bestimmten Glauben kämpft, sondern weil sie verfolgt und mit jeglichen Mitteln zu zerstören sucht, jede Art von religiösen Glauben und Verehrung. Kirchen werden zerstört oder zu weltlichen Zwecken verwendet. Diener der Kirche und treue Gottgläubige werden ins Gefängnis

---

[1] Nathan Söderblom's ecumenical collection B 4, UUB, typewritten letter: carbon copy of the German translation from the original English.

[2] With the final establishment of Stalin's absolute power at the end of 1929, terror against Christians and other religious groups in the Soviet Union increased considerably. Especially clergymen, nuns, and monks were murdered or sentenced to forced labor in Siberia, incredible atrocities were committed, churches and monasteries were vandalized and destroyed. During the »Great Purge« of the 1930s, the situation was aggravated still more. Only the German invasion in 1941 forced Stalin to change his anti-religious policies. – Up to this day, little is known in the West about that persecution, not least because the leaders of the Orthodox Church at the time were forced to deny all such allegations in their official statements.

geworfen, getötet, in entlegene Gegenden entführt und der Möglichkeit beraubt, sich die notwendigste Nahrung zu verschaffen, obwohl sie nicht das geringste gegen die Gesellschaft getan haben, sondern nur versucht haben, dem Gebote ihres Gewissens folgend, Gott zu gehorchen und ihre Brüder zu lieben und ihnen zu helfen.

1: Wir, die Präsidenten des Ökumenischen Rates für praktisches Christentum, unternehmen es daher, uns in erster Linie an die Mitglieder der Sowjet-Regierung zu wenden und sie aufzufordern, zu erwägen, nicht nur wie nutzlos und unmöglich eine solche Verfolgung sein muss, selbst wenn sie mit jeglicher Energie und Gewalt durchgeführt wird, sondern auch in welchem Widerspruch eine solche Handlung gegen alle zivilisierten und menschlichen Vorstellungen über die Freiheit des Geistes und die Würde des Menschen steht. Wenn die Sowjetregierung eine glückliche Zukunft für Russland erstrebt, so sind wir überzeugt, dass Religionsfreiheit hierzu als eine der elementarsten Bedingungen angesehen werden muss.

2: Wenden wir uns an den Völkerbund in Genf und an alle verantwortlichen Staatsmänner in der Welt und fordern sie auf, das Wohl der Menschheit im Auge zu behalten und zu erwägen, wie notwendig die Beendigung einer solchen Verfolgung des Glaubens und einer solchen Verneinung der heiligsten und elementarsten Menschenrechte ist. Es scheint uns, dass die Entwicklung des Verkehrs zwischen Sowjet Russland und der übrigen westlichen Zivilisation wünschenswert sein muss, da gegenseitige Kenntnis und Vertrauen zwischen den Nationen zu unserer Christenpflicht gehört, aber selbst wirtschaftlicher Austausch und jegliche Art von Verkehr scheint gehemmt und getrübt, wenn unsere Brüder in Russland und die Glieder jeglicher Art ehrenwerten christlichen oder anderen religiösen Glaubens unfähig sind, das zu erfüllen, was für sie die heiligste aller menschlichen Pflichten ist.

3: Aber ganz besonders wenden wir uns an unsere christlichen Brüder überall in der Welt, von jeglicher Konfession und Gemeinschaft und fordern sie auf zu wachen und zu beten und ihre Herzen mit ganzem Ernst auf das unsagbare Elend und die Pein zu lenken, die unsere christlichen Brüder und die anderen gottesfürchtigen Männer und Frauen im russischen Staate heute martern, mit uns zusammen Gott für sie anzuflehen und die richtigen friedlichen Mittel zu finden, um die Herrscher von Russland zu überreden, die Verfolgungen aufzugeben und den Untertanen geistige Freiheit zu geben und die Freiheit, die heiligen Pflichten des Glaubens und er Liebe zu erfüllen.

Lasst uns unsere leidenden Brüder und Märtyrer mit beständiger und warmer Fürsprache[3] unterstützen. Und lasst uns uns alle in unserer Fürsprache vereinigen am Sonntag Estomihi, der der Beginn der Fastenzeit ist, wenn wir mit der andächtigen Betrachtung des Leidens unseres Herrn beginnen.

Ihr aufrichtig ergebener

gez. Nathan Söderblom

---

[3] In this sentence and the next, Söderblom by »Fürsprache« means: Fürbitte, intercessory prayer.

327. To Birger Forell[1]

Upsala den 24 febr. 1930

Bäste Herr Kyrkoherde!

Hjärtligt tack för det vänliga och intressanta brevet. Särskilt gläder det mig att Ni arbetar för en församlingssyster. Jag vill gärna stödja Eder anhållan hos Röda Korset. Låt mig veta när Ni skickar in ansökan, så att min rekommendation icke kommer för tidigt, ty då bortglömmes den.

Professor Ottos tyska utvidgade upplaga av föreläsningarna här har jag läst med levande intresse. Hans förtrogenhet med indisk religion och hans principiella syn på religionen ställa honom i främsta ledet bland religionens kännare och forskare. Men hans idé om att giva den anglikanska kyrkan en särskild ställning är högst olycklig och bevisar hans brist på verklighetssinne. Lyckligtvis tror jag inte att något sådant kommer att kunna genomföras annat än vid skrivbordet. Men skulle en utsöndring av anglikanismen i den ekumeniska väckelsen ske, så blir den omedelbara följden att även lutherdomen måste stå för sig själv. Ty avståndet mellan lutherdomen och en hel del protestantiska religionsformer är vida större än avståndet mellan lutherdomen och anglikanismen.

Jag hoppas nu kunna hålla visitation i Berlin 4–6 april och installera Eder Femte i Fastan. Giv mig ett förslag till program. Lördag förmiddag kunna vi samla skolbarnen i kyrkan. Lördag eftermiddag bör väl upptagas med sammanträde med kyrkorådet och allt vad därtill hör. När är högmässotiden? Skulle det löna sig med en ytterligare gudstjänst på aftonen för dem, som till äventyrs icke få rum vid installationen på förmiddagen? Med stor försiktighet hoppas jag kunna klara saken. Det ojämförligt svåraste för mig är sällskaplig samvaro med många människor. Jag ber Eder därför avstyra dylika större tillställningar. Samtidigt skriver jag till envoyén. Till installationen böra naturligtvis inbjudas Generalsuperintendenten för Berlin, som skall stå bredvid mig framför altaret, vidare lokalförsamlingens kyrkoherde. Hur skulle det vara att be Deissmann och Siegmund-Schultze att assistera? Kanske är det för mycket begärt att en sådan man som Deissmann skall assistera. De båda kunna ju också inbjudas utan att assistera. Förmodligen kommer någon av sjömansprästerna. Kyrkvärdarna skulle också assistera, och vi behöva egentligen icke flera än fyra assistenter. Men inbjudan bör väl riktas även till presidenten Kapler, Dr. W. Simons etc. Giv mig ett förslag även härom.

Med goda önskningar
Eder tillgivne

---

[1] Nathan Söderblom's collection of letters, to Swedes and foreigners, UUB, typewritten letter (carbon copy).

Uppsala, February 24, 1930

Dear Reverend,

Many thanks for your kind and interesting letter. It is particularly pleasing to me that you are working to get a nurse for the congregation. I shall be glad to support your request at the Red Cross. Let me know when you send your application, so that my recommendation does not arrive too early, for then it would fall into oblivion.

I read Professor Otto's enlarged German edition of his lectures here with lively interest. His familiarity with Indian religion and his basic view of religion place him in the foremost rank among experts and scholars of religion. But his idea of granting a special position to the Anglican church is quite unfortunate and proves his lack of a sense of reality. Fortunately I do not believe that anything of the kind can be realized anywhere but at a study's desk. If, however, a singling out of Anglicanism does happen in the ecumenical awakening, the immediate consequence then would be that Lutheranism too must stand by itself. For the distance between Lutheranism and a fair number of Protestant forms of religion is far greater that the distance between Lutheranism and Anglicanism.

I am now hoping to be able to conduct an inspection in Berlin on April 4-6 and to install you on the fifth Sunday of Lent.[2] Make a suggestion for the program. On Saturday morning we could assemble the schoolchildren in the church. Saturday afternoon will probably have to be absorbed by a meeting with the church council and all that goes with it. At what time is the worship service? Would it be worthwhile to have another service in the evening for those who perchance did not get in for the installation in the morning? By being very cautious I hope I will manage the thing. What is incomparably most difficult for me is social gatherings with many people.[3] I therefore ask you to prevent any such larger arrangements. I simultaneously write to the Envoy. The Generalsuperintendent of Berlin[4] who shall stand beside me at the altar must of course be invited for the installation, moreover the pastor of the local congregation. How about requesting Deißmann and Siegmund-Schultze to assist? Perhaps it is asking too much that a man like Deißmann should assist. The two can of course also be invited without assisting. Presumably one of the sailors' chaplains is going to come. The church elders should also assist; actually, we do not need more than four assistants. But an invitation must probably also be directed to President Kapler, Dr. W. Simons, etc.[5] Make a suggestion for me about this too.

With good wishes
yours sincerely

---

[2] April 4-6, 1930, are Friday through Sunday, so the inauguration is planned for April 6.

[3] It is distressing to see what his heart condition has done to this man who for all his life had thrived with people and their company.

[4] Otto Dibelius, cf. letter no. 173, n. 2. His official designation was Generalsuperintendent of Kurmark.

[5] For Hermann Kapler, see letter no. 239, n. 3. Walter Simons (1861-1937) was Foreign Secretary in 1920/21. He worked for a realistic regulation of war reparations and resigned when this proved unachievable. From 1922-1929, he was President of the German *Reichsgericht* (Supreme Court), as such acting President of the republic for three months after Friedrich Ebert's death in February, 1925. His serving as President of the *Evangelisch-Sozialer Kongress* (cf. letter no. 14, n. 2) from 1925-1936 is the reason for Söderblom's suggestion.

Upsala 11 VI 30

Hochverehrte Frau von Harnack!

Wie kann ein solcher Mensch sterben? Ist es möglich dass ein solcher Mensch überhaupt stirbt? Solche waren die Aufrufe meiner Frau und meiner Tochter diesen Morgen, als wir erfuhren, dass der Theologus laureatus unsrer Epoche das irdische Dasein verlassen hat.[2] Das war auch mein erster Eindruck. Und die Frage bleibt nicht ohne Antwort. Ein Geist wie Adolf von Harnack gehört zu den tatsächlichen Beweisen des ewigen Lebens. Man vergass vor ihm die Armseligkeit unsres Daseins und sogar das Elend der Welt. Er war bei uns während der Hungerzeit. Von notwendigen Pflichten in Anspruch genommen konnte ich leider nicht so wie ich wollte seine Gegenwart in jeder Stunde geniessen. Eines Tagen [sic] kam meine Frau, wie selten entrüstet, empört zu mir, Sie hatte allein mit Ihm gefrühstückt. »Eine Welt, in der Harnack nicht Butter und Ei bekommen kann, ist verkehrt, muss geändert werden«! Aber er war heiter und gross. Sein Geist wie immer sprudelnd, frei und überlegen. Als ich zum ersten Mal nach dem Kriege an einem grossen Diner in Lambeth Palace beim Erzbischof von Canterbury theilnahm, wollte man vor Allem wissen: wie geht es Harnack. Erzählen Sie uns etwas von Harnack.

Schon als ich Student war, öffnete seine Dogmengeschichte meinem jugendlichen Geiste neue und weite Horizonte. Mit welcher Begeisterung habe ich nicht in unsrem akad[emischen] theolog[ischen] Vereine[3] das Werk zu beschreiben versucht. Nach unsrer Hochzeit fuhren wir direkt nach meiner Pfarrei in Paris. Meine Frau hat mich öfters dafür geneckt, dass ich unsre wenige Stunden in Berlin auf unsrer Hochzeitsreise dazu benutzt habe, Harnacks Vorlesung zu besuchen. Als sie Ihn gesehen, gelesen und getroffen hat, hat meine Frau meine Begeisterung geteilt.[4] Wenn wir von Harnack reden und jetzt von seinem Hinscheiden hören, werden unsre müden, alten Gemüter frisch und jung. Es ist eine Gottesgabe, einen Menschen so sein Leben lang bewundern und lieben zu dürfen. Verschiedenheit in Meinungen bedeutet dabei nichts. Ich sage oft: »Die Grossen, die Genien haben recht, auch wenn sie sich widersprechen.« Das Herz ist voll, ich schreibe ohne Ordnung. Er war eine Offenbarung des Geistes, eine Erscheinung von Esprit und Geist ebenso wie von Pneuma. Er hatte, wie die ganz Grossen, Zeit und Interesse für Alle. Bei wichtigen Epochen meines Lebens hat er bisweilen Worte entscheidender Wichtigkeit geschrieben oder gesprochen. Mit Stolz bewahre ich den Brief in welchem er mich fragte, ob ich nach Berlin kommen wollte.[5] Die Entscheidung war schwierig; wurde mir aber völlig

---

[1] Amalie von Harnack, nee Thiersch (1858–1937), wife of Adolf von Harnack. – Harnack's papers – letters, Staatsbibliothek zu Berlin, Preußischer Kulturbesitz, handwritten letter.
[2] Adolf von Harnack had died in Heidelberg on June 10.
[3] On the Theological Association at Uppsala University, cf. Sundkler, op. cit., 23 f.
[4] Cf. letter no. 5.
[5] Not found in UUB. But cf. letter no. 51.

klar. Sodann wurde Lehmann gerufen. Niemand hat wie Harnack an die Weltkirchenkonferenz geschrieben, die in Stockholm 1925 tagte.[6] Hier an unsrem Tische sprach er Worte die ich nie vergessen kann. Das schöne Bild von ihm haben unsre Kinder Harnack nennen gelernt als sie zu sprechen begannen.

Er war der letzte und der Primus inter pares der grossen Geister der Religionsforschung die eine für die Uneingeweihten rätselhafte Freude und Reichtum unsrem Leben geschenkt hat. In seinem Marcion[7] hat er die ganz tiefen Töne der Religion angeschlagen.

Die Erde wird jetzt ärmer. Aber der Geist besiegt das Vergängliche.

Als eine hohe Gnade Gottes betrachte ich seine Freundschaft. Ach, es war mir vergönnt, Ihn noch einmal in Berlin in April zu sehen und zu sprechen.

Ich denke an das lange Lebensglück, das Sie Ihm bereitet haben. Gott segne Sie und Ihre Lieben!

Ihr ehrfurchtsvoll ergebenster
Nathan Söderblom

329. To GUSTAF AULÉN[1]

Upsala den 11 sept. 1930

Käre Vän!

Gärna hade jag velat stanna över i Lund för att träffa Yngve och Dig. Men jag måste ila hem. Orsaken varför jag skriver är den Brittisk-Nordiska Teologkonferensen som hölls i Cambridge i fjol, och som väl nu är i tur att anordnas i Sverige. Orsaken varför jag besvärar Dig och inte Yngve i saken är den, att Du står som medlem av Teologkommissionen, vilken gjort ett ypperligt arbete. Det är förträffligt att nu också Faith and Order insatt en teologkommission, ty, som betonades vid Ekumeniska Rådets sammanträde i Chexbres, dessa teologiska kolloquier utgöra ett uttryck för att både Life and Work och Faith and Order bygga på vår kristna gemenskap. Och hur skulle etiska grundsatser kunna utvinnas utan grundliga studier av uppenbarelsen och dess historia och tankevärld? Nu har också Studentrörelsen lagt sig till med teologiska kolloquier. Jag har försökt få dem anordnade i samband med Deissmanns och Bells teologkommission. Men den första är nu redan utsatt, och sådana teologiska samtal kunna ju icke vara för många.

. . .

Med goda hälsningar
Din tillgivne

---

[6] Letter no. 255.
[7] Cf. letter no. 211, n. 3.

[1] Nathan Söderblom's collection of letters, to Swedes and foreigners, UUB, typewritten letter (carbon copy).

Uppsala, September 11, 1930

Dear friend,

I would have loved to stay over in Lund to meet Yngve[2] and you. But I had to hurry home. The reason for my writing is the British-Nordic conference of theologians which was held in Cambridge last year, and whose arrangement would now be Sweden's turn. The reason for my troubling you and not Yngve is that you are in the position of being a member of the committee of theologians which has done an outstanding job. It is splendid that Faith and Order has now also installed a committee of theologians, because, as was emphasized at the Ecumenical Council's meeting at Chêxbres,[3] these theological colloquies give expression to the fact that both Life and Work and Faith and Order are based on our Christian fellowship. How could ethical principles be arrived at without a thorough study of revelation and its history and world of ideas? Now the Student Movement too has taken to theological colloquies. I tried to have them arranged in connection with Deissmann's and Bell's committee of theologians. But the former has now already been fixed, and there surely cannot be too many of such theological discourses.

... [On some of the details of organizing the Swedish conference]

Yours sincerely

330. From STRENOPOULOS GERMANOS[1]

Saint-Étienne, le 29 Novembre 1930

Eminence et cher frère et ami

Ici où je me trouve depuis quelques jours en tournée pastorale, je lis dans le »Temps« que le prix Nobel de la paix pour l'année 1930 a été decené [sic; lis: décerné] à Vous, mon cher ami.

Je ne peux pas Vous exprimer la grande joie que je sentis en lisant cette nouvelle! S'il y a une personnalité qui a bien mérité de ce prix pour ses efforts pacifistes, c'est vous, mon cher ami. Pour nous qui nous travaillons à coté de Vous depuis plusieurs années il est aussi un grand honneur et un encouragement que notre oeuvre trouve un echo dans le monde entier. Je vous felicite de tout mon coeur et je vous souhaite longues et prospères années en bon [sic] santé pour la continuation de votre activité admirable.

J'ose vous offrir ces lignes de la part aussi de S.S. du Patriarche Oecuménique, qui va se réjouir, je suis bie [bien] sûr, en apprenant par son delegué accredité auprès de Votre Eminence, le chef de l'Eglise de la Suède, la bonne nouvelle.

Encore une fois felicitations cordiales

Votre bien aimé frère en Jesus-Christ

+Germanos Metropolite de Thyateira

---

[2] Yngve Brilioth who at the time was professor in Lund; cf. letter no. 141, n. 6.

[3] At this conference in September, 1930, the Universal Council for Life and Work was formed, here referred to as Ecumenical Council, which was to become common phraseology. It turned out to be the predecessor of the World Council of Churches.

[1] Nathan Söderblom's collection of letters, from foreigners, UUB, handwritten letter.

Saint-Étienne, November 29, 1930

Your Eminence and dear Brother and friend,

Here where I have now been spending several days on a pastoral tour, I have read in »Temps« that the Nobel Peace Prize for the year 1930 has been awarded to You, my dear friend.[2]

I cannot express the great joy that I felt when reading this news! If there is a personality who well deserved this prize for his pacifist endeavors, it is you, my dear friend. For us who have been working beside You for many years, it also is a great honor and an encouragement that our work finds an echo all over the world. I congratulate you of all my heart, and I wish you long and prosperous years in good health for the continuation of your admirable activity.

I dare to present these lines to you also on behalf of His Holiness the Ecumenical Patriarch who, I am quite sure, will rejoice when learning the good news from his delegate accredited with Your Eminence the leader of the Church of Sweden.

Once more cordial congratulations
Your beloved Brother in Jesus Christ
+Germanos Metropolitan of Thyateira

331. To Amalie von Harnack[1]

Uppsala, den 30 dec. 1930

Excellenz.

Hier steht wirklich »Gestorben am 10. Juni 1930«. Ich kann das nicht richtig fassen noch anerkennen. Oder vielmehr es bewährt sich hier mit seltener Frische und Stärke das alte schon in der Lehre des Heilands und in der Predigt des Paulus vorhandene Wort, dass für den Christen nicht der Tod, sondern die lebendigmachende Erfahrung von und Gemeinschaft mit Gott durch Christus die entscheidende Zweiteilung des Daseins macht. Was für ein Wort ist mir stets in den Gedanken gekommen als ich Adolf von Harnack gelesen oder was leider nur allzu wenige Male geschehen ist, gehört habe, oder wenn ich an Ihn gedacht habe oder wenn wir meine Frau und ich und unsere Söhne und Töchter und andere Gleichgesinnte Freunde oft und gern zu der Erhebung unsrer Herzen und zur Stärkung unserer Lebenswanderung mit Freude von Ihm gesprochen haben? Das ist das Wort: Geist. Er war ja geistreich, sprudelnd von Esprit noch als ich das ersehnte hohe Privilegium hatte Ihn mit meiner Tochter noch einmal im Leben beim schwedischen Gesandten in Berlin in diesem Jahre zu treffen und zu hören. Bei aller trüben und schweren und langweiligen sogenannten Frömmigkeit und Philiströser theologischer Zunftmässigkeit ist es doch eine herrliche Gottesgabe gewesen Ihn unter uns gehabt zu haben. Und doch denke ich hier nicht dar-

---

[2] It should be mentioned in this connection that Söderblom was the only winner of this prize who had known Alfred Nobel in person: Nobel had been one of Söderblom's parishioners in the years of his pastorate in Paris. Cf. Sundkler, op. cit., 392.

[1] Nathan Söderblom's collection of letters, to Swedes and foreigners, UUB, typewritten letter (carbon copy).

an, sondern an die geistige Kraft die Ihn beseelte und die Seinen Worten und Schriften Flügel gibt. Ach, was für eine Gnade jung gewesen zu sein als Ihr Herr Gemahl die volle Kraft seines Genius entfaltete. Ach, wie schwelgte ich in seiner Dogmengeschichte. Sie war mir wie vielen anderen eine Offenbarung der wunderbaren Schicksale des christlichen Gedankens und auch und besonders der Herrlichkeit der echten kongenialen religiösen Forschung. Ich weiss nicht was mich am meisten in jenem Riesenwerke gefesselt hat, vielleicht die Darstellung des Neuplatonismus. Die Grundthese und auch einzelne Behauptungen habe ich schon damals nicht annehmen können. Aber wissen Sie, Frau Excellenz, völlige Übereinstimmung in der Theorie garantiert in keiner Weise die unbeschreibliche geistige Gemeinschaft welche Herz und Seele erquickt. Schon damals habe ich auch das Wort Ihres verewigten Gemahles verstanden, dass die Freude die uns den priviligierten, das heisst den wissenschaftlichen Forschern auf dem wunderbarsten aller Gebiete, der Religion wie ein Mysterium zuteilkommt, von der Frömmigkeit leicht als eine Art Weltlichkeit missverstanden wird, wohl aber tatsächlich ein heliger [sic] Gottesdienst ist. Es wäre töricht hier sagen zu wollen was ich Alles dem Theologo laureato unserer Epoche verdanke.

Eine herzergreifende Offenbarung der suveränen Macht des Geistes war die Erscheinung Harnacks hier bei uns in der Hungerzeit. Meine Frau kam eines Tages und sagte im gewaltsamer[2] Empörung: »was haben die Menschen für eine Welt zubereitet in welcher ein Harnack nicht das nötige kräftige Essen bekommen kann«? Und doch Er war der freieste und freudigste unter uns allen. Er sprach nicht von dem Elend. Er lebte nicht in einem Weltfremden, künstlichen Dünkel, wohl aber wirklich im ewigen Leben des Geistes. Eines Abends sollten meine Frau und ich irgend wo bei Freunden sein, die es als die höchste Ehre betrachtet hätten Harnack empfangen zu dürfen. Aber wir dachten Er sollte zu Hause ausruhen. Als wir abends zurückkamen herrschte im Wohnzimmer eine Heiterkeit welche für die jungen Anwesenden unvergesslich bleibt. Der große Theologe, der Fürst der Wissenschaft hatte die Kinder dort aufgesucht und unterhielt sich mit ihnen in einer Weise, die [lies: wie] nur die von Goethe geschilderte und verwirklichte Wesentlichkeit und Einfachheit des Genius es versteht. Wir glaubten kaum unsere Augen. Dieser Gelehrte mit den gewaltigen Kenntnissen konnte den Mensch, das heisst das Kind im Menschen finden. Seine Gegenwart lockte das Beste im Menschen hervor.

Daher bleibt Er auch uns allen die wir das Privilegium [hatten] Ihn persöhnlich erleben zu dürfen ein lebendiger Beweis des Geistes und des ewigen Lebens.

Ich glückwünsche den Heimgegangenen[,] Seinen Herrn Sohn Professor Axel von Harnack, Sie gnädigste Frau und uns alle zu dem Erscheinen dieses Buches das Sie die ungemein große und unverdiente Güte gehabt haben

---

[2] Swedish: *våldsam*; the German equivalent would be »heftig«.

mir zu schenken.[3] Wenn ich beginnen wollte die Stellen anzuführen, die mich und meine Söhne gepackt und erleuchtet haben, würde ich zu lang werden. Zum Beispiel Seite 15 der erste Satz[4] oder 167 der letzte Satz den wir jetzt uns einprägen sollen, gestärkt von Seinem prophetischen Glauben (S. 170).[5] Wie freigiebig war Er. Wie pietätvoll hat Er den vor Ihm von diesem Leben Wegberufenen Freunden und Mitarbeitern von dem Reichtum Seines Geistes Nachrufe gespendet, die klassisch sind. Wie unwürdig bin ich Seiner Mühe an mich zu schreiben und über mich zu schreiben. Ein Buch von Ihm in die Hand zu nehmen und durchzublättern in dem man bei beliebten Stellen gern verweilt[,] ist auf einmal[6] erweckend und befestigend. Man wird demütig, wach und froh. Richtlinien hat Er uns gegeben auf vielen Gebieten. Man lese S. 81, für die Ekumenische Arbeit vorbildlich[7]. Nein, ich muss zu Ende kommen. Ich betrachte es als eine hohe Gnadengabe des himmlischen Vaters, dass ich Adolf von Harnack kennen dürfte. Ich könnte einige wenige deutsche Namen nennen welche in einer trüben verzweiflender Zeit wie Sternen geleuchtet haben.

Gott segne Sie Frau Excellenz in dem neuen Jahre, Ew. Excellenz selbst und alle Diejenigen die Ihrem Herzen lieb und nahe sind.

Ich bin Ew. Excellenz verehrungsvoll und tief dankbar ergebener

332. From Rudolf Otto[1]

Marburg, i3 i 3i

Verehrter Herr Erzbischof.

Zunächst meine herzlichsten Glückwünsche zu der so verdienten Ehrung, die Ihnen durch den Nobelpreis zu teil geworden ist. Und fast noch mehr zu Ihrer Genesung, von der mir Birger Forel berichtet.

Sodann die Bitte, dass Sie meinem Kollegen Frick erlauben wollen, Ihren Namen unter den beiliegenden Aufruf zu setzen.[2] Wir wollen nicht nur Deutsche für unser Unternehmen interessieren, und es soll wahrlich nicht

---

[3] Adolf von Harnack, *Aus der Werkstatt des Vollendeten*, ed. by Axel v. Harnack, Gießen 1930. Written in the last year of his life, the following selection of references made by Söderblom can in hindsight also be read as his own legacy.

[4] The worst of sins is wasting one's time with dawdling.

[5] German idealism had inaugurated an era of the spirit (*Geist*) which was then delayed for several decades, Harnack writes, but is gaining new momentum now as the futility of the intervening materialism has become obvious.

[6] Swedish: *på en gång*; in German here: *zugleich*.

[7] Pages 81–83: It is not organizational or doctrinal unity the ecumenical movement should strive for, but cooperation of the different churches in trying to solve the urgent social problems. This could then lead to an interdenominational federation. Cf. letters no. 244, n. 2, and 251, n. 2.

[1] Nathan Söderblom's collection of letters, from foreigners, UUB, typewritten letter.

[2] I have not been able to find the text of this appeal. The continuation of this letter shows that it concerns the raising of funds for the Marburg collection of specimens from the history of religion. – For Heinrich Frick, cf. letter no. 305, n. 2.

nur Deutschen dienen, sondern uns ist es sehr Ernst mit unserer internationalen Aufgabe, und mit unserer interkonfessionellen und interreligiösen.
Wir haben Katholiken und Juden unter unseren Mitunterzeichnern, und
auch einen Buddhisten aus China und die beiden grossen Guru)s aus Myso-
re, und last not least Rabindranath Tagore.

Frick geht jetzt nach Amerika, um dort unter den alten Freunden Mar-
burgs und dann unter reicheren Deutsch-amerikanern für unsere Sammlung
Interesse zu wecken. Der Kultusminister hat sein Interesse an der Sache erklärt, und der frühere Kultusminister Becker ist unter unsern Direktoren
und Mitunterzeichnern.[3]

Ihr Name würde uns und unsern Freunden eine Ermutigung und unserm
Unternehmen eine wesentliche Hilfe sein. Dass Ihr Interesse unserer Sammlung sicher ist, das weiss ich ja schon.

Unser erstes Ziel ist, das herrliche Schloss in Marburg zu erwerben, damit wir Platz bekommen.[4] Wir haben unsere Sammlungstätigkeit schon vorläufig einstellen müssen, da uns einfach der Platz fehlt.

Da Frick im Begriffe der Abreise ist, erbitte ich eine recht umgehende
Antwort.

...

Bestätigen Sie mir auch die guten Nachrichten über Ihre Genesung, die
mir die liebsten sein werden. Ich selber habe recht schwere Zeiten durchzu-
machen gehabt, und soll im Februar an den Lago maggiore, »in die Sonne«,
die leider gewöhnlich nicht scheint, sobald ich einmal in den Süden fahre.

...

Mit meinen ergebenen Grüssen auch an Frau Erzbischof,
bin ich Ihr
R. Otto

333. From Strenopoulos Germanos[1]

London, April 8th 1931
My dear Brother in Christ,
I express my heartfelt thanks to Your Grace for sending me the copy of
Your telegram to His Holiness, the Oecumenical Patriarch.[2]

I am always ashamed when I read the great eulogies You are so good as
to make to my authorities for my humble person and for the remembrance

---

[3] Carl Heinrich Becker (1876-1933), Islam scholar and Orientalist, professor in Hamburg
1908 and later in Berlin, Prussian sescretary of education in 1921 and 1925-1930.

[4] This ambitious plan apparently did not succeed; today, the collection ist housed in a
building right across the street from the castle.

[1] Nathan Söderblom's collection of letters, from foreigners, UUB, handwritten letter.

[2] The Ecumenical Patriarch had congratulated Söderblom on being awarded the Nobel
Peace Prize.

of my name in every occasion.[3] May God bless Your labours for the reunion of the Christian Churches.

On the great festival of Easter I do reciprocate Your wishes as well as those of Your family and I wish the risen Lord may give You all strength and rejoicing.

Yours sincerely
+Germanos of Thyateira

334. From EIVIND BERGGRAV[1]

Tromsø 22. April 1931.

Kjære Erkebiskop.
Med ditt idag hitkomne Nobel-foredrag har jeg gjennemlevet en utvikling som vilde forekommet mig utrolig, hvis den ikke ver sann. Hvad kunde vi ane i 1917 av dette? Absurdum var dengang monumentalt, credo var et se-nepskorn. Og nu synger en fugleskare i treets grener.

Som du kan tenke dig har ditt notat av min far for mig vært noget dypt bevegende, vemodig och lykkelig. *Ditt øie så* ham. Og du tendte noget hos ham, – som hos så mange av oss. Du sendte ham et telegram dengang til Hamar under Uppsalakonferansen, som var en av de siste lykkelige ord han mottok. Du takket for at hans sønn var med, och mor skrev til mig og for-talte hvad far hadde sagt da han leste det.

Om vi utenom det program-fremstøt og den verdensomspennende utvik-ling som den sak har hatt, som Du reiste i 1914, tenker på alle de personlige solstråler du har spredt i enkeltvise sinn verden over, så tror jeg vi ser noget også av grokraftens hemmelighet i selve saken.

God reise til Skotland – jeg har en privatdetektiv i Sv. D. som holder mig underrettet om dine skritt!

Din ærbødig hengivne
Eivind Berggrav

Tromsø, April 22, 1931.

Dear Archbishop,
By means of your Nobel address that arrived today, I have relived a development which would have seemed unlikely to me, if it were not true. What could we surmise of this in 1917? *Absurdum* was monumental then, *credo* was a mustard seed. And now a flock of birds is singing on the tree's branches.[2]

---

[3] Söderblom was known for his generous recognition of the achievements of others.

[1] Nathan Söderblom's collection of letters, from foreigners, UUB, typewritten letter.

[2] Allusion to the famous dictum ascribed to Tertullian, »Credo quia absurdum«, I believe because it is absurd. (Actually, this is not a quote from Tertullian. The closest equivalent is *De carne Christi* 5,4: »credibile est quia ineptum est«, it – namely, the death of Christ – is credible because it is foolish. This is a polemic statement against Marcion who excluded any connection of God with human death.) The metaphor of the mustard seed is taken from Matth. 13:31 f. –

Believe me that your note of my father[3] was something deeply moving for me, melancholic and gladdening. *Your* eye *did see* him. And you lit something in him – as in so many of us. You sent him a cable to Hamar during the Uppsala conference, which was one of the last happy words he received. You thanked him that his son participated, and Mother wrote to me, telling what Father had said when he read it.

Quite apart from the programmatic step forward and the world-encompassing development this cause has undergone which you raised in 1914: I believe that if we think of all those personal rays of sunshine you have spread in individual souls all over the world, we also see something of the mystery of the vigor of growth in that cause itself.

Have a good trip to Scotland[4] – I have a private detective at *Sv[enska] D[agbladet]*[5] who will keep me informed as to your steps!

Reverently yours,
Eivind Berggrav

In hindsight, it would almost seem as if Berggrav had a premonition here that Söderblom did not have much time left in life; he died on July 12. Be that as it may, for anyone interested in the relationship between the two men, reading Berggrav's moving commemoration of his Swedish friend is recommended: *N. Söderblom. Geni og karakter*, Oslo 1931.

[3] Otto Jensen (1856–1918), pastor, and bishop of Hamar 1917–1918. His son adopted the older family name of Berggrav.

[4] Söderblom was to travel to Edinburgh to give his Gifford Lectures on *The Living God*. He was able only to deliver the first part before he died. It was published posthumously in Swedish, *Den levande Guden. Grundformer av personlig religion*, Stockholm 1932, in English, Oxford 1933, and in German in 1942.

[5] One of the leading Swedish newspapers.

Index of Names

The numbers refer to the letters, not the pages of this edition, unless they are preceded by »p.« which indicates the pages of the introduction. Numbers in bold print refer to letters written by or to the respective person, numbers in ordinary print to their being mentioned in the text, numbers in italics to footnotes (whose number is added). The first mention of a name in a letter leads to information about the person in question (exceptions noted below). Biblical names, translators and editors are not listed, nor (with a few exceptions) those only mentioned in square brackets. Indirect references to a person (e. g., »the Kaiser«) are put in round brackets. – The letters ä, å, ö, ø, ü are treated like a, o, u, in the alphabetical order.

527

Acknowledgments

The heirs to the following authors of letters to Söderblom have kindly granted
permission for printing:
For Paul Althaus (letter no. 253): Prodekan em. Gerhard Althaus, Planegg, Germany
For Gustaf Aulén (letters no. 44. 62. 198. 213. 272): Dr. Gustaf Aulén. Växjö, Sweden
For Eivind Berggrav (letters no. 267. 301. 307. 313. 334): Mrs. Marit Berggrav, Hørvik,
   Norway
For Torsten Bohlin (letters no. 182. 306. 318): Harald Bohlin, Uppsala, Sweden
For Adolf Deißmann (letters no. 59. 92. 101. 125. 163. 293): Dr. Gerhard Deißmann,
   Bremen, Germany
For Nils Johan Göransson (letters no. 27. 30. 32. 40. 73): Mrs. Kerstin Göransson Dahne,
   Uppsala, Sweden
For Sven Hedin (letter no. 282): Sven Hedins Stiftelse, Stockholm, Sweden
For Friedrich Heiler (letters no. 116. 118. 122. 123. 138. 140. 147. 149. 153. 159. 166. 168.
   170. 172. 174. 177. 181. 191. 203. 221. 225. 228. 232. 234. 261. 268. 283. 289): Mrs.
   Birgitta Hartog, Bad Oeynhausen, Germany
For Albert Hellerström (letters no. 129. 136): Mr. Klas Hellerström, Håverud, Sweden
For Selma Lagerlöf (letters no. 235. 241. 247. 256): Sveriges Författarförbund,
   Stockholm, Sweden
For Gerardus van der Leeuw: (letter no. 145): Dr. Gerardus van der Leeuw, Jr.,
   Bennekom, The Netherlands
For Rudolf Otto (letters no. 17. 142. 150. 155. 160. 167. 180. 188. 238. 277. 279. 285. 295.
   296. 303. 308. 312. 324. 332): Marburger Universitätsbund, Marburg, Germany

In the case of Alfred Loisy, inquiries for surviving heirs have unfortunately not been
   successful.

***

The photograph of Söderblom and the facsimile of his handwriting were kindly presented
   to the editor by Dr. Staffan Runestam, Uppsala, Sweden. The facsimile is the dramatic
   postcard written to Nils Johan Göransson just a few days after the outbreak of World
   War I; the printed version is letter no. 70 in the present edition.